*

*Chronicle of
the Living Christ*

Chronicle
of the
Living Christ

The Life and Ministry of Jesus Christ:

Foundations of Cosmic Christianity

Robert A. Powell

& Anthroposophic Press

Copyright © Robert A. Powell, 1996

Published by Anthroposophic Press
RR 4, Box 94 A-1, Hudson, NY 12534

Library of Congress Cataloging-in-Publication Data

Powell, Robert (Robert A.)
  Chronicle of the living Christ : the life and ministry of Jesus Christ :
foundations of cosmic Christianity / by Robert A. Powell.
      p.   cm.
  Includes bibliographical references and index.
  ISBN 0-88010-407-4 (paper)
  1. Jesus Christ—Chronology—Miscellanea.
  2. Jesus Christ—Anthroposophical interpretations.
  3. Jesus Christ—Biography—Miscellanea.
  4. Emmerich, Anna Katharina, 1774–1824.   I. Title.
BP596.J4P68   1996   95–47063
299'.935—dc20   CIP

10 9 8 7 6 5 4 3 2 1

Printed in the United States of America

Contents

This book is dedicated to all seekers of star wisdom,
and in particular to Willi Sucher (1902–1985), who set me on
the path of research into the cosmic mysteries of the life of Christ Jesus.
Willi Sucher, Anne Catherine Emmerich, and Rudolf Steiner
have been my guides.

* * *

Special thanks are due to James Wetmore for his extensive and helpful comments,
to Christopher Bamford of Anthroposophic Press for his encouragement and edi-
torial advice, to Marie Carmichael and Reid Shaw of the Sophia Foundation,
and to Richard Bloedon, Gerhild Powell, Bradley Rader, and Jussi and Raija
Timgren for their generous support. To Mary Giddens for her careful and patient
help in typesetting the manuscript and the many others who have assisted in the
production of this book in one way or another I also extend my sincerest thanks;
especially to Peter Treadgold for his help with the computation of the horoscopes
and the tabulation of dates for the end of the century.

*

Abbreviations

Books frequently referred to in the text:

BL   *Das bittere Leiden unsers Herrn Jesu Christi nach den Betrachtungen der gottseligen Anna Katharina Emmerich*, Clemens Brentano, *Complete Works,* vol. 26 (Stuttgart: Kohlhammer, 1980)

HDK *Die heiligen Drei Könige*, Helmut Fahsel (Basel: Ilionverlag, 1941)

LBVM *The Life of the Blessed Virgin Mary from the Visions of Anne Catherine Emmerich,* transl. Sir Michael Palairet (Rockford, Illinois: Tan Books, 1970)

LHHJC *Das Leben unseres Herrn und Heilandes Jesu Christi nach den Geschichten der gottseligen Anna Katharina Emmerich aufgeschrieben von Clemens Brentano,* 3 volumes (Regensburg, 1858–1860)

LIFE *The Life of Anne Catherine Emmerich* by the Very Reverend Carl E. Schmöger, C.SS.R., 2 volumes (Rockford, Illinois: Tan Books, 1976)

LJ i   *Lehrjahre Jesu. Teil I: Mai 1821 bis Juli 1822,* Clemens Brentano, *Complete Works* vol. 24.1 (Stuttgart: Kohlhammer, 1983)

LJ ii   *Lehrjahre Jesu. Teil II: August bis Dezember 1822,* Clemens Brentano, *Complete Works* vol. 24.2 (Stuttgart: Kohlhammer, 1985)

LJC   *The Life of Jesus Christ, and Biblical Revelations, From the Visions of the Venerable Anne Catherine Emmerich,* 4 volumes (Rockford, Illinois: Tan Books, 1979)

MKF *Öffnet Eure Herzen MARIA, der Königen des Friedens,* Slavko Barbaric and Tomislav Vlasic (Jestetten, Germany: Rosenkranz Aktion, 1987)

TC   *The Time of Christ,* Ormond Edwards (Edinburgh: Floris Books, 1986)

WJW *Der Wandel Jesu in der Welt,* Helmut Fahsel (Basel: Ilionverlag, 1942)

Foreword

by James Wetmore

THE BOOK YOU HOLD in your hands makes extraordinary claims, and it does so on the basis of what may at first seem a highly unlikely pair of informants: one a venerated daughter of the Catholic Church, whose writings have provided spiritual sustenance to a great number of believers; the other a man who, having first established himself as a rising philosopher in the intense intellectual ferment of late nineteenth century Germany, went on to became the most prolific esotericist of the twentieth century. I refer, respectively, to Anne Catherine Emmerich, the nun who beheld the life of Christ in interior vision with such exactitude that her account has guided archeologists to long-forgotten sites such as Mary's house in Ephesus, and Rudolf Steiner, epistemologist, scholar of Goethe, founder of anthroposophy, and guiding force behind a host of related movements — including Waldorf education, biodynamic agriculture, and anthroposophical medicine.

Two primary influences on this book have been mentioned, but it is the author who coordinates these initially disparate sources from a highly original, creative, synthetic viewpoint. Robert Powell establishes here what he believes are accurate coordinates in time and space for Jesus Christ and other figures in the New Testament. Such coordinates have never been reliably determined before. To make his claims, he presents various views on the subject, from both ancient and modern sources, and then introduces the results of his own far-reaching research based on Rudolf Steiner and the visions of Anne Catherine Emmerich. These visions include extensive geographical and calendrical indications, as well as references to phases of the Moon. Having once established a correlation between events in Jesus' life and spatio-temporal coordinates, much else then falls into place. Various difficulties are raised and dealt with, some in considerable detail. Ultimately, however, the author is able to establish the necessary calibration — first, at a few significant points where relatively complete data is at hand, and then by filling in gaps through ingenious cross-referencing.

On the basis of his investigations, Powell provides dates for the pivotal events of the historic ministry of Jesus Christ. He believes, moreover, that the fate of our contemporary world depends on the extent to which we can inwardly participate in these events which, he maintains, are particularly relevant for the last three and one-half years of the twentieth century. Indeed, the whole second part of the book consists of a synopsis of Anne Catherine Emmerich's chronicle of the life of Christ, set out in chronological order with calendrical references and geographical maps, to serve not merely as a guidebook to the daily life of Jesus Christ, but as a meditative breviary. Taken together with the Tabulation of Dates for the End of the Century, this represents a sacred calendar aimed at nothing less, in the final analysis, than the realization of St. Paul's challenging words, "Not I, but Christ in me."

While this book may be said to have some antecedents, in the sense that the author relies on certain sources, it has no real *precursors* (excepting perhaps the work of Willi Sucher, whom Powell cites as an early mentor). Hence there exists no community of colleagues or experts in the field who could be drawn upon to assess the work within a larger context. It is unique both in its contents and its conclusions; and should be read with an open mind.

Introduction

THIS BOOK TELLS the dramatic story of what its author believes to be the determination of a precise chronology for the life of Christ. The universal significance of this chronology, if true, requires that the presentation be scientific, even though the *subject matter* is at the same time a spiritual reality. This means that the science involved must be approached differently than would a physical science involved in and limited to the investigation of natural phenomena.

The life of Christ Jesus has been the subject of many thousands of books, each with its own perspective and intent; but most of these have ignored the epistemological conditions that the spiritual reality of Christ's life inevitably imposes upon a sincere researcher in this field. Among those who have made real and significant contributions to our understanding of the spiritual conditions surrounding this historical reality, I have found two to be especially useful: Rudolf Steiner and Anne Catherine Emmerich.

My interest in investigating the life of Christ was first awakened by Rudolf Steiner, who stressed the central importance of the Incarnation and the Mystery of Golgotha for the whole of evolution. His inspiring picture of cosmic evolution, along with his remarkable spiritual scientific investigations into the spiritual events underlying the Gospel stories underscored the need for a deeper understanding of the historical reality of the Christ Event. Rudolf Steiner, whose teaching focuses upon preparations for and the consequences of this event, and who sought to recreate the ancient mysteries out of the Christ Impulse, led me to Anne Catherine Emmerich and what he called her "exceptionally accurate account." It was given to Anne Catherine Emmerich (about whom more will be said shortly) to be so attuned to the life of Christ as a mystical reality that her comprehensive vision encompassed even minute details of time and place—testable "coordinates," in fact.

My first encounter with Anne Catherine Emmerich's work raised the question: How is it possible that this woman, who never left the area in which she was born (Germany), could describe in such detail the geography and topography of Palestine and the customs and habits of people living there? To answer this, I undertook an exhaustive analysis of her work, gradually penetrating the historical reality underlying Christ's life, as will be described in the following pages.

I am not the first person to have traveled this road. The French priest, Abbé Julien Gouyet of Paris, after reading an account of Anne Catherine Emmerich's visions concerning the death of the Virgin Mary near Ephesus, traveled there and searched the whole area. On October 18, 1881, guided by various particulars in her account, he discovered the ruins of a small stone building on a mountain (*Bülbül Dag*, "Mount Nightingale") overlooking the Aegean Sea, with a view across to the remains of the ancient city of Ephesus. He was convinced that this was the house described in her visions as the dwelling place of the Virgin Mary during the last years of her life. He was ridiculed at first, but several years later the ruins were independently discovered again by two Lazarist missionaries who had undertaken a similar search on the basis of Anne Catherine Emmerich's visions. They ascertained that the building had been a place of pilgrimage in earlier times for Christians descended from the church of Ephesus, the community referred to by Saint John (Rev. 2:1–7). The building had been known in those days as *Panaya Kapulu*, the House of the Blessed Virgin, and was revered as the place where she had died. According to tradition, the date of her death, August 15, was the very day of the annual pilgrimage to *Panaya Kapulu*.

Following this discovery, a commission from the nearby Turkish city of Izmir determined that the foundation of the original house dated back to the first century A.D. It noted that the structure of the house conformed exactly to Anne Catherine Emmerich's detailed description. The house has since been restored and is now a place of pilgrimage. At a ceremony to commemorate the hundredth anniversary of its restoration, Archbishop Bernardini made this statement: "Dear brothers and sisters, all our bishops agree that the Virgin Mary died here. September 28 and May 12 are very significant holy days for us, for on September 28, 1890, it was confirmed that the Blessed Virgin lived and died here, and on May 12, 1891, the first religious ceremony was held here in her honor. This house is the only known surviving building in which the Blessed Virgin lived."

This remarkable example demonstrates the authenticity of Anne Catherine Emmerich's visions. That her visions provide spiritual nourishment had long been the experience of many spiritual seekers, but the discovery of Panaya Kapulu confirmed that her visions were objectively authentic and accessible (at least in part) to corroboration along conventional lines of research. This latter point will be further demonstrated in the present work, which proposes, with the help of Anne Catherine Emmerich's account, to establish an accurate historical dating of the life of Christ against the background presented by Rudolf Steiner's indications.

Led by these two guides, our quest will resemble the pilgrimage of the Magi who, guided by what they had read in the stars, came to pay homage to the Jesus Child.[1] For our path will be determined—as was theirs—by the stars. But we will be led backward in time, not forward in space. Like the Magi, our path will lead to the Nativity—and beyond that to the births of the Virgin Mary and John the Baptist as well. You, the reader, are invited to join in this quest and to undertake a spiritual journey illumined by the light of a Christian star wisdom similar to that which, two thousand years ago, led the Magi to Bethlehem.

A Note on Anne Catherine Emmerich and Rudolf Steiner

For the benefit of readers unacquainted with Anne Catherine Emmerich and Rudolf Steiner, a brief outline of their biographies follows, for it is largely through them that the discovery of the dates of the birth of Christ Jesus and of many events during His ministry has been made possible.

* * *

Anne Catherine Emmerich was born September 8, 1774, at Flamske, not far from Coesfeld, Germany. From early childhood she was blessed with the gift of spiritual sight (clairvoyance) and lived almost constantly in inner vision of scenes represented in the Old and New Testaments. As a child, her visions were predominantly of pre-Christian scenes, but these grew less frequent with the passing years, and, by the time she had become, at twenty-nine, an Augustinian nun at the order's convent in Dülmen, Germany, her visions had become concerned primarily with the life of Christ. Because of difficult political circumstances, her convent was disbanded on December 3, 1811, and one by one the nuns in residence were obliged to leave. Anne Catherine—already

---

1. See also Robert Powell, *Christian Hermetic Astrology: The Star of the Magi and the Life of Christ.*

very ill—withdrew to a small room in a house in Dülmen. By November, 1812, her illness had grown so severe that she was permanently confined to bed. Shortly thereafter, on December 29, 1812, she received the *stigmata*, a manifesting of the wounds suffered on the Cross, and the highest outward sign of inner union with Christ. Unable to assimilate any form of nourishment, for the rest of her life she was sustained almost exclusively by water and the Eucharist. As news spread that she bore the stigmata (which bled on Fridays), more and more people came to see her. For us, the most significant of these was the poet Clemens Brentano, who visited her on the morning of Thursday September 24, 1818. He was so impressed by the radiance of her being that he decided to move nearby in order to record her visions. Anne Catherine had already had a presentiment that someone—whom she called "the pilgrim"—would come to preserve her revelations. The moment Clemens Brentano entered her room, she recognized him as this "pilgrim."

Brentano, a novelist and romantic poet then living in Berlin, was associated with leading members of the Romantic Movement in Germany. Earlier (1806–1808), his association with Achim von Arnim had resulted in their famous compilation of folk literature, *Des Knaben Wunderhorn* (*The Boy's Magic Horn*). He settled his affairs and moved from Berlin to Dülmen early in 1819. He visited Anne Catherine every morning, noting down briefly all that she related to him; then, after writing out a full report at home, he returned later the same day to read it back to her. She would then often expand upon certain points, or, if necessary, correct details.

On July 29, 1820, Anne Catherine began to communicate visions concerning the day-to-day life of Christ Jesus that she had witnessed each preceding day. These visions encompassed the better part of Christ's ministry, and she was able to describe in extraordinary detail the places Christ visited, his miracles and healings, his teaching activity in the synagogues and elsewhere, and the people around him. She not only named and described many of these people with astonishing concreteness but spoke also of their families, their occupations, and other intimate, biographical details.

Anne Catherine was called to relate the day-by-day details of the life and ministry of Christ Jesus, and Brentano was called to record all that she communicated of her visions. They worked together daily until her death on February 9, 1824, except for one period of six months, during which Brentano was away, and several shorter periods when, mainly due to illness, it was impossible for Anne Catherine to communicate her visions. Although she had already recounted various details—the life of the Virgin Mary and the visit of

the three kings, among other things, during 1819 and the early part of 1820—
the real start of the revelation bestowed on Anne Catherine was July 29, 1820,
when she began describing the ministry of Our Lord *day by day*. This revelation continued until her death some three and one-half years later—although
only three years were actually recorded because Clemens Brentano had to
leave Dülmen for six months in 1823. Brentano (and others) believed that the
three years of Christ's ministry had been revealed almost in their entirety in the
daily chronicle extending from four months before the Baptism to the Ascension. As we shall see, however, the revelation was not complete. As long as the
belief persisted—as it has until now—that the account as recorded was more
or less complete, it was not possible to establish a true chronology of Jesus
Christ's life. Only now, with the discovery of a gap in the visionary account,
are we in a position to establish the actual chronology of Christ's ministry.

*   *   *

Rudolf Steiner (1861–1925) was a twentieth-century clairvoyant and spiritual teacher of enormous probity, depth of perception, and scope. Like
Anne Catherine Emmerich, Rudolf Steiner was clairvoyant from childhood.
As a young man, he studied philosophy and various sciences in order to ac-
quire a thorough grasp of the modern scientific world-view and method and
to discipline his natural clairvoyance with a trained intellectual consciousness. Thus Steiner did not remain either at the level of intellectual "scientific" consciousness or at that of natural clairvoyance, but went on to develop
a "scientific clairvoyance"—or spiritual science—in place of the natural
clairvoyance of his youth.

   According to Steiner's own account, scientific clairvoyance may be developed through an intensification of the power of *thinking* in such a way that
thinking develops into spiritual vision. This is achieved by practicing the
ability to focus attention—in thought—upon the active, living, but elusive
point at which thinking itself emerges into consciousness. Steiner elaborated the foundations for his view in early philosophical and epistemological
works such as *Truth and Science, Intuitive Thinking as a Spiritual Path: A
Philosophy of Freedom*, and *The Science of Knowing*.[2] The essential point that
Steiner seeks to establish is that, *in principle*, no limits to knowledge exist.
These works go beyond philosophy in that they can be taken as manuals for

---

2. See Bibliography.

meditative experience which, in turn, can serve for the attainment of "scientific clairvoyance." But this description, by itself, does not do full justice to Steiner's accomplishment, for he was able to describe precisely differentiated levels of consciousness that can no longer be characterized simply by the word *clairvoyance*. For *clairvoyance* (in the sense of *scientific clairvoyance*), he substituted the term *Imagination*, and, for the two higher levels of consciousness beyond this, he used the terms *Inspiration* and *Intuition*, to which he attached very specific meaning in all three cases.

Steiner devoted considerable attention to the development of these three higher states of consciousness, beyond modern scientific-intellectual consciousness while always taking the latter as his starting point. His book *How to Know Higher Worlds*[3] describes this process very precisely. This element of scientific precision in Steiner's path is characterized by the term *spiritual science*. It is particularly remarkable that Steiner was able to apply this spiritual science—which he also called *anthroposophy*—successfully to various practical domains, providing new spiritually-based procedures in many different areas. In the field of education, for example, he pioneered the worldwide Waldorf (Steiner) education movement; in the realm of healing, he developed anthroposophical medicine; in agriculture, he introduced organic (biodynamic) farming; and in the care of the handicapped and maladjusted, he introduced new methods that are now practiced in Camphill villages (and elsewhere) around the world. This list of his innovations in the fields of science, social development, and the arts, all of which result from the application of spiritual science as he developed it, could be extended considerably.

In the sphere of the arts, for example, he founded a new kind of architecture, which is exemplified in the building of the Goetheanum in Dornach, Switzerland; at the same time, together with the sculptress Edith Maryon, he sculpted a remarkable statue of Christ (*The Representative of Humanity*), which is housed there; moreover, besides producing a number of extraordinary paintings and drawings, Steiner introduced a new way of painting (based on an extension of Goethe's theory of color) that is now taught at a number of art schools around the world. Again, in addition to composing mantric verses of spiritual poetry, Steiner also revived the ancient art of recitation ("speech formation") and wrote four *Mystery Plays* that are performed regularly by actors practicing this new form of speech. Further,

---

3. See Bibliography.

Steiner resurrected ancient temple dance, in a new form, as an art of movement ("eurythmy") based on cosmic-spiritual principles. This is taught in
Waldorf schools around the world and is practiced both as a performing art
and as a new form of movement therapy ("curative eurythmy").

Another key element of Steiner's spiritual research, one which proved indispensable for the present work, is his detailed exposition of cosmic cycles.
In this domain, his teaching concerning the second coming of Christ and the
significance of the 33 1/3-year cycle in this connection provides a fundamental key that allowed the door leading to the results presented here to open.

For the research presented in this book, it is Steiner's spiritual-scientific
findings in the realm of Christology that are particularly significant. Without
them, the research would not have been undertaken in the first place. One
of the most extraordinary discoveries made by Rudolf Steiner is that *two* children named Jesus were born. One of them was paid homage to by the three
kings as described in the Gospel of Saint Matthew, while the other was visited with great reverence by the shepherds, as described in the Gospel of
Saint Luke. This finding, discovered by Rudolf Steiner through his faculty
of conscious clairvoyance, is central to the content of this book. Before proceeding to examine the nature and implications of these discoveries, however, it is perhaps interesting to review his remarks (and those of other
anthroposophical researchers) concerning Anne Catherine Emmerich's
visions—since they, too, play a significant part in the narrative to follow.

When he was asked about the visions of Anne Catherine Emmerich as
recorded by Clemens Brentano, Steiner said—implying that he himself had
investigated Anne Catherine's work and confirmed it for himself to some
extent—"These contain the visions of an extraordinarily good somnambu-
list. Namely, these are the parts which relate to mirror vision. Without a
doubt, they contain exceptionally accurate material."[4] Elaborating upon
this, Georg Goelzer writes:

Anne Catherine Emmerich's vision of Golgotha is most interesting....
This Christian mystic, although she did not possess the faculty of
reading the past directly in face of the Sun of the timeless spirit, was

---

4. Rudolf Steiner's original statement concerning Anne Catherine Emmerich, upon which
Georg Goelzer elaborates, was in answer to a question following his lectures in September,
1908. The lectures were those published in English as *Egyptian Myths and Mysteries*
(Anthroposophic Press, Hudson, NY, 1971). Unfortunately, this edition, like the German,
does not contain the question and answer which is available in manuscript only.

undoubtedly able to behold the mirroring of this Sun reality on the waves of life in the light of the soul. Even though illusory thoughts and the soul's stormy emotional waves may distort the pure mirror image and cause confusion, nevertheless, when the soul is pure, its eye may receive individual visions of extraordinary depth. Nevertheless, in the case of such images, true knowledge is possible only in the light of the unified panorama of spiritual science itself. (Especially significant is [Emmerich's] description of the peculiar condition of the youth of Nain at his death, which is in surprising agreement with Rudolf Steiner's . . . indications.)[5]

This passage from Georg Goelzer's book is followed by a lengthy quotation from Anne Catherine Emmerich's description of the crucifixion on Golgotha. Ita Wegman, the physician who collaborated with Rudolf Steiner in pioneering a new form of medicine based on Steiner's anthroposophical spiritual science, was also interested in these descriptions. Liane Collot d'Herbois offers this personal recollection:

Dr. Madeleine van Deventer had two books in which Ita Wegman showed great interest. These were the volumes of *The Life of Christ Jesus according to the Visions of the Blessed Anne Catherine Emmerich*, the work of a mystic who experienced the whole of Christ's life in visions and who died in 1824. Besides much else, Emmerich also gave a very realistic description of the crucifixion. One day Ita Wegman disappeared into her room with these two large volumes. She was so deeply impressed by them that she did not see anyone for three days. She read the descriptions from beginning to end and scarcely allowed herself an hour's sleep.[6]

Many others have been impressed and deeply affected by Anne Catherine's account of the life of Christ (for example, Gerard Manley Hopkins and Jacques Maritain), yet until now it has been generally viewed merely as useful for the edification of the soul. However, as we shall see, Emmerich's account is not only edifying and uplifting but also, on the whole, *true*. I say "on the

---

5. Georg Goelzer, *Palladion, Gral und Grundstein* (Verlag am Goetheanum: Dornach/ Switzerland,1989), pp. 78–79.
6. Liane Collot d'Herbois, "Persönliche Erinnerungen an Ita Wegman," *Mitteilungen aus der anthroposophischen Arbeit in Deutschland*, vol. 44 (Stuttgart, Michaelmas, 1990), p. 203.

whole," because it would be nearly impossible to check every detail. What can be said is that, at least with respect to space (the geography and topography of Palestine) and time (the historical dating of the Christ events), Anne Catherine Emmerich's account of the life of Christ is very accurate indeed, and from this it follows that considerable confidence may be placed in her visions as a whole.

We are currently nearing the 2,000th anniversary of the birth of Jesus: December 6, 1999, or, cosmically, December 31/January 1, 1999/2000, when the Sun will return for the 2,000th time to the zodiacal position it held at the birth of Jesus, as will be discussed in the following pages. The question thus arises whether modern astronomical-chronological research can help determine this date with the same degree of certainty as that of his death. I believe that this date—and the dates of other major events in Christ's life— have in fact now been established, as will be set forth in what follows. With the help of Anne Catherine Emmerich's descriptions (supplemented by the Gospels and the indications of Rudolf Steiner), it has proved possible, furthermore, to reconstruct a day-by-day chronicle of Christ's life for much of His ministry. The authenticity of Anne Catherine's chronicle can, moreover, be independently verified by applying astronomical chronology to her calendar indications. The results of such astronomical-chronological research show that Anne Catherine's descriptions of the life of Christ during his ministry are consistent throughout with respect to the calendar, thus providing an internal control on the chronological validity of her descriptions of the rest of the life of Christ.

Using the information made available by Anne Catherine Emmerich and Rudolf Steiner to establish precise coordinates for Christ's life—and employing Steiner's indication concerning the significance of the 33 1/3-year cycle—we shall be in a position at the end of this work (see Afterword) to provide historical evidence to further support the accuracy of the claims made in this book.

Chapter One

Historical Overview

INTRODUCTORY REMARKS

By the very nature of its subject matter, much of this book is concerned with dates. In carrying out the research leading to the dating of events in the life of Christ, my motivation was not simply to determine these dates but rather, having determined them, to *apply* them. An immediate application was the computation of planetary positions on various dates with a view to unveiling the mystery of the star of the Magi and other cosmic mysteries. The importance of this approach is evident from the following statement by Rudolf Steiner:

> In Palestine, during the time when Jesus of Nazareth walked on Earth as Christ Jesus — during the three years of his life, from his thirtieth to his thirty-third year — the entire Being of the Cosmic Christ was acting uninterruptedly upon him, and was working into him. The Christ always stood under the influence of the entire cosmos. He made no step without this working of the cosmic forces into and in him.... It was always in accordance with the collective Being of the whole Universe, with whom the Earth is in harmony, that all that Christ Jesus did took place.[1]

One way of exploring the truth of this assertion is to compute planetary positions against the background of the signs of the zodiac for major events in the life of Christ, and to see whether a cosmic harmony prevailed between these configurations of the heavenly bodies above and the events and miracles of the earthly life of Christ below. This task has already been undertaken,

1. Rudolf Steiner, *The Spiritual Guidance of the Individual and Humanity.*

and the results show that there definitely is a striking correspondence between planetary configurations and the Christ events.[2] However, in order to compute these planetary configurations, the relevant dates had first to be established. Once discovered, these dates — or rather, their connection with certain time intervals in Christ's life — reveal a profound wisdom that sheds new light upon the very nature of Christ's life, as will emerge during the course of this book.

One could argue, of course, that Christianity has managed very well until now without knowing the exact dates of Christ's life and that such details are in any case irrelevant to the central mysteries of salvation and redemption. Without claiming in any way that such knowledge is necessary, or even important, for the salvation of the human being or the redemption of the Earth, the point of this book is that these dates, once known, can be applied, worked with, and understood in such a way that a deeper relationship to Christ is made possible; indeed, they open the door to a completely new perspective on Him. This new aspect has to do with the Cosmic Christ, who is revealed in the solar system as a whole (which can be regarded as an outer expression of the kingdom of heaven). As we consider this, however, we must at the same time bear in mind that Christ himself said: "My kingdom is not of this world" (John 18:36). In other words, there is a certain validity in regarding the Sun, Moon, and planets — the domain of the Cosmic Christ — as an outer manifestation of the kingdom of heaven, a point that will be developed further during the course of this book.

Paradoxical though it may seem, it is precisely knowledge of the concrete details of Christ's life that enables us to comprehend the Cosmic Christ. These details (more especially the dates) enable us to explore the heavenly correspondences that existed during Christ's life on Earth. At the same time, they open a new dimension of Christianity, one attuned to Christ as a *cosmic* reality, and it is upon this reality that this book aspires to shed some light. With the closing of two millennia of Christianity, it would seem that the time has come for humanity to approach the mystery of the Cosmic Christ. Here we may recall Christ's words concerning "the sign of the Son of Man in heaven" (Matthew 24:30), which imply a cosmic dimension of Christianity and call for humanity to look to the signs in the heavens and to begin to decipher them, as did the Magi of old. We can begin by contemplating the movements of the Sun, Moon, and planets against the background of the

2. Robert Powell, *Christian Hermetic Astrology: The Star of the Magi and the Life of Christ.*

signs of the zodiac in relation to corresponding stellar events during the life of Christ.[3] To lay a firm foundation for Cosmic Christianity, however, we must first establish secure dates for the life of Christ. To begin, then, let us consider the date of birth of Jesus, for this is the obvious starting point for our whole inquiry.

The Date of Birth

The birth of Jesus is traditionally celebrated by the Church on December 25. Prior to A.D. 354, however, the chosen date was January 6. Both of these dates, as shown below, are based on correspondences, that is, they are symbolical, and not *necessarily* based on historical fact. Our first inquiry, then, will examine the underlying significance of these traditional dates.

Let us first consider January 6, which is, incidentally, the date of the nativity still celebrated in the Armenian Church. This date was chosen in the course of the third century A.D. as the day on which to commemorate the birth of Jesus. Who made this choice and why?

To answer these questions, we must imagine the climate of early Christianity in Egypt — for it was above all in Alexandria, the city founded by Alexander the Great in 332 B.C., that the Church flourished most vigorously at that time. Here the ancient mystery-wisdom tradition of Egypt and the newly-emerging Christian religion met and clashed. Among the Church fathers who lived and worked in Alexandria were Clement of Alexandria (ca. 150–215 A.D.) and Origen (ca. 185–254 A.D.), two of the greatest teachers in the early history of the Church.

These and other early Church fathers were faced with a multitude of religious cults that derived from various ancient mystery traditions. As "apologists," they undertook the task of representing Christianity, which, they argued, differed from all pagan cults in its claim to *historicity*. Whereas the traditional mystery cults were directed primarily to polytheistic worship, Christianity emphasized the worship of the One — the Son of God, who had lived on Earth as a human being. Christianity is in fact centered on the being of Christ, the Second Person of the Godhead, who passed through *birth* and *death*. This distinguishes Christianity from all other religions, cults, and beliefs: Christianity has its basis in *the historical fact* of the life, death, and resurrection of Christ Jesus.

---

3. Robert Powell and Michael Brinch, *Christian Star Calendar.*

Although Christianity rests squarely on this historical event, and is unique among religious traditions in this regard, the *dates* of Christ's birth and death were not transmitted — at least no record of them has yet been discovered. The only two calendrical details recorded in the Gospel of Saint John set the crucifixion on the day of preparation for the Passover, which is said to have fallen on a Friday, that is, the day before the Sabbath, that year (i.e.,with the Sabbath, starting Friday evening). Nor is much help with dating to be expected from Jewish or Roman historians. To those in power at that time in Jerusalem (Pontius Pilate, Herod Antipas, and the priests and Pharisees comprising the Sanhedrin), Jesus was only a carpenter's son from Nazareth who — because he had taught and healed throughout the land and had agitated the people, drawing a following largely from the commonfolk — had died a common criminal's death upon a cross. No official source bothered to record anything more concerning Jesus of Nazareth. The startling paradox, then, is that the *historical fact* upon which Christianity rests — and it is precisely this historicity that sets Christianity apart — is nowhere documented, with the exception of the witness borne later by the four Gospels. Yet none of these mentions any explicit dates, even though they do contain a few calendrical indications. The early Church fathers were thus faced with solemnizing an historical fact for which they had no exact date. They wished, quite naturally, to celebrate the birth and death of the Messiah each year, but in the absence of any transmitted dates how could they proceed?

In the case of the death and resurrection, the solution was straightforward. Since the resurrection took place on the Sunday following the feast of the Passover, the annual commemoration of this event was specified to take place on the Sunday after the spring Full Moon, for the latter always coincided more or less with the onset of the Passover festival. In fact, in the year A.D. 33 the spring Full Moon (the first Full Moon after the vernal equinox) fell on Friday, April 3, the day of the crucifixion. The actual moment of the Full Moon was 7:45 P.M. Jerusalem time, and the Passover festival began at sunset (around 6:00 P.M.). By fixing Easter Sunday as the Sunday after the first spring Full Moon, the "archetype" established in the year A.D. 33 recurs each year, although usually only approximately, since the spring Full Moon falls on a Friday only once every seven years (on the average). It should be noted here, however, that only in the twentieth century have we been able, through astronomical chronology, to accurately establish the true historical date of the crucifixion (see Appendix I). Prior to this, the above-mentioned rule had been applied to determine the date of Easter Sunday without any definite knowledge, generally speaking, of the original date (April 5, A.D. 33) on which the resurrection in fact took place.

But what of the commemoration of the birth of Christ Jesus? The Alexandrian Church fathers in the third century chose January 6, and this date spread then throughout the Church. Their choice was influenced by the mystery cults prevailing in Egypt at that time. For instance, Saint Epiphanius of Salamis (ca. 315–403 A.D.) wrote concerning the festival in Alexandria dedicated to the goddess Koré, which was celebrated each year on the night of January 5/6: "On this night Koré—the Virgin—gave birth to Aion" (*Panarion* 51, 22, 10). This festival was essentially a solar cult, for Aion was identified with Helios, the Sun, believed by the Egyptians to be born (or reborn) on January 5/6. But why was this date chosen for the birth of Jesus?

Evidently the sages then living in Egypt believed that, in the Julian calendar (introduced by Julius Caesar in 46 B.C.), the winter solstice occurred on January 5/6. This was for them the date transmitted by tradition as the longest night of the year. In actual fact the longest night of the year at the time of Christ was December 22/23, but this was apparently not generally known to the people of Alexandria, who adhered to the traditional date. It is difficult to believe, however, that the reason for the two-week discrepancy between the traditional date and the actual date for the celebration of the winter solstice was entirely due to ignorance of the astronomical facts. Perhaps it was due to an error that arose with the introduction of the Julian calendar in place of the traditional Egyptian calendar. However that may be, the early Christians did take note of the solar phenomenon of the winter solstice, and we must remember that there was a natural correspondence for them between Christ and the Sun. Anastasios Sinaita of the Eastern Church wrote, for example:

> Helios (the Sun) has the first place in the sky and leads the heavenly dance. So is Christ, who is the spiritual Sun, placed above all the heavenly hierarchies and powers, for He is the leader, the door to the Father. (*Hexaemeron* 5)

To early Christians the identification of Christ with the spirit of the Sun was self-evident. For them, Christ was the Sun of righteousness, and the physical Sun was his outward symbol. Such analogic thinking was also prevalent in Egypt at that time and has been called the *hermetic* mode of thought, after the Egyptian sage Hermes. The presiding axiom of this mode of thinking is summarized in the so-called Emerald Table: "That which is above is like unto that which is below, and that which is below is like unto that which is above."[4] Early Christians living in Egypt and influenced by this hermetic mode of thought conceived of the physical Sun as an outer manifestation, or symbol, of the spiritual Sun (Christ). Just as the physical Sun was thought to be born (or reborn) each year on January 6, so did the Church fathers of Alexandria believe that the birthdate of Christ must have fallen on this day.

The Church fathers in the *West* arrived at the date of December 25 for the nativity by the same reasoning, for it was believed in Rome that the winter solstice — the longest night of the year — fell on December 24/25. Although more accurate than the traditional date of January 5/6 celebrated in Egypt, the longest night of the year at the time of Christ was in fact December 22/23. Nevertheless, the Roman followers of Mithras held their festival dedicated to the Invincible Sun on December 25. Each year, on this day, they celebrated the triumph of the Sun over the powers of darkness, which they held to be at their height on the night of December 24/25, the longest night of the year according to their belief. Just as the Sun (Helios) was thought to be born (or reborn) on December 25 of each year, after which its light and warmth would begin to increase, so the Roman Christians, since they had no historical testimony regarding the actual day of Christ's birth, considered that it too must have taken place on this day. The parallel is clear: the birthday of the physical Sun, Helios, ought to fall on the same day as that of its archetype, the spiritual Sun — Christ. Thus, by A.D. 354, December 25, previously the festival of the Invincible Sun, was being celebrated as the day of the nativity:

> But they name this day (December 25) also "the birthday of the Invincible Sun." Truly, who is as invincible as Our Lord, who cast down and triumphed over death? And if they call this day "the birthday of the Sun" then He is the Sun of righteousness, of whom the prophet Malachi said: "to the God-fearing His name will arise as the Sun of righteousness, and salvation is beneath His wings." (From a homily by Saint John Chrysostom; cf. A. Wilmart; "La collection des 38 homélies latines de St. Jean Chrysostome," *Journal of Theological Studies*, vol. 19, 1918, pp. 305–327.)

---

4. Anonymous, *Meditations on the Tarot. A Journey into Christian Hermeticism* (Rockport, MA: Element Books, 1993). Chapter 1 discusses the full text of the Emerald Table and describes in detail the analogical hermetic mode of thought.

We see then that the traditional dates assigned to the nativity were derived by way of *analogy*. In both cases the nativity was determined to coincide with the longest night of the year, *symbolizing* the birth of the Christ Sun. The actual moment of birth was (and still is) celebrated at midnight: December 24/25 in the West; January 5/6 in the East. If the underlying symbolism is understood, December 25 is still an appropriate date to celebrate the birth (or rebirth) of the spiritual Sun (Christ), for December 25 comes just three days after the winter solstice, which at the present time falls on December 21/22.

When, in the fourth century, Roman Christians adopted December 25 (in preference to January 6) as the date of the nativity, they nevertheless still continued to celebrate January 6, regarding it then as the date of the baptism in the Jordan rather than of the birth of Jesus. Moreover, since the three kings were believed to have visited the newborn child shortly after his birth, January 6 came to be celebrated also as the date of the Adoration of the Magi. The term *epiphany*, meaning "appearance," was associated with January 6, for it was believed that on this day, the star appeared over the place of Jesus' birth *and* that on this same day thirty years later the dove appeared above Him at the baptism.

The tradition of celebrating January 6 as the date of the baptism in the Jordan appears to derive from the gnostic Basilides, who taught in Alexandria in the second century A.D. Clement of Alexandria mentions a gnostic sect, followers of Basilides that celebrated the baptism on this day (*Stromata* I, 146, 1,2). It was certainly again by way of analogy with the mystery cult of Koré in Alexandria that the gnostics adopted January 6 as the date of the baptism: for them, the *baptism of Jesus* was actually the *birth of Christ*. This was their interpretation of the words the Father pronounced at that moment: "Thou art my Son whom this day I have begotten" (Luke 3:22). The gnostics maintained therefore that the real birth of Christ occurred at the baptism and that the date of January 6 corresponded to the baptism — the descent of Christ onto Earth — rather than to the physical birth of *Jesus*. They believed that, at the baptism, the *divine* being of Christ united with the *human* being of Jesus and was "born" at that moment. And so, they celebrated this "birth," i.e., the baptism, each year on that day. This practice spread subsequently to Rome, and January 6 is still celebrated by the Church as the date of the baptism. As we shall see, the historical baptism actually occurred in autumn, not in the middle of winter, a point to which we shall return later in greater detail in connection with the day-by-day chronicle of Christ's ministry. But first we will turn our attention to the determination of the true birth date of Jesus.

* * *

The visions of Anne Catherine Emmerich, as recorded by Clemens Brentano in *The Life of the Blessed Virgin Mary*, include detailed descriptions of the nativity itself, as well as precise geographical indications of its location in a cave at the south end of a hill to the east of Bethlehem. The Constantine-Basilica, which Saint Helena had built above the cave of the nativity, still stands on this very spot today. Anne Catherine communicated the following about the timing of the birth:

> The Blessed Virgin spent the Sabbath in the Cave of the Nativity in prayer and meditation.... In the *afternoon of the Sabbath*, when it is the Jewish custom to go for a walk, Joseph took the Blessed Virgin through the valley behind the cave to the tomb of Maraha, Abraham's nurse.... Mary had told Joseph that *tonight at midnight* would be the hour of the child's birth, for then the nine months since the Annunciation would have been completed.... [That night] I saw the radiance around the Blessed Virgin ever growing greater.... Meanwhile the Blessed Virgin, borne up in ecstasy, was now gazing downwards, adoring her God, whose Mother she had become and who lay on the Earth before her in the form of a helpless newborn child. I saw our Redeemer as a tiny child, shining with a light that overpowered all the surrounding radiance, and lying on the carpet at the Blessed Virgin's knees. (LBVM pp. 191–193) [author's emphasis]

According to this description, the birth took place around midnight on the day after the Sabbath. Since the Jewish Sabbath falls on Saturday, and the Jewish day begins at sunset, the Sabbath day extends from sunset Friday to sunset Saturday. The birth took place, therefore, around the midnight between Saturday and Sunday. This is the first detail to take note of.

Anne Catherine's visions indicate also that the birth took place during the Jewish month of Kislev. This is evident from her description of events following the birth. She states that the child was circumcised at dawn the day after the Sabbath following the birth, that is, Sunday morning, one week after the birth (cf. Luke 2:21). Regarding the next Sabbath, and the beginning of the Feast of the Dedication of the Temple, she says:

> This feast really begins on the 25th day of the month of Kislev, but as this fell on the evening of Friday. . . in the year of Jesus' birth, that is

to say, on the eve of the Sabbath, it was postponed to the evening of Saturday. . . or the 26th day of Kislev. It lasted eight days. [Thus the sixth day after the circumcision was the 25th day of Kislev, so that the circumcision happened on the nineteenth day of Kislev and the birth of Jesus on the twelfth day of Kislev.] (LBVM pp. 240–241)

Readers already familiar with the writings that describe Anne Catherine's visions will realize that I have omitted reference to the calendar dates on which she had the relevant visions. I have done this because these dates are not directly related to their calendar equivalents at the time of Christ (Friday, December 7, and Saturday, December 8), and they are misleading when it comes to dating the birth of Jesus. It is only the *Jewish* calendar dates and festivals communicated by Anne Catherine that are relevant, not the modern calendar dates on which she experienced the visions. If we do not understand that, we could easily conclude that the beginning of the Feast of the Dedication, two weeks after the birth of Jesus, fell on December 7/8, simply because this was the calendar date on which her vision of this event occurred. This indeed was the error Helmut Fahsel made in his monumental work *Der Wandel Jesu in der Welt*,[5] where he simply transposed the day-by-day account of Christ's ministry (as revealed by Anne Catherine) back in time to the years A.D. 31–34. In fact, the weekdays of the Julian calendar then in use in the Roman Empire for these particular years did partly coincide with the weekdays of the modern calendar on which Anne Catherine communicated her daily visions of the ministry (1821–1824). The concordance was even exact for the year A.D. 31 and for the first two months of the year A.D. 32; but from March, A.D. 32 onward an error of one day slipped in, because A.D. 32 was a leap year, whereas 1822 was not.

Despite this fallacy in Fahsel's transposition of dates, I take this opportunity to express grateful acknowledgment and deep indebtedness to Helmut Fahsel for arranging Anne Catherine Emmerich's visions of the ministry according to weekdays and calendar dates. In his work, Fahsel also reckoned the duration of Jesus' travels from town to town. His chronicle proved an indispensable resource for the chronological research into Christ's ministry presented in this book. Nevertheless, his simple calendrical transposition of 1821–1824 to A.D. 31–34 does not stand the test when comparing the Jewish calendar for A.D. 31–34 with the Jewish calendrical indications given by Anne Catherine Emmerich.

---

5. WJW pp. 93ff.

At the time of Christ, the Jewish calendar, not the Julian calendar employed by the Romans, was in use in Palestine. Hence it is clearly the Jewish calendar that is of primary importance in all chronological matters pertaining to the life of Christ. Thus the date of the crucifixion mentioned in the Gospel of Saint John refers to the Jewish calendar: namely, the day of preparation for the Passover, the 14th day of the month of Nisan. In A.D. 33, this was the same as April 3 in the Julian calendar. However, the date "April 3" would have been meaningless for the majority of Jews living in Palestine at that time. For them, this day was "Nisan 14." Their calendrical reference was naturally the days and months of the Jewish calendar. Similarly, the date Kislev 25 was known throughout Palestine as the start of the Feast of the Dedication. Indeed, it is the communication of this date in relation to the Sabbath that provides a key to the dating of the birth of Jesus. Assuming that Anne Catherine Emmerich's indication is correct, the birth took place thirteen days before this feast, on Kislev 12, around midnight Saturday/Sunday. For astronomical chronology, then, the problem is to determine when, historically, for those years in which the birth of Jesus might have taken place, Kislev 25 coincided in fact with the Sabbath (Friday/Saturday); or, which leads to the same result, when Kislev 12 coincided with Saturday/Sunday.

Knowledge of the Jewish calendar is obviously necessary to answer this question. It will also provide an essential guideline for the chronological research undertaken in this book. Here it suffices to point out that the occurrence of the New Moon more or less coincided with the start of a new month in the calendar of ancient Israel. A New Moon festival was celebrated on the evening of the first day of the new month, and the months were reckoned as "hollow" or "full," depending on whether they comprised 29 or 30 days (these usually alternated). In this way, the months corresponded closely with the phases of the Moon, for on average 29 1/2 days (actually 29.53 days) elapse from one New Moon to the next.

At some time in the history of Israel, a set of rules for specifying the Jewish calendar was devised, primarily to reconcile the inevitable discrepancies between solar and lunar reckoning. In principle, the first (Nisan), third (Sivan), fifth (Ab), seventh (Tishri) and eleventh (Shebat) months were consistently full, each containing 30 days, while the second (Iyyar), fourth (Tammuz), sixth (Elul), and tenth (Tebeth) months were consistently hollow, each containing 29 days. The remaining months — the eighth (Heshvan or Marcheshvan), the ninth (Kislev), and the twelfth (Adar) — could be either full or hollow. As we shall see when we look into Anne Catherine's calendar indications, these rules seem to have been applied in general — but not rigorously — by the time of Christ. (See Appendix II for a discussion of the Jewish calendar, and Appendix III for an investigation into Anne Catherine Emmerich's calendar indications.)

A study of the Jewish calendar dates indicated by Anne Catherine discloses that the beginning of a new month did, in fact, closely correspond to the astronomical New Moon. Often, indeed, the start of a new month fell on the same day as the New Moon, as may be seen from the reconstruction of the Jewish calendar for the time of Christ in Appendix III. Since the Jewish day began at sunset, the New Moon often took place a few hours before sunset. Frequently, too, the first day of the new month fell one day (sometimes two) after the day of the astronomical New Moon, in which case the new sickle of the Moon would generally have been already visible on the western horizon at sunset. This was the natural start of the lunar month for the people in ancient times who viewed the appearance of the sickle of the New Moon on the western horizon at sunset as the "birth" (or "rebirth") of the Moon, which heralded the start of the new month.

This method of counting alternate months of the year as either full (30 days) or hollow (29 days) did not guarantee that the months would remain precisely in step with the phases of the Moon. However, it was possible to regulate the sequence of months to coincide with the phases of the Moon — especially in the eighth and ninth months, Heshvan and Kislev, which could be either full or hollow. Therefore we can understand that, by the eighth or ninth month (Heshvan or Kislev), the occurrence of the New Moon could sometimes fall *after* the start of the new month. The month of Kislev in which Jesus was born actually started one and one-third days before the astronomical New Moon. But how is it possible to establish this?

To do so, we need to know in what *year* the birth of Jesus fell. For this, the following statement by Anne Catherine Emmerich provides the necessary clue: "Christ reached the age of thirty-three years and three times six weeks. I say three times six, because that figure was in that moment shown to me three times one after the other" (LBVM p. 145). Assuming that the crucifixion took place on Friday, April 3, A.D. 33 (as established in Appendix I), the birth must have occurred in the year 2 B.C., which is also the year favored by some early Christian writers, among them Epiphanius. To be precise, the birth took place, according to Sister Emmerich, on Kislev 12 in 2 B.C., and it follows from this that Christ Jesus attained the age of thirty-three on Kislev

12 in A.D. 32.[6] Since the astronomical New Moon at the start of the month of Kislev in A.D. 32 took place on November 21 at 9:15 P.M. Jerusalem time, the first day of the month of Kislev could possibly have started at sunset the following day, November 22, in which case Kislev 1 that year would equate with November 22/23. This means that Kislev 12, eleven days later, may well have coincided with December 2/3 in the year A.D. 32, exactly four calendar months prior to the crucifixion on April 3 of the following year. Even if Kislev 12 did not coincide precisely with December 2/3, A.D. 32, it must have been within a day or two of this date. Counting from Tuesday, December 2, A.D. 32, to Friday April 3, A.D. 33, gives seventeen full weeks plus a fraction (Tuesday to Friday), corresponding closely with the indication that "Christ reached the age of thirty-three years and three times six weeks." In other words, thirty-three years elapsed between Kislev 12, 2 B.C., and Kislev 12, A.D. 32; and a further eighteen weeks elapsed before the crucifixion.

Having provisionally established 2 B.C. as the birth year, the task remains to determine the Julian calendar date of Kislev 12 *in that year*. The New Moon at the start of the month of Kislev in 2 B.C. occurred at 1:20 A.M. Jerusalem time on November 27. Very often the first day of the Jewish month began at sunset on the same calendar date following the occurrence of the astronomical New Moon. In this case, Kislev 1 would equate with November 27/28, and Kislev 12 with December 8/9. However, since December 8 in 2 B.C. was a Monday, it does not fulfill the first condition referred to above, namely, that in the birth year of Jesus, Kislev 12 coincided with Saturday/Sunday. To fulfill this condition in 2 B.C., Kislev 12 must correspond to Saturday/Sunday, December 6/7. Thus, in the light of Anne Catherine Emmerich's indications, the birth of Jesus took place around midnight December 6/7 2 B.C. (see Table 1).

TABLE 1

THE BIRTH OF JESUS

The New Moon denoting the start of the month of Kislev took place at 1:20 A.M. Jerusalem time on November 27, 2 B.C. However, Kislev 1 had already started at sunset on November 25, 1 1/3 days prior to this. (* denotes Sabbath)

6. Note that in the historical method of dating there is no year 0, and the count goes straight from 1 B.C. to A.D. 1. Someone born in 2 B.C. would have attained the age of 1 in 1 B.C., the age of 2 in A.D. 1, and the age of 3 in A.D. 2, etc., and the age of 33 in A.D. 32.

Kislev 1	Tue/Wed	25/26 November	New Moon Festival
Kislev 2	Wed/Thu	26/27 November	
Kislev 3	Thu/Fri	27/28 November	
*Kislev 4	Fri/Sat	28/29 November	
Kislev 5	Sat/Sun	29/30 November	
Kislev 6	Sun/Mon	30/ 1 December	
Kislev 7	Mon/Tue	1/ 2 December	
Kislev 8	Tue/Wed	2/ 3 December	
Kislev 9	Wed/Thu	3/ 4 December	
Kislev 10	Thu/Fri	4/ 5 December	
*Kislev 11	Fri/Sat	5/ 6 December	
Kislev 12	Sat/Sun	6/ 7 December	Birth of Jesus
Kislev 13	Sun/Mon	7/ 8 December	
Kislev 14	Mon/Tue	8/ 9 December	
Kislev 15	Tue/Wed	9/10 December	
Kislev 16	Wed/Thu	10/11 December	
Kislev 17	Thu/Fri	11/12 December	
*Kislev 18	Fri/Sat	12/13 December	
Kislev 19	Sat/Sun	13/14 December	Circumcision
Kislev 20	Sun/Mon	14/15 December	
Kislev 21	Mon/Tue	15/16 December	
Kislev 22	Tue/Wed	16/17 December	
Kislev 23	Wed/Thu	17/18 December	
Kislev 24	Thu/Fri	18/19 December	
*Kislev 25	Fri/Sat	19/20 December	Feast of the Dedication
Kislev 26	Sat/Sun	20/21 December	of the Temple started

The sequence of days in the month of Kislev, 2 B.C., is listed in Table 1, where the day count shows that Kislev 1 fell on November 25/26. The preceding month of Heshvan, having completed 29 (or more likely 30) days, the New Moon festival of Kislev could have been celebrated on the evening of Tuesday, November 25 in 2 B.C. Assuming that dusk, which denoted the start of the new day, occurred around 5:20 P.M. Jerusalem time on November 25, the New Moon then fell 32 hours later, at 1:20 A.M. Jerusalem time on November 27. Thus Kislev 1 started 32 hours (= 1 1/3 days) prior to the astronomical New Moon. By counting 30 days in that month of Kislev, making it a "full" month, the start of the next month (Tebeth) would have been brought back closer into step with the Moon's phases.

*   *   *

Using Anne Catherine Emmerich's indications as a basis for research, we can establish that the birth of Jesus took place around midnight between Saturday and Sunday, December 6/7, in 2 B.C.[7] This result differs by one year and eighteen days from the most famous dating of Jesus' birth, that made by Dionysius Exiguus in A.D. 525. Dionysius concluded that the birth took place on December 24/25, 1 B.C., that is, just one week prior to January 1, A.D. 1, the date that Dionysius chose as the beginning of the Christian era. Considering that Dionysius had little upon which to base his study, apart from a few remarks by the early Church fathers, the date he arrived at for the birth of Jesus is remarkably close to the actual historical date of December 6/7, 2 B.C., which it has been only recently possible to determine.

Many readers may object that December 6/7, 2 B.C., is untenable as the birth date of Jesus, since Herod the Great is generally held to have died in 4 B.C. This assumption is the primary reason that most modern biblical chronologists place the birth of Jesus before 4 B.C. Without tackling the problem of dating the death of Herod at this point, it will have to suffice to refer to the work of the theologian Florian Riess (*Das Geburtsjahr Christi*, Freiburg, 1880), supported more recently by Ormond Edwards (*The Time of Christ*, Floris Books, Edinburgh, 1986), both of whom conclude that Herod died no more than three months after the lunar eclipse on January 10 in 1 B.C. Ormond Edwards bases his conclusion on evidence presented by coins minted close to the beginning of Herod's reign, combined with a new consideration of the Jewish historian Josephus' count of the years of his reign.

In a previous work, *The Star of the Magi and the Life of Christ*, I undertook an investigation of Herod's death in connection with the star of the Magi and came to the same conclusion as Ormond Edwards regarding the death of Herod in 1 B.C. At that time, I examined the whole question of the life of Herod in relation to the birth of Jesus as described in the Gospel of Saint

---

7. Elsewhere Anne Catherine Emmerich said: "The actual date of Christ's birth, as I always see it, is four weeks earlier than its celebration by the Church" (LBVM p. 165). This remark holds true if the *original* date of birth celebrated by the Church is taken (i.e., January 6.), for the historical date was December 6 (or rather the night of December 6/7). Interestingly, the date December 6 — Saint Nicholas Day — is celebrated in many countries as a presentiment of Christmas day, and in some countries children receive presents this day. In my book *The Star of the Magi and the Life of Christ,* I have shown that December 6 was the actual date of the birth of Jesus, since the birth occurred shortly before midnight on the night of December 6/7.

Matthew (taking into account Anne Catherine's indications concerning the star of the Magi). Here it is worth noting that the visit of the Magi (which obviously took place before Herod's death) is not mentioned in the account of the birth given in the Gospel of Saint Luke, to which we have been directing our attention in the foregoing. The nativity described in the Gospel of Saint Matthew will be considered later.

The Date of the Baptism

The first two verses of the second chapter of the Gospel of Saint Luke state:

> 1. In those days a decree went out from Caesar Augustus that all the world should be enrolled.
> 2. This was the first enrollment, when Quirinius was governor of Syria.

This reference to Quirinius was examined thoroughly by Emil Schürer in his book, *The History of the Jewish People in the Age of Christ Jesus*. According to Schürer, Quirinius was very likely governor of Syria in 3–2 B.C., and definitely so in A.D. 6–7. Our date for the birth — December 6/7, 2 B.C. — fits well, then, with this chronological indication given in the Gospel of Saint Luke.

Two further important chronological indications are given in the third chapter of the Gospel of Saint Luke:

> 1–3. In the fifteenth year of the reign of Tiberius Caesar, Pontius Pilate being governor of Judea, and Herod being tetrarch of Galilee . . . the word of God came to John the son of Zechariah in the wilderness; and he went into all the region about the Jordan, preaching a baptism of repentance for the forgiveness of sins.
> 21–22. Now when all the people were baptized, and when Jesus also had been baptized and was praying, the heaven was opened . . . Jesus, when he began his ministry, was about thirty years of age.

Let us combine these references with Anne Catherine's indications and see whether we can close in on the date of the baptism in the Jordan. Here Luke's statement regarding " the fifteenth year of the reign of Tiberius" is of central importance. According to J. K. Fotheringham, who applied astronomical chronology to establish the date of the crucifixion as April 3, A.D. 33:

Technical chronology proves just as decisively that the fifteenth year of Tiberius was the year A.D. 28–29. . . . The only question is whether the fifteenth year of Tiberius began in Nisan (spring) of A.D. 28 or in the autumn of that year. (TC p. 146)

Subsequently Ormond Edwards was able to establish from evidence provided by the dating of a coin that the fifteenth year of Tiberius in fact extended from the autumn of A.D. 28 to the autumn of A.D. 29. The specification of the fifteenth year of Tiberius thus tallies precisely with Anne Catherine Emmerich's indication that "the word of God" came to John during the month of Nisan. As we shall see, the Nisan concerned was in the year A.D. 29. In other words, John began his baptizing activity after the month of Nisan (spring) of A.D. 29.

The Gospel of Saint Luke states that, at the baptism, Jesus "was about thirty years of age." According to our calculations, Jesus turned thirty on Kislev 12, A.D. 29. If Luke's "about thirty years" is interpreted in a strict sense, the baptism must have taken place towards the end of the year 29 (since Kislev 12 corresponded approximately to December 5/6 that year). With the help of Anne Catherine's indications, however, it is possible to arrive at an exact date.

As in the case of her description of the birth of Jesus, where the date Kislev 12 in the Jewish calendar was found by counting back from the beginning of the Feast of the Dedication (Kislev 25), so the date of the baptism can be determined by counting back from the beginning of the Feast of Tabernacles (Tishri 15) in the autumn of A.D. 29. In her day-by-day account of the travels of Jesus in the period after the baptism, Anne Catherine mentions *three* Sabbaths before the beginning of the Feast of Tabernacles, when Jesus approached the town of Dibon on the east side of the Jordan (northeast of the place of baptism). Again it is the Sabbath — the seventh day — that provides the key to the specification of the weekdays, for Anne Catherine beheld the start of the Feast of Tabernacles as on the third day after the Sabbath, that is, Tuesday (starting Monday evening), since the Sabbath is Saturday (starting Friday evening). This means, according to her account, that Tishri 15 fell on Monday/Tuesday in the year of the baptism.

In A.D. 29, the New Moon at the start of the month of Tishri occurred at 5:00 P.M. Jerusalem time on Monday, September 26. At sunset on this date, the first day of Tishri must have begun; and then, fourteen days later, at sunset on Monday, October 10, the fifteenth day of Tishri would have begun. Since Tishri is the seventh month of the year, it is reckoned as a "full" month

(30 days) and the preceding month (Elul) as "hollow" (29 days). Counting back three Sabbaths (Saturdays) from Monday, October 10, we arrive at Saturday, September 24, in the year 29 A.D., which means that the Sabbath would have started at sunset on Friday, September 23. This Sabbath was the twenty-seventh day of the month of Elul (Elul 27, see Table 2).

TABLE 2

THE BAPTISM OF JESUS

The New Moon denoting the start of the month of Tishri took place at 5:00 P.M. Jerusalem time on September 26, A.D. 29. The first day of the month of Tishri (Tishri 1) started at sunset on this day. (*denotes Sabbath)

Elul 26	Thu/Fri	22/23 September	Baptism
*Elul 27	Fri/Sat	23/24 September	
Elul 28	Sat/Sun	24/25 September	
Elul 29	Sun/Mon	25/26 September	
Tishri 1	Mon/Tue	26/27 September	New Moon Festival
Tishri 2	Tue/Wed	27/28 September	
Tishri 3	Wed/Thu	28/29 September	
Tishri 4	Thu/Fri	29/30 September	
*Tishri 5	Fri/Sat	30/1 October	
Tishri 6	Sat/Sun	1/2 October	
Tishri 7	Sun/Mon	2/3 October	
Tishri 8	Mon/Tue	3/4 October	
Tishri 9	Tue/Wed	4/5 October	
Tishri 10	Wed/Thu	5/6 October	
Tishri 11	Thu/Fri	6/7 October	
*Tishri 12	Fri/Sat	7/8 October	
Tishri 13	Sat/Sun	8/9 October	
Tishri 14	Sun/Mon	9/10 October	
Tishri 15	Mon/Tue	10/11 October	Start of the Feast of Tabernacles

We turn now to Anne Catherine's description of the events surrounding the baptism:

Jesus, walking more quickly than Lazarus, reached John's place of baptism two hours before him. . . . A crowd more numerous than usual was assembled to whom John was with great animation preaching of the nearness of the Messiah and of penance, proclaiming at the same time that the moment was approaching for him to retire from his office of teacher. Jesus was standing in the throng of listeners. John felt His presence. He saw Him also, and that fired him with zeal and filled his heart with joy. But he did not on that account interrupt his discourse, and when he had finished he began to baptize. He had already baptized very many and it was drawing on ten o'clock, when Jesus in His turn came down among the aspirants to the pool of baptism. John bowed low before Him, saying "I ought to be baptized by Thee, and comest Thou to me?" Jesus answered: "Suffer it to be so now, for so it becometh us to fulfill all justice that thou baptize Me and I by thee be baptized." He said also: "Thou shalt receive the baptism of the Holy Spirit and of blood." [After the baptism] Jesus journeyed that same day with His followers the distance of a couple of hours towards Jerusalem to a little, obscure place whose name sounded like Bethel. . . . Jesus celebrated the Sabbath in this place. (LJC i. pp. 438, 444–445)

From the above description, it is evident that Jesus was baptized on the morning of the day preceding the Sabbath, i.e., at 10:00 A.M. on Friday morning. Since this was the first of *three* Sabbaths that elapsed in the period from the baptism to the start of the Feast of Tabernacles, it must have been the Sabbath of Friday/Saturday, September 23/24. The baptism therefore took place at 10:00 A.M., on Friday, September 23, A.D. 29 — or Elul 26 in the Jewish calendar (see Table 2).

From Elul 26 to Kislev 12 is two and one-half months, which means that Jesus was two and one-half months short of his thirtieth birthday when he was baptized. This fits the chronological indication, given by Saint Luke, that Jesus was about thirty years of age; and it concurs with the supposition of many early Christian authors that the baptism took place in the autumn. Having established the date of the baptism — and therewith the start of the ministry — to be Friday September 23, A.D. 29, we are now in a position to reconstruct Christ's ministry on the basis of Anne Catherine Emmerich's daily communications. But before we undertake this, we must look in detail at the question of the *duration* of the ministry.

The Duration of Christ's Ministry

Throughout the history of Christianity, many theories have been put forward concerning the length of Christ's ministry. The estimates most frequently referred to are:

(1) a one-year ministry, advocated by Clement of Alexandria and Origen (second/third centuries), since only *one* Passover is mentioned in the synoptic gospels (Mark 14:1);

(2) a two-year ministry, supported by Epiphanius (fourth century), since the Gospel of Saint John mentions *three* Passovers;

(3) a three-year ministry, propounded by Eusebius (third/fourth centuries), who thought that in addition to the three Passovers mentioned in the Gospel of Saint John (2:13; 6:4; 11:55), there was an *extra year* of Christ's ministry between the Passovers mentioned in 2:13 and 6:4.

In each of these three estimates, the actual duration is usually reckoned as somewhat longer than the exact period in years. Thus, if the traditional date of the baptism (January 6) is taken as the date of baptism, then the Passover follows about three months later, since the Passover coincides more or less with Easter. This means that the duration of the ministry would have been reckoned to be one and one-quarter, two and one-quarter, or three and one-quarter years.

In the light of Anne Catherine's indications, as we have shown, the baptism occurred on the morning of Friday, September 23, A.D. 29, when Jesus was approaching thirty years of age. Moreover, as shown in Appendix I, the crucifixion took place on the afternoon of Friday, April 3, A.D. 33, when he was thirty-three years and eighteen weeks old. From these dates it is possible to establish that the duration of Christ's ministry was approximately three and one-half years. This length of time is indicated indirectly also in a passage of the Gospel of Saint Luke that immediately follows the account of the baptism and the temptation in the wilderness. After the temptation, Luke reports that Jesus went up to Galilee, and

came to Nazareth, where he had been brought up; and he went to the synagogue, as his custom was, on the Sabbath day. And he stood up to read; and there was given to him the book of the prophet Isaiah. He opened the book and found the place where it was written: "The Spirit of the Lord is upon me, because he has anointed me to preach good news to the poor. He has sent me . . . to proclaim the acceptable year of the Lord." And he closed the book, and gave it back to the attendant, and sat down; and the eyes of all in the synagogue were fixed on him. And he began to say to them, "Today this scripture has been fulfilled in your hearing." . . . And he said, "Truly, I say to you no prophet is acceptable in his own country. But in truth I tell you, there were many widows in Israel in the days of Elijah, when the heaven was shut up for *three years and six months.*" (Luke 4:16–25)

This chronological indication of three and one-half years in the Gospel of Saint Luke can be interpreted as an indirect reference to the duration of Christ's ministry. We also read in the Letter of James: "Elijah was a man of like nature with ourselves and he prayed fervently that it might not rain, and for three years and six months it did not rain on the Earth" (James 5:17). Christ, however, came as the "wellspring of the water of eternal life" (John 4:14), which gushed forth during the three and one-half years of his ministry, thus "balancing out" the three and one-half years of Elijah. The drought in the days of Elijah, "when the heaven was shut up for three years and six months," was compensated during the ministry of Christ, who said to the Samaritan woman at Jacob's well: "Every one who drinks of this water will thirst again, but whoever drinks of the water that I shall give him will never thirst; the water that I shall give him will become in him a spring of water welling up to eternal life" (John 4:13–14).

An interval of about three and one-half years is also referred to in the Book of Daniel (12:11), where a period of desolation lasting 1290 days is mentioned. Again, in the Book of Revelation, an interval of three and one-half years is mentioned several times:

(i) "[T]hey will trample over the holy city for forty-two months" (11:2);
(ii) "And I will grant my two witnesses power to prophesy for 1,260 days" (11:3);
(iii) "And the woman fled into the wilderness, where she has a place prepared by God, in which to be nourished for 1,260 days" (12:6);
(iv) "And the beast . . . was allowed to exercise authority for forty-two months" (13:5).

Since three and one-half years amounts to 1,278 days, the period of 1,260 days is slightly less, and that of 1,290 days slightly more, than three and one-half years, whereas forty-two months is exactly three and one-half years. The time-periods given in Apocalypse texts (i) and (ii) are more or less identical. Here the principle of "balancing out" is indicated, which can be thought of in terms of cosmic scales of justice. If the Antichrist is "allowed to exercise authority for forty-two months," this is because Christ's influence held sway on Earth for the three and one-half years between the baptism in the Jordan and the resurrection.

A further indication of the working of the cosmic scales of justice is that, according to (i), the anti-Christian powers despoil that which is holy for three and one-half years, and according to (ii), the two witnesses of God are able to prophesy for three and one-half years. Furthermore, the "forty-two months" of the Antichrist concurs with the "period of desolation" of 1,290 days spoken of by the prophet Daniel. On a cosmic scale, the three and one-half "years of grace" of Christ's ministry balance out the three and one-half years during which the Antichrist will be allowed to exercise his authority on Earth. It is quite extraordinary also that, when the number of days is counted from the baptism (Friday, September 23, A.D. 29) to the resurrection, (Sunday, April 5, A.D. 33), the same 1,290 days appears again!

The Gap in Anne Catherine Emmerich's Account of the Ministry

As mentioned earlier in the biographical sketch, Anne Catherine Emmerich began to communicate her day-by-day account of the ministry of Christ to Clemens Brentano on July 29, 1820. Counting the days from then till her death on February 9, 1824, yields 1,290 days, the same period of approximately three and one-half years again! Theoretically, therefore, it would have been possible for her to relate the *entire* 1,290 days of the ministry of Christ, from the baptism up to the resurrection, assuming that she was attuned to Christ's life day by day in her own life, which, as will emerge in the following, was indeed the case. In fact, however, owing to a six-month period in 1823 during which Clemens Brentano was away, and owing to shorter periods of illness during which she was unable to relate anything, the period of 1,290 days was reduced to less than three years of reported visions. This must be taken into account in reconstructing Christ's ministry from her communications, for it implies that there must be a gap in her account. But where does this gap lie? And why did it escape the notice of Clemens Brentano and others who have occupied themselves with Anne Catherine Emmerich's visions?

To answer these questions, it will be helpful to provide an overview of these visions. From the start of her daily communications concerning Christ's ministry, which began on July 29, 1820, six main periods can be distinguished:

(a) July 29, 1820–March 29, 1821: The last eight months of the ministry, leading up to the crucifixion.
(b) March 30, 1821–June 1, 1821: The crucifixion, the resurrection, and subsequent events.
(c) June 2, 1821–April 28, 1823: The four months prior to the baptism; then from the baptism to the sending out of the apostles.
(d) April 29, 1823–October 21, 1823: No communication (due to Clemens Brentano's absence).
(e) October 22, 1823–January 8, 1824: Reconstruction of the first eleven weeks of period (d), from the sending out of the apostles onward.
(f) January 9, 1824–February 9, 1824: Day-by-day communications concerning the ministry resumed, then discontinued (due to ill health).

These six periods do not take into account brief interruptions in the visions owing to illness or other causes, nor are all the boundaries between the periods exact. For example, after the start of the day-by-day account of the four months prior to the baptism (period [c], which began on June 2, 1821), communication of details of events following the resurrection (period [b]) intervened for two months, until August 4, 1821. There was thus an overlap of two months during which period (b) extended into period (c). Similarly, much that Anne Catherine related concerning the Passion was revealed during the Easter week of other years, not just 1821.

When Clemens Brentano returned after his six-month absence (period [d]) he found, much to his disappointment, that during this time Anne Catherine Emmerich had continued to receive a day-by-day revelation of Christ's ministry throughout the period. On Tuesday, October 21, 1823, he read to her his last notes, which had ended on April 28, at the point where, in the mountains northwest of Garisma, Christ was teaching the disciples in preparation for their apostolic missions. When Brentano finished reading these notes, Anne Catherine Emmerich said that she saw everything again with her spiritual vision and promised that she would continue the revelation as best she could from the point at which it had been broken off. Thus she resumed on Wednesday, October 22, with the vision that belonged to Wednesday, April 30, communicating all she had then beheld after the dispersion of the apostles. She proceeded in this way, reconstructing a period of almost eleven weeks, until Thursday, January 8, 1824, after which she stopped communicating the "lost" day-by-day ministry any further, thus leaving a gap in the record. But during this period (October 22 to January 8) she was able to communicate almost eleven weeks of the revelation that she had originally received from Wednesday, April 30, to Sunday, July 13, 1823.

Brentano believed that the revelation up to July 13, 1823 completed the cycle that Anne Catherine Emmerich had begun on July 29, 1820. From this date onward, until March 29, 1821, she had revealed, day by day, the last eight months of the ministry up to the crucifixion. He was convinced that the revelation of the *entire* ministry had been given him at this point, excepting fifteen missing days (July 14 to July 28). The fact is, however, that 313 days were missing, not fifteen days, and this can be shown by reference to Anne Catherine's own communications.

With the publication in Germany, beginning in 1980, of Clemens Brentano's original notes, new insight into the duration of Christ's ministry was made possible. A three-volume edition of *The Life of Our Lord and Saviour Jesus Christ* (based on Clemens Brentano's notes) had been published after Brentano's death by Carl Schmöger. The fact that Schmöger changed an important detail in the course of his editing only came to light with the publication of the original notes. This detail was communicated by Anne Catherine on Tuesday, September 11, 1821, and relates to the period preceding the baptism in the Jordan. Her account of the baptism itself followed seventeen days later, on Friday, September 28, 1821.

According to our earlier investigations, the historical date of the baptism was Friday, September 23, A.D. 29, which corresponds to Elul 26 in the Jewish calendar. By subtracting seventeen days from the date that Anne Catherine Emmerich communicated the detail in question, September 11, 1821, we arrive at Tuesday, September 6, A.D. 29, which corresponds to Elul 9 that year. On Elul 9, Anne Catherine saw Jesus and five disciples travel after dark (the night of Monday/Tuesday) from Kisloth (near Mount Tabor) to Nazareth. Instead of entering Nazareth, however, they stayed with a small community of Essenes living close by. Jesus was put up in the house of an old Essene named Eliud. During the course of the day (Tuesday), his mother, Mary, came to the house of Eliud and talked with Jesus. The English translation of Schmöger's edition reads:

Jesus talked much with His Mother on this day, for she came to Him two or three times. He told her that He would go up to Jerusalem *three* times for the Passover, but that the last time would be one of great affliction for her. (LJC i p. 366) [Italics are author's emphasis.]

According to the original notes, however, Jesus told Mary that he would travel to Jerusalem *four* times for the Passover (LJ i pp. 90–91). Historically, these four journeys took place during the month of Nisan in the spring of the years A.D. 30, 31, 32, and 33. At the fourth Passover, on the day of preparation (Nisan 14, A.D. 33), the crucifixion took place. If this indication concerning four Passovers had been taken seriously, and not been changed to three, the true duration of the ministry (three and one-half years) would have been discovered long ago.[8] But why was it changed to three?

Anne Catherine's report that Jesus said he would go to Jerusalem four times for the Passover was changed because Clemens Brentano, and later Carl Schmöger, believed that her two and one-half year day-by-day revelation gave a complete account of the ministry, apart from a short fifteen-day gap. For this reason Clemens Brentano wrote in a footnote: "She made a slip of the tongue; it should be three times" (LJ i p. 90); and Carl Schmöger changed the text accordingly from four to three. However, when various statements made by Anne Catherine Emmerich are taken in conjunction with certain indications given in the Gospel of Saint John, it becomes evident that the gap was in fact about ten months (313 days) in length, that the ministry therefore lasted three and one-half years, and that there were four Passovers rather than three.

In the tenth chapter of the Gospel of Saint John, prior to the raising of Lazarus, it is written that Jesus was in Jerusalem for the Feast of the Dedication: "It was the Feast of the Dedication at Jerusalem; it was winter, and Jesus was walking in the temple, in the portico of Solomon" (John 10:22–23). Now, the Feast of the Dedication of the Temple, as referred to earlier, began

---

8. Further corroboration that the ministry lasted three and one-half years is given in Anne Catherine Emmerich's account of the words spoken by Jesus on October 6, A.D. 29, two weeks after the baptism. "They then spoke of John's great zeal, and remarked upon the handsome and strong appearance of Jesus. Jesus answered that in three and one-half years' time they would see nothing more of strength and beauty in his appearance; his body would become so disfigured as to be unrecognizable." This reference, shortly after the baptism, to the disfiguring of his body through the crucifixion, clearly indicates a period of three and one-half years for the ministry.

on Kislev 25, falling in December or late November. But in Anne Catherine Emmerich's day-by-day descriptions of the travels of Jesus, she nowhere describes him as visiting Jerusalem at this time of the year. The following observations regarding the four Feasts of the Dedication can be made on the basis of her descriptions:

First Feast of the Dedication. The evening of the day after the Sabbath, Sunday evening, December 18, A.D. 29, was the start of Kislev 25 in the Jewish calendar. On that evening Jesus celebrated the beginning of the Feast of the Dedication in the synagogue at Thebez in Samaria (present-day Tubas, about nine miles northeast of Jacob's well). He was on his way to Galilee for the wedding at Cana. (LJC ii p. 33)

Second Feast of the Dedication. On the evening of the start of the Sabbath, Friday evening, December 8, A.D. 30, Kislev 25 began. On that evening Jesus taught in the synagogue at Capernaum, on the north side of the Sea of Galilee (Lake Tiberius). During the following period (lasting over two weeks), he visited various towns to the northwest of the Sea of Galilee. (LJC iii p. 93)

Third Feast of the Dedication. Missing from Anne Catherine Emmerich's account.

Fourth Feast of the Dedication. In November and December, A.D. 32, Jesus was crossing the Arabian desert after visiting Chaldea, prior to returning to Palestine in January, A.D. 33, for the three months leading up to the crucifixion. (LJC iii p. 519–579)

It is evident from the above that the reference in the Gospel of Saint John to Jesus' presence in Jerusalem at the Feast of the Dedication can only refer to A.D. 31. As if he were somehow aware of this, Helmut Fahsel, in his description of Anne Catherine's account of the Tuesday prior to Passion week (historically Tuesday, March 24, A.D. 33), wrote the following:

Early that morning He taught the disciples (in Bethany) in the house where they were staying (belonging to Lazarus). During the day He spoke in the Temple (in Jerusalem), without the presence of the Pharisees. The disciples, stimulated by what He had taught them, asked

Him concerning the meaning of "Thy Kingdom come." Jesus spoke at length about this, and also that He and the Father are one (John 10:30), and that He would go to the Father (John 16:16)—all of which He had already touched upon once before in Jerusalem at the Feast of the Dedication. (WJW p. 377)

This must refer to Jesus' presence in Jerusalem at the Feast of the Dedication in A.D. 31. In that year, Kislev 25 started on the evening of November 28. With the help of Saint John's Gospel, then, a detail belonging to the "missing year" (missing from Anne Catherine Emmerich's account of the ministry) is filled in, allowing us to deduce that Jesus was in Jerusalem for the Feast of the Dedication at the end of November/start of December in the year 31.

The only further relevant information provided in the Gospel of Saint John is that Jesus "went away again [after the Feast of the Dedication] across the Jordan to the place where John at first baptized, and there he remained. And many came to him; and they said, 'John did no sign, but everything that John said about this man was true.' And many believed in him there" (John 10:40–42).

Chapter 11 begins with the account of Lazarus' illness, death, and resuscitation from the dead by Jesus. Now, according to Anne Catherine's account of the last period of Christ's ministry, the raising of Lazarus occurred at the end of the month of Tammuz in A.D. 32 (see Appendix IV, where the date of the raising of Lazarus is identified as July 26, A.D. 32, which corresponds to Tammuz 28). This implies that there is a gap of almost eight months in the Gospel of Saint John, separating chapter 10 and chapter 11: from the Feast of the Dedication, which ended on December 5, A.D. 31, to the raising of Lazarus on July 26, A.D. 32. All that we are told by Saint John about Jesus' activity during this period is that "he went across the Jordan to the place where John first baptized" (John 10:40).

Most of this eight-month period falls in the "missing period" (the 313 days lacking in Anne Catherine Emmerich's account). In fact, the missing period starts in the summer of A.D. 31 and extends to a point several weeks before the raising of Lazarus. But, apart from Jesus' visit to Jerusalem for the Feast of the Dedication in A.D. 31, can we establish that any other event took place during this missing period?

Here again the Gospel of Saint John can support us. Comparing this Gospel with Anne Catherine's description, we can see that the two accounts agree chronologically—as is made clear in the chronicle of the ministry presented in Part II of this book. It emerges that the other three Gospels are not arranged strictly chronologically and that the order of certain events they present is occasionally displaced. The Gospel of Saint John, in contrast, is chronologically accurate; and the sequence of events it presents conforms to the historical account given by Anne Catherine Emmerich. More than any other gospel, the Gospel of Saint John should be able, then, to help us fill in details of the missing period of the ministry.

We have shown above that the presence of Jesus in Jerusalem at the Feast of the Dedication, as described in the Gospel of Saint John, belongs to the missing year. Although Anne Catherine Emmerich nowhere recounts this event directly in her day-by-day account of the ministry, she nevertheless refers to it (as a forthcoming event) toward the end of the period prior to the missing ten months:

> When He and the disciples started for Bethsaida, they directed their steps to the south of the Jordan bridge. On their way they came, this side of Bethsaida, to an inn where His mother, the widow of Nain, Lia, and two other women, were waiting to take leave of Him, because He was now going to teach on the other side of the Jordan. Mary was very much afflicted. She had a private interview with Jesus, in which she shed abundant tears and begged Him not to go to Jerusalem for the Feast of the Dedication of the Temple.... He told her that He must fulfill the mission for which His Father had sent Him. (LJC iii p. 461)

This reference to Jesus' intention to travel to Jerusalem for the Feast of the Dedication could have made it clear to Clemens Brentano, and also to Carl Schmöger, that her revelation of the ministry was incomplete. Taken together with her indications concerning four Passovers, they could have deduced that a period amounting to somewhat less than one year was missing from her account of the ministry. Unfortunately, neither took the necessary step. But let us return to the Gospel of Saint John in order to determine what else of the missing period may be revealed there.

To orient ourselves, let us turn to chapter 6. There it is mentioned that "the Passover, the feast of the Jews, was at hand" (John 6:4). Following this, Saint John describes the feeding of the five thousand, the walking on the water, and the sermon in the synagogue at Capernaum where Jesus referred to himself as the bread of life. All of this accords with Anne Catherine Emmerich's account. According to the chronicle of the ministry established on the basis of her account (presented later in this book), the feeding of the five thousand took place on the afternoon of Monday, January 29, A.D. 31, on a mountain close to the town of Bethsaida-Julius; that night—Monday/ Tuesday—the walking on the water occurred; and, after visiting some places around the Sea of Galilee, Jesus then arrived in Capernaum on the last day of January and began his teaching concerning the bread of life. On the evening of the Sabbath, Friday evening, February 2, A.D. 31, he continued this teaching in the synagogue at Capernaum (John 6:52–59). On the next day, Saturday, February 3, A.D. 31, he taught again in the synagogue, and there arose a great dispute with some of his disciples who sided with the Pharisees (John 6:60–66). Jesus then withdrew from the synagogue and met with his close disciples that evening on a hill at the north end of the town. It was here that he spoke the words recorded at the close of chapter 6: "Did I not choose you, the twelve, and one of you is a devil?" (John 6:70) Chapter 7 then starts: "After this Jesus went about in Galilee; he would not go about in Judea, because the Jews sought to kill him. Now the Jews' Feast of Tabernacles was at hand. . . . After his brothers had gone up [to Jerusalem] to the feast, then he also went up, not publicly but in private" (John 7:1–2, 10).

As the Feast of Tabernacles was celebrated in the autumn, beginning on Tishri 15, there is a gap of 7 1/2 months between chapter 6 and chapter 7 of Saint John's Gospel. The period extending from the evening of Saturday, February 3, A.D. 31, to the evening of Wednesday, September 19 (Tishri 15), A.D. 31, is unaccounted for, but it was during this period of 7 1/2 months that the Passover referred to in chapter 6 ("the Passover, the feast of the Jews, was at hand" John 6:4) must have taken place. Anne Catherine in fact described Jesus' presence in Jerusalem for this Passover festival, as well as his subsequent journey back to Galilee, where the transfiguration on Mount Tabor took place on the night April 3/4, A.D. 31, exactly two years before the crucifixion on April 3, A.D. 33.

Following the transfiguration, Anne Catherine continued her day-by-day description of the ministry through April, May, June, and part of July, reaching the point where Jesus visited the ruined citadel of Datheman close by the so-called "Way of David" (LJC iii p. 469). At this point, Sunday, July 8, A.D. 31, her narrative broke off, and here the missing period begins, extending to the point where she renewed her daily account of the ministry several weeks before the raising of Lazarus. As the raising of Lazarus occurred on July 26, A.D. 32, the missing period must have lasted until the summer of A.D. 32— more precisely, until May 16. The events related in chapters 7, 8, 9, and 10 of Saint John's Gospel fall within this missing period (July 9, A.D. 31 to May 16, A.D. 32). Summarizing these chapters briefly from a chronological point of view:

CHAPTER 7 describes Jesus in Galilee and then recounts his presence in Jerusalem at the Feast of Tabernacles, relating historically to the week Wednesday, September 19 to Wednesday, September 26, A.D. 31 (Tishri 15–22); the last day of the feast, referred to in John 7:37 as "the great day," might have been Tishri 23 (sometimes called "the day of joy").

CHAPTER 8 describes Jesus teaching in the temple at Jerusalem.

CHAPTER 9 relates the healing of the man born blind.

CHAPTER 10 describes Jesus' presence in Jerusalem at the Feast of the Dedication, historically the week of Wednesday, November 28 to Wednesday, December 5, A.D. 31 (Kislev 25–Tebeth 2), and indicates that, after this, Jesus went "across the Jordan to the place where John at first baptized." (John 10:40)

Of the missing period (summer A.D. 31 to summer A.D. 32), which chapters 7 through 10 of Saint John's Gospel refer to, Anne Catherine Emmerich's day-by-day account mentions only the forthcoming Feast of the Dedication in the late autumn of A.D. 31. Here the only precise chronological references—either from Anne Catherine Emmerich or Saint John's Gospel—are those concerning the Feast of Tabernacles and the Feast of the Dedication. Thus the missing ten month period of Christ's ministry is really more or less completely lost to us due to various circumstances that hindered Anne Catherine from giving the full revelation before she died.

Having established the date of the birth of Jesus, the date of the baptism in the Jordan, the length of the ministry, and the dates of the missing period (ten months) in Anne Catherine Emmerich's account, we now find it possible to construct a daily chronicle of Christ's ministry, following the life of Christ day by day from the baptism (Friday, September 23, A.D. 29) to the crucifixion (Friday, April 3, A.D. 33), with the exception of the missing ten-month period extending from July 9, A.D., 31 to May 16, A.D. 32. Except for such events as the healing of the man born blind, which took place during these missing ten months, we can now date most of the events in the ministry of Christ Jesus with a high degree of accuracy. The dates of major events thus established are as follows:

TABLE 3
DATES OF SOME OF THE MAJOR EVENTS

Birth of Jesus	midnight	December 6/7	2 B.C.
Baptism in the Jordan	10:00 A.M.	September 23	A.D. 29
Start of the Forty days in wilderness	dusk	October 21	A.D. 29
End of the Forty days in wilderness	sunset	November 30	A.D. 29
Wedding at Cana (Jn.2:1–12)	morning	December 28	A.D. 29
Healing of nobleman's son (Jn.4:43–54)	1:00 P.M.	August 3	A.D. 30
Raising of youth of Nain (Lk.7:11–17)	9:00 A.M.	November 13	A.D. 30
Raising of Jairus' daughter (Mk.5:35–43)	evening	December 1	A.D. 30
Beheading of John the Baptist	evening	January 3	A.D. 31
Healing of the paralyzed man (Jn.5:1–14)	evening	January 19	A.D. 31
Feeding of the Five Thousand (Jn.6:16–21)	4–6:00 P.M.	January 29	A.D. 31
Walking on the water (Jn.6:16–21)	night	January 29/30	A.D. 31
Transfiguration (Mk.17:1–8)	midnight	April 3/4	A.D. 31
Raising of Lazarus (Jn.11:1–44)	morning	July 26	A.D. 32
Triumphant entry / Jerusalem (Mk.21:1–11)	morning	March 19	A.D. 33
Crucifixion	3:00 P.M.	April 3	A.D. 33
Resurrection	dawn	April 5	A.D. 33
Ascension	noon	May 14	A.D. 33
Whitsun (Pentecost)	dawn	May 24	A.D. 33

These dates serve as a basis for the description of the life of Christ—considered especially in connection with the movements of the stars—outlined in my book *The Star of the Magi and the Life of Christ*. In that book, I elucidate both the "Star of the Magi," viewed in relation to the triple conjunction of Jupiter and Saturn in 7 B.C., and the "Star of the Shepherds" in 2 B.C. The present work goes a stage further: not only are the horoscopes of the conception and birth of Jesus (from 7/6 B.C. and 2 B.C.) presented, but the horoscopes of the conception and birth of Mary as well (from 22/21 B.C. and 18/17 B.C.). In addition, the horoscopes of the conception and birth of John the Baptist—insofar as it has been possible to determine them by means of spiritual-astrological research—are given in Appendix V. Moreover, the horoscopes at the death of Jesus, Mary, and John are also published in this book.

At first sight, it may seem that the findings presented in this work are of a speculative nature. This impression may easily arise due to its rather rapid and concise manner of presentation. To describe the findings adequately would necessitate writing a volume much longer than the present one, as the findings required both a long process of preliminary research and the establishment of new hermeneutic principles. Only at the end of this process did I feel sufficiently confident of the accuracy of these conclusions to sketch them here. Readers wishing to achieve this degree of certainty for themselves must carefully weigh the results presented, mindful that a wealth of description had to be omitted. In other words, readers should realize that the description of the actual course leading to the discovery of these research findings has been reduced to a minimum. Nevertheless, I believe that these findings, if carefully and conscientiously evaluated, will reveal their truth.

Readers will then find that perhaps the most significant horoscopes in human history are put at their disposal. An interpretation of these horoscopes is not undertaken in the following pages, for this would entail a study of a different kind. At the same time, however, to arrive at these horoscopes, some of the deeper mysteries surrounding the life of Christ Jesus will necessarily come to light. At first reading, many may be shocked by these findings; but if approached in the right spirit, they can contribute to an immeasurable enhancement of our understanding of the life of Christ Jesus.

The findings offered here present also a foundation for a Cosmic Christianity in the spirit of Rudolf Steiner's indication, cited at the beginning of this chapter, that the Cosmic Christ worked uninterruptedly into Jesus from the baptism on, and that all the events in the life of Christ Jesus stood in harmony with the whole cosmos. If this statement is true, it means that every one of Christ's deeds corresponded to the prevailing configuration in the heavens. But how is it possible to know what the heavenly configurations were at the various epochs in the life of Christ? This is only possible if the dates of these events can be determined, for it is from these dates that the planetary configurations are computed.

We have shown how it is possible to find the dates of the birth and baptism of Jesus on the basis of the Jewish calendar dates of these events communicated by Anne Catherine Emmerich. The question arises: How trustworthy are her visions? Why should any degree of confidence be placed in her communications?

An answer to this question is provided by the fact that, if all of Anne Catherine's statements concerning the Jewish calendar are considered in connection with the particular days of the week on which the events she describes occurred, a remarkable agreement with the reconstructed Jewish calendar for the period A.D. 29–33 is apparent. A detailed analysis of this is given in Appendix III. From this analysis we can see clearly that Anne Catherine could not possibly have contrived these dates. In Table 2, for example, concerning the Feast of Tabernacles, which always begins on the evening of Tishri 15 in the Jewish calendar, it is apparent that the start of Tishri 15 fell on a Monday evening, exactly as Anne Catherine described. In this case, the likelihood of her accuracy with regard to the weekday of this Jewish date was one in seven, so this one statement alone cannot be taken as unusually significant — it could simply have been a fortunate coincidence. However, to be accurate thirteen times consecutively (see Appendix III) is a different matter altogether, for the probability in this case is one in 96,889,010,407 or almost one in 100 billion. The only possible conclusion to be drawn is that she was speaking the truth, bearing in mind that she was a simple, uneducated woman who knew nothing about the intricacies of the Jewish lunar calendar, which modern astronomical computational methods are now able to compute back two thousand years with a high degree of accuracy. From the standpoint of probability theory, it is clear that, at least with respect to dates, she was speaking the truth (leaving aside the intriguing question of *how* this was possible).

Apart from dates, however, there are other points to be considered. One is that her account of the life of Christ agrees by and large with the testimony of the four Gospels, the primary historical source, of course, for facts of Christ's life. Anyone familiar with the account in the Gospels will recognize it, greatly expanded and in much more detailed form, in Anne Catherine's description, thus supporting the authenticity of her visions. Her descriptions of Jewish customs at the time of Christ are recognized by experts as being, on the whole, remarkably precise. "Archeologists were frequently amazed at the accuracy and exactitude with which Emmerich described the household fittings and utensils and customs of the people of Israel" (WJW, 11). And in the Foreword to his book *Die Reiche der heilige drei Könige* ("The Kingdoms of the Three Kings"), Anton Urbas writes:

> Since Anne Catherine Emmerich names the places visited by the Saviour on His journeys and describes them in such precise detail, I took recourse to travel guides and atlases of Palestine so as to check the accuracy of her indications. The more comparisons I made, the more I came to the conclusion that Anne Catherine Emmerich had greater knowledge of the Holy Land and knew more concerning Jewish

customs than all the geographers and archeologists in the whole world. (quoted in WJW, p. 11)

This brings us to the next point: the geography and topography of the Holy Land as described in Anne Catherine's account of Jesus' daily travels. These descriptions are very precise, as often as not giving the geographical *direction* in which Jesus traveled and the *length of time* he took to journey from one place to the next. Helmut Fahsel gathered all these descriptions together and found that they were mutually consistent and agreed precisely with the actual topography of Palestine. On the basis of Anne Catherine's indications, Fahsel was able to construct detailed maps of Palestine for the time of Christ. These maps were published in his monumental *Der Wandel Jesu in der Welt* (WJW). They present clear, consistent solutions to archeological riddles to which only vague, uncertain proposals have been given up until now.

For example, among archeologists there is no agreement on the location of Bethsaida, the hometown of the disciples Peter, Andrew, and Philip. Some modern archeologists identify Bethsaida with Bethsaida-Julias, the ruins of which have been located on the hill et-Tell, just east of the Jordan and some two and one-half miles north of where the Jordan flows into the Sea of Galilee. Anne Catherine, however, clearly situated Bethsaida-Julias at the site of et-Tell, but sees Bethsaida as a little fishing village on the north shore of the Sea of Galilee, about two and one-half miles southeast of Capernaum (WJW, 459). In light of this description, the ruins of Bethsaida would now lie beneath the waters of the lake, since the ruins of Capernaum have been located on the present northern lake shore of the Sea of Galilee. She even explained that a shift in the geography of the lake shore arose on account of an earthquake (WJW, 466).

Many other examples could be given regarding the solution, or possible solution, of archeological riddles on the basis of Anne Catherine Emmerich's visions. (The discovery of the site of Mary's house near Ephesus, referred to in the Foreword, is a most striking example.) Her indications concerning the locations of various miracles are especially significant. Fahsel's detailed research makes it possible to accurately locate most of these places. One example is the Mount of Beatitudes, where the sermon on the mount (Matthew 5:1–7:28) and the feeding of the five thousand (John 6:1–15) took place. Despite the explicit reference in John's Gospel that before the feeding of the five thousand "Jesus went to the other side of the Sea of Galilee" (John 6:1) and in the Gospel of Mark that after the miraculous feeding Jesus and the disciples crossed back across the lake and "came to land at Gennesaret" (Mark 6:53), most archeologists now locate the Mount of Beatitudes close to Gennesaret on the northwest side of the Sea of Galilee. Each year hundreds of thousands of tourists visit the Church of the Beatitudes (built upon the hillcrest of Eremos at the supposed site of the sermon on the mount) and the Church of the Loaves and Fishes at Tabgha at the foot of Eremos (the supposed location of the miracle of the feeding of the five thousand) in the belief that these were the actual historical sites. Anne Catherine's account of the geographical location of the Mount of Beatitudes, however, in agreement with the Gospels of Mark and John, points to a site on the other side of the Sea of Galilee. Her description is so detailed that Fahsel was able to identify the site of the hill quite precisely on the northeast side of the lake, overlooking the Sea of Galilee. (See Fahsel's maps in Part II of this book.)

Considering these points as a whole, there is good reason to place considerable confidence in Anne Catherine Emmerich's visions. This does not mean that *everything* she described is wholly accurate. She was human, not infallible. The same can be said of Clemens Brentano, who wrote down her visions as she described them. It is quite possible that mistakes in his transcription of her account occurred and that, for one reason or another, errors crept into the text. Nevertheless, as far as the dates communicated by Anne Catherine Emmerich are concerned, the probability of error is extraordinarily low (as has been shown), and this seems justification enough for accepting her calendar indications as a reliable basis for dating the life of Christ.

On the basis of these dates, a new approach to Cosmic Christianity opens up, as will become clear in the following pages. This approach depends in part on an accurate determination of the horoscopes of Jesus and the Virgin Mary. The starting point for this research is again Anne Catherine Emmerich's account, but now combined with Rudolf Steiner's finding that there were *two* children born with the name "Jesus" — a spiritual scientific observation that was substantiated many years after his death by the discovery of the Dead Sea Scrolls. It is not possible here to go into the fascinating story told by the Dead Sea Scrolls of two Messiahs — a priestly one and a kingly one — and of their forerunner, the prophet.[9] Suffice it to say that the perspective of two Messiahs opened up by the Dead Sea Scrolls in the second half of the twentieth century had been described in detail by Rudolf Steiner on the basis of his exact clairvoyance in the first quarter of the century.

9. Elizabeth Weymann, *Zepter und Stern* (Stuttgart: Urachhaus, 1993).

Without Rudolf Steiner's indications, the research leading to the discovery of the horoscopes of the two Jesus children would hardly have been possible.

Readers who wish to learn more of the astronomical and astrological details that also contributed to the findings sketched in this volume may wish to consult my earlier works (see Bibliography).

Chapter Two

The Genealogies of Jesus

At the beginning of our era, Jesus Christ was born. This was an event that, perhaps more than any other, dramatically altered human history, and yet, paradoxically, only the most fragmentary biographical or historical references to him exist. To complicate matters, the few references found in the New Testament seem contradictory. For example, Saint Matthew's Gospel gives a quite different genealogy for Jesus than is given in the Gospel of Saint Luke. In Matthew, the genealogy passes from David through Solomon and culminates with "Jacob the father of Joseph the husband of Mary, of whom Jesus was born, who is called Christ" (Matthew 1:16). In Luke, it descends from David through Nathan and culminates with Jesus, "being the son (as was supposed) of Joseph, the son of Heli" (Luke 3:23). What are we to make of this discrepancy in genealogies? According to Anne Catherine Emmerich:

> I saw the line of the Messiah proceeding from David and dividing into two branches. The right-hand one went through Solomon down to Jacob, the father of Saint Joseph. I saw the figures of all Saint Joseph's ancestors named in the Gospel on this right-hand branch of the descent from David through Solomon. This branch has the greater significance of the two. . . . The right-hand and left-hand branches met several times, and they crossed each other at a point a few generations before the end. I was given an explanation about the higher significance of the line of descent through Solomon. It had in it more of the spirit and less of the flesh, and had some of the significance belonging to Solomon himself. I cannot express this. The left-hand line of descent went from David through Nathan down to Heli, which is the real name of Joachim, Mary's father, for he did not receive the name of Joachim till later, just as Abram was not called Abraham until later. In my visions I often hear

Jesus called after the flesh a son of Heli. I saw this whole line from David through Nathan flowing at a lower level. . . . At a point three or four generations above Heli or Joachim, the two lines crossed each other and rose up, ending with the Blessed Virgin. (LBVM, 56–58).[1]

If Anne Catherine's account is true, it means that Joseph descended from Solomon, as described in the Gospel of Saint Matthew, and that Mary descended from Nathan, as described in the Gospel of Saint Luke. This would mean that Jesus, the son of Joseph and Mary, descended from Solomon on his father's side and from Nathan on his mother's. This would explain the two different genealogies given in Matthew and Luke. As we shall see, there is an element of truth in this explanation, but it is not the whole truth, for there is a deeper, more profound significance to the two genealogies, which was discovered and made public by Rudolf Steiner at the beginning of this century. Through his extraordinary faculty of spiritual vision, Steiner beheld the two lines of descent described in the Gospel of Saint Matthew and the Gospel of Saint Luke. But he saw these two lines culminating with the births of *two* children, *each* named Jesus:

We learn from the Bible that David had two sons, Solomon and Nathan. Thus two lines of descent, the "Solomon line" and the "Nathan line" stemmed from David. Leaving aside the intermediate members, we can say: At the beginning of our era, descendants both of the Solomon line and of the Nathan line of the House of David were living in Palestine. In Nazareth there lived a man named "Joseph," a descendant of the Nathan line; he had a wife, "Mary." And in Bethlehem there lived a descendant of the Solomon line, also named "Joseph." It is not in the least surprising that there were two men of David's lineage named Joseph and that each was married to a Mary as the Bible says. Thus at the beginning of our era there were two couples in Palestine, both bearing the names "Joseph" and "Mary." The Bethlehem couple traced its origin back to the "Solomon" or kingly line of the House of

---

1. Clemens Brentano commented: "Catherine Emmerich no doubt meant by this the connection between the line of David through Nathan and that through Solomon. In the third generation upwards from Joachim, Saint Joseph's grandmother (who had married as her first husband Matthan, of the line of Solomon, and had by him two sons, one of whom was Jacob, the father of Saint Joseph) took as her second husband Levi, of the line of Nathan, and had by him Matthat, the father of Heli or Joachim" (LBVM, 58, fn.1).

David and the other (the Nazareth couple) to the "Nathan" or priestly line. To this latter couple (of the Nathan line) was born the child described to you. . . . At the time when the child was due to be born, this couple of the Nathan lineage journeyed from Nazareth to Bethlehem, as Saint Luke relates, "to be taxed." The genealogical table is given in his Gospel. The other couple did not originally reside in Nazareth but in Bethlehem; this is related by the writer of the Gospel of Saint Matthew. This couple of the Solomon line also had a child named "Jesus." . . . The births of the two Jesus children were separated by a period of months. But Jesus of The Gospel of Saint Luke and John the Baptist were both born too late to have been victims of the so-called "massacre of the innocents." Has the thought never struck you that those who read about the Bethlehem massacre must ask themselves: How could there have been a John? But the facts can be substantiated in all respects. The Jesus of Saint Matthew's Gospel was taken to Egypt by his parents, and John, supposedly, was born shortly before or about the same time. According to the usual view, John remained in Palestine, but in that case he would certainly have been a victim of Herod's murderous deed. You see how necessary it is to devote serious thought to these things; for if all the children of two years old and younger were actually put to death at that time, John would have been one of them. But this riddle will become intelligible if . . . you realize that the events related in the Gospels of Saint Luke and Saint Matthew did not take place at the same time. The Nathan Jesus was born after the Bethlehem massacre; so too was John. (Rudolf Steiner, *Gospel of Saint Luke*, pp. 90–95)

Since the time Rudolf Steiner first spoke of the two Jesus children (1909), confirmation of an expectation of two Messiahs—one priestly, one kingly—has been provided by the Dead Sea Scrolls, discovered in 1947. These scrolls of an Essene community at Qumran, "show with complete unanimity the expectation of *two* Messiahs, one a high priest from the tribe of Levi, and one royal from the tribe of Judah. The priestly Messiah receives the highest place, the royal Messiah ranks second." (Karl Georg Kuhn, "The Two Messiahs of Aaron and Israel," p. 57).

The idea of two Jesus children, which on first hearing sounds distinctly heretical, if not incredible, gains in plausibility when the Gospel accounts themselves are studied from this point of view. After the birth of Jesus, the

Gospel of Saint Matthew describes the visit of three wise men from the East: "[G]oing into the house they saw the child with Mary his mother, and they fell down and worshipped him" (Matthew 2:11). In Saint Luke's Gospel, however, there is no mention of a house. Instead, after his birth, Jesus is described as having been laid in a manger (Luke 2:7); and the child is visited, not by wise men ("kings"), but by humble shepherds.

According to Steiner's spiritual research, we are confronted here with two different individualities. The term "individuality" rather than "personality" is appropriate, as it invokes the idea of reincarnation. As many traditions attest (and Steiner's research, in particular, substantiates), it is the *individuality* that reincarnates in a succession of earthly lives, manifesting as a new *personality* in each incarnation. The only example of reincarnation referred to in the Gospels is that of Elijah as John the Baptist: "But I tell you Elijah has already come, and they did not know him, but did to him whatever they pleased. So also the Son of Man will suffer at their hands. Then the disciples understood that he was speaking to them of John the Baptist" (Matthew 17:12–13). Here it is a matter of the same individuality (spirit) who lived first of all some eight centuries before Christ as the prophet Elijah and then reincarnated at the beginning of the Christian era as John the Baptist. Elijah can be thought of as an historical personality and John the Baptist as a different historical personality; but Jesus revealed to the disciples that both were manifestations, in successive earthly incarnations, of one and the same individuality. Assuming the reality of reincarnation, then, one may ask which individuality reincarnated as Jesus of the Solomon line, and which as Jesus of the Nathan line.

We may note first that a qualitative difference between the two is evident from the Gospel accounts. One was of a kingly nature. He was born in a house and visited by wise men or Magi ("kings"). Indeed, such was his status that he was felt to be a threat to the king of Israel, Herod the Great. The other was born in lowly circumstances (described as a cave by Anne Catherine Emmerich), and visited by humble shepherds. The royal quality of wisdom is evinced in the one account, whereas the other is imbued with qualities of the heart, such as "peace" and "goodwill." ("Glory to God in the highest, and peace on Earth to people of goodwill" are the words spoken by the Angel at the proclamation to the shepherds of the birth of the Saviour, as described in chapter two of the Gospel of Saint Luke.) This qualitative difference gives an indication of the nature of the two individualities, the Jesus of the Solomon line and the Jesus of the Nathan line. The genealogies themselves bear this out. Whereas

Nathan is described simply as a "son" (1 Chronicles 14:4), Solomon is called the "wisest of all kings" (1 Chronicles 9:22): "And the Lord gave Solomon great repute in the sight of Israel, and bestowed upon him such royal majesty as had not been seen on any king before him in Israel" (1 Chronicles 29:25). As Anne Catherine expressed it, the line of descent through Solomon "had some of the significance belonging to Solomon himself."

It is also interesting to note a statement made by Rudolf Steiner concerning Hiram Abiff, the master craftsman who built Solomon's temple: "Hiram Abiff, the lonely hermit, stood at the threshold of initiation. In his next incarnation he was initiated. He was then named 'Lazarus'; for Lazarus was Hiram Abiff in his foregoing incarnation." (Rudolf Steiner, *Zur Geschichte und aus den Inhalten der erkenntnis-kultischen Abteilung der E.S.* 1904–1914, p. 409).

Now, from the descriptions of Anne Catherine Emmerich, it emerges that Lazarus was wealthy and that it was he who looked after the finances of Jesus and the disciples. This relationship between Jesus and Lazarus bears a similarity to that between Solomon and Hiram Abiff—which is not surprising if in fact Lazarus had been Hiram Abiff, the builder of Solomon's temple, in his preceding incarnation. Just as Hiram Abiff had made it possible for Solomon to build the House of the Lord in Jerusalem, so Lazarus of Bethany (near Jerusalem) made it possible for Jesus to carry out his work of laying the foundations for a new kingdom and ushering in a new era upon the Earth.

Rudolf Steiner not only spoke of Lazarus as the reincarnated Hiram Abiff, but also of the Jesus of Saint Matthew's Gospel as the reincarnated Zarathustra (Greek, Zoroaster):

> You will learn to understand the Jesus of the Gospel of Saint Matthew in the light of the more intimate facts. In this boy was reincarnated the Zarathustra-Individuality, from whom the people of ancient Persia had once received the teaching concerning Ahura Mazdao, the great Sun Being. . . . Six hundred years before our era, Zarathustra was born again in ancient Chaldea as Zaratas, who became the teacher of the Chaldean mystery schools; he was also the teacher of Pythagoras. . . . Deep and fervent attachment to the individuality [not the personality] of Zarathustra prevailed in the mystery schools of Chaldea. These wise men of the East felt that they were intimately connected with their great leader. They saw in him the "star of humanity," for "Zoroaster" means "golden star," or "star of splendor." They saw in him a reflection of the

Sun itself. And with their profound wisdom they could not fail to know when their Master was born again in Bethlehem. Led by their "star," they brought as offerings to him the outer symbols for the most precious gifts he had been able to bestow upon men.... Thus by appearing before their Master when he was born again in Bethlehem, the Magi gave evidence of their union with him. The writer of the Gospel of Saint Matthew relates what is literally true when he describes how the wise men (among whom Zarathustra had once worked) knew that he had reappeared among men, and how they expressed their connection with him through the three symbols of gold, frankincense and myrrh— symbols of the precious gifts he had bestowed upon them. The need now was that Zarathustra, as Jesus of the Solomon line of the House of David, should be able to work with all possible power in order to give again to men, in a rejuvenated form, everything he had already given in earlier times.... Jesus of the Solomon line of the House of David, the reincarnated Zarathustra, was led to Egypt.... Hence the "flight into Egypt" and its spiritual consequences: the absorption of all the forces he now needed in order to give again to men in full strength and in rejuvenated form what he had bestowed upon them in past ages. Thus the history of the Jesus whose parents resided originally in Bethlehem is correctly related by Saint Matthew. Saint Luke relates only that the parents of the Jesus of whom he is writing resided in Nazareth, that they went to Bethlehem to be "taxed" and that Jesus was born during that short period. The parents then returned to Nazareth with the child. In the Gospel of Saint Matthew we are told that Jesus was born in Bethlehem and that he had to be taken to Egypt. It was after their return from Egypt that the parents settled in Nazareth, for the child who was the reincarnation of Zarathustra was destined to grow up near the child who represented the other stream. (Rudolf Steiner, *Gospel of Saint Luke*, pp. 95–102)

Having considered the individuality of the Solomon Jesus, the reincarnated Zarathustra, we must now turn to the question of the individuality of the Nathan Jesus of Saint Luke's Gospel. Who had the Nathan Jesus been in a previous incarnation?

As mentioned above, the Solomon Jesus was the leading representative of the stream of wisdom, while the Nathan Jesus represented a spiritual stream that is characterized rather by "peace and goodwill." In fact, according to the spiritual researches of Rudolf Steiner, the Nathan Jesus was a representative of the Indian spiritual stream—in contrast to the Persian spiritual stream of Zarathustra. In Buddhism—regarded by many as the highest flowering of India's spirituality—the central impulse is not so much the acquisition of wisdom (such as that of the Magi), but rather the development of inward, heart qualities such as compassion. Just as the Solomon Jesus, the reincarnated Zarathustra, was the leader of the "wisdom stream" stemming back to the Persian culture of the Magi, so the Nathan Jesus was the leader of the Hindu spiritual stream exemplified by Krishna in the Bhagavad Gita, the stream that later brought forth the great teacher of compassion, Gautama Buddha. According to Rudolf Steiner, however, whereas the individuality of the Solomon Jesus had incarnated repeatedly, the individuality of the Nathan Jesus had never incarnated before, apart from an "embodiment" in Krishna.[2] In the Nathan Jesus, the "sister soul" of Adam, a soul that (unlike Adam) had not passed through the Fall, was present. This soul, having never been fully incarnated, was untainted by the consequences of the Fall. It was free of "sin," including the "original sin" incurred through the Fall:

> In the Luke Jesus boy lived a part of man's being that had never before entered human evolution on Earth.... It was held back in the soul world, apart from the stream of incarnation. Only those initiated in the mysteries could have any connection with this sister soul.... This sister soul remained in the soul world. It was also the one incarnated in the Luke Jesus boy. But this was not the first time, in the strict sense of the word, that this soul was embodied as physical man . . . This sister soul of Adam was embodied, so to say, in Krishna, the only time that it had become physically visible; and then again it was embodied in the Luke Jesus boy. (Rudolf Steiner, *The Bhagavad Gita and the Epistles of Paul*, pp. 93–98)

The sister soul of Adam, incarnated as the Nathan Jesus, was endowed with childlike innocence, strength of compassion, and a remarkable capacity for self-sacrifice. But this Jesus was not endowed with the remarkable intelligence and wisdom of the other Jesus and did not possess the same ability to

---

2. The term "embodiment" is used, as distinct from "incarnation," to signify a "partial incarnation" in which the spirit manifests *through* the body rather than being incarnated *in* the body. In Hindu doctrine precise distinctions are made between differing degrees of the "descent of Avatars."

learn. The two Jesus children came into contact with each other, however, when, after their return from Egypt, the Solomon Jesus and his family settled in Nazareth. As discussed in my *Christian Hermetic Astrology*, this took place in September, A.D. 2. And so, from this moment on, the two Jesus children grew up in close proximity.

The parents of the Nathan Jesus had no more children, whereas those of the Solomon Jesus had six more: James, Joseph, Judas, Simon and two daughters (Mark 6:3 and Matthew 13:55–56). Thus the Nathan Jesus was an only child, while the Solomon Jesus was the eldest of seven siblings.

It was the custom in Palestine at the Feast of the Passover (Easter) to journey to the Temple in Jerusalem. In A.D. 8, when the Nathan Jesus reached the age of eight, he made this journey to Jerusalem with his parents for the first time, and he returned thereafter every year. In A.D. 12, Passover—as far as is possible to determine on the basis of modern astronomical chronology—started on the evening of Saturday, March 26, and ended at sunset on Sunday, April 3. The Gospel of Saint Luke describes the Feast of the Passover in A.D. 12 as follows:

Now his parents went to Jerusalem every year at the Feast of the Passover. And when he was twelve years old, they went up according to custom; and when the feast was ended, as they were returning, the boy Jesus stayed behind in Jerusalem. His parents did not know it, but supposing him to be in the company they went a day's journey, and they sought him among their kinsfolk and acquaintances; and when they did not find him, they returned to Jerusalem, seeking him. After three days they found him in the Temple, sitting among the teachers, listening to them and asking them questions; and all who heard him were amazed at his understanding and his answers. (Luke 2:41–47)

It is evident that something remarkable had happened to the Nathan Jesus child: a transformation from a simple, loving child to one of profound wisdom. What took place? Rudolf Steiner's spiritual researches revealed the following:

In the case of the twelve-year-old Jesus, the following happened. The Zarathustra-Ego which had lived hitherto in the body of the Jesus belonging to the kingly or Solomon line of the House of David . . . left that body and passed into the body of the Nathan Jesus who then appeared as one transformed. (Rudolf Steiner, *The Gospel of Saint Luke*, pp. 106–107)

According to this description, the spirit of the Solomon Jesus (Zarathustra) passed out of his body at some time around Sunday, April 3, A.D. 12, and united with the Nathan Jesus, bringing about a profound transformation. This mysterious occurrence is depicted artistically by the Italian Renaissance painter Borgognone in his painting "The Twelve-year-old Jesus in the Temple" in the church of Saint Ambrosius, Milan. The Nathan Jesus sits in the center on a raised seat holding a discourse, surrounded by the doctors and scribes. His gaze is directed toward another child—the Solomon Jesus—on the left side of the painting. Whereas the Nathan Jesus basks in an aura of radiance arising through his inner union with the spirit of Zarathustra ("golden star"), the Solomon Jesus looks pale and weak, bereft of spirit, and appears to be making his way, in a dream-like state, away from the Nathan Jesus. A reproduction of this painting, together with many others purportedly showing the two Jesus children, is to be found in Hella Krause-Zimmer's book *Die zwei Jesusknaben in der bildenden Kunst* [The Two Jesus Children in Pictorial Art].

Bereft of spirit, the Solomon Jesus could not live for long. As will be shown in the next section, where we consider the dates of birth of the two Jesus children, the death of the Solomon Jesus in fact occurred only two months or so later. Another two months later, the mother of the Nathan Jesus died as well. According to Rudolf Steiner, the father of the Solomon Jesus had already passed away before the Passover festival, and the widowed (Solomon) Mary, left alone with so many children, then married Joseph of Nazareth, whose son, the Nathan Jesus, thereby gained four step-brothers and two step-sisters. In this way, the spirit of the Solomon Jesus, now indwelling the body of the Nathan Jesus, was reunited with his mother, brothers, and sisters.

The next important event in the life of Jesus was the Baptism in the Jordan, which, according to the research presented in Chapter One, took place two and one-half months prior to Jesus' thirtieth birthday. On the evening before the baptism, according to Anne Catherine Emmerich, Jesus had a long and profound conversation with Mary at the home (actually more of a castle) of Lazarus in Bethany. During the course of this conversation the spirit of the Solomon Jesus (Zarathustra) left the Nathan Jesus after having been united with him for some eighteen years, and departed the earthly plane. That very night, accompanied by Lazarus, Jesus made his way to the place on the banks of the Jordan where John was baptizing. They arrived there around the break of day, and at about ten o'clock that morning the baptism took place; that is, Christ, the Logos descended to indwell the body vacated by the spirit of the Solomon Jesus. This moment signifies the *birth* of the cosmic being Christ, as indicated by the words of Saint Luke:

> And when Jesus also had been baptized and was praying, the heaven was opened, and the Holy Spirit descended upon him in bodily form, as a dove, and a voice came from heaven, "Thou art my beloved Son; today I have begotten thee." (Luke 3:21–22)[3]

The translation, "Today I have begotten thee," is nowadays usually rendered as "With thee I am well pleased." The deeper sense, however, expressed by the first translation, is of a birth. This was the moment when the Christ descended from cosmic realms to take up his dwelling place on Earth and begin his three and one-half year ministry in the body of Jesus. Thus a new being was born: Jesus Christ, the union of the human being Jesus with the cosmic being Christ. The earthly life of Jesus Christ ended with the death on the cross at Golgotha on the afternoon of Friday, April 3, A.D. 33, exactly twenty-one years after the event in the Temple at which the spirit of the Solomon Jesus had united with the twelve-year-old Nathan Jesus.

Such are the main stages of the life of Jesus as portrayed by Rudolf Steiner on the basis of his spiritual research. Together with the detailed visions of Anne Catherine Emmerich, these form the basis for the historical-chronological references and research findings that are presented below and in my other work, *Christian Hermetic Astrology: The Star of the Magi and the Life of Christ,* where, in addition, "astrosophical" principles are invoked. It will be evident to those readers who have followed the text so far that profound mysteries underlie the life of the Messiah. Unfortunately, it has been possible to give only the briefest indications of these mysteries. The interested reader is referred to the works of Rudolf Steiner where this subject is expounded at greater length.[4]

---

3. See footnote to this passage in the Gospel of Saint Luke from the Revised Standard Version of the Holy Bible: "Other ancient authorities read: *Today I have begotten thee.*"
4. See Bibliography.

It will also be apparent from the above that there must be two horoscopes for Jesus: one for the Solomon Jesus and one for the Nathan Jesus. In what follows I shall describe how it was possible to determine not only both of these birth horoscopes, but also the horoscopes of the two conceptions, as well as the two deaths (of the Solomon Jesus in A.D. 12; of the Nathan Jesus at the Mystery of Golgotha in A.D. 33). Further, there are two horoscopes for Mary: one for the mother of the Solomon Jesus and one for the mother of the Nathan Jesus. In the section on the Virgin Mary, I shall indicate how it proved possible to determine the horoscopes for both Marys, including their horoscopes of conception and death (of the Nathan Mary in A.D. 12; of the Solomon Mary in A.D. 44).

The research outlined in the following pages is based, on the one hand, on the spiritual visions of Anne Catherine Emmerich and, on the other, on the spiritual research presented by Rudolf Steiner. Each has contributed in a remarkable way to a deeper understanding of the mysteries surrounding the life of Jesus Christ. The clairvoyance of Anne Catherine Emmerich and of Rudolf Steiner, taken in conjunction with astronomical-chronological research, enables us to penetrate these mysteries in a way never before possible, as will soon be evident.

Chapter Three

The Solomon Jesus

A key to establishing the birthdate of the Solomon Jesus is the "Star of the Magi" spoken of in the Gospel of Saint Matthew. According to the German astronomer Kepler, in his work *De Stella Nova*, the Star of the Magi was bound up with the triple conjunction of the planets Jupiter and Saturn in the year 7 B.C. The birth of Jesus was announced shortly thereafter, when Mars also entered into conjunction with Jupiter and Saturn.

Another astronomical phenomenon frequently referred to in connection with dating the birth of Jesus is "Herod's eclipse." The Jewish historian Josephus, writing in the first century A.D., reported that Herod the Great died after an eclipse of the Moon shortly before the Feast of the Passover. A lunar eclipse visible in Jerusalem did occur on the night of March 12/13 in 4 B.C., and this has been taken by some to mean that the birth of Jesus occurred prior to this date, in 5, 6 or 7 B.C. Such a view tends to support Kepler, who looked to the conjunction of Mars, Jupiter, and Saturn in March, 6 B.C., as announcing the birth of the Messiah. The following research fully confirms Kepler's thesis. Before considering this question in further detail, however, it will be helpful to look at the various possible candidates for Herod's eclipse.

LUNAR ECLIPSES VISIBLE IN JERUSALEM
(time given is that of central eclipse)

7 B.C. None
6 B.C. None
5 B.C. Total eclipse on March 23 at 8:43 P.M.
5 B.C. Total eclipse on September 15 at 10:45 P.M.
4 B.C. Partial eclipse on March 13 at 3:18 A.M.
3 B.C. None
2 B.C. None
1 B.C. Total eclipse on January 10 at 1:31 A.M.

The table above shows that from 7 B.C. to 1 B.C. there were four lunar eclipses visible in Jerusalem, as may be seen in *Solar and Lunar Eclipses of the Ancient Near East* by M. Kudlek and E. Michler.

Two tendencies are apparent among modern scholars who have occupied themselves with the problem of dating the birth of Jesus: that of writers such as K. Ferrari d' Occhieppo, Roy A. Rosenberg, and David Hughes, who follow Kepler in identifying the triple conjunction of Jupiter and Saturn in 7 B.C. as the Star of the Magi, and therefore place the birth of Jesus in the period preceding the lunar eclipse of 4 B.C.; and those, such as Ernest L. Martin and Ormond Edwards, who make a case for the lunar eclipse of January, 1 B.C., as "Herod's eclipse," and thus date the birth of Jesus to 2 B.C., in agreement with most ancient authorities (Edwards actually dates the birth to January 6, 1 B.C. See below).

According to the research findings that will be presented here, Kepler's date—March, 6 B.C.—is correct for the birth of the *Solomon* Jesus, and the year 2 B.C. is correct for the birth of the *Nathan* Jesus. Thus, both groups of modern scholars are right, but only in light of the births of *two* Jesus children can this be recognized.

Of the above-mentioned scholars, only Ormond Edwards—a priest in the Christian Community (a denomination founded in collaboration with Rudolf Steiner)—has taken the existence of two Jesus children into account. In his book *The Time of Christ* Edwards dates the birth of the Solomon Jesus to January 6, 1 B.C., and that of the Nathan Jesus to December 25, 1 B.C. Moreover, he places the death of Herod "certainly early in 1 B.C., and probably on Shebat 2, January 28, 1 B.C." (TC, 59). Edwards thus accommodates Rudolf Steiner's statements that "the Nathan Jesus was born after the Bethlehem massacre" and "the births of the two Jesus children were separated by a period of months." Moreover, Edwards accepts "the Messianic significance of the triple conjunction in that year, without being prepared to accept that 7 B.C. was the year in which the Magi made their journey" (TC, 65). He considers it possible that the Magi believed that the triple conjunction between Jupiter and Saturn in 7 B.C. heralded the birth of the Messiah, but then followed the movement of Jupiter until it "came to rest in Virgo, at which time the Magi paid homage to the newborn son of the House of David" (TC, 89). According to Edwards, this would mean that the arrival of the Magi in Jerusalem occurred some time between December 24, 2 B.C., and January 3, 1 B.C. (TC, 67).

For many years, I considered Ormond Edward's dates for the births of the two Jesus children to be plausible. I was deeply impressed by his scholarship and thorough grasp of the intricacies of Biblical chronology. Nevertheless, I felt compelled to research further. I was struck by the fact that the date put forward by Edwards as the birth of the Nathan Jesus (December 25, 1 B.C.,) agreed exactly with Dionysius Exiguus (6th Century A.D.), the Christian monk and scholar who introduced this date for the birth of Jesus Christ as the starting point of our modern chronology. Dionysius placed the birth of Jesus on December 25, 1 B.C., and specified that the civil reckoning should begin seven days later on January 1 A.D. 1, to agree with the start of the ordinary Roman year.

Since Ormond Edwards dates the Crucifixion to April 3, A.D. 33, in agreement with Rudolf Steiner and the majority of modern scholars, this implies a lifespan for the Nathan Jesus (December 25, 1 B.C., to April 3, A.D. 33) of 32 years and 99 days, or approximately 32 1/4 years. This, however, does not agree with the two most reliable clairvoyant sources at our disposal: both Rudolf Steiner and Anne Catherine Emmerich state that the life of Jesus Christ lasted *at least* 33 years. Steiner indicates 33 1/4 (or 33 and 1/3) years,[1] while Anne Catherine Emmerich says: "Jesus, when put to death, was thirty-three years, four months, and two weeks old" (LJ i, 196). This statement that the Nathan Jesus lived 33 1/3 years, together with two other indications by Anne Catherine Emmerich, enabled me to situate the birth of the Nathan Jesus on the night of December 6/7 in 2 B.C. An analysis of Anne Catherine's indications, leading to the discovery that December 6/7, 2 B.C., was the birth date of the Nathan Jesus, was given in Chapter One. I will now present the reasons for pinpointing the exact time of the birth to December 6, shortly before midnight.

Taking the birth year of the Nathan Jesus of the Luke Gospel as 2 B.C. resolves one of the major problems of New Testament chronology: namely,

---

1. Rudolf Steiner, *Et incarnatus est* (lecture: Basel, December 23, 1917), GA 118. There is some ambiguity in Rudolf Steiner's formulation. He seems to imply that the rhythm of the life of Jesus Christ is one-third of a century, but on the other hand he speaks of the interval from Christmas to Easter thirty-three years later. This has even led some to interpret his words as signifying that the length of the life of Jesus Christ was 32 1/4 years; but this is a false interpretation, as has been shown in Ellen Schalk's essay on the 33-year life of Jesus Christ in *Beiträge zu einer Erweiterung der Heilkunst* (Goetheanum, Dornach, Switzerland, 1983, pp. 1–6). This false interpretation rests on an example Rudolf Steiner employed once when he spoke of Easter 1917 in relation to the Christmas festival thirty-three years earlier in 1884. If this is interpreted as December 25, 1884, the interval to Easter 1917 is indeed only 32 1/4 years; but in this lecture Rudolf Steiner used the term "Christmas-year," i.e., the year *beginning at Christmas* rather than on New Year's day. The Christmas-year 1884 *began* on December 25, 1883, and the interval—he says expressly "thirty-three years"—to Easter 1917 is indeed 33 1/4 years.

the problem raised by the words, "In those days a decree went out from Caesar Augustus that all the world should be enrolled. This was the first enrollment, when Quirinius was governor of Syria" (Luke 2:1–2). Now, there were official censuses, as recorded by Augustus (*Res. Gestae Divi Augusti*, II, 8), in 28 B.C., in 8 B.C., and in A.D. 16; but none is recorded for the period when the birth of Jesus Christ occurred. In 2 B.C., however, the Silver Jubilee of Augustus' rule over the empire took place; and on February 5, 2 B.C., the Senate awarded him the title *Pater Patriae* ("father of the country"). Celebrations were held in Rome and it is not unreasonable to suppose that an oath of allegiance was demanded not just of the citizens of Rome, but of those in the provinces as well. Such an oath, entailing an enrollment of names, could be described as a "census":

> If the oath of loyalty is what brought Joseph and Mary to Bethlehem, then it makes sense why Mary had to accompany Joseph. For a regular census Mary would not have needed to go with Joseph, nor would Joseph have needed to travel so far. But both Joseph and Mary were descendants of David, and were legitimate claimants to the throne of Israel (had such a throne existed), and we can easily imagine why Mary, as well as Joseph, was expected to sign the oath of loyalty to Augustus. (Ernest L. Martin, *The Birth of Christ Recalculated*, pp. 70–71)

In his *The History of the Jewish People in the Age of Jesus Christ*, Emil Schürer examines the second point raised by Luke, the reference to Quirinius. He concludes that Quirinius was probably governor of Syria in 3/2 B.C. and was definitely so in A.D. 6/7. Ernest Martin also presents considerable evidence to support his claim that Quirinius was temporary governor of Syria in 2 B.C.

The two references in Luke regarding the timing of the baptism in the Jordan fit well if the birth year of Jesus was 2 B.C. (The references are Luke 3:1: "In the fifteenth year of the reign of Tiberius . . ." and Luke 3:23: "Jesus, when he began his ministry was about thirty years of age.") The few available chronological indications provided by Saint Luke point, therefore, to 2 B.C. as the birth year of the Nathan Jesus, supporting the date December 6, 2 B.C., derived from Anne Catherine Emmerich's statements.

Astrosophically, the moment of *conception* is of prime importance and, like the moment of birth, has a profound astrological significance, as will be described in the following pages. For this reason, it is not only Jesus' hour of birth that is of interest but also the time and date of his conception. We will show in the next section, on the basis of astrological considerations, that March 6, 2 B.C. was the date of conception of the Nathan Jesus. Thus, just as the birth on December 6 occurred historically eighteen days prior to the traditional date of December 24/25, so the annunciation occurred on March 5/6, nineteen days earlier than the traditional date of March 24/25.

In the case of the Solomon Jesus, whose birth took place earlier than that of the Nathan Jesus, we must look further back in time than 2 B.C. The only real reference point here is the Star of the Magi. Anne Catherine's statements are again most helpful:

> At the hour when the child Jesus was born I saw a wonderful vision which appeared to the three holy kings. These kings were star-worshippers and had a tower shaped like a pyramid with steps. It was made partly of timber and was on the top of a hill; one of them was always there, with several priests, to observe the stars. They always wrote down what they saw and communicated it to each other. . . . They saw a beautiful rainbow over the Moon, which was in one of its quarters. Upon the rainbow a Virgin was enthroned; her right foot was resting on the Moon. (LBVM, 200–201)

Anne Catherine goes on to describe a wondrous vision of the spirit of a child coming forth from a chalice in front of the Virgin. But the main point here, according to Anne Catherine's descriptions, is that at the birth of the Solomon Jesus, as witnessed in the stars by the three kings, the Moon was in the constellation Virgo, and "was in one of its quarters." Normally this could be interpreted as signifying First Quarter or Last Quarter; but, reading Anne Catherine's vision more closely, we find that she speaks of a "transparent disk" above the child, which made her think of the eucharistic wafer. The whole impression conveyed by her vision is that of the Full Moon, and her statement that the Moon was visible in one of its quarters, I believe, is meant in the sense that it was in one of its main visible phases: First Quarter, Full Moon, or Last Quarter. (At the New Moon, of course, the Moon is not visible.)

Looking back before 2 B.C., the Moon was full in the middle of Virgo on the night March 5/6, 6 B.C. If this was the night of the birth of the Solomon Jesus, as beheld in a vision in the stars by the three kings, the Solomon Jesus would have been born exactly four years before the conception of the Nathan Jesus. This relationship between the birth and conception dates could signify a deep connection between the two Jesus children, as will emerge later in connection with the *hermetic rule* linking conception and birth.

To explore this question, we must begin to think astrosophically. This implies paying close, even meditative, attention to the definite relationship between the human being and the heavens as expressed in the movements of the Sun, Moon, and planets against the background of the signs of the zodiac. A central astrosophical image is that of the human soul descending into a prevailing heavenly configuration appropriate to the fulfillment of its destiny. This image is elaborated in great depth and through numerous examples in Volumes I and II of my *Hermetic Astrology*. The significance of the heavenly configuration at conception is also discussed there.

The stellar configuration at *conception* relates more to the *body*, the formation of the physical embryo beginning at this moment, whereas the positions of the stars at *birth* have to do more with the destiny of the *soul*, which begins unfolding at the moment of birth. The zodiacal position of the Sun at birth is connected with the spirit, signifying in the present case that the spirit of the Solomon Jesus chose to be born with the Sun in the middle of the constellation Pisces, opposite the Full Moon in the middle of Virgo. Exactly four years later, the Sun was again in the middle of Pisces at the conception configuration of the Nathan Jesus. Moreover, it was the New Moon, so the Moon (connected especially with the life forces) was also in the middle of Pisces. Since the Sun and Moon at the conception of the Nathan Jesus were at the same point in the zodiac as the Sun at the birth of the Solomon Jesus, there is, astrologically speaking, a deep relationship between the spirit of the Solomon Jesus and the body (including the life forces) of the Nathan Jesus. This sheds a clear light on the event in the Temple in A.D. 12, when the spirit of the Solomon Jesus passed over into the body of the Nathan Jesus. But what else may be said about the night of March 5/6, 6 B.C., with the Full Moon rising in Virgo?

The three kings would have seen the Full Moon rising in the middle of Virgo on this evening; and in the preceding morning they would certainly have observed Mars drawing into conjunction with Jupiter. Let us recall again that Kepler dated the birth of Jesus as March, 6 B.C., on account of the meeting of Mars with Saturn and Jupiter. A conjunction between Mars and Saturn took place on February 20 at 25° Pisces, followed by a conjunction of Mars and Jupiter on March 5 at 4 1/2° Aries. In light of Kepler's indication, the birth of the Solomon Jesus took place on this day — conception having occurred at the conjunction between Jupiter and Saturn nine months previously, when Mars was in opposition to them. Since the Sun was in the middle of Pisces on March 5 (assuming this to have been the date of the birth of the Solomon Jesus), it would have necessarily been in the middle of Gemini at his conception (counting back nine months), allowing for a normal embryonic period. In fact, on June 7, 7 B.C., the Sun was in the middle of Gemini, and Saturn and Jupiter were in conjunction at 25° Pisces, opposite Mars at 23° Virgo. On the preceding May 29, the day of the New Moon, the first of the three conjunctions between Jupiter and Saturn in 7 B.C. had taken place. It was this event, the first conjunction between the two largest planets, that heralded the approaching conception of Zarathustra ("golden star"). From this moment on, the Magi were alerted to the descent into incarnation of their master.

Here we come to the essence of the astrosophical approach to the soul's incarnation. Readers to whom such considerations are new might find them complicated or even initially unintelligible. In this case, a certain amount of patience is called for to bear with the astrosophical approach, and if the following proves too difficult to grasp at first reading, the reader should not feel discouraged. The relatively few purely astrosophical passages in this book need not detract from the overall objective of the work, which is to lay the foundations for Cosmic Christianity on the basis of a precise knowledge of the life of Christ.

It is appropriate here to mention Willi Sucher (1902–1985) again, who pioneered astrosophy as a foundation for Cosmic Christianity.[2] Whereas in traditional astrology the whole focus of attention is on the birth horoscope, Willi Sucher's astrosophical research opened up an entirely new perspective, one that focuses on the whole period between conception and birth, so that the birth horoscope emerges as the culmination of an entire process of incarnation extending through the embryological period. This new astrosophical science is sometimes referred to as "astrological biography" because it delineates an astrological prefiguration of the biography on the basis of events in the embryonic period. Another significant discovery of Sucher's is that it is not the traditional geocentric, "Earth-centered" horoscope alone that must be considered but also the heliocentric, "Sun-centered" horoscope. Sucher's work is amply confirmed in my *Hermetic Astrology* trilogy, which introduces the more complex hermetic "helio-geocentric" horoscope in which heliocentric planetary positions are considered from a geocentric

2. Willi Sucher, *Cosmic Christianity and the Changing Countenance of Cosomology.*

point of view. This is essentially nothing other than an application of the astronomical system of the Danish astronomer Tycho Brahe (1546–1601)—about which more later. But what is the relevance of this?

For the incarnated human personality, this planet is the center of the universe, in the sense that it is here one's destiny unfolds between birth and death. Although the Sun is considered the center of the solar system in a physical sense, the Earth is central for the evolution of the soul's destiny. Yet, at the same time, the Sun is central for the human spirit or higher self, although this statement should be qualified in light of the significance of the pivotal period in the history of the Earth that the ministry of Jesus Christ—culminating in the Mystery of Golgotha—represents. According to Rudolf Steiner's spiritual research, Christ departed from the Sun and united with Jesus at the baptism in the Jordan in order to pass through the Mystery of Golgotha at the end of his three and one-half year ministry. Before the Incarnation, Christ was spiritually centered in the Sun; but since the Mystery of Golgotha he is united with the Earth. On a spiritual level, therefore, through Christ's sacrifice, the Earth has become central, replacing the Sun as the center. Though it acknowledges the heliocentric perspective in relation to the human individuality (or higher self), the Earth-centeredness brought about by Christ is taken into account in the hermetic horoscope, which, in combining Sun-centeredness and Earth-centeredness, takes the Mystery of Golgotha fully into account. Most modern astrologers focus solely on the geocentric horoscope and pay no attention to the heliocentric, let alone the hermetic horoscope. Yet, as my *Hermetic Astrology* trilogy shows, the heliocentric and hermetic perspectives are of the utmost significance. In the following pages there will be occasional reference to this new field, as well as to the fundamental principles of astrological biography as they pertain to the process of human incarnation.

It is a basic principle of astrosophy that the incarnation of a human being unfolds in accordance with the movements of the Sun, Moon, and planets against the background of the fixed stars of the zodiac during the period between conception and birth. The Moon's orbit through the signs of the zodiac is especially significant in this context: one lunar orbit requires 27 1/3 days, so ten orbits amount to 273 days, which corresponds to an average embryonic period. Willi Sucher discovered that each lunar sidereal orbit during the embryonic period corresponds to seven years of life—from which it follows that the entire embryonic period (on average ten lunar orbits) corresponds to one lifetime (on average seventy years). The destiny for the first seven years is "woven from the stars" during the Moon's first orbit of the zodiac following conception. This first orbit is completed when the Moon returns to its zodiacal position at conception 27 1/3 days later; during the second orbit the soul's destiny is woven for its life between 7 and 14 years—and so on. The Moon's position in the sidereal zodiac at the moment of conception is therefore of great significance, for the Moon's return to this position every 27 1/3 days during the embryonic period signifies the start of a new phase in the weaving of the incarnating soul's destiny. Moreover, according to the "rule of Hermes," the Ascendant (or sometimes the Descendant) at birth is the same as the Moon's zodiacal position at conception; and conversely, the Ascendant (or Descendant) at conception is identical to the Moon's zodiacal location at birth.[3] Using the hermetic rule, together with the correspondence between the planetary movements during the embryonic period and the soul's ensuing destiny, it has proven possible to determine not only that the birth of the Solomon Jesus took place on the evening of March 5, 6 B.C., but also that his conception occurred on June 7, 7 B.C.; moreover, it has proven possible to determine the exact times of his conception and birth.

Painstaking research was required to arrive at such results. In the course of this research, which included establishing also horoscopes of conception and birth for the Nathan Jesus, it proved invaluable to consider what was known about the two Jesus children *in relation to each another*. A starting point was provided by the birth of the Nathan Jesus, which Anne Catherine Emmerich described taking place at midnight on the night following the close of the Sabbath. Together with other indications that she gave, this led to the discovery that the birth of the Nathan Jesus took place around midnight Saturday/Sunday on December 6/7, 2 B.C. A horoscope cast for that midnight locates the Ascendant in the middle of Virgo and the Moon at about 12° Aries.

Owing to the relationship between the two Jesus children, it was not surprising to find an astrological reciprocity between the birth horoscopes of the Nathan Jesus and the Solomon Jesus. This is expressed in the fulfillment of the hermetic rule between their horoscopes (the interchange of Moon and

3. The rule of Hermes is an ancient astrological rule for determining the horoscope of conception retrospectively from the day and hour of birth. As cited by Porphyry: "Petosiris says that the place where the Moon stands at conception becomes the Ascendant, or the point lying opposite, at birth. However, the place where the Moon stands at birth was the Ascendant at conception." See *Hermetic Astrology*, vol. I, Appendix I, for a description of the hermetic rule in a historical context.

Ascendant). At the birth of the Nathan Jesus, the Ascendant was in the middle of Virgo, exactly in the position occupied by the Full Moon on the night of the birth of the Solomon Jesus. Similarly, the zodiacal position (12° Aries) of the Moon at the birth of the Nathan Jesus also represents the Ascendant-Descendant axis at the birth of the Solomon Jesus. Since the hermetic rule establishes the axis without indicating whether the Ascendant or Descendant is involved in a given case, the question remains: Was the Ascendant at the birth of the Solomon Jesus 12° Aries, or was it 12° Libra?

Let us consider both of these possibilities in connection with the Full Moon in Virgo on the night March 5/6, 6 B.C. The actual moment of the Full Moon was twenty minutes past midnight (12:20 A.M. local time in Bethlehem) on March 6. At this moment the Sun was at 15 1/2° Pisces, the Moon at 15 1/2° Virgo, and the Ascendant in Bethlehem at 7° Sagittarius. Going back approximately 4 1/2 hours to 7:58 P.M. in the evening of March 5, the Ascendant in Bethlehem was 12° Libra; going forward approximately 7 1/2 hours to 7:41 A.M. on the morning of March 6, it was 12° Aries.

If we now compare these results with Anne Catherine's vision of the three kings beholding the Moon in Virgo on the night of Jesus' birth, we can rule out the second possibility—for 7:41 A.M. was after sunrise, and the Moon had already set. This means that the first possibility is the only plausible one; that is, that the birth of the Solomon Jesus occurred at 7:58 P.M. on March 5, 6 B.C., when the Ascendant in Bethlehem was 12° Libra (see Chart 1). With this established, it becomes possible to determine the date and the time of conception of the Solomon Jesus. "Astrological biography," as will be shown shortly, further confirms these horoscopes of conception and birth.

Let us first apply the hermetic rule to the birth of the Solomon Jesus, in order to find his horoscope of conception, bearing in mind that the hermetic rule is the astrological rule connecting conception and birth. In other words, given the birth horoscope, the hermetic rule can be applied to find the conception horoscope. In the present case we have established the date and time of the birth of the Solomon Jesus. Now to apply the hermetic rule it is necessary to know the position of the Moon at birth, which specifies the Ascendant-Descendant axis at conception, and the position of the Ascendant-Descendant axis at birth, which specifies the Moon at conception. Applying the hermetic rule is a matter of using the Ascendant-Descendant axis, so that the Ascendant and the Descendant are equivalent in status. At the birth of the Solomon Jesus the Moon was at 15° Virgo and the Ascendant at 12° Libra. According to the hermetic rule, therefore, the Ascendant at conception was 15° Virgo (or possibly 15° Pisces), and the Moon was at 12° Libra (or possibly 12° Aries). As already mentioned, if we follow the Sun back nine months from its position in the middle of Pisces at birth, we locate its position at conception in the middle of Gemini. This, of course, assumes a normal embryonic period of nine months. Earlier in this chapter the date June 7, 7 B.C., was suggested as a possible date of conception, at which time the Sun was in the middle of Gemini (16° Gemini), while Jupiter and Saturn were in conjunction (25° Pisces) opposite Mars at 23° Virgo. Now, at 11.41 A.M. local time, on June 7, 7 B.C., the Moon was at 12° Libra and the Ascendant in Bethlehem was 15° Virgo, thus fulfilling the hermetic rule (see Chart 2) and strongly confirming that this was indeed the moment when the Solomon Jesus was conceived. Further confirmation by way of astrological biography now follows.

Chapter Four

Astrological Biography

Astrological biography is the study of the unfolding of destiny through seven-year cycles between birth and death as prefigured in the heavenly configurations between conception and birth. During the embryonic period, the "web of destiny"—which begins to unfold from the moment of birth onward—is woven in such a way that it reflects the configurations in the heavens between conception and birth. Astrological biography is concerned with reading the meaning of these heavenly configurations for the human being's biography between birth and death. For example, if a striking planetary configuration occurs midway between conception and birth, assuming a normal length embryonic period of 273 days, it prefigures a human being's destiny around the age of 35, since according to astrological biography 273 days corresponds to 70 years of life.[1]

In the following application of astrological biography to the time between conception and birth of the Solomon Jesus, let us try to consider the cosmic situation at that time as it might have been viewed by the three kings. The most spectacular event in the heavens in that year (7 B.C.) was the triple conjunction between Jupiter and Saturn on May 29, October 1, and December 5, with the two planets remaining in close proximity to one another throughout this period and for several weeks before the first conjunction and after the third. The three kings could have easily observed Saturn and Jupiter drawing closer to one another toward the end of May, since they were visible high in the sky in the constellation Pisces in the hours preceding sunrise. On May 29, the New Moon took place in Gemini, and, on this moonless night, Saturn and Jupiter could have been observed very close together. On the following nights the waxing crescent of the Moon emerged,

---

1. Robert Powell, *Hermetic Astrology*, vol. II: *Astrological Biography* gives a number of examples.

passing from Gemini, through Cancer, Leo, and Virgo into Libra. At the same time, Mars in Virgo was drawing into opposition with Saturn and Jupiter. On the morning of June 7, 7 B.C., according to the above application of the hermetic rule, the conception of the Solomon Jesus occurred.

In his book *Der Stern der Weisen* [The Star of the Magi], Konradin Ferrari d' Occhieppo points out that Babylon was the only center in Mesopo-tamia where computations of the movements of the heavenly bodies were still being carried out at the time of Christ. Uruk, formerly a great center of astronomical observation, had been destroyed in 141 B.C. Moreover, despite the foundation of the city of Seleucia on the banks of the Tigris (ca. 300 B.C.), which attracted much of the population of Babylon, the priestly caste that carried out the observation and computation of astronomical events remained in Babylon, the holy city of Marduk. (Marduk, the god of Jupiter, was the leader of the Babylonian pantheon of planetary gods.[2]) Cuneiform tablets excavated in Babylon show that the conjunction of Jupiter and Saturn in 7 B.C. had been computed in advance, as well as the following astronomical events of the early part of 6 B.C.:

ASTRONOMICAL EVENT	DATE COMPUTED BY BABYLONIANS	DATE ACCORDING TO MODERN COMPUTATION
The entrance of Jupiter into the sidereal sign of Aries	February 12, 6 B.C.	February 13, 6 B.C.
The entrance of Mars into the sidereal sign of Aries	February 26, 6 B.C.	February 27, 6 B.C.
The conjunction of Jupiter and Mars	March 5, 6 B.C	March 5, 6 B.C.

Thus, the very date that (according to the research presented in this book) represents the birth date of the Jesus of Saint Matthew's Gospel had been computed in advance in Babylon—from which city, according to many researchers (including K. Ferrari d' Occhieppo), the three kings came! Although this date was not originally computed as the birthdate of the Solomon Jesus, it nevertheless represents a striking coincidence. According to Anne Catherine Emmerich, the names of the three kings were Theokeno (traditionally Caspar), Mensor (traditionally Melchior), and Sair (traditionally Balthasar). She

---

2. See Robert Powell, *History of the Planets*, p. 4.

describes the kings as friends but as coming from three different countries: Theokeno from Media, Mensor from Chaldea, and Sair from another country ("Partherme"?) (LBVM, 232). From her description, the home of Mensor has been identified as the island fortress Achaiachala (HDK, 63), some two hundred miles up the Euphrates from Babylon. The Roman emperor Julian the Apostate (A.D. 363) later visited this fortress on one of his campaigns.[3] Perhaps Mensor was one of the Babylonian priestly caste who had moved from Babylon to Achaiachala. Or perhaps he was in touch with the Babylonian priestly caste. In either case, it is quite conceivable that he knew of these computations and could thus have been alerted in advance to the conjunction of Mars and Jupiter in Aries on March 5, 6 B.C. Nevertheless, Anne Catherine Emmerich makes it quite clear that it was on the basis of a visionary experience from the world of stars that the three kings knew of the birth of the Messiah. At the time of this vision, on the night of the birth, Sair was visiting Mensor. But Theokeno, who lived about five days' journey from Mensor, also had the same vision at the hour of the birth of Jesus, and set off to meet up with the other two kings. From Anne Catherine's descriptions, it has proven possible to date the visit of the Magi to Bethlehem, which took place several months after the birth.

At this juncture, it should be pointed out that Anne Catherine did not distinguish between the Solomon Jesus and the Nathan Jesus. When she related her visions to Clemens Brentano, while on the whole she recounted the visit of the Magi (to the Solomon Jesus) quite separately from the shepherd's adoration (of the Nathan Jesus), she sometimes mixed together elements of the two. The two births, however, must be strictly separated to arrive at the truth. Nevertheless, the fact of the births of two Jesus children was not revealed to her, and so it is quite natural that her accounts are somewhat tangled. But why, we may ask, was the fact of two births and two holy families concealed from her when so much was revealed? Why did this mystery have to wait until the time of Rudolf Steiner to be discovered?

During the period (1819–1824) that Anne Catherine was telling her visions to Clemens Brentano, there was virtually no knowledge of reincarnation in the West. It would therefore have been something quite inexplicable, and very confusing, if she had spoken of two Jesus children—since an understanding of reincarnation makes up an important part of the background needed to comprehend the fact of their existence. Almost a hundred years

---

3. Ammianus Marcellinus, *Res Gestae* xxiv, ii, 2.

had to elapse, until the time of Rudolf Steiner's teaching activity (1900–1925), before this mystery could be unveiled; for it was in the context of reincarnation that Rudolf Steiner spoke of this mystery, referring to the Solomon Jesus as the reincarnation of Zarathustra and the Nathan Jesus as the incarnation of the "sister soul" of Adam.

Even now that knowledge of reincarnation has become more widespread than in Rudolf Steiner's day, the idea of two Jesus children may be radically new for many readers. Some might feel that, since reincarnation is not accepted or taught by traditional Christianity, it is a false doctrine, and contradicts Christianity's teaching of salvation by way of the resurrection of the body at the end of time. However, it is possible to view reincarnation positively, in a Christian way, by looking at the succession of lives (earthly incarnations) as a means or path of development eventually leading toward the resurrection of the body as the goal of Christian evolution. In this case, there is no contradiction with traditional Christianity. On the contrary, much appears clearer in the light of reincarnation, for which reason Rudolf Steiner's unveiling of the mystery of two Jesus children against this background helps to open up completely new perspectives—perspectives that are fundamental for Cosmic Christianity and for the research presented in this book.

On the basis of Rudolf Steiner's descriptions, taken in conjunction with the visions of Anne Catherine Emmerich, many details concerning the life of Jesus Christ become clear. One instance of this, particularly rich in historical incident, is the visit of the Magi to Bethlehem to pay homage to their reincarnated master Zarathustra.

> I always saw the kings approaching Bethlehem when I was putting out the crib in the convent—that is to say, about December 25. (LBVM, 219)

In 1821, Anne Catherine described at length the journey of the three holy kings to Bethlehem, beginning with their departure from Achaiachala and including their twenty-eight day camel journey across the desert to Bethlehem. Fortunately, her account contains sufficient reference to Jewish weekdays and festivals for us to confidently assign specific dates to key events here also. For example, she related that Herod returned from Jericho to Jerusalem while the kings were on their way "in order to take part in the feast of the Dedication of the Temple on the 25th day of the month Kislev" (LBVM, 254). Now, in the year 6 B.C., Kislev 25 fell on December 6 or 7, so this indicates that the three kings were on their way by December 6/7 at least. According to Anne Catherine the "star" that led the kings was the soul of Zarathustra ("radiant star") himself. [Etymologically the word Zarathustra means "radiant star."] However, according to her account, this spiritual guidance disappeared as the kings approached Jerusalem on the Sabbath. They arrived at the city on Saturday evening. After describing the encounter with Herod, who had summoned the three kings to his palace early on Sunday morning, the Magi traveled on, reaching Bethlehem at dusk that evening. Thus, it was *shortly after dusk* that "they saw a light shining in the sky beside Bethlehem, as though the Moon were rising" (LBVM, 258). If, indeed, it was the Moon rising shortly after dusk, this tells us that the Full Moon rose that evening, for the Moon can only rise *just after sunset* at the time of the Full Moon, or shortly thereafter. Indeed, on Sunday, December 26, 6 B.C., the Moon became full in the constellation of Cancer shortly after midnight (12:14 A.M. Bethlehem time); and that evening, shortly after sunset, the Full Moon rose across the eastern horizon a little before six o'clock (5:40 P.M. Bethlehem time). That same evening the three kings found Joseph, Mary, and the child, just as they had seen them in their visions. The evening of Sunday, December 26, 6 B.C., some nine and one-half months after the birth, was therefore the night of the Adoration of the Magi.

This conclusion admittedly depends upon interpreting Anne Catherine Emmerich's rather uncertain formulation "as though the Moon were rising" as referring to the actual Moon. Yet accepting this to be so leads to December 26 as the date of the Adoration of the Magi, which agrees with her previous statement that she always saw the three kings approaching Bethlehem around December 25. This lends justification to the interpretation of her words about the Moon as actual and not merely symbolic. Note that here again, as with almost all of Anne Catherine's remarks about the calendar, her indication concerning the day of the week—in this case, Sunday—is of major significance in pinpointing the date.

According to Anne Catherine's account, the three kings remained in Bethlehem for the whole of the following day (Monday), and were warned by an angel that night not to return to Herod but to go to Chaldea through the desert, passing south of the Dead Sea (LBVM, 267). Before leaving, the kings warned the Holy Family, but Mary and Joseph did not flee with the child Jesus immediately. Meanwhile, Herod had become exceedingly uneasy on account of the visit of the three kings to his palace in Jerusalem on December 25/26 in search of a "newborn king." Therefore, when the kings did not return to him to report whether or not they had found the child, he spread abroad a rumor that the Magi had not returned because they had been mistaken and had failed to find the child they were looking for. Nevertheless, Herod was agitated and suspected that he had somehow been outwitted by the Magi. His disquiet increased, until he finally ordered the massacre of the innocents.

Prior to this terrible event, Joseph was warned by an angel to flee with Mary and Jesus to Egypt. "The day he started on the flight was what is now February 29th" (LBVM, 295). Since February 29 occurs only once every four years, Anne Catherine's indication permits us to date the flight into Egypt to February 29, 5 B.C., since this was a leap year. This was two months after the departure of the Magi from Bethlehem, and by this time the child Jesus was about one year old. Anne Catherine then describes how the Holy Family journeyed to Heliopolis. "Toward the middle of Jesus' second year the Blessed Virgin was told of Herod's massacre of the innocents by an angel appearing to her in Heliopolis" (LBVM, 318). Jesus was one and one-half years old in September, 5 B.C., so (if Anne Catherine Emmerich's account is correct) it must have been around this time that the massacre of the innocents took place. Herod's delay in taking action explains why he ordered that all male children in Bethlehem up to *two* years of age be put to death (Matthew 2:16). As indicated in the table of lunar eclipses given earlier, there was a total eclipse of the Moon visible in Jerusalem on the evening of September 15, 5 B.C.; and it seems likely that the massacre of the innocents took place around this time.

> After staying in Heliopolis for a year and a half, until Jesus was about two years old, the Holy Family left the city, because of lack of work and various persecutions. They moved southwards in the direction of Memphis.... They had to cross a small arm of a river or canal, and came to a place whose name as it was at that time I cannot remember; afterwards it was called Matarea, and was near Heliopolis.... The first time that the child Jesus went alone to the Jewish settlement (I am not sure whether it was in his fifth or seventh year) . . . he knelt down to pray on the way, and I saw two angels appearing to him and announcing the death of Herod the Great. (LBVM, 323–324, 333)

Anne Catherine describes how an angel later came to Joseph in a dream, saying that those who had sought the life of the child were now dead and that it would be safe to journey back to Israel:

Joseph . . . wished to settle in his ancestral home of Bethlehem. He was, however, still irresolute, since on arriving in the Promised Land he heard that Judea was governed by Archeleus, who like Herod was very cruel. I saw that the Holy Family stayed about three months in Gaza, where there were many heathen. Here an angel again appeared to Joseph in a dream and commanded him to go to Nazareth, which he did at once. . . . The return from Egypt happened in September. Jesus was nearly eight years old. (LBVM, 344–345)

This indicates that the Solomon Jesus child and his family went to live in Nazareth, after returning from Egypt in September, A.D. 2, when Jesus was seven and one-half years old. Shortly thereafter, in December, A.D. 2, the Nathan Jesus child reached the age of three; and from this time on the two Jesus children grew up in close proximity to one another.

It is difficult to arrive at a precise date for the death of Herod from Anne Catherine's communications. She relates:

Herod reigned forty years in all until his death. He was, it is true, only a vassal-king for seven years, but harassed the country grievously and committed many cruelties. He died about the time of Christ's sixth year. I think that his death was kept a secret for some time. His end was dreadful, and in the last days of his life he was responsible for many murders and much misery. I saw him crawling about in a room padded with cushions. He had a spear, and stabbed at anyone who came near him. Jesus must have been born about the thirty-fourth year of Herod's reign. (LBVM, 205–206)

Emmerich refers here to the death of Herod in the "fifth or seventh year" of the child Jesus. But this contradicts most historians, who regard "Herod's eclipse" as that of March 12/13, 4 B.C., and therefore place Herod's death in the intervening period before the start of the Feast of the Passover on April 11, 4 B.C. However, as mentioned above, two modern historians, Ernest L. Martin and Ormond Edwards, present considerable evidence in favor of regarding the total eclipse of January 9/10, 1 B.C., as Herod's eclipse, thus dating Herod's death to the period before the Feast of the Passover that started on April 10, in 1 B.C. Both Martin and Edwards believe that the most likely date for the death of Herod was January 28, 1 B.C. Just over two months later, then, on March 5, 1 B.C., the Solomon Jesus child would have attained the age of five years, which would fit well with Anne Catherine Emmerich's statement that in his fifth year ("fifth or seventh year") two angels appeared to him to announce the death of Herod the Great. This was six years after the triple conjunction of Jupiter and Saturn in 7 B.C. with which the incarnation of the Solomon Jesus began, his conception having taken place shortly after the first conjunction of Jupiter and Saturn.

Apart from Anne Catherine's statement and the researches of Martin and Edwards, there is another reason for believing that Herod lived on beyond 4 B.C. Since, according to the research presented in Chapter One, the birth of the Nathan Jesus took place on December 6, 2 B.C., it follows that the birth of John the Baptist took place "at the end of May or the beginning of June" (LBVM, 163) and that John's conception would have occurred some nine months earlier, around the beginning of September, 3 B.C. Describing the conception of John the Baptist, the Gospel of Saint Luke refers to Zechariah, the father of John: "In the days of Herod, king of Judea, there was a priest named Zechariah. . . ." (Luke 1:5). Thus, it would seem that Herod the Great was still alive in September, 3 B.C. Nevertheless, according to Rudolf Steiner, the births of John the Baptist and the Nathan Jesus took place *after* the massacre of the innocents. Assuming that this took place in (or around) September, 5 B.C., the Nathan Jesus would then have been born in Bethlehem over three years later.

There still remains Rudolf Steiner's statement that the births of the two Jesus children were separated by "a period of months." We have made a strong case that the Solomon Jesus was born on March 5, 6 B.C., and the Nathan Jesus on December 6, 2 B.C. Therefore four years and nine months— or 57 months—elapsed between the two births. "A few years" would thus have been a more accurate expression. We must now try to resolve this apparent discrepancy.

Readers acquainted with Rudolf Steiner's works will recall his descriptions of the event of the twelve-year-old Jesus in the Temple, when the two Jesus children united to become one:

> This is magnificently presented to us in the Gospel of Saint Luke, in the passage referring to the astounding scene where the twelve-year-old Jesus is sitting among the learned Rabbis and saying things that sound utterly strange. How could Jesus of the Nathan line be capable of this? The explanation is that at that moment the Zarathustra-individuality had passed into him. . . . We have followed Zarathustra from his birth

as the Jesus of Saint Matthew's Gospel to his twelfth year, when he left his original body and passed into the bodily constitution of the Nathan Jesus.... He of whom the early chapters of Saint Matthew's Gospel speaks—Jesus of the Solomon line—wasted away and died, comparatively soon after his twelfth year. At first there were two boys; then the two became one. (Rudolf Steiner, *The Gospel of Saint Matthew*, pp. 112–116)

This description seems to imply that the Solomon Jesus and the Nathan Jesus were both twelve years old (or in their twelfth year). As discussed in the previous chapter, the event in the Temple took place immediately following the Feast of the Passover in A.D. 12, which ended at sunset on Sunday, April 3, A.D. 12. However, according to the research presented here, the Nathan Jesus was then twelve years and four months old, and the Solomon Jesus seventeen years and one month old. It is therefore quite correct to speak of the twelve-year-old Jesus with respect to the *Nathan* Jesus, and the expression "twelfth year" used by Rudolf Steiner is certainly to be understood in the sense of the "twelve-year-old Jesus," as implied in the above quotation. However, in light of the research presented in this book this term cannot be applied to the Solomon Jesus child. Why, then, did Rudolf Steiner do so?

As far as it is possible to judge, Rudolf Steiner's spiritual vision was focused on the fact of the two Jesus children becoming one. Just as two drops of water, when they coalesce, become indistinguishable, so with the union of the two Jesus children: they became one entity. In Steiner's spiritual perception of this event in the Temple, of which he spoke many times, he understood the age to have been twelve years, but his attention may very well have been focused on the twelve-year-old *Nathan* Jesus, with whom the Solomon Jesus merged. When he said, "Jesus of the Solomon line wasted away and died comparatively soon after his twelfth year," the word "his" most likely refers to the Nathan Jesus. Recall, too, that the Solomon Jesus *died* when the Nathan Jesus was twelve years old. In the light of the research presented in this book, we feel confident that this is how Rudolf Steiner's words are to be understood.

Indirect evidence that this interpretation may be correct is also provided by a reference by Steiner to Mary's age at the time of the baptism in the Jordan. This will be discussed at greater length in the section on Mary. Here it must suffice to quote Steiner's words:

At the moment of the baptism in the Jordan, the mother [i.e., Mary, the mother of the Solomon Jesus] too was aware of something like the climax of the change that had come about in her. She was then between her forty-fifth and forty-sixth years. She felt as though permeated by the soul of that mother who had died, the mother of the Jesus child who in his twelfth year had received the Zarathustra-Ego. Thus the spirit of the other mother had come down upon (her). . . and she felt herself as the young mother who had once given birth to the Jesus child of Saint Luke's Gospel. (Rudolf Steiner, *The Fifth Gospel*, pp. 92–93)

Here it emerges that, at the time of the baptism in the Jordan, an event took place analogous to the merging of the two Jesus children at the end of the Passover festival in A.D. 12. The spirit of the Nathan Mary (the mother of the Nathan Jesus) united with the Solomon Mary (the mother of the Solomon Jesus), and the two became one. It was to this *union* of the two Marys that Steiner's attention must have been drawn. For, as will be discussed in the section on Mary, the Solomon Mary was forty-nine years old at the time of the baptism in the Jordan, while the Nathan Mary would have been forty-five years and two months old had she lived to that time. Rudolf Steiner's words seem to indicate that the Solomon Mary was forty-five to forty-six years old at the time of the baptism; but they actually apply to the mother of the *Nathan* Jesus, who had *united* spiritually with the Solomon Mary. This apparent discrepancy can be plausibly explained only by Steiner's focus on the *union* of the two Marys, just as in his descriptions of the twelve-year-old Jesus in the Temple, where the age of twelve applies to the Nathan Jesus, although the *Solomon* Jesus is in fact being referred to.

The research presented in this book thus leads to the conviction that, at the event in the Temple at the end of the Passover festival (Sunday, April 3) in A.D. 12, the Solomon Jesus was seventeen years and one month old. Consideration of his family situation supports this conclusion. For, according to Rudolf Steiner, the father of the Solomon Jesus had already died prior to the Passover. At his death, he left Mary a widow with seven children, of whom Jesus was the eldest. It is unlikely that these seven children were born in such rapid succession that at their father's death the eldest child was only twelve years old, whereas the age of seventeen years is quite plausible. Although not a definite proof, consideration of the family situation—taken in conjunction with other factors—lends further support to the more mature age.

Moreover, astrological confirmation that the age of the Solomon Jesus at the time of the Temple event was seventeen years and one month is provided by the method of "astrological biography." But, before applying this method, let us turn our attention to the remaining question of the date of the Solomon Jesus' death. Research of the same kind that led to the determination of the dates and times of the Solomon Jesus' conception and birth leads to the dating of his death to June 5, A.D. 12, two months after the Temple event. However, it has not yet proven possible to determine the exact hour of death on this date. It may very well have been shortly after midnight, however, for the following significant astrological configurations obtained at that time: three-quarters of an hour after midnight (12:45 A.M., Nazareth time) on June 5, A.D. 12, Venus and Mars, themselves in exact conjunction (at 16° Gemini), were also in conjunction with the Sun (14° Gemini); and Saturn (3° Scorpio) was in opposition to the Moon (6° Taurus) in the Pleiades (see Chart 3). At that time, the Solomon Jesus was seventeen years and three months old.

At first sight, the dating of the death of the Solomon Jesus to June 5, A.D. 12, might seem to rest upon nothing more than astrological considerations. Having once determined that the date of the union of the two Jesus children at the Temple was April 3, A.D. 12, and given Rudolf Steiner's indication that the young Solomon Jesus died "in a comparatively short time,"[4] it is a question as to how long after April 3 this was. If a "comparatively short time" is interpreted as a matter of months, then the period May/June, A.D. 12, cannot be too far off. Looking at the various planetary configurations during this time, that of June 5 is the most striking. In the last analysis, however, in this case there is no certainty that the date June 5, A.D. 12, is truly the correct date of death of the Solomon Jesus. It could be that the remarkable fit in this instance of applying astrological biography (see following) is the result of chance coincidence.

Now let us turn to the application of astrological biography in the life of the Solomon Jesus. Since the Solomon Jesus continued his spiritual activity after the death of his body by indwelling the Nathan Jesus, it is logical to look at major events—such as the baptism in the Jordan and the death on the cross at Golgotha—in the context of the "biography" of the "dead" Solomon Jesus now active in the body of the Nathan Jesus. Taking account of this, the most important events in this biography are:

---

4. Rudolf Steiner, *The Fifth Gospel*, p. 116.

(1) the flight into Egypt, which began around February 29, 5 B.C.;

(2) the birth of the Nathan Jesus on December 6, 2 B.C.;

(3) the union with the Nathan Jesus (at the end of Passover) on April 3, A.D. 12;

(4) the death of the Solomon Jesus on June 5, A.D. 12;

(5) the baptism in the Jordan on September 23, A.D. 29 (this is the date determined, on the basis of Anne Catherine Emmerich's statements, in Part I of this book);

(6) the crucifixion on Golgotha on Friday, April 3, A.D. 33.

The method of astrological biography is discussed at length in my book *Hermetic Astrology, vol. II: Astrological Biography.* The underlying principle is the correspondence between the embryonic period and the course of life, where the Moon's position in the sidereal zodiac at each moment in time during the embryonic period corresponds to a definite moment in the unfolding of the biography. It was Willi Sucher who first discovered the principle of this correspondence: i.e., that one orbit of the Moon around the sidereal zodiac during the embryonic period prefigures seven years of life. In this way, once the age at a given event in life is known, the corresponding "embryonic age" can be found in terms of the Moon's position in the sidereal zodiac. For the six events listed above, the following table gives the biographic age at each event and the corresponding embryonic age in terms of the Moon's position in the sidereal zodiac.

AGE	MOON'S POSITION IN SIDEREAL ZODIAC	CORRESPONDING DATE IN EMBRYONIC PERIOD
1) almost one year	0 orbits + 51° = 3° Sagittarius	June 11, 7 B.C., 4:30 A.M.
2) 4 years 9 months	0 orbits + 244 1/4° = 16 1/2° Gemini	June 26, 7 B.C., 9:00 A.M.
3) 17 years 1 month	2 orbits + 158 1/2° = 20 1/2° Pisces	August 12, 7 B.C., 9:30 P.M.
4) 17 years 3 months	2 orbits + 167° = 29° Pisces	August 13, 7 B.C., 2:30 P.M.
5) 34 years 6 1/2 months	4 orbits + 336 1/2° = 18 1/2° Virgo	Oct 20, 7 B.C., 6:00 P.M.
6) 38 years 1 month	5 orbits + 158 1/2° = 20 1/2° Pisces	Nov 2, 7 B.C., 5:30 P.M.

By way of explanation, let us consider entry (1) in the above table. At the start of the flight into Egypt, the Solomon Jesus child was almost one year old. Since seven years of life correspond to one orbit (360 degrees) of the Moon around the sidereal zodiac, one year amounts to one-seventh of the lunar orbit, or 51 degrees (to the nearest degree). The embryonic prefiguration of period (1) can therefore be determined—under the assumption that the Moon at conception was located at 12° Libra. Adding 51 degrees, gives 3° Sagittarius. In other words, the Moon started out at the conception on June 7, 7 B.C., at 12° Libra, and, in the early hours of June 11, 7 B.C., it reached 3° Sagittarius.

Looking at the planetary configuration on June 11, 7 B.C., we see that Mars drew into exact opposition with Saturn on this day (recall that Mars was approaching opposition to Saturn and Jupiter on the day of conception). With the entry of the Moon into Sagittarius and with the exact opposition between Mars and Saturn, the Solomon Jesus child was then obliged to flee Palestine to escape the Massacre of the Innocents—Herod being the "hunter" and the Solomon Jesus the "quarry." Sagittarius is the zodiacal sign traditionally connected with hunting and the lunar Sagittarius period, which started in the life of the Solomon Jesus child in February, 5 B.C. and lasted seven months until September, 5 B.C., was probably the time during which the Massacre of the Innocents took place. It is perhaps worth mentioning that there are also *seven-month* zodiacal periods (i.e., 1/12th of the *seven year* cycles "governed" by each lunar orbit during the embryonic period) corresponding to the Moon's passage through each sign of the sidereal zodiac during the embryonic period. This correspondence also plays a role in astrological biography and helped to corroborate the research results presented here.

The next lunar zodiacal period of special interest to us in the biography of the Solomon Jesus child is that of Gemini, for it was during this time that the birth of the Nathan Jesus took place. At the conception of the Solomon Jesus child, the Sun was in the middle of Gemini, and so the passage of the Moon through Gemini during the embryonic period was of deep significance. In fact, as may be seen from event (2) in the above table, the Moon was at 16 1/2° Gemini, and therefore in conjunction with the zodiacal location where the Sun had been at conception (16° Gemini).

The age of seven—in A.D. 2—corresponds to the completion of the Moon's first orbit of the sidereal zodiac during the embryonic period. Since the Moon at conception stood at 12° Libra (corresponding to birth), its return to 12° Libra at the end of its first orbit corresponded to the age of seven. During this time, the lunar zodiacal period of Libra, the decision was made by the Holy Family to return from Egypt to Palestine.

The next seven-year period, from seven to fourteen (during which time, in the corresponding part of the embryonic period, the Moon passed once again around the sidereal zodiac to return to 12° Libra for the second time), was spent at Nazareth in close proximity to the Nathan Jesus child. Prior to the middle of the following seven-year period, from fourteen to twenty-one, there came the event in the Temple (3) and the death of the Solomon Jesus (4), both events taking place in the lunar zodiacal period of Pisces.

The special significance of this Piscean period is indicated by the fact that the Sun stood in the middle of Pisces at the birth of the Solomon Jesus. At event (3) the Moon's corresponding position in the embryonic period was 20 1/2° Pisces, in conjunction with the heliocentric zodiacal locations of Jupiter (19 3/4° Pisces) and Saturn (20 1/2° Pisces), and close to (orb 3°) the position taken up by the Sun at birth (15 1/2° Pisces). At event (4) the Moon's corresponding position in the embryonic period was 29° Pisces, conjunct Jupiter (27° Pisces) and Saturn (24° Pisces). Thus death on the spiritual level, at the event in the Temple, took place when the Moon's zodiacal location was equivalent to that of Saturn and Jupiter considered *heliocentrically*; death then followed on the physical level, event (4), when the Moon was conjoined with the *geocentric* locations of Jupiter and Saturn. The interested reader is referred to the author's other works for the principles involved here.

In the case of a highly developed individuality such as Zarathustra, who was incarnated in the Solomon Jesus, death signifies merely a translation of activity from one realm to another. This individuality worked on, after the death of the body on June 5, A.D. 12, in union with the Nathan Jesus. (We have already seen that he had begun to indwell the physical body of the younger Jesus child sometime around April 3, A.D. 12.) Thus, the Solomon Jesus was active in preparing the way for the unfolding of the earthly mission of Jesus Christ—the mission which began with the baptism in the Jordan and culminated in the death on the cross on Golgotha.

Looking at these two major events from the point of view of the astrological biography of the Solomon Jesus—i.e., viewing them in relation to the corresponding moments of his embryonic period—the relationship of the Moon to the planets Saturn and Jupiter (in the embryonic period) again stands out, as in event (3). At event (5), the baptism in the Jordan, the corresponding position of the Moon during the embryonic period was 18 1/2° Virgo. Here the Moon was more or less opposite the position taken up by the Sun at birth (15 1/2° Pisces) and loosely in conjunction with the position taken up by the Moon at birth (15 Virgo)—this latter also representing the zodiacal position of the Ascendant at conception (15° Virgo). More striking, however, is the fact that, at the moment in the embryonic period corresponding to the baptism in the Jordan, the Moon (18 1/2° Virgo) was in opposition to a conjunction of Jupiter (19° Pisces) and Saturn (19° Pisces).

Lastly, at event (6), the crucifixion, the Moon (20 1/2° Pisces) was in conjunction with Jupiter (18° Pisces) and Saturn (18 1/2° Pisces). So we see the beginning and end of the three and one-half year period of Christ's ministry prefigured in the embryonic period of the Solomon Jesus by the opposition of the Moon to Jupiter and Saturn, corresponding to the baptism in the Jordan, and the conjunction of the Moon with Jupiter and Saturn, corresponding to the death on the cross on Golgotha.

It is also instructive to note that the Moon's position in the embryonic period corresponding to the death on the cross (20 1/2° Pisces) was identical to the Moon's position in the embryonic period at event (3), the event in the Temple, when the Solomon Jesus "died spiritually"—leaving his own body to unite with that of the Nathan Jesus. Astrologically, this can be understood as a consequence of the fact that *exactly* twenty-one years had elapsed between the two events (April 3, A.D. 12–April 3, A.D. 33). Since twenty-one years comprise three seven-year periods, and since one seven-year period is delineated in the embryonic period by one orbit of the Moon around the sidereal zodiac, it follows that after three seven-year periods, the Moon will have returned to the same position in the sidereal zodiac that it had occupied three orbits earlier in the embryonic period. In the biography of the Solomon Jesus this signified that his "spiritual death" at the end of the Passover festival in A.D. 12 was a "microcosmic reflection" of, and preparation for, the great event of the sacrifice of Jesus Christ on the cross on the day of preparation for the Passover festival in A.D. 33.

More elaborate details have been omitted here in order not to make the description too complicated. For more details the reader is referred to *Hermetic Astrology, vol. II: Astrological Biography*. Nevertheless, it should be possible from the above outline to gain some idea of the overview of destiny that may be provided by astrological biography. The entire application depends, of course, on the validity of the birth and conception horoscopes, and one of the conclusions that may be drawn from the above application is that the birth and conception horoscopes of the Solomon Jesus, as given in Charts 1 and 2, are evidently correct. This conclusion follows from the remarkable concordance between major events in the biography and the corresponding events in the embryonic period. Hopefully other researchers will be able to follow up this study to arrive at independent confirmation of these findings.

To summarize our main findings concerning the Solomon Jesus: we have shown that Kepler's indication of March, 6 B.C., as the birth month of Jesus (the Solomon Jesus) is correct, the exact date being March 5, the day of the conjunction between Mars and Jupiter. To be more precise, the birth occurred that evening, when the Full Moon appeared in the middle of the constellation Virgo. The conception, as determined by the hermetic rule, took place nine months earlier, on June 7, 7 B.C., shortly after the first of the three conjunctions that took place between Jupiter and Saturn in Pisces as Mars was coming into opposition to them. On the basis of astrological considerations, it would appear that the Solomon Jesus died on June 5, A.D. 12, almost exactly eighteen years after his conception, as the Sun, Mars, and Venus were in conjunction in the middle of Gemini. But this physical death was preceded two months earlier—on April 3, A.D. 12 —by the "spiritual death" of the Solomon Jesus that took place in the event of his uniting with the twelve-year-old Nathan Jesus in the Temple in Jerusalem.

We shall now focus our attention upon the astrological biography of the Nathan Jesus.

Chapter Five

The Nathan Jesus

The starting point for the research presented in this book was a study of the life of Christ Jesus on the basis of Anne Catherine Emmerich's spiritual visions and Rudolf Steiner's spiritual research. However, due to the importance of Anne Catherine's visions for the present book, a closer consideration of her contribution will hopefully not be taken amiss.

Anne Catherine's visions were attuned in a wonderful and mysterious way to the actual historical life of the Messiah. She was blessed from earliest childhood onward with continued visions of scenes recorded in the Old and New Testaments. After receiving the stigmata—on December 29, 1812—she remained permanently bedridden, and practically the whole of her waking and sleeping existence was then given up to beholding the life of Christ Jesus in spiritual vision. She lived from that time almost exclusively on water and the holy sacrament, which she received daily.

During the last five years of Anne Catherine's life the poet Clemens Brentano sat each day at her bedside (apart from short periods when he was absent for one reason or another) and recorded her visions as she recounted them. On July 29, 1820, she began to communicate to him the day-by-day life of Christ Jesus, from shortly before the baptism in the Jordan up to the Mystery of Golgotha. The attunement of her visions with the actual historical life of Christ was such that there was a concordance between the weekdays at the time of Christ and those on which she had her visions. For example, every Friday evening she experienced the onset of the Sabbath in the life of Christ at the historical point in time at which she was beholding it.

The Jewish Sabbath extends from dusk on Friday evening to sunset on Saturday evening, and this weekly rhythm of the Sabbath was seen and experienced by Anne Catherine Emmerich week after week throughout the ministry of Christ Jesus. She also reported the occurrence of Jewish festival days—such as the Feast of the Passover (Easter), the Feast of Weeks (Pentecost), the Feast of Tabernacles (Autumn Thanksgiving), the Feast of the Dedication of the Temple (Christmas), and the Feast of Purim (Lent Carnival)—as well as other festivals, such as celebrations of the New Moon at the end of one Jewish month and the start of the next. Since the Jewish calendar is related to the phases of the Moon, where the start of the first day of a new month generally coincides with the first appearance of the New Moon at sunset, it is not at all difficult to apply modern astronomy to compute the days of the Jewish months at the time of Christ. Indeed, just this procedure was applied in Chapter One where, using Anne Catherine Emmerich's references to the Jewish festivals in combination with her specification of the weekdays (given by the Sabbath rhythm), we were able to date not only the birth of the Nathan Jesus but also the baptism in the Jordan and most of the major events in the life of Christ.

Anne Catherine's calendar and weekday references are internally consistent and agree with the actual historical period from the baptism in the autumn of A.D. 29 to the crucifixion on Friday, April 3, A.D. 33. Considering that she was a simple peasant woman who could scarcely read or write, it is unthinkable that she had any knowledge of the Jewish calendar. Yet it is a fact that the many references she made to this calendar (in terms of the Jewish festival days) fit exactly with the actual historical period of Christ's life (see Appendix III). It would have been impossible for Anne Catherine to fabricate such accurate calendrical reference points. We can therefore draw the conclusion that she was accurately describing the life of Christ, that she could somehow behold his life as it actually happened.

In Chapter One we determined the birth time of the Nathan Jesus to be about midnight Saturday/Sunday, December 6/7, 2 B.C. We can now also apply the hermetic astrological rule, as we did in the case of the Solomon Jesus, to determine the conception horoscope of the Nathan Jesus. At his birth on December 6/7 the Sun was located in the middle of the sidereal sign of the Archer, at 16° Sagittarius, the Ascendant was close to the middle of Virgo, and the Moon was at 12° Aries. Assuming a normal gestation period, nine months previously the Sun was in the middle of Pisces on March 6, 2 B.C. This was the day of the New Moon, so the Moon was also in the middle of Pisces. This zodiacal location of the Moon fulfills the specification of the hermetic rule that the Moon at conception indicates the Ascendant-Descendant axis at birth. Since the Ascendant was in Virgo, the Moon at conception must also have been in Virgo, or in Pisces.

The hermetic rule similarly states that the zodiacal location of the Moon at birth aligns with the Ascendant-Descendant axis at conception. Since the Moon was at 12° Aries at birth, the Ascendant at conception must therefore have been either 12° Aries or 12° Libra. In fact, approximately one hour after sunrise (at 7:39 A.M. Nazareth time) on March 6, 2 B.C., the Ascendant in Nazareth was 12° Aries (see Chart 5). At this moment, the Moon was at 12° Pisces. The Ascendant at the birth of the Nathan Jesus was therefore 12° Virgo, which enables us to determine the exact time of birth: 11:31 P.M., Bethlehem time, on December 6, 2 B.C., when the Ascendant was 12° Virgo (see Chart 4). Applying astrological biography, we shall see that these birth and conception horoscopes of the Nathan Jesus can indeed be strongly confirmed. But before taking this step, let us first consider the *contrast* between the births of the two Jesus children.

The Solomon Jesus was born in a house in Bethlehem on March 5, 6 B.C., an event that was beheld that evening as a spiritual vision in the stars by the three kings in the East who visited the child about nine and one-half months later. At his birth, on the night of the Full Moon in Virgo, the planets Jupiter and Mars were in conjunction, close to Saturn. Four years later, on Thursday, March 6, 2 B.C., the annunciation, or conception, of the Nathan Jesus occurred in Nazareth. Nine months later, on Saturday, December 6, 2 B.C., the Nathan Jesus child was born in Bethlehem. On that night an angel appeared to shepherds in the fields near Bethlehem, proclaiming, "Be not afraid; for behold, I bring you good news of a great joy which will come to all the people; for to you is born this day in the city of David a Saviour, who is Christ the Lord. And this will be a sign for you: you will find a babe wrapped in swaddling cloths and lying in a manger," (Luke 2:8–12).

Anne Catherine describes this birth as taking place in a cave on the outskirts of Bethlehem. The shepherds made their way from the hill where they had been with their flocks—not immediately, but "in the early dawn . . . to arrive at the crib early in the morning" (LBVM, 197). If, on their way down, the shepherds had looked toward the eastern horizon shortly before sunrise, they would have seen the planets Mars (3° Scorpio) and Venus (2° Scorpio) in conjunction in Scorpio. Similarly, had they looked to the east a few minutes after the birth of the Nathan Jesus, they would have seen Jupiter, close to the middle of Virgo, rising across the eastern horizon.

Returning to the annunciation, celebrated by the Church on March 25, the conception took place, according to the hermetic rule, not on March 25, but on March 6 (to be precise, at 7:39 A.M.) in Nazareth. Anne Catherine Emmerich, however, saw the mystery of the Annunciation as occurring at midnight. This would have been the midnight of March 5/6, 2 B.C. She describes Mary retiring to her room long before midnight to pray. That evening, March 5, 2 B.C., was exactly four years after the birth of the Solomon Jesus child.

> I saw her fervently praying for a long time, with her face raised to heaven. She was imploring God for redemption, for the promised King, and beseeching Him that her prayer might have some share in sending Him. She knelt long in an ecstasy of prayer. . . . (LBVM, 142)

Anne Catherine then describes an infusion of light in the room with the appearance of the Angel Gabriel, and Mary answering the Angel Gabriel with the words "Behold, I am the handmaid of the Lord; let it be to me according to your word" (Luke 1:38).

> As soon as the Blessed Virgin had spoken the words, "Be it done unto me according to thy word," I saw the Holy Spirit in the appearance of a winged figure, but not in the form of a dove as usually represented. The head was like the face of a man, and light was spread like wings beside the figure, from whose breast and hands I saw three streams of light pouring down towards the right side of the Blessed Virgin and meeting as they reached her. This light streaming in upon her right side caused the Blessed Virgin to become completely transfused with radiance. . . . After the angel had disappeared, I saw the Blessed Virgin wrapped in the deepest ecstasy. I saw that she recognized the Incarnation of the promised Redeemer within herself in the form of a tiny human figure of light. . . . It was at midnight that I saw this mystery happen. . . . Towards morning I saw her go to bed. (LBVM, 142, 144)

Here there seems to be a discrepancy between the time of conception as seen in spiritual vision by Anne Catherine and the time computed by the hermetic rule. However, it is important to bear in mind—as described in *Hermetic Astrology, vol. II: Astrological Biography*—that the moment of conception, as calculated by applying the hermetic rule, is the moment at which begins the formation of the body of life forces (known in esotericism as the *etheric body*). It is from this moment of *etheric conception* that the destiny of the approaching life on Earth is woven into the etheric body, and it is with this phenomenon, taking place throughout the embryonic period, that astrological biography is concerned.

The moment of etheric conception is the culmination of the descent into incarnation, and although it is close in time to physical conception, it need not coincide with it exactly. In the case of the annunciation, the Angel Gabriel first appeared to announce the conception, and only when Mary had given her assent did the *sister soul* of Adam—borne down to Mary by the Holy Spirit—enter into incarnation and unite with the Virgin. It was this union on the level of the soul and spirit that took place at midnight March 5/6, 2 B.C., as described by Anne Catherine. This process of incarnation, culminating on the morning of March 6 with the union on the level of the etheric (life forces), is signified by the horoscope of conception of the Nathan Jesus. The incarnation of the Nathan Jesus was directed to the goal of birth, but already at the annunciation the spirit-being of the Nathan Jesus entered into union with the Virgin Mary. Mary remained in a condition of ecstasy that night, and only when she retired to bed "toward morning" did the etheric conception take place.

At the time of the annunciation, the angel told Mary that her aunt Elizabeth at Jutta (present-day Yattah, near Hebron) had conceived a child in her old age and was now six months pregnant. Mary felt a great longing to visit Elizabeth, but this meant a long journey from Nazareth to Jutta, which lies south of Jerusalem. According to Anne Catherine Emmerich, however, since the Passover was drawing near (it was due to start on Nisan 15, which in the year 2 B.C. began on the evening of March 21) Mary decided to accompany Joseph to Jerusalem for this feast and planned to go on then to visit Elizabeth at its conclusion. Now Zechariah, the husband of Elizabeth, had been struck dumb more than six months previously because of his disbelief when the Angel Gabriel appeared to him to announce the conception of John the Baptist. On account of his wife's advanced age, Zechariah had not believed that Elizabeth could conceive a child (Luke 1). Anne Catherine's account shows that when Joseph and Mary came to Jerusalem, Zechariah was also there to celebrate the holy feast. With the close of the Sabbath on the last day (Saturday, March 29) Zechariah left and returned home, not knowing anything of the intended visit to Jutta by Joseph and Mary, who then made their way from Jerusalem on the morning after the Feast of the Passover had ended. On the basis of Emmerich's description it can be deduced that they arrived in Jutta late in the day on Sunday, March 30, 2 B.C. Elizabeth had had a presentiment that her cousin Mary,[1] whom she knew of but had not yet met, was coming to visit her, and she set out from her house to meet her.

> They greeted each other warmly with outstretched hands, and at that moment I saw a shining brightness in the Blessed Virgin and as it were a ray of light passing from her to Elizabeth, filling the latter with wonderful joy.... Mary and Elizabeth, after passing through the housedoor, came into a hall which, it seemed to me, was also the kitchen. Here they took each other by both arms, Mary greeted Elizabeth very warmly and each pressed her cheek against the other's. Again I saw a radiance stream from Mary into Elizabeth, whereby the latter was transfused with light. Her heart was filled with holy joy. She stepped back, her hand raised, and exclaimed full of humility, joy, and exaltation: "Blessed art thou among women and blessed is the fruit of thy womb. And whence is this to me that the mother of my Lord should come to me? For behold as the voice of thy salutation sounded in my ears, the infant in my womb leapt for joy. And blessed art thou that hast believed, because those things shall be accomplished that were spoken to thee by the Lord." (LBVM, 150)

As recorded in the Gospel of Saint Luke, Mary then spoke the Magnificat (Luke 1:46–55). Now, Anne Catherine related this account of the visitation on Monday, July 2, 1820, but she said that it referred to what she had seen on the previous day (Sunday)—July 2 being the Feast Day of the Visitation in the Church. It is evident from her account that, historically, the visitation occurred on Sunday, March 30, 2 B.C., the day after the completion of Passover that year. On that day, twenty-four days after the annunciation, the first act of worship took place, an act that was to be repeated each day during Mary's stay with Elizabeth.

> Every morning and evening they joined together in prayer and recited the Magnificat, which Mary had received from the Holy Spirit at Elizabeth's greeting of her. With the angel's salutation the Blessed Virgin was consecrated as the Church. With the words "Behold the handmaid of the Lord, let it be done to me according to thy word," the Word entered into her, saluted by the Church, by His maidservant. God was

---

1. Elizabeth was a cousin of Mary's mother Anna.

now in His Temple, Mary was now the Temple and the Ark of the New Covenant. Elizabeth's greeting and the movement of John beneath his mother's heart was the first act of worship of the community in the presence of this Holy Thing. When the Blessed Virgin uttered the Magnificat, the Church of the New Covenant, of the new Espousals, celebrated for the first time the fulfillment of the divine promises of the Old Covenant.... (LBVM, 153)

This sublime vision makes evident the profound spiritual significance of the visitation. According to Rudolf Steiner's account in the fifth lecture of *The Gospel of Saint Luke*, the embryo of John the Baptist was quickened through the visit of Mary. What Anne Catherine saw as a "ray of light" streaming from Mary to Elizabeth was a blessing proceeding from the Nathan Jesus, in Mary's womb, to John the Baptist, in Elizabeth's womb. This is the deeper significance underlying the words, "The babe leapt in her womb" (Luke 1:41).

The Blessed Virgin remained with Elizabeth until the birth of John "at the end of May or the beginning of June" (LBVM, 163). Available evidence suggests that this birth took place on June 4, 2 B.C., shortly after midnight (12:37 A.M. in Jutta), at which time the Sun was at 12 1/2° Gemini, the Ascendant at 16° Pisces, and the Moon (at 3° Cancer) in conjunction with Mercury (0° Cancer) and Mars (2° Cancer). (See Appendix V for a discussion of the conception, birth, and death horoscopes of John the Baptist.) At the birth of John the Baptist, the Nathan Jesus embryo was almost exactly three months old; and this, I believe, is what is meant by the words: "Mary stayed for three months with Elizabeth, until after the birth of John, but was not present on the occasion of his circumcision" (LBVM, 163). That is, Mary stayed with Elizabeth until after the birth of John, by which time the embryo within her was three months old. John's circumcision, according to Jewish custom, must have taken place one week after the birth, but by this time Mary had returned to Nazareth. Here she remained for most of the remaining six months of her pregnancy, before setting off for Bethlehem, where the birth of the Nathan Jesus child took place on December 6, 2 B.C.

Anne Catherine Emmerich said: "The actual date of Christ's birth, as I see it, is four weeks earlier than its celebration by the Church; it must have happened on Saint Catherine's feast day" (LBVM, 165). Saint Catherine's day is November 25, which is four weeks prior to the traditional date of celebration of Christmas, December 25. Note, however, that what Anne Catherine indicates by "it must have happened" is based on supposition, rather than clairvoyant vision. A careful examination of her description reveals that it was on Saint Catherine's day—the evening of Tuesday, November 25, 2 B.C.—that Joseph and Mary set forth from Nazareth on their journey to Bethlehem. It is interesting to note, in the light of Anne Catherine's statement, that the Church Fathers celebrated the birth of Christ Jesus on January 6, so that the actual date of Christ's birth (December 6) is four weeks earlier than that of its celebration by the early Church. It was only in the fourth century A.D., in Rome, that December 25, the day of the "Invincible Sun" (at that time the winter solstice was believed to occur on that day), came to be celebrated as the birthday of Christ Jesus. This tradition then spread from Rome to the rest of the Christian world. However, the date December 25 is really nothing other than the celebration of the Invincible Sun, understood in a Christian sense, with Christ as the Spirit of the Sun.

The shepherds' visit took place at daybreak Sunday, December 7, 2 B.C., the day after the birth. The circumcision followed one week later, at dawn on Sunday, December 14, in accordance with the law that newborn boys be circumcised on the eighth day after their birth (Leviticus 12:3). Priests came to the cave of the nativity to perform the rite, and it was at this ceremony that the child was named Jesus.

> Although I know that the angel had told Joseph that the child was to be called Jesus, yet I remember that the priest did not at once approve of this name, and therefore fell to praying. I then saw a shining angel appear before the priest, holding before his eyes a tablet [like that on the cross] with the name of Jesus. I do not know whether he or any of the other priests saw this angel as I did, but he was awe-struck, and I saw him writing this name by divine inspiration on a parchment. The infant Jesus wept loudly after the sacred ceremony.... (LBVM, 215)

On the Friday evening (December 19) following the circumcision, the Feast of the Dedication of the Temple should have begun, for this was the start of Kislev 25 in the Jewish calendar. But, as this was the eve of the Sabbath, it was postponed to the evening of Saturday, December 20, 2 B.C., and lasted until the following Sabbath. From this it is evident that the birth of Jesus took place on Kislev 12 in the Jewish calendar—December 6/7 in the year 2 B.C. Recall that it was Anne Catherine's communication concerning the start of the Feast of the Dedication of the Temple on Kislev 26,

on Saturday night, two weeks after the birth, that first enabled us to identify the date of birth with certainty as Saturday evening, December 6.

After the Feast of Dedication on the Sabbath (December 26/27, 2 B.C.),
the Holy Family remained in Bethlehem until the time approached when,
according to the Law, the sanctification of the firstborn should take place.
This was traditionally the fortieth day after birth (Leviticus 12:2–8). At
dawn on Monday, January 12, 1 B.C., the Holy Family left Bethlehem, and
traveled to Jerusalem, where they stayed with an old couple on the outskirts
of the city. On the morning of Thursday, January 15—being the fortieth
day after the birth on December 6—Joseph and Mary took the child Jesus
to the Temple in Jerusalem.[2] It was still dark when they arrived. As they
were going into the Temple, they were met by the old priest, Simeon, who
had been instructed by an angel the previous evening that the first child to
be presented in the morning would be the Messiah. Mary was then guided
to the place where the ceremony was to take place, and was received by the
aged prophet Anna.

> At the close of the ceremony, Simeon came up to where Mary was
> standing, took the infant Jesus from her into his arms, speaking long
> and loudly over Him in raptures of joy and thanking God that He had
> fulfilled His promise. He ended with his *Nunc Dimittis* (Luke 2:29–
> 32). After the presentation Joseph came up, and he and Mary listened
> with great reverence to Simeon's inspired words to Our Lady (Luke
> 2:34). When Simeon had finished speaking, the prophet Anna was also
> filled with inspiration, and spoke long and loudly about the infant
> Jesus, hailing His mother as blessed. (LBVM, 287)

According to Anne Catherine, the presentation in the Temple ended at
about nine o'clock that morning. The Holy Family then journeyed back to
Nazareth. Simeon fell ill immediately after returning home from the Temple

---

2. It should be noted that the date January 15, 1 B.C., refers to the day of the presentation of
the Nathan Jesus in the temple forty days after his birth. Anne Catherine Emmerich pointed
out that the Solomon Jesus was presented in the Temple on the *forty-third* day after his birth,
i.e., on April 17, 6 B.C. Of course, she does not use the expression "Solomon Jesus," but in this
case the Jesus of the Gospel of Saint Matthew is unmistakably identified by her description of
Mary's presentation to the temple of "five triangular pieces of gold from the kings' gifts"
(LBVM, 286, fn.1). Similarly, the date of circumcision of the Solomon Jesus was probably
March 13, 6 B.C., eight days after his birth on March 5.

on the day of the presentation and died the next day, Friday, January 16, 1 B.C. That same evening he was buried.

It should be pointed out that, in general, Anne Catherine's visions of events such as the visitation of Mary to Elizabeth and the presentation in the Temple took place on the Church festival days during which these events are celebrated—that is, she saw the visitation on July 2, and the presentation in the Temple on February 2, and these are the corresponding dates in the Church calendar. The dates we have established—such as March 30 for the visitation, and January 15 for the presentation in the Temple—were derived from Anne Catherine's references to festivals in the Jewish calendar, as well as from the weekdays given by the Sabbath rhythm. For example, she describes the presentation in the Temple on February 2 in the year 1821, which was a Thursday. Here she is clearly describing the Nathan Jesus child, who was brought to the Temple on the fortieth day after his birth. Thus, Thursday, February 2, corresponds to Thursday, January 15, 1 B.C. (this being forty days after Saturday, December 6, 2 B.C.). In this case the weekdays are in agreement, since the day on which she had the vision was in fact Thursday. Later, on Friday, January 17, 1823, she said that she saw Christ Jesus in Hebron during the third year of his ministry, teaching about the redemption of the firstborn. She recounted once again the presentation of Jesus in the Temple:

> The Blessed Virgin did not present Our Lord in the Temple until the forty-third day after his birth. Because of the feast, she waited for three days with the good people of the inn outside the Bethlehem gate of Jerusalem. Besides the customary offering of doves, she presented to the Temple five triangular pieces of gold from the kings' gifts." (LBVM, 286, fn. 1)

The mention of the kings here makes it obvious that she is referring to the *Solomon* Jesus child. Adding forty-three days to his birth on Friday, March 5, 6 B.C., we arrive at Saturday, April 17, 6 B.C., as the day of his presentation in the Temple. The remarkable thing about the date (January 17) on which she had this vision is that it nearly coincides with the historical date (January 15) of the presentation in the Temple of the Nathan Jesus.

When the Holy Family returned to Nazareth after the presentation of the Nathan Jesus in the Temple (January, 1 B.C.), the Solomon Jesus child, who was still living with his parents in Egypt, was not quite five years old. At the age of seven and one-half (in September, A.D. 2), he and his parents returned from Egypt to Palestine; but instead of returning to Bethlehem, they went to live in Nazareth. According to Rudolf Steiner, the family of the Solomon Jesus became quite large. Jesus (the eldest) eventually acquired four brothers (James, Joseph, Simon, and Judas) and two sisters, whose names are unknown (Matthew 13:55–56). The Nathan Jesus, however, remained an only child. The two families became friends, and the Nathan Jesus found playmates among the other children. Perhaps this is what Anne Catherine refers to in the following:

> There lived in Nazareth an Essene family related to Joachim. They had four sons, a few years older or younger than Jesus, named respectively Cleophas, James, Judas, and Japhet. They too were playmates of Jesus, and with their parents were in the habit of making the journey to the Temple along with the Holy Family. These four brothers became, at the time of Jesus' baptism, disciples of John, and after his murder, disciples of Jesus. . . . They were among those disciples of John whom Jesus took with him to the marriage feast at Cana. Cleophas is the same to whom, in company with Luke, Jesus appeared at Emmaus. (LJC i, 325)

Although there is admittedly only circumstantial evidence that the four brothers referred to above are the younger brothers of the Solomon Jesus, let us consider the hypothesis further. It is clear that Anne Catherine's spiritual gaze was directed toward the four brothers at a later period; and, if they were indeed the brothers of the Solomon Jesus, perhaps it was concealed from her that there had been a fifth, oldest brother named Jesus who had died at the age of seventeen years and three months. Of the four brothers, she describes two—James and Judas—as having the same names as two of the brothers of the Solomon Jesus, as listed in the Gospels. But it could well have been that the other two were named, for example, Joseph Cleophas and Simon Japhet. In other words, the divergence in the names of the four brothers as given on the one hand by Anne Catherine Emmerich and on the other in the Gospels does not necessarily mean that two different families, each with four sons, are being referred to. The Gospels themselves are in agreement with regard to three of the four names, as the Gospel of Saint Matthew refers to James, Joseph, Simon, and Judas, whereas the Gospel of Saint Mark lists James, Joses, Judas, and Simon (Mark 6:3). Evidently, Joses is the same as Joseph.

Anne Catherine speaks in the above quotation of the family being "related to Joachim." From her precise and detailed accounts of family trees, it emerges that Joachim was a cousin of the Joseph from Bethlehem, who was the father of the Solomon Jesus and the four brothers named in the Gospels. Since Joachim was the grandfather of the Nathan Jesus, the two Jesus children were distantly related. The relationship between Joachim and Joseph of Bethlehem helps to explain why, when Joseph was returning with his family from Egypt, he decided to go to Nazareth rather than return to Bethlehem. The relationship between Joachim and Joseph of Bethlehem derived from the fact that Joachim's grandmother's first husband was Matthan, the father of Jacob, the father of Joseph of Bethlehem (see the genealogy of the "Solomon line" in the Gospel of Saint Matthew), and her second husband was Levi, the father of Matthat, the father of Joachim (see the genealogy of the "Nathan line" in the Gospel of Saint Luke). Thus Joachim and Joseph of Bethlehem were cousins.

GENEALOGICAL TABLE

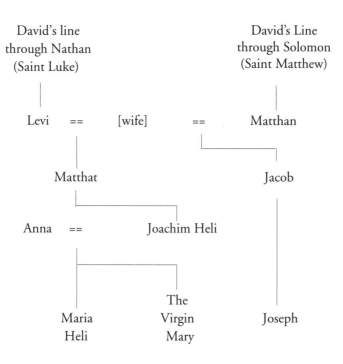

Anne Catherine's remark that the family (related to Joachim) was Essene is not directly relevant here, for nothing is known concerning any affiliation of Joseph or Mary of Bethlehem with the Essenes, although there may have been such an affiliation. On the other hand, her remark about their having accompanied the Holy Family (Joseph and Mary of Nazareth and the Nathan Jesus) on the journey to the Temple each year at the Passover festival is most significant. For it was on the occasion of the Passover festival in A.D. 12 that the union of the two Jesus children occurred. We can imagine that, on the journey to the Temple in A.D. 12, by which time Joseph of Bethlehem had died, his children (those who were old enough) traveled with their relatives Joseph and Mary of Nazareth, together with the Nathan Jesus child. After the death of the Solomon Jesus on June 5, A.D. 12, followed by the death of Mary of Nazareth two months later, it is easily understandable that Joseph of Nazareth would have married Mary of Bethlehem to provide a family life for the Nathan Jesus child together with the six remaining children of Mary of Bethlehem.

Next to nothing is known about the life of Jesus between the ages of twelve and thirty, so only descriptions by genuine seers can help us here. Anne Catherine does not describe anything of significance during this period, except the death of Joseph, which she places around the start of the month of Nisan (ca. April 2, A.D. 29) when Jesus was twenty-nine years old. Rudolf Steiner, who provides many useful and inspiring indications concerning these lost years in his lecture cycle entitled *The Fifth Gospel*, also mentions the death of Joseph: "The father died about this time—it was when Jesus of Nazareth was in his twenty-fourth year, or thereabouts."[3]

There is an apparent discrepancy between what Rudolf Steiner and Anne Catherine have to say about Jesus' age at the time of Joseph's death. Anne Catherine has Joseph's death at the time of Jesus' *Saturn return*, at the age of twenty-nine years and four months (Saturn takes 29 1/2 years to complete a cycle of the sidereal zodiac). Rudolf Steiner, on the other hand, places the death of Joseph at the time Jesus would have been in his twenty-fourth year, at his second *Jupiter return* (Jupiter takes 23 3/4 years to complete its second cycle of the sidereal zodiac).

Just as a "Sun birthday" is celebrated each year with the solar return, so a "Jupiter birthday" takes place every twelve years with the Jupiter return. Thus the event of the union of the Solomon Jesus with the twelve-year old Nathan Jesus in the Temple took place not long after the Jupiter birthday.

---

3. Rudolf Steiner, *The Fifth Gospel*, p. 73.

Similarly, a "Saturn birthday" occurs every 29 1/2 years with the Saturn return. And so the baptism in the Jordan followed shortly after the first Saturn birthday in the life of the Nathan Jesus. However, it still remains to determine whether the death of Joseph of Nazareth took place at the second Jupiter return (according to Steiner) or at the first Saturn return (according to Anne Catherine).

Despite the five-year discrepancy just described, both seers agree that Joseph died before Jesus' baptism in the Jordan. His death meant that the Nathan Jesus was bereft of both natural parents, though there remained his stepmother (Mary of Bethlehem, the mother of the Solomon Jesus), and his foster brothers and sisters. The higher significance of Joseph's death is that the way opened then for Jesus to devote himself fully to the mission of his *heavenly* Father, now that his *earthly* father was no longer living.

In his lectures on *The Fifth Gospel* Rudolf Steiner spoke about some of the experiences undergone by Jesus of Nazareth from the age of twelve until the baptism. During this time there were three main influences on him: (1) the Hebrew wisdom; (2) the pagan mysteries; and (3) the Essenes. In each case, according to Steiner's description, Jesus was led into deep despair; for he came to see that the tradition of Hebrew wisdom was nearing its end, and that the voice of the Bath-Kol (the mysterious inspiration heard by the learned Jewish doctors and scribes) would soon cease to speak. He also experienced the decadence of the pagan mysteries, by then obsessed with conjuring demonic beings. Lastly, although he had gained profound wisdom from the Essenes, he came to realize that the group's pure, semi-monastic way of life, although helpful in *their* own attainment to the spirit, did not help others, but rather drove impure spirits to plague non-Essenes all the more. Jesus powerfully experienced the decline of Judaism, the fall of paganism, and the isolationism of the Essenes, and came to the realization that something completely new was needed to save humanity and the Earth. Through these deep, painful experiences, Jesus was prepared for his mission as the bearer of the Christ, a mission soon to begin at the baptism in the Jordan.

In Chapter One, we were able, on the basis of Anne Catherine's indications, to determine the exact date (and time) of the baptism in the Jordan: ten o'clock on the morning of Friday, September 23, A.D. 29. Both Steiner and Anne Catherine agree that preceding the baptism a significant conversation took place between Jesus and Mary. According to Anne Catherine, this conversation occurred in Bethany at the home of Lazarus on the afternoon of the day preceding the baptism.

Jesus retired for an interview with the Blessed Virgin. He told her most earnestly and lovingly that he was about to begin his career, that he was now going to John's baptism. . . . Henceforth she should not seek to deter him by human considerations, for he must accomplish what was marked out for him; a very different life was now about to commence for him, and they who would adhere to him must suffer with him; that he must now fulfill his mission, and she must sacrifice all purely personal claims upon him. He added that although he would love her as ever, yet he was now for all humankind. She should do as he said and his heavenly Father would reward her, for what Simeon had foretold was about to be fulfilled, a sword would pierce her soul. The Blessed Virgin listened gravely. She was very much troubled, though at the same time strong in her resignation to God, for Jesus was very tender and loving. (LJC i, 405–406)

Describing this same conversation in *The Fifth Gospel*, Rudolf Steiner points out that Jesus communicated to his stepmother Mary the essence of his experiences of suffering in connection with the decline of Judaism, the fall of paganism, and the isolationism of the Essenes.

The words which Jesus spoke to his stepmother were not words in the ordinary sense; they were like living beings, passing over from him to his stepmother, and the forces of his own soul lent wings to his words. During this conversation, everything he had suffered with such intensity passed over with the words into the soul of his stepmother. His own I (self) accompanied every word. It was not a mere exchange of words or thoughts, but his soul passed over into her soul on the wings of the words which told of his infinite love but also of his infinite pain. And so he was able to unfold to her, as in a great panorama, what he had experienced three times over. What passed between them was yet further heightened in that Jesus allowed the conversation to lead over gradually to the realization that had come to him from his threefold suffering in connection with the decline that was perceptible in humankind. (Rudolf Steiner, *The Fifth Gospel*, p. 129)

According to Steiner, during this conversation the Zarathustra/Solomon Jesus individuality departed the body of the Nathan Jesus, who then journeyed in a dreamlike state to the place of baptism. According to Anne

Catherine, he was accompanied by Lazarus, with whom he walked through the night from Bethany, arriving at the place of baptism around sunrise the next morning. That morning John the Baptist preached and baptized with more zeal than ever before, sensing the presence of the Messiah, who then came down to the baptismal pool at about ten o'clock to be baptized. It was at this moment, as he was baptized, that the cosmic being of Christ descended to unite with the Nathan Jesus.

> They were just mounting the steps when the voice of God came over Jesus who was still standing alone and in prayer upon the stone. There came from heaven a great, rushing wind like thunder. All trembled and looked up. A cloud of white light descended, and I saw over Jesus a winged figure of light as if flowing over him like a stream. . . . Jesus was perfectly transparent, entirely penetrated by light. One could scarcely look at him. (LJC i, 441–442)

As previously noted, the words spoken at the baptism by the voice of God are usually rendered as "Thou art my beloved Son, with whom I am well pleased" (Luke 3:22); but, according to some ancient authorities, they should read, "Thou art my beloved Son; today I have begotten thee." The latter is, in fact, closer to the true significance of the moment of the baptism, for the baptism was at the same time truly the *birth* of Christ, that is, his union with the earthly Jesus. At this moment Jesus becomes *Christ* Jesus. The baptism signifies the start of the divine mission, the ministry of Christ Jesus, which continued for three and one-half years, leading to the death on the cross on Friday, April 3, A.D. 33 (see Chart 6).

The chronicle of the three and one-half years of the ministry, apart from the "missing period" (July 9, A.D. 31 to May 16, A.D. 32) may be followed day by day from the baptism on September 23, A.D. 29 (actually from four months previously: May 29, A.D. 29) up to the crucifixion on April 3, A.D. 33. The significance of the planetary positions in the sidereal zodiac at the most important events in the life of Christ are discussed in *Christian Hermetic Astrology: The Star of the Magi and the Life of Christ*.[4] Here it should be noted that the basic outline of Christ's life given in this book is in close agreement with ancient authorities. Consider, for example, the three and one-half year duration of the ministry. As Jack Finegan writes "Taken as it

---

4. See Bibliography.

stands, the Fourth Gospel appears to require a ministry of three years plus a number of months, and there is some support for a duration of some such magnitude in Epiphanius and Eusebius" (*Handbook of Biblical Chronology*, p. 285). Or again, consider our finding that Jesus was twenty-nine years and ten months old at the baptism (actually 29 years 9 1/2 months, from the birth on December 6, 2 B.C., to the baptism on September 23, A.D. 29): "Epiphanius then explains that Jesus was in fact, at the time of his baptism, twenty-nine years and ten months of age, which might be called 'thirty years, but not full' " (ibid, p. 252). Moreover, Epiphanius, like some other ancient authorities, dates the baptism to the autumn: "Jesus was baptized, Epiphanius says, according to Egyptian reckoning on Hathyr 12 and according to Roman reckoning on the sixth day before the Ides of November. These dates are both equivalent to November 8" (ibid., p. 251). Lastly, nearly all the ancient authorities date the birth of Jesus to 3 or 2 B.C. (ibid, p. 229).

Harold W. Hoehner and Ernest L. Martin are contemporary biblical scholars who have arrived at results similar to those summarized in this book. Martin's research agrees that John the Baptist began preaching in the spring of A.D. 29, probably in the month of Nisan:

> This evidence clearly points to John the Baptist beginning his preaching in the spring of A.D. 29. John was of Levitical descent and the Old Testament legislated that Levitical duties were to begin when a man reached thirty years of age (Numbers 4:3). John started his preaching about the month of Nisan in A.D. 29 (as allowed for in the Law, Exodus 40:1, 12–17)—early spring. Christ was about six months younger than John (Luke 2:36) and Luke tells us that Christ began his ministry when he was "about thirty years of age" (Luke 3:23). The apostle John indicates that Christ preached for three and one-half years, dying in the Passover season. Thus, Christ's ministry began near autumn of A.D. 29. Professor Hoehner in his new book *Chronological Aspects of the Life of Christ* has admirably demonstrated that Christ began his ministry near the Autumn of A.D. 29, and was crucified at the Passover season in A.D. 33. But what year was Christ's birth? This should be simple to figure. One needs to subtract thirty years from A.D. 29. This leads directly to 2 B.C. If one is willing to believe Luke, this is the year which should be accepted. (Ernest L. Martin, *The Birth of Christ Recalculated*, pp. 51–52)

Let us continue our study of the life of the Nathan Jesus by summarizing the most significant dates in his life:

(1) the event in the Temple at the age of twelve, on April 3, A.D. 12;
(2) the baptism in the Jordan on the morning of September 23, A.D. 29; and
(3) the death on the cross on the afternoon of April 3, A.D. 33.

To apply the method of astrological biography, we need only compute the *biographic* points corresponding to the relevant *embryonic* points (in terms of the Moon's position in the sidereal zodiac at the corresponding date in the embryonic period).

AGE	MOON'S POSITION IN SIDEREAL ZODIAC	CORRESPONDING DATE IN EMBRYONIC PERIOD
1) 12 years 4 months	1 orbits + 274° = 16° Sagittarius	April 23, 2 B.C., 11:30 A.M.
2) 29 years 9 1/2 months	4 orbits + 92 1/2° = 14 1/2° Gemini	June 30, 2 B.C., 5:00 A.M.
3) 33 years 4 months	4 orbits + 274° = 16° Sagittarius	July 14, 2 B.C., 7:00 A.M.

In each case, the Moon's position is on the axis passing through the middle of the signs Gemini and Sagittarius. This is significant, especially as the Sun at the birth of the Nathan Jesus (16° Sagittarius) is aligned with this axis.

Let us now consider event (1) in greater detail. At the conception of the Nathan Jesus on March 6, 2 B.C., Jupiter, close to Regulus, was moving retrograde in Leo, and continued so to move until the end of March. During April, Jupiter moved forward again and returned to its starting point (4° Leo) exactly on April 23—the exact date in the embryonic period that corresponds to event (1). Recalling the words in the Gospel of Saint Luke after the Temple event—"Jesus increased in wisdom" (Luke 2:52)—it seems clear that they indicate the significance of Jupiter, the planet of wisdom, which began to play a major role in the life of Jesus from this point onward. Also significant is the position of the *Sun* on April 23, 2 B.C., at 3° Taurus, for this was exactly opposite the zodiacal location of the striking conjunction between Venus (2° Scorpio) and Mars (3° Scorpio) at the birth of the

Nathan Jesus. Looking now to the heliocentric (Sun-centered) planetary configuration on April 23, 2 B.C., Venus (16 1/2° Leo) was heliocentrically in conjunction with Jupiter (14 1/2° Leo), close to the position of heliocentric Mercury at the conception (18° Leo). The conjunction of *Venus* and *Jupiter* points to the uniting of *Love* and *Wisdom*, as represented by the two Jesus children.

In the case of event (2), the baptism in the Jordan, the corresponding date in the embryonic period was June 30, 2 B.C. On this date Mercury arrived at 4° Leo, Jupiter's position at the conception, as referred to above. Moreover, Mercury was heliocentrically in conjunction with Neptune (18° Scorpio). This emphasis on Mercury is interesting, for at the moment of the baptism in the Jordan (10:00 A.M. on September 23, A.D. 29), Mercury and Saturn were heliocentrically in exact conjunction. Mercury, the planet of the healer, points to the beginning of Christ Jesus' healing mission, which began with the baptism. Practically the whole three and one-half year ministry was devoted to healing the sick and driving out demons. The zodiacal location of the Sun (7° Cancer) on June 30 is also interesting. This corresponds to the deepest point, the *midnight position* in the conception horoscope of the Nathan Jesus, since the highest point, the Midheaven, was 8° Capricorn at the moment of conception. Jesus reached this midnight position of the baptism at the time of the profoundly significant conversation he had with his stepmother the day before. It was at this *midnight hour* in the destiny of Jesus of Nazareth that the Solomon Jesus withdrew to make way for the coming of the cosmic being of Christ, who descended to unite with Jesus at the baptism.

We now turn to (3), the Mystery of Golgotha. Here the corresponding date in the embryonic period was July 14, 2 B.C.; and again, the position of the Sun (21° Cancer) is highly significant. For this was the zodiacal axis of the Moon's nodes at the birth of the Nathan Jesus (21° Capricorn to 21° Cancer = true Moon node axis). The Moon's nodes represent "gateways" to the cosmic world, and the position of the Sun on this axis indicates, in the life of the Nathan Jesus, the time of departure from earthly life, when his spirit-being (represented by the Sun) was to leave the earthly plane through the "gate of death" (represented in this case by the nodal axis). On July 14, Mars (27 1/2° Cancer) was approaching the nodal axis (29 1/2° Capricorn to 29 1/2° Cancer), which could be interpreted as "death by violence," signifying here the crucifixion. And in the hermetic configuration for July 14, Mercury (29° Sagittarius) and Venus (27° Sagittarius) were in conjunction, symbolizing the "healing through love" that this sacrificial death on the cross accomplished.

As in the case of the Solomon Jesus, astrological biography, when applied to the birth and conception configurations of the Nathan Jesus, conforms remarkably to the three events described above and lends additional confirmation to the validity of the birth and conception configurations (Charts 4 and 5) put forward in this book. It would be possible to go into much greater detail concerning the astrological biography of the Nathan Jesus, but the foregoing should suffice to provide a general outline.

Chapter Six

The Nathan Mary

Readers who are aware of the appearances of Mary in the nineteenth and twentieth centuries—for example, Lourdes in 1858, Fatima in 1917, and so on—may be aware of a more recent series of visions that began on Saint John's Day, 1981, in Medjugorje, Yugoslavia, and still continues. At the first appearance on June 24, 1981, Mary appeared to five young people and identified herself with the words: "I am the Queen of Peace. I have come to bring peace to Earth" (MKF, 105). Since then, the revelation has continued with regular appearances, in the course of which Mary has revealed ten mysteries concerning the future, not yet made public. Several million people have visited Medjugorje. The Virgin's central message is that a renewal of religious life, a new turning toward God, is necessary if the world is to be saved. This renewal is to be attained, above all, through prayer, which, Mary stresses, means "prayer of the heart":

Pray with the heart. Do not let prayer and fasting become a routine or a matter of habit. (MKF, 110)

It is natural, upon hearing of such appearances, to question their authenticity. Can the several young people, to whom Mary has reportedly appeared numerous times at Medjugorje, really be trusted? This question can be approached from two sides: from the standpoint of the young people themselves, and from the standpoint of the question, "Are the appearances authentic?" And if the appearances are authentic, do the young people faithfully transmit what is revealed to them without any distortion?

These two questions are central to all *private revelations*. For example, they apply also to the revelation of the life of Jesus Christ received by Anne Catherine Emmerich. In her case, however, since she made explicit remarks concerning Jewish feast days and other specific events during the time of Christ, it is possible to *test* her revelation, and this has been done as shown in Appendix III. The results of this testing are clear; at least with respect to her calendar indications, Anne Catherine's revelation is authentic. And, since it is authentic in this regard, the whole of her revelation gains credibility.

The communications—purportedly from the Virgin Mary—related by the young people in Medjugorje are, on the whole, not readily accessible to objective scrutiny. There is one communication of a quite explicit nature, however, and this *does* lend itself to investigation. It was made in August, 1984, when Mary's 2000th birthday supposedly occurred. According to the young people, the Virgin made it known to them that, on August 5, she would celebrate her birthday of two thousand years ago (MKF, 86). This communication leads to the conclusion that Mary was born on the historical date August 5, 17 B.C. — i.e., on August 5 in the year -16 (using the astronomical designation).[1] But can this be established as true?

The question is somewhat complicated when we recall that we are investigating the birth of *two* Marys, not one. We shall refer to these simply as the *Nathan Mary* and the *Solomon Mary*. If the revelation is authentic, then we can further ask if the Mary currently manifesting in Medjugorje is the mother of the Nathan Jesus, or the mother of the Solomon Jesus?

We can turn first to the indications of Rudolf Steiner and Anne Catherine Emmerich. Taken together with the astronomical-astrological mode of investigation we have already employed, we can determine the birth and conception dates of the two Marys. With this data, we are in a position to judge the communication from Medjugorje concerning the birth date of Mary on August 5, 17 B.C.

Let us first consider Rudolf Steiner's communications concerning the Nathan Mary, who could also be called *Mary of Nazareth*. From Steiner's descriptions it is clear that this Mary had a deep affinity with the Nathan Jesus, who was the *sister soul* of Adam, and whose sole historical manifestation (though not a physical incarnation) was as Krishna.[2] She was connected with the spiritual stream of love and compassion that attained its high point in Hinduism with Krishna and, in Buddhism, with Gautama Buddha. She was a deeply loving and compassionate soul, who had developed the capacity

---

1. The two modes used to designate pre-Christian dates are *historical* and *astronomical*: the use of the designation "B.C." is *historical*, and the use of a minus sign ("-16," for example) is *astronomical*.

2. Rudolf Steiner, *The Bhagavad Gita and the Epistles of Paul* (Hudson, NY: Anthroposophic Press, 1971), p. 98.

for love and self-sacrifice to a high degree. This, rather than spiritual wisdom, predominated in her personality. At an early age, she married Joseph of Nazareth, and bore one child, Jesus of Nazareth. In early childhood, this Nathan Jesus spoke the long-lost primal language, which his mother could understand through her faculty of love. Not long after the event in the Temple at the Passover of A.D. 12, she died. Rudolf Steiner describes how, seventeen years later, at the baptism in the Jordan, the Nathan Mary was spiritually united with the Solomon Mary.

> At the moment of this baptism in the Jordan, the mother (the Solomon Mary) was aware of something like the climax of the change that had come about in her. She was then between her forty-fifth and forty-sixth years. She felt as though pervaded by the soul of that mother (the Nathan Mary) who had died, the mother of the Jesus child who in his twelfth year had received the Zarathustra individuality. Thus the spirit of the other mother had come upon the mother with whom Jesus had held that conversation. And she felt herself as the young mother who had once given birth to the Jesus child of Saint Luke's Gospel. (Rudolf Steiner, *The Fifth Gospel*, p. 93)

Since the baptism took place on September 23, A.D. 29, Steiner's narration here indicates that Mary was born in 17 B.C. Indeed, if the birth date had been August 5, 17 B.C. (astronomically the year -16), then she would have been forty-five years old on August 5, A.D. 29. To investigate this further, we now turn to Anne Catherine Emmerich's account.

Unlike Rudolf Steiner, Anne Catherine does not distinguish between the two Marys. Her statements must be carefully examined to discern which Mary is being referred to. Through her identification of Joachim, the father of Mary, with Heli of the Nathan line in the Gospel of Saint Luke, the parents of the Nathan Mary are identified as Joachim and Anna. Now, in the description of her vision of the "immaculate conception" of Mary in the womb of Anna, Anne Catherine gives a calendar indication that refers of course to the conception of the *Nathan* Mary:

> It was near the time of the Feast of Tabernacles ... as Joachim was praying I saw an angel appear to him, telling him to journey to the Temple, for his sacrifice would be accepted and his prayers granted. ... He arrived in Jerusalem on the fourth day of the feast, and stayed in his

usual lodgings near the Temple. Anna arrived in Jerusalem also on the fourth day of the feast and stayed with Zechariah's relations by the fish-market. She did not meet Joachim until the end of the feast.... She had been bidden by an angel to meet her husband under the Golden Gate.... Joachim went through a little door; the passage sloped downwards.... Here he was met by Anna, radiant with joy. They embraced each other with holy joy.... They were in a state of ecstasy and enveloped in a cloud of light. I saw this light issuing from a great host of angels.... Anna and Joachim . . . were enveloped in a glory of brightness. I understood, that as a result of the grace here given, the conception of Mary was as pure as all conceptions would have been but for the Fall. I had at the same time an indescribable vision. The heavens opened above them, and I saw the joy of the Holy Trinity and of the angels, and their participation in the mysterious blessing bestowed on Mary's parents. Anna and Joachim returned, praising God, to the exit under the Golden Gate. They came into a kind of chapel under a beautiful and high arch, where many lights were burning. Here they were received by priests who led them away. (LBVM, 32, 40)

According to Leviticus 23: 34–36, the Feast of Tabernacles is celebrated for seven days—Tishri 15–21, with an eighth festival day on Tishri 22—therefore, the conception of the Nathan Mary must have taken place after Tishri 22. In fact, it actually took place, as we shall see, at the New Moon on the night of Tishri 29 or Tishri 30. (The astronomical New Moon generally falls on day 29 or day 30 of the Jewish lunar month, and day 1, starting at dusk, usually coincides with the first appearance of the thin crescent of the New Moon on the western horizon.) But why should the conception have taken place at the astronomical New Moon?

Here we must consider more closely the term *immaculate conception*. It will be helpful to refer to the vision of Saint John in the twelfth chapter of the Book of Revelation:

And a great portent appeared in heaven, a woman clothed with the Sun, with the Moon under her feet, and on her head a crown of twelve stars. (Revelation 12:1)

This vision could be interpreted as a picture of the cosmic forces at work in the soul at the time of the astronomical New Moon, when the Sun forces are most powerful and those of the Moon are at a minimum. In the cosmic "language of the soul," the Moon is "underfoot" at the time of the New Moon. This is an image of purity; the lunar forces are connected with the lower nature in contrast to the solar (or spiritual) nature of the human being. In this sense, the astronomical New Moon is an appropriate time for an immaculate conception, such as Anne Catherine describes.[3] It should be remembered, from Chapter Five, that the conception of the Nathan Jesus— also immaculately conceived—took place at the New Moon in Pisces on March 6, 2 B.C., the day of the annunciation. If we accept this interpretation, the conception of the Nathan Mary took place at the astronomical New Moon at the end of the month of Tishri. (Tishri falls in September or October.) But the *year* remains to be determined.

After describing the annunciation of Jesus' conception, Anne Catherine remarked that "Mary at this time was a little over fourteen years old" (LJC i, 196). Here she is obviously referring to the conception of the Nathan Jesus, for, as she says, it took place in the house in Nazareth, and at the time Mary's mother Anna was visiting her. If August 5, 17 B.C., had been Mary's birth date, she would have been fourteen years and seven months old at the annunciation on March 6, 2 B.C.—which fits with Anne Catherine's statement. This seems to indicate that it was the Nathan Mary who was born in 17 B.C. and whose 2000th birthday was celebrated in 1984, as referred to in the communication from Medjugorje.

The astronomical New Moon at the end of the month of Tishri in 18 B.C. occurred late on the evening of October 24—that is, Tishri 29 (or possibly Tishri 30). This, then, was the time of the conception of the Nathan Mary, if we accept the foregoing interpretation of "immaculate conception." Using the hermetic-astrological rule linking conception and birth, we can then extrapolate from this date to arrive at likely birth dates. In doing so, however, we must remember that the conception date referred to is the *cosmic conception*, as determined by the hermetic rule, which does not necessarily coincide exactly with the physical conception. Proceeding from the astronomical New Moon on the evening of October 24, 18 B.C., it is obviously, in this case, a matter of cosmic conception.

When seventeen weeks and five days after the conception of the Blessed Virgin had gone by (that is to say, five days before Anna's pregnancy

---

3. Obviously this is only one aspect of an immaculate conception, and we cannot here go into a more prolonged discussion of this mystery.

was half accomplished), I saw Our Lady's holy mother lying asleep in her bed in her house near Nazareth. Then there came a shining light above her, and a ray from this light fell upon the middle of her side, and the light passed into her in the shape of a little shining human figure. In the same instant I saw Our Lady's holy mother raise herself on her couch surrounded by light. She was in ecstasy, and had a vision of her womb opening like a tabernacle to enclose a shining little virgin from whom humanity's whole salvation was to spring. I saw that this was the instant in which for the first time the child moved within her. . . . It was made known to me that the Blessed Virgin's soul was united to her body five days earlier than with other children, and that her birth was twelve days earlier. (LBVM, 73–74)

This indication by Anne Catherine is not quite clear, for "seventeen weeks and five days" amounts to only four calendar months, whereas the midpoint of a normal embryonic period occurs at 4 1/2 months. Be that as it may, it is evident that she is referring to the *quickening* (the union of the soul with the body, coinciding with the first movement of the child in a mother's womb) as having occurred approximately at the midpoint of the embryonic period. Furthermore, in the case of the Nathan Mary, the quickening—and the birth—took place earlier than usual. If this is true, August 5 would be disqualified as a possible birth date, since the interval from the date of conception (October 24) to August 5 amounts to 285 days, suggesting a birth twelve days *late*—taking the mean length of the embryonic period to be ten lunar sidereal revolutions (10 x 27 1/3 days = 273 days). A full-length term of 273 days, measured from October 24, gives us a birth date of July 23. So, in the event of a premature birth, the birth date must have been prior to July 23, 17 B.C.

Anne Catherine adds that the birth of the Nathan Mary occurred around midnight (LBVM, 75). This indication is helpful in applying the hermetic-astrological rule, which in turn suggests that the birth took place around midnight on July 17/18; that is, 267 days from the moment of conception. Applying the hermetic-astrological rule linking conception and birth to this data gives us the exact times of conception and birth, as shown below.

The conception took place in Jerusalem at 11:26 P.M. local time on October 24, 18 B.C. The Sun (2° Scorpio) was in conjunction with the Moon (4° Scorpio) and the Ascendant was 6° Leo (see Chart 8). Here it is interesting to note that, at the birth of the Nathan Jesus, Venus (2° Scorpio) in conjunction with Mars (3° Scorpio) occupied the same zodiacal locations as the Sun and Moon at Mary's immaculate conception. Two hundred and sixty-seven days later the birth of the Nathan Mary took place in Nazareth at 11:50 P.M. local time on July 17, 17 B.C., with the Ascendant at 4° Taurus (opposite the Moon at conception) and the Moon at 6° Leo (identical to the Ascendant at conception), in accordance with the hermetic rule (see Chart 7).

Most striking with regard to the birth configuration is the conjunction of the Moon, Venus, and Mars with Regulus (the Lion's heart at 5° Leo)—a most extraordinary planetary/stellar configuration, indicating remarkable heart forces (Leo being the zodiacal sign corresponding to the heart). The birth, as well as the conception, thus took place on the day of the astronomical New Moon. But, as the conjunction of the Sun and Moon had been at about six o'clock that morning, by the time of the birth at midnight the Moon had separated from the Sun by eleven degrees (Sun at 25° Cancer; Moon at 6° Leo).

It still remains to examine the date August 5, 17 B.C., which was communicated at Medjugorje. The *year* of birth (17 B.C.) has been shown to be correct; but the birth occurred *eighteen full days* earlier, according to our reckoning. Nevertheless, further investigation reveals that August 5 was a profoundly significant date for the Nathan Mary; for it was on this day in A.D. 12 that the Nathan Mary died, at the age of twenty-eight years and eighteen days. It is possible, therefore, that the young seers of Medjugorje communicated Mary's date of death as that of her birth. Let us now, therefore, look at the events leading up to the death of the Nathan Mary.

Here it is helpful to recall Rudolf Steiner's description of the sequence of events in A.D. 12. First, on April 3, at the end of the Passover, the event in the Temple during which the Zarathustra/Solomon Jesus individuality united spiritually with the Nathan Jesus took place. This was followed two months later by the death of the Solomon Jesus youth on June 5. Shortly thereafter (in fact, according to the research presented in this book, two months later), the Nathan Mary died. But what did Anne Catherine say about Mary's death?

> Now I will tell you of the death of the Blessed Virgin. . . . After a pause she continued, marking on her fingers the figures she mentioned: See this number, a stroke I and then a V, does not this make four? Then again V and three strokes, does not this make eight? This is not properly written out; but I see them as separate figures. . . . (LBVM, 367)

Anne Catherine herself interpreted this to mean that the Virgin Mary died in the year A.D. 48, but it seems more likely that the real significance of these figures is the date August 4, that is, the *fourth* day of the *eighth* month in this case; it was on the night of August 4/5, A.D. 12 that the Nathan Mary died. Taking midnight to be the approximate time of death, a remarkable configuration of planets is evident (see Chart 9). Saturn (3° Scorpio) was at the same point in the zodiac where the Sun (2° Scorpio) and Moon (4° Scorpio) stood at the immaculate conception. Further, the Moon (24° Cancer) was in conjunction with Mercury (27° Cancer) and Mars (25° Cancer) at exactly the place in the zodiac where the Sun (25° Cancer) stood at Mary's birth. Of course, it could be that her death did not take place at midnight, but later, on August 5—for example, around dawn, when the Moon was between Mars and Mercury in Cancer.

Here I must apologize for the condensed data I am presenting— interested readers are again referred to my other works where the matter is gone into more fully.[4] Suffice it to say that I am convinced that the date, August 5, communicated by the Virgin Mary at Medjugorje is of profound significance and agrees with the date communicated by Anne Catherine Emmerich. Furthermore, this date refers to the *Nathan* Mary, lending support to our view that the appearances at Medjugorje are a revelation from her. However, August 5, 17 B.C., was eighteen full days *after* the birth of the Nathan Mary at midnight on July 17/18. In conclusion, the real significance of August 5 is as the date of *death* of the Nathan Mary.

The German Romantic poet and visionary philosopher, Friedrich von Hardenberg, called Novalis, wrote: *"When a spirit dies, it becomes a human being. When a human being dies, he or she becomes spirit"* (*Novalis*, p. 436). Here, birth and death are linked metaphorically. This does not mean to imply that Mary communicated her death date as her birth date but, rather, that the seers did not communicate her message fully, leading to a confusion between the two dates; at least, this is one solution to this riddle.

This work is concerned with laying the foundations of an approach to Cosmic Christianity—and not just with the determination of the historical dates of conception, birth, and death for the sake of mere curiosity, although

---

4. Robert Powell. *Hermetic Astrology: Towards a New Wisdom of the Stars; Volume 1, Astrology and Reincarnation.* and *Volume 2, Astrological Biography.* (Kinsau, Germany: Hermetika Verlag, 1987, 1989).

without such data we cannot proceed. But, having ascertained these historical dates, we can move on to consider their *cosmic* aspect.

By way of illustration, let us relate the conception, birth, and death of the Nathan Mary to a simple, but highly significant cosmic phenomenon, namely, the passage of the Sun around the zodiac. Let us recall that the cosmic significance of celebrating a birthday is that it represents the Sun's completion of one orbit of the zodiac and, thus, its return to the position in the zodiac it occupied at birth. The date of birth—indicating, within a day or so, the Sun's return to the birth position in the zodiac—is valid as long as a person is living. In a cosmic sense, however, its validity does not hold for much longer than the person's life span, since the date of return of the Sun to its birth position in the zodiac gradually *shifts* in relation to the historical date of birth. This gradual shift is the result of the so-called "precession of the equinoxes," as indicated by the retrograde motion of the vernal point backward through the zodiac at a rate of one degree in 72 years. It is this phenomenon that gives rise to the various zodiacal ages. For example, since the location of the Sun on the day of the vernal equinox (March 21) is now in Pisces, the present age is referred to as the *Age of Pisces*. Since calendar dates are specified by the Sun's position in relation to the vernal point, and since the vernal point moves retrograde through the zodiac, it follows that this movement must be taken into account when considering the Sun's position in the zodiac for a given historical date. Let us now consider this retrograde movement more closely, since it affects the dates of commemoration of the conception, birth, and death of the Nathan Mary.

Here we come to a distinction that is most important for the right understanding of Cosmic Christianity: namely, that the level with which Cosmic Christianity deals must be distinguished from the level of historical Christianity. For historical Christianity, and in the light of the research presented in this book, the dates of the Nathan Mary's conception, birth, and death are October 24/25, July 17/18, and August 4/5. These are the *historical* dates of these events and deserve commemoration as such. However, from the perspective of *Cosmic* Christianity, the memory of these events is indicated primarily by the location of the Sun in the sidereal zodiac at the Nathan Mary's conception, birth, and death. This location is a cosmic reality—but it is a reality that is now commemorated on an entirely different set of dates than the original historical dates. How should this be understood?

The principle underlying Cosmic Christianity is that all historical events are "remembered" by the cosmos by being inscribed in the so-called "akasha chronicle" or "akashic record," whose outer expression is the sidereal zodiac. Everything is recorded in the stars. Of the multitude of memories imprinted in the starry heavens, however, some are more important than others. The most important memories of historical events are those connected with the life of Christ. This is because, to use a phrase coined by Rudolf Steiner, the incarnation, life, death, and resurrection of Christ signify the "turning point of time," the pivotal axis upon which the whole of history turns. These events, and all related events (such as, for instance, the conception, birth, and death of Mary), are truly worthy of commemoration. On a cosmic level, they are commemorated whenever the Sun, which is also a fixed star, crosses over ("transits") that part of the sidereal zodiac where the event in question is imprinted, the original imprint having taken place primarily through the Sun—because of the Sun's relationship (as a star) to the stars comprising the sidereal zodiac. This is the principle underlying the *Sun Chronicle* of the dates of commemoration (in terms of cosmic memory) of the Christ events as listed in *Christian Hermetic Astrology*, Volume Three. And it is this same principle of Cosmic Christianity that now underlies the following considerations concerning the determination of the "cosmic dates" of commemoration for the conception, birth, and death of the Nathan Mary.

From a cosmic standpoint, owing to the lapse of two thousand years and the corresponding precession of the equinoxes during this time, the celebration dates have shifted. For example, after seventy-two years, owing to precession—which proceeds at a rate of one degree in seventy-two years—the Sun returns to the same point in the sidereal zodiac one day later than the original birth date. After seventy-two years, a "birthday," from an astronomical viewpoint, should be celebrated a day *later*. After one hundred and forty-four years the shift will amount to two days, and after two thousand years, it becomes almost twenty-eight (28 x 72 = 2,016). For this reason, the cosmic commemoration of the death of the Nathan Mary currently occurs twenty-eight days after the death date of August 4/5. A further correction must be made, however: August 4/5 in the Julian calendar at the time of Christ corresponds to August 2/3 in the Gregorian calendar. (The Gregorian calendar, still in use, was introduced by Pope Gregory XIII in 1582.Unless otherwise stated, all dates in this book are in the Julian calendar used at the time of Christ.) Adding twenty-eight days to August 2/3, we find that the cosmic celebration of the *death* of the Nathan Mary occurs at the present time (in the modern Gregorian calendar) on August 30/31. This means that the Sun returns to the same degree in the sidereal zodiac it occupied at the Nathan Mary's death (12 1/2° Leo) each year on August 30/31.

Similarly, adding twenty-eight days to the date of birth of the Nathan Mary (July 17/18 = July 15/16 in the Gregorian calendar), we arrive at August 12/13 as the modern (Gregorian) date of the cosmic celebration of the *birth* of the Nathan Mary at the present time. On this date the Sun returns to the same degree in the sidereal zodiac (25° Cancer) where it stood at her birth in 17 B.C.

And finally, adding twenty-eight days to the date of conception of the Nathan Mary (October 24/25 = October 22/23 in the Gregorian calendar), we come to November 19/20 as the date of the cosmic celebration of the *immaculate conception* of the Nathan Mary at the present time. On November 19/20, the Sun returns to 2° Scorpio in the sidereal zodiac, where it was at the conception in 18 B.C.[5]

---

5. In the above computations *twenty-six days* have been added to each of the original dates. This arises through the simultaneous *addition* of twenty-eight days, on account of precession, and the *subtraction* of two days, because of the change from the Julian to the Gregorian calendar. The original dates and the corresponding modern dates, together with the Sun's longitude in the sidereal zodiac, are tabulated on page 143.

Chapter Seven

The Solomon Mary

The mother of the Solomon Jesus, Mary of *Bethlehem*, was an extraordinarily *wise* woman. In contrast to the childlike Nathan Mary, who had developed a remarkable capacity for *love* and *compassion*, the Solomon Mary possessed a highly developed, wisdom-filled *intelligence*. There was thus a deep affinity between her and her profoundly wise son, the Zarathustra/Solomon Jesus individuality. Like the Nathan Mary, the Solomon Mary married at an early age and bore her first son, Jesus, not long after. As discussed in Chapter Three, the conception of the Solomon Jesus took place on June 7, 7 B.C., and the birth on March 5, 6 B.C. The visit of the Magi took place just over nine and one-half months later, on December 26/27, 6 B.C. According to Anne Catherine Emmerich:

> The Magi celebrated a three-day feast starting from today, December 8. On this night, fifteen years before Christ's birth, they had seen for the first time the star promised by Balaam rise in the sky [Numbers 24:17: "A star shall rise out of Jacob"] —the star for which they and their forefathers had waited so long, scanning the heavens in patient watchfulness. They discerned it in the picture of a virgin, bearing in one hand a scepter and in the other a balance. The scales were held even by a perfect ear of wheat in the one and a cluster of grapes in the other. Therefore, every year since their return from Bethlehem they kept a three-day feast beginning with this day. I saw, too, that as a result of this vision on the day of the conception of Mary, fifteen years before the birth of Christ, the star-worshippers did away with a terrible religious custom of theirs. . . . (LBVM, 66)

Anne Catherine is clearly referring to the Solomon Mary. And the reference to the date of conception of the Solomon Mary is very specific: December 8, fifteen years before the birth of the Solomon Jesus. This means that the birth of the Solomon Mary—assuming that it took place approximately nine months after conception—occurred on or near September 8. If this is correct, then the Solomon Mary was about fourteen years and six months old at the birth of the Solomon Jesus, whereas at the birth of the Nathan Jesus, the Nathan Mary was fifteen years, four months and twenty days old. It is also interesting to note that December 8 and September 8 are the festival days in the Catholic Church when the conception and birth of Mary are traditionally celebrated. The Catholic Church celebrates the dates of the conception and birth of the *Solomon* Mary, rather than those (October 25 and July 18) of the Nathan Mary.[1]

Looking at the planetary configuration for the conception of the Solomon Mary on December 8, 22 B.C., we find that this was the day of a New Moon. The conception of the Solomon Mary was thus an immaculate conception, as were those of the Nathan Mary and the Nathan Jesus.(Here again this refers only to the *astronomical* aspect and not to the deeper mystery of an immaculate conception.) By applying the hermetic-astrological rule, the *exact* times of conception and birth of the Solomon Mary were as follows.

Conception took place at 8:10 A.M., almost precisely at the time of the astronomical New Moon on December 8, 22 B.C. At this moment, the Ascendant was 4° Capricorn, and the Sun and the Moon were both at 18/19° Sagittarius (see Chart 11). Twenty years later, at the birth of the Nathan Jesus on December 6/7, 2 B.C., the Sun was at 16° Sagittarius, almost identical to its zodiacal position at the conception of the Solomon Mary. There is thus a deep affinity between the Solomon Mary and the Nathan Jesus. Remember that it was she, known as the "Mother of the Lord," who became his stepmother after A.D. 12, and who stood under the cross at his crucifixion.

In accordance with the hermetic-astrological rule, the birth of the Solomon Mary took place in Bethlehem shortly before midnight, September 7/8, 21 B.C. The Moon was at 4° Capricorn, identical to the Ascendant at the conception; and the Ascendant at birth was 19° Gemini, opposite the Moon's sidereal longitude at conception (see Chart 10). The actual moment of birth was 10:57 P.M. on September 7, 21 B.C. Thus, though the birth date

---

1. The actual dates of the conception and birth of the Nathan Mary were October 24 and July 17—each shortly before midnight. Similarly, the birth of Jesus is traditionally celebrated at midnight, December 24/25. Nevertheless, the festival day is December 25, since this day is believed to be the first day of his life. Analogously, October 25 and July 18 are the festival days of the conception and birth of the Nathan Mary.

was September 7, the festival day celebrating the first day of life of the new-born child is September 8 (as celebrated in the Church), since the birth occurred near midnight.

The Sun at the birth of the Solomon Mary stood at 16° Virgo in the sidereal zodiac. The designation *Virgin Mary* is therefore truly appropriate in a cosmic sense, and the cosmic celebration of the birth of the Virgin Mary rightly takes place each year when the Sun returns to 16° Virgo. At the present time, the Sun returns to this zodiacal degree each year on October 3/4. Indeed, the 2,000th anniversary of the cosmic celebration of the birth of the Virgin Mary was on October 3, 1980. Similarly, the cosmic celebration of the Virgin's immaculate conception takes place each year when the Sun returns to 17 1/2° Sagittarius (January 2/3 at the present time). The 2,000th anniversary of the cosmic celebration of the conception of the Solomon Mary was on January 3, 1980. (See table at the end of this book for a tabulation of these dates.)

How is it possible that the Catholic Church came to celebrate December 8 and September 8 as the festival days of the conception and birth of Mary? We must remember that at the time of Christ the people of Israel used the Jewish calendar, and that dates recorded in the Jewish calendar are not easily transposable to the corresponding dates in the Gregorian calendar. For example, knowing that the Nathan Jesus was born on Kislev 12 does not help us to determine that this was December 6/7 in the Julian calendar, unless the year (2 B.C.) is also known. It is something quite remarkable then that the actual Julian dates of conception and birth of the Solomon Mary came to be celebrated by the Church. Anne Catherine described how this occurred in the case of the Virgin's birth (the date of December 8 for the conception was presumably specified simply by going back exactly nine calendar months):

> I saw a pious pilgrim, two hundred and fifty years after Mary's death, traversing the Holy Land, visiting and venerating all the places connected with the actions of Jesus while on Earth. He was supernaturally guided. Sometimes he tarried several days together in certain places in which he tasted extraordinary consolation. There he prayed and meditated, and there also he received revelations from On High. For several years he had, from the 7th to the 8th of September, noticed a great jubilation in nature and heard angelic voices singing in the air. He prayed earnestly to know the meaning of all this, and it was made known to him in a vision that it was the birthnight of the Blessed Virgin Mary.

He was on his way to Mount Sinai when he had this vision. In it he was informed also of the existence of a chapel built in Mary's honor in a cave of the prophet Elijah. He was told to reveal this as well as the circumstances of Mary's birthnight, to the hermits on Mount Sinai.... I saw that in consequence of the pilgrim's communication, the 8th of September was here first celebrated in the year 250, and that later it was introduced into other parts of the Church. (LJC i, 147)

Our next task will be the determination of the date of *death* of the Solomon Mary. But first, let us consider Rudolf Steiner's remarks concerning the designation, *Virgin Mary*. Strictly speaking, since the Solomon Mary was the mother of seven children, she cannot be called virgin. But there is a deeper sense to the title *Blessed Virgin Mary*, explained by Rudolf Steiner in connection with a mysterious occurrence that took place at the time of the baptism in the Jordan:

Then the immortal part of the original mother of the Nathan Jesus descended from the spiritual world and transformed the mother who had been taken into the house of the Nathan Joseph, making her again virginal. Thus the soul of the mother whom the Nathan Jesus had lost was restored to him at the time of the baptism in the Jordan. The mother who had remained to him harbored within her the soul of his original mother, called in the Bible, the "blessed" Mary. (Rudolf Steiner, *The Gospel of Saint Luke*, p. 108)

According to this description, the two Marys were spiritually united at the baptism in the Jordan in A.D. 29, just as the two Jesus children had been spiritually united at the event in the Temple following Passover in A.D. 12. The Nathan Mary, who had departed earthly life and entered the spiritual world on August 4/5, A.D. 12, descended from spiritual realms at the baptism on September 23, A.D. 29 to unite spiritually with the Solomon Mary. Through this union, the Solomon Mary became "again virginal." This could be interpreted to signify that the vibrant, youthful quality of the Nathan Mary's soul so impressed itself upon the Solomon Mary that the latter became inwardly like a young maiden again, but there is also a more profound meaning to becoming "again virginal," relating to overcoming the consequences of the Fall.

But how old was the Solomon Mary at the baptism? From her birth on September 7/8, 21 B.C., until the baptism on the morning of September 23, A.D.

29, forty-nine years and fifteen full days had elapsed. This seems to contradict Rudolf Steiner's statement, quoted earlier, that at the baptism Mary was between the ages of forty-five and forty-six. This statement would be appropriate in the case of the Nathan Mary, however, had she lived beyond A.D. 12. At her death, on August 4/5 A.D. 12, she was twenty-eight years and eighteen days old; had she lived until the baptism on September 23 A.D. 29, she *would have been* forty-five years and two months old. One possible explanation for Rudolf Steiner's statement is that his clairvoyant vision of the fusion of the two Marys—the "two became one"—was such that it was difficult to distinguish the two. We have already pointed out that something similar evidently obtained in the case of the two Jesus children, when the Nathan Jesus was twelve years old and the Solomon Jesus seventeen, although Rudolf Steiner always spoke of the "twelve-year-old Jesus" even when referring to the *Solomon* Jesus.

The exceptional quality of the Solomon Mary, even as a young girl, was enhanced when she joined the Temple virgins in Jerusalem. According to Anne Catherine, "Mary was three years and three months old when she made the vow to join the virgins in the Temple" (LJC i, 156), and this was "eleven years before the birth of Christ" (LJC i, 178). These statements, taken together, agree with our finding that the Solomon Mary was fourteen and one-half years old at the birth of Jesus.

The Solomon Mary reached the age of three years and three months on December 8, 18 B.C., and so it must have been around this time that she was presented in the Temple. (The festival day commemorating Mary's "presentation in the Temple" at the age of three is celebrated in the Catholic Church on November 21.) According to another statement made by Anne Catherine Emmerich, "Two years before the entry of Mary into the Temple, just seventeen years before the birth of Christ, Herod ordered that work should be done on the Temple" (LBVM, 206). In this case, "seventeen years before the birth of Christ" apparently refers to the birth of the Nathan Jesus in 2 B.C.; seventeen years would lead us back to 19 B.C. Josephus informs us that Herod the Great began rebuilding the Temple in his eighteenth year, 20/19 B.C., and that work continued for one and a half years (*Antiquities* XV, xi, 1,6). This agrees with Anne Catherine's statement. The symbolic significance of the rebuilding of the Temple, seen in relation to Mary's entry as a Temple virgin, is that Mary herself was to become the *temple of God*, the *ark of the covenant*. Later, at the time of the first Passover festival of his ministry, in the spring of A.D. 30, Jesus Christ referred to the "temple of his body" in a similar sense:

The Jews then said to him, "What sign have you to show us for doing this?" Jesus answered them, "Destroy this temple, and in three days I will raise it up." The Jews then said, "It has taken forty-six years to build this temple, and you will raise it up in three days?" But he spoke of the temple of his body. (John 2:18–21)

Going back forty-six years from the spring of A.D. 30 leads us to the spring of 17 B.C., when the Solomon Mary was three and one-half years old and had already been presented in the Temple. With regard to the forty-six years of work on the Temple, which seems to contradict Josephus' statement that work continued for one and a half years, Anne Catherine reports that by the time Mary came into the Temple the rebuilding of the inner Temple was complete, but that outer work continued. She also described something of Mary's stay in the Temple:

I saw the Blessed Virgin living in the Temple in a perpetual ecstasy of prayer. Her soul did not seem to be on the Earth, and she often received consolation and comfort from heaven. She had an endless longing for the fulfillment of the Promise, and in her humility hardly ventured on the wish to be the lowliest maidservant of the Mother of the Redeemer. Mary's teacher and nurse in the Temple was called Noemi; she was a sister of Lazarus' mother and was fifty years old. She and the other Temple women belonged to the Essenes. Mary learned from her how to knit and helped her when she washed the blood of the sacrifices from the vessels and instruments, or when she cut up and prepared certain parts of the flesh for the Temple women and priests; for this formed part of their food. Later on Mary took a still more active part in these duties. (LBVM, 117)

The fact that Lazarus' aunt Noemi was the foster-mother of Mary during her stay at the Temple probably indicates how the relationship between Lazarus and the Holy Family came about. But how long did Mary stay in the Temple? Since the Solomon Jesus was born when she was fourteen and one-half years old, she must have left the Temple before then. According to Anne Catherine, "the Blessed Virgin had reached the age of fourteen and was to be dismissed from the Temple with seven other maidens to be married" (LBVM, 127). The Solomon Mary reached the age of fourteen on September 7/8, 7 B.C. But, as shown in Chapter One, the conception of the Solomon Jesus took place on June 7, 7 B.C. If Anne Catherine's indication is correct, the conception must have taken place while she was still a Temple virgin, at the age of thirteen years and nine months. In support of this, it should be pointed out that Anne Catherine beheld the annunciation to the Solomon Mary in the Temple, but not knowing of the *two* Marys, rejected this vision of the annunciation because of the annunciation to the Nathan Mary in Nazareth that took place later.

> Hereupon I saw the Blessed Virgin supplicating God with great fervor in her praying cell [in the Temple]. . . . She heard there a voice (unaccompanied by any visible appearance) and received a revelation which comforted her and gave her strength to consent to her marriage. This was not the annunciation, for I saw that happen later in Nazareth. I must, however, once have thought that I saw the appearance of an angel here too, for in my youth I often confused this vision with the Annunciation and thought I saw the latter happening in the Temple. (LBVM, 129–130)

To understand the mysterious circumstances surrounding the conception of the Solomon Jesus while Mary was still a Temple virgin, we must take Mary's betrothal to Joseph into account. This Joseph, who could be called *Joseph of Bethlehem* (since it was Joseph of Nazareth who married the Nathan Mary), was the son of Jacob, referred to in the Gospel of Saint Matthew. Anne Catherine added:

> Joseph, whose father was called Jacob, was the third of six brothers. His parents lived in a large house outside Bethlehem, once the ancestral home of David. . . . He left the house at night in order to earn his living in another place by carpentry. He might have been eighteen to twenty years old at that time. . . . Later still I saw him working in Tiberias for a master-carpenter. He might have been as much as thirty-three years old at that time. . . . Joseph was very devout and prayed fervently for the coming of the Messiah . . . [He] gave himself up to continual prayer, till he received the call to betake himself to Jerusalem to become by divine decree the spouse of the Blessed Virgin. (LBVM, 118–123)

How did this call take place? According to Anne Catherine, messengers from the Temple in Jerusalem were sent out to summon all the unmarried men of the line of David. The Solomon Mary was then presented to them. A high priest handed a branch to each man, bidding him hold it between his hands during the sacrifice and prayer that followed. Afterward, the branches were laid on the altar and it was announced that the one whose branch blossomed would be the one chosen by the Lord to marry the maiden Mary. None of the branches blossomed, however, and the priests of the Temple then searched further through the ancestral rolls until they found that of the six brothers from Bethlehem, one was missing. A search was made for Joseph and he also came to the Temple. During the prayer and sacrifice he also held a branch, and as he was about to lay it upon the altar, it blossomed like a lily, designating him as Mary's bridegroom (LBVM, 131–132).

But was there more to this betrothal of Joseph to Mary in the Temple? Had the conception already taken place by this time? Emil Bock indicates that just as the priests of the Temple arranged the marriage of Joseph and Mary, so also the conception of Jesus occurred in such a way that neither Joseph nor Mary were truly conscious of what had happened. Due to a so-called "temple sleep," the conception of the Solomon Jesus apparently took place in the Temple when Mary was betrothed to Joseph at the age of thirteen years and nine months, so that when Mary left the Temple at the age of fourteen, she was already three months with child.

> How it came about that Mary—scarcely having left the protective enclosure of the Temple—felt herself becoming a mother, is shrouded in mystery. Perhaps this mystery is related to that which already was woven about the circumstances leading to the "temple marriage" between Joseph and Mary. Those who, out of eugenic aims and insights led the parents together, might have done so in accordance with an age-old tradition in which, in certain cultures, every union through marriage was brought about by priests in such a way that the conception of the first-born child took place in a kind of "temple sleep" without the parents being fully conscious of it. (Bock, 79–80)

This would help to explain Joseph's attitude, referred to in the Gospel of Saint Matthew, where he was obviously perplexed to discover that Mary was expecting a child:

> When his mother Mary had been betrothed to Joseph, before they came together she was found to be with child of the Holy Spirit; and

her husband Joseph, being a just man and unwilling to put her to shame, resolved to divorce her quietly. (Matthew 1: 18–19)

We can surmise that Mary was betrothed to Joseph and that an annunciation had taken place at which an angel, as an emissary of the Holy Spirit, announced the conception of her child to her. This does not preclude Joseph's possible role in the conception, but he had no knowledge of it because of the "temple sleep." In any case, Joseph was clearly upset when he learned that Mary was with child. Whatever the true explanation of this passage from Saint Matthew, it seems there were *two* annunciations: one by an angel to the Solomon Mary in the Temple, and one by the Angel Gabriel to the Nathan Mary in Nazareth.

The further life and destiny of the Solomon Mary after the birth of Jesus was highly eventful: the visit of the Magi to the house of Joseph and Mary in Bethlehem, the flight to Egypt, the return to Israel, the start of a new life in Nazareth, the birth of six further children, the death of her husband before Passover in A.D. 12, followed by the death of her seventeen-year-old son Jesus in June, A.D. 12. A new life began for her and the remaining six children when she married Joseph of Nazareth, who had been left a widower with one child, the twelve-year-old Nathan Jesus, following the death of the Nathan Mary, August 4/5, A.D. 12. The combined family lived in Nazareth, where Jesus later attracted the hostility of the Pharisees because of his extraordinary wisdom and highly developed faculties, which often led him into variance with established teachings. Following the death of Joseph of Nazareth, which, according to Anne Catherine, took place before Passover of A.D. 29, a wealthy man named Levi who lived in Capernaum offered Jesus a house near the town (LJC i, 330–331). Levi was a friend of the Holy Family who, when he saw the difficulties Jesus endured in Nazareth at the hands of the Pharisees, provided him this house to live in undisturbed. The house was situated between Capernaum and Bethsaida on the Sea of Galilee, and Jesus moved into it after Passover in A.D. 29, at the age of twenty-nine. Mary also came to live there, leaving the rest of her family in Nazareth. By this time she had recognized that God had chosen Jesus for an extraordinary mission and felt called to devote herself to helping him fulfill it.

On Sunday, May 29, A.D. 29, after Passover and before the baptism in the Jordan on September 23, AD 29, Jesus, who was preparing for his mission, set off on his first journey to Hebron, to visit the area where John the Baptist had grown up. John had already received the Word of God in the wilderness not far from Mount Lebanon, where he had been living. "He went into all the region about the Jordan preaching a baptism of repentance for the forgiveness of sins" (Luke 3:3). About three months before the baptism of Jesus, John began baptizing at a certain place on the banks of the Jordan. During the time leading to Jesus' baptism, the Nathan Mary was drawing spiritually nearer to the Solomon Mary. The two Marys united at the time of the baptism, so that from that time, the Nathan Jesus "regained" his natural mother in the being of his stepmother. Thus an even closer bond developed between Jesus and Mary.

During the three-and-a-half-year ministry, Mary lived in the house between Bethsaida and Capernaum, to which Jesus always returned from his travels. This house therefore became the center of his activities, and Mary was usually there to receive guests—the disciples and holy women. Mary often traveled in the company of other women, such as Lazarus' sister Martha, to hear Jesus preaching. She was present at the wedding at Cana, for example, not long after the start of the ministry, where the miracle of the transformation of water into wine took place (John 2:1–12). She was also present when Jesus taught in the Temple near the end of his ministry, and also witnessed his triumphant entry into Jerusalem before his crucifixion.

Jesus often sent women who had undergone conversion—such as Mary Magdalene and the Samaritan woman Dina—to his mother for instruction, and he also introduced his disciples to her. There was an understanding between Jesus and Mary that she should be a spiritual mother to the community of his followers. Mary took his disciples and the holy women into her heart and prayers and bestowed spiritual blessings upon them. Each time Jesus introduced a new disciple to her, it was a sacred act to which Mary responded with inner intensity and holiness of purpose.

Following the crucifixion, at which she was present, Mary acquired a new role: she increasingly became the central figure among the disciples. This came to expression most strongly at Whitsun, on Sunday, May 24, A.D. 33, fifty days after the resurrection, when she was present in the midst of the Twelve.

How long after Whitsun did Mary live? When Anne Catherine Emmerich was asked how old Mary was at her death, she replied, "She reached the age of sixty-four years all but three and twenty days" (LBVM, 346). This very precise statement enables us to determine the exact date of her death. She would have reached the age of sixty-four on September 7/8, A.D. 44. Going back twenty-three full days leads us to August 15, which is the *traditional* date of

Mary's death and assumption, as celebrated in the Catholic Church. According to Anne Catherine, "The Blessed Virgin died after the ninth hour, at the same time as Our Lord" (LBVM, 372), or three o'clock in the afternoon—to which she adds, that the death took place in Ephesus. This information is sufficient to cast a horoscope for the hour of death of the Virgin Mary at Ephesus, at 3:00 P.M. on August 15, A.D. 44. In this horoscope (see Chart 12), the Sun is at 22 1/2° Leo, the Ascendant at 21° Sagittarius, and the Moon is culminating at 11° Libra. It is interesting that the position of the Moon at the death of the Virgin is close to the sidereal location of Saturn (9 1/2° Libra) at the birth of the Solomon Mary. Similarly, at the moment of death, Mars (4 1/2° Leo) was conjunct the Moon's descending node (4 1/2° Leo) at Mary's birth, and opposite the position of Mars (5° Aquarius) at Mary's conception. In the *hermetic* (heliocentric) chart at Mary's death, Mars (24° Cancer) was close to its sidereal location (26° Cancer) at Mary's birth.

Anne Catherine's visions indicate that, after the ascension of Christ Jesus, Mary lived for three years in Jerusalem in a house on Mount Zion, and for another three years at the home of Lazarus in Bethany; and "when half of the time of Mary's life after Christ's ascension had elapsed, about the sixth year after that event, the apostles were again assembled in Jerusalem" (LJC iv, 7). She then traveled with John the Evangelist to Ephesus, where she settled in a dwelling on a hill some three-and-a-half hours south of Ephesus (LBVM, 346–347).[2] Christ told John from the cross, "Behold, your mother!" ("And from that hour the disciple took her to his own home" John 19:27.) The.

---

2. In 1891, after reading Anne Catherine Emmerich's description of Mary's home at Ephesus, two Lazarite priests from Smyrna set off to search for it. After five days' search in the mountainous area south of Ephesus they were guided by some local people to a ruined building located on the summit of an isolated hill. The site, and also the plan of the house, exactly fitted Anne Catherine Emmerich's description. The priests learned that the place had been venerated down through the ages as Panaya Kapulu ("The House of the Holy Virgin"). Local villagers made annual pilgrimages there each year on August 15, the Festival of the Assumption of the Blessed Virgin Mary. Subsequent archeological investigations have confirmed the authenticity of Panaya Kapulu. The foundations of the original house date back to the first century. In the seventh century the building appears to have been enlarged and converted into a chapel in which Mary's Oratory became the main altar. At that time the entry was added and the fireplace wall removed. In 1898 the original hearthstones were discovered under the existing floor, still containing some ashes, petrified with age. In 1951 the Turkish government built a road up to the Holy Hill and the Society of Panaya, founded by the Archbishop of Smyrna, completely restored the ruins in accordance with the description in Sister Emmerich's visions. In 1954 the Little Brothers of Jesus accepted the post of serving at Panaya Kapulu, now known as the Shrine of Our Lady of the Assumption (See note by Robert Larson, LJC iv, 473–476).

statement that John went to Ephesus lends support to Anne Catherine's statement that Mary settled down in Ephesus.

Concerning the extraordinary circumstances surrounding Mary's death in Ephesus, Anne Catherine gives the following account:

> A short time before the Blessed Virgin's death, as she felt the approach of her reunion with her God, her Son, and her Redeemer, she prayed that there might be fulfilled what Jesus had promised to her in the house of Lazarus at Bethany on the day before his ascension. It was shown to me in the spirit how at that time, when she begged him that she might not live for long in this vale of tears after he had ascended, Jesus told her in general what spiritual works she was to accomplish before her end on Earth. He told her, too, that in answer to her prayers the apostles and several disciples would be present at her death, and what she was to say to them and how she was to bless them.... After the Blessed Virgin had prayed that the apostles should come to her, I saw the call going forth to them in many different parts of the world.... I saw all, the farthest as well as the nearest, being summoned by visions to come to the Blessed Virgin.... (LBVM, 363–364)

Anne Catherine Emmerich described where each apostle was when the summons to travel to Ephesus was received. All but Thomas, who was in India, gathered together at the house of Mary as she lay on her death bed. Thomas did not arrive until after her death.

We are now in a position to specify the annual cosmic celebration not only of the conception and birth of the Solomon Mary, but also of her death. This latter is the date on which the Sun returns to its sidereal location at her death, 22 1/2° Leo. At present the Sun returns there each year on September 9/10, so the 2000th anniversary of the Mary's death will take place on September 9/10 in the year 2044.

To conclude this study of the Blessed Virgin, let us now apply the principles of astrological biography to consider four of the most important events in her life:

(1) The birth of the Solomon Jesus: March 5, 6 B.C.
(2) The baptism in the Jordan: September 23, A.D. 29
(3) The crucifixion/resurrection: April 3/5, A.D. 33
(4) The death of Mary: August 15, A.D. 44

As stated, the basic principle in astrological biography is the correspondence between the embryonic period and the subsequent course of life. It is necessary to determine, from Mary's age at each of the above four events, the corresponding *embryonic age* represented by the Moon's longitude in the sidereal zodiac. The following table lists the results thus obtained:

AGE	MOON'S POSITION IN SIDEREAL ZODIAC	CORRESPONDING DATE IN EMBRYONIC PERIOD
1) 14 years 6 months	2 orbits + 25 1/2° = 14 1/2 ° Capricorn	January 6, 21 B.C., 5:00 P.M.
2) 49 years 15 days	7 orbits + 2 ° = 21° Sagittarius	June 16, 21 B.C., 10:30 P.M.
3) 52 years 7 months	7 orbits + 184° = 23° Gemini	June 29, 21 B.C., 11:30 P.M.
4) 63 years 11 months and 8 days	9 orbits + 48° = 7° Aquarius	August 14, 21 B.C., 00:45 A.M.

Looking at the planetary positions on the dates given in the right-hand column above, it is clear that the conception configuration is very important.

(1): The Moon at 14 1/2° Capricorn was in conjunction with the sidereal location (13° Capricorn) of Venus at the conception; Venus (19° Aquarius) was in conjunction with the zodiacal location (19° Aquarius) not only of the Moon's node at conception but also of heliocentric Venus at conception; and heliocentric Mercury (19° Sagittarius) was in alignment with the conception position of heliocentric Jupiter (19° Sagittarius).

(2): The Moon at 21° Sagittarius was in conjunction with Jupiter (18 1/2° Sagittarius) at the conception, and in conjunction with the Sun (17 1/2° Sagittarius) and the Moon (19° Sagittarius) at conception. At the same time, Mars (21° Gemini) and Venus (23 1/2° Gemini) were approximately opposite the foregoing, and heliocentric Mars (18 1/2° Gemini) was more or less exactly opposite heliocentric Jupiter (18 1/2° Sagittarius) at conception. The position of Jupiter (7° Capricorn) was opposite the sidereal location (7 3/4° Capricorn) of Uranus at conception.

(3): Heliocentric Mercury (17° Sagittarius) was in conjunction with the locations of the Moon (19° Sagittarius), the Sun (17 1/2° Sagittarius) and Jupiter (18 1/2° Sagittarius) at conception; and Venus at 17° Gemini was opposite the Moon (19° Sagittarius), the Sun (17 1/2° Sagittarius), and Jupiter (18 1/2° Sagittarius) at the conception. Jupiter (5 1/2° Capricorn) was opposite the Sun

(7 3/4° Cancer), and the latter was exactly opposite the zodiacal location (7 3/4° Capricorn) of Uranus at the conception.

(4): The Moon at 7° Aquarius, in the Moon's node at 6° Aquarius, was conjunct the sidereal location (5° Aquarius) of Mars at conception. Jupiter (1 1/4° Capricorn) was in conjunction with its sidereal location (1° Capricorn) at birth.

While such particulars may prove wearisome for non-specialists, these few examples of astrological biography—drawn from four of the most important events in the life of the Blessed Virgin—should illustrate the principles involved and make clear why the author feels that they strongly confirm the validity of the birth, conception, and death horoscopes determined in this chapter. All three of these dates turn out to be identical with the festival dates celebrated in the Catholic Church: December 8, September 7/8, and August 15. These are of course the historical dates; the corresponding dates of the "cosmic celebration" of these events, when the Sun returns to the same sidereal locations, are January 2/3, October 3/4, and September 9/10.

What is the respective validity of these two sets of dates— historically and cosmically? The fact that the Church celebrates the death of Mary on August 15 means that this event lives in the minds and hearts of a vast number of people on that day each year. This is a spiritual reality, as attested by the fact that Anne Catherine Emmerich's visions of the death of Mary generally took place on or around August 15 each year. But here we must distinguish between the *cosmic* and *earthly* celebrations of events. The earthly celebration of the death of Mary takes place each year on August 15, but the cosmic celebration follows twenty-five or twenty-six days later, on September 9 or September 10. Just as incarnated human beings commemorate the death of Mary on August 15, so we may conceive of non-incarnated souls, together with angelic beings, commemorating this event when the Sun is at 22 1/2° Leo in the sidereal zodiac (at the present time, September 9/10).[3] It is quite possible for human beings to attune themselves to this cosmic-spiritual reality—in fact, this book is primarily intended to serve this end, by paying

---

3. For those readers familiar with traditional western astrology, based on the tropical zodiac, the relationship between the tropical and sidereal zodiac may be clarified with reference to the above-mentioned cosmic and earthly celebration of events. The tropical zodiac provides an *earthly* frame of reference, since it is related to the cycle of nature, whereas the sidereal zodiac refers to heavenly, *spiritual* reality; and since human beings, when they incarnate upon the Earth, come from spiritual realms, the frame of reference for incarnation is necessarily the sidereal zodiac.

attention to the cosmic celebration of such events to establish a greater orientation for Cosmic Christianity.

We find a striking example of the irruption of cosmic-spiritual reality in Anne Catherine's own life. Each year Christians celebrate the birth of Jesus on December 25. However, as referred to in Chapter One, the historical date of birth of the Nathan Jesus was December 6/7. On the night of this birth, the Sun was at 16° Sagittarius in the sidereal zodiac. In our time the Sun returns to this position on January 1, but in Anne Catherine Emmerich's day it was December 29. Anne Catherine had long prayed to her *heavenly bridegroom*, Jesus Christ, that she might partake of his suffering. And at three o'clock on the afternoon of Tuesday, December 29, 1812, as she was lying in bed, Christ appeared to her in a figure of light and bestowed upon her the stigmata. At this moment the Sun was at 15 1/2° Sagittarius in the sidereal zodiac, just where it had been at the birth of the Nathan Jesus.

Other examples of this "breaking-through" of divine-spiritual reality into the earthly world in connection with the dates of the *cosmic celebration* of the conception, birth, and death of both Jesus and Mary could be given, but this one instance must suffice here. Surely it illustrates something of the significance of knowing the dates of cosmic celebration. For the sake of easy reference, other relevant dates have been tabulated on page 143 of this book. May they help to provide an orientation for living, throughout the course of the year with the spiritual reality of Cosmic Christianity.

*

Interlude

EXCURSUS TABLE

Dates of conception (ø), birth (*), and death (+)
of Mary, Jesus, and John

EVENT	ORIGINAL DATE	SUN'S LONGITUDE IN SIDEREAL ZODIAC	CORRESPONDING MODERN DATE	2000TH ANNIVERSARY
ø Nathan Mary	October 24/25, 18 B.C.	2 1/2° Scorpio	Nov. 19/20	Nov. 19, 1983
* Nathan Mary	July 17/18, 17 B.C.	25 1/2° Cancer	August 12/13	August 12, 1984
+ Nathan Mary	August 4/5, A.D. 12	12 1/2° Leo	August 30/31	August 30, 2012
øSolomon Mary	December 8, 22 B.C.	17 1/2° Sagittarius	January 2/3	January 3, 1980
* Solomon Mary	September 7/8, 21 B.C.	16° Virgo	October 3/4	October 3, 1980
+ Solomon Mary	August 15, A.D. 44	22 1/2° Leo	Sept. 9/10	Sept. 9/10, 2044
ø John the Baptist	September 9, 3 B.C.	17° Virgo	October 4/5	October 5, 1998
* John the Baptist	June 3/4, 2 B.C.	12 1/2°Gemini	June 28/29	June 29, 1999
+ John the Baptist	January 3/4, A.D. 31	14 1/2° Capricorn	January 29	January 29, 2031
ø Solomon Jesus	June 7, 7 B.C.	16° Gemini	July 2/3	July 2, 1994
* Solomon Jesus	March 5, 6 B.C.	15 1/2° Pisces	March 30/31	March 31, 1995
+ Solomon Jesus	June 4/5, A.D. 12	14° Gemini	June 30/July 1	June 30, 2012
ø Nathan Jesus	March 6, 2 B.C.	16° Pisces	March 31/April 1	March 31, 1999
* Nathan Jesus	December 6/7, 2 B.C.	16° Sagittarius	January 1	January 1, 2000
+ Nathan Jesus	April 3, A.D. 33	14° Aries	April 28/29	April 28/29, 2033

ASTROLOGICAL CHARTS

A Note Concerning the Zodiac

It should be noted that all zodiacal longitudes indicated in the text and presented in the following horoscopes are in terms of the sidereal zodiac, which has to be distinguished from the tropical zodiac in widespread use in contemporary astrology in the West. The tropical zodiac was introduced into astrology in the middle of the second century A.D. by the Greek astronomer Claudius Ptolemy. Prior to this the sidereal zodiac was in use. Such was the influence of Ptolemy upon the western astrological tradition that the tropical zodiac become substituted for the sidereal zodiac used by the Babylonians, Egyptians, and early Greek astrologers. Yet the astrological tradition in India was not influenced by Ptolemy, and so the sidereal zodiac is still used to this day by Hindu astrologers.

The sidereal zodiac originated with the Babylonians in the sixth/fifth centuries B.C. and was defined by them in relation to certain bright stars. For example, Aldebaran ("the Bull's eye") is located in the middle of the sidereal sign/constellation of the Bull at 15° Taurus, and Antares ("the Scorpion's heart") is in the middle of the sidereal sign/constellation of the Scorpion at 15° Scorpio. The sidereal signs, each thirty degrees long, coincide closely with the twelve astronomical zodiacal constellations of the same name. Whereas the signs of the tropical zodiac, since they are defined in relation to the vernal point, now have little or no relationship to the corresponding zodiacal constellations. This is because the vernal point, the zodiacal location of the sun on March 21, shifts slowly backwards through the sidereal zodiac at a rate of one degree in seventy-two years ("the precession of the equinoxes").

When Ptolemy introduced the tropical zodiac into astrology, there was an almost exact coincidence between the tropical and the sidereal zodiac, as the vernal point, which is defined to be 0° Aries in the tropical zodiac, was at 1° Aries in the sidereal zodiac in the middle of the second century A.D. Thus, there was only one degree difference between the two zodiacs. So, it made hardly any difference to Ptolemy or his contemporaries to use the tropical zodiac instead of the sidereal zodiac. But now— the vernal point, on account of precession, having shifted back from 1° Aries to 5° Pisces—there is a 25 degree difference and so there is virtually no correspondence between the two. Without going into further detail concerning the complex issue of the zodiac, as I have shown in my *Hermetic Astrology* trilogy, the sidereal zodiac is the zodiac used by the three Magi, who were the last representatives of the true star wisdom of antiquity. For this reason the sidereal zodiac is used throughout this book.

A Note Concerning the Astrological Charts

Each chart indicates the positions in the sidereal zodiac of the Sun, Moon, Moon's nodes and planets (plus the Ascendant and the Midheaven in cases where the time is known). The data is based on computer calculations of the planetary positions, geocentric and heliocentric, at the conception (ø), birth (*) and death (+) of the person under consideration. The charts comprise an outer and an inner circle. The outer circle is the "hermetic" chart, based on the heliocentric system of Tycho Brahe (1546-1601); the inner circle gives the traditional geocentric horoscope. Thus the heliocentric/hermetic chart (outer circle) is superimposed on the geocentric (inner circle). All planetary positions are listed in the sidereal zodiac to degree and minute; all dates are given in terms of the Julian calendar in use at the time of Christ; and all times are given as local time in the 24-hour system. (See bibliography of works by Robert Powell for information concerning the astronomical basis of these charts).

* * *

15 horoscopes relating to the conception (ø), birth (*), death (+) of five individuals:

Solomon Jesus • Nathan Jesus • Solomon Mary • Nathan Mary • John the Baptist

Plus 18 astrological charts of the most important Christ events from the Baptism to the event of Pentecost (see Table 3)

With grateful acknowledgment to Peter Treadgold, who produced the table of dates relating to the three and one-half years of Christ's ministry (Appendix VI) and printed out the horoscopes with his "Triform Chart and Ephemeris Program." For anyone interested in working with or carrying out research in the field of Astrosophy, this program is ideal, enabling one to produce charts such as the horoscopes in this book or such as those of Willi Sucher and other contributors to Astrosophy.[1]

---

1. With this program one can:

*compute birth charts in a large variety of systems (tropical, sidereal, geocentric, heliocentric, hermetic, etc.)
*calculate conception charts using the hermetic rule, in turn applying it for correction of the birth time
*produce charts for the period between conception and birth
*print out an "astrological biography" for the whole span of life
*work with the geocentric, heliocentric (and even lemniscatory) planetary system
*work with the sidereal zodiac according to the definition of your choice (Babylonian sidereal, Indian sidereal, unequal-division astronomical, etc.)
*work with planetary aspects with orbs of your choice

Included are eight house systems and a variety of chart formats, one of which was used to produce the horoscopes in this book. It also includes an ephemeris program with search facility.

If you are interested, please write for further details: Peter Treadgold, Triform, Costa Brava 9, Pt. 2-2a, 28034 Madrid, Spain.

The program runs under Microsoft Windows.

CHART 1

Birth of the Solomon Jesus

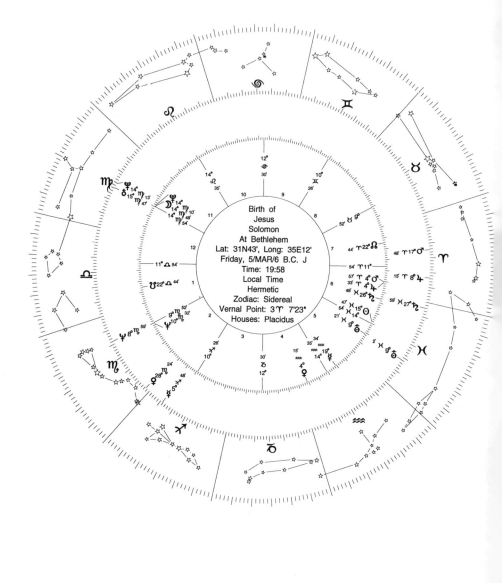

Birth of
Jesus
Solomon
At Bethlehem
Lat: 31N43', Long: 35E12'
Friday, 5/MAR/6 B.C. J
Time: 19:58
Local Time
Hermetic
Zodiac: Sidereal
Vernal Point: 3♈ 7'23"
Houses: Placidus

CHART 2

Conception of Solomon Jesus

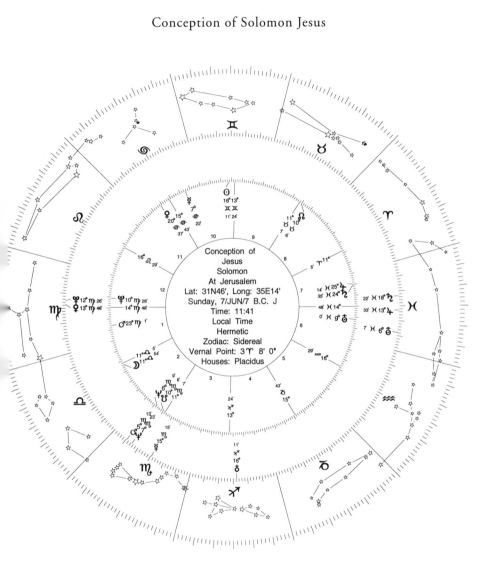

Conception of
Jesus
Solomon
At Jerusalem
Lat: 31N46', Long: 35E14'
Sunday, 7/JUN/7 B.C. J
Time: 11:41
Local Time
Hermetic
Zodiac: Sidereal
Vernal Point: 3♈ 8' 0"
Houses: Placidus

CHART 3

Death of Solomon Jesus

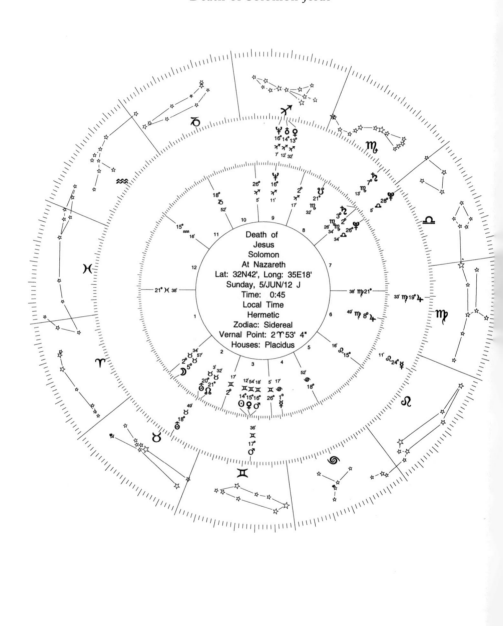

Death of
Jesus
Solomon
At Nazareth
Lat: 32N42', Long: 35E18'
Sunday, 5/JUN/12 J
Time: 0:45
Local Time
Hermetic
Zodiac: Sidereal
Vernal Point: 2 ♈ 53' 4"
Houses: Placidus

CHART 4

Birth of Nathan Jesus

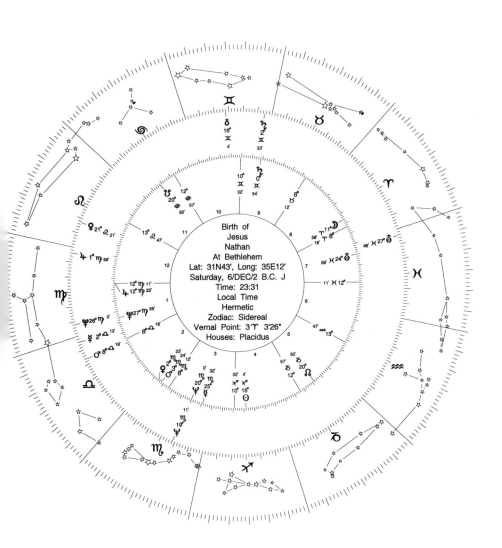

CHART 5

Conception of Nathan Jesus

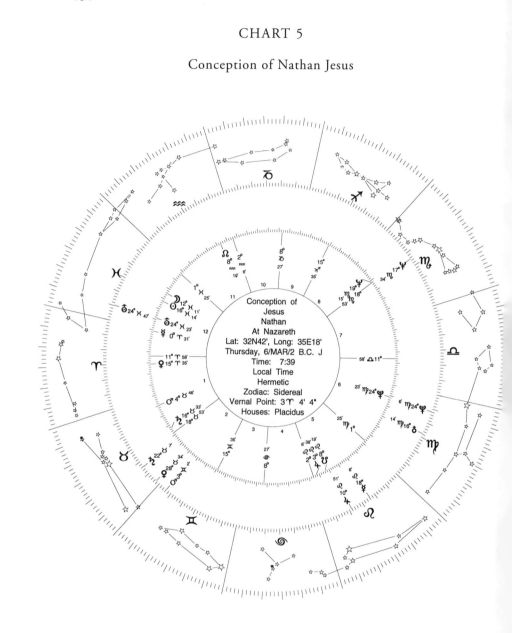

Conception of
Jesus
Nathan
At Nazareth
Lat: 32N42', Long: 35E18'
Thursday, 6/MAR/2 B.C. J
Time: 7:39
Local Time
Hermetic
Zodiac: Sidereal
Vernal Point: 3♈ 4' 4"
Houses: Placidus

CHART 6

Death (Crucifixion) of Nathan Jesus

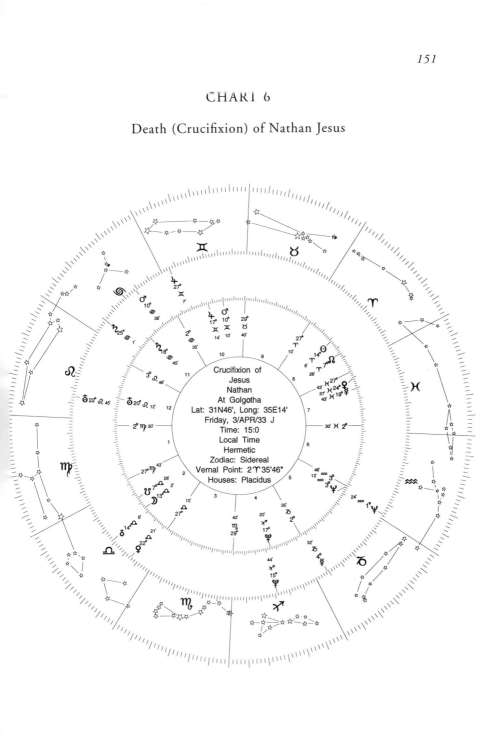

Crucifixion of
Jesus
Nathan
At Golgotha
Lat: 31N46', Long: 35E14'
Friday, 3/APR/33 J
Time: 15:0
Local Time
Hermetic
Zodiac: Sidereal
Vernal Point: 2♈35'46"
Houses: Placidus

CHART 7

Birth of Nathan Mary

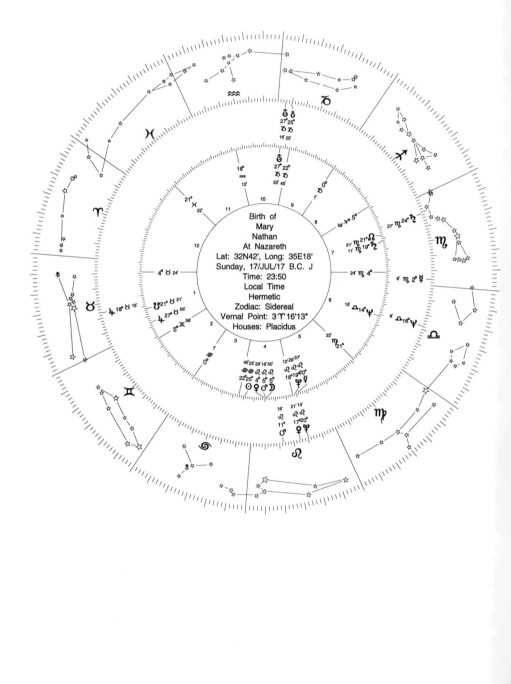

Birth of
Mary
Nathan
At Nazareth
Lat: 32N42', Long: 35E18'
Sunday, 17/JUL/17 B.C. J
Time: 23:50
Local Time
Hermetic
Zodiac: Sidereal
Vernal Point: 3 ♈ 16'13"
Houses: Placidus

CHART 8

Conception of Nathan Mary

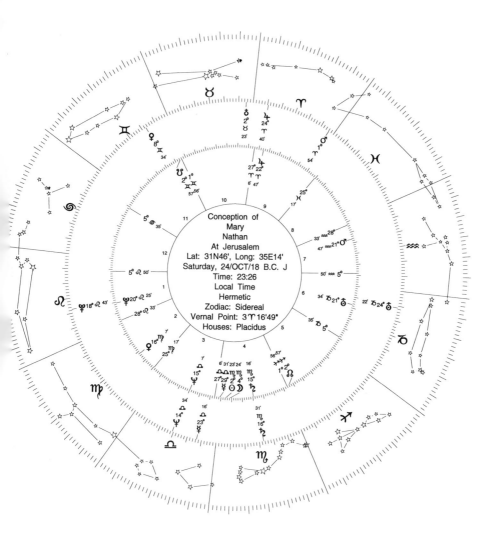

Conception of
Mary
Nathan
At Jerusalem
Lat: 31N46', Long: 35E14'
Saturday, 24/OCT/18 B.C. J
Time: 23:26
Local Time
Hermetic
Zodiac: Sidereal
Vernal Point: 3♈16'49"
Houses: Placidus

CHART 9

Death of Nathan Mary

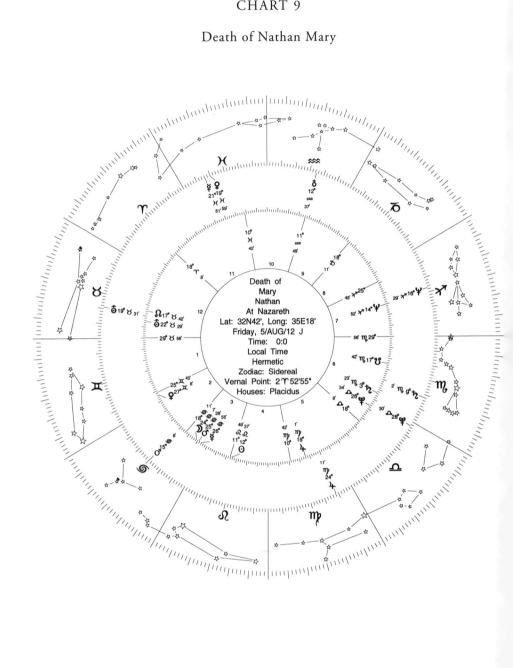

CHART 10

Birth of Solomon Mary

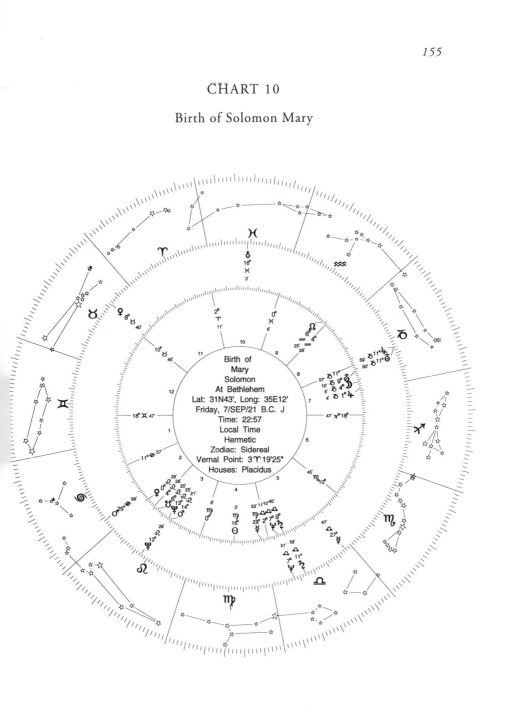

Birth of
Mary
Solomon
At Bethlehem
Lat: 31N43', Long: 35E12'
Friday, 7/SEP/21 B.C. J
Time: 22:57
Local Time
Hermetic
Zodiac: Sidereal
Vernal Point: 3♈19'25"
Houses: Placidus

156

CHART 11

Conception of Solomon Mary

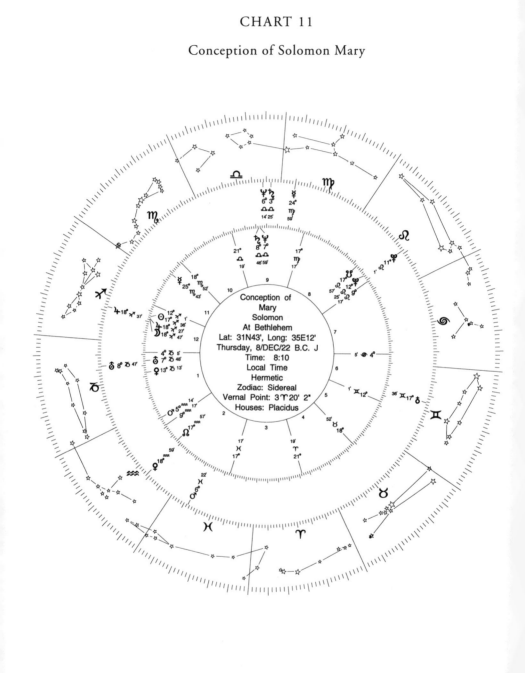

CHART 12

Death of Solomon Mary

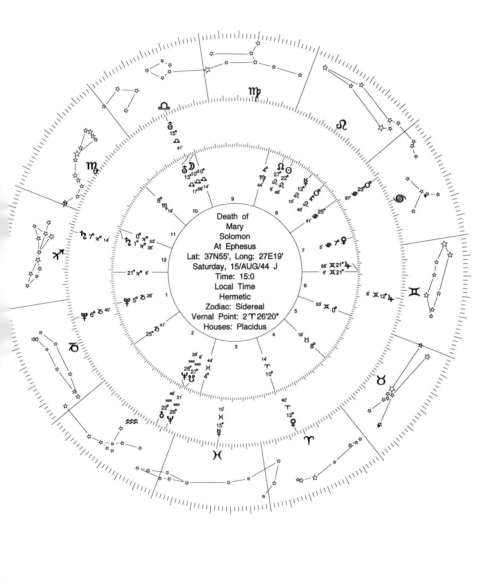

Death of
Mary
Solomon
At Ephesus
Lat: 37N55', Long: 27E19'
Saturday, 15/AUG/44 J
Time: 15:0
Local Time
Hermetic
Zodiac: Sidereal
Vernal Point: 2♈26'20"
Houses: Placidus

CHART 13

Birth of John the Baptist

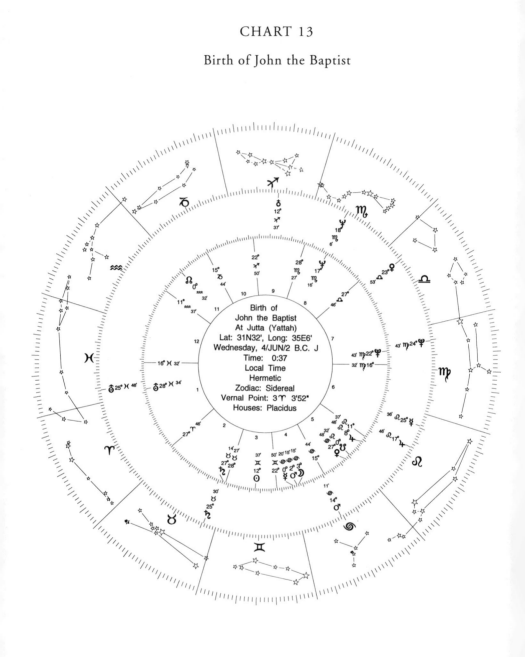

Birth of
John the Baptist
At Jutta (Yattah)
Lat: 31N32', Long: 35E6'
Wednesday, 4/JUN/2 B.C. J
Time: 0:37
Local Time
Hermetic
Zodiac: Sidereal
Vernal Point: 3♈ 3'52"
Houses: Placidus

CHART 14

Conception of John the Baptist

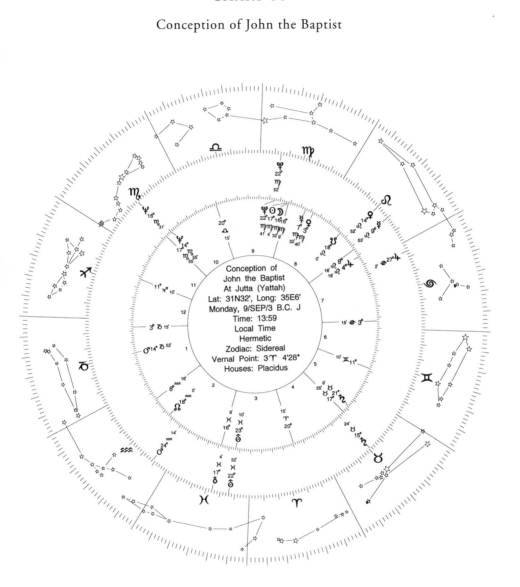

Conception of
John the Baptist
At Jutta (Yattah)
Lat: 31N32', Long: 35E6'
Monday, 9/SEP/3 B.C. J
Time: 13:59
Local Time
Hermetic
Zodiac: Sidereal
Vernal Point: 3 ♈ 4'28"
Houses: Placidus

CHART 15

Death of John the Baptist

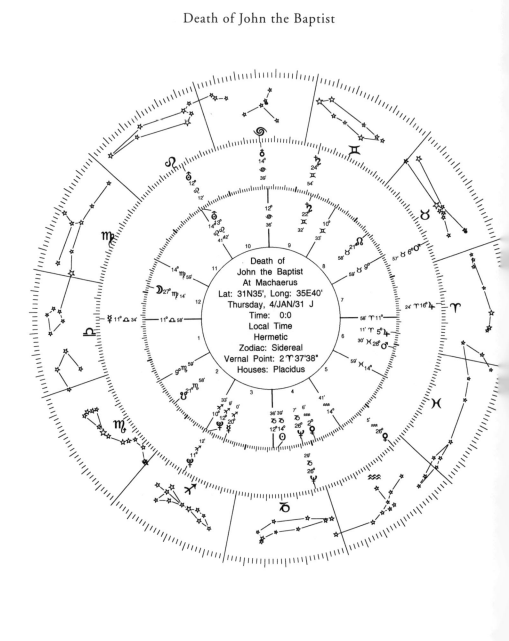

Death of
John the Baptist
At Machaerus
Lat: 31N35', Long: 35E40'
Thursday, 4/JAN/31 J
Time: 0:0
Local Time
Hermetic
Zodiac: Sidereal
Vernal Point: 2 ♈ 37'38"
Houses: Placidus

1. Baptism of Jesus Christ

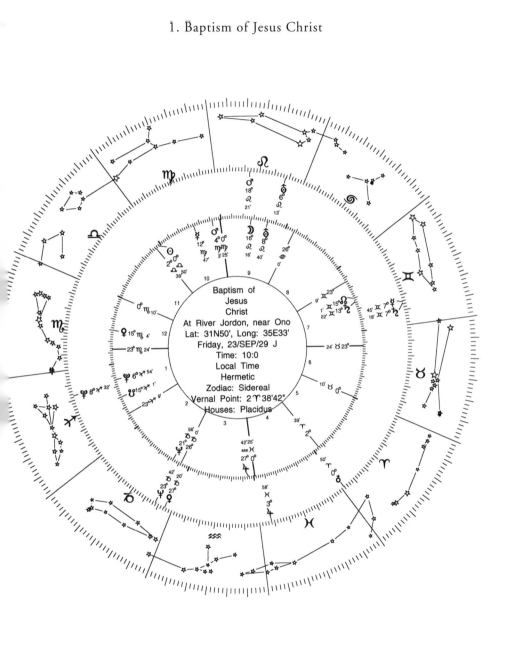

Baptism of
Jesus
Christ
At River Jordon, near Ono
Lat: 31N50', Long: 35E33'
Friday, 23/SEP/29 J
Time: 10:0
Local Time
Hermetic
Zodiac: Sidereal
Vernal Point: 2 ♈ 38'42"
Houses: Placidus

2. Temptations of Jesus Christ (Start)

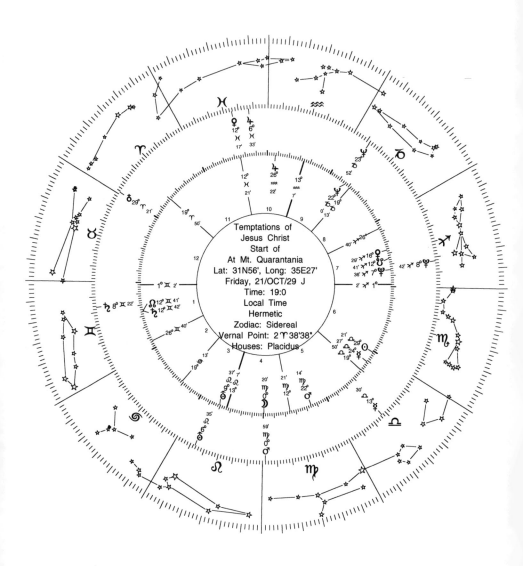

Temptations of
Jesus Christ
Start of
At Mt. Quarantania
Lat: 31N56', Long: 35E27'
Friday, 21/OCT/29 J
Time: 19:0
Local Time
Hermetic
Zodiac: Sidereal
Vernal Point: 2 ♈ 38'38"
Houses: Placidus

3. Temptations of Jesus Christ (End)

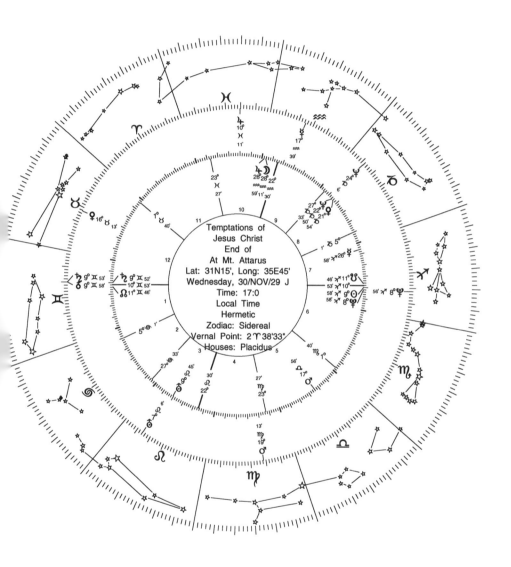

Temptations of
Jesus Christ
End of
At Mt. Attarus
Lat: 31N15', Long: 35E45'
Wednesday, 30/NOV/29 J
Time: 17:0
Local Time
Hermetic
Zodiac: Sidereal
Vernal Point: 2♈38'33"
Houses: Placidus

4. Miracle of Water into Wine at the Wedding in Cana

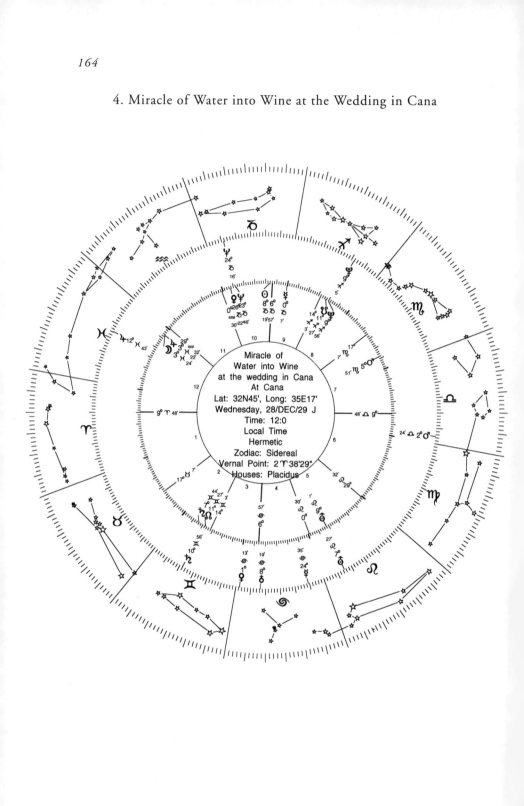

5. Healing of the Nobleman's Son

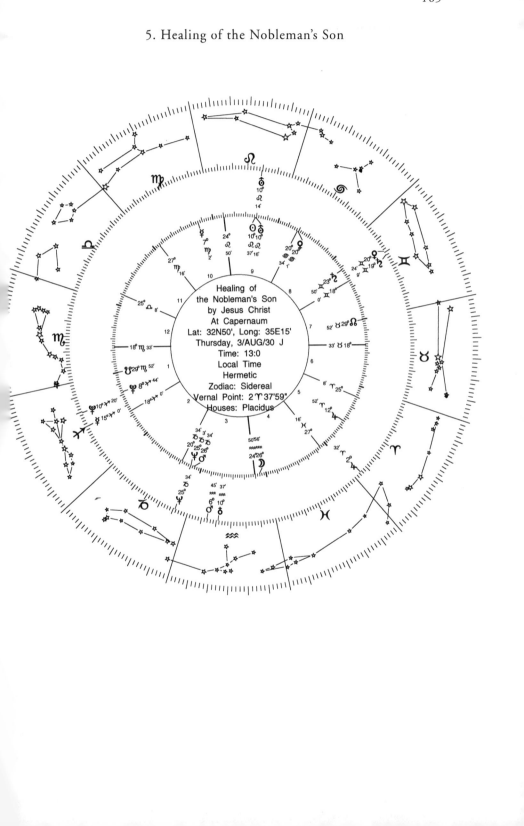

Healing of
the Nobleman's Son
by Jesus Christ
At Capernaum
Lat: 32N50', Long: 35E15'
Thursday, 3/AUG/30 J
Time: 13:0
Local Time
Hermetic
Zodiac: Sidereal
Vernal Point: 2♈37'59"
Houses: Placidus

6. Raising of the Youth of Nain

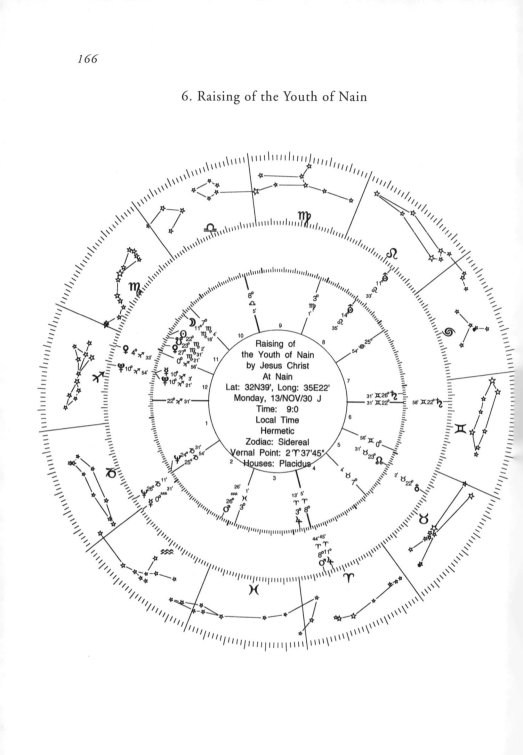

Raising of
the Youth of Nain
by Jesus Christ
At Nain
Lat: 32N39', Long: 35E22'
Monday, 13/NOV/30 J
Time: 9:0
Local Time
Hermetic
Zodiac: Sidereal
Vernal Point: 2 ♈ 37'45"
Houses: Placidus

7. Raising of Jairus' Daughter

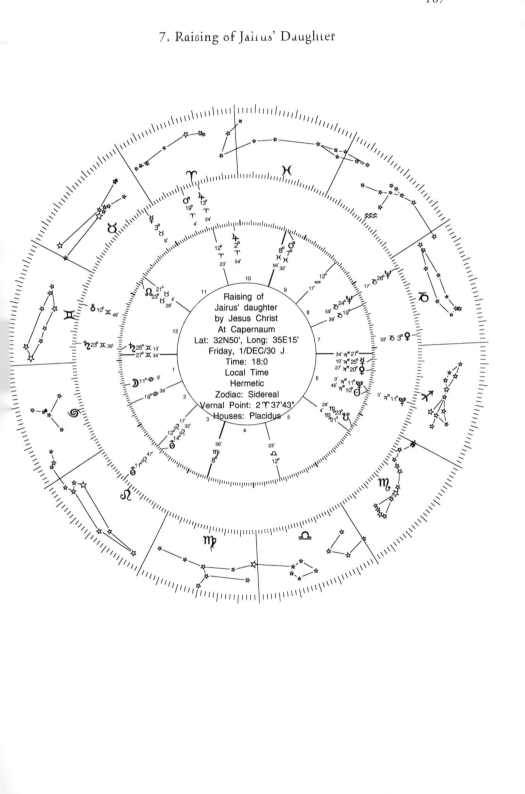

Raising of
Jairus' daughter
by Jesus Christ
At Capernaum
Lat: 32N50', Long: 35E15'
Friday, 1/DEC/30 J
Time: 18:0
Local Time
Hermetic
Zodiac: Sidereal
Vernal Point: 2♈37'43"
Houses: Placidus

8. Death of John the Baptist

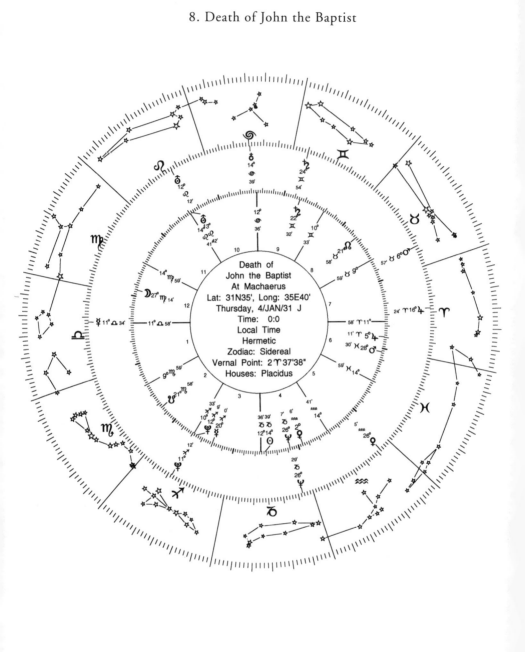

Death of
John the Baptist
At Machaerus
Lat: 31N35', Long: 35E40'
Thursday, 4/JAN/31 J
Time: 0:0
Local Time
Hermetic
Zodiac: Sidereal
Vernal Point: 2♈37'38"
Houses: Placidus

9. Healing of the Paralyzed Man

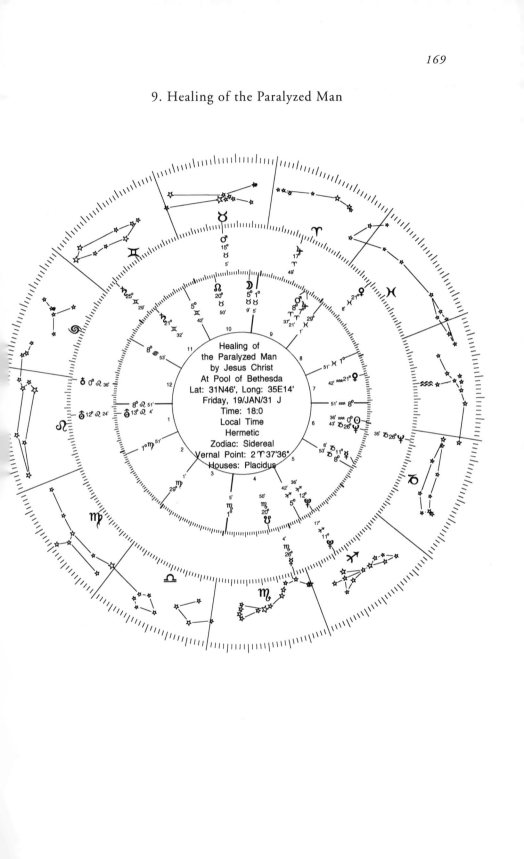

10. Feeding of the Five Thousand

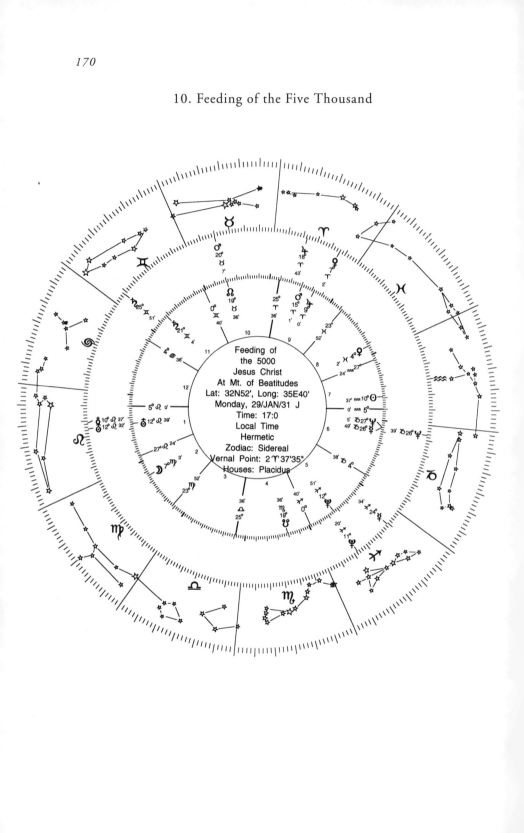

Feeding of
the 5000
Jesus Christ
At Mt. of Beatitudes
Lat: 32N52', Long: 35E40'
Monday, 29/JAN/31 J
Time: 17:0
Local Time
Hermetic
Zodiac: Sidereal
Vernal Point: 2♈37'35"
Houses: Placidus

11. Miracle of Walking on the Water

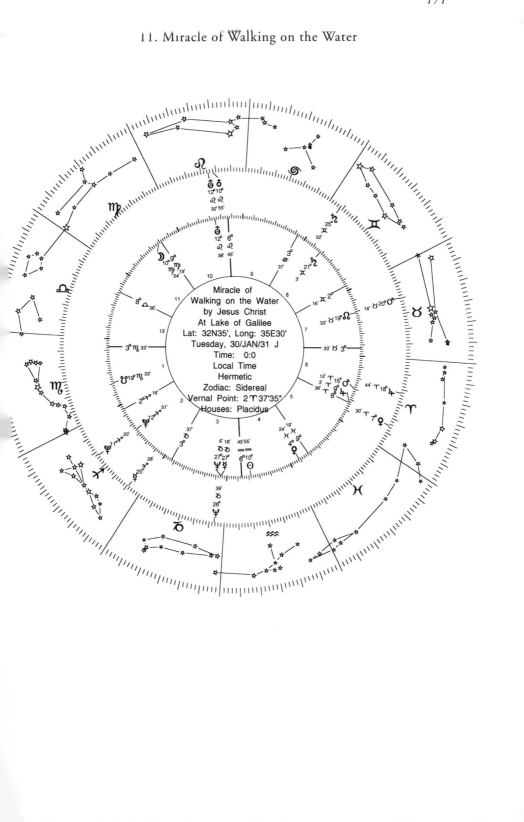

12. Transfiguration of Jesus Christ

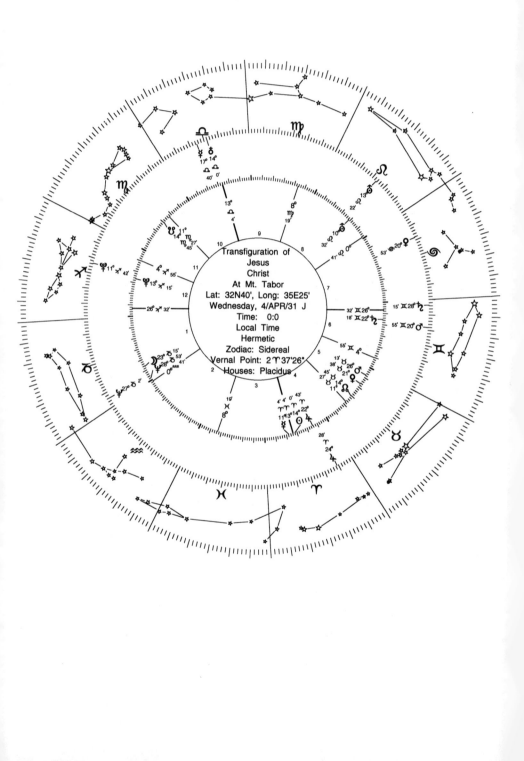

Transfiguration of
Jesus
Christ
At Mt. Tabor
Lat: 32N40', Long: 35E25'
Wednesday, 4/APR/31 J
Time: 0:0
Local Time
Hermetic
Zodiac: Sidereal
Vernal Point: 2♈37'26"
Houses: Placidus

13. Raising of Lazarus

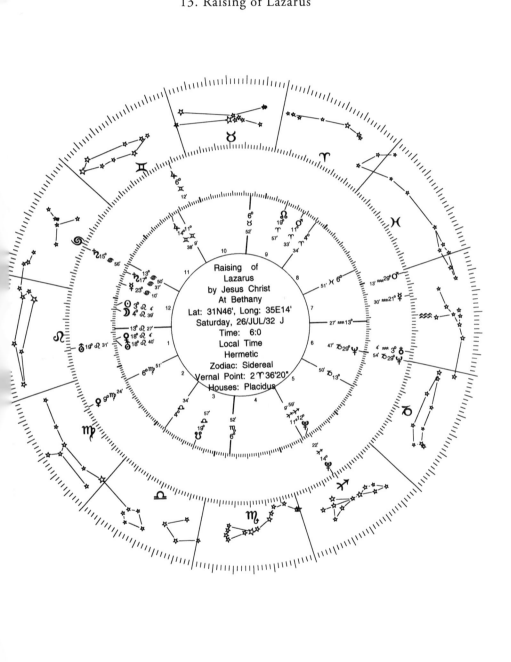

Raising of
Lazarus
by Jesus Christ
At Bethany
Lat: 31N46', Long: 35E14'
Saturday, 26/JUL/32 J
Time: 6:0
Local Time
Hermetic
Zodiac: Sidereal
Vernal Point: 2♈36'20"
Houses: Placidus

14. Entry of Jesus Christ into Jerusalem

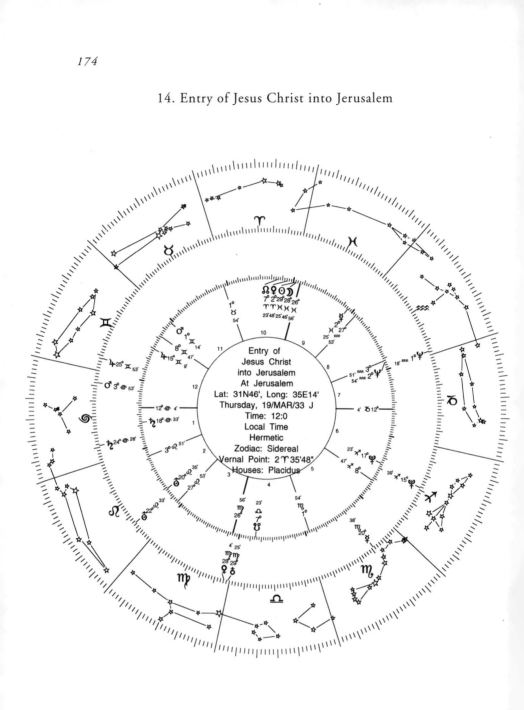

Entry of
Jesus Christ
into Jerusalem
At Jerusalem
Lat: 31N46', Long: 35E14'
Thursday, 19/MAR/33 J
Time: 12:0
Local Time
Hermetic
Zodiac: Sidereal
Vernal Point: 2♈35'48"
Houses: Placidus

15. Crucifixion of Jesus (Nathan) Christ

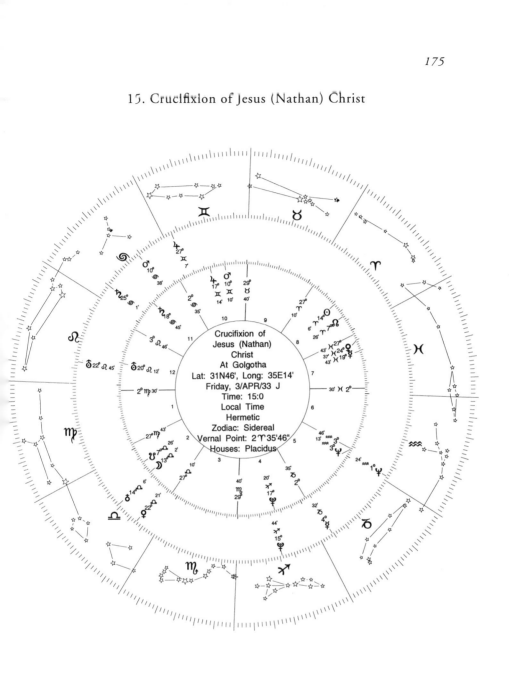

Crucifixion of
Jesus (Nathan)
Christ
At Golgotha
Lat: 31N46', Long: 35E14'
Friday, 3/APR/33 J
Time: 15:0
Local Time
Hermetic
Zodiac: Sidereal
Vernal Point: 2♈35'46"
Houses: Placidus

16. Resurrection of Jesus Christ

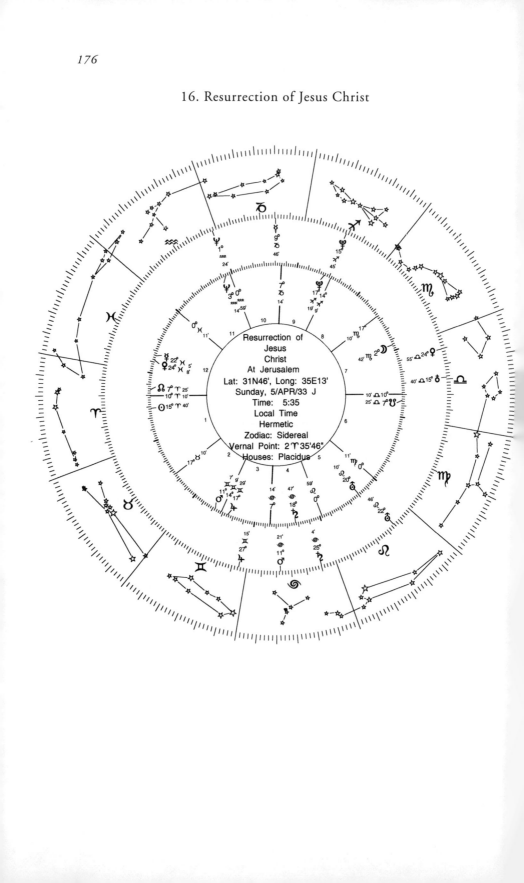

17. Ascension of Jesus Christ

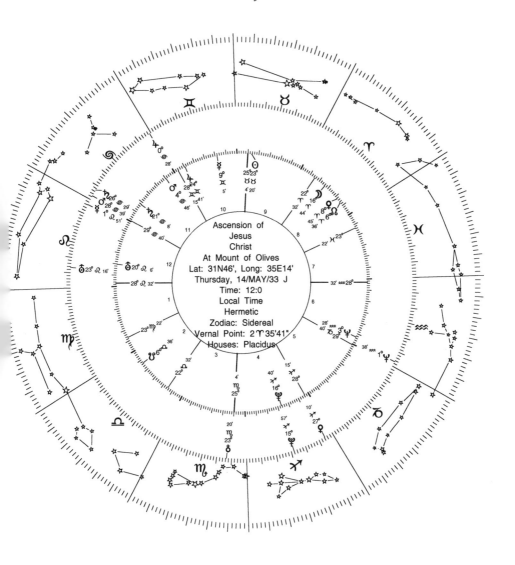

Ascension of
Jesus
Christ
At Mount of Olives
Lat: 31N46', Long: 35E14'
Thursday, 14/MAY/33 J
Time: 12:0
Local Time
Hermetic
Zodiac: Sidereal
Vernal Point: 2♈35'41"
Houses: Placidus

18. Event of Pentecost (Whitsun)

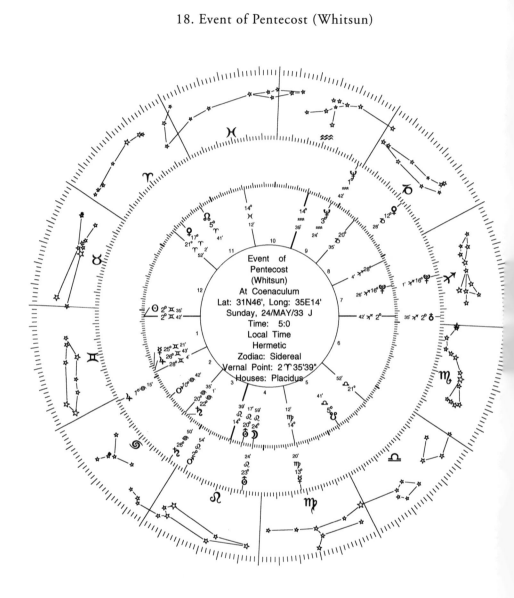

Event of
Pentecost
(Whitsun)
At Coenaculum
Lat: 31N46', Long: 35E14'
Sunday, 24/MAY/33 J
Time: 5:0
Local Time
Hermetic
Zodiac: Sidereal
Vernal Point: 2♈35'39"
Houses: Placidus

Introduction

THE FOLLOWING DIARY or chronicle of Christ's ministry (excluding about ten months from A.D. 31 to summer, A.D. 32) is based primarily on the visions of Anne Catherine Emmerich, which she communicated daily to Clemens Brentano for almost three years. The Chronicle begins historically on Sunday, May 29, A.D. 29, four months prior to the baptism, i.e., four months before the start of the three and one-half year ministry, and ends, when Jesus is 33 1/3 years old, with the crucifixion on Friday, April 3, A.D. 33—a date that coincides with Rudolf Steiner's indication for the date of the crucifixion (see Appendix 1). Indeed, as already noted in Part I, there is generally speaking a remarkable agreement between Rudolf Steiner's spiritual scientific research and Anne Catherine Emmerich's visionary descriptions of the life of Christ, and both of these, in turn, are in harmony with the four Gospels. These, naturally, are primary sources for the Chronicle and are frequently referred to in it.

The dates given in the Chronicle are not the dates on which Anne Catherine Emmerich's visions took place, but rather the actual historical dates of the events related. Nevertheless, there is a fairly close relationship between Anne Catherine's calendar dates (on which she had her visions) and the actual historical dates, the difference between them generally amounting to not more than five days. The actual historical dates were again discovered by applying astronomical chronology to Anne Catherine's communications concerning the Jewish calendar, feast days, and the like (see Appendices III and IV). Additional help was provided by her consistent reference every seven days to the Sabbath, on which, almost without exception, she saw Jesus celebrating the Sabbath (from Friday evening until Saturday evening) wherever he was at that time. The remaining days of the week—Sunday, Monday, Tuesday, Wednesday, Thursday—are usually easily recognizable from the terms used by Anne Catherine such as "yesterday afternoon," "this morning," "on the next day," and so on. In this way, the exact day—and often the time—of events was able to be found.

Together with Anne Catherine Emmerich's occasional references to the Jewish months or to the festival days (specified in terms of the Jewish months), her regular mention of the ever-recurring Sabbath enabled the daily chronicle of Christ's ministry to become historically identified. The Sabbaths and the Jewish months form the backbone to the Chronicle, which is thereby internally consistent. Moreover, Anne Catherine's references perfectly match with the actual Jewish calendar for the historical period A.D. 29–33. We were able to establish this "match" here for the first time only because we were able to identify the "missing period" (summer A.D. 31 to summer A.D. 32), which allowed us to realize that Anne Catherine's account of the ministry over two and one-half years was incomplete (i.e., it should have been three and one-half years).

The Names of Places

The place names given in the Chronicle were communicated by Anne Catherine Emmerich. Her geographical descriptions were sufficiently detailed to enable these places—most of which are now completely unknown—to be located fairly accurately. In his monumental work *Der Wandel Jesu in der Welt*, Helmut Fahsel drew up a series of detailed maps of Palestine. He related each map to a specific period covered in Christ's ministry and entered onto it the places named by Anne Catherine Emmerich that Jesus visited during the period in question. These maps, which are extremely helpful for an orientation while following the Chronicle, serve as the basis for the maps reproduced here (see pages 375–414).

As a help in comparing with present-day maps of Palestine, the modern names (usually Arabic) of mountains, plains, and valleys have been entered on the maps. The dotted lines indicate the approximate route taken by Jesus on his travels during the period in question. The small half-circle denotes the beginning and the arrowhead the end of each particular journey. The subsequent map then continues the route taken during the next period of time.

The Structure of the Chronicle

The most obvious structure underlying the life of Christ is that given by the yearly celebration of the Passover festival in Jerusalem. Christ's earthly life ended on the day of preparation for the Passover (Nisan 14) in A.D. 33 and the "word of God" came to John the Baptist in the wilderness during the second half of the month of Nisan in the spring of A.D. 29. The Chronicle is concerned with the span of time from Nisan 15, A.D. 29 to Nisan 14, A.D. 33, which comprises four years in the Jewish calendar, each year commencing with the Feast of the Passover on Nisan 15. Note that this specification of the year from Passover to Passover corresponds more or less exactly with the Christian year measured from Easter to Easter.

> Year 1: Nisan 15, A.D. 29, to Nisan 14, A.D. 30
> Year 2: Nisan 15, A.D. 30, to Nisan 14, A.D. 31
> Year 3: Nisan 15, A.D. 31, to Nisan 14, A.D. 32
> Year 4: Nisan 15, A.D. 32, to Nisan 14, A.D. 33

In the reconstruction of the months of the Jewish calendar during these four years—in relation to the Julian calendar in use in the Roman Empire at the time of Christ—it is possible that an error of one or two days may have occurred. As far as possible, though, the dates have been controlled against the calendar indications given by Anne Catherine Emmerich (see Appendix III). Alongside each Julian calendar date is listed (in brackets) the corresponding Jewish calendar date. Note that the Julian date starts at midnight, whereas the Jewish date always starts at dusk on the evening before and ends at sunset on the given Julian date. The complete tabulation of the reconstructed Jewish calendar for the period in question is given in Appendix III. This tabulation gives the exact time of conjunction of Sun and Moon (New Moon), whereas the times of the New Moon at the start of each Jewish lunar month in the Chronicle are rounded to the nearest quarter of an hour.

How to read the Chronicle

The Chronicle provides an outline of the life of Christ—more or less a condensed extract based on Anne Catherine Emmerich's descriptions. In reading it, a reader can always refer back to her original, complete description or to the account given in the Gospels. Indeed, because of the schematic nature of the Chronicle, many other kinds of collateral reading may also be helpful in allowing a fully imagined, meditative re-creation of the day in question.

Above all, perhaps, the Chronicle invites the reader to enter into it from the perspective of a silent participant or eyewitness to the events in question. This, of course, requires an inner activity of the soul whereby one immerses oneself profoundly and participates intensely in the events. Rudolf Steiner writes:

> When a person's development is sufficiently advanced so that he or she can receive an impulse from the Christ that is strong enough to influence his or her circulation . . . —that is, when the Christ impulse can extend its influence into the physical body, even for a short time—then that person is in a position to be initiated in the physical body. . . . *Those who can intensively immerse themselves in the events that occurred at that time in Palestine through Jesus Christ and the Mystery of Golgotha so that they can live with these events as in an objective spiritual reality manifesting itself to them in a living way, can attain by this experience the same as was once attained in ancient initiation ceremonies. . . .* (Rudolf Steiner, *The Gospel of Saint John in Relation to the other Gospels*)

Thus, the reader is invited to enter livingly into the daily events of Christ's life. More than this, with the help of the tabulation in Appendix VI, it is possible to relive the three and one-half years of Christ's ministry day by day as these events themselves are being remembered or reactivated as described in the introduction to Appendix VI. In this process, the divine (Christ) and the human (Jesus) come together in a remarkable way. For, as we follow the daily travels of Jesus, we shall find the Son of God continually present and active in and through Jesus' human nature. Jesus, the perfect human being, fulfills a divine archetype, while the Christ, who is one with the Father, embodies all levels of existence reaching down from the Father to the level of the perfect human being, Jesus.

We catch a glimpse of one such divine archetype that is fulfilled by Jesus if we consider the figure of Cheiron, the teacher of Jason and the Argonauts, who was represented in classical mythology as half-human, half-horse. Cheiron appears in the heavens in the zodiacal sign of Sagittarius. Also, at the birth of Jesus, as we have seen, the Sun stood in the middle of Sagittarius. Therefore we shall not be surprised to find Jesus, like Cheiron, traveling from place to place with untiring energy, *teaching and healing* wherever he went.

As a silent eyewitness to this and other extraordinary activity, the reader is now invited to accompany the God-Man on his wanderings and enter into his healing ministry.

CHRONICLE

YEAR 1

Nisan 15, A.D. 29, to Nisan 14, A.D. 30
April 16/17, A.D. 29, to April 4/5, A.D. 30

NISAN (30 days): April 2/3 to May 1/2 A.D. 29
Nisan New Moon: April 2 at 10:30 P.M. Jerusalem time

Around the start of the month of Nisan, Joseph died, which signified Jesus' spiritual coming of age. Since the age of eight, Jesus had attended the Passover festival in Jerusalem every year with Joseph and Mary. Now, twenty-one years later, in A.D. 29 (aged 29), he went to Jerusalem accompanied only by Mary. We can imagine what a solemn event this visit to the temple must have been and how, from this time on, the Heavenly Father filled his attention, his earthly father having passed away.

The Passover festival lasted a week, from Nisan 15 to Nisan 21. On the day corresponding historically to the last day of the Passover festival (April 24, A.D. 29), Anne Catherine Emmerich had a vision of John the Baptist in the wilderness, not far from Mount Lebanon. The "word of God" came to John. It was the fifteenth year of the reign of Tiberius. John left the wilderness and "he went into all the region about the Jordan, preaching a baptism of repentance for the forgiveness of sins" (Luke 3:3).

In a subsequent vision, relating to June, A.D. 29, which was about the time John attained the age of 30, Anne Catherine saw him travel through Galilee and Samaria, visiting Bethsaida, Capernaum, Tiberius, Nazareth, Jericho, and his birthplace Juttah, near Hebron. Everywhere he introduced himself as Zechariah's son, and spoke of himself as a forerunner of Jesus. He traveled back up the east side of the River Jordan to the Sea of Galilee. Crossing the Jordan, he visited Bethsaida, Capernaum, and Nazareth again. Then he returned through Samaria to a place on the banks of the Jordan near where the River Zarqa flows into the Jordan, between Ainon and Salem. Here he remained, teaching and baptizing.

Thus, about three months before the baptism, John traveled *twice* through Palestine, proclaiming the one who was to come, whose way he prepared.

IYYAR (29 days): May 2/3 to May 30/31, A.D. 29
Iyyar New Moon: May 2 at 1:20 P.M. Jerusalem time

After returning from the Passover, around the start of the month of Iyyar, Jesus and Mary moved from Nazareth to a house near the town of Capernaum. The house was made available to them by a wealthy friend, a man called Levi, who lived in Capernaum. Levi saw that Jesus had difficulties in Nazareth because he was frequently at variance with the teachings of the Pharisees there. Levi provided Jesus with a house so that he could have a place to go where, without fear of disturbance, he could gather his followers around him. The house was situated outside the town, between Capernaum and Bethsaida, not far from the Sea of Galilee. The house was large enough to accommodate not only Jesus and Mary but also guests. It was even possible to hold small gatherings there. Levi also saw to it that his servants regularly brought provisions for Jesus and Mary from Capernaum and that the house was properly cared for, and that it was protected when both Jesus and Mary went away.

Toward the end of the month of Iyyar, Jesus began his travels, which, from this time on and for almost four years, were to take him through the length and breadth of Palestine and beyond. On the first journey, which signified the start of his public teaching, he went by way of Nazareth to the region of Hebron in the south, where John the Baptist had grown up. It was with this journey that Anne Catherine's day-by-day communications concerning the ministry of Jesus Christ began. Although, strictly speaking, the ministry began some four months later, with the baptism in the Jordan, the daily Chronicle of Jesus' public teaching starts here. . . .

MAP 1: *Journey to the Place Where John the Baptist Grew Up*

Sunday, May 29, A.D. 29 (Iyyar 27) This morning Jesus set off from Capernaum on his journey to the region of Hebron in Judea. For the first part of the journey, as far as Nazareth, he was accompanied by Mary. Between Capernaum and Nazareth, they passed through Bethulia. There Nathanael Chased was deeply moved by the gaze that Jesus cast in his direction. Mary then remained in Nazareth with her niece, Mary Cleophas. She would await Jesus' return there. Jesus continued on his way that same evening, accompanied by two young friends from Nazareth, Parmenas and Jonadab.

Monday, May 30, A.D. 29 (Iyyar 28) Jesus and his two friends traveled the whole day, without stopping, through Samaria, directing their steps toward Jerusalem.

SIVAN (30 days): May 31/June 1 to June 29/30, A.D. 29
Sivan New Moon: June 1 at 2:15 A.M. Jerusalem time

Tuesday, May 31, A.D. 29 (Iyyar 29) Today, they arrived at Lazarus' castle in Bethany. After talking with Lazarus, Jesus and his two friends visited the temple in Jerusalem. That evening (the start of the first day of Sivan) they traveled further, journeying through the night to Hebron.

Wednesday, June 1, A.D. 29 (Sivan 1) In Hebron, Jesus, saying he wanted to visit a friend, parted company with Parmenas and Jonadab. They did not become Jesus' disciples until much later. Jesus then went into the desert region south of Hebron and found his way to the cave ("Elizabeth's cave") where the young John the Baptist had stayed, having been brought thither by his mother Elizabeth.

Thursday, June 2, A.D. 29 (Sivan 2) In the wilderness south of Hebron, Jesus remained alone in prayer, preparing for his mission.

Friday, June 3, A.D. 29 (Sivan 3) Traveling eastward, Jesus came to the shores of the Dead Sea. There was a storm, and some people were in difficulty on their raft. Jesus helped them to land. He then made his way to Hebron for the Sabbath. That evening, he visited the synagogue for the evening Sabbath celebration.

Saturday, June 4, A.D. 29 (Sivan 4) After the morning service at the synagogue, Jesus visited the sick to console and help them, but he did not heal anyone. Wherever he went, he evoked wonder and amazement, for he appeared to all as a wonderful and benevolent person. Even those possessed grew quiet in his presence. Some people thought at first that he was John the Baptist, but then they realized that he was another prophet, as yet unknown. That evening, Jesus left Hebron and traveled by night to the Jordan.

Sunday, June 5, A.D. 29 (Sivan 5) Early in the morning, Jesus arrived at the point where the Jordan flows into the Dead Sea. Crossing the River Jordan by boat, he then proceeded northward, on the east side of the Jordan.

Monday, June, 6 A.D. 29 (Sivan 6) In the region north of Pella, on the east side of the Jordan, Jesus visited many sick people, consoling them, and exhorting them to prayer. In response to a question, he taught concerning the nearness of the Messiah and gave indications as to how one would be able to recognize him.

Tuesday, June 7, A.D. 29 (Sivan 7) Today, he reached a place south of Gergesa, east of the Sea of Galilee, through which the Hieromax flows. There, he helped some men who were at work repairing their boats.

Wednesday, June 8, to Tuesday, June 14, A.D. 29 (Sivan 8–14) For several days, Jesus remained on the east side of the Jordan. Everywhere he went, he helped others. Then he crossed the Jordan and went to the little town of Dothaim, west of the Sea of Galilee.

Wednesday, June 15, A.D. 29 (Sivan 15) Jesus visited the madhouse in Dothaim. There a number of people were raging uncontrollably. As Jesus began to speak to them, they became quiet. When they were thus calmed, Jesus sent them back to their homes. The people of Dothaim were astonished and invited him to attend a wedding on the following day.

Thursday, June 16, A.D. 29 (Sivan 16) Jesus attended the wedding in Dothaim, speaking at the celebration in a friendly manner. Afterward, he addressed some words of wisdom to the bride and groom, who later, after the resurrection, joined the community of Christians.

Friday, June 17, A.D. 29 (Sivan 17) Today, Jesus was in Nazareth. He received a cool reception when he visited various acquaintances of his parents. He wanted to attend the evening Sabbath service in the synagogue to teach there, but he was turned away. Instead, he addressed a crowd of people in the marketplace, including Pharisees and Sadducees. He spoke of the Messiah, saying that he would be different than anyone imagined him to be. He also spoke of John the Baptist as a voice in the wilderness.

Saturday, June 18, and Sunday, June 19, A.D. 29 (Sivan 18–19) Jesus remained in Nazareth.

Monday, June 20, or Tuesday, June 21, A.D. 29 (Sivan 20–21) Together with Mary, Mary Cleophas, the parents of Parmenas, and others—altogether a group of about twenty people—Jesus left Nazareth and set off in the direction of Capernaum.

Wednesday, June 22, A.D. *29 (Sivan 22)* Jesus and Mary were at their house between Capernaum and Bethsaida. Mary Cleophas stayed at a house nearby, and Parmenas' parents also stayed in the neighborhood. At this time, John the Baptist was becoming renowned throughout the land, owing to his activity of teaching and baptizing on the east bank of the Jordan between Ainon and Salem. He had already been baptizing for several weeks, and his fame had spread to Herod Antipas, who sent messengers to him from his castle at Callirhoe, east of the Dead Sea, where he was staying. Herod invited John to visit him, but John turned the invitation down. About this time Herod traveled in his coach, together with some of his soldiers, to a place about five hours south of Ainon, and invited John to visit him there. John came to a hut nearby, and Herod went alone to talk to him. Herod asked John why he chose to live in a miserable hut (near Ainon), saying that he would have a large house built for him. John replied that he did not need a house; he had all that he needed, and his sole will was to serve God. He spoke solemnly and decisively, standing at some distance from Herod, and then left to return to the place of baptism.

Thursday, June 23, to Wednesday, June 29, A.D. *29 (Sivan 23–29)* Jesus went from place to place, especially visiting those places through which John the Baptist had passed several weeks earlier on his journey through Palestine. Everywhere he went, Jesus taught in the synagogues and consoled the sick but did not perform any healing miracles. During the first part of this one-week period, Anne Catherine saw Jesus teaching at the synagogue of a small place concerning the nearness of the Messiah, the baptism of John, and the need for repentance. The people started to voice their disapproval. They whispered, mockingly, "Three months ago his father, the carpenter, was still alive. He worked with him. Now he has traveled about and returned to impart his wisdom."

On Saturday, June 25, A.D. 29, Anne Catherine saw John baptizing the three sons of Mary Cleophas—the future apostles Simon, James the Lesser, and Judas Thaddeus—at Ainon. These three were the sons of Mary Cleophas by her first marriage to Alphaeus, who had died. Their half-brother Joses Barsabbas—the son of Mary Cleophas and her second husband, Sabbas—was also baptized then. Two other future apostles, Andrew and Philip, had already become followers of John the Baptist, and Andrew (and probably Philip) had also been baptized. Andrew and Philip had since returned to their place of work at Bethsaida. By now, John had about twenty disciples.

Wednesday, June 29, A.D. 29 (Sivan 29) Today, Jesus was in Cana, where he visited his widowed cousin Mary, the daughter of Sobe and the sister of Mary Salome. (Mary Salome was married to Zebedee—their children, James and John, afterward became apostles—whereas Mary of Cana was also the aunt of the bridegroom Nathanael who, six months hence, married the daughter of the wealthy Israel of Cana. See Wednesday, December 28, A.D. 29 for the wedding at Cana, which Jesus attended.) Here, in Cana, Jesus was not accompanied by any of those who were to become disciples.

> *TAMMUZ (29 days): June 30/July 1 to July 28/29, A.D. 29*
> *Tammuz New Moon: June 30 at 1:30 P.M. Jerusalem time*

> MAP 2: *Journey to Sidon, Mount Carmel, and Jacob's Well*

Friday, July 1, A.D. 29 (Tammuz 1) At this time, Anne Catherine saw Jesus, accompanied by one other person, on the high road between Samaria and Nazareth. In a place shaded from the heat of the sun, four men were waiting who later became disciples. These men had recently been baptized by John at the place of baptizing near Ainon. As Jesus approached them, they went up to him and told him of their baptism and of John's discourses concerning the nearness of the Messiah.

Saturday, July 2, to Tuesday, July 5, A.D. 29 (Tammuz 2–5) During this period, Jesus made his way through Galilee in the direction of Capernaum. Here and there, in the region on the west side of the Sea of Galilee, he taught about the Messiah. From time to time, too, one of the possessed would call out after him. He cast out a demon from one of them. On the way, he met six more of the Baptist's disciples, among whom was Levi, who later became an apostle and was named Matthias. Kolaja and Eustachius, who were distantly related to Jesus, were also among these six. They had heard of Jesus, and suspected that he might be the one of whom the Baptist prophesied. Kolaja and Eustachius accompanied Jesus along the way, speaking to him of John, and of Lazarus and his sisters. They marveled at Jesus and were filled with wonder both at his manner of speaking and at what he said.

Wednesday, July 6, A.D. 29 (Tammuz 6) Unaccompanied, Jesus went through a fence enclosing a fishery on the Sea of Galilee. Five boats were there, and several huts for the fishermen. The fishery belonged to Peter, the later apostle. He and his brother Andrew were in one of the huts. James and John, together with their father Zebedee and several other fishermen, were on the boats. Passing between the huts, Jesus exchanged words with Andrew and possibly also with Peter. Jesus said that he would return to them again. He then left the lake shore.

Thursday, July 7, A.D. 29 (Tammuz 7) Today, Jesus was on his way northward through Galilee, accompanied by about half-a-dozen people. People were impressed by his teaching on the way. Some felt he might be the one spoken of by John the Baptist.

Friday, July 8, A.D. 29 (Tammuz 8) Having continued on his way northward through the night, Jesus went on this morning, accompanied by about ten people. He taught as he went, stopping now and then to address people in various places they passed through. Later in the day, they crossed a spur of the Lebanon foothills and beheld the city of Sidon on the coast of the Mediterranean. The city was large and bustling with life; there were innumerable ships on the sea. Jesus and his group made their way toward the city. Not only pagans—gentiles—lived there, but also some Jews. That evening, the Sabbath began. Jesus taught in the synagogue of the Jewish community. He spoke of the coming of the Messiah and of the downfall of idolatry. Leaving his companions behind, Jesus left the city, proceeding southward to the town of Sarepta, where he stayed overnight in a dwelling built into the city walls. An elderly man lived there. This was the same dwelling where the widow had lived who had once given food to Elijah (1 Kings 17:9).

Saturday, July 9, A.D. 29, to Tuesday, July 19, A.D. 29 (Tammuz 9–19) Jesus decided to remain in Sarepta for several days. He stayed with the pious old Jews living in the city walls who revered Elijah and were occupied with interpreting the prophecies concerning the coming of the Messiah. Jesus also visited the synagogue and taught the children. He spent much time, too, alone in prayer in the forest around the town. Sometimes he remained there all night. He also visited some of the surrounding pagan places and admonished the Jews not to mix with the pagans. Toward the end of this period, John the Baptist and his followers left the place of baptism near Ainon and went south to a new place, near Gilgal. After baptizing there only for a short time, John then continued on to a third place of baptism on the west side of the Jordan, near a village called Ono. It was here that Jesus himself was later baptized.

Wednesday, July 20, A.D. 29 (Tammuz 20) Around this time, Jesus left Sarepta and went north to a place not far from a battlefield where in a vision Ezekiel had beheld the bones of the dead that were gathered together and restored to life (Ezekiel 37). Jesus taught and consoled the people living there, teaching them that Ezekiel's vision was about to be fulfilled (meaning that the breathing of new life into the dead was a vision referring to the sending of the Holy Spirit).

Thursday, July 21, A.D. 29 (Tammuz 21) Jesus traveled further north to a little shepherd community situated close to a small stream. Naomi and her daughter Ruth had stayed here for a length of time (Ruth 1:19). Jesus taught the shepherds, and then set off back toward Sarepta again, passing by Sidon on the way.

Friday, July 22, and Saturday, July 23, A.D. 29 (Tammuz 22–23) Jesus taught and celebrated the Sabbath in Sarepta. Then he departed and walked through the night, traveling southward toward Mount Carmel, where the prophet Elijah had once been.

Sunday, July 24, and Monday, July 25, A.D. 29 (Tammuz 24–25) Jesus continued on his way. After visiting Mount Carmel, he traveled eastward toward Mount Tabor. At the foot of the west side of Mount Tabor was the little town Kisloth-Tabor. Here Jesus taught in the synagogue concerning the baptism of John. Five people accompanied Jesus here, among them some future disciples. One of the holy women, Veronica, together with her son Amandor and her friend Joanna Chuza, left Jerusalem at this time to travel to Capernaum. From there they were to go with Mary to Nazareth, where they expected Jesus to arrive when he returned from his journey to Lebanon.

Wednesday, July 27, A.D. 29 (Tammuz 27) The Sanhedrin met in Jerusalem and decided to take action. They sent out couriers with letters to all the main towns of Palestine, warning the rabbis and overseers of the synagogues to be on their guard against a certain person prophesied by John the Baptist. The intention of the Sanhedrin was to collect information concerning this supposed Messiah.

AB (30 Days): July 29/30 to August 27/28, A.D. 29
Ab New Moon: July 29 at 11:10 P.M. Jerusalem time

Friday, July 29, and Saturday, July 30, A.D. 29 (Tammuz 29–Ab 1) Before returning to Nazareth, Jesus, with his five traveling companions, visited Jacob's well near Sychar in Samaria. He taught here and there as he went, celebrating the Sabbath in the neighborhood.

Sunday, July 31, and Monday, August 1, A.D. 29 (Ab 2–3) Jesus and those accompanying him returned to Nazareth. Mary set out to greet him on his way into the town, but when she saw that he was in the company of others, she returned to Nazareth without greeting him. Jesus taught in the synagogue, and the holy women attended.

Tuesday, August 2, A.D. 29 (Ab 4) Jesus taught in the synagogue at Nazareth. At least twenty people he knew from his childhood and youth were present, but the holy women were not there. Some of the crowd began to whisper mockingly, "Perhaps now his intention will be to take over the place of baptism near Ainon, recently vacated by John, and give himself out for one like unto the Baptist; but we will not be deceived by this imposter, whom we know only too well."

Wednesday, August 3, A.D. 29 (Ab 5) Today, Anne Catherine saw a group of about twenty arrive at John's place of baptism near Ono. They had been sent from Jerusalem by the Sanhedrin. They told John that he should present himself in Jerusalem. But John replied that soon the one he proclaimed would come to him. He described the one-to-come quite clearly, saying that he had been born in Bethlehem and raised in Nazareth but that he had never seen him.

MAP 3: *Travels in Southern Galilee*

Thursday, August 4, A.D. 29 (Ab 6) Jesus spoke with his mother at the house where she was staying and where the other holy women and friends were also gathered. Jesus explained that, because of the hostility and rejection he had encountered in Nazareth, he would return to Capernaum and Bethsaida to teach. He left the house with Veronica's son Amandor, the Essene youth Eustachius, and the son of the widow Lea, Kolaja. Amandor, Eustachius, and Kolaja were his first three disciples.

Friday, August 5, A.D. 29 (Ab 7) As the Sabbath began this evening, Jesus went to the synagogue in Bethsaida. He spoke very powerfully, advocating repentance and the baptism by John. Many people were present, including the future apostle Philip.

Sunday, August 7, A.D. 29 (Ab 9) Jesus made his way from Bethsaida to Capernaum, teaching on the way. He was accompanied by Amandor, Eustachius, and Kolaja.

Monday, August 8, A.D. 29 (Ab 10) Today, Jesus taught for the first time in the synagogue at Capernaum. Among the large crowd were also the future apostles Peter and Andrew.

Tuesday, August 9, A.D. 29 (Ab 11) Jesus stayed in Capernaum.

Wednesday, August 10, A.D. 29 (Ab 12) Today, Jesus taught at a place on the west shore of the Sea of Galilee, two hours south of Capernaum. The three disciples who had accompanied him to Bethsaida and Capernaum were still with him.

Thursday, August 11, A.D. 29 (Ab 13) Jesus traveled southward through Lower Galilee in the direction of Samaria. Then he turned toward the north again.

Friday, August 12, and Saturday, August 13, A.D. 29 (Ab 14–15) Jesus celebrated the Sabbath at a village located about midway between Nazareth and Sephoris. He spoke at the little synagogue there. News of his coming had spread. As well as the holy women from Nazareth, some future apostles were there: Peter, Andrew, James the Lesser, and Philip, all of whom were already followers of John the Baptist.

Sunday, August 14, A.D. 29 (Ab 16) With his three disciples, Jesus went to Sephoris, about four hours from Nazareth. There he visited his great-aunt Maraha, who had a daughter and two sons. The Virgin Mary, Mary Cleophas, and some other women had also made their way to Sephoris. They ate together with Jesus in Maraha's house, where he stayed overnight.

Monday, August 15, to Wednesday, August 17, A.D. 29 (Ab 17–19) Jesus taught at two synagogues in Sephoris. In the larger one, where the holy women were able to attend, there were some Pharisees present who began voicing their disapproval of Jesus' teachings. In the smaller one, where there was no place for women, Jesus was accorded a friendly reception.

Thursday, August 18, A.D. 29 (Ab 20) Today, Jesus taught at the synagogue of the Sadducees in Sephoris. Next to the synagogue was a madhouse, and inmates were obliged to attend the synagogue, accompanied by custodians. As Jesus taught, one or the other of the inmates began to speak out loud: "This is Jesus of Nazareth, born in Bethlehem, visited by wise men from the east." "His mother is with Maraha." "He is bringing a new teaching," and so on. Jesus spoke the words: "The spirit that speaks this is from below and should return there." At this, all the inmates became quiet and were healed. Afterward a great uproar broke out in Sephoris, forcing Jesus to hide in a house. That night, he left the town, as did his three disciples and the two sons of Maraha (Arastaria and Cocharia). Later, the five met up with Jesus by some trees outside the town, on the way from Sephoris to Bethulia. They then proceeded together to Bethulia.

Friday, August 19, A.D. 29 (Ab 21) Mary and the holy women also made their way to Bethulia. The town was much visited on account of its springs; it was a kind of bathing resort. Jesus and his five companions went to an inn on the outskirts of town. Mary went to see him there. That evening, as the Sabbath began, Jesus taught in Bethulia.

Saturday, August 20, A.D. 29 (Ab 22) That morning, and also at the close of the Sabbath, Jesus taught in the synagogue at Bethulia. Many people came from the surrounding area, and he was well received.

Sunday, August 21, A.D. 29 (Ab 23) Jesus proved to be so popular that he was asked by various people in Bethulia if he would lodge with them. Jesus' five disciples were also offered living quarters in the town.

Monday, August 22, A.D. 29 (Ab 24) So many people thronged into Bethulia to hear him that Jesus went to teach in a valley south of the town. In addition to the five disciples, about twenty others followed him there. The holy women had by this time already returned to Nazareth.

Tuesday, August 23, and Wednesday, August 24, A.D. 29 (Ab 25–26) During the day, Jesus taught in the same valley south of Bethulia to a group of about thirty people. Here there was a place for teaching, used by the Essenes, that went back to the days of the prophets. Toward sunset, Jesus went to a small place in the valley of Zabulon consisting of a number of villas. It was about an hour north of Nazareth. There, Jesus taught that evening in the synagogue, where he received a friendly welcome.

Thursday, August 25, A.D. 29 (Ab 27) Today, Jesus was in the neighborhood of Cedes (Kision), a small place southeast of Nazareth, near Mount Tabor. He preached on a hill and spoke of his coming baptism.

Friday, August 26, A.D. 29 (Ab 28) Speaking here and there, Jesus wandered through an area where there were many shepherds. As the Sabbath began, he arrived in the town Jezrael, south of Mount Tabor.

MAP 4: *Travels with Eliud in Lower Galilee*

Saturday, August 27, A.D. 29 (Ab 29) In his Sabbath teaching, Jesus warned against setting oneself apart from others through pride. His attention was directed especially to those of the Nazarite sect, many of whom were living in Jezrael, who had set themselves apart from others living in the town who had married pagans.

Sunday, August 28, A.D. 29 (Ab 30) The Nazarites invited Jesus to eat with them. During the course of the meal, some Nazarites spoke about circumcision. Jesus declared that circumcision would soon be replaced by baptism (through the Holy Spirit) as the sign of the new covenant.

ELUL (29 Days): August 28/29 to September 25/26, A.D. 29
Elul New Moon: August 28 at 8:00 A.M. Jerusalem time

Monday, August 29, A.D. 29 (Elul 1) Today, Jesus visited a group of rich tax collectors living between Jezrael and Apheke. They had their own synagogue, where Jesus taught.

Tuesday, August 30, A.D. 29 (Elul 2) Jesus continued to teach the tax collectors, exhorting them to receive the baptism of John.

Wednesday, August 31, A.D. 29 (Elul 3) The tax collectors offered Jesus presents. However, he declined them. Accompanied by several people who wanted to go to John the Baptist, Jesus passed through the neighborhood of Dothaim. Passing a madhouse, he calmed and freed the inhabitants. That evening, he arrived at Kisloth-Tabor, where the Pharisees took exception to his entourage of tax collectors, healed lunatics, and other hangers-on. Jesus taught in the synagogue, saying much that did not please the Pharisees.

Thursday, September 1, A.D. *29 (Elul 4)* The Pharisees invited Jesus to a meal, so that they could ensnare him with his own words. On arriving, the first thing that Jesus did was to ask where the poor were. To the displeasure of the Pharisees, Jesus then sent out his disciples to round up the poor of the town and bring them to the meal. The same night, he left Kisloth.

Friday, September 2, A.D. *29 (Elul 5)* After leaving Kisloth, Jesus passed through the Edron valley, accompanied by some followers. He came to the shepherd village of Chimki. That evening, he celebrated the Sabbath and taught in the synagogue there.

Saturday, September 3, A.D. *29 (Elul 6)* Jesus again taught in the synagogue, expounding several parables, which the Pharisees mocked as childish. That night, Jesus stayed with a poor family and healed the mistress of the house who was suffering from dropsy.

Sunday, September 4, A.D. *29 (Elul 7)* This evening, in the synagogue, the Pharisees were greatly angered at Jesus' teaching, which warned against taking life too lightly as had been done at the time of Noah or Lot. The Pharisees accused Jesus of speaking as if he were the Messiah himself, and—amid uproar—they put out the lights. That night, Jesus and his disciples left Chimki and went northward.

Monday, September 5, A.D. *29 (Elul 8)* Jesus and his traveling companions went to a shepherd village between the Edron valley and Nazareth. There they ate with some shepherds. Jesus healed two people who had been smitten with leprosy. He and his five disciples then went on to Nazareth and put up in a community of Essenes on the outskirts of the town. Jesus stayed with the venerable Eliud, an elderly Essene widower, who was cared for by his daughter.

Tuesday, September 6, A.D. *29 (Elul 9)* While the five disciples visited friends and relatives in Nazareth, Jesus talked with the aged Eliud, who had had many deep mystical experiences. The Holy Virgin and Mary Cleophas visited Jesus. In the course of conversation with his mother, Jesus told her that he would go to Jerusalem four times for the Passover festival, but that the last time would be one of great affliction for her.

Wednesday, September 7, A.D. 29 (Elul 10) Jesus spent much of the day in deep conversation with Eliud. This pious and devout Essene told Jesus of his mystical experiences concerning the coming of the Messiah. Jesus was able to interpret these experiences for Eliud and to answer many of his questions regarding the things he had seen in vision. That evening, Jesus and Eliud visited the place where Joseph had worked as a carpenter.

Thursday, September 8, A.D. 29 (Elul 11) Together with Eliud, Jesus set off on a journey southward from Nazareth, passing through the valley of Esdrelon, and then turning eastward in the direction of Endor. They arrived at a small village close to a well-known spring. At the synagogue, Jesus taught concerning the Messiah and the Kingdom of God, which he affirmed was not of this world. He also expounded many passages from the prophets. That night, he and Eliud stayed at an inn near the synagogue.

Friday, September 9, A.D. 29 (Elul 12) Setting off early, Jesus and Eliud journeyed around Mount Hermon and came to Endor. There they visited a sanatorium—a bathing spot for invalids—where Jesus taught the sick and told two parables. There was no synagogue in Endor, so, for the Sabbath, they returned to the synagogue at the village where they had been the previous day.

Saturday, September 10, A.D. 29 (Elul 13) After the Sabbath morning service in the synagogue, Jesus and Eliud returned to Endor. The inhabitants of the town were Canaanites, some of whom secretly worshipped an idol of the goddess Astarte. Jesus reprehended them for this practice. Then, accompanied by Eliud, he returned to the synagogue for the service at the close of the Sabbath. That evening, he and Eliud set off back to Nazareth.

Sunday, September 11, A.D. 29 (Elul 14) Jesus and Eliud arrived back at Eliud's home in the early hours of the morning. Jesus' disciples, a number of Essenes, and some other people—including two Pharisees from Nazareth—gathered together to hear his discourses. The Pharisees invited Jesus to come to them and later conducted him to the synagogue. There, he taught concerning Moses and the prophecies of the coming of the Messiah. That night, he stayed at an inn nearby, together with his five disciples.

Monday, September 12, A.D. 29 (Elul 15) Today, Jesus addressed a group of tax collectors who were on their way to be baptized by John. Afterward, in the synagogue, he taught a parable and then, on his way out, blessed some children. To the small group of five followers, four others were now added as disciples; these four were friends of or were related to the Holy Family.

Tuesday, September 13, A.D. 29 (Elul 16) Three youths from wealthy families in Nazareth were sent by their parents to the synagogue to hear a dispute between Jesus and some learned men of Nazareth. This dispute was arranged by the Pharisees to test Jesus' wisdom. Jesus displayed such an extraordinary knowledge that all present were excited by his teaching. Urged on by their parents, who thought that their sons could benefit from absorbing Jesus' wisdom, the three youths then sought to become Jesus' pupils; but Jesus rejected them, which incensed their parents. That night, Jesus stayed again at Eliud's home.

Wednesday, September 14, A.D. 29 (Elul 17) The three youths returned to Jesus to request that they might become his pupils. Again, Jesus sent them away. Later, he explained to his disciples that the three youths sought to follow him on account of what they might be able to gain for themselves and were not willing to sacrifice all for love. He then sent the disciples on in advance to the place of baptism, instructing them to travel via Capernaum to let his mother know that he himself would soon go to be baptized. That night, he set off with Eliud for the little town of Chim, southwest of Nazareth.

Thursday, September 15, A.D. 29 (Elul 18) At daybreak, Jesus and Eliud reached Chim. Not far from the town was a small pool in which the lepers of the place washed themselves. Jesus went into a leper's hut and healed him. He and Eliud then made their way south through the valley of Esdrelon. They continued walking after dark, deep in conversation. Around midnight, Jesus said to Eliud that he would reveal himself, and—turning toward heaven—he prayed. A cloud of light enveloped them both and Jesus became radiantly transfigured. Eliud stood still, utterly entranced. After a while, the light melted away, and Jesus resumed his steps, followed by Eliud, who was speechless at what he had beheld.

Friday, September 16, A.D. 29 (Elul 19) At dawn, they approached the huts of some shepherds. The shepherds already knew Jesus. Leading Jesus and Eliud to a shed, they washed the feet of the two guests and prepared a meal for them. Afterward, Jesus took leave of Eliud, first blessing him and then embracing him before going on his way. Jesus then traveled to the mountain village of Gur. He celebrated the Sabbath there alone in his room at an inn, having requested a roll of the Scriptures to be brought to him from the synagogue.

Saturday, September 17, A.D. 29 (Elul 20) On this day, the last Sabbath prior to his baptism, Jesus spent the whole day in his room alone in prayer.

MAP 5: *Journey to the Baptism in the Jordan*

Sunday, September 18, A.D. 29 (Elul 21) Jesus arose before daybreak and proceeded further. Toward evening, he arrived at Gophna on Mount Ephraim, north of Jerusalem. After eating a meal at an inn, he was escorted by some relatives and a couple of Pharisees to a house where he stayed overnight.

Monday, September 19, A.D. 29 (Elul 22) Jesus went to the synagogue and asked for the scriptures of one of the prophets. He then interpreted the prophecies, saying that the time had arrived for the coming of the Messiah. After spending much of the day teaching in the synagogue, Jesus departed from Gophna. That evening, he arrived at the shepherd village of Bethel, where he met up with two groups of people on their way to be baptized by John the Baptist. The patriarch Jacob had lived for a time in the neighborhood of Bethel.

Tuesday, September 20, A.D. 29 (Elul 23) Jesus went to the synagogue and taught concerning baptism and the nearness of the Messiah. At the evening meal at the inn where he was staying, some of the guests denounced Herod's unlawful connection with his brother's wife. Jesus concurred but said that whoever judged others would himself be judged also. On this day, Anne Catherine also saw Mary, the mother of Jesus, and four of the holy women journeying towards Bethany.

Wednesday, September 21, A.D. 29 (Elul 24) Jesus left Bethel early and arrived that evening at a little village called Giah on Mount Amma, facing the Gibeon desert. There, he ate a meal and talked with several people who asked him about the prophet from Nazareth. Then he continued on his way, arriving that night at Lazarus' castle in Bethany. He was greeted not only by Lazarus but also by Nicodemus, John Mark, and the aged Obed (a relative of the prophetess Anna), who were guests of Lazarus in Bethany. Among the women gathered there as guests of Martha were Veronica, Mary Mark, and Susanna of Jerusalem. Jesus greeted them all, and they took a meal together before retiring for the night.

Thursday, September 22, A.D. 29 (Elul 25) During the morning, Jesus walked about in the courtyards and gardens of the castle, teaching those who were present. Then Martha took Jesus to visit her sister Mary, known as Silent Mary, who lived by herself like a hermit in part of the castle. Jesus was left alone to talk with Silent Mary, who lived in continuous vision of heavenly things. Normally silent in the presence of other people, Mary began to speak of the mysteries of Jesus' incarnation, passion, and death. After saying some prayers, Jesus returned to talk with Martha, who expressed her deep concern regarding her other sister, Mary Magdalene. At about half-past one, the Holy Virgin Mary arrived, accompanied by Mary Chuza, the widow Lea, Mary Salome, and Mary Cleophas. After a light meal, Jesus and his mother, Mary, retired to talk with one another. In this conversation, Jesus told Mary that he was now going to be baptized and that his real mission would begin with this event. He said that they would meet again briefly in Samaria after the baptism, but that he would then go into the desert for forty days. Mary was much troubled when she heard this, but Jesus answered by saying that he must now fulfill his mission and that she should renounce all personal claims upon him. That evening, Lazarus gave a feast for all who were present. During the meal, Jesus again alluded to the persecutions that lay ahead of him, saying that those who allied themselves with him would suffer with him. The same night, Jesus, accompanied by Lazarus, set off in the direction of Jericho to make his way to the place of baptism.

Friday, September 23, A.D. 29 (Elul 26) Jesus went on ahead of Lazarus and arrived at the place of baptism some two hours before him. This place of baptism (the third, as John originally began to baptize further north, near Ainon, and then baptized for a short time near Gilgal) was located on the west side

of the Jordan, just south of the village called Ono. A large crowd had already
assembled there to hear John's preaching when Jesus arrived around daybreak. John felt Jesus' presence among the crowd. He was fired with zeal and
preached with great animation concerning the nearness of the Messiah.
Then, he started baptizing. By ten o'clock he had already baptized many people. Jesus now came down to the baptizing pool where John was being helped
by Andrew, later the apostle, and by Saturnin, a young Greek of royal blood
from the city of Patras, who later was one of Jesus' closest disciples. At the
moment of baptism, a voice of thunder spoke the words, "This is my beloved
Son in whom I am well pleased," and Jesus became transparent with radiant
light. Meanwhile, Nicodemus, Obed, John Mark, and Joseph of Arimathea
had also arrived to join Lazarus in witnessing the baptism of Jesus. John then
told Andrew to announce the baptism of the Messiah throughout Galilee.
He himself then continued baptizing and preaching, while Jesus journeyed
with his followers in the direction of Jerusalem, traveling until he reached a
little place called Bethel, where there was a kind of hospital. (Anne Catherine
Emmerich was not sure of the name of this Bethel, east of Jerusalem, which
is not to be confused with the shepherd village Bethel, north of Jerusalem,
where Jesus had been a few days previously, on Elul 23). In Bethel, Andrew
and Saturnin baptized a number of people, following Jesus' instructions.
This baptism as Jesus gave it differed in several respects from John's baptizing. Jesus and his disciples then celebrated the Sabbath in Bethel.

Saturday, September 24, A.D. 29 (Elul 27) After the close of the Sabbath, Andrew took leave of Jesus and departed for Galilee, to proclaim the baptism
of the Messiah there. Jesus and those with him then went to the town of
Luz.

Sunday, September 25, A.D. 29 (Elul 28) In the synagogue at Luz, Jesus held
a lengthy discourse, interpreting many things from the Old Testament. He
also spoke of the need to forsake all to follow the Messiah and to have no
great concern for one's daily needs. Lazarus, who had accompanied Jesus
thus far, now parted company with him and returned to Bethany.

Monday, September 26, A.D. 29 (Elul 29) Accompanied by twelve disciples,
Jesus traveled southward from Luz, healing several sick people on the way.
When the group arrived at the little village of Ensemes, Jesus was given a
warm welcome. The people there had already heard of the new prophet.

Jesus spoke in the synagogue. He repeated John's words concerning the relation of his baptism to the Messiah's (Matthew 3:11), adding: "Whoever despises the Precursor's baptism will not honor the Messiah's." That evening Jesus ate a meal with his disciples. Afterward, they prayed together, for it was the close of the month of Elul and the start of the first day of Tishri, the beginning of the civil year in the Jewish calendar.

MAP 6: *Visit to the Valley of the Shepherds Near Bethlehem*

TISHRI (30 days): September 26/27 to October 25/26, A.D. 29
Tishri New Moon: September 26 at 5:00 P.M. Jerusalem time

Tuesday, September 27, A.D. 29 (Tishri 1) News of John's baptism of Jesus had spread and there was talk of it everywhere, especially in Jerusalem. Because of this, Jesus avoided the larger towns. He intended to make his public appearance only after the forty days in the wilderness. Before going into the desert, however, he wanted to retrace the steps of Joseph and Mary as they had journeyed to Bethlehem almost thirty years before. Accompanied by his followers, he took the byways Joseph and Mary had taken, stopping occasionally at the places where his parents had halted on their journey. Jesus and his disciples spent the night in a shepherd's house.

Wednesday, September 28, A.D. 29 (Tishri 2) Jesus and his disciples continued on their journey, stopping here and there to teach the workers in the fields. Jesus spoke in terms of the parables of plowing, sowing, and reaping (Luke 9:62; Mark 4:26–29; Matthew 13:24–30). On the way, he appointed Saturnin and another disciple to baptize in the Jordan. Soon, they were to begin to give the baptism of Jesus. That afternoon, Jesus and his followers arrived at the little town of Betharaba. Jesus taught some people who were gathered there in an open square. That evening, he set off again, traveling with his disciples through the night.

Thursday, September 29, A.D. 29 (Tishri 3) As the sun was rising, Jesus and his disciples made their way down to the valley of the shepherds near Bethlehem. He was seen from afar by some shepherds, who beheld him in the glory of the light of the rising sun. They quickly summoned more shepherds, who gathered together to greet Jesus and praise him with verses from the Psalms. Jesus told them that he had come to visit them because of the homage the shepherds had paid to him as an infant in the crib. He also recounted the parable of the good shepherd (John 10:1–18).

Friday, September 30, A.D. 29 (Tishri 4) The shepherds conducted Jesus and the disciples in the direction of Bethlehem. They arrived at the dwellings of the sons of the three shepherds who had visited him at his birth. These three shepherds had in the meantime died. Their burial place was an isolated hill where there was a vineyard. After visiting their graves, Jesus and his followers, accompanied by some shepherds, visited the cave where he had been born. As it was now evening, lamps were lit in the cave, where they celebrated the beginning of the Sabbath together.

Saturday, October 1, A.D. 29 (Tishri 5) With his disciples, Jesus visited numerous dwellings in and around the valley of the shepherds. Saturnin baptized some of the more elderly shepherds who could not go to the baptism in the Jordan. Anne Catherine noted that Jesus himself never baptized, but always baptized through his disciples.

Sunday, October 2, A.D. 29 (Tishri 6) Jesus took leave of the shepherds and of his disciples, saying that he now wanted to be alone for a while, and would visit some people by himself. He arranged to meet with his disciples in a valley on Mount Ephraim in two days' time. He then set off alone, southward.

Monday, October 3, A.D. 29 (Tishri 7) Passing through a wild region, Jesus came to an inn belonging to a man called Reuben, who had been there at the time of the Holy Family's flight into Egypt. Jesus greeted and blessed Reuben, and then healed Reuben's grandchildren, some of whom were sick with leprosy, some of whom were lame.

Tuesday, October 4, A.D. 29 (Tishri 8) The disciples met Jesus in a valley on Mount Ephraim, some five miles east of Hebron. He conducted them to a nearby cave, where they spent the night. The disciples lit a fire, and Jesus recounted all that had taken place in the cave: that David had been there before his fight with Goliath, and that the Holy Family had spent a night there on the way to Egypt.

Wednesday, October 5, A.D. 29 (Tishri 9) Jesus and his followers made their way northward. They visited an inn near Bethlehem and ate a meal there. Traveling further, they went around Jerusalem on the west side of the city until they reached the town of Mizpah, where Judas Maccabeus once had been (1 Maccabees 3:46). Jesus taught in the synagogue. Some of the members of the Sanhedrin had come from Jerusalem as agents. They listened with great interest to what Jesus had to say. After leaving the synagogue, Jesus and his companions journeyed eastward about one hour to the home of Aminadab and Manasseh, who had already been baptized. Here they stayed the night.

Thursday, October 6, A.D. *29 (Tishri 10)* Jesus and his disciples traveled on a couple of hours eastward until they reached a farmhouse, which had been one of the last stopping places of the Holy Family on their way to Bethlehem. The lady of the house, who had been a young woman at the time of Joseph and Mary's visit thirty years before, was now blind and almost bent double. She confessed her sins to Jesus, who instructed her to bathe in some water that he had just used. As she did so, she recovered her sight, was healed, and became upright. The people of this place asked Jesus who was the greatest, John the Baptist or himself. Jesus replied: "He to whom John bears witness." Then they spoke of John's great zeal, and remarked upon Jesus' strong and handsome appearance. Jesus answered that in three-and-a-half years' time they would see no more strength and beauty in his appearance; his body would become so disfigured as to be unrecognizable.

Friday, October 7, A.D. *29 (Tishri 11)* At daybreak, Jesus and his followers set off in the direction of the Jordan. They came close to the place of baptism where John was preaching to the assembled crowd. (This was now John's new place of baptism, somewhat south of the place where he had baptized Jesus.) At that moment, John turned, pointing in the direction of Jesus, who—although far away in the distance—was just visible. He said: "Behold the Lamb of God, who bears the sins of the world." He continued with the words recorded in John 1:30–34. Jesus, however, did not draw nearer but made his way northwest. Nevertheless, two pupils of John — the brothers Aram and Themeni, nephews of Joseph of Arimathea—followed Jesus until they caught up with him and joined his group of disciples. When they arrived at the town of Gilgal, Saturnin and two other disciples began baptizing there. Amid much jubilation from the people of the place, Jesus and his disciples went to the synagogue to celebrate the Sabbath.

Saturday, October 8, A.D. *29 (Tishri 12)* Jesus remained for the Sabbath in Gilgal. Lazarus, Joseph of Arimathea, and some other friends arrived from

Jerusalem to hear him preach. The mood was joyful, and as Jesus was leaving the synagogue the crowd shouted: "The covenant is fulfilled!" Lazarus and the friends from Jerusalem left, and Jesus sent a message through them to his mother in Galilee that she should expect him at Great Chorazin (about ten miles east of Capernaum) at the Feast of Tabernacles.

Sunday, October 9, A.D. 29 (Tishri 13) Agents reported back to the Sanhedrin in Jerusalem about the jubilation Jesus evoked at Gilgal and his baptizing activity there. The Sanhedrin, composed of seventy-one priests and scribes, appointed a committee of twenty to investigate Jesus. They concluded that Jesus was in league with the devil. On this day, Jesus and about twenty followers left Gilgal. Traveling eastward, they crossed the Jordan on a large raft. Coming to a place where many tax collectors lived—they had already been baptized by John—Jesus taught them the parable of the sower (Matthew 13).

Monday, October 10, A.D. 29 (Tishri 14) After giving further teaching to the tax collectors, Jesus set off in the direction of Dibon. At the outskirts of the town, he paused to teach. That evening was the start of the Feast of Tabernacles—to celebrate the gathering in of the fruits of the fields—and little booths (tabernacles) had been erected and festooned with bushes, bunches of grapes, and so forth. Jesus and his disciples were offered refreshment. That night, they stayed at an inn not far from the synagogue of Dibon.

Tuesday, October 11, A.D. 29 (Tishri 15) After teaching in the synagogue, Jesus found that some sick people had been brought there into the open court. They cried out: "Lord, thou art a prophet! Thou hast been sent from God! Thou canst help us! Help us, Lord!" He healed many of them. That evening, he was received at a banquet in his honor. Afterward, Jesus arranged with the disciples to meet him on the following morning at a place outside the town. Then Jesus left the inn where they were staying and went to pray alone on the mountain.

MAP 7: *The Forty Days in the Wilderness*

Wednesday, October 12, A.D. 29 (Tishri 16) Early in the morning the disciples met up with Jesus and journeyed with him northward from Dibon. They passed through Bethsob and paused briefly in Ainon before arriving that evening at the town of Succoth, where Jesus taught in the synagogue, and Saturnin—together with four other disciples—baptized a number of people.

Thursday, October 13, A.D. 29 (Tishri 17) After teaching and healing in Succoth, Jesus and his disciples journeyed further north through the region known as the Decapolis.

Friday, October 14, A.D. 29 (Tishri 18) They passed by Gerasa and arrived at the town of Great Chorazin, where they celebrated the Sabbath.

Saturday, October 15, A.D. 29 (Tishri 19) Jesus taught in the synagogue until the close of the Sabbath. Then he went to the inn where the Holy Virgin Mary together with Peter's wife, Susanna of Jerusalem, and several other holy women were waiting in expectation of his arrival. The sixth day of the week-long Feast of Tabernacles was just beginning, and the women had decorated their rented rooms at the inn accordingly. Jesus talked with his mother and again told her that after going to Bethany he would go alone into the wilderness.

Sunday, October 16, A.D. 29 (Tishri 20) Today, Jesus taught upon a hill. Many men and women from the neighborhood came to hear him. He spoke of his imminent departure and foretold that John's baptizing would soon cease. He also referred to the hard trials that would beset him and his followers. That evening, Jesus set off in a southwesterly direction accompanied by about twenty traveling companions. They journeyed through the night.

Monday, October 17, A.D. 29 (Tishri 21) The whole day through, Jesus and the disciples continued on their way. In the evening, they arrived at the town of Aruma, where they stayed at an inn that had been made ready for them by Martha and Susanna of Jerusalem. Some Essenes living nearby came to eat with Jesus and his disciples. That evening, Jesus taught in the synagogue. Judas Iscariot was among the crowd of those who listened.

Tuesday, October 18, A.D. 29 (Tishri 22) Jesus taught again in the synagogue. Later, he went to the town of Phasael and visited the Essene Jairus (not the Jairus mentioned in the Gospels). He ate with Jairus and spent the night at his house.

Wednesday, October 19, A.D. *29 (Tishri 23)* Jesus remained in Phasael, teaching, and then—accompanied by Jairus—visited the sick. He comforted them and promised to return in four months' time to heal them That evening, Jesus and his disciples journeyed further in the direction of Bethany.

Thursday, October 20, A.D. *29 (Tishri 24)* Toward evening, Jesus and his disciples arrived at a hostel near Bethany that had been put at their disposal by Lazarus. Lazarus came to greet them. Talking with the disciples, Jesus spoke of the dangers facing those who follow him. He said that each should consider carefully—during the coming period of separation from him— whether he really wanted to continue being a disciple. Jesus then took leave of them and made his way to Lazarus' castle at Bethany, accompanied by Lazarus and the two nephews of Joseph of Arimathea, Aram and Themeni. Here many friends from Jerusalem were expecting him.

Friday, October 21, A.D. *29 (Tishri 25)* Jesus interpreted various passages from the scriptures to the friends gathered together. Later, he had a conversation with Silent Mary, whom he blessed. He then set off in the direction of Jericho. For the first part of the journey, Jesus was accompanied by Lazarus. Lazarus went with Jesus as far as a hostel (that he owned) close to the wilderness. Here they parted company, and Jesus continued on his way alone and barefoot. As the Sabbath began, he climbed a mountain—Mount Quarantania—about one hour's distance from Jericho. Here he started his forty-day fast and spent the night in prayer in a cave. Jesus knelt with outstretched arms and prayed to his heavenly Father for strength and courage in all the trials that awaited him.

Saturday, October 22, A.D. *29 (Tishri 26)* For the whole of the Sabbath and the following night, Jesus remained in prayer. A vast cloud of light descended upon him, and he received consolation from on high. Jesus offered up to the Father the fruits of all his future labors and sufferings so that these fruits should benefit his faithful followers in all ages to come. So intense was Jesus' praying that Anne Catherine saw him sweat blood.

Sunday, October 23, A.D. *29 (Tishri 27)* Jesus descended from the mountain (Mount Quarantania) before sunrise. He walked toward the Jordan, which he crossed on a beam of wood, and journeyed east of the town of Bethabara into the wilderness beyond the Dead Sea. Eventually, he reached a very wild mountain range east of Callirrhoe where he ascended the forbidding Mount Attarus. This savage, desolate mountain lay about nine hours' distance from Jericho. Here he continued to pray and fast, spending the night in a narrow cave near the summit of the mountain.

Monday, October 24, to Wednesday, November 30, A.D. *29 (Tishri 28–Kislev 6)* Throughout this period Jesus stayed at the mountain cave on Mount Attarus, praying and fasting. Here he was tempted. The three temptations described in Matthew 4:1–11 and Luke 4:1–13 actually took place on the last three days of the forty-day period (November 27–29). Throughout the whole period, however, Anne Catherine beheld how Jesus was daily submitted to temptation that then culminated in the three temptations described in the Gospels. On Wednesday, November 30, when Jesus had overcome the last temptation, the twelve angels of the twelve apostles served him heavenly food. These twelve angels were accompanied in turn by the seventy-two angels of the seventy-two disciples. An indescribable blessing and consolation emanated from this heavenly celebration of Jesus' triumphant victory over temptation—a blessing and consolation that was transmitted by the angels to the apostles and disciples.

HESHVAN (29 days): October 26/27 to November 23/24, A.D. *29*
Heshvan New Moon: October 26 at 3:00 A.M. *Jerusalem time*

[*Note concerning the calendar:* The forty days in the wilderness were "Jewish days," in which the day began at dusk and extended until the following sunset. The 40-day period began with the onset of the Sabbath evening of Friday, October 21, which was the beginning of Tishri 26 in the Jewish calendar. The last of the forty days—which equated with Kislev 6 in the Jewish calendar—ended on the evening of Wednesday, November 30. That evening, as Jesus descended from the mountain, Kislev 7 began. Jesus then traveled through the night until he reached the river Jordan.]

KISLEV (30 days): November 24/25 to December 23/24, A.D. *29*
Kislev New Moon: November 24 at 2:00 P.M. *Jerusalem time*

MAP 8: *At the Second Place of Baptism*

Thursday, December 1, A.D. 29 (Kislev 7) At daybreak, Jesus arrived at the Jordan at the spot where he had crossed some five weeks previously. He walked along the banks of the river until he came to the place of baptism. John the Baptist beheld Jesus on the opposite side of the river and spoke to those assembled to hear him: "Behold the Lamb of God!" (John 1:36). Jesus, however, withdrew from the river bank and went in the direction of Bethabara. Andrew and Saturnin, who were standing with John, set off to follow him (John 1:35). They crossed the Jordan together with three other disciples of John. Eventually, they caught up with Jesus. He turned to them and asked: "What do you seek?" Andrew answered joyfully: "Master, where are you staying?" Whereupon he said: "Come and see" (John 1:37–39). The Saviour then conducted them to an inn at Bethabara and told them that his teaching activity would now begin and that he intended to gather more disciples. Andrew was the first of the future apostles to join Jesus as a disciple.

Friday, December 2, A.D. 29 (Kislev 8) Jesus traveled with his five disciples to the place of the tax collectors where he had been on Tishri 13–14. After teaching there and at another place, he returned to Bethabara for the beginning of the Sabbath.

Saturday, December 3, A.D. 29 (Kislev 9) Jesus celebrated the Sabbath in Bethabara and taught in the synagogue there.

Sunday, December 4, A.D. 29 (Kislev 10) Jesus made his way up the Jordan to the second place of baptism (near Gilgal), where John had baptized for only a short time. Jesus blessed the water. Andrew and Saturnin baptized, and Jesus taught from a nearby grassy mound concerning repentance, baptism, and the coming of the Holy Spirit. Those who came were mainly disciples of John the Baptist. But other followers of John complained about the rivalry presented by Jesus' baptizing. John reminded them that he was merely the Forerunner (John 3:26–36). Jesus returned to Bethabara, staying there overnight.

Monday, December 5, A.D. 29 (Kislev 11) Early in the day, Jesus made his way to Ophra, south of Gilgal. He was accompanied by about twenty people, among then Andrew, Saturnin, and the two nephews of Joseph of Arimathea (Aram and Themeni). As he entered the town, some of those possessed cried out: "Here comes the prophet, the Son of God, Jesus Christ, our enemy; he will cast us out!" Jesus commanded them to be silent, whereupon they all became quiet and followed him to the synagogue. He taught there until evening and then retired to an inn.

Tuesday, December 6, A.D. 29 (Kislev 12) Jesus and his traveling companions walked from Ophra to the second place of baptism near Gilgal. Andrew and Saturnin again baptized, while Jesus taught those who came.

Wednesday, December 7, A.D. 29 (Kislev 13) Accompanied by three disciples, Jesus journeyed from Bethabara to Dibon, where he had been at the start of the Feast of Tabernacles (Tishri 15). There he taught at the synagogue and also addressed some workers in the fields, speaking of the parable of the sower (Matthew 13:2).

Thursday, December 8, A.D. 29 (Kislev 14) Jesus taught all day in a valley near Dibon. Andrew, Saturnin, and the other disciples returned to Ophra to encourage those who had been awakened there by Jesus' teaching.

Friday, December 9, A.D. 29 (Kislev 15) Together with some seven disciples, Jesus walked from Dibon to Eleale, where he stayed with one of the Elders of the synagogue. That evening, the Sabbath began and Jesus taught in the synagogue.

Saturday, December 10, A.D. 29 (Kislev 16) Jesus remained in Eleale for the Sabbath and the following night.

Sunday, December 11, A.D. 29 (Kislev 17) Today, Jesus journeyed about three hours from Eleale to Bethjesimoth, a small place on the east side of a mountain. On the way, he was joined by Andrew and Saturnin. In Bethjesimoth, he healed some of those who were possessed. He caused the chains in which they were fettered to fall miraculously to the ground. Afterward, he visited and cured many of the sick in their homes.

Monday, December 12, A.D. 29 (Kislev 18) Jesus stayed in Bethjesimoth all day, teaching and healing.

Tuesday, December 13, A.D. 29 (Kislev 19) Accompanied by Andrew, Saturnin, Aram, Themeni, and about eight other disciples, Jesus journeyed northwestward. Together, they crossed the Jordan at the crossing-point near Dibon and traveled on to a shepherd place west of Phasael. Here Jesus taught in the open air, on a small elevation upon which a teacher's chair—made of stone—had been erected.

Wednesday, December 14, A.D. 29 (Kislev 20) Toward evening, Jesus and his companions arrived at the town of Shiloh where there were two synagogues — one belonging to the Pharisees and the other to the Sadducees. A group of Pharisees and Sadducees gathered to dispute with Jesus. They spoke of the voice of thunder at his baptism. Jesus replied that this was the voice of his heavenly Father—the Father of all who repent their sins and are born again through baptism. His hearers were furious at the things he spoke of and left seething with rage.

Thursday, December 15, A.D. 29 (Kislev 21) Jesus taught in the synagogue at Shiloh concerning reverence for the old and love of one's parents.

Friday, December 16, A.D. 29 (Kislev 22) This morning, Andrew, Saturnin, Aram, and Themeni took leave of Jesus and set off for Galilee. Andrew went to his brother Simon Peter (John 1:41). Jesus and the remaining disciples journeyed to Kibzaim for the Sabbath. There, they met Lazarus and his servant, together with Martha, Joanna Chuza, and Simeon's son, who were all on their way to the wedding at Cana.

Saturday, December 17, A.D. 29 (Kislev 23) After the Sabbath morning service, Jesus healed by word of command several people who had been carried to a place in front of the synagogue. He was invited to a meal at the home of a distinguished Levite. At the close of the Sabbath, Jesus went to Sichem (Sychar) where he stayed the night at an inn.

Sunday, December 18, A.D. 29 (Kislev 24) Early this morning, Jesus left Sychar and traveled to Thebez. As he entered the town, those possessed cried out: "Here comes the prophet of Galilee! He has power over us! He will cast us out!" Jesus commanded them to be quiet and they became silent. He taught in the synagogue, healing many. That evening—the start of Kislev 25 in the Jewish calendar—the Feast of the Dedication of the Temple began, which Jesus celebrated here.

Monday, December 19, A.D. *29 (Kislev 25)* Before daybreak, Jesus left Thebez and traveled north toward Galilee. On the way, he paused briefly in Abel-Mehola, the birthplace of the prophet Elisha, and then continued on again. On the road leading to Tarichea, Jesus encountered Andrew, Simon Peter, and John. Andrew introduced his brother to Jesus. Jesus looked at him and said: "Thou art Simon, the son of Jonas; thou shalt be called Cephas" [which means Peter, the rock] (John 1:42). To John, he said something about seeing him again another time. Peter and John then journeyed on to Gennabris while Jesus, together with his disciples (including Andrew), continued on their way toward Tarichea. By this time, John the Baptist had abandoned his third place of baptism (near Ono) and returned to the second place (near Gilgal), where Jesus had instructed his disciples to baptize.

MAP 9: *The Wedding at Cana*

Tuesday, December 20, A.D. *29 (Kislev 26)* Jesus and his traveling companions did not go into Tarichea, but stayed at an inn just outside the town. Jesus was visited there by Lazarus, Saturnin, Simeon's son, and the bridegroom Nathanael, who was to be married at the wedding at Cana. Nathanael invited Jesus and everyone else to attend his wedding. That evening, they remained at the inn and celebrated the Feast of the Dedication of the Temple, which lasted from the evening of December 18 (start of Kislev 25) to the evening of December 26 (end of Tebeth 2).

Wednesday, December 21, A.D. *29 (Kislev 27)* Today, Jesus wandered about in the neighboring hills with some of his disciples. That evening, they gathered at the inn and prayed together, lighting the candles for the Feast of the Dedication. Andrew busied himself writing letters with a reed upon strips of parchment. These were to be sent by messengers to Philip, Peter, and his stepbrother Jonathan, notifying them that Jesus would be in Capernaum for the Sabbath.

Thursday, December 22, A.D. *29 (Kislev 28)* Today, Jesus went to Capernaum accompanied by Andrew, Saturnin, Obed, and several other disciples. On the way, Andrew parted company with Jesus and went to meet his stepbrother Jonathan, who was with Philip. He told them that Jesus was truly the Messiah. In Capernaum, Jesus and his traveling companions stayed at a house belonging to Nathanael, the bridegroom. Here a messenger from Cades came to see Jesus. His master's son was very ill, and he begged Jesus to come and heal the child. Jesus gave instructions to be followed, whereupon the child was healed without his direct presence.

Friday, December 23, A.D. 29 (Kislev 29) That evening, at the start of the Sabbath, Jesus taught in the synagogue. Many friends and relatives were in attendance, including the Holy Virgin Mary. In connection with the lighting of candles at the Feast of Dedication, Jesus spoke of the light that should not be hidden under a bushel (Matthew 5:17).

Saturday, December 24, A.D. 29 (Kislev 30) Jesus taught again, morning and afternoon, in the synagogue. At the close of the Sabbath, he and his disciples went for a walk in the little vale nearby. Philip, who was modest and humble, hung back. Jesus turned and said to him: "Follow me" (John 1:43), whereupon Philip, filled with joy, joined the other disciples. That evening, after returning to the town, Jesus visited his mother—several other relatives were also gathered there—and together they celebrated the New Moon festival (start of the month of Tebeth).

TEBETH (29 days): December 24/25, A.D. 29, to January 21/22, A.D. 30
Tebeth New Moon: December 24 at 2:45 A.M. Jerusalem time

Sunday, December 25, A.D. 29 (Tebeth 1) The Holy Virgin and her companions set off along the road leading to Cana. Jesus and his disciples went a more circuitous route. They traveled through Gennabris, where Jesus taught in the synagogue. While he did so, Philip sought out Nathanael Chased, who worked in Gennabris as a clerk. Philip found Nathanael and said to him: "We have found him of whom Moses in the law and also the prophets wrote, Jesus of Nazareth, the son of Joseph." Nathanael replied: "Can anything good come from Nazareth?" Philip then said to him: "Come and see" (John 1:45–46). Philip and Nathanael then set off along the road to Cana, and soon caught up with Jesus. Philip called out: "Master! I bring you here one who has asked: Can anything good come from Nazareth?" Jesus, turning to the disciples, said, as Nathanael came up to them, "Behold, a true Israelite in whom there is no guile!" (John 1:47). Then followed the exchange of words between Jesus and Nathanael Chased reported in John 1:48–51. Everyone then went on to Cana, where Jesus was received by the bridegroom, Nathanael, and by the bride's father, Israel, by her mother, and the Holy Virgin.

Monday, December 26, A.D. 29 (Tebeth 2) In Cana, Jesus stayed at a house belonging to one of Mary's cousins. This cousin was the daughter of Anne's sister Sobe and was also an aunt of Nathanael the bridegroom. Today, Jesus spent much time walking and talking with those disciples who later became his apostles.

Tuesday, December 27, A.D. 29 (Tebeth 3) About a hundred guests had gathered in Cana to attend the wedding. That evening, Jesus taught in the synagogue concerning the significance of marriage, husbands and wives, continence, chastity, and spiritual union. Later, Jesus addressed the bridal pair.

Wednesday, December 28, A.D. 29 (Tebeth 4) Today, on the third day (in terms of Jewish days) after Jesus's arrival in Cana, the marriage ceremony took place at about nine o'clock in the morning. Afterward, the guests left the synagogue and assembled for the wedding banquet. Jesus had taken responsibility for arranging the banquet. However, when Mary saw that there was no wine, she said to him: "They have no wine." There then followed the sequence of events that culminated in the miracle of the transformation of water into wine (John 2:4–11). This miracle gave interior strength to all those present who drank of the wine. All became convinced of Jesus' power and of the lofty nature of his mission. Faith entered their hearts, and they became inwardly united as a community. Here, for the first time, Jesus was in the midst of his community. He wrought this miracle on their behalf. This was his first miraculous sign, which found its octave subsequently in the last miracle, that of the Last Supper, at which the apostles received inner strength for their mission. After the banquet, Nathanael the bridegroom had a private conversation with Jesus in which he expressed his desire to lead a life of continence. His bride came to Jesus with the same wish. Kneeling before Jesus, they took a vow to live as brother and sister for a period of three years. He bestowed his blessing upon them.

Thursday, December 29, A.D. 29 (Tebeth 5) Jesus taught in the house where the wedding banquet had taken place. Several guests, including Lazarus and Martha, departed from Cana. That evening, in a festive procession, the bride and bridegroom were conducted to their house.

Friday, December 30, A.D. 29 (Tebeth 6) Today, most of the remaining guests, including Mary and the other holy women, left Cana. In the evening, with the beginning of the Sabbath, Jesus taught in the synagogue concerning the marriage ceremony and the devout sentiments of the bridal pair.

Saturday, December 31, A.D. 29 (Tebeth 7) Jesus taught morning and afternoon in the synagogue. When he came out of the synagogue, in the presence of the priests, he healed six people and raised from the dead a man who had died as a consequence of falling from a tower. After the close of the Sabbath, Jesus and his remaining disciples set off for Capernaum (John 2:12).

Sunday, January 1, and Monday, January 2, A.D. 30 (Tebeth 8–9) Jesus stayed in Capernaum, teaching in the synagogue and fasting. (The actual day of fasting celebrated at this time in the Jewish calendar is Tebeth 10. The fast commemorates the beginning of the siege of Jerusalem—see 2 Kings 25:1. This year, A.D. 30, Tebeth 10 began on Monday evening, and the fast ought to have begun at sunrise on the following day. Anne Catherine, however, referred to two days of fasting). Here in Capernaum, Jesus healed the sick. In between periods of teaching, he remained with his mother.

MAP 10: *The First Sermon on the Mount*

Tuesday, January 3, A.D. 30 (Tebeth 10) Jesus sent Andrew, Saturnin, Aram, Themeni, and Eustachius to the third place of baptism, near Ono, which had since been abandoned by John. After accompanying them part of the way, Jesus went with three other disciples to Bethulia, where again he healed the sick and taught.

Wednesday, January 4, A.D. 30 (Tebeth 11) Jesus, accompanied by the three disciples, walked to Hanathon, seven or eight hours northwest of Capernaum. Near Hanathon, there was a mountain used by the prophets in former times. Jesus sent out his three disciples to let the people of the town know that on the following day he would teach on the mountain.

Thursday, January 5, A.D. 30 (Tebeth 12) Jesus was on the mountain near Hanathon. Addressing the assembled crowd, he referred to the spirit one receives through baptism. This is the spirit in which—through penance, making amends, and reconciliation—all people can be united and become one with the Father in heaven. He also spoke concerning some of the petitions of his prayer (the Our Father), but without giving the entire prayer. He taught from noon until evening. Then he made his way to Bethanat.

Friday, January 6, A.D. 30 (Tebeth 13) In Bethanat, Jesus and his three disciples were joined by five of John's disciples. Together, they walked southward in the direction of Capernaum. Pausing on a hill about half an hour from the Sea of Galilee, they could see Peter, James, and John in their fishing boats. Jesus indicated that these three fishermen would also join him. After paying a brief visit to his mother at her house between Bethsaida and Capernaum, Jesus and the disciples went to the synagogue in Capernaum to celebrate the start of the Sabbath.

Saturday, January 7, A.D. 30 (Tebeth 14) Jesus taught in the synagogue at Capernaum until the close of the Sabbath.

Sunday, January 8, A.D. 30 (Tebeth 15) Jesus visited his mother and talked with her until deep into the night. He said that he would first journey to the place of baptism, then celebrate the Passover in Jerusalem, and afterward summon his apostles and make his public appearance.

Monday, January 9, A.D. 30 (Tebeth 16) Before sunrise, Jesus set off with his eight disciples to journey to the place of baptism. Passing around the north side of the Sea of Galilee, they then went down the east side, staying overnight at Hippos.

Tuesday, January 10, A.D. 30 (Tebeth 17) Today, they journeyed on. As they approached Gadara, Jesus healed a man possessed. Toward evening, they reached Jezrael. Here Jesus publicly healed several people in front of the synagogue. However, after only a few hours in Jezrael, they set off on their way again.

MAP 11: *At the Place of Baptism*

Wednesday, January 11, A.D. 30 (Tebeth 18) Today, Jesus and his disciples arrived at Akrabis, a shepherd place. Jesus taught in the open air.

Thursday, January 12, A.D. 30 (Tebeth 19) Toward evening, Jesus arrived in Hay, not far from Bethel, where he healed several people. He taught, and a number of Pharisees disputed with him, putting such questions as: "When will the Messiah come?"

Friday, January 13, A.D. *30 (Tebeth 20)* Toward noon, Jesus and his disciples arrived at the place of baptism near Ono. There he gave instruction to the people who had come to be baptized. That evening, he celebrated the Sabbath at the synagogue in Ono.

Saturday, January 14, A.D. *30 (Tebeth 21)* Today, Jesus taught in the synagogue. He spoke of himself as continuing the work begun by John. He also healed several people.

Sunday, January 15, A.D. *30 (Tebeth 22)* While Andrew and Saturnin were baptizing, Jesus gave instruction to the people who had come to the place of baptism. Many had been sent by John, who was now at the second place of baptism, on the east side of the Jordan. John had stopped baptizing, and now only preached, speaking always of Jesus. He also denounced Herod Antipas as an adulterer, thus arousing the fury of Herodias.

Monday, January 16, A.D. *30 (Tebeth 23)* Jesus continued to teach at the place of baptism. He spoke of his baptism as a cleansing, while John's baptism had been one of penance. He also referred to a baptism by fire (from the Holy Spirit), which was to come. John's baptism had used the words: "May Yahveh through the ministry of his Seraphim and Cherubim pour out his blessing upon thee with wisdom, understanding, and strength." In contrast, Jesus' baptism was in the name of the Father, the Son, and the Holy Spirit.

Tuesday, January 17, A.D. *30 (Tebeth 24)* Jesus went with several disciples to the ruined city of Hazezon-Thamar on the west side of the Dead Sea, not far from Engaddi. The people living there—slaves belonging to wandering tribes—were very poor and humble. They gratefully received Jesus in their midst, and he healed a number of them.

Wednesday, January 18, A.D. *30 (Tebeth 25)* Jesus made his way through the valley of the shepherds, where he had been one week after his baptism.

Thursday, January 19, A.D. *30 (Tebeth 26)* As Jesus approached Bethabara, many who were possessed ran about, calling out that Jesus was coming. Jesus cast the evil spirits out of these people. Then he and his disciples put up at an inn.

Friday, January 20, A.D. 30 (Tebeth 27) Andrew and five disciples had come from the place of baptizing. Also Lazarus, Joseph of Arimathea, and some others had come from Jerusalem to hear Jesus teach in the synagogue on the Sabbath. The people of Bethabara were well disposed toward Jesus.

Saturday, January 21, A.D. 30 (Tebeth 28) At the close of the Sabbath, Jesus set off to return to the place of baptizing. On the way, he passed through Bethagla. Meanwhile, Lazarus and Joseph of Arimathea traveled to Jerusalem.

Sunday, January 22, A.D. 30 (Tebeth 29) Today was the Feast of the New Moon (close of the month of Tebeth/start of the month of Shebat). It was a day of rest—a joyous festival—and thus there was no baptizing. Jesus taught in the synagogue at Ono.

SHEBAT (30 days): January 22/23, to February 20/21, A.D. 30
Shebat New Moon: January 22, at 4:30 P.M. Jerusalem time

Monday, January 23, A.D. 30 (Shebat 1) Because of the New Moon festival there was no baptizing today, but to prepare those who were going to be baptized Jesus taught at the place of baptism. In the evening, at the start of the second day of the month of Shebat, a feast was celebrated to commemorate the death of the wicked king Alexander Jannaeus. Lazarus and Obed arrived.

Tuesday, January 24, A.D. 30 (Shebat 2) Early this morning, Andrew and Saturnin began baptizing. Jesus set off with Lazarus and Obed in the direction of Bethlehem, taking a course between Bethagla and Ophra. Lazarus told Jesus of the reports concerning him that were circulating in Jerusalem. They spent the night with some shepherds.

Wednesday, January 25, A.D. 30 (Shebat 3) Jesus, Lazarus, and Obed started out in the direction of Ono. Lazarus and Obed left Jesus on the way and returned to Jerusalem. Jesus went on, visiting and healing some sick people on the way. He reached the place of baptism, Ono, around 3.00 P.M. that afternoon.

Thursday, January 26, A.D. 30 (Shebat 4) Jesus taught again today, while Andrew and Saturnin continued to baptize.

MAP 12: *A Raising from the Dead*

Friday, January 27, A.D. 30 (Shebat 5) Jesus and many of his disciples walked through Bethagla to Adummin. Here they visited the spot where the parable of the good Samaritan had taken place. Jesus taught this parable to his disciples and to those people from the neighborhood who had come to hear him. In the evening, Jesus celebrated the Sabbath in Adummin.

Saturday, January 28, A.D. 30 (Shebat 6) Jesus taught in the synagogue and also healed many people. At the close of the Sabbath, he and the disciples returned to the place of baptism.

Sunday, January 29, A.D. 30 (Shebat 7) Jesus taught, while Andrew and Saturnin baptized. In the evening, Jesus went with some disciples to Nebo, situated at the foot of Mount Nebo. The disciples brought some water from the baptismal pool in leathern bottles.

Monday, January 30, A.D. 30 (Shebat 8) Jesus sat on a special chair—for teachers—in the open air, and prepared people for baptism. They were then baptized with water drawn from the place of baptism.

Tuesday, January 31, A.D. 30 (Shebat 9) This morning Jesus and the disciples left Nebo. They stopped at a place between Nebo and the Jordan. Here Jesus taught. Later that evening, they returned to their inn near the place of baptism.

Wednesday, February 1, A.D. 30 (Shebat 10) Jesus taught various people in the district surrounding the place of baptism.

Thursday, February 2, A.D. 30 (Shebat 11) At the house of a rich peasant, about half an hour from Ono, Jesus taught a parable concerning sowing and harvesting (Matthew 13:3, 24).

Friday, February 3, A.D. 30 (Shebat 12) Jesus went from house to house in Ono, urging the people to pay their tithes. The feast of the fruits of trees was shortly to begin. He reminded the people of the custom of donating alms at the time of this feast. That evening, he celebrated the Sabbath in the synagogue.

Saturday, February 4, A.D. 30 (Shebat 13) Throughout the day, Jesus taught in Ono concerning the threefold meaning of the approaching feast. Firstly, it commemorated the rising of the sap in the trees; secondly, the tithes were paid at this time; and lastly, it was a feast of thanksgiving for the fertility of the soil.

Sunday, February 5, A.D. 30 (Shebat 14) The preparations for the new year's "fruits of the trees" festival continued. That evening, with the start of Shebat 15, the festival began. Jesus preached again concerning its meaning.

Monday, February 6, A.D. 30 (Shebat 15) On the occasion of the festival, fruits were distributed to the poor. Jesus received about twenty new disciples today. Together, they left Ono and set off in the direction of Galilee.

Tuesday, February 7, A.D. 30 (Shebat 16) When Jesus arrived at Aruma, a messenger came to him from Phasael sent by Jairus, the Essene. The messenger told Jesus that Jairus' daughter had died. Jesus left his disciples, arranging to meet them in two days' time in Jezrael, and went with the messenger to Phasael. When he arrived at the home of Jairus, the daughter lay bound in sheets and wrappings ready for burial. Jesus ordered the bindings to be loosened. Then he took the girl's hand, commanding her to rise. She sat up, and rose to stand before him. She was about sixteen years old. Jesus warned those present not to speak of what they had witnessed. (This miracle is not to be confused with the raising from the dead of the daughter of Jairus of Capernaum reported in Mark 5:35–43—see Kislev 3/Kislev 16, A.D. 30).

Wednesday, February 8, A.D. 30 (Shebat 17) Jesus went eastward from Phasael, crossed the Jordan and walked northward. Then he re-crossed the Jordan north of Salem, and made his way to Jezrael. Thus, he avoided passing through Samaria.

Thursday, February 9, A.D. 30 (Shebat 18) In Jezrael, where one month before he had publicly healed the sick, Jesus now taught and performed a number of miracles. A large crowd assembled, including his disciples from Galilee: Nathanael Chased, Nathanael the bridegroom, Peter, James, John, and the sons of Mary Cleophas. Lazarus, Martha, Veronica, and Joanna Chuza came from Jerusalem. The women had persuaded Mary Magdalene also to come with them to see Jesus. She came, although she was still leading a dissolute life. As she stood at the window of the inn where she was staying, she saw Jesus walking by with his disciples. He glanced in her direction, and his look penetrated to the depths of her soul. Overwhelmed by her own misery, Mary Magdalene rushed to a leper house to take refuge. She felt deeply moved by the soul-searching glance Jesus had cast upon her. Martha and Lazarus came to fetch her. They calmed her and then traveled back with her to Magdalum, where they celebrated the Sabbath together.

Map 13: First Journey with the Future Apostles

Friday, February 10, A.D. *30 (Shebat 19)* After visiting his mother on the way, Jesus arrived in Capernaum at the beginning of the Sabbath. He taught that evening, and stayed overnight in a house belonging to Nathanael the bridegroom.

Saturday, February 11, A.D. *30 (Shebat 20)* Jesus taught until the close of the Sabbath. Many sick and possessed people were brought to him from the neighborhood. In public, before a large crowd, Jesus then healed the sick and cast out devils.

Sunday, February 12, A.D. *30 (Shebat 21)* So many people flocked to hear him that Jesus left Capernaum early in the morning, accompanied by some disciples. Jesus withdrew to pray alone in the hills. Then the disciples went down to some dwellings close to the Sea of Galilee to tell the fishermen living there about Jesus. That evening, Jesus returned to his mother's house between Capernaum and Bethsaida. There he met Lazarus and Martha, who had traveled from Magdalum to say goodbye to Jesus prior to their departure for Jerusalem.

Monday, February 13, A.D. *30 (Shebat 22)* Jesus went to the synagogue in Capernaum and taught there. Some Pharisees objected to his teaching, saying that the whole land was unsettled and in a state of commotion on his account. Jesus rebuked them severely. That night, Jesus went to an inn in Gennabris (Nathanael Chased's hometown), accompanied by Nathanael Chased and seven future apostles: Andrew, Peter, the brothers James and John, and the sons of Mary Cleophas (Judas Thaddeus, Simon, and James the Lesser).

Tuesday, February 14, A.D. *30 (Shebat 23)* Jesus taught in Gennabris, healing some of those who were possessed. In addition to Nathanael Chased and the seven future apostles, Jonathan—the stepbrother of Peter and Andrew—was also in Gennabris.

Wednesday, February 15, A.D. *30 (Shebat 24)* Jesus and the disciples journeyed to Bethulia, where Jesus taught the parable of the grain of corn (John 12:24–26) in the synagogue. He stayed that night in an inn.

Thursday, February 16, A.D. *30 (Shebat 25)* The Pharisees in Bethulia feared that Jesus would celebrate the Sabbath in their town. Because of this, Jesus left the town and taught at a nearby place where there was a teacher's chair made of stone. During the afternoon he made his way to the town of Kisloth at the foot of Mount Tabor. Word had got around that he would celebrate the Sabbath there, and therefore many people flocked to Kisloth to hear him. Andrew and some other disciples had gone on ahead and reserved rooms at an inn for Jesus and his traveling companions. They set up a space in front of the inn, using thick ropes that were run through stakes to hold the crowd back. That evening, Jesus preached from there. Among those listening were several rich merchants of Kisloth. Jesus taught concerning the dangers attached to acquiring wealth. Pointing to one of the thick ropes, made of camel hair, he said: "A rope like this would pass more easily through the eye of a needle than a rich man into the kingdom of heaven" (cf. Matthew 19:24).

Friday, February 17, A.D. *30 (Shebat 26)* Kisloth was a Levitical town, renowned for its large and magnificent synagogue. Jesus taught in the synagogue most of the day and also that evening. In front of the synagogue, he healed a number of children who were brought to him. He also cured several women. After preaching that evening, he and his disciples ate a meal together at the inn where he was staying.

Saturday, February 18, A.D. *30 (Shebat 27)* Today, Jesus healed many sick people in front of the synagogue. After the close of the Sabbath, a Pharisee, who was so moved by what he had heard of Jesus' teaching that he was converted, invited Jesus and his disciples to dine with him.

Sunday, February 19, A.D. *30 (Shebat 28)* Today, a great banquet was held in Jesus' honor at the public festival hall. Jesus and his disciples attended. Jesus also taught here. That evening, he left Kisloth to travel to Jezrael, about three hours away.

Monday, February 20, A.D. 30 (Shebat 29) In Jezrael, Jesus' relatives—as well as the disciples from Bethsaida (including Andrew and Nathanael)—took leave of Jesus in order to visit their homes. They arranged to meet up again in three days in the town of Ulama. About fifteen disciples remained with Jesus. He taught in the synagogue concerning the vineyard of Naboth (1 Kings 21).

Tuesday, February 21, A.D. 30 (Shebat 30) Today, Jesus taught in the open at a place about an hour and a half east of Jezrael. Later in the day, Jesus and his disciples made their way to Sunem. That evening, at the inn where they were staying, they celebrated the New Moon festival denoting the start of the month of Adar.

> *ADAR (29 days): February 21/22, to March 21/22, A.D. 30*
> *Adar New Moon: February 21 at 7:15 A.M. Jerusalem time*

Wednesday, February 22, A.D. 30 (Adar 1) A multitude of people gathered at Sunem to hear Jesus. There was great jubilation at the appearance of the new prophet, sent by God. Jesus taught in the synagogue and visited some homes to heal the sick.

Thursday, February 23, A.D. 30 (Adar 2) This morning Jesus went with his disciples to a teacher's chair on the top of a hill. There was great excitement, and he healed many sick people who had been brought there. Jesus spoke of the necessity of repenting, doing penance, and fulfilling the commandments. That afternoon he proceeded to Ulama, where he met up with his other disciples. On his way to the inn, where they were to stay, he healed several people who were possessed.

MAP 14: *Travels in Galilee*

Friday, February 24, A.D. 30 (Adar 3) Today, Jesus visited the sick in their homes to comfort and heal them. At the start of the Sabbath, he taught in the synagogue, referring to the commandment "honor thy parents."

Saturday, February 25, A.D. 30 (Adar 4) At the close of the Sabbath, Jesus was invited to attend a banquet in his honor.

Sunday, February 26, A.D. 30 (Adar 5) Around nine o'clock in the morning, Jesus and his disciples walked to a place about a quarter of an hour from the town. Many people had already gathered there to hear him; also many sick people had been brought, whom he healed. Jesus taught concerning the death of Moses, which was to be celebrated on Adar 7, a day of fasting. Afterward, he went to a place where those who were possessed dwelt and cured them.

Monday, February 27, A.D. 30 (Adar 6) Jesus taught in the synagogue at Ulama. Around midday, he left town and traveled in the direction of Capernaum, journeying through the night.

Tuesday, February 28, A.D. 30 (Adar 7) Early this morning, he arrived at his mother's house in Capernaum. She and the other holy women gathered there were veiled because of the fast day commemorating the death of Moses. Jesus talked privately with Mary. He told her that he would soon leave for Judea in order to be in Jerusalem for the Passover. Today, too, Jesus taught in the synagogue in Capernaum.

Wednesday, March 1, A.D. 30 (Adar 8) Jesus taught again in the synagogue at Capernaum. In the evening, he took leave of many of his disciples, as he intended to travel to Judea with a small group of only twelve disciples.

Thursday, March 2, A.D. 30 (Adar 9) Mary and several holy women accompanied Jesus and a small group of disciples as far as the little place called Dothaim. Entering the town, they were welcomed by a group of men, some of them priests, who invited them to a meal. Jesus told the story of Joseph, who had been sold at a well nearby (Genesis 37:17–28). After the meal, Jesus took leave of his mother, who wept. Then Jesus went with his disciples and some people of Dothaim to Joseph's well and blessed it. Traveling further, Jesus and his disciples arrived toward evening at Sephoris. Here he stayed with his great-aunt Maraha.

Friday, March 3, A.D. 30 (Adar 10) That evening, at the start of the Sabbath, he preached in the synagogue. However, he was not well received by the learned teachers there who criticized his wandering about the land instead of staying with his mother.

Saturday, March 4, A.D. 30 (Adar 11) Jesus taught again in the synagogue in Sephoris and visited various homes—mostly of Essene families—to offer encouragement and support to his followers. He spoke with great affection, his words full of love. That night a great storm arose. Jesus prayed with outstretched arms that danger might be averted. Thus, he protected the ships on the Sea of Galilee from afar.

Sunday, March 5, A.D. *30 (Adar 12)* Jesus and his disciples made their way to Nazareth. In the evening, Jesus taught at the synagogue. It was the start of the fast day (Adar 13) commemorating Esther. That night another storm arose, and Jesus—through prayer—again helped to avert the danger threatening the people aboard ships on the Sea of Galilee.

Monday, March 6, A.D. *30 (Adar 13)* Today, Jesus was visited by the three rich youths who had sought him out on Elul 16/17. Jesus again refused their request to become his disciples. In the afternoon, he taught in the synagogue. That evening, with the start of Adar 14, the Festival of Purim—a festival of joy—began. Jesus visited the home of the old Essene Eliud, talking with him late into the night.

Tuesday, March 7, A.D. *30 (Adar 14)* The Festival of Purim was celebrated today with scenes from the Book of Esther enacted by children and maidens. There was also a great banquet, which Jesus attended, and presents were given to the poor.

Wednesday, March 8, A.D. *30 (Adar 15)* Today, the Festival of Purim continued to be celebrated. This morning Jesus went with his disciples and some priests to the pleasant gardens near Nazareth, where passages from the Book of Esther were read aloud.

Thursday, March 9, A.D. *30 (Adar 16)* This morning, Jesus was in the synagogue, where a kind of thanksgiving service took place. Afterwards, he disputed with some priests. In the afternoon, he went with his disciples to Apheca.

Friday, March 10, to Sunday, March 12, A.D. *30 (Adar 17–19)* In the course of the day, Jesus returned to Nazareth, where he celebrated the Sabbath. During the night from Sunday to Monday, he made his last visit to the home of the old Essene Eliud, who was close to death.

Monday, March 13, A.D. *30 (Adar 20)* This morning, Jesus and his disciples left Nazareth. Priests accompanied them part of the way. Some were secretly envious of Jesus because of his knowledge and how he taught. Jesus then set off on the same route that the Holy Family had taken on the flight to Egypt. He passed first through the little place Nazara. Here he performed a miracle:. He bought bread and multiplied it in his hands and distributed it to the poor. Then he made his way to Lazarus' villa near Ginnim. He was met by Lazarus, John Mark, Obed, and four other disciples. Together they stayed overnight at Lazarus' villa.

Tuesday, March 14, A.D. 30 (Adar 21) Today, Jesus taught in the synagogue at Ginnim.

Wednesday, March 15, A.D. 30 (Adar 22) This evening, with the start of Adar 23, Jesus celebrated the beginning of the Feast of the Dedication of the Temple of Zorobabel. It was Zorobabel—of the house of David—who had laid the foundation stone of the temple around 519 B.C. (Ezra 3). However, this dedication feast was not given the same significance as the Feast of the Maccabees that began on Kislev 25 and lasted for a whole week.

Thursday, March 16, A.D. 30 (Adar 23) For most of the day, Jesus celebrated the Temple feast in the synagogue. That evening, he and the disciples continued on their way, walking through the night.

MAP 15: *The First Passover*

Friday, March 17, A.D. 30 (Adar 24) On the way to Bethany, a young man from Samaria approached and cast himself down at Jesus' feet, saying, "Savior of humanity, thou who wilt free Judea and restore her to her former glory . . ." He begged to become a disciple of Jesus. He was an orphan who had inherited much from his father, and he held some kind of office in Samaria. Jesus said he would talk with him again later. (This second meeting, which took place on Iyyar 17, A.D. 32, is recorded in Matthew 19:16–22). At the beginning of the Sabbath, they arrived at the shepherd's inn where Mary and the holy women had stayed (prior to baptism) on their way to Bethany. Jesus celebrated the Sabbath there.

Saturday, March 18, A.D. 30 (Adar 25) Jesus and the disciples remained at the inn, where they celebrated the Sabbath. After the close of the Sabbath, they continued on their way to Bethany. That night Jesus stayed at Lazarus' castle.

Sunday, March 19, A.D. 30 (Adar 26) This morning Jesus and Lazarus went to Jerusalem. By midday, the holy women and friends of Jesus from Jerusalem were gathered together at the house of Mary Mark. They ate a meal together with Jesus, who spoke of the nearness of the kingdom of heaven. That evening, Jesus and Lazarus returned to Bethany.

Monday, March 20, A.D. 30 (Adar 27) Jesus went to Jerusalem again. He visited Obed, the son of Simeon, and ate a meal there. After eating, he walked the streets of Jerusalem. That evening, he returned to Bethany, where Saturnin and some of John's disciples came to him. Nicodemus also came from Jerusalem to hear Jesus.

Tuesday, March 21, A.D. 30 (Adar 28) This morning Jesus went to Simon the Pharisee's inn in Bethany. Many disciples and holy women gathered there and ate together with Jesus, who spoke of the fulfillment of the prophecies.

Wednesday, March 22, A.D. 30 (Adar 29) Accompanied by Lazarus and Saturnin, Jesus visited the homes of the sick in Bethany and healed a number of people. That evening, with the start of the first day of Nisan, the New Moon festival was celebrated in the synagogue.

> *NISAN (30 days): March 22/23 to April 20/21, A.D. 30*
> *Nisan New Moon: March 22 at 10:45 P.M. Jerusalem time*

Thursday, March 23, A.D. 30 (Nisan 1) Together with Lazarus, Saturnin, Obed, and several other disciples, Jesus was present at the service in the temple at Jerusalem. Jesus' presence evoked mixed emotions in the people there, ranging from deep sympathy to hatred.

Friday, March 24, A.D. 30 (Nisan 2) Jesus taught his disciples in the great hall at Lazarus' castle. He spoke about his youth. Among other things, he said: "It is now exactly eighteen years since a *bachir* (youth) in the temple argued most eloquently with the doctors of the law, who were filled with wrath against him." Jesus then related what the *bachir* had taught. That evening, he celebrated the Sabbath in the synagogue at Bethany.

Saturday, March 25, A.D. 30 (Nisan 3) This morning Jesus went to celebrate the Sabbath in the temple at Jerusalem. He wore a white woven robe with a girdle and a white mantle. He chanted and sang in turn with the others. Around two o'clock in the afternoon, he and his disciples ate a meal together at a place adjoining the temple. Jesus remained at the temple for the rest of the day, returning to Bethany at about nine o'clock in the evening.

Sunday, March 26, A.D. 30 (Nisan 4) Jesus was in the temple again this morning, accompanied by about twenty disciples. Afterward, he taught in the house of John Mark. Then he returned to Bethany, where he and Lazarus shared a meal with Simon the Pharisee.

Monday, March 27, A.D. 30 (Nisan 5) This morning, Jesus visited the temple. During the afternoon, he and his disciples went to the house of Joseph of Arimathea, where Jesus taught. Joseph of Arimathea's house was located beyond the city walls, in the northeast, near to the house of John Mark (not to be confused with the house in which the Last Supper took place, which belonged to Joseph of Arimathea and Nicodemus).

Tuesday, March 28, A.D. 30 (Nisan 6) Jesus was in the temple. The Pharisees were angered to see him again. Afterward, he returned to the home of Joseph of Arimathea. Everywhere, preparation was underway for the approaching Feast of the Passover.

Wednesday, March 29, A.D. 30 (Nisan 7) This morning, Jesus taught and healed in Bethany. During the afternoon he went to the temple, remaining there for the evening service. When it was over, and most of the people had gone, Jesus taught his disciples concerning the nearness of the fulfillment of all the prophecies. He hinted at the deeper mystery underlying the sacrifice of the paschal lamb. That night, he traveled southward to John the Baptist's hometown (Juttah).

Thursday, March 30, A.D. 30 (Nisan 8) Jesus went from Juttah to Hebron, where he taught and healed many sick people.

Friday, March 31, A.D. 30 (Nisan 9) Around midday, Jesus left Hebron and made his way back to Bethany in time for the start of the Sabbath.

Saturday, April 1, A.D. 30 (Nisan 10) Jesus went to the temple for the Sabbath. Together with Obed, he entered the inner court, where the priests and

Levites were holding a discourse concerning the Passover festival. The whole assembly was thrown into consternation by the appearance of Jesus, who started to put questions that they could not answer. Jesus told them that the sacrifice of the paschal lamb—meaning the Lamb of God—would soon be fulfilled, so that the temple and its services would then come to an end. The Pharisees were angry and astounded at his whole bearing. They did not undertake anything against him. Although it was forbidden to ordinary people to come into this part of the temple, Jesus had entered it in his capacity as a prophet. That evening, after the close of the Sabbath, he returned to Bethany and talked with Lazarus' sister, Silent Mary, about the nearness of the kingdom of God. He blessed her, for she was close to death.

Sunday, April 2, A.D. 30 (Nisan 11) This morning, Jesus healed publicly in Bethany. Among those who came to be healed were some who were blind and some who were lame. In the afternoon, he taught again in the temple. That evening, a group of Jesus' friends and supporters from Galilee arrived to celebrate the Passover in Jerusalem. Mary and the holy women also arrived and stayed at the home of Mary Mark.

Monday, April 3, A.D. 30 (Nisan 12) Jesus and his disciples went to the temple. There Jesus found vendors ranged around the court selling their wares. He admonished them in a friendly manner and bade them to retire with their goods to the court of the Gentiles. He and the disciples helped them move their tables. Today, for the first time, Jesus healed the sick in Jerusalem.

Tuesday, April 4, A.D. 30 (Nisan 13) A great multitude of people were gathered in Jerusalem. Arriving at the temple, Jesus and his disciples again found the vendors there. Jesus admonished them more severely this time, and set about forcibly removing their tables to the outer court. Some pious Jews approved of his action and called out: "The prophet of Nazareth!" The Pharisees, put to shame by Jesus' action, were angered by the crowd's response. Later, as Jesus left the temple, he healed a cripple. All was quiet on the streets of Jerusalem that evening, for people were busy in their homes cleansing out the leaven and preparing the unleavened bread.

Wednesday, April 5, A.D. 30 (Nisan 14) Jesus remained in Bethany today, the day of preparation for the Passover. In the temple, the vendors gathered again. In the afternoon, the paschal lambs were slaughtered. Lazarus, Obed, and Saturnin slaughtered the three lambs that Jesus and the disciples were to eat. The Passover meal took place in the great hall at Lazarus' castle. Jesus taught, and they sang and prayed together until late into the night.

YEAR 2
Nisan 15, A.D. 30, to Nisan 14, A.D. 31
April 5/6, A.D. 30, to March 26/27, A.D. 31

Thursday, April 6, A.D. 30 (Nisan 15) Having prayed for much of the night on Mount Zion, at daybreak Jesus and his disciples went to the temple. Jesus taught in the forecourts. Vendors had again erected tables to sell their wares, and Jesus demanded that they withdraw. When they refused, he drew a cord of twisted reeds from the folds of his robe. With this in hand, he overturned their tables and drove the vendors back, assisted by the disciples. Jesus said: "Take these things away; you shall not make my Father's house a house of trade." They replied: "What sign have you to show us for doing this?" Jesus answered them: "Destroy this temple, and in three days I will raise it up." They said: "It has taken forty-six years to build this temple, and you will raise it up in three days?" But he spoke of the temple of his body (John 2:13–21). All this occurred between seven and eight o'clock in the morning.

Friday, April 7, A.D. 30 (Nisan 16) This afternoon, Jesus healed about ten people—some crippled, some dumb—in the forecourt of the temple, giving rise to much excitement and jubilation. Summoned to answer for his action, he rebuked his interrogators severely. He then returned to Bethany, where he celebrated the Sabbath.

Saturday, April 8, A.D. 30 (Nisan 17) Jesus remained for the whole day at Lazarus' castle. At the close of the Sabbath, some Pharisees went to the home of Mary Mark, thinking to find Jesus there. They wished to take him into custody. However, they found only his mother, Mary, and the holy women. After addressing the women sharply and telling them to leave the city, the Pharisees went away. The women then hurried to Bethany, where they found Martha together with Silent Mary. The latter died just a few hours later, in the presence of the Holy Virgin. That same night Nicodemus came to Bethany and talked privately with Jesus through the night (John 3:1–21).

Sunday, April 9, A.D. 30 (Nisan 18) Before daybreak, Jesus and Nicodemus went to Jerusalem to Lazarus' house on Mount Zion. Joseph of Arimathea joined them there. Later, a whole group of about thirty disciples came. Jesus gave instructions about what the disciples should do during the coming period.

Monday, April 10, to Monday, April 17, A.D. 30 (Nisan 19–26) Jesus remained concealed at Bethany for part of this week and for the rest of the time at a little place called Bahurim, about one hour's distance north of Bethany.

Tuesday, April 18, to Tuesday, April 25, A.D. 30 (Nisan 27–Iyyar 4) Jesus traveled northward through Samaria to the southern end of the Sea of Galilee. He crossed over to the east side of the Jordan and journeyed south of Succoth to the region of Ainon, where John the Baptist had first started baptizing. John himself had now returned to this first place of baptism. Jesus taught some of John's disciples during these days, but he did not meet John.

IYYAR (30 days): April 21/22 to May 20/21, A.D. 30
Iyyar New Moon: April 21 at 2:30 P.M. Jerusalem time

Wednesday, April 26, to Tuesday, May 2, A.D. 30 (Iyyar 5–11) Jesus returned to Bethany and remained concealed at Lazarus' castle, where he was visited again both by Nicodemus and by Joseph of Arimathea.

Wednesday, May 3, A.D. 30 (Iyyar 12) Around this time (about three weeks after the Passover festival), Jesus went to the place of baptism near Ono, where he himself had been baptized. (This was the third place of baptism chosen by John the Baptist.) His disciples had gathered there, and many people came to hear him. While Jesus was teaching, a messenger from King Abgaras of Edessa arrived. The messenger asked Jesus to accompany him back to Edessa, or—if not—if he could at least paint a portrait of him. He produced a letter from the king in which the king described that he was ill, and believed in Jesus as God or the Son of God, and requested to be healed. Jesus replied to the king's letter by miraculously causing a perfect likeness of his countenance to be imprinted on the messenger's paper. The sight of this image later effected a deep transformation in the king's life.

Thursday, May 4, to Sunday, May 21, A.D. 30 (Iyyar 13–30) After leaving the third place of baptism near Ono, Jesus crossed the Jordan and went to the second place of baptism near Gilgal. Many people were baptized there during this period by Andrew, Saturnin, Peter, and James the brother of John (John 3:22). John the Baptist remained at the first place of baptism near Ainon (John 3:23). Several of John's disciples traveled down the Jordan to join Jesus, and a controversy arose between these disciples of John and one who had been baptized by Jesus' disciples—a controversy concerning the difference between the baptisms with regard to purification (John 3:25). Furthermore, as Jesus now had so many disciples, John's remaining disciples complained that everyone was going over to Jesus (John 3:26). John's reply that he had come to bear witness as the forerunner of the Messiah is reported in John 3:26–36. All of these events—the controversy, the testimony of John the Baptist, the multitude that flocked to be baptized by Jesus' disciples—aroused fresh excitement among the Pharisees. They dispatched letters to the Elders of all the synagogues in the land, directing them to take Jesus and his disciples into custody.

SIVAN (30 days): May 21/22 to June 19/20, A.D. 30
Sivan New Moon: May 21 at 6:00 A.M. Jerusalem time

Around the beginning of the month of Sivan, Jesus left the place of baptism, and his disciples returned to their homes in different parts of the country. (At the same time, Herod Antipas imprisoned John the Baptist in his castle at Callirrhoe but let him go again six weeks later, around the middle of the month of Tammuz.) Jesus crossed the Jordan and made his way through Samaria toward Tyre.

MAP 16: *Travels in Northern Galilee*

While Jesus was crossing through West Galilee, Andrew brought Bartholomew to meet him. Jesus said: "I know him; he will follow me. I see good in him, and in due course of time I shall call him." Jesus traveled further up the coast of the Mediterranean, passing by Tyre and teaching here and there in the region lying inland between Tyre and Sidon. Later, he turned south again and visited his mother near Capernaum. Then, accompanied by Saturnin and some other disciples, he went to the towns of Adama and Seleucia close to Lake Merom. Here he taught various people privately, rather than appearing publicly in the synagogues. He also healed many.

Tuesday, June 20, A.D. 30 (Sivan 30) Toward the end of the month of Sivan, accompanied by a few disciples, Jesus made his way to the city of Tyre. This evening he went to stay at an inn on the outskirts of the city. Here he and his disciples celebrated the New Moon festival that signified the end of the month of Sivan and the beginning of the month of Tammuz.

TAMMUZ (29 days):June 20/21 to July 18/19, A.D. 30
Tammuz New Moon: June 19 at 8:45 P.M. Jerusalem time

Wednesday, June 21, A.D. 30 (Tammuz 1) Today, about twenty of Jesus' disciples arrived at Tyre, having traveled from Galilee. In the evening, they met together with Jesus. He greeted each one of them warmly and told the assembled disciples that he would soon take up his public teaching again.

Thursday, June 22, A.D. 30 (Tammuz 2) Today, the Galilean disciples set off back to Galilee. Jesus went with Saturnin and another disciple to a fruit plantation some two hours northeast of Tyre. Jesus taught the workers there. That night, he stayed in one of their huts.

Friday, June 23, A.D. 30 (Tammuz 3) Jesus returned to Tyre. In the evening, he celebrated the Sabbath in the Jewish meeting house in Tyre.

Saturday, June 24, and Sunday, June 25, A.D. 30 (Tammuz 4–5) On Saturday, Jesus celebrated the Sabbath in Tyre. On Sunday, he healed people in the bathing garden of the Jewish meeting house there. Many people were baptized by Saturnin.

Monday, June 26, A.D. 30 (Tammuz 6) Jesus sent Saturnin and the other disciple with messages to Capernaum and Ainon. Jesus then went alone to the town of Sichor-Libnath, where there was a rich man named Simeon, who revered Jesus greatly. Simeon welcomed Jesus, and they dined together.

Tuesday, June 27, A.D. 30 (Tammuz 7) Jesus taught at Simeon's house and in a public place in the town.

Wednesday, June 28, A.D. 30 (Tammuz 8) Having sent disciples from Capernaum to Ainon, as Jesus had instructed, Saturnin and the other disciple arrived this morning from Capernaum. In Sichor-Libnath, Jesus continued his teaching.

Thursday, June 29, A.D. 30 (Tammuz 9) Jesus and the two disciples went north of Sichor-Libnath to an inn where they met up with Peter, Andrew, James the Lesser, and Nathanael Chased. That evening they returned together to Sichor-Libnath. It was a beautiful moonlit night, and Jesus paused from time to time to pray or teach.

Friday, June 30, A.D. 30 (Tammuz 10) Jesus and his disciples all stayed with Simeon at his house where they celebrated the start of the Sabbath that evening.

Saturday, July 1, A.D. 30 (Tammuz 11) Although it was the Sabbath, Jesus and his disciples set off early in the morning to journey to a little town in the land of Chabul. They traveled through mountain passes some five or six hours north of Sichor-Libnath. Arriving at their destination—a town where many Jewish exiles lived—Jesus healed about twenty people. He also taught concerning the prophet Elisha. That night, Jesus and his disciples stayed at an inn in the mountains about two hours from the town.

Sunday, July 2, A.D. 30 (Tammuz 12) Today, Jesus taught and healed a number of people—mainly non-Jews—who came to the inn where he was staying. Toward evening, he and the disciples made their way back to Sichor-Libnath.

Monday, July 3, A.D. 30 (Tammuz 13) Many people were baptized with water from a basin in the court of Simeon's mansion in Sichor-Libnath. Jesus blessed the water and instructed the people. They were then baptized by Andrew, Peter, or Saturnin. Toward evening, Jesus and the disciples left and traveled eastward in the direction of Adama. That night they rested under some trees where there was much high grass.

Tuesday, July 4, A.D. 30 (Tammuz 14) Around midday, they arrived in Adama. After being given a meal by some of the most respected people of the town, Jesus was conducted to the synagogue. Here he spoke of the fulfillment of the divine covenant.

Wednesday, July 5, A.D. 30 (Tammuz 15) The disciples went from house to house inviting people to attend a discourse that Jesus would give the following day. That evening, a great banquet was held at the public hall in honor of Jesus.

Thursday, July 6, A.D. 30 (Tammuz 16) Jesus discoursed for much of the day—
from around nine in the morning to four in the afternoon—at a place on a
hill with a stone teacher's chair overshadowed by a tree. First, he prayed to the
heavenly Father; then, he spoke of penance and baptism, and of Moses and the
giving of the Law. At the end of his discourse, when many people had already
left, an elderly man with a long beard stepped forward and said: "Allow me
now to speak with you. You have enumerated twenty-three truths when, in reality, there are twenty-four." He then proceeded to relate them one after the
other. Jesus replied: "You say that there are twenty-four truths and that I have
taught only twenty-three. But you have already added three to my number, for
I taught only twenty." And Jesus counted up twenty truths according to the
letters of the Hebrew alphabet. But the old man would by no means acknowledge his error. Jesus spoke of the evil of obstinacy and of the disastrous consequences attached to making arbitrary additions to the truth. As he spoke, the
old man turned pale, then yellow, and became shrunken on one side. Bewail-
ing his plight, the old man acknowledged his error and implored Jesus to have
mercy on him. Jesus responded to his entreaties, restoring him to his former
condition. The old man cast himself down at Jesus' feet and—as a result of
this conversion—became one of Jesus' most faithful followers.

Friday, July 7, A.D. 30 (Tammuz 17) Today was a day of fasting to commemorate the breaking of the Tablets of the Law and also the breaking down of
the walls of Jerusalem by the Babylonians (2 Kings 25:4). Jesus taught in the
synagogue at Adama. That evening, with the start of the Sabbath, he again
taught in the synagogue.

Saturday, July 8, A.D. 30 (Tammuz 18) Jesus taught in the synagogue. After
the close of the Sabbath, he went with his disciples and about ten other people to a house in the mountains north of Adama, where they shared a meal.
He told them that he would soon leave Adama. He recounted, among other
things, the parable of the unjust steward (Luke 16:1).

Sunday, July 9, A.D. 30 (Tammuz 19) Jesus and the disciples went from house
to house in Adama, inviting the people to be baptized and to attend the discourse in two days' time.

Monday, July 10, A.D. 30 (Tammuz 20) Jesus gave instruction to the people
who came to be baptized. Following the instruction, four of the disciples
baptized them at a reservoir that served as a baptismal well.

Tuesday, July 11, A.D. 30 (Tammuz 21) At daybreak, the disciples crossed the lake to Seleucia, a fortified town inhabited by Roman soldiers and a few oppressed Jews. The disciples invited the people to attend a discourse of Jesus. The people assembled at a teaching place on a hill at some distance from the town. When Jesus arrived, he spoke concerning nourishment of the body and the soul. Afterward, he went to Seleucia, where he was served a meal as a guest of the most distinguished people of the town. Here he taught: "Not what goes into the mouth defiles a person, but what comes out" (Matthew 15:11). The inhabitants of Seleucia were deeply impressed by his teaching and asked him to stay. He did not stay there himself but allowed Andrew and Nathanael Chased to do so.

Wednesday, July 12, A.D. 30 (Tammuz 22) Jesus preached again in Adama and people continued to be baptized. That evening Andrew and Nathanael Chased returned from Seleucia.

Thursday, July 13, A.D. 30 (Tammuz 23) Peter, Andrew, and some other disciples went off to visit other places in the region to invite people to attend a sermon that Jesus would give on a mountain near Berotha on the day following the Sabbath. Jesus stayed in Adama and, accompanied by Saturnin and the remaining disciples, visited the sick to heal and comfort them.

Friday, July 14, A.D. 30 (Tammuz 24) This evening, Jesus celebrated the Sabbath at the large synagogue in Adama.

Saturday, July 15, A.D. 30 (Tammuz 25) After the close of the Sabbath, Jesus, at a meal, was asked by some of the town elders what he thought of the Essenes. Jesus answered that there was nothing to reproach in their way of life.

Sunday, July 16, A.D. 30 (Tammuz 26) Before daybreak, Jesus and his disciples left Adama and went to a nearby mountain, where it had been made known beforehand that he would teach on the day after the Sabbath. A multitude had already gathered there and, as Jesus arrived, he was greeted with cries such as: "Thou art the true prophet, the helper!" Shortly after nine, Jesus began to teach. He spoke of, among other things, the parable of the sowing of the seed (Matthew 13:24–30). He taught until evening. After a communal meal, he blessed the people and left. Peter, Andrew, James the Lesser, and Nathanael Chased then returned to Capernaum and

Bethsaida. After parting company with them, Jesus, Saturnin, and the other remaining disciple made their way to Zedad, where they stayed that night at an inn.

Monday, July 17, A.D. *30 (Tammuz 27)* For the entire day and through the following night Jesus and the two disciples continued on their way. That night, John the Baptist was arrested again by Herod's soldiers at the place of baptism near Ainon. He was locked up, first in the tower of Herod's castle at Hesebon, and then was brought to Machaerus.

Tuesday, July 18, A.D. *30 (Tammuz 28)* After visiting some small shepherd places, Jesus, Saturnin, and the other disciple arrived at Gaththepher. Here Jesus continued his healing work. Then he traveled to Capernaum, arriving at his mother's house that evening. There Mary and about seven holy women, together with Lazarus, Obed, Aram, Themeni, Nathanael the bridegroom, and several other disciples awaited him. They discussed John's imprisonment. Jesus spoke of it as a sign for the beginning of his public work, the next step of which would be his going to Bethany.

Wednesday, July 19, A.D. *30 (Tammuz 29)* This morning, Jesus comforted Mary and told her not to be downcast about his coming journey to Judea. Around midday, he set off with Lazarus and about five other disciples. They passed by Bethulia and continued on their way southward. At dusk, the New Moon festival was celebrated at synagogues throughout the land, indicating the start of the month of Ab. Jesus and his companions walked through the night.

AB (30 days): July 19/20 to August 17/18, A.D. *30*
Ab New Moon: July 19 at 9:45 A.M. *Jerusalem time*

MAP 17: *The Conversation at Jacob's Well*

Thursday, July 20, A.D. *30 (Ab 1)* Early this morning, Jesus and his disciples arrived at an inn, east of Jezrael, belonging to Lazarus. There, they breakfasted before traveling on. Later in the day, they passed by Salem and, further south, crossed the Jordan. That night, they slept at a shepherd's place not far from the river, more or less west of Dibon.

Friday, July 21, A.D. 30 (Ab 2) Jesus and Lazarus re-crossed the Jordan before the sun rose. Proceeding onward, they reached Bethany late that afternoon. The entire group of Jesus' friends and supporters were gathered at Lazarus' castle, expectantly awaiting their arrival. After eating together, they celebrated the start of the Sabbath. That night, when all was still in the castle, Jesus went to the Mount of Olives, to the cave in the garden of Gethsemane, where he was to pray on the night before the Passion began. Now he prayed to his heavenly Father for strength to fulfill his mission. He returned to Lazarus' castle before daybreak.

Saturday, July 22, A.D. 30 (Ab 3) Jesus and his disciples remained for the Sabbath and the following evening at Lazarus' castle. Jesus spoke of his experiences in Adama. He also related the parable of the good Samaritan (Luke 10:25–27). That night, he prayed again alone on the Mount of Olives.

Sunday, July 23, A.D. 30 (Ab 4) Today, as Jesus explained his intention to teach throughout the land, Lazarus and the women made plans how best to help Jesus in his mission. They thought of setting up inns for Jesus and the disciples at certain places and of supplying provisions and clothes. After eating a meal together, everyone gathered in the castle's subterranean hall. Here Jesus spoke of how God in his mercy had sent to his people one prophet after another, but each had been disowned and mistreated. Now, however, the people would reject the supreme grace: Jesus predicted what would befall them. He summarized this teaching in the parable of the vineyard owner and the evil tenants (Matthew 21:33–43). Later, he told the parable of the lost coin and also hinted at Mary Magdalene when he referred to the "joy before the angels of God over one sinner who repents" (Luke 15:8–10). Jesus then retired to pray alone again on the Mount of Olives. He returned shortly before midnight and—with Lazarus and Saturnin—set off for Bethoron, where he was expected to teach the following day.

Monday, July 24, A.D. 30 (Ab 5) Early this morning, on the outskirts of Bethoron, they met up with Peter, Andrew, James the Greater, John, Judas Thaddeus, James the Lesser, and Philip. Around eight o'clock, Jesus and his disciples came to the synagogue. It was already full of people waiting in expectation to hear him. He spoke of the persecution of the prophets and the imprisonment of John the Baptist. He spoke too of his own future persecution and of the judgment and woe that would come upon Jerusalem. After healing various people in the town, Jesus and his disciples left Bethoron and journeyed to Kibzaim. That night, they stayed at a large house belonging to a shepherd.

Tuesday, July 25, A.D. 30 (Ab 6) Jesus and the disciples journeyed on, passing through Gabaa and Najoth. Jesus taught and healed as he traveled on his way. That night, they stayed again at a shepherd's place.

Wednesday, July 26, A.D. 30 (Ab 7) While the other disciples were otherwise engaged, Jesus went to Jacob's well, accompanied by Andrew, James the Greater, and Saturnin. Toward midday, they arrived at the hill on which the well-house was located. Jesus sent the three disciples to Sychar to buy provisions and sat down near the well. Then there took place the encounter with the Samaritan woman—named Dina—as described in the Gospel of Saint John 4:1–42.

Thursday, July 27, A.D. 30 (Ab 8) Jesus taught at Sychar for the whole day, expounding again upon the theme of the persecution of the prophets that is summarized in the parable of the vineyard owner and the evil tenants (Matthew 21:33–43). Dina, the Samaritan woman, spoke to Jesus concerning her future, for she had resolved to dedicate herself to his work, to help Jesus and the disciples in whatever way she could.

Friday, July 28, A.D. 30 (Ab 9) This morning, having stayed the night at an inn outside Sychar, Jesus taught at the inn and later on the surrounding hills. In the afternoon, he journeyed to Ginnim accompanied by his disciples. The Sabbath had already begun when they arrived, so they went straight to the synagogue. After the service, they made their way to a place belonging to Lazarus situated some three-quarters of an hour south of Ginnim. They stayed overnight there.

Saturday, July 29, A.D. 30 (Ab 10) Jesus preached at the synagogue in Ginnim, and entered into a dispute with twelve Pharisees, who asked him what it meant that Jonah was three days and three nights in the belly of the whale. Jesus explained that it meant that the Messiah would be slain and would remain three days in the grave, and then arise again from the dead (Matthew 12:38–42).

MAP 18: *The Healing of the Nobleman's Son*

Sunday, July 30, A.D. 30 (Ab 11) As Jesus taught this morning, many children were gathered in a park close by the place belonging to Lazarus where Jesus was staying. Around midday, he set off together with three disciples to Atharot, where a group of Sadducees tried to trick Jesus into raising from the dead someone who had been dead already eight days. Jesus exposed their plot, however. He then traveled on to a place on a hill near Engannim, where he stayed overnight.

Monday, July 31, A.D. 30 (Ab 12) Jesus and three of his disciples went to Engannim, where he had some distant relatives who were Essenes. He taught in the synagogue and was well received.

Tuesday, August 1, A.D. 30 (Ab 13) Many came to hear Jesus speak today as he taught in the synagogue. He spoke of the deeds of Elijah, and mentioned the three holy kings who had come from the East. When he had finished speaking, he healed many sick people. Later, he slipped away from the crowd and withdrew to pray alone in the hills.

Wednesday, August 2, A.D. 30 (Ab 14) Accompanied by three disciples, Jesus went to the town of Nain. There he met the widow of Nain—Maroni—whose sister was married to James the Greater. Maroni introduced Jesus to another widow who, like herself, wished to serve his work and help the community of his followers.

Thursday, August 3, A.D. 30 (Ab 15) This morning Jesus arrived at Cana. He stayed near the synagogue with a doctor of the law. While he was teaching those who had gathered in the forecourt of the house where he was staying, a messenger from Zorobabel, a high-ranking official of Capernaum, arrived with a message saying that his son was dying. There then occurred, at a distance, the miraculous healing of the boy, as described in John 4:46–54. This was the second sign that Jesus did upon coming up from Judea to Galilee (the first being the turning of water into wine at the wedding at Cana).

Friday, August 4, A.D. 30 (Ab 16) Jesus and the three disciples made their way to Capernaum, where they were greeted by Zorobabel and members of his family. Jesus laid his hand on the child's head and gave him the name Jesse (before he had been called Joel). After visiting his mother, Jesus went to the synagogue for the start of the Sabbath. Afterward, he healed the sick.

Saturday, August 5, A.D. 30 (Ab 17) On the way to the synagogue, Jesus healed many who were sick. After the morning service, two adulterous women approached him, wanting to repent publicly of their sins. Jesus forgave them. And for this, and for healing on the Sabbath, he was called to account by the Pharisees. That evening the Pharisees met with the town elders, including Zorobabel, to discuss what to do about Jesus. Zorobabel was able to exert a calming influence.

Sunday, August 6, A.D. 30 (Ab 18) Today, Jesus walked to the Sea of Galilee, where he met with Peter and Andrew. He taught at their fishery and then— together with Peter—visited the latter's home.

Monday, August 7, A.D. 30 (Ab 19) This morning, Jesus taught in the synagogue at Bethsaida. Afterward, he went with Saturnin and another disciple to a home for lepers and simpletons. Jesus consoled and healed many of them, then returned to Andrew's home to dine.

MAP 19: *The Healings at Capernaum*

Tuesday, August 8, A.D. 30 (Ab 20) Accompanied by Tharzissus and Aristobolus, Jesus made his way to Lower Sephoris.

Wednesday, August 9, A.D. 30 (Ab 21) This evening, Jesus spoke at the synagogue in Lower Sephoris concerning marriage and divorce.

Thursday, August 10, A.D. 30 (Ab 22) Jesus went to a house between Lower and Upper Sephoris where he cured an old woman of dropsy and healed a boy—about eight years old—who had been blind from birth. Saturnin was with him now, and when they proceeded to the valley of Zabulon they were joined by Jesus' childhood companion, Parmenas.

Friday, August 11, A.D. 30 (Ab 23) This morning, Pharisees from Upper and Lower Sephoris drew Jesus into a great dispute concerning the strict teaching on marriage and divorce that he had recently expounded in Lower Sephoris (Matthew 19:3–9). That afternoon, Jesus went to Nazareth and taught in the synagogue at the start of the Sabbath. He spoke of the passage in Isaiah 61:1–2 and of its fulfillment, as narrated in Luke 4:16–22.

Saturday, August 12, A.D. 30 (Ab 24) Jesus taught again in the synagogue at Nazareth and sharply reproached the Pharisees for their misinterpretation of the law. At midday, he dined with an Essene family. He then returned to teach at the synagogue again (Luke 4:23–28). At the close of the Sabbath, when Jesus came out of the synagogue, he was immediately surrounded by about twenty Pharisees. They began to lead him out of the town toward a nearby hill, for they intended to cast him down from the brow of the hill. Suddenly, however, Jesus stopped, stood still, and with the help of angelic beings passed—as if invisible—through the midst of the crowd to his escape (Luke 4:29–30).

Sunday, August 13, A.D. 30 (Ab 25) This morning Jesus met up with four disciples—Saturnin, Parmenas, and the Greek brothers Tharzissus and Aristobolus—on their way from Nazareth to Tarichea. They walked together, arriving around four o'clock that afternoon. Here in Tarichea Jesus healed five lepers. He and the four disciples then proceeded on to the Jordan, which they crossed that night.

Monday, August 14, A.D. 30 (Ab 26) Jesus and the four disciples made their way to Galaad, where they stayed at an inn on the outskirts of town.

Tuesday, August 15, A.D. 30 (Ab 27) Today they went northward to the town of Gerasa, where they arrived that evening. Here he received a message sent by the Holy Virgin on behalf of a widow of Nain who was possessed. This widow was an acquaintance of Maroni, the widow of Nain whom Jesus had visited there on Ab 14. Receiving the message, Jesus healed the possessed woman from a distance.

Wednesday, August 16, A.D. 30 (Ab 28) After teaching some unbelievers on a mountainside near Gerasa, Jesus journeyed to a place on the northeast side of the Sea of Galilee, where a boat sent by Peter and Andrew was waiting to collect him. He traveled across the lake and landed near Bethsaida. Peter, Andrew, John, James the Greater, James the Lesser, and Philip met him there. They all went with him to Peter's house, where the Holy Virgin and some of the holy women were waiting. All expressed their concern about the vehemence of the Pharisees directed toward Jesus, and said it would be better for him not to teach in Capernaum, where fifteen Pharisees had been sent to investigate the new prophet. Jesus, however, dismissed their worries with a few words.

Thursday, August 17, A.D. 30 (Ab 29) Jesus healed many people on his way to Bethsaida and in the town itself. That night he returned to Peter's house again.

Friday, August 18, A.D. 30 (Ab 30) After healing many in Bethsaida, Jesus made his way to the synagogue in Capernaum. It was the start of the Sabbath, and also the beginning of the month of Elul. In Capernaum, many Pharisees, including the fifteen newcomers who were there to investigate him, listened to Jesus' teaching. They were astounded at his interpretation of the prophet Isaiah (Ch. 49), whispering to one another: "Never before has a prophet taught like this!" (Mark 1:21–22). But they had no reply to Jesus' sermon. Then Jesus left the synagogue. Outside he healed the sick and, afterward, returned to Peter's house, where he healed more people.

ELUL (29 days): August 18/19 to September 15/16, A.D. 30
Elul New Moon: August 17 at 9:15 P.M. Jerusalem time

Saturday, August 19, A.D. 30 (Elul 1) Jesus went again to the synagogue in Capernaum to teach. It was the Sabbath. And there took place the scene, described in Mark 1:23–27 and Luke 4:31–36, where Jesus healed a man who was possessed. After further healings, around midday, Jesus went to Peter's house in Bethsaida where he healed Peter's mother-in-law, who had a raging fever. She rose immediately from her bed and helped the other women serve the next meal (Luke 4:38–39; Matthew 8:14–15; Mark 1:29–31). Jesus then healed many more people who were brought to him at Peter's house (Mark 1:32–34). Later, after teaching again in the synagogue, Jesus withdrew to a lonely place where he spent the night in prayer.

Sunday, August 20, A.D. 30 (Elul 2) Early this morning Peter and the other disciples came to Jesus and told him that many sick people were waiting for him (Mark 1:36–37). Jesus replied that he would return another time and took leave of the disciples. Later he met up again with Saturnin, Parmenas, Tharzissus, and Aristobolus and they continued together to Bethulia. That evening, he put up at an inn, where he taught.

Monday, August 21, A.D. 30 (Elul 3) Jesus taught in Bethulia today.

Tuesday, August 22, A.D. 30 (Elul 4) This morning, Jesus taught and healed in Bethulia. And in the afternoon he and his disciples went to the nearby town of Jotopata. Here there were many Herodians. (The Herodians were a secret brotherhood opposed to Roman rule; they had the support of Herod Antipas.) Jesus taught in the synagogue. The Herodians tried to trap him into saying that he was the Messiah, but Jesus exposed them, and proclaimed their secrets to the assembled people.

Wednesday, August 23, A.D. 30 (Elul 5) It was harvest time. Jesus and the disciples walked from field to field. Here and there, he held a discourse with the workers.

Thursday, August 24, A.D. 30 (Elul 6) Today, Jesus continued on his way toward Gennabris.

Friday, August 25, A.D. 30 (Elul 7) Andrew, James, and John came to Jesus to conduct him to Gennabris. They arrived in Gennabris at the start of the Sabbath. Jesus taught in the synagogue, which was very full. Afterward, he was invited to a meal by a Pharisee.

Saturday, August 26, A.D. 30 (Elul 8) Jesus taught again this morning in the synagogue. Herod Antipas had sent some spies to Galilee to hear what Jesus was preaching. Jesus referred to them in these words: "When they come, you may tell the foxes (spies) to take word back to that other fox (Herod) not to trouble himself about me. He may continue his wicked course and fulfill his designs with regard to John the Baptist. For the rest, I shall not be constrained by him. I shall continue to teach wherever I am sent in every region, and even in Jerusalem itself when the time comes. I shall fulfill my mission and account for it to my Father in heaven." That evening, after the close of the Sabbath, Jesus was invited to a banquet to celebrate the completion of the harvest. He spoke of Isaiah 58:7 ("Share your bread with the hungry, and bring the poor and homeless into your house . . .") and asked whether it was not customary to invite the poor to such feasts of thanksgiving. Jesus expressed this by saying: "Where are the poor?" Then he sent his disciples out to bring in the poor from the streets.

Sunday, August 27, A.D. 30 (Elul 9) This morning, Jesus healed many people in Gennabris. In the afternoon, he and his disciples set off in a southerly direction and stayed overnight in an empty shed not far from Ulama.

MAP 20: *Journeys in Perea and Galaaditis*

Monday, August 28, A.D. *30 (Elul 10)* Continuing southward, Jesus and the disciples arrived around two o'clock this afternoon at Abel-Mehola. Here he healed many sick people. This was frowned upon by the disapproving Pharisees.

Tuesday, August 29, A.D. *30 (Elul 11)* Jesus and his disciples visited a school for orphans in Abel-Mehola, where he told the children the story of Job as it actually took place. (According to Anne Catherine, Job was Abraham's great-great-great-grandfather.) Jesus spent the whole day with the children and took an evening walk with them.

Wednesday, August 30, A.D. *30 (Elul 12)* This morning, Jesus taught in the synagogue. Here some Pharisees and Sadducees disputed with him. He also healed a man whose arms and hands were paralysed. During the afternoon and evening, Jesus performed more cures.

Thursday, August 31, A.D. *30 (Elul 13)* After revisiting the children at the school in Abel-Mehola, Jesus and his disciples made their way to Bezech.

Friday, September 1, A.D. *30 (Elul 14)* Many disciples from Ainon and Jerusalem met up with Jesus in Bezech. Altogether about thirty disciples were present. In the morning, Jesus taught on a hill in the middle of Bezech and, later in the day, he healed many people. That evening, he taught in the synagogue as the Sabbath began.

Saturday, September 2, A.D. *30 (Elul 15)* Jesus taught in the synagogue until the close of the Sabbath. That evening he healed many who were sick, and then dined with his disciples.

Sunday, September 3, A.D. *30 (Elul 16)* Jesus and the disciples made their way to the Jordan, which they crossed with the ferry near Salem. They stayed the night in tents between Succoth and Ainon.

Monday, September 4, A.D. *30 (Elul 17)* This morning, in Ainon, Jesus healed many people. Then, toward midday, he went to the place of baptism, where he taught and also prepared those waiting to be baptized. Around three o'clock in the afternoon he returned to Ainon and went to the home of Mara the Suphanite, to exorcise her (she was possessed) and to forgive her sins. After, at a festive meal held in honor of Jesus, Mara the Suphanite and her three children entered and presented Jesus with costly spices.

Tuesday, September 5, A.D. 30 (Elul 18) Jesus instructed Andrew, James, and John and some other disciples to remain at Ainon to baptize those who came there for baptism. Meanwhile, accompanied by about twelve disciples, Jesus went to Kamon. Here he taught and healed. Then he crossed the Jabbok where the patriarch Jacob had once been (Genesis 32:2), and entered the town of Mahanaim. Here he held a discourse on Jacob. Afterward, he went on to Ramoth-Galaad where, that evening, he taught in the synagogue on commemorating the sacrifice of Jephthah's daughter (Judges 11:29–40).

Wednesday, September 6, A.D. 30 (Elul 19) Jesus attended the festival to commemorate the sacrifice of Jephthah's daughter. This lasted until late afternoon. That evening, Jesus healed many sick people and taught in the synagogue about the sale of Joseph by his brothers.

Thursday, September 7, A.D. 30 (Elul 20) This morning Jesus preached in the non-Jewish quarter of Ainon. Several heathens immediately decided to become baptized. In the afternoon, Jesus taught again in the synagogue. Then, following a meal with some Levites, Jesus left the town and went to an inn near the town of Arga.

Friday, September 8, A.D. 30 (Elul 21) Jesus taught in the synagogue at Arga today and again this evening at the beginning of the Sabbath. He spoke of the slaying of Zimri and the Midianite woman by Phinehas the grandson of Aaron (Numbers 25:6–15).

Saturday, September 9, A.D. 30 (Elul 22) Jesus taught morning and afternoon in the synagogue. During the day, he met with a group of pagans, who asked to be baptized.

Sunday, September 10, A.D. 30 (Elul 23) Jesus gave instruction to the heathens. They were then baptized by Saturnin and Judas Barsabbas. In the afternoon, Jesus went to the little town of Azo, where, in the evening—with the start of Elul 24—a festival was celebrated to commemorate Gideon's victory over the Midianites. It was from Azo that Gideon set out with three hundred men to do battle (Judges 7:7–25). In the synagogue, Jesus spoke of this historical event.

Monday, September 11, A.D. 30 (Elul 24) This morning Jesus took part in a gathering to commemorate Gideon's victory. In the afternoon, another gathering was held, during which Jesus told the parable of the prodigal son to a group of poor people there.

Tuesday, September 12, A.D. 30 (Elul 25) After teaching in the synagogue and healing many people, Jesus and the disciples—together with about thirty people from Azo—walked to a small fishing lake. Jesus and the disciples then made their way to the town of Ephron.

Wednesday, September 13, A.D. 30 (Elul 26) In Ephron, there were Levites who belonged to an ancient sect called Rechabites. Jesus reproached them for the severity of their interpretation of the Law, and instructed the people not to heed their harsh interpretation.

Thursday, September 14, A.D. 30 (Elul 27) After healing the sick of Ephron, Jesus and the disciples made their way to Betharamphtha.

Friday, September 15, A.D. 30 (Elul 28) At Betharamphtha, there was a castle. Here Abigail, the divorced wife of the tetrarch Philip, lived with her five daughters. The people of Betharamphtha held Abigail in high esteem for her goodness and benevolence. Here, in Betharamphtha, Jesus too was received hospitably by the people. That evening, with the onset of the Sabbath, he taught in the synagogue.

Saturday, September 16, A.D. 30 (Elul 29) Jesus taught again in the synagogue this morning, and then cured many sick people. Abigail, having heard of Jesus' presence in the town, sent gifts from her castle so that the townspeople could all the more honorably welcome Jesus and his disciples. That evening, trumpets were blown from the roof of the synagogue to mark the start of Tishri 1, signifying the beginning of the civil year (the religious year began with Nisan1).

TISHRI (30 days): September 16/17 to October 15/16, A.D. 30
Tishri New Moon: September 16 at 8:00 A.M. Jerusalem time

Sunday, September 17, AD 30 (Tishri 1) The festival celebrating the start of the civil year continued today. At an open place in the town, Jesus and his disciples met Abigail, accompanied by her five daughters. She cast herself down at Jesus' feet and invited him to an entertainment she had arranged in his honor. Jesus accepted the invitation. After the meal, he talked with Abigail in the portico of her castle. She was full of anxiety because of her tragic destiny and hoped for pardon for her wrongdoings. Jesus comforted her, saying her sins would be forgiven.

Monday, September 18, A.D. 30 (Tishri 2) This morning, after healing many people, Jesus spoke in the synagogue. He taught about Isaac's sacrifice (Genesis 22), which was associated with the two-day New Year festival at the start of the month of Tishri. Leaving Betharamphtha, Jesus and his disciples then proceeded to Abila, where he taught at an open place where there was a pillar erected in memory of Elijah.

Tuesday, September 19, A.D. 30 (Tishri 3) This morning Jesus was conducted by Levites to a home for the blind and the deaf-and-dumb, whom he healed, causing great jubilation in Abila. Afterward, he taught again from the pillar of Elijah and spoke about the prophet's life.

Wednesday, September 20, A.D. 30 (Tishri 4) After teaching in the synagogue and healing a number of people, Jesus and his disciples—accompanied by some Levites and Rechabites and other inhabitants of the town—went for a walk, passing through some vineyards on the way. As they walked, Jesus interpreted several passages from the prophets concerning the Messiah.

Thursday, September 21, A.D. 30 (Tishri 5) Again Jesus taught in the synagogue and healed. Then he and the disciples made their way to Gadara, arriving there that evening.

Friday, September 22, A.D. 30 (Tishri 6) Jesus taught in the synagogue at Gadara for much of the day. As the Sabbath began that evening, he taught about the renewal of God's covenant through Moses (Deuteronomy 29ff.).

Saturday, September 23, A.D. 30 (Tishri 7) This morning, after healing the sick, Jesus taught again in the synagogue. In the afternoon, at the request of a pagan priestess whose child had just died, he went to her house in the pagan quarter of the town and raised the child from the dead. Then he healed many other pagan children, who were all suffering because of their parents' worship of Moloch. Jesus exorcised the priestess and then revealed to the assembled people the nature of their idolatry. The people believed; they determined to renounce the worship of Moloch and turn to the God of Israel. That evening, with the start of Tishri 8, there began a day of fasting in penance for the worship in ancient days of the golden calf (this fast-day normally fell on Tishri 7, but was shifted to Tishri 8 this year as Tishri 7 coincided with the Sabbath).

Sunday, September 24, A.D. 30 (Tishri 8) After further teaching and healing this morning in Gadara, Jesus and his disciples left, traveling southward toward Dion. They stayed overnight at an inn some distance north of the town.

Monday, September 25, A.D. 30 (Tishri 9) Jesus and the disciples arrived at Dion about ten o'clock this morning. He began immediately to heal the sick, continuing to do so for much of the afternoon. Great jubilation broke out on account of these healings. The people sang: "Blessed is he who considers the poor . . ." (Psalm 41). Jesus and those with him then went to the synagogue and thanked God. Afterward, they ate a meal together. That evening, everyone returned to the synagogue in mourning garments for the great Feast of Atonement then starting (Tishri 10).

Tuesday, September 26, A.D. 30 (Tishri 10) Today, for the Feast of Atonement, Jesus taught in the synagogue regarding penance. He spoke against those who practiced only bodily purification and did not restrain those desires of the soul that were evil.

Wednesday, September 27, A.D. 30 (Tishri 11) This morning, after teaching in the synagogue, Jesus and the disciples left Dion. They went southward to Jogbeha, where members of the Karaites sect, descended from Jethro, the father-in-law of Moses, lived. They led a plain, simple life. Because they rejected all oral traditions relating to the Law, the Karaites were the sworn enemies of the Pharisees. They lived in expectation of the coming of the Messiah, and regarded Jesus as a prophet. They received Jesus with great reverence. During his instruction, Jesus commended them for their charitable way of life.

Thursday, September 28, A.D. 30 (Tishri 12) Today Jesus taught in Jogbeha, and healed many sick people. He and the disciples then went to Succoth, where they stayed overnight.

Map 21: Travels in Samaria

Friday, September 29, A.D. 30 (Tishri 13) Jesus and his disciples proceeded from Succoth to Ainon, where Mara the Suphanite, whom he had healed on Elul 17, had prepared a festive welcome for him. After conversing with Mara at her home, Jesus went to the place of baptism and met with Andrew, James, and John, who had stayed there baptizing since Elul 18. Jesus addressed the assembled people. Among those present were Lazarus, Joseph of Arimathea, and some other disciples from Jerusalem, who had traveled there for the special Sabbath preceding the Feast of Tabernacles. That evening, as the Sabbath began, Jesus taught in the synagogue at Ainon. Afterward, there was a banquet at the public hall arranged by Mara the Suphanite in honor of Jesus.

Saturday, September 30, A.D. 30 (Tishri 14) Jesus taught in the synagogue, healed many of the sick, and then told the parable of the prodigal son (Luke 15:11–32). That evening, after the close of the Sabbath, everyone gathered at a place on the outskirts of the town. Here tabernacles had been erected, for it was the commencement of the Feast of Tabernacles (Tishri 15), which was to last for seven days (Leviticus 23:33–43). The meal lasted until late that night. Jesus went from table to table instructing the guests.

Sunday, October 1, A.D. 30 (Tishri 15) After teaching and healing this morning in Ainon, Jesus and the disciples made their way slowly to Succoth, arriving there around five in the afternoon. In the large synagogue at Succoth an adulteress pressed through the crowd listening to Jesus and begged for mercy. She confessed her shame. Jesus said: "Your sins are forgiven! Arise, child of God!" Then he reconciled her with her husband.

Monday, October 2, A.D. 30 (Tishri 16) This morning Jesus returned from Succoth to the place of baptism near Ainon, where he healed the sick. He received the confessions of many people, granting them absolution from their sins.

Tuesday, October 3, A.D. 30 (Tishri 17) This morning, after talking with Mara at her house in Ainon, Jesus left the town and proceeded to the shepherds' settlement called Akrabis.

Wednesday, October 4, A.D. 30 (Tishri 18) Jesus walked around Akrabis, pausing at each entrance gate, where tabernacles had been erected. He healed many people as he went. After a festive meal, he and the disciples went on to Shiloh, arriving there toward evening. He taught in the open air from a teacher's chair carved from stone.

Thursday, October 5, A.D. 30 (Tishri 19) This morning Jesus taught again in Shiloh from the stone teacher's chair. He spoke of God's mercy to the people of Israel, the destruction of the temple, and the present time of grace, whereby he made it quite clear that it was he himself who was to bring salvation.

Friday, October 6, A.D. 30 (Tishri 20) Jesus went this morning from Shiloh to Korea. There he healed the blind youth Manahem, who had the gift of prophecy. That evening, with the beginning of the Sabbath, he spoke in the synagogue about Noah, the ark, and the rainbow as the sign of God's mercy.

Saturday, October 7, A.D. 30 (Tishri 21) Jesus taught in the synagogue and healed many sick people. This evening, with the close of the Sabbath, the Feast of Tabernacles also drew to a close.

Sunday, October 8, A.D. 30 (Tishri 22) After visiting Manahem's parents, Jesus and about seven disciples went to Ophra. During the afternoon, Jesus visited several houses in Ophra and healed the sick. That evening, in the synagogue, a celebration took place in connection with the "day of joy" following on from the Feast of Tabernacles.

Monday, October 9, A.D. 30 (Tishri 23) In the synagogue Jesus spoke about Adam and Joshua. He taught concerning worldly cares and referred to the lilies of the field (Matthew 6:25–34). Then he spoke of Daniel and Job. That evening, he received a visit from a messenger of the pagan Cyrinus of Cyprus inviting Jesus to Cyprus.

Tuesday, October 10, A.D. 30 (Tishri 24) Today Jesus and the disciples left Ophra. On the way they visited some farms. They stayed overnight at a farmhouse where some shepherds were living.

Wednesday, October 11, A.D. 30 (Tishri 25) Jesus and the disciples continued on, arriving at the town of Salem early in the afternoon. After healing the sick, Jesus taught at the synagogue. He spoke of Melchizedek of Salem, and also of the prophet Malachi, who had once stayed there.

Thursday, October 12, A.D. 30 (Tishri 26) Jesus was a guest at a festive meal in his honor at one of the inns in Salem. Some Pharisees from the neighboring town of Aruma were present at the banquet, and they invited Jesus to Aruma for the Sabbath.

Friday, October 13, A.D. 30 (Tishri 27) Jesus and the disciples traveled to Aruma. That evening, with the onset of the Sabbath, he spoke at the synagogue about the sacred Hebrew language, Abraham's ancestors, and God's call to Abraham (Genesis 12).

Saturday, October 14, A.D. 30 (Tishri 28) Jesus taught again in the synagogue, and later visited a home for old people, whom he comforted and consoled. After a banquet given in his honor, he taught again that evening in the synagogue, where the festival of the consecration of Solomon's temple was being commemorated (1 Kings 8:65–66). He referred to the destruction of the temple, and that it would be rebuilt in three days.

Sunday, October 15, A.D. 30 (Tishri 29) This morning Jesus exchanged words with the Pharisees, who defended their adherence to outer customs and forms. Jesus pointed out to them that this was of no use because they had in fact lost the inner spirit of their religion. He and the disciples then proceeded to an inn near Thanat-Silo, which Lazarus had put at their disposal.

Monday, October 16, A.D. 30 (Tishri 30) This evening, with the New Moon festival celebrating the start of the month of Heshvan, Jesus taught in the synagogue at Thanat-Silo.

HESHVAN (30 days): October 16/17 to November 14/15, A.D. 30
Heshvan New Moon: October 15 at 6:45 P.M. Jerusalem time

Tuesday, October 17, A.D. 30 (Heshvan 1) Jesus healed the sick in Thanat-Silo and then went into the fields, which were being harvested. There he taught, again referring to unnecessary and exaggerated concern for the cares of life (Matthew 6:25–34).

Wednesday, October 18, A.D. 30 (Heshvan 2) This morning Jesus healed again in Thanat-Silo. He left the town around midday, proceeding on to Aser-Michmethat. That night he stayed with the family of Obed, who owned a large estate outside of the town.

Thursday, October 19, A.D. 30 (Heshvan 3) This morning about four hundred people gathered to hear Jesus on a grass terrace, near a well at the entrance to the town. Jesus spoke of his mission and also about baptism and repentance. He then prepared some of those in the audience for baptism. He spent much of the rest of the day with Obed, who had eighteen children, and who modeled his life after Job.

Friday, October 20, A.D. 30 (Heshvan 4) After confessing their sins to Jesus, a number of people were baptized by Saturnin and Judas Barsabbas. That evening, as the Sabbath began, Jesus taught in the synagogue about the miraculous deeds of the prophet Elisha.

Saturday, October 21, A.D. 30 (Heshvan 5) Jesus taught again in the synagogue and then healed the sick. At a meal held in his honor, he told the Pharisees the parable of the unjust steward (Luke 16:1–15). That evening, a fast-day began to commemorate the blinding of Zedekiah by Nebuchadnezzar (2 Kings 25:7).

Sunday, October 22, A.D. 30 (Heshvan 6) As usual on a fast-day, the people went for a walk. Jesus went, too, and taught as he walked. When he reached the town well, he said that the kingdom of God would pass from the Jews to the world. Later, he recounted the parable of the talents (Matthew 25:14–30) to Obed. Toward evening, he instructed a group of women, recounting the parable of the wise and foolish virgins (Matthew 25:1–13).

Monday, October 23, A.D. 30 (Heshvan 7) This morning Jesus left Aser-Michmethat, accompanied by five disciples. Teaching as he walked, Jesus arrived at Meroz during the afternoon. In the evening, he taught in the synagogue. Afterward, he and the disciples went to an inn belonging to Lazarus outside—to the east—of the town. There he was visited by Bartholomew,

Simon, Judas Thaddeus, and Philip. They stayed the night with him. Bartholomew and Simon recommended that Jesus accept Judas Iscariot as a disciple, whereupon Jesus sighed and appeared to be troubled.

Tuesday, October 24, A.D. 30 (Heshvan 8) This morning Jesus and the disciples went to the town well and healed the sick who had gathered there. Afterward, he healed some of those who were possessed and visited the leper-house to cure the lepers. That afternoon, Bartholomew and Simon introduced Judas Iscariot to Jesus. Jesus was friendly, but filled with indescribable sorrow. Judas bowed and said: "Master, I pray thee allow me to join your teaching." Jesus replied gently and with the prophetic words: "You may have a place among my disciples, unless you would prefer to leave it to another." Later, Jesus taught from a mountain located between Meroz and Atharot, for it had been announced to the people in both towns that he would teach here today.

Wednesday, October 25, A.D. 30 (Heshvan 9) Today Jesus continued his teaching from the mountain. Disputing with the Pharisees, he referred to the two commandments: Love of God and love of neighbor (Matthew 22:36–40). Later in the day, while healing the sick, he was approached by a rich pagan widow from Nain, called Lais. She sought Jesus' aid on behalf of her two daughters, Sabia and Athalia, both of whom had stayed in Nain because they were possessed. Jesus exorcised Lais' daughters from afar and told her to purify herself, saying: "The sins of the parents are on these children." After this healing, Manahem, the blind youth whose sight Jesus had restored in Korea, returned from delivering a message to Lazarus in Bethany and came to Jesus. Manahem was accompanied by the nephews of Joseph of Arimathea, Aram, and Themani.

Thursday, October 26, A.D. 30 (Heshvan 10) Jesus continued his teaching from the mountain. Later, as he was coming down from there, he was approached by Lais and her two healed daughters, whom she had brought from Nain. They cast themselves down at Jesus' feet and gave thanks. He commanded them to rise and told them that they now belonged to the community of his heavenly Father.

Friday, October 27, A.D. 30 (Heshvan 11) After visiting Simon of Iscariot, the uncle of Judas, in Iscariot, Jesus and the disciples made their way to Dothan for the Sabbath. Here he was joined by some other disciples, including Nathanael the bridegroom. That evening, he taught in the synagogue.

Saturday, October 28, A.D. 30 (Heshvan 12) This morning, after teaching in the synagogue, Jesus visited Issachar of Dothan, a rich man of about fifty, who had recently married his brother's widow, Salome, who was twenty-five years old. Issachar lay ill with dropsy, and Jesus healed him. That evening, Issachar and Salome held a banquet at their home for Jesus and the disciples. Thomas, the future disciple, who was well known to Issachar, attended the banquet. Bartholomew, Judas Iscariot, and James the Lesser were also present.

Sunday, October 29, A.D. 30 (Heshvan 13) This morning, while Jesus was walking with the disciples, Thomas asked Jesus if he could become a disciple. Then two of John the Baptist's disciples approached him. They had been sent by John, who was in prison at Machaerus (see Matthew 11:2–6 and Luke 7:18–23). After teaching again in the synagogue, Jesus and the disciples left Dothan and went to stay the night at an inn near Sunem.

Monday, October 30, A.D. 30 (Heshvan 14) Jesus did not enter Sunem but, passing by Endor, went on to an inn in the valley between Abez and Mount Gilboa. Here he was met by a group of about fifteen elderly people, family relatives. Jesus spoke much with these pious, simple-hearted people, who expressed their concern on account of the Pharisees' hostility toward Jesus.

Tuesday, October 31, A.D. 30 (Heshvan 15) Jesus began the morning talking with his elderly relatives, then he traveled with his disciples to Abez. Here, after teaching at the well (Saul's well) east of the town, Jesus blessed a number of children, and then taught in the synagogue.

Wednesday, November 1, A.D. 30 (Heshvan 16) Jesus taught again at Saul's well. That afternoon, he and the disciples walked to Dabrath, where they stayed overnight at an inn outside town.

MAP 22: *Travels in Southern Galilee*

Thursday, November 2, A.D. 30 (Heshvan 17) In Dabrath, Jesus visited his relative Jesse, who requested that his two sons—Kaleb and Aaron—be taken as disciples. Later, Jesus healed the sick and taught in the synagogue.

Friday, November 3, A.D. 30 (Heshvan 18) Jesus was teaching before the synagogue when he was approached by a rich widow—Noemi of Dabrath—who had deceived her husband by committing adultery, causing him to die of grief. She cast herself at Jesus' feet and confessed her sins. Jesus said: "Arise! Your sins are forgiven!" With the start of the Sabbath, Jesus entered the synagogue and taught there. He stayed overnight in the house of Jesse.

Saturday, November 4, A.D. 30 (Heshvan 19) This morning, Jesus visited the school in Dabrath. He addressed the children and blessed them. At the close of the Sabbath he taught again in the synagogue, speaking of the patriarchs Isaac and Jacob and referring to the prophet Malachi's prophecy (1:11). That night, back at Jesse's house, he was visited by Cyrinus of Cyprus and talked with him until dawn.

Sunday, November 5, A.D. 30 (Heshvan 20) Jesus and the disciples went to Gischala, a stronghold garrisoned by Roman soldiers, whom Herod had to pay for. Jesus gave instruction to his disciples in which he mentioned three "men of zeal" from Gischala. The first was the founder of the Sadducees, who had lived over two hundred years before Christ. The second was John of Gischala, who subsequently fomented an uprising in Galilee and actively resisted the Romans at the siege of Jerusalem. The third was Saul, who later became the apostle Paul, now living with his parents at Tarsus, but who had been born in Gischala.

Monday, November 6, A.D. 30 (Heshvan 21) Today a Roman officer—named Achias—who was living in the house vacated by Saul and his parents, came to Jesus, bowed down before him, and said: "Master, reject not your servant! Have pity on my little son lying sick at home!" After exchanging a few words, Jesus said: "Your faith has saved you!" Jesus then entered the house where Saul had been born and Achias now lived and healed his son who was dumb and paralyzed. Afterward, he and the disciples left Gischala and went on to Gabara, where Jesus taught in the synagogue.

Tuesday, November 7, A.D. 30 (Heshvan 22) Today Jesus prepared for the Sermon on the Mount that he would deliver the following day. He sent out his disciples to the neighboring places to make it known that he would give instruction on the mountain beyond Gabara. Some sixty disciples, friends, and relatives of Jesus came to Gabara in expectation of this occasion.

Among them was Mary Magdalene, who had been persuaded to come by her sister Martha.

Wednesday, November 8, A.D. 30 (Heshvan 23) Around ten o'clock Jesus arrived at the mountain, where there was a teacher's chair. He delivered a powerful discourse, culminating with the words: "Come! Come to me, all who are weary and laden with guilt! Come to me, O sinners! Do penance, believe, and share the kingdom with me!" At these words, Mary Magdalene was deeply moved inwardly, and Jesus, perceiving her agitation, addressed his hearers with some words of consolation—words actually meant for Mary Magdalene—and she was converted. That evening, a Pharisee named Simon Zabulon invited Jesus to a banquet. During the meal, Mary Magdalene entered the room carrying a flask of ointment, with which she anointed Jesus' head. (This scene and the ensuing dispute with Simon Zabulon is described in Luke 7:36–50).

Thursday, November 9, A.D. 30 (Heshvan 24) Jesus and his disciples went to the estate of Zorobabel, the high-ranking official of Capernaum, whose son Jesus had healed on Ab 15.

Friday, November 10, A.D. 30 (Heshvan 25) This morning, in Capernaum, Jesus was approached by the Roman centurion Cornelius, whose servant was desperately ill. Jesus praised Cornelius for his faith and healed the servant from afar (Matthew 8:5–13 and Luke 7:1–10). Next, Jesus went to a leper's hut and healed the leper, as described in Mark 1:40–45. Then, leaving the leper's hut, he went to an inn in the Valley of the Doves, south of Capernaum, where he met Maroni, the widow of Nain, who begged him to come and heal her twelve-year-old son. In the afternoon, he returned to Capernaum and taught in the synagogue as the Sabbath began. Suddenly a man who was possessed ran in and caused a great commotion. Jesus healed him (Mark 1:21–28). Seeing this, the Pharisees—utterly astounded—gave up their plan to lay hands on Jesus.

Saturday, November 11, A.D. 30 (Heshvan 26) Today Jesus taught in parables (Matthew 13:18–30, 34–43). After the close of the Sabbath, the Pharisees began to dispute with him in the forecourt of the synagogue. They accused him of blasphemy for having forgiven Mary Magdalene her sins three days before at the meal arranged by the Pharisee Simon Zabulon. Their accusations caused a great uproar, during which Jesus left quietly. He went to his mother's house and talked with her and the other women there.

Sunday, November 12, A.D. *30 (Heshvan 27)* Jesus and his disciples walked in the direction of Nain. On the way, Jesus taught how to distinguish true teachers from false (Matthew 7:15–20). That night, he stayed with his disciples at a shepherd's inn three or four hours from Nain.

Monday, November 13, A.D. *30 (Heshvan 28)* At around nine in the morning, as Jesus and the disciples were approaching Nain, they met a funeral procession emerging from the city gate. Jesus commanded the coffin bearers to stand still and set the coffin down. He raised his eyes to heaven and spoke the words recorded in Matthew 11:25–30. There then occurred the miraculous raising from the dead of the youth of Nain—the twelve-year-old Martialis, son of the widow Maroni—described in Luke 7:11–17.

Tuesday, November 14, A.D. *30 (Heshvan 29)* This morning, news of the miracle spread rapidly and many sick people came to be healed. Jesus also spoke of the sanctity of marriage, and helped to reconcile several couples whose wives were seeking divorce from their husbands. Around midday, Jesus left Nain, accompanied by his disciples, and went to Megiddo, where he stayed the night at an inn on the outskirts of the town.

Wednesday, November 15, A.D. *30 (Heshvan 30)* During the afternoon Jesus wandered in the fields east of Megiddo teaching the workers who were busy sowing seeds. He taught them in parables. As he was thus engaged, some disciples of John the Baptist arrived and accompanied Jesus into Megiddo. Many sick people were gathered there: lame, blind, dumb, deaf, and others. Jesus cured them all and then addressed John's disciples with the words in Matthew 11:2–6 (also Luke 7:18–23). After John's disciples had left, Jesus spoke to those who remained (Matthew 11:7–15; also Luke 7:24–29). That evening, the New Moon festival to celebrate the commencement of the month of Kislev took place.

KISLEV (30 days): November 15/16 to December 14/15, A.D. *30*
Kislev New Moon: November 14 at 5:30 A.M. *Jerusalem time.*

Thursday, November 16, A.D. *30 (Kislev 1)* Today, Jesus and the disciples left Megiddo in the direction of Mount Tabor. Jesus taught as they went. Toward evening, they arrived at a small shepherds' place at the foot of the northwest side of the mountain. Here Jesus taught. They all stayed there overnight.

Friday, November 17, A.D. 30 (Kislev 2) This morning Jesus went to the home of a leper, whom he healed. Then Jesus and his disciples walked in the direction of Capernaum, arriving there shortly after the beginning of the Sabbath. They went to the synagogue, where Jesus taught. As he was leaving the synagogue, two lepers came to him and—trembling—sank down on their knees before him. Jesus laid his hands upon them, breathed upon the face of each, and said: "Your sins are forgiven!" The Pharisees protested loudly because he had healed on the Sabbath and questioned by what right he was able to forgive sins. Without uttering a word, Jesus passed through their midst. He went to his mother's house. After consoling his mother and the other women there, Jesus went out and spent the night in prayer.

Saturday, November 18, A.D. 30 (Kislev 3) After healing some people at Peter's house, Jesus instructed some fifty people waiting to be baptized. These were then baptized by Andrew and Saturnin. Later, Jesus went to the synagogue in Capernaum and healed a number of sick people who were waiting outside. Here he was approached by Jairus, the chief of the synagogue. Jairus pleaded with Jesus to come and heal his daughter, Salome, who was on the point of death (Mark 5:21–24). Jesus agreed to go with Jairus, but on the way a messenger came to relate the news that Salome was already dead. Jesus, in his mercy, performed the miracle of raising Salome from the dead. Because of her parents' attitude toward Jesus, which the girl imitated, this led again to her illness and death on Kislev 16/17 (See second raising of Salome from the dead on this date).

MAP 23: *The Sermons on the Mount*

Sunday, November 19, A.D. 30 (Kislev 4) After being present for the baptism of a number of people this morning, Jesus taught from the banks of the Sea of Galilee. As the throng of people grew, Jesus and some of his disciples climbed aboard a ship placed at his disposal, and Jesus taught from there. The other disciples boarded Peter's ship. This then hooked up Jesus' ship, towing it across the lake while Jesus continued to teach on the way. Around four o'clock that afternoon they reached the eastern shore and went to a nearby place of tax collectors where Matthew (then called Levi) lived. He cast himself down before Jesus. Jesus said: "Levi (Matthew), arise, and follow me!" (Matthew 9:9). That night, Jesus stayed at an inn in the town of Bethsaida-Julias.

Monday, November 20, A.D. 30 (Kislev 5) Today Jesus and the disciples visited Matthew at his house and welcomed him as a disciple. Judas Thaddeus, Simon, James the Lesser, and Joses Barsabbas were especially overjoyed at this—Matthew was their stepbrother—and embraced him warmly. Jesus spoke with Matthew's wife and blessed the children. Then Matthew knelt before him, and Jesus—laying his hand upon him—blessed him and gave him the name Matthew (he had been called Levi before). Following this, there was a banquet in Matthew's home at which a large number of tax collectors and Pharisees were present, as described in Luke 5:29-39. Jesus stayed overnight at Matthew's house, while the disciples slept on their boats.

Tuesday, November 21, A.D. 30 (Kislev 6) This morning, from the shore of the Sea of Galilee, Jesus called to Peter and Andrew, who were casting a net into the lake, "Come and follow me, I will make you fishers of men." A little further down the shore he called also to the brothers James and John (Matthew 4:18-22). Peter and Andrew baptized today, and also Saturnin. That evening, as crowds thronged around him, Jesus and the future twelve apostles boarded Peter's boat, and Jesus gave instructions to go over to the other side of the lake in the direction of Tiberius (Matthew 8:18). In the middle of the lake a great storm arose, which Jesus calmed (Matthew 8:23-27; Luke 8:22-25). Then he commanded the disciples to sail back in the direction from which they had come, toward Chorazin (as the neighborhood was called on account of the town Great Chorazin).

Wednesday, November 22, A.D.30 (Kislev 7) Jesus taught today from the side of a mountain about one hour southwest of Great Chorazin. He healed many people and blessed the children who were brought to him. Many Gentiles were present, and all those seeking baptism were baptized. That evening, in Matthew's house, Jesus told the disciples the parable of the hidden treasure (Matthew 13:44), which he interpreted as the Gentiles' longing for salvation.

Thursday, November 23, A.D. 30 (Kislev 8) After teaching and healing on the shore of the lake, Jesus and the twelve sailed back to Bethsaida, arriving there around four o'clock. They were met by his mother, accompanied by the widow of Nain (Maroni) and her son Martialis.

Friday, November 24, A.D. 30 (Kislev 9) Jesus' fame had spread, so that large crowds flocked to Capernaum hoping to see him. As a result, about twelve thousand people were now gathered there. As the Sabbath began, Jesus taught in the synagogue, and healed a possessed man who had been brought there.

Saturday, November 25, A.D. 30 (Kislev 10) Mary Cleophas lay desperately ill at Peter's house. After teaching at the synagogue in Capernaum, Jesus went to Peter's house and healed her.

Sunday, November 26, A.D. 30 (Kislev 11) After he and the disciples had distributed gifts and alms to the poor, Jesus taught on the shore of the lake. As the crowd grew very large, he and the disciples boarded a boat moored close by. From there, Jesus continued to teach the crowds on the shore. A scribe—Saraseth of Nazareth—came up and declared his readiness to follow him. Jesus replied: "Foxes have holes, and birds of the air have nests; but the Son of man has nowhere to lay his head" (Matthew 8:19–20). As evening approached, Jesus instructed Peter to row his boat out upon the lake and to cast out the nets. A great shoal of fish filled them (Luke 5:4–5) so that it was not until the early hours of the following morning, between three and four o'clock, that Peter and his helpers were able to land the fish. Jesus was waiting on the shore, where the exchange of words given in Luke 5:6–10 took place.

Monday, November 27, A.D. 30 (Kislev 12) Today Jesus went up a mountainside with Saturnin and Amandor. He taught them about prayer. Meanwhile the disciples, selling the fish in Capernaum and elsewhere, recounted the miracle of the huge shoal of fish.

Tuesday, November 28, A.D. 30 (Kislev 13) Jesus and the disciples sailed across the Sea of Galilee. After disembarking, they went to a mountain near Bethsaida-Julias, where many people were gathered to hear Jesus teach. Here began the "Sermon on the Mount" referred to in Matthew 5 and Luke 6. This sermon lasted some fourteen days, but its conclusion was not delivered until three months later, on Nisan 2. To begin with, Jesus spoke of the first beatitude (Matthew 5:3). The instruction lasted the whole day.

Wednesday, November 29, A.D. 30 (Kislev 14) Today Jesus began to teach concerning the second beatitude (Matthew 5:4). Five holy women were present, including the Holy Virgin Mary, Mary Cleophas, and Maroni of Nain, and also all the twelve disciples who later became apostles. After the sermon, Jesus taught the disciples as indicated in Matthew 5:14–20.

Thursday, November 30, A.D. 30 (Kislev 15) Jesus continued to teach the second beatitude. He also explained many teachings of the prophets.

Friday, December 1, A.D. 30 (Kislev 16) Jesus preached today concerning the third beatitude. But because the Sabbath was approaching, he broke off early and sailed back toward Capernaum. There he taught near the south gate, in a house that Peter had rented. It was here that the healing of the paralytic described in Mark 2:1–2, Luke 5:17–26, and Matthew 9:1–9 occurred. After this, Jesus went to the synagogue, where he taught—this time without disruption. Jairus, whose daughter (Salome) Jesus had raised from the dead on Kislev 3, was there. As Jesus left, Jairus approached him to ask help for Salome, who was again close to death. Jesus agreed to go. On their way, the message of Salome's death reached them. But they continued on. Then occurred the healing of the widow Enue from Caesarea Philippi, who had been suffering from a flow of blood for twelve years (Matthew 9:20–22, Mark 5:25–34, and Luke 8:43–48). Reaching Jairus' home Jesus then repeated the raising of Salome from the dead (Matthew 9:23–25, Mark 5:35–43, and Luke 8:49–56). Afterward, Jesus left the house. On his way through the streets of Capernaum he was approached by two blind men, whom he healed (Matthew 9:27–30). Following this, Jesus healed Joas the Pharisee, who was possessed (Matthew 9:32–34).

Saturday, December 2, A.D. 30 (Kislev 17) Today Jesus visited the centurion Cornelius. Then he went to Jairus' house and cautioned Salome to follow the word of God. At the close of the Sabbath, he taught in the synagogue. The Pharisees left early, and Jesus continued teaching the disciples, as indicated in Matthew 5:27–37. The Pharisees then returned with a man whose hand was withered, whom Jesus healed.

Sunday, December 3, A.D. 30 (Kislev 18) Jesus taught again in the house near the south gate of Capernaum and spoke of the beatitudes. Among the hearers was Lea, the sister-in-law of Enue, whom he had healed two days before. As Jesus was saying the sixth beatitude, "Blessed are the pure in heart, for they shall see God", Mary and four holy women entered the room. Lea called out: "Blessed is the womb that bore you, and the breasts that you sucked!" Jesus replied: "Blessed rather are those who hear the word of God and keep it!" (Luke 11:27–28). Later, Jesus taught again from a boat at the shore of the lake. It was here that he spoke the words in Luke 9:59–62. He then sailed across to the region of Great Chorazin.

Monday, December 4, A.D. 30 (Kislev 19) Today Jesus continued the Sermon on the Mount near Bethsaida-Julias. He spoke on the fourth beatitude. Afterward, he went with the twelve to a place on the east shore of the lake. There he gave the twelve authority to cast out unclean spirits (Matthew 10:1–4). Jesus then sailed with the twelve and about five other disciples to Magdala, where he exorcised some people who were possessed. Peter, Andrew, James, and John also cast out unclean spirits. Jesus and the disciples then spent the night on board the boat.

Tuesday, December 5, A.D. 30 (Kislev 20) On an incline east of Magdala, Jesus healed two possessed youths from Gergesa. Later, he and the disciples boarded their boat and sailed out upon the lake, where they spent the night.

Wednesday, December 6, A.D. 30 (Kislev 21) Today there occurred the healing of the two possessed men from Gergesa whose demons Jesus drove out into a great herd of swine, which then plunged down into the lake (Mark 5:1–20).

Thursday, December 7, A.D. 30 (Kislev 22) Jesus taught and healed for much of the day. Then he instructed the disciples to sail back to Bethsaida, while he withdrew into the hills alone to pray. That night, the disciples saw Jesus walking across the water toward them. (This was not the walking on the water described in Matthew 14:22–33, which took place later, on Shebat 16/17).

Friday, December 8, A.D. 30 (Kislev 23) Soon after Jesus and the disciples landed at Bethsaida, two blind men approached him. Jesus healed them. The people knew that Jesus had come for the Sabbath. Indeed, so many came to him that he did not have time even to eat (Mark 3:20–21). Not far from Capernaum, a person who was blind and dumb and filled with demons was brought to Jesus. Jesus healed him, evoking the crowd's astonishment (Matthew 12:22–23). But the Pharisees said that Jesus drove out demons with the help of the devil (Matthew 12:24). That evening, as the Sabbath began, Jesus taught undisturbed in the synagogue, answering the Pharisees' accusation with the words reported in Matthew 12:25–30. That night, again, he stayed at Peter's house.

Saturday, December 9, A.D. *30 (Kislev 24)* While Jesus visited the homes of Jairus, Cornelius, and Zorobabel, the disciples baptized at Peter's house. Jesus then visited his mother, telling her that next day he would be departing. He also comforted Martha, who was deeply saddened by Mary Magdalene's relapse. Before the Sabbath ended, Jesus again taught the beatitude: "Blessed are the poor in spirit." At the end of the Sabbath, he returned to the synagogue, inveighing against the Pharisees' teaching that he drove out devils with the help of devils (Matthew 12:31–37).

Sunday, December 10, A.D. *30 (Kislev 25)* Today there occurred—for the first time—the sending out of the disciples. At about ten o'clock in the morning, with the twelve and about thirty other disciples, Jesus left Capernaum and went north in the direction of Saphet and Hanathon, accompanied by a large crowd. Around three in the afternoon, they approached Hanathon. Here Jesus and the disciples climbed a mountain used in former times by the prophets. Jesus had taught there less than one year ago, on Tebeth 12. This time, however, the crowd did not go up the mountain. On the mountain, Jesus addressed the disciples, giving them instructions and sending them out into the world with the words found in Matthew 9:36–10:16. Each of the twelve had a small flask of oil, and Jesus taught them how to use it for anointing and also for healing. Afterward, the disciples knelt in a circle around Jesus, and he prayed and laid his hands upon the head of each of the twelve. Then he blessed the remaining disciples. After embracing one another, the disciples set off, having received indications from Jesus as to where they should go and when they should return to him. Peter, James the Lesser, John, Philip, Thomas, Judas, and twelve other disciples remained with him. They all came down the mountain together. At the bottom, they met up with a crowd of people returning home from Capernaum. That night Jesus stayed in Bethanat (Matthew 11:1).

MAP 24: *The Journey through Middle Galilee*

Monday, December 11, A.D. *30 (Kislev 26)* Jesus and the disciples who were with him journeyed to a place called Hucuca. Not far from there was a well, where Jesus healed a blind man and also several people who were lame. Afterward, he taught in the synagogue at Hucuca, speaking of the beatitudes and telling several parables. Jesus and the disciples then stayed the night with the chief elder of the synagogue.

Tuesday, December 12, A.D. 30 (Kislev 27) Jesus healed many sick people in Hucuca. In the synagogue, he spoke of the Messiah and of the significance of prayer. He said that the Messiah was already here; indeed, that they were living at the time of the Messiah, and that he, Jesus, was proclaiming the Messiah's teachings. He taught them devotion to God in spirit and in truth. The doctors of the synagogue asked Jesus, in a friendly way, whether he himself were the Messiah, the Son of God. Jesus did not answer directly. He said that they should not inquire into his origin but consider his teachings and actions. He spoke of the will of the Father (Matthew 12:50; John 5:30). That night, Jesus and the disciples stayed again at the house of the chief elder of the synagogue.

Wednesday, December 13, A.D. 30 (Kislev 28) This morning, again, Jesus taught in Hucuca. Around midday, he set off in the direction of Bethanat. Not far from the town, he was met by an old blind man, named Ctesiphon, led by two youths. Ctesiphon beseeched Jesus to have mercy on him. Jesus led him to a nearby fountain and commanded him to wash his eyes, after which Jesus anointed his forehead, temples, and eyes with oil. Ctesiphon's sight was immediately restored, and he gave profound thanks. Reaching Bethanat, Jesus taught at the synagogue, where he was well received by the people. There were no Pharisees in Bethanat.

Thursday, December 14, A.D. 30 (Kislev 29) Jesus and his disciples made their way north toward Galgala, where Jesus taught in the synagogue. He spoke of the prophet Malachi's prophecy concerning the coming of the Messiah and his forerunner, saying that the time of fulfillment had come. Afterward, Jesus went on to the town of Elkese, the birthplace of the prophet Nahum. Here he taught and cured eight lepers at the local leper house. Later, toward evening, he went to Bethan, and visited a niece of Elizabeth, who lived there with her husband and five children. They were Essenes. The sons later became disciples and were among the original seventy-two.

Friday, December 15, A.D. 30 (Kislev 30) This morning Jesus spoke in the synagogue about the second beatitude. In the afternoon, he taught again, and some Pharisees from Saphet came to hear him. They invited him to Saphet for the Sabbath, and Jesus accepted their invitation. He was received with much ceremony, and went straightaway to the synagogue, where a great crowd had assembled. It was not only the start of the Sabbath but also the close of the Feast of Lights; at the same time, it was the New Moon Festival denoting the beginning of the month of Tebeth.

TEBETH (29 days): December 15/16, A.D. *30, to January 12/13,* A.D. *31*
Tebeth New Moon: December 13, A.D. *30 at 4:30* P.M. *Jerusalem time*

Saturday, December 16, A.D. *30 (Tebeth 1)* This morning Jesus healed the sick, the deaf, the blind, the palsied, and the lame. Some Pharisees and Sadducees, visiting Saphet from Jerusalem, were scandalized at what they saw. They could not tolerate such a disturbance on the Sabbath and therefore began to dispute with Jesus, saying that he did not observe the Law. Jesus reduced them to silence by writing an account of their secret sins and transgressions on a wall in Old Hebrew, which only they could read. Then he asked them whether they wanted the writing to remain on the wall and become known publicly, or whether they would allow him to continue his work in peace, in which case they could efface the writing. Thoroughly frightened, they rubbed out the writing and went away to leave him to continue his work of healing the sick.

Sunday, December 17, A.D. *30 (Tebeth 2)* About midday, after healing people on the outskirts of Saphet, Jesus went on to Carianthaim. Before entering the town, he blessed a group of children. Then he made his way to the synagogue, healing the sick on the way. In the synagogue Jesus again taught the beatitudes and—addressing the Levites—interpreted a passage from 1 Kings 6:15–19.

Monday, December 18, A.D. *30 (Tebeth 3)* Jesus taught in the town park. Peter and James the Lesser, assisted by some other disciples, baptized about a hundred people. That evening, Jesus taught in the synagogue on the beatitudes.

Tuesday, December 19, A.D. *30 (Tebeth 4)* Today Jesus and his disciples went southward from Carianthaim, toward a place called Naasson, where there was a sugar-cane plantation, where Jesus paused to teach. Then he made his way to Abram, and taught there that evening. After teaching, he retired to an inn outside of the town.

Wednesday, December 20, A.D. *30 (Tebeth 5)* This morning the steward of the inn laid a dispute before Jesus and begged him for a decision. The dispute concerned a well, used by cattle from two different tribes. At issue was the question as to which tribe was really entitled to use the well. Jesus replied that each side should set an equal number of cattle free, and from whichever side the greater number went to the well of their own accord, this side should have the greater right to use of the well. He then employed this as an analogy for the living water that the Son of Man would give—that it would belong to those who most earnestly desired it. Then, around ten o'clock, Jesus went into Abram. On the way to the synagogue in Abram, Jesus cured many of the sick and crippled who were lying in the street. Reaching the synagogue, he taught there, but only in the Pharisees' synagogue, not in the Sadducees' synagogue. That evening, he went to an inn at the southern end of the town. This inn had been placed at the disposal of Jesus and the disciples by Lazarus.

Thursday, December 21, A.D. *30 (Tebeth 6)* All morning, Jesus taught and healed at the inn. He continued his healing activity and preached again at the synagogue, where the Pharisees treated him with respect.

Friday, December 22, A.D. *30 (Tebeth 7)* At a house in Abram, Jesus gave instruction on the meaning of the state of marriage to three couples, who were about to be married. He spoke of the Law, but now the situation was different, Jesus said. The time of fulfillment had come and grace should take the place of the Law. As Jesus delivered this instruction, not only were the three bridal couples present but also their parents, relatives, and some Pharisees. That evening, while he was teaching at the synagogue, the Pharisees attacked Jesus for his teaching concerning marriage.

Saturday, December 23, A.D. *30 (Tebeth 8)* After teaching again this morning in the synagogue in Abram, Jesus first visited a school for boys and youths and then a school for girls, where he taught and blessed the young people. At the service at the close of the Sabbath, Jesus spoke again and took leave of the people of Abram, who were deeply moved and begged him to stay. That evening, before returning to his inn, he took part in the wedding festivities.

Sunday, December 24, A.D. *30 (Tebeth 9)* Jesus went to Dothaim. Arriving at the outskirts of town, he was met by a group of people, including some

Pharisees. On the whole, however, he received a cool reception. That night, he stayed at an inn put at his disposal by Lazarus.

Monday, December 25, A.D. 30 (Tebeth 10) At the inn in Dothaim, Jesus met Martha and Lazarus and some other women and disciples from Jerusalem. Martha went from Dothaim to Magdalum, to try and persuade her sister Mary Magdalene to come and hear Jesus speak the next day on a hill near Azanoth.

Tuesday, December 26, A.D. 30 (Tebeth 11) Jesus made his way to the hill near Azanoth, where he had announced that he would teach. On the way, he met his mother and some of the holy women—among them were Anna Cleophas, Susanna Alpheus, Susanna of Jerusalem, Veronica, Joanna Chuza, Mary Mark, Maroni, Mara the Suphanite, and Dina the Samaritan. Martha had succeeded in persuading Mary Magdalene to come—it had taken great patience—and she arrived with great pomp and ceremony at the hill. After healing many sick people, Jesus spoke concerning the woe that would befall the towns of Chorazin, Bethsaida, and Capernaum (Matthew 11:20). Many children who were present then began calling out: "Jesus of Nazareth! Most holy prophet! Son of David! Son of God!" Many listeners, including Magdalene, were deeply moved by this. Jesus then spoke the words recorded in Matthew 12:43. Magdalene was truly shocked. Turning to different parts of the crowd, Jesus commanded the devils to depart from all those who sought freedom from their possession. As the devils departed, many, including Mary Magdalene, sunk to the ground. Three times in all, as she took in Jesus' powerful and moving words, Mary Magdalene fell unconscious to the ground. Coming to after the third occasion, she wept bitterly and asked Martha to bring her to join the holy women. Lazarus and Martha then brought her to the inn where the holy women were staying. Meanwhile, Jesus came down to Azanoth and went to the synagogue to teach. Mary Magdalene came too. He spoke again in her direction. As he looked at her, she fell unconscious again and another devil departed from her. Later, she cast herself at his feet, begging for salvation. Jesus comforted her, saying she should repent with all her heart, and that she should have faith and hope.

Wednesday, December 27, A.D. 30 (Tebeth 12) During the night, because of the great crowd in Azanoth, Jesus and his disciples left and made their way to Damna. In the morning, Jesus continued his teaching on a hillside near

Damna. Many from Azanoth, including Mary Magdalene and the holy women, came to hear him. First, he spoke of sin, then of God's mercy and the present time of grace. He besought his listeners to accept this grace. During this discourse, he looked directly at Mary Magdalene three times, and each time she fainted. After the third time, she appeared pale and weak, as if annihilated, and was scarcely recognizable any more. Her tears flowed incessantly. Jesus came to her to comfort her. She asked him: "Lord, is there still salvation for me?" Jesus forgave her her transgressions and promised to save her from further relapses. Then he blessed her and commended her to his mother. He told her to turn to the Virgin for advice and comfort. Then Jesus said to the holy women: "Mary Magdalene has been a great sinner, but for all future time she will be a model for all penitents." This was the second—and final—conversion of Mary Magdalene.

MAP 25: *The Third Journey to Hebron*

Thursday, December 28, A.D. 30 (Tebeth 13) After staying overnight at an inn near a cave known as "the cave of John," Jesus today went to the town of Gath-Hephter, where the prophet Jonah had been born. As he approached the synagogue, he found many mothers and children awaiting him. Jesus blessed them and then went on to heal the sick. In the synagogue, he taught concerning the patriarch Joseph and spoke also of the dignity and worth of children. After visiting some homes, he went to the town of Kisloth at the foot of Mount Tabor.

Friday, December 29, A.D. 30 (Tebeth 14) This morning Jesus received a visit from some Pharisees from Nazareth, who invited him to come there. Jesus and his disciples set off and arrived at Nazareth around midday. They went to the home of the widowed mother of his childhood friend Jonadab. Jesus then visited the sick and healed them. That evening, after teaching in the synagogue, Jesus ate at Jonadab's home and stayed there overnight.

Saturday, December 30, A.D. 30 (Tebeth 15) Today, Jesus taught in the synagogue twice, in the morning and again in the evening. In his evening sermon, he spoke of God as his heavenly Father and of the judgment that would come upon Jerusalem. He warned his disciples of the persecution they would receive, exhorting them to perseverance and faithfulness (Matthew 10:5-42). The Pharisees then began to create an uproar, calling out:

"Who is he? Who does he pretend to be? Where did he get his teaching? Is he not from here? His father was a carpenter, and his relatives, brothers, and sisters are all from here!" (Matthew 13:53-56). Jesus did not reply, but continued to instruct his disciples. After further insolent remarks from the Pharisees, Jesus spoke the words recorded in Matthew 13:57-58. That night, Jesus and the disciples ate with some Essenes, the same with whom he had been last time he was in Nazareth.

Sunday, December 31, A.D. 30 (Tebeth 16) Jesus left Nazareth around one o'clock in the morning. He went toward Mount Tabor. On the way, around dawn, he healed a number of lepers. Reaching Mount Tabor, he went up to the prophet's teaching chair and, after healing the sick, spoke of the first four beatitudes and recounted some parables. Around midday Jesus gathered the twelve and all the other disciples together. After giving them instructions, he sent them out in pairs (Matthew 9:36-38; 10:5-16). Peter, John, and a few other disciples remained with him. Together, they made their way to Sunem. They got there around sunset. Here Jesus healed a dumb, lame, epileptic boy. That evening, in Sunem, Jesus spoke alone with the boy's father, for it was his sin that had led to his son's condition. Jesus said that he should repent.

Monday, January 1, A.D. 31 (Tebeth 17) This morning, Jesus healed the brother and two sisters of the child whom he had cured yesterday. All three were feeble-minded. Laying his hands upon them, he restored them to normalcy. The three children were astounded, awaking as if from a dream. They had always believed that people wanted to kill them, and they were particularly afraid of fire. Jesus then taught on the street, and blessed and healed many children. Afterward, accompanied by Peter and John, he set off toward Samaria. They traveled quickly for the rest of the day and on through the whole night. On the way, Jesus told them that John the Baptist would soon meet his end, and that he wanted to go to Hebron to comfort the Baptist's relatives.

Tuesday, January 2, A.D. 31 (Tebeth 18) Early this morning Jesus met up with three Egyptian youths who had recently become disciples at Dothaim. After breakfasting with them, he taught the workers in the fields, speaking in parables. Jesus and the disciples then traveled on to Thanat-Silo.

Wednesday, January 3, A.D. 31 (Tebeth 19) This morning Jesus taught in the synagogue. Afterward, some people from Jerusalem told him of the sudden collapse of a wall and a tower in Jerusalem two days before. As a result, a crowd of laborers, including eighteen master workers sent by Herod, had been buried beneath the falling debris (Luke 13:4). Herod's workmen had engineered the accident to stir up the people against Pontius Pilate. But their plan had backfired, resulting in their own deaths. Jesus expressed his compassion for the innocent laborers, but added that the sin of the master workers was not greater than that of the Pharisees, Sadducees, and others who labored against the Kingdom of God. These later would also be buried one day under their own treacherous structures. After healing the sick, Jesus and the disciples made their way to Antipatris, where they stayed overnight in an inn. That night, during the festivities to celebrate Herod's birthday at Machaerus, John the Baptist was beheaded at the request of Herodias' daughter, Salome. After witnessing the spectacle of Salome dancing before him, Herod had said to her: "Ask what you will, and I will give it to you. Yes, I swear, even if you ask for half my kingdom, I shall give it to you." Salome hurriedly conferred with her mother, who told her to ask for the head of John the Baptist on a dish (Mark 6:17–29).

Thursday, January 4, A.D. *31 (Tebeth 20)* This morning Jesus entered the town of Antipatris, and visited the house of the chief magistrate, whose name was Ozias. Ozias had sent for Jesus because his daughter, Michol, about fourteen years old, was very sick. Jesus healed the girl, who was paralyzed, by anointing her with oil. She arose at Jesus's command, and she and her parents were filled with joy at this miracle. In the synagogue, Jesus told the parables of the good shepherd (John 10:1) and the wicked vine-dressers (Matthew 21:33). Afterward, he healed the sick and then set off for Ozensara, where he arrived late that evening.

Friday, January 5, A.D. *31 (Tebeth 21)* Jesus journeyed on from Ozensara to Bethoron, where he had already taught on Ab 5. This evening, at the start of the Sabbath, he taught in the synagogue. Afterward he healed the sick, but the Pharisees objected to his healing on the Sabbath, saying that the Sabbath belonged to God. Jesus replied: "I have no other time and no other measure than the will of the Father in heaven." Afterward, when Jesus ate a meal with the Pharisees, they reproached him for allowing women of bad repute to follow him. They meant Mary Magdalene, Dina the Samaritan, and Mara the Suphanite (Luke 8:1–3). Jesus answered: "If you knew me, you would speak differently. I have come out of compassion for sinners."

Saturday, January 6, A.D. 31 (Tebeth 22) Today Jesus taught and healed again on the Sabbath and had to put up with the Pharisees' objections.

Sunday, January 7, A.D. 31 (Tebeth 23) Journeying on, Jesus passed through Anathot, the birthplace of the prophet Jeremiah. He then went on to Bethany, where Mary Magdalene was now living. She had moved into the living quarters of her sister, Silent Mary, who had died on Nisan 18. Mary Magdalene set off to meet Jesus, before he arrived at Bethany. She cast herself down at his feet, shedding tears of repentance and gratitude. Jesus raised her up and spoke tenderly to her, saying that she should follow in the footsteps of her departed sister who, although she had not sinned, had done penance. At Bethany, Jesus met with his mother, who had traveled with some of the holy women to see him there. Jesus spoke with her privately about the death of John the Baptist—about which she already knew by inner revelation.

Monday, January 8, A.D. 31 (Tebeth 24) Jesus left Bethany and crossed the Mount of Olives. Weeping, he turned to those with him and said: "If this city (Jerusalem) does not accept salvation, its temple will be destroyed like this building that has tumbled down. A great number will be buried in the ruins." He referred to the recent catastrophe of the collapsing building as an example that should serve to the people as a warning (Luke 13:3–5). He visited the laborers' hospital at the southern foot of the Mount of Olives, healing the sick there and also those who had been wounded in the catastrophe. Then he went to Bethlehem and visited an inn, not far from the city gate, frequented by Essenes and other holy people. Afterward, he set off in the direction of Hebron, making his way to Zacharias' house at Juttah. Since Zacharias and Elizabeth had died, a cousin of John the Baptist lived in the house. Here Jesus met up with his mother, the holy women, and others from Jerusalem, who had traveled on ahead. They exchanged greetings. Jesus then went to the synagogue in Juttah, where he spoke of David, who had been born in Hebron.

Tuesday, January 9, A.D. 31 (Tebeth 25) Jesus and his disciples spent the day in and around Juttah, teaching and healing. That evening, after the other women had retired, Jesus and his mother, accompanied by Peter, John, and the three sons of Mary Heli (who had been disciples of the Baptist), went into the room where John the Baptist had been born. Kneeling together with the others, on a large rug, the Holy Virgin, Jesus' mother, recounted events from the Baptist's life. Then Jesus told them that John had been put to death by Herod. Stricken with grief, they shed tears of lamentation on the rug. Jesus consoled them with earnest words. He said that silence should be maintained, at least for the time being. For, with the exception of his murderers, apart from them, none knew of John the Baptist's death.

Wednesday, January 10, A.D. 31 (Tebeth 26) This morning, with his disciples, Jesus visited the cave of Machpelah near Hain Mambre where Abraham, Sarah, Isaac, and Jacob were buried. All entered the cave barefoot and stood in reverential silence. Only Jesus spoke. Then they visited the town of Bethain, where Jesus taught and healed.

Thursday, January 11, A.D. 31 (Tebeth 27) Jesus went to Hebron, where he taught in the synagogue, where the festival of the expulsion of the Sadducees from the Sanhedrin was being celebrated. He spoke out forcefully against the Sadducees for denying the resurrection of the dead. Afterward, he healed several people at their homes.

Friday, January 12, A.D. 31 (Tebeth 28) Jesus spent the whole day healing the sick and teaching at the entrance to the synagogue in Hebron. That evening, with the onset of the Sabbath, he spoke in the synagogue about the institution of the Paschal lamb. At one point in his talk, he said: "When the Sun and Moon are darkened, the mother brings the child to the temple to be redeemed." He also alluded to John the Baptist and spoke of the martyrdom of many of the prophets. A profound silence spread through the synagogue, affecting all deeply and causing many to shed tears. At this moment, too, several of John's relatives and friends received an interior revelation of John the Baptist's death, and many fainted from grief. Afterward, Jesus shared a meal with them and related the details of John's murder. He spoke comforting words to all present.

Saturday, January 13, A.D. 31 (Tebeth 29) This morning, after teaching in the synagogue at Juttah, Jesus healed a number of people in the neighborhood around the town. After the close of the Sabbath, Joseph of Arimathea, who had come from Jerusalem, invited Jesus to heal there before returning to Galilee.

SHEBAT (30 days): January 13/14 to February 11/12, A.D. 31
Shebat New Moon: January 12 at 3:45 A.M. Jerusalem time

Sunday, January 14, A.D. 31 (Shebat 1) Today Jesus visited the grave of Zecharias. It was decided that John's body should be brought from Machaerus and buried in Juttah. Then Jesus left, escorted by about twenty friends and disciples. That evening everyone went to an inn near Libnah.

Monday, January 15, A.D. 31 (Shebat 2) Today Saturnin, Judas Barsabbas, and two other disciples arrived from Galilee at the inn near Libnah. In the evening, a group of disciples left the inn and went to Machaerus to collect John the Baptist's body.

Tuesday, January 16, A.D. 31 (Shebat 3) Today Jesus went from Libnah to Bethzur, where he was well received. Lazarus and some other friends from Jerusalem were already waiting for him in the inn near the synagogue.

Wednesday, January 17, A.D. 31 (Shebat 4) Jesus healed some sick people in their homes. Then he visited a school, where he blessed the children.

Thursday, January 18, A.D. 31 (Shebat 5) Martha, Mary Magdalene, and the widow Mary Salome, who was living in Bethany as a guest of Martha, came to meet Jesus on his way to Bethany. That evening Jesus and his friends and disciples shared a meal in Bethany. After everyone had gone to bed, Jesus went alone to pray on the Mount of Olives.

Friday, January 19, A.D. 31 (Shebat 6) This morning Jesus and a group of disciples went to Jerusalem, first visiting the house of Joanna Chuza. Around ten in the morning, he went to the temple and taught there without arousing any opposition. After sharing a small meal with his disciples in the early afternoon at the house of Joanna Chuza, Jesus and the disciples went to the pool of Bethesda, where Jesus imparted instructions to the sick, healing a number of them. On the way out, he healed the paralyzed man who had been ill for thirty-eight years (John 5:1–15). By then, the Sabbath had already begun. So Jesus went to the temple and taught there again. In the evening, around sunset, John the Baptist's body was buried at Juttah, in the vault of Zecharias, the disciples having returned from Machaerus with it the day before.

Saturday, January 20, A.D. 31 (Shebat 7) Jesus and the disciples healed the sick this morning at the Coenaculum on Mount Zion. That afternoon they ate there, and then Jesus went to the temple. Once again, he was able to teach without encountering any opposition. That evening he and the disciples ate at the house of Simon the Pharisee in Bethany. Afterward, at Lazarus' castle, Jesus said goodbye to Lazarus, Martha, and Mary Magdalene.

Sunday, January 21, A.D. 31 (Shebat 8) Early this morning Jesus and the disciples left Bethany. They journeyed without stopping for about eleven hours until they reached Lebona on the southern slope of Mount Garizim.

Monday, January 22, A.D. 31 (Shebat 9) Journeying further, they arrived at Thirza.

Tuesday, January 23, A.D. 31 (Shebat 10) Jesus visited the hospital and prison in Thirza and healed the sick. Later, he taught in the synagogue concerning the fifth beatitude and the parable of the prodigal son (Luke 15:11).

Wednesday, January 24, A.D. 31 (Shebat 11) Today Jesus and the disciples traveled further, reaching Bethulia that evening.

Thursday, January 25, A.D. 31 (Shebat 12) Around noon, Jesus arrived at an inn near Damna, where he met with his mother and some of his disciples. Their joy at seeing one another again was diminished when those who had not yet heard of the circumstances surrounding John the Baptist's death were told. After eating a meal together, everyone went on in the direction of Capernaum. That night, Jesus stayed at his mother's home.

Friday, January 26, A.D. 31 (Shebat 13) Capernaum was full of visitors who had come from far and wide to hear Jesus. In addition, a group of sixty-four Pharisees had also gathered, having come from all around to investigate the carpenter's son from Nazareth. Jesus visited the homes of Zorobabel, Cornelius, and Jairus. Jairus had lost his position as chief elder at the synagogue and had been persecuted because of his contact with Jesus. Now Jairus committed himself wholly to the service of Jesus. Jesus then began healing and continued to heal throughout the morning. Around midday, he withdrew to a hall to preach. Then, as the Sabbath began, he went to the synagogue. He had to make his way through a great crowd before he could begin to teach.

When the Pharisees asked him if it was allowed to heal on the Sabbath, he answered by healing a man with a withered hand (Matthew 12:9) and by driving out a devil from one who was deaf, mute, and possessed, and whose hearing and speech were immediately restored. Witnessing this, the Pharisees accused Jesus of being in league with the devil (Matthew 9:32–34). Jesus, however, defended himself with the words spoken in Matthew 12:33–37. Amid the uproar, Jesus and the disciples withdrew. That night, Jesus stayed at Peter's house.

Saturday, January 27, A.D. 31 (Shebat 14) This morning, at Peter's house, the twelve and the other disciples reported their experiences from their missionary travels since Kislev 25 (Mark 6:30). Jesus listened to their doubts and to the problems they had encountered, giving practical instructions for the future. That night, Jesus and his disciples sailed across the Sea of Galilee and landed between Matthew's custom house and Little Chorazin.

MAP 26: *First Journey to Ornithopolis*

Sunday, January 28, A.D. 31 (Shebat 15) Many people had followed Jesus from Capernaum and Bethsaida. As a result, early this morning, a large crowd had already assembled on the mountain above Matthew's custom house. They had come to hear Jesus speak. Still more people came from the surrounding area, bringing with them the sick and the possessed. In the afternoon, after healing and teaching, Jesus dismissed the crowd, saying that he would teach next morning on the mountain near Bethsaida-Julias. Jesus, the twelve, and the seventy-two disciples then withdrew to a shaded, solitary place. Jesus then gave them instruction along the lines of Matthew 10:1–42. He arranged them in ranks as follows: the twelve apostles two by two headed by Peter and John; the older disciples formed a circle around them, and then came the younger ones according to the rank he assigned to them. He set the apostles over the disciples, saying that the former should send and call the latter, just as he sent and called the apostles.

Monday, January 29, A.D. 31 (Shebat 16) Today a large crowd of some five thousand people assembled on the mountain near Bethsaida-Julias. It was here, last Kislev 13, that Jesus had started to teach the "Sermon on the Mount." In the months since Kislev 13, Jesus had continued to teach the beatitudes and the Our Father prayer. Now Jesus taught and healed; and the apostles baptized many people. And again, the main content of Jesus' teaching was the beatitudes and the Lord's Prayer. Between four and six o'clock in the afternoon, there took place the miraculous feeding of the five thousand (John 6:5–15 and Mark 6:35–44). In the evening Jesus withdrew alone (Matthew 14:22–23), while the apostles sailed on Peter's ship back toward Bethsaida. A great storm arose on the Sea of Galilee, and there then took place the second miracle of the walking on the water (Matthew 14:25–33), which had taken place for the first time on the night of Kislev 22–23.

Tuesday, January 30, A.D. 31 (Shebat 17) At sunrise, Peter's ship landed near Dalmanutha (Mark 8:10). Here Jesus healed and continued his teaching concerning the beatitudes and the Lord's Prayer. He and the twelve then sailed over to Tarichea. After healing, he resumed teaching. It was here that he healed some children and spoke of the value of children, along the lines of Matthew 18:3–4. Toward evening, he set sail again.

Wednesday, January 31, A.D. 31 (Shebat 18) Early this morning, Jesus and the disciples landed again between Matthew's custom house and Little Chorazin, where Jesus addressed a crowd of about a hundred people. About noon, he sailed back toward Bethsaida. On landing, he went to Peter's house. Here he was greeted by Lazarus, who had come to see him. Veronica's son Amandor and one or two others had also come. Then Jesus went to a place on the road leading into Bethsaida, where a group of people had gathered. Here he began his great teaching concerning the eucharistic bread of life, which is summarized in John 6:25–34. On this occasion, Jesus did not however say that he himself was the bread of life.

Thursday, February 1, A.D. 31 (Shebat 19) Jesus continued the teaching on the bread of life at the same place on the road leading into Bethsaida, this time saying quite plainly that he was the bread of life (John 6:35–51). Some two thousand people were present.

Friday, February 2, A.D. 31 (Shebat 20) Still at the same place on the road into Bethsaida, Jesus taught on the same theme as the "Sermon on the Mount" (Matthew 5:3–12; 6:9–13). He spoke of the beatitudes and the Lord's Prayer. In the evening, with the start of the Sabbath, he went to the synagogue. As he was teaching, he was interrupted with the question: "How can you call yourself the bread of life come down from heaven, since every one

knows where you come from?" Jesus then taught again concerning the bread
of life (John 6:52–59). This caused a great uproar. The Pharisees cried out:
"How can he give us his body (flesh) to eat?" Jesus replied that he would give
them the food of which he spoke "in its own time" (in 113 weeks).

Saturday, February 3, A.D. 31 (Shebat 21) Today Jesus taught in the synagogue concerning the sixth and seventh petitions of the Our Father and the
first beatitude. He was questioned about his discourse of the day before on
the bread of life, concerning the eating of his flesh and the drinking of his
blood. He repeated in strong and precise terms all that he had said about this.
Then even some of his disciples began to complain: "This saying is hard, and
who can bear it?" (John 6:60). Jesus replied that they should not be scandalized, and that they would witness quite other things. He also predicted that
he would be persecuted, that even his most faithful disciples would desert
him, and that he would be put to death. Yet, he added, he would not desert
them. His spirit would be with them (John 6:61–65). As he was leaving the
synagogue, the Pharisees and certain disloyal disciples tried to detain him
with further questions, but the apostles and loyal disciples surrounded him
and escorted him from the synagogue amid much noise, shouting, and confusion. Jesus and his accompanying disciples then withdrew to a hill at the
north end of the town. There he asked the twelve whether they too would
leave him. Peter answered on behalf of all: "Lord, to whom shall we go? You
have the words of eternal life. And we believe and know that you are the Holy
One of God." Jesus replied: "Have I not chosen you twelve? And yet one
among you is a devil"—meaning Judas Iscariot (John 6:67–71).

Sunday, February 4, A.D. 31 (Shebat 22) Following an invitation from Nathanael (the bridegroom of the wedding at Cana), Jesus, the twelve apostles and
the loyal disciples set off for Cana, on the first stage of a journey through Galilee (John 7:1).

Monday, February 5, A.D. 31 (Shebat 23) While they were walking this morning in the neighborhood of Gischala, Jesus revealed to the twelve the disposition and character of each, and arranged them correspondingly in three
groups or rows: in the first row—Peter, Andrew, John, James the Greater
and Matthew; in the second row—Judas Thaddeus, Bartholomew, and
James the Less; and in the third row—Thomas, Simon, Philip, and Judas Iscariot. Judas Barsabbas stood at the head of the remaining disciples, nearest

to the twelve, and Jesus then placed him in the second row together with Thaddeus, Bartholomew and James.

Tuesday, February 6, A.D. 31 (Shebat 24) Jesus and the disciples visited Cydessa, where many Gentiles lived.

Wednesday, February 7, A.D. 31 (Shebat 25) After healing the sick of Cydessa, Jesus taught in the synagogue. He spoke of the duration of the descent of the Son of Man into the earth's womb, saying it was the same as Jonah had endured in the whale's belly (Matthew 12:38–40). Continuing northward, Jesus then conferred new power upon the twelve and the disciples for healing the sick and exorcising the possessed. Anne Catherine saw rays of different colors streaming out from Jesus into each disciple according to his disposition.

Thursday, February 8, A.D. 31 (Shebat 26) Today Jesus taught in the synagogue at Nephthali, the birthplace of Tobias. In the evening, he arrived at Elkasa.

Friday, February 9, A.D. 31 (Shebat 27) This morning Jesus healed and taught in various homes in Elkasa. As the Sabbath started, he taught in the synagogue, speaking of the building of Solomon's temple. Afterward, the Pharisees invited him to a meal in the town hall. There a dispute broke out. The Pharisees complained to Jesus that his disciples did not observe the Law, for they did not wash their hands before coming to the table (Mark 7:1–13). Jesus replied with the words recorded in Mark 7:14–16. Later, Jesus explained to the disciples the nature of the Pharisees' spiritual impurity (Matthew 15:12–20).

Saturday, February 10, A.D. 31 (Shebat 28) Jesus continued to teach in the synagogue, urging both Jews and unbelievers to become baptized. Again, the Pharisees reproached him, this time saying that his disciples did not fast regularly. Jesus replied: "The disciples eat after long labor, and then only if others are supplied. But if these latter are hungry, they give them what they have, and God blesses it." Here Jesus was referring to the feeding of the five thousand, where the disciples had given bread and fish to the hungry multitude. Then Jesus and the disciples left the town and made their way northwestward. On the way, he gave instruction concerning prayer, referring especially to the Lord's Prayer.

Sunday, February 11, A.D. *31 (Shebat 29)* Proceeding on further toward the northwest and continuing his discourse on prayer, Jesus with his disciples finally reached the city of Dan, also known as Lais. Here they stayed the night at an inn.

Monday, February 12, A.D. *31 (Shebat 30)* In the company of Peter, John, and James the Greater, Jesus healed the sick at many homes in Dan. He was followed by an old pagan woman from Ornithopolis, who was crippled on one side. Jesus seemed to ignore her, for he was concerned solely with healing the Jews. Nevertheless, she begged him to come and heal her daughter, who was possessed. Jesus replied that it was not yet time, that he wanted to avoid giving offense, and that he would not help the pagans before the Jews. Later that afternoon, the Syrophoenician woman from Ornithopolis approached Jesus and again begged him to drive the unclean spirit out of her daughter. There then followed the exorcism of her daughter, as described in Matthew 15:21–28. Jesus asked her whether she herself wished to be healed, but the Syrophoenician woman replied that she was not worthy, and that she asked only for her daughter's cure. Then Jesus laid one hand upon her head, the other on her side, and said: "Straighten up! May it be done to you as you also will it to be done! The devil has gone out of your daughter." The woman stood upright and cried out: "O Lord, I see my daughter lying in bed well and at peace!" That evening, Jesus and the disciples dined at the home of an old man of the Nazarite sect, a friend of Lazarus and Nicodemus. It was the celebration of the New Moon festival at the start of the month of Adar.

ADAR (29 days): February 12/13 to March 12/13, A.D. *31*
Adar New Moon: February 10 at 3:00 P.M., *Jerusalem time*

Tuesday, February 13, A.D. *31 (Adar 1)* This morning, Jesus healed in the town market-place. Among those who came to him was a relative of the Syrophoenician woman. Jesus cured his crippled arm and deaf-and-dumbness. The man who had been healed then turned to the pagans and Jews around him and began to speak prophetically: "The food that you, the children of the house, reject, we outcasts shall gather up. We shall live upon it and give thanks. What you allow to go to waste of the bread of heaven will be to us the fruit of the crumbs that we gather up." There was a great power of inspiration in his words, and much agitation arose among the crowd. Then Jesus withdrew into the mountains west of Dan. He met with the apostles and disciples, and they all spent the night there.

Wednesday, February 14, A.D. *31 (Adar 2)* Jesus and the disciples journeyed toward Ornithopolis, where Jesus had been invited to go by the Syrophoenician woman. They stayed the night at an inn on the way.

Thursday, February 15, A.D. *31 (Adar 3)* Jesus healed many people this morning at a place near the inn. Then, after giving instruction concerning various passages from the prophets, he and the disciples traveled on to Ornithopolis, where their arrival had been prepared for by the Syrophoenician woman. They were given a festive reception, including a banquet at which Jesus was anointed with a flask of costly ointment by the Syrophoenician woman's daughter.

Friday, February 16, A.D. *31 (Adar 4)* Today, after healing and teaching the Jews in and around Ornithopolis, Jesus and the disciples were again guests at the home of the Syrophoenician woman. She begged Jesus to visit and help the people of Sarepta, saying: "Sarepta, whose poor widow shared all she had with Elijah, is itself now a poor widow threatened with starvation. You, the greatest of prophets, have pity on her! Forgive me, a widow and once poor, to whom you have restored all, if I may be so bold as to plead also for Sarepta." Jesus promised that he would visit the town.

Saturday, February 17, A.D. *31 (Adar 5)* After visiting a school in Ornithopolis this morning, Jesus and the disciples set off for Sarepta, the town where the widow had dwelt at the time of Elijah (1 Kings 17:10). Arriving at the Jewish settlement on the outskirts of Sarepta, they were given a joyful reception.

Sunday, February 18, A.D. *31 (Adar 6)* The apostles brought bread and clothing from Sarepta to be distributed to the poor Jews in the settlement. After teaching and comforting the people of the settlement, Jesus and the disciples went eastward to a hill near a pagan town. Some pagans were awaiting him, and he taught there before journeying on further.

Monday, February 19, A.D. *31 (Adar 7)* Jesus traveled on today until he arrived at the town of Rechob.

MAP 27. *Journey to Gessur and Travels in Gaulanitis*

Tuesday, February 20, A.D. 31 (Adar 8) Leaving Rechob, Jesus walked for several hours in a northeasterly direction to Gessur, where he stayed the night with some tax collectors.

Wednesday, February 21, A.D. 31 (Adar 9) This morning Jesus taught in the quarter where the tax collectors lived. An aged great-uncle of the apostle Bartholomew came to hear Jesus and invited him to dine at his home the next day.

Thursday, February 22, A.D. 31 (Adar 10) Jesus followed the invitation and was received magnificently in the pagan style, being presented with a sumptuous meal. He healed some people in front of the house, and addressed those who were gathered there.

Friday, February 23, A.D. 31 (Adar 11) Today, the tax collectors with whom Jesus was staying distributed their wealth to the poor and needy. They were moved to do so by Jesus' teaching. Jesus taught at the tax collectors' custom house before a crowd of both Jews and pagans. Some Pharisees, who were visiting Gessur for the Sabbath, criticized Jesus for mixing with tax collectors and pagans. That evening, he taught at the synagogue. Again a dispute arose with the Pharisees.

Saturday, February 24, A.D. 31 (Adar 12) Today Bartholomew's great-uncle and about sixteen other elderly men were baptized by Judas Barsabbas. After dining again with Bartholomew's great-uncle, Jesus preached in the synagogue at the close of the Sabbath. Then he left Gessur, traveling to a fishing village on Phiala Lake. He arrived there late that night.

Sunday, February 25, A.D. 31 (Adar 13) After teaching in the synagogue, Jesus and the disciples visited various shepherd dwellings scattered around the lake. In the evening, accompanied by John, Bartholomew, and another disciple, Jesus went south toward Nobah and stayed there at an inn frequented by Pharisees.

Monday, February 26, A.D. 31 (Adar 14) Today Jesus taught and prepared a number of people for baptism. John and Bartholomew then performed the baptism. Jesus was well received in Nobah by the people, but at a banquet given that evening in the public hall the Pharisees began to argue with him about his disciples' conduct. During the discussion, Jesus told the parable of the laborers in the vineyard (Matthew 20:1–6) and also that of the rich glutton and poor Lazarus (Luke 16:19–31). Finally, he reproached the Pharisees for not having invited the poor, and sent out the disciples to round up the poor and bring them to the banquet. Today the Purim festival began.

Tuesday, February 27, A.D. 31 (Adar 15) The Purim festival (Adar 14/15) continued. As usual during this festival, the entire Book of Esther was read in the synagogue. Jesus went around visiting the homes of the sick and aged, reading to them from a scroll of the Book of Esther and healing some who were sick.

Wednesday, February 28, A.D. 31 (Adar 16) Accompanied by some of his disciples, Jesus walked to Gaulon, where he taught and healed. Then he continued on until he reached Regaba. Here he met up with the remaining disciples who had gone on ahead.

Thursday, March 1, A.D. 31 (Adar 17) Today Jesus visited people at their homes in Regaba, teaching and comforting them.

Friday, March 2, A.D. 31 (Adar 18) For the Sabbath, a great crowd of people came to Regaba from the surrounding area. Among them were many lame, blind, dumb, and other sick people. The crowd pressed around Jesus so much that after the evening service in the synagogue Jesus withdrew to a mountain outside of town.

Saturday, March 3, A.D. 31 (Adar 19) Today, a crowd of people sought out Jesus on the mountain. He taught them about the Lord's Prayer, and healed many of the sick. Afterward he continued on his way with the disciples, speaking about the great trials that the future would bring.

Sunday, March 4, A.D. 31 (Adar 20) Today Jesus and the disciples arrived at Caesarea-Philippi around midday. He stayed at an inn belonging to the Pharisees, close to the synagogue.

Monday, March 5, A.D. 31 (Adar 21) Jesus taught and healed on a hill outside Caesarea-Philippi. That evening, he dined with the Pharisees, who asked him provocative questions.

Tuesday, March 6, A.D. *31 (Adar 22)* This morning Jesus continued his healing and teaching activity outside Caesarea-Philippi. Meanwhile some more disciples arrived, bringing the total number to about sixty. Around midday, Jesus and these disciples went to the house of Enue's uncle, who was a pagan. (It was Enue who had been cured of the issue of blood when she touched Jesus' garment at Capernaum on Kislev 16, as he was on his way to raise the daughter of Jairus from the dead.) The widow Enue and her daughter conducted Jesus to her aged uncle. Jesus spoke with Enue's uncle and the others there who desired to be baptized. They were then baptized by Saturnin, with water blessed by Jesus. At the meal that followed the baptism, Enue's twenty-one-year-old daughter approached Jesus from behind, anointing his head with a costly mixture of essence of oils.

Wednesday, March 7, A.D. *31 (Adar 23)* This morning, Jesus and some disciples visited Enue's house, where they were given something to eat. Jesus directed that bread, grain, clothing, and blankets be sent to the town gate and distributed to the poor and needy. Then he went to the synagogue, where a dispute arose with the Pharisees. Following this, Jesus left Caesarea-Philippi and made his way to Argob.

Thursday, March 8, A.D. *31 (Adar 24)* Today Jesus taught in a public square in Argob. He also healed a number of people. In the afternoon, he left Argob, traveling through a mountainous region to a shepherd community. He stayed there in an inn.

Friday, March 9, A.D. *31 (Adar 25)* Today Jesus traveled to the stronghold of Regaba. Here a great multitude had gathered, including some Pharisees from Capernaum, who had come for the Sabbath to hear Jesus preach. In the evening, Jesus taught in the crowded synagogue concerning the building of Solomon's temple (1 Kings 6 & 7).

Saturday, March 10, A.D. *31 (Adar 26)* Today Jesus healed many blind people in Regaba. He also drove out demons from a number of those who were possessed. That evening, in the synagogue, the Pharisees accused him of driving out devils by the power of Beelzebub. Replying, Jesus called them children of "the father of lies." In the presence of the Pharisees, he warned his disciples to beware of them. Then he and his disciples withdrew into the desert, where they spent the night.

Sunday, March 11, A.D. 31 (Adar 27) Today they journeyed on to Chorazin. As Jesus approached the town, he healed many who were sick.

Monday, March 12, A.D. 31 (Adar 28) Today in Chorazin, teaching in the synagogue, Jesus was again subject to violent attacks by the Pharisees. As he left the town, several of them even followed him. But Jesus and the disciples walked on. Then the disciples brought a pious shepherd to him who was deaf and dumb. Jesus healed the shepherd in the presence of the Pharisees, so that they might see that he healed by way of prayer and faith in the heavenly Father, and not through the devil (Mark 7:31–37). Jesus and the disciples then went on to the tax-collecting place where Matthew's custom house was. After a while, they withdrew from the crowd there, staying until nightfall at the foot of the Mount of Beatitudes near Bethsaida-Julias. That night, they crossed the Jordan and visited the house of Andrew in Bethsaida.

Tuesday, March 13, A.D. 31 (Adar 29) Today Jesus and the disciples returned to the mountain ridge above Matthew's custom house. Here Jesus delivered a discourse to the crowd and healed many (Matthew 15:29–31). He spoke the words recorded in Matthew 7:7–11. That evening the month of Nisan began. Jesus stayed overnight in Matthew's old house.

NISAN (30 days): March 13/14 to April 11/12, A.D. 31
Nisan New Moon: March 12 at 3:15 A.M. Jerusalem time

Wednesday, March 14, A.D. 31 (Nisan 1) Early this morning, Jesus and the disciples went to a mountain northeast of the Mount of Beatitudes. A considerable crowd had assembled to hear him. Jesus spoke concerning the last two beatitudes. He spent that night on Peter's ship.

Thursday, March 15, A.D. 31 (Nisan 2) Today Jesus delivered the so-called "Sermon on the Mount" (Matthew 5:1–7; 29), signifying the conclusion of his presentation of the beatitudes, which had begun on the Mount of Beatitudes on Kislev 13. Then toward evening, there took place the feeding of the four thousand (Matthew 15:32–39). Jesus took leave of the people, who shed tears of thanks. He made his way back to the lake with the disciples. Before they could board their ship, they were met by a group of Pharisees who demanded Jesus to show them a sign from heaven. He replied as recorded in Matthew 16:1-4, saying that, after a certain number of weeks (actually 107), they would be given the sign of Jonah (Matthew 12:40). Jesus and the disciples then boarded Peter's ship and rowed out onto the lake, where they spent the night.

Friday, March 16, A.D. 31 (Nisan 3) Still on board Peter's ship, Jesus taught the disciples concerning the persecution and suffering that he would endure. He warned them to beware of the Pharisees and Sadducees (Matthew 16:5-12). Around noon, they landed at Bethsaida and went to eat at Andrew's house. As Jesus was leaving the house, he healed an old blind man (Mark 8:22-26). Then Jesus and the disciples rowed back to the east side of the Sea of Galilee and went to the town of Bethsaida-Julias for the Sabbath. That evening he preached in the synagogue on the deeper meaning of the commandment "Honor thy father and mother."

Saturday, March 17, A.D. 31 (Nisan 4) After the Sabbath morning service in the synagogue, Jesus visited various places in Bethsaida-Julias. When he was shown some newly constructed buildings, he told the parable of the house built on sand and the other built on rock (Matthew 7:24–27). He also spoke of the foundation stone that the builders would reject (Matthew 21:42). On his way back to the Sabbath closing service, he healed several people.

Sunday, March 18, A.D. 31 (Nisan 5) Jesus and the disciples left Bethsaida-Julias and journeyed to Sogane, where he taught and healed until late afternoon. Then they went to a hill outside of the town, and Jesus taught the disciples and listened to their accounts of the experiences they had undergone when on their missionary travels. That night, Jesus withdrew alone to pray.

Monday, March 19, A.D. 31 (Nisan 6) Before dawn, Jesus returned to the disciples, and they prayed together. The twelve stood around him in a circle and the other disciples around them. Jesus asked: "Who do the people say I am?" The reply to this question is recorded in Matthew 16:13–14. Then Jesus asked: "But who do you say that I am?" Peter, taking a step forward, declared: "Thou art Christ, the Son of the living God!" At this very moment, the Sun was rising, and Jesus spoke the words recorded in Matthew 16:17–20. He told the disciples that he was the promised Messiah, applying all the relevant passages from the prophets to himself. He announced that now the time had come for them to journey to Jerusalem for the Passover. Traveling through the day, that evening they arrived at Bethulia. Here Lazarus was waiting for Jesus. Lazarus had come to warn him that an insurrection against Pontius Pilate was planned and that this threatened to disrupt the Passover festival. The revolt would be led by Judas of Gamala, who had the support of a large number of Galileans. Lazarus said that it would therefore be advisable for Jesus to hold back from the celebrations in Jerusalem. But Jesus replied that this uprising would be the forerunner of a far greater one that would take place at a later time, meaning that which would accompany his future trial and persecution.

MAP 28: *Journey to the Second Passover*

Tuesday, March 20, A.D. *31 (Nisan 7)* Jesus and the disciples split up into different groups for the journey to Bethany. Jesus was accompanied by Simon, Judas Thaddeus, Nathanael Chased, and Judas Barsabbas. They made rapid progress, arriving that night at Lazarus' estate near Ginnim.

Wednesday, March 21, A.D. *31 (Nisan 8)* Continuing their journey, Jesus and his four traveling companions reached the town of Lebonah this evening.

Thursday, March 22, A.D. *31 (Nisan 9)* After healing some people in Lebonah, Jesus and the four disciples traveled on to Korea, where he healed several people.

Friday, March 23 A.D. *31 (Nisan 10)* As Jesus and the disciples were approaching Ephron, they were met on the way by Mary Magdalene and the widow Salome who had come together from Bethany to greet Jesus. After resting and talking with the two women, Jesus and the four disciples continued on their way. (The two women returned to Bethany by another route.) When Jesus and the disciples arrived at Bethany, they were welcomed by Lazarus. His mother, the Holy Virgin, was also there, and other disciples and friends had already arrived. That evening, Jesus and all those gathered together in Bethany celebrated the Sabbath in the great hall of the castle. He spoke much about the paschal lamb and about his future suffering.

Saturday, March 24, A.D. *31 (Nisan 11)* Jesus taught this morning and afternoon (at the close of the Sabbath) in the castle. In between, he walked in the garden. Mary Magdalene followed him everywhere, full of love and contrition. She sat at his feet to take in his words. Since her final conversion, she had changed greatly in her countenance and bearing. That evening, there was a meal attended by all, including friends and disciples from Jerusalem.

Sunday, March 25, A.D. 31 (Nisan 12) Around ten o'clock in the morning Jesus and the disciples crossed the Mount of Olives and went to the temple. Here Jesus taught the disciples and a crowd of people who had gathered around. However, as there were several teaching chairs set up, Jesus did not arouse too much attention. After about an hour, he and the disciples returned to Bethany. That afternoon, about fifty Galileans—followers of Judas of Gamala—were seized by Roman soldiers, as Pontius Pilate had been informed that they would try to start an insurrection. However, the people rebelled, attacking the soldiers, and managed to free the captives. Several people died in the mêlée.

Monday, March 26, A.D. 31 (Nisan 13) News had spread that Jesus was in Jerusalem for the Passover, and many sick people came to the temple to be healed by Jesus. As he was entering the temple, Jesus caught sight of the man whom he had healed at the pool of Bethesda. (He had been paralyzed for thirty-eight years.) Jesus called out to him: "See, you are well! Sin no more, that nothing worse befall you." This person had not known who had healed him. But now he made it his business to tell the Pharisees that it was Jesus who had healed him on the Sabbath (John 5:14–15). Immediately the Pharisees gathered around Jesus, charging him with breaking the Sabbath, but no great disturbance arose, and Jesus continued to teach concerning the Paschal sacrifice. The Pharisees asked scornfully whether he—the prophet—would do them the honour of eating the paschal lamb with them. Jesus replied: "The Son of Man is himself a sacrifice for your sins!" In the end, as Jesus continued teaching, the Pharisees became so exasperated that they raised a great commotion. But Jesus managed to slip away and disappear into the crowd, returning to Bethany where preparations were underway for the feast on the following day.

Tuesday, March 27, A.D. 31 (Nisan 14) Today, Jesus and his friends and disciples walked together on the Mount of Olives. Meanwhile, the healed man from the pool of Bethesda continued to go around telling the Pharisees that it was Jesus who had cured him. The Pharisees then determined to take Jesus into custody. In the afternoon, the slaughter of the paschal lambs in the temple began—at 3:00 P.M. and not at 12:30 P.M. as was the case on the day of the crucifixion. (On the day of the crucifixion the earlier start was occasioned by the onset of the Sabbath a few hours later.) That evening, all Jesus' friends and disciples gathered in the great hall at Lazarus' castle to share the Passover feast. During the meal, Jesus spoke of the Son of Man as the true vine and referred to his disciples as the grapes on the vine (John 15:1–8). The festivities, with singing from the Psalms, lasted until late into the night.

YEAR 3
Nisan 15, A.D. 31, to Nisan 14, A.D. 32
March 27/28, A.D. 31, to April 13/14, A.D. 32

Wednesday, March 28, A.D. 31 (Nisan 15) Early this morning Jesus and the disciples went to the temple. They stood among the crowd from sunrise until about eleven o'clock. Then there was a pause in the reception of the offerings. Jesus went up to the great teacher's chair in the court before the sanctuary. A large crowd gathered around, including many Pharisees and also the man who had been healed at the pool of Bethesda. The Pharisees accused Jesus of breaking the Sabbath because he had healed this man on the Sabbath. Jesus replied that the Sabbath was made for humanity, not humanity for the Sabbath. He then recounted the parable of the sick man and poor Lazarus. This so outraged the Pharisees that they pressed around and sent for the temple guards to take Jesus into custody. At the height of the uproar, it suddenly grew dark. Jesus looked up to heaven and said: "Father, render testimony to thy Son!" A loud noise like thunder resounded and a heavenly voice proclaimed: "This is my beloved son in whom I am well pleased!" Jesus' enemies were terrified. The disciples then escorted Jesus from the temple to safety. They then proceeded northward from Jerusalem until they reached Rama, where they stayed the night at an inn.

Thursday, March 29, A.D. 31 (Nisan 16) Leaving Rama early this morning, Jesus and the disciples made their way to Thanat-Silo. Here Jesus was given a warm reception. All the Pharisees were away in Jerusalem. Today, Pontius Pilate issued an order forbidding all Galileans from leaving the city without his permission.

Friday, March 30, A.D. 31 (Nisan 17) Jesus and the disciples left Thanat-Silo and went on to Atharot, where Jesus taught on a hill outside of the town and healed the sick. Later, after the Sabbath had begun, Jesus taught in the synagogue. During the course of the evening, he healed a widow crippled at the waist for eighteen years. She was used to going bent double, almost touching the ground. Jesus summoned her to him and laid his hand on her back, saying: "Woman, be freed from your infirmity!" She rose up straightway and gave thanks to God. An aged Pharisee, who was also a cripple and for this reason had not gone to Jerusalem, presided over the synagogue. When the healing of the crippled widow took place, he turned to the people and said: "There are six days upon which we may work. Come then and be healed, but not on the Sabbath." Jesus replied: "You hypocrite! Does not everyone loose his ox or ass from the manger on the Sabbath and lead it to water? And shall not this woman, a daughter of Abraham, be loosed from the bond in which Satan has bound her for eighteen years?" (Luke 13:10–17).

Saturday, March 31, A.D. *31 (Nisan 18)* After healing many people yesterday in Atharot, Jesus was invited to the home of the widow whom he had healed the evening before. Later, some of the disciples were spotted plucking ears of corn as they walked. This was reported to the Pharisees and led, a few days later (Nisan 23/24), to a renewed attack on Jesus in Dothaim and Capernaum (Matthew 12:1–2). After the Sabbath had ended, Jesus and the disciples went to Lazarus' estate near Ginnim and stayed there overnight.

MAP 29: *Second Journey to Ornithopolis*

Sunday, April 1, A.D. *31 (Nisan 19)* Jesus and the disciples journeyed to Hadad-Rimmon, where he healed the sick and taught concerning the resurrection from the dead, the last judgment, and God's mercy. Today it was learned that Pontius Pilate had ordered Judas of Gamala and many of his followers to be put to death. This was the way that Pilate took revenge for the collapse of the tower and wall that had occurred at the instigation of Herod Antipas two months before.

Monday, April 2, A.D. *31 (Nisan 20)* Today Jesus spoke before a large crowd in Hadad-Rimmon.

Tuesday, April 3, A.D. *31 (Nisan 21)* From the inn at Hadad-Rimmon where he had been staying, Jesus went to Kisloth at the foot of Mount Tabor. Here he taught and healed. Around three o'clock in the afternoon, he went with Peter, John and James the Greater up Mount Tabor. Around midnight, the transfiguration took place (Matthew 17:1–8).

Wednesday, April 4, A.D. 31 (Nisan 22) Early in the morning, Jesus and the three disciples came down the mountain and met up again with the other disciples. There then followed the healing of the possessed boy whom the disciples had been unable to heal (Mark 9:14–27). After healing several more people, Jesus and the disciples continued on their way until they reached Dothaim. As they walked, the three disciples who had witnessed the transfiguration asked Jesus questions concerning what he had said about the resurrection of the Son of Man and the words in the scripture about the resurrection of Elijah. Jesus answered them as recorded in Matthew 17:9–13 and Mark 9:9–13. He also taught the disciples as stated in Luke 12:22–53. In Dothaim, they met up with some other disciples who had already arrived. As these listened to the account of the healing of the possessed child whom the disciples could not heal, the question arose as to why they had been unable to do so. Jesus replied as found in Matthew 17:19–21. That evening, Jesus and the disciples were guests at a meal given by the Pharisees, who attacked them for breaking the Sabbath, that is, for plucking ears of corn on the Sabbath. Jesus replied in the words given in Matthew 12:2–8.

Thursday, April 5, A.D. 31 (Nisan 23) This morning, after teaching in Dothaim, Jesus made his way to Capernaum. There he and the disciples were guests at a feast in honor of their homecoming. Some Pharisees were also present. These Pharisees again accused Jesus of sanctioning the violation of long-established customs, charging that the disciples had broken the Sabbath, plucked corn, neglected handwashing, and so on.

Friday, April 6, A.D. 31 (Nisan 24) This morning, at Peter's house, there occurred the exchange concerning the payment of tax (Matthew 17:24–27). Jesus told Peter that he would find a shekel in the mouth of the first fish that he would catch. Peter then went to the lake and caught a large fish, in whose mouth was a shekel. He used it to pay his and Jesus' tax. The fish was large enough to be then eaten by Jesus and the disciples for lunch. After the meal, Jesus spoke the words recorded in Mark 9:33–35. Then he went with the disciples to Capernaum. There he addressed a crowd of people at the marketplace. What he said is recorded in Mark 9:36–50 and in the entire eighteenth chapter of the Gospel of Saint Matthew. At the start of the Sabbath, he went to the synagogue in Capernaum and taught there.

Saturday, April 7, A.D. *31 (Nisan 25)* This afternoon Jesus was in Bethsaida and spoke with the disciples who had returned from their missionary journeys. Altogether about seventy disciples were gathered. As Jesus helped at the reception of the disciples, Peter said: "Lord, do you want to serve? Let us serve!" Jesus replied that he had been sent to serve. He spoke again of humility and said that whoever would be first must be the servant of all. Then he spoke of certain deeper mysteries, saying that his conception had been not human but divine, from the Holy Spirit. He spoke with great reverence of his mother, calling her the purest vessel and holiest of created beings. Also, he referred to the Fall and the ensuing separation from God. He said that now he had come to restore the relationship with God. His words were spoken with great solemnity and earnestness, so that the disciples were deeply moved.

Sunday, April 8, A.D. *31 (Nisan 26)* Today Jesus and the disciples walked in the region north of Capernaum. Jesus paused occasionally to teach the disciples or the laborers in the fields. That evening he stayed at a shepherd settlement. He told the shepherds the parable of the lost sheep (Matthew 18:12) and spoke of the good shepherd (John 10:1).

Monday, April 9, A.D. *31 (Nisan 27)* Jesus and the disciples continued on their way, arriving this afternoon at Leccum.

Tuesday, April 10, A.D. *31 (Nisan 28)* In Leccum, Jesus visited the aged and the sick, several of whom he healed. Then he taught at the marketplace. He spoke about marriage, making use of all kinds of analogies, including that of the son of the vineyard owner (Matthew 21:37–39). The people were deeply moved by Jesus' words. As evening approached, he went with the disciples to Bethsaida-Julias.

Wednesday, April 11, A.D. *31 (Nisan 29)* Today, in Bethsaida-Julias, there was talk of the murder of the Galileans that had occurred in the temple at Jerusalem. Jesus then spoke as recorded in Luke 13:1–5. He also referred to the parable of the unfruitful fig tree (Luke 13:6–9).

Thursday, April 12, A.D. 31 (Nisan 30) Jesus and the disciples spent the whole day walking in the neighborhood surrounding the Mount of Beatitudes. That evening, they crossed the Jordan and returned to Bethsaida.

> *IYYAR (29 days): April 12/13 to May 10/11, A.D. 31*
> *Iyyar New Moon: April 10 at 4:30 P.M., Jerusalem time*

Friday, April 13, A.D. 31 (Iyyar 1) After the evening Sabbath sermon in the synagogue, Jesus accepted the invitation of a well-to-do Pharisee to dine with him at his house. Here took place the healing of a man with dropsy, which scandalized the Pharisees (Luke 14:1–14). Jesus then told the parable of the great feast (Luke 14:15–24) and asked that the poor be invited to join with them in their meal.

Saturday, April 14, A.D. 31 (Iyyar 2) As usual on the Sabbath, Jesus and the disciples went for a walk. They went to a deserted region between Tiberius and Magdalum and were followed by a large crowd. Jesus spoke to the crowd (Luke 14:25–33).

Sunday, April 15, A.D. 31 (Iyyar 3) Jesus sent out the disciples to invite the people to a sermon on the mountain near Gabara, which would begin on Iyyar 6.

Monday, April 16, A.D. 31 (Iyyar 4) As Jesus arrived at the outskirts of Tarichea, several lepers called out to him. He healed them and then went on to heal many sick people who were brought to him.

Tuesday, April 17, A.D. 31 (Iyyar 5) This morning, Jesus visited a sanatorium south of Tarichea and healed the sick there. Then he and the disciples went to a hostel close to the mountain where he would teach next day. Many people were already on their way to this event—so many, in fact, that the Pharisees complained to Jesus that the entire land was in disturbance.

Wednesday, April 18, A.D. 31 (Iyyar 6) At about ten in the morning Jesus arrived at the mountain near Gabara where the new "Sermon on the Mount" was to begin. Many Pharisees, Sadducees, and Herodians were among the people gathered there to hear him. After beginning with a prayer, Jesus began to teach about prayer and the love of one's neighbor (Matthew 5:38-6:8). He also warned against the Pharisees and false prophets. Jesus taught without interruption until evening. Then he descended the mountain to return to where he was staying. Among those who came to meet him there were Lazarus, Martha, Dina the Samaritan, Mara the Suphanite, Maroni of Nain and his mother, Mary.

Thursday, April 19, A.D. 31 (Iyyar 7) Today, Jesus continued his "Sermon on the Mount." The Pharisees began to proclaim Jesus as a "disturber of the peace," saying that they had the Sabbath, the festival days, and their own teaching, and that they did not need the innovations of this upstart. They threatened to complain to Herod—who would certainly put a stop to Jesus' activities. Jesus answered that he would continue to teach and heal, in spite of Herod, until his mission was complete. Eventually, the pressure of the crowd forced the Pharisees to leave so that Jesus could continue his teaching undisturbed. After the sermon had ended and the crowd had dispersed, Jesus taught the disciples concerning the character of the Pharisees and how they should conduct themselves in relation to them. That evening, as Jesus and the disciples ate together, Lazarus told of the journey the women had made to Machaerus from Hebron and Jerusalem. Indeed, one of them, Joanna Chuza, had just succeeded in recovering the head of John the Baptist from Herod's castle.

Friday, April 20, A.D. 31 (Iyyar 8) This morning Jesus and the twelve apostles healed the sick who were gathered at the foot of the mountain. The remaining disciples and holy women dispensed food and clothing to the poor. This was the cause of much joy and thanksgiving. Afterward, the people dispersed to return to their home towns in time for the Sabbath. Jesus and the disciples then made their way to Garisma. On the way, they passed through Capharoth. In Capharoth, some Pharisees, who were well-disposed to Jesus, warned him that Herod was out to imprison him and deal with him as he had done with John the Baptist. Jesus replied that he had nothing to fear from "the fox," and that he would do what his Father had sent him to do (Luke 13:31–33). Reaching Garisma, Jesus and the disciples went to the synagogue for the start of the Sabbath.

Saturday, April 21, A.D. 31 (Iyyar 9) Jesus taught the disciples openly on a hill, speaking of the lost sheep (Luke 15:3–7), the lost coin (Luke 15:8–10), and the ten virgins (Matthew 25:1–13). Some Jews from Cyprus —on their return journey there from Jerusalem—came to Jesus and told him how much the Jewish colony on Cyprus longed to hear him.

Sunday, April 22, A.D. 31 (Iyyar 10) This morning Jesus continued his instruction to the disciples. That afternoon, they went to a deserted region northwest of Garisma, and stayed there overnight in the mountains.

Monday, April 23, A.D. 31 (Iyyar 11) Here, in the mountains, Jesus gave his blessing to the disciples and sent them out on missionary journeys. This was the third such occasion on which they were sent out. In so doing, he laid his hands upon the apostles and the disciples of long standing, filling them with new strength.

Tuesday, April 24, A.D. 31 (Iyyar 12) Proceeding further, around midday, Jesus and the few remaining disciples crossed the River Leontes and came to an inn. Here they were well received, and Jesus taught the people who had come to hear him.

Wednesday, April 25, A.D. 31 (Iyyar 13) Today, Jesus and his few disciples— James the Lesser, Barnabas, Mnason, Azor, the two sons of Cyrinus and a youth from Cyprus—continued further toward Ornithopolis. They halted their journey at a small place about an hour east of Ornithopolis, where Jesus taught in the synagogue. Then they proceeded to Ornithopolis, where they went to the home of the Syrophoenician woman. Here Jesus healed some people and then took part in a feast held in his honour by the Syrophoenician woman and her daughter. Around four in the afternoon Jesus and his companions left and went to the harbor north of Ornithopolis. Close to the harbor there was a synagogue where Jesus taught. That night, as Jesus and the disciples boarded boats to set sail to Cyprus, the moon was full and the stars were shining. Altogether there were ten rowing boats, each equipped with sails (like Peter's boat on the Sea of Galilee).

MAP 30: *The Journey to Cyprus*

Thursday, April 26, A.D. 31 (Iyyar 14) The sea was calm, and the passage proceeded so rapidly that the sailors called out: "O, what an auspicious voyage! This is thanks to thee, O prophet!" Jesus stood at the mast. He bid them to be silent and to give thanks only to God. Toward evening they landed at

Salamis. Here Jesus went to the synagogue in the Jewish quarter, where he healed some people who were suffering from dropsy.

Friday, April 27, A.D. 31 (Iyyar 15) This morning Jesus healed the sick at the local hospital. After teaching at an open square, Jesus and the disciples ate a meal held in his honour. At the start of the Sabbath, he taught in the synagogue.

Saturday, April 28, A.D. 31 (Iyyar 16) This morning he taught in the synagogue, which was completely full, and visited the hospital again. Then he dined as guest of honour at the house of Cyrinus. At the close of the Sabbath, he taught in the synagogue concerning the Law and true sacrifice. At the same time he gave instructions to prepare those wanting to be baptized.

Sunday, April 29, A.D. 31 (Iyyar 17) After healing some people who were then baptized by the disciples, he taught on a hill. A large crowd gathered to hear him. The Roman governor of Salamis sent an invitation to Jesus, which Jesus accepted. At the governor's palace Jesus answered the questions that were put to him. He emphasized that his kingdom was not of this world. The governor was astonished at Jesus' words, at the content of his wisdom, and invited Jesus to return and speak again. Around two in the afternoon Jesus arrived at the home of the father of his disciple Jonas. Jonas' father was an Essene and lived a pious and simple life. Here Jesus gave instruction to a number of people waiting to be baptized. Barnabas, James the Lesser, and Azor then baptized them.

Monday, April 30, A.D. 31 (Iyyar 18) This morning Jesus taught close to the place of baptism. Among the crowd—of both Jews and pagans—were some pagan philosophers. They questioned Jesus. Then, in the afternoon, Jesus visited some private homes where he healed the sick. That evening, he dined with the rabbis as their guest of honour. Later, when he and the disciples had returned to their inn, a pagan lady—her name was Mercuria—came to speak with Jesus. Mercuria confessed her sins and Jesus spoke earnestly with her. His words were full of compassion. He commanded her to renounce her way of life and told her of God the Almighty.

Tuesday, May 1, A.D. 31 (Iyyar 19) The disciples continued to baptize, while Jesus taught and healed the sick. Jesus then began to teach the pagan philosophers about the nature of their cults and the arising of false gods.

Wednesday, May 2, A.D. 31 (Iyyar 20) Today, Jesus set off, going from field to field, instructing the workers as he went. It was during one such instruction that he spoke the words recorded in Luke 8:18. That night he stayed at an inn near the Roman way.

Thursday, May 3, A.D. 31 (Iyyar 21) Today Jesus traveled further and arrived at an inn on the outskirts of Chytroi, where he was greeted by the father of Barnabas.

Friday, May 4, A.D. 31 (Iyyar 22) This morning Jesus visited an iron mine near Chytroi. He addressed the workers and spoke the words recorded in Luke 6:31. He then entered the town and was greeted by the Jewish elders and also by two of the philosophers from Salamis. It was the start of the Sabbath. Therefore, Jesus taught in the synagogue. Many pagans listened from the terrace outside. At one point, a lame rabbi called out for help, and Jesus healed him on the spot. Afterward, Jesus shared a meal at the house of Barnabas' father and stayed the night there.

Saturday, May 5, A.D. 31 (Iyyar 23) This morning Jesus taught on a hill near Chytroi. In the afternoon, he healed the sick and then preached again in the synagogue for the close of the Sabbath.

Sunday, May 6, A.D. 31 (Iyyar 24) Accompanied by about one hundred people, Jesus went to a place near Chytroi where bees were kept. Here he taught about the Lord's Prayer and the beatitudes.

Monday, May 7, A.D. 31 (Iyyar 25) Jesus continued teaching at the same place as yesterday. Meanwhile, the crowd of listeners had increased to several hundred. He spoke about the prophet Malachi. In the afternoon, he returned to the house of Barnabas' father.

Tuesday, May 8, A.D. 31 (Iyyar 26) Jesus taught at a well near Chytroi and prepared the listeners for baptism. The Jews and pagans were separated. Jesus spoke about circumcision, saying that it could not be demanded of pagans; pagan converts should be circumcised only if they themselves requested it. On the other hand, it could not be expected of the Jews that they should permit pagans to enter the synagogue. Trouble should be avoided, and one should thank God for those who renounced idolatry and sought salvation.

Wednesday, May 9, A.D. *31 (Iyyar 27)* Jesus continued to teach at the well while the disciples baptized. Around noon, Jesus set off for Mallep, a village built by Jews for their colony. He was received there with much joy and celebration. In the synagogue Jesus taught concerning the petition "Thy Kingdom Come" of the Lord's Prayer.

Thursday, May 10, A.D. *31 (Iyyar 28)* At the midday meal, three blind boys were led into the room where Jesus and the disciples were eating. They were playing flutes. Jesus asked them if they would like to see the light, and then—much to their joy—he healed them. As the news of this miracle spread, the whole town began to rejoice. That evening, Jesus taught again in the synagogue.

Friday, May 11, A.D. *31 (Iyyar 29)* Today, Jesus and the disciples took a walk with seven (formerly pagan) philosophers who had received baptism. The latter asked him about the Persian King Djemschid, who had received a golden blade from God with which he had divided many lands and shed blessings everywhere. Jesus replied that Djemschid had been a leader who was wise and intelligent in things of the sense world. He spoke of Djemschid as a false type of Melchizedek, who was truly a priest and a king to whom they should turn their attention. The sacrifice of bread and wine which Melchizedek had offered would be fulfilled and perfected and would endure until the end of the world. They returned to the synagogue in Mallep for the start of the Sabbath.

SIVAN (30 days): May 11/12 to June 9/10, A.D. *31*
Sivan New Moon: May 10 at 7.00 A.M., *Jerusalem time*

Saturday, May 12, A.D. *31 (Sivan 1)* This morning Jesus continued teaching in the synagogue. He spoke of the Sabbath year and the Jubilee (Leviticus 25). Then he went with a large crowd of people to the bathing gardens on the outskirts of the town. Here he taught and prepared people for baptism. James the Lesser and Barnabas then baptized. Many people accompanied Jesus today for the Sabbath-day walk, which he took in the valley of Lafina, before returning to the synagogue for the close of the Sabbath. Afterward, he discoursed late into the night with some of the philosophers.

Sunday, May 13, A.D. *31 (Sivan 2)* Today, again, Jesus taught at the place of baptism. Several bridegrooms were present. Jesus gave them instruction concerning marriage. They then received baptism. Afterward, Jesus accepted an invitation to dine at the house of a rabbi in the village of Leppe, west of Mallep. The bridegrooms were also invited, together with their brides-to-be. Following the meal, Jesus spoke of the sacredness of marriage. It was already dark when he and the disciples returned to Mallep to sleep.

Monday, May 14, A.D. *31 (Sivan 3)* Today Jesus was present at the wedding celebration of the bridegrooms and their brides. After the festivities were over, he went for a walk with the philosophers. That evening, he taught again in the synagogue concerning the significance of marriage.

Tuesday, May 15, A.D. *31 (Sivan 4)* Jesus and a disciple, Mnason, accompanied by the philosophers, made their way through the fields, going from farm to farm. Here and there Jesus taught concerning the Feast of Weeks (the Jewish festival corresponding to Whitsun, seven weeks after the Passover), which was approaching. He spoke of the Feast of Weeks as a festival of remembrance of the giving of the Law to Moses on Mount Sinai.

Wednesday, May 16, A.D. *31 (Sivan 5)* Jesus taught again today about the Feast of Weeks, about the giving of the Law on Mount Sinai, and about baptism. The Feast of Weeks began that evening. There was a torchlight prayer-procession, which Jesus joined. Afterward, he retired to pray alone.

Thursday, May 17, A.D. *31 (Sivan 6)* This morning Jesus took part in the ceremonies to celebrate the Feast of Weeks in the synagogue. He walked at the head of the column of rabbis as they proceeded around the synagogue blessing the land, the sea, and all regions of the earth. There then followed the reading. It had to do with the period between the exodus from Egypt and the giving of the Law on Mount Sinai on the fiftieth day after the Passover.

Friday, May 18 A.D. *31 (Sivan 7)* Jesus and the disciples visited the homes of various people to teach, comfort, and heal. He spoke with several women about their marriage difficulties. That evening, with the beginning of the Sabbath, Jesus spoke in the synagogue with tremendous power and earnestness. He spoke of the breaking of the commandments and of adultery. Afterward, he prayed alone all night.

Saturday, May 19, A.D. 31 (Sivan 8) Many came to visit Jesus at his inn. They sought comfort after the mighty speech that he had delivered the evening before. Jesus comforted and instructed many people, one of whom invited him to dine. Everyone was astonished at the remarkable effect that Jesus had in helping people right their life situations.

Sunday, May 20, A.D. 31 (Sivan 9) Jesus spent the whole day visiting people at their homes. Everywhere he recommended the Jews to move from Cyprus to Palestine, prophesying future catastrophes that would take place on Cyprus.

Monday, May 21, A.D. 31 (Sivan 10) Jesus and the disciples journeyed some seven hours to a miners' village near Chytroi. The family of Barnabas had invited him here. He taught on the way.

Tuesday, May 22, A.D. 31 (Sivan 11) Jesus taught on the village square. The disciples distributed clothes and provisions to the people. Afterward, all took part in a meal together.

Wednesday, May 23, A.D. 31 (Sivan 12) Today Jesus accompanied a cousin of Maroni, the widow of Nain, to the harbor at Kition, and gave him a message for his mother, and some of the apostles.

Thursday, May 24, A.D. 31 (Sivan 13) Early this morning Jesus and the disciples left the miners' village near Chytroi. Around four in the afternoon they arrived at the family home of his disciple Mnason, three quarters of an hour from Keryneia.

Friday, May 25, A.D. 31 (Sivan 14) Jesus went to the synagogue in Keryneia for the beginning of the Sabbath with the disciples and with Mnason's family. There, Jesus spoke against idolatry.

Saturday, May 26, A.D. 31 (Sivan 15) This morning Jesus taught about fifty people who were awaiting baptism. They were then baptized. At the close of the Sabbath, he taught again in the synagogue at Keryneia. Later, he returned with the disciples to Mallep.

Sunday, May 27, A.D. 31 (Sivan 16) Jesus announced today that he would soon be leaving Cyprus to return to Palestine.

Monday, May 28, A.D. 31 (Sivan 17) This morning Jesus visited some farms east of Mallep. He taught there and healed the sick, including a blind child. Later, there was a festive meal in Mallep, to which Jesus invited the poor and needy. Afterward, he taught concerning the meaning of the word "Amen." That night, he and the disciples left Mallep.

Tuesday, May 29, A.D. 31 (Sivan 18) Around two in the afternoon, Jesus and the disciples arrived back in Salamis. Here Jesus met again with the Roman governor of the town, who decided to convert. The pagan priestess Mercuria also converted. Jesus discussed with her her plans to leave Cyprus and move to Palestine.

Wednesday, May 30, A.D. 31 (Sivan 19) At dawn, the Roman governor bade farewell to Jesus, who then made his way to the harbor at Kition, about two hours from Salamis. After eating a meal at the harbor, Jesus and his traveling companions—now about twenty-seven in number—set off from Cyprus on board three ships.

MAP 31: *Travels in Middle and Southern Galilee*

Thursday, May 31, A.D. 31 (Sivan 20) After an uneventful crossing, the three ships arrived at the bay between Akko (Ptolemais) and Hepha (Haifa). Jesus and his companions landed east of Hepha, at the estuary of the river Kison. Disciples were waiting to greet Jesus as he and the others disembarked.

Friday, June 1, A.D. 31 (Sivan 21) Jesus and the disciples went northward and crossed the River Belus. They then went eastward to the town of Misael, where Elizabeth, the mother of John the Baptist, had grown up. That evening, with the start of the Sabbath, Jesus and the disciples went to the synagogue in Misael. Here Levites were responsible for the services.

Saturday, June 2, A.D. 31 (Sivan 22) Jesus went with some Levites to visit Elizabeth's birthplace. Afterward, Jesus went to heal the sick in their homes. At the close of the Sabbath, he preached in the synagogue. He taught of Samson and his deeds, as an example of a forerunner of the Messiah.

Sunday, June 3, A.D. 31 (Sivan 23) Early this morning Judas Iscariot, Thomas, and several other disciples went to Hepha to make arrangements for the new disciples who were expected to arrive from Cyprus. Jesus went with them as far as the bridge over the River Belus. Then he turned toward the southeast and came to a place with a synagogue. Here he preached to a crowd of people who had come from all around.

Monday, June 4, A.D. 31 (Sivan 24) Today Jesus visited the place where Elizabeth had spent most of her youth. Some of her relatives were still living there. After healing some sick people, Jesus went to a place with a synagogue between Sephoris and Nazareth.

Tuesday, June 5, A.D. 31 (Sivan 25) Today Jesus traveled to Thaanach. Here he healed a Pharisee who had been part of the committee investigating Jesus and had fallen seriously ill after speaking out against him. When the Pharisees of Thaanach saw their healed colleague, they did not dare to take any steps against Jesus, who was therefore able to teach in the synagogue undisturbed. He spoke out clearly concerning the Messiah, and the Pharisees had an inkling he was referring to himself.

Wednesday, June 6, A.D. 31 (Sivan 26) In Thaanach, Jesus visited the carpenter's workshop where Joseph had worked. Afterward, he went south to Sion, where he taught in the synagogue. He rebuked the Pharisees for subjugating the people with the heavy duties that they themselves did not perform.

Thursday, June 7, A.D. 31 (Sivan 27) Jesus visited Sion to comfort the poor and oppressed. In the morning, he healed the sick, while the disciples distributed what money and goods they had to the poor. In the afternoon, Jesus and the disciples went to Nain. Here, on Heshvan 28, he had raised the youth Martialis from the dead. Martialis' mother—the rich widow Maroni—had put one of her properties at Jesus' disposal to be used by him and his disciples as an inn. Jesus and the disciples visited this house. Martha, Mary Magdalene, Veronica, Joanna Chuza, and Mara the Suphanite were waiting there. Jesus told them of his visit to Cyprus, speaking with special warmth of the Roman governor in Salamis.

Friday, June 8, A.D. 31 (Sivan 28) Jesus visited several people in Nain and then went to Maroni's garden. Here he gave the holy women advice about their inner life and their work serving the community of Christians. Then, for the start of the Sabbath, Jesus and the disciples went to the synagogue.

The rabbis invited him to read the holy scripture that evening. The texts included a reading from the prophet Zechariah in which some passages referred to the vocation of the Gentiles and to the Messiah. Jesus spoke about this, saying that many Gentiles would gain entrance to the kingdom of the Messiah. Then, addressing the Pharisees in particular, he said that they would not recognize the Messiah, for he would appear quite differently than they expected. At this, three Pharisees began to protest violently against Jesus, saying that he should not disturb the Sabbath by healing—indeed, that he should cease his activity altogether. Jesus replied that he would fulfill his office, which was to teach and to heal, until the chosen time had come.

Saturday, June 9, A.D. 31 (Sivan 29) Jesus and the disciples took a Sabbath walk together through the fields around Nain. Jesus spoke earnestly with the disciples about his future. He promised them that, if they would remain true to him, his power would always be with them. Later, on the way to the synagogue for the close of the Sabbath, he healed some sick people, again provoking cries of protest from the approaching Pharisees, who objected to the disturbance of the day of rest. Jesus reduced them to silence by accusing them of hypocrisy and oppression of the poor.

Sunday, June 10, A.D. 31 (Sivan 30) Jesus left Nain, going northward to Rimon, where he taught in an open place. Then he went on to Beth-Lechem, where he healed several people. Proceeding further, at sunset, he reached an inn on the outskirts of Azanoth.

TAMMUZ (29 days): June 10/11 to July 8/9, A.D. 31
Tammuz New Moon: June 8 at 10:00 P.M., Jerusalem time

Monday, June 11, A.D. 31 (Tammuz 1) After teaching in the synagogue at Azanoth, Jesus walked on to Damna, where he was greeted by Lazarus and the two nephews of Joseph of Arimathea. He spoke at length with Lazarus about accommodating those who would be arriving from Cyprus.

Tuesday, June 12, A.D. 31 (Tammuz 2) Jesus, together with Lazarus and the disciples, visited the village belonging to the Centurion Zorobabel of Capernaum where there was an inn that had been put at the disposal of Jesus and the disciples. At the inn, Jesus was met, among others, by Nathanael of Cana. Later, Zorobabel and Cornelius came and took a walk with Jesus before they returned to Capernaum. Then Jesus and the accompanying disciples went to the house of Mary, his mother. He dined alone with her and told her of his journey to Cyprus. The Holy Virgin spoke of her concern for his future. Jesus said she should think only of God's plan, which he would fulfill.

Wednesday, June 13, A.D. 31 (Tammuz 3) Today, many disciples from Bethsaida, Capernaum, and the surrounding region came to see Jesus. They greeted him and spoke with him. News was delivered that ships had arrived from Cyprus with about two hundred Jews, who needed to be accommodated. They had arrived in Joppe where they were met by Barnabas and Mnason.

MAP 32: *Travels in Galilee and Gaulanitis*

Thursday, June 14, A.D. 31 (Tammuz 4) This morning Jesus and some disciples visited Peter's wife, mother-in-law, and daughter. Jesus healed some sick people. Then he went on to Capernaum where he healed some children who later became disciples. In the afternoon, at Peter's house, Jesus met together with the disciples. He introduced them to three of the philosophers from Salamis. They had just arrived in Capernaum with James the Lesser and Judas Thaddeus. After dining together, Jesus and the disciples went to Andrew's house, where accounts were given of the various missionary journeys undertaken by each. (Most of the apostles, however, had not yet returned.) That evening, Jesus returned to his mother's house, where he introduced the newly converted disciples to her. Jesus and his mother had an inner accord that he should introduce his new disciples to her. This was so that, as their "spiritual mother," so to speak, she could find a place for each in her heart and in her prayers and bestow her blessing upon them.

Friday, June 15, A.D. 31 (Tammuz 5) This morning Jesus went with some disciples to the leper hospital north of Bethsaida. Here he healed and taught. Then he returned to Peter's house, where he healed a number of sick people who had been brought there. As the Sabbath began, he taught in the synagogue. He spoke out sharply against the Pharisees who were there to spy on him, and also interpreted the parable of the king's wedding feast (Matthew 22:1–14).

Saturday, June 16, A.D. 31 (Tammuz 6) Jesus and some disciples visited the homes of various people in Capernaum. He healed many children who were

ill, as there was an epidemic of scarlet fever. Then he visited Jairus, Zorobabel, and Cornelius. At the close of the Sabbath, he returned to preach in the
synagogue, addressing the Pharisees severely on account of their hypocrisy.
That evening, he dined at the home of Mary, his mother, the Holy Virgin;
also present were several apostles and disciples who had returned from their
journeys.

Sunday, June 17, A.D. *31 (Tammuz 7)* This morning Jesus taught the disciples
about their mission, work, attitudes, errors. He mentioned their future persecution and spoke at length about the parable of the workers in the vineyard
(Matthew 20:1–16). That afternoon, Peter, James the Greater, and Matthew
returned. All gathered in Peter's house, where they listened to Jesus' account
of his journey to Cyprus.

Monday, June 18, A.D. *31 (Tammuz 8)* Jesus and the disciples set sail on the
Sea of Galilee. It was a beautiful day and Jesus sat at the mast and taught.

Tuesday, June 19, A.D. *31 (Tammuz 9)* The Holy Virgin Mary and the holy
women went to Cana, where Mary Cleophas was living. Jesus followed with
nine apostles, Nathanael of Cana, and a few others.

Wednesday, June 20, A.D. *31 (Tammuz 10)* Many friends and relatives came
to see Jesus in Cana. They warned him of the bitterness of the Pharisees
toward him, saying that it was becoming more and more dangerous for him
to continue teaching. Jesus then taught them about his mission. He said that
he would do nothing except follow the will of his Father. Then, with the nine
apostles and some disciples, he went to Mount Tabor, where they were
reunited with the three remaining apostles—Thomas, John, and
Bartholomew—who had now returned from their missionary journeys.
They all went back to Cana together and dined at the house of Israel, the
father of the bride at the wedding (John 2:1–11). Present were: the twelve
apostles, the seventy disciples who had been sent out together with the apostles on their missionary journeys, the holy women, and many other friends
and relatives. It was a kind of feast of remembrance of the wedding at Cana,
and it was a great joy for all to be together again.

Thursday, June 21, A.D. *31 (Tammuz 11)* Jesus went with the apostles and
disciples to a hill about two hours' walk from Cana in the direction of

Gabara. Jesus asked them to tell what they had experienced on their missionary journeys. He said: "Now will be seen who has loved me—and, in me, my heavenly Father—and who has spread the word of salvation and healed, not for his own sake, and not for the sake of vain renown, but on my account." As Peter spoke enthusiastically about casting out demons from those possessed, Jesus bade him to be silent and, looking up to heaven, spoke the words recorded in Luke 10:18–20. As Jesus spoke, Anne Catherine saw a cloud of light shining around him; he prayed joyfully and addressed the disciples and apostles with the words recorded in Luke 10:21–24. Later, they all proceeded to the foot of the mountain near Gabara, where they ate a meal of fish, bread, honey and fruit. Afterward, they went up the mountain, and Jesus taught lessons related to what they had told him. Then they made their way to Capernaum, arriving there late at night.

Friday, June 22, A.D. 31 (Tammuz 12) This morning Jesus ate with his mother. In the afternoon, he taught the apostles and disciples. Then they all went together to the synagogue in Capernaum for the Sabbath. Here he taught concerning Korah and Abiram (Numbers 16) and spoke of Samuel's resigning from his judicial office (I Samuel 12). The Pharisees reproached Jesus for his disciples' failure to observe the Law. At this, Jesus again delivered a severe discourse against the Pharisees. He was interrupted by a young Pharisee suddenly crying out in a loud voice: "Truly this is the Son of God! The Holy One of Israel! He is more than a prophet!" A great commotion arose, and two Pharisees ejected the young man from the synagogue. Later, as Jesus was leaving, the young Pharisee cast himself down at his feet and begged to become a disciple. Jesus assented and introduced him to some of his disciples.

Saturday, June 23, A.D. 31 (Tammuz 13) Jesus taught in Bethsaida this morning. In the afternoon, he returned to Capernaum, where he and the disciples went to the synagogue before the close of the Sabbath. Jesus taught of the need to be awake at the coming of the Son of Man (Luke 12:35–40). Then, in answer to Peter's question as to whether he spoke for everyone or only for the disciples, Jesus replied as in Luke 12:41–59. After the close of the Sabbath, Jesus and some disciples were invited to dine with the Pharisees. Here, again, a dispute broke out (Luke 11:37–52). Afterward, Jesus was approached by a young man from Nazareth who had often sought to become a disciple. Then the exchange about the good Samaritan recounted in Luke 10:25–37 took place.

Sunday, June 24, A.D. 31 (Tammuz 14) Jesus and the disciples went to the mountain near Hanathon. Here they were joined by some people from the neighborhood. Jesus taught about the petitions of the Lord's Prayer (Luke 11:1–4). That night Jesus, the disciples, and others—in all, some fifty people—remained in prayer on the mountain.

Monday, June 25, A.D. 31 (Tammuz 15) This morning Jesus ended his teaching on prayer with a talk on the significance of the word *Amen*. Jesus received an invitation to go to Bethsaida-Julias. On the way, he went to an inn where the Holy Virgin and some of the holy women were waiting for him. Mary was downcast and begged Jesus not to go to Jerusalem for the Feast of the Dedication of the Temple. Jesus comforted her, saying that he would complete the work of his Father, and that she should be courageous and should strengthen and encourage the others. Jesus and the disciples then continued on to Bethsaida-Julias. There he dined with the Pharisees. That evening, he taught in the synagogue.

Tuesday, June 26, A.D. 31 (Tammuz 16) This morning Jesus climbed the mountain northeast of Bethsaida-Julias, where the feeding of the five thousand had occurred. Besides the apostles and disciples, people from Capernaum, Caesarea Philippi, and other places had gathered together to hear him. Jesus taught for about three hours (Matthew 5:10–20; 6:1–34; 7:1–27). Then, toward evening, he went to the town of Argob and stayed there overnight at an inn.

Wednesday, June 27, A.D. 31 (Tammuz 17) Today Jesus taught again on the mountain where he had been yesterday. A great multitude had now assembled, and Jesus taught in part what is recorded in Luke12. He also healed the sick and drove devils out of the possessed. The crowd was jubilant. Jesus pronounced woe upon Chorazin, Bethsaida, Capernaum (Luke 10:13–15) and also upon Jerusalem (Luke 13:34–35). Finally, he sent out the newly converted disciples, two by two. That evening, he returned to the inn at Argob.

Thursday, June 28, A.D. 31 (Tammuz 18) This morning Jesus took leave of most of the remaining apostles and disciples. Only Peter, James, John, Matthew, and a few disciples remained with him. They went to Matthew's custom house. Here several friends from Capernaum (Jairus, Zorobabel, Cornelius, and some others) were waiting for him. Jesus taught and consoled them before traveling on by boat to Dalmanutha, where he taught that evening.

MAP 33: *The Journey Through Auranitis*

Friday, June 29, A.D. 31 (Tammuz 19) Today, accompanied by Peter, James, and John, Jesus went to Edrai. With the beginning of the Sabbath they went to the synagogue, where he taught.

Saturday, June 30, A.D. 31 (Tammuz 20) Jesus taught again in the synagogue, interpreting various passages from the holy scripture (Numbers 19–21; Judges 11). He also healed many people.

Sunday, July 1, A.D. 31 (Tammuz 21) Today Jesus and the three apostles journeyed further eastward in the direction of Bosra. On the way, Jesus paused to teach. He also healed the sick and the possessed.

MAP 34: *The Journey in Hauran*

Monday, July 2, A.D. 31 (Tammuz 22) Bosra was a Levitical town where many pagans lived. Jesus spent some time with the Levites and then traveled further to Nobah, arriving there late at night.

Tuesday, July 3, A.D. 31 (Tammuz 23) In Nobah, Jesus healed many people who were possessed. Peter, James, and John also taught and healed.

Wednesday, July 4, A.D. 31 (Tammuz 24) Today Jesus and his companions traveled to a shepherd settlement called the "field of Jacob's peace," where Jesus healed some who were sick. Then, on a hill nearby, Jesus spoke to the shepherds, referring to the star of Jacob foretold by the prophet Balaam. He also spoke of the journey of the three kings from the East. After speaking of the fulfillment of John the Baptist's testimony concerning the Messiah, Jesus told the parable of the good shepherd (John 10:1–18).

Thursday, July 5, A.D. 31 (Tammuz 25) This morning Jesus visited the huts of some of the shepherds, teaching and consoling them. He then went to Salcha, arriving there around midday. He was well received. Many were baptized, the sick were healed, and children were blessed. Jesus also taught in the synagogue.

Friday, July 6, A.D. *31 (Tammuz 26)* Before noon, Jesus and his traveling companions left Salcha and walked westward along what is called the "Way of David" on account of David's having hidden himself in this region near Mizpeh (1 Samuel 22). Jesus told his companions how Abraham had approached the promised land along David's Way and how the procession of the three holy kings had also traveled the same path. Then, after a time, they left the Way of David and went southward to the town of Thantia, arriving there at the onset of the Sabbath. In the synagogue, Jesus spoke of Balaam and the star of Jacob (Numbers 24:17) and of Micah's prophecy concerning Bethlehem (Micah 5:2).

Saturday, July 7, A.D. *31 (Tammuz 27)* Today, in Thantia, Jesus healed several people in their homes, and the disciples baptized many converts. Jesus taught again concerning the star of Jacob, Micah's prophecy, and the journey of the three kings—all of this in relation to the coming of the Messiah.

Sunday, July 8, A.D. 31 (Tammuz 28) Jesus traveled from Thantia to Datheman, where there was a ruined citadel, used in the war of the Maccabees (1 Maccabees 5:9). Nearby was the mountain where Jephthah's daughter and her twelve maiden-companions had lamented for two months before Jephthah was put to death (Judges 11:29–40). Balaam had also been on this mountain when he was summoned by the King of Moab (Numbers 22:4–5). Jesus ascended the mountain and taught. That evening, he went to Datheman.

*   *   *

This entry for Sunday, July 8, A.D. 31 (Tammuz 28) was the last of the daily accounts of Anne Catherine's visions that Clemens Brentano entered into his notebooks. He added: "What a pity! What a shame! Everything is lost!" Brentano wrote his entry on the evening of January 8, 1824. From then on, owing to unspeakable suffering, although she continued to live in visions of the day-by-day life of Christ, Anne Catherine was unable to communicate anything further. On January 14, she uttered the words, recorded by Clemens Brentano: "O, now I would soon be finished with relating the life of Jesus! And now I am in this wretched condition!" Within a month, however, on February 9, 1824, she was dead.

In fact, as mentioned earlier (in Chapter One), 313 days are missing from Anne Catherine's account—from where she left off (July 8, A.D. 31) to the period shortly before the raising of Lazarus. Historically, these 313 days run from July 9, A.D. 31 to May 16, A.D. 32. In other words, Anne Catherine's daily chronicle of Christ's ministry begins again on May 17, A.D. 32.

As explained in Chapter One, all that we know of the missing period comes from the Gospel of Saint John. This may be summarized as follows:

(1) Jesus was in Galilee before the Feast of Tabernacles; his brothers advised him to go to Judea (John 7:1–9).

(2) Jesus attended the Feast of Tabernacles (September 19–26, A.D. 31) in Jerusalem (John 7:10–36).

(3) On the last day of the Feast, he spoke the words: "If anyone thirst, let him come to me and drink," and the Pharisees tried to have him arrested (John 7:37–52).

(4) In the temple, Jesus pardoned the woman who had committed adultery (John 8:1–11).

(5) In the temple, Jesus referred to himself with the words: "I am the light of the world" (John 8:12). The Pharisees disputed with him and took up stones to throw at him, but Jesus hid himself and left the temple (John 8:13–59).

(6) Near the pool of Siloam in Jerusalem, Jesus healed the man born blind (John 9). As this healing took place on the Sabbath, i.e. between Friday evening and Saturday evening, it must have been on one of the following dates in A.D. 31: October 5/6, October 12/13, October 19/20, October 26/27, November 2/3, November 9/10, November 16/17 or November 23/24.

(7) Jesus told the parable of the good shepherd (John 10:1–21).

(8) Jesus attended the Feast of the Dedication of the Temple in Jerusalem (November 28 –December 5, A.D. 31), where the Pharisees tried to arrest him again (John 10:22–39).

(9) He went to the place on the Jordan between Ainon and Salem, where John had first baptized (John 10:40).

(10) Although not mentioned in the Gospel of Saint John, it is almost certain that Jesus attended the Feast of the Passover in Jerusalem in the month of Nisan A.D. 32, which started on Nisan 15, equating historically with April 14/15, A.D. 32, and lasted for one week.

*   *   *

YEAR 4
Nisan 15, A.D. 32, to Nisan 14, A.D. 33
April 14/15, A.D. 32, to April 2/3, A.D. 33

MAP 35: *Travels in Ammonitis and Judea*

Saturday, May 17, A.D. 32 (Iyyar 17) Accompanied by Peter, James, and John, Jesus went to Bethabara, where he was joined by Matthew and another apostle. A large crowd had gathered. Jesus healed a great many people. It was here that Jesus spoke of marriage, blessed the children brought to him (Matthew 19:10–15), and advised the rich youth (Matthew 19:16–26). This last incident was followed by the exchange of words between Peter and Jesus recorded in Matthew 19:27–30. Then, toward evening, Jesus went to dine in a house where about ten of the holy women were gathered. These included Martha, Mary Magdalene and her maidservant Marcella, Mary Salome, Mary Cleophas, Veronica, and Mary Mark of Jerusalem. Jesus continued to teach.

Sunday, May 18, A.D. 32 (Iyyar 18) This evening, after the close of the Sabbath, Jesus with the five apostles traveled eastward from Bethabara. Not far from Nebo he was met by some people who asked him to visit a house where ten lepers lay. He went to the house and healed the lepers, instructing them to bathe in a nearby pool and to present themselves to the priests to show that they were healed. As Jesus then continued on his way, one of the lepers ran after him, cast himself down and gave thanks. (A similar incident repeated itself later on Sivan 14 and is described in Luke 17:11–19).

Monday, May 19, A.D. 32 (Iyyar 19) Jesus and the five apostles traveled southward in the direction of Madian. On the way, they were joined by four other apostles and several disciples.

Tuesday, May 20, A.D. 32 (Iyyar 20) They did not enter Madian. Instead, they went to a Jewish settlement on the outskirts of the town. Here Jesus taught.

Wednesday, May 21, A.D. 32 (Iyyar 21) Today Jesus and his traveling companions made their way northward from Madian in the direction of Jericho. They stayed the night with some shepherds.

Thursday, May 22, A.D. 32 (Iyyar 22) Not far from the Jordan there was a large house where a shepherd family lived. Jesus went into the house. Here he recounted the parable of the unmerciful servant (Matthew 18:23–35) and spoke the words: "Those who say they are chaste, but who eat and drink only what pleases their appetite, are like those who try to extinguish a fire with dry wood."

Friday, May 23, A.D. 32 (Iyyar 23) Jesus and nine apostles and many disciples made their way to Bethjesimoth, where Jesus was awaited by the other apostles (Bartholomew, Judas and another) and several disciples. With the onset of the Sabbath, he taught in the synagogue at Bethjesimoth. He also healed a crippled woman. And again the Pharisees protested against healing on the Sabbath.

Saturday, May 24, to Tuesday, May 27, A.D. 32 (Iyyar 24–27) Jesus remained these four days in Bethjesimoth. The Pharisees tried to prevent him from going into the synagogue, but Jesus walked through them and entered the holy building, where he taught in parables.

Wednesday, May 28, A.D. 32 (Iyyar 28) Today, on the way to Jericho, the apostles and disciples related their experiences and what they had done on their travels in Jesus' name. Jesus said: "Now you cling to me, because you fare well. In the time of need, you will act otherwise. Even those who bear a mantle of love toward me will let it fall and will flee." He was referring to John on the night of Gethsemane (Mark 14:51–52).

Thursday, May 29, A.D. 32 (Iyyar 29) Not far from Jericho, four Pharisees approached Jesus and warned him not to come, as Herod sought to kill him. Jesus replied as recorded in Luke 13:31–35. Then two brothers from Jericho came to him to ask him to divide their inheritance (Luke 12:13–34). Jesus also blessed many of the children of the city who came to see him.

SIVAN (30 days): May 29/30 to June 27/28, A.D. 32
Sivan New Moon: May 28 at midnight (0 hours), Jerusalem time

Friday, May 30, A.D. 32 (Sivan 1) A large crowd gathered on the outskirts of Jericho to see Jesus. The chief tax collector, Zacchaeus, also wanted to see him and, because he was small in stature, climbed a sycamore tree for a better view.

There then took place the exchange between Zacchaeus and Jesus as recorded in Luke 19:1–10. Then, at the start of the Sabbath, Jesus and the disciples went to the synagogue. Afterward, they dined at an inn. Zacchaeus came too.

Saturday, May 31, A.D. 32 (Sivan 2) Today, Jesus taught in the synagogue in Jericho. After the close of the Sabbath, he and the apostles went to Zacchaeus' house, where they dined. Jesus told the parable of the fig tree (Luke 13:6–9) and other parables. He then stayed the night with Zacchaeus. It was about this time that Lazarus became deathly ill.

Sunday, June 1, to Tuesday, June 3, A.D. 32 (Sivan 3–5) Jesus and the disciples stayed in Jericho.

Wednesday, June 4, A.D. 32 (Sivan 6) Today Jesus and his disciples were invited to dine with the Pharisees. During the meal, they accused Jesus of breaking the Law by healing on the Sabbath. Jesus replied in words similar to those recorded in Luke 14:1–24. Today, many people in Jericho were baptized by James and Bartholomew.

Thursday, June 5, A.D. 32 (Sivan 7) Jesus taught in the synagogue and on the streets of Jericho. Many tax collectors and sinners came to hear him, and the Pharisees plotted against him (Luke 15:1–2). The disciples were unhappy that Jesus associated with tax collectors and sinners. Because of this, Jesus told them the parables recorded in Luke 15:3–32.

Friday, June 6, A.D. 32 (Sivan 8) After healing a woman with an issue of blood this morning, Jesus taught concerning repeated and constant prayer. Later, messengers came from Bethany requesting Jesus to go there and heal Lazarus. But Jesus replied that the time was not yet ripe and that he would travel first to Samaria.

Saturday, June 7, A.D. 32 (Sivan 9) Today, on the Sabbath, Jesus taught and healed, going from house to house. It was the end of his stay in Jericho, and he wished to pour out the fullness of his love upon the people there.

Sunday, June 8, A.D. 32 (Sivan 10) Jesus taught and healed and also drove out demons from those possessed. He sent out the apostles and disciples, two by two.

Monday, June 9, A.D. 32 (Sivan 11) About one hundred Pharisees from various places came to Jericho. Together with the local Pharisees, they questioned Jesus. Jesus replied with such powerful words that they were reduced to silence.

Tuesday, June 10, A.D. 32 (Sivan 12) Today Jesus left Jericho and went to a village about an hour north of the city. On the way, he passed two blind people sitting at the roadside and restored their sight to them (Matthew 20:29–34).

Wednesday, June 11, A.D. 32 (Sivan 13) In the village north of Jericho many sick people had gathered. Jesus healed them. He also taught there.

Thursday, June 12, A.D. 32 (Sivan 14) Not far from the village were ten lepers in a tent. Jesus healed them, but only one ran after Jesus to thank him (Luke 17:11–19). The leper who ran after Jesus later became a disciple. Shortly afterward, as they passed along, a man came out of a shepherd settlement and begged Jesus to come because his daughter had just died. Jesus, accompanied by Peter, James, and John went with the shepherd to his house. His daughter, who was about seven years old, lay dead. Looking up to heaven, Jesus placed one hand on her head and the other on her breast and prayed. The child then rose up, alive. Jesus told the apostles that—in his name—they should do as he did.

Friday, June 13, to Tuesday, June 17, A.D. 32 (Sivan 15–19) Still among the shepherds, Jesus and the three apostles went from dwelling to dwelling and healed many who were sick.

Wednesday, June 18, A.D. 32 (Sivan 20) Today, Jesus went into the mountainous region near Hebron. Here he and Peter attended a wedding celebration in a shepherd's dwelling. Jesus then healed many weak and sickly children.

Thursday, June 19, A.D. 32 (Sivan 21) Today, Jesus went southward toward Juttah, accompanied by some of the wedding guests. As he went, he was joined by three more apostles, among them Andrew. On the way, he healed more children.

Friday, June 20, A.D. 32 (Sivan 22) At the onset of the Sabbath, Jesus went to the synagogue of a small village in the mountains near Juttah. The priests did not want him to teach there but were obliged to let him do so.

Saturday, June 21, A.D. 32 (Sivan 23) Today, on the Sabbath, Jesus taught again in the village synagogue. He spoke about not being able to serve two masters (Matthew 6:24).

Sunday, June 22, to Tuesday, June 24, A.D. 32 (Sivan 24–26) Jesus taught again in the village. He said that he had come to bring a sword (Matthew 10:34–36). The disciples were confused by this utterance, but Jesus explained to them that he meant the renunciation of all evil.

Wednesday, June 25, A.D. 32 (Sivan 27) Jesus sent off most of the apostles and disciples. He left the village and went north to Bethain, where he taught under a tree.

*   *   *

Note: Owing to great suffering, at this point Anne Catherine was unable to communicate anything for thirteen days. During this time it is possible that Jesus journeyed northward to Capernaum and was returning back through Samaria when Anne Catherine resumed her account. At first, she was able to communicate only fragments from the period we are now entering that leads up to the raising of Lazarus.

*   *   *

MAP 36: *The Raising of Lazarus*

Wednesday, July 9, A.D. 32 (Tammuz 11) Jesus stayed at a little village in Samaria. His mother, accompanied by her elder sister, Mary Heli, and Mary Heli's daughter, Mary Cleophas, were on their way from Bethany to meet him and urge him to come to Bethany and heal Lazarus.

Thursday, July 10, A.D. 32 (Tammuz 12) The three holy women came to Jesus today and told him of Martha and Mary Magdalene's request that he come to Bethany, as Lazarus lay seriously ill (John 11:6).

Friday, July 11, to Saturday, July 12, A.D. 32 (Tammuz 13–14) Having talked with Jesus, the three holy women decided to stay in the little village to celebrate the Sabbath there. Jesus himself went to another place with a large synagogue. Here he taught and healed and blessed some children.

Sunday, July 13, to Tuesday, July 15, A.D. 32 (Tammuz 15–17) During these days Jesus taught concerning the good Samaritan (Luke 10:30–37) and the lost coin (Luke 15:8–10). He also healed the sick and blessed many children.

Wednesday, July 16, A.D. 32 (Tammuz 18) Jesus, accompanied by some apostles, returned to the little village, where the three holy women were waiting for him. Together they received the news of Lazarus' death. It was here that Jesus spoke the words: "Our friend Lazarus has fallen asleep" (John 11:7–13).

Thursday, July 17, A.D. 32 (Tammuz 19) Toward evening, Jesus, accompanied by the three holy women and the apostles, set off for Bethany. They traveled that night by moonlight to Lazarus' country estate near Ginnim. Here Martha and Mary Magdalene were waiting for him.

Friday, July 18, A.D. 32 (Tammuz 20) The holy women stayed at Lazarus' estate. Jesus and the apostles went to Ginnim for the Sabbath. Jesus taught in the synagogue.

Saturday, July 19, A.D. 32 (Tammuz 21) After the close of the Sabbath, Jesus and the apostles returned to Lazarus' estate. Mary Magdalene came to meet Jesus on the way. She lamented over the death of Lazarus, saying that if Jesus had been there he would not have died. Jesus replied that his time had not yet come. They then ate at Lazarus' estate and Jesus taught. He asked Martha and Mary Magdalene to allow all of Lazarus' effects to stay in Bethany, saying that he would come there in a few days. It was now that he told the apostles that Lazarus was dead (John 11:14–16).

Sunday, July 20, A.D. 32 (Tammuz 22) This morning, the holy women set off back to Bethany. Jesus and the apostles returned to Ginnim.

Monday, July 21, A.D. 32 (Tammuz 23) Today, Jesus and the apostles journeyed towards Bethany.

Tuesday, July 22, A.D. 32 (Tammuz 24) Toward evening they reached the inn of a little place near Bahurim. Here Jesus taught concerning the laborers in the vineyard (Matthew 20:1–16). Mary Salome, the mother of James and John, approached him to request that her two sons be allowed to take a place beside him in his kingdom (Matthew 20:20–21).

Wednesday, July 23, A.D. 32 (Tammuz 25) Jesus taught in the synagogue. He reproached the disciples for being impatient with him because he had delayed so long in going to Bethany. Jesus said that he was like a person who could not give an account of his views and actions, because they would not be understood.

Thursday, July 24, A.D. 32 (Tammuz 26) In this little place near Bahurim there were Pharisees who reported back to Jerusalem concerning Jesus. Mary Salome again approached Jesus on account of her two sons, James and John, but he rebuked her sternly.

Friday, July 25, A.D. 32 (Tammuz 27) Jesus and the apostles made their way to Bethany. As he walked, Jesus taught. Mary Salome went on ahead, arriving in Bethany toward evening. She went first to Martha to tell her that Jesus was approaching. Mary Magdalene went with Mary Salome to greet him, but she returned without having spoken to him. Then Martha went to meet him. In the exchange that took place between Martha and Jesus, Jesus spoke the words: "I am the resurrection and the life" (John 11:17–27). It was dusk. Martha hurried back and spoke with Mary Magdalene, who went up to Jesus, casting herself at his feet and saying: "Lord, if you had been here, my brother would not have died." Jesus wept (John 11:28–37). Jesus then taught about death late into the night.

Saturday, July 26, A.D. 32 (Tammuz 28) In the early hours of the morning, Jesus went to Lazarus' grave. He was accompanied by the apostles, seven holy women, and many other people. He went into the vault where Lazarus' tomb was. Lazarus had been dead for several days, and his corpse had lain for some days before being entombed, for it had been hoped that Jesus would come and wake him from the dead. As Jesus instructed the apostles to remove the stone from the grave, Martha said: "Lord, by this time there will be an odor, for he has been buried for four days." There then took place the raising of Lazarus from the dead, as described in John 11:38-44. After the cloths and winding-sheet had been removed, Lazarus climbed out of his coffin and came out from the tomb. He tottered on his feet and looked like a phantom. He went past Jesus through the door of the vault. His sisters and the other holy women stepped back, as if he were a ghost. Jesus followed him from the vault into the open air, went up to him, and took hold of both his hands in a gesture of friendship. A great crowd of people, who beheld Lazarus in fear and wonder, thronged around. Jesus walked with Lazarus to his house. The apostles and the holy women went with them. A great tumult arose among the crowd. Inside the house, the women went to prepare a meal, leaving Jesus and the apostles alone with Lazarus. The apostles formed a circle around Jesus and Lazarus. Lazarus kneeled before Jesus who blessed him, laying his right hand on Lazarus' head and breathing upon him seven times. Thus, he consecrated Lazarus to his service, purifying him of all earthly connections and infusing him with the seven gifts of the Holy Spirit, which the apostles would receive only later, at Whitsun. Afterward, all dined together. Jesus taught, and Lazarus sat next to him. Because there was a great commotion outside, Jesus sent the apostles to disperse the crowd. He continued to teach that evening.

Sunday, July 27, A.D. 32 (Tammuz 29) Before daybreak, Jesus, accompanied by John and Matthew, went to Jerusalem to the house on Mount Zion where later the Last Supper would take place. This house belonged to Nicodemus. Jesus remained there for the whole day and that night. Mary Mark, Veronica, and about a dozen other friends came to visit him. He taught and consoled them. Meanwhile, a meeting of the Pharisees and high priests was being held to discuss the raising of Lazarus by Jesus. The Pharisees feared that Jesus might awaken all the dead and that this would lead to great confusion. In Bethany, a great tumult arose. Lazarus was forced to hide and the ten apostles left.

AB (30 days): July 27/28 to August 25/26, A.D. 32
Ab New Moon: July 26 at 5:00 A.M. Jerusalem time

Monday, July 28, A.D. 32 (Ab 1) Before sunrise, Jesus, John, and Matthew left Jerusalem. They crossed the Jordan and traveled in a northeasterly direction. That evening, they met up with six other apostles, who had journeyed from Bethany.

Tuesday, July 29, A.D. *32 (Ab 2)* Traveling on, Jesus healed a blind man, a shepherd from the region of Jericho, who immediately wanted to become a disciple. Reaching a small village, Jesus taught in a hall.

Wednesday, July 30, A.D. *32 (Ab 3)* On the way toward a small town, Jesus passed by a fig tree that had no figs on it and cursed it, just as he did later on the way to Jerusalem on Adar 29, after his triumphant entry into Jerusalem (Matthew 21:18–20). Reaching the town, Jesus taught in the synagogue and spoke of the significance of the barren fig tree (Luke 13:6–9).

Thursday, July 31, A.D. *32 (Ab 4)* Jesus and his traveling companions made their way northward through Perea. He began to instruct the disciples regarding what they should do when he would be away. That night, Jesus stayed with some shepherds.

Friday, August 1, A.D. *32 (Ab 5)* Jesus wanted to hold the Sabbath in the town of Great Chorazin. He dismissed most of the apostles. Then, around noon, he went into the town, accompanied by Andrew, Peter, and Philip. He taught in the synagogue.

Saturday, August 2, A.D. *32 (Ab 6)* This morning, Jesus taught again in the synagogue. About midday, a man from Capernaum came to him, begging him to come and heal his son, who was dangerously ill. Jesus told him to re-turn to Capernaum where he would find that his son was well. After healing the boy from a distance, Jesus then healed many other sick people. Later, fol-lowing the close of Sabbath, Jesus and the apostles left the town. They crossed the Jordan on a raft formed of beams strung together. They then traveled by moonlight to Bethsaida. Here they went to Andrew's house.

Sunday, August 3, A.D. *32 (Ab 7)* Today, Jesus visited another house in Beth-saida. Here some of the holy women had gathered. Later, Jesus and the three apostles left Bethsaida and went to a house north of the town. Here he taught a group of disciples. Then Jesus, accompanied by Andrew, Peter and Philip, traveled further, crossing back across the Jordan.

Monday, August 4, A.D. *32 (Ab 8)* Jesus and the three apostles journeyed for the whole day and night through the region known as Basan, east of the Sea of Galilee.

Tuesday, August 5, A.D. *32 (Ab 9)* At around five this morning, after having slept apart, Jesus and the three apostles met at a prearranged place. They then journeyed on together. As they went, Jesus taught. In the evening, they stopped at an inn, where Jesus told them of his plans for the coming journey. He said that only three disciples would accompany him: Eliud, Silas, and Eremenzear. These were three shepherd youths, sixteen, seventeen, or eighteen years of age. Jesus told the others to meet him, on his return, at Jacob's well near Sychar. He indicated when this would be (Tebeth 22). In the intervening period, the disciples were to continue their work.

MAP 37: *The Journey to Chaldea and Egypt*

Wednesday, August 6, A.D. *32 (Ab 10)* At daybreak, Jesus and the three shepherd youths parted company with the apostles and disciples, who were saddened by the departure. Andrew, Peter, and Philip returned to their homes. The remaining disciples split up and went in various directions. Jesus and his traveling companions meanwhile journeyed eastward, Jesus teaching as they went. That night, they stayed at a house. Jesus did not say who he was and was taken to be a traveling shepherd. He taught in parables but did not heal anyone.

Thursday, August 7, A.D. *32 (Ab 11)* This morning, Jesus traveled on in a southeasterly direction. He and the three young shepherds stayed the night with some shepherds they met on the way. Anne Catherine tells that there had been a great uproar in Jerusalem about the raising of Lazarus and that Jesus had left Judea in order to be forgotten. This journey outside of Palestine, accompanied by only the three shepherd youths, was not recorded, as no apostle was present, and no one really knew where he was.

Friday, August 8, A.D. *32 (Ab 12)* Today, before the onset of the Sabbath, Jesus and the three youths reached the town of Cedar, one of the last towns east of Palestine where there was a Jewish settlement. Cedar was divided into a heathen and a Jewish quarter. Jesus and the youths went to the synagogue for the celebration of the Sabbath. There, Jesus was held to be a prophet.

Saturday, August 9, and Sunday, August 10, A.D. *32 (Ab 13–14)* Jesus taught in Cedar, where he was invited to various homes. He also taught in the open by the town well.

Monday, August 11, A.D. 32 (Ab 15) This morning, Jesus was still in Cedar. The people had asked him to remain until the next Sabbath and to teach in the synagogue. That evening, he went to a little village east of Cedar to which he had been invited. He stayed there overnight.

Tuesday, August 12, A.D. 32 (Ab 16) This evening, he returned to Cedar.

Wednesday, August 13, A.D. 32 (Ab 17) Today, Jesus and the three youths journeyed eastward to Edon. On the way, Jesus healed a bedridden married couple in their home. The couple then followed Jesus to Edon.

Thursday, August 14, A.D. 32 (Ab 18) This afternoon, Jesus and his traveling companions reached Edon. They went to a wedding celebration to which Jesus had been invited. It was in progress when they arrived. News of Jesus had spread from Cedar and he was received as a prophet. At the wedding feast, Jesus taught, telling of a man who had changed water into wine at a wedding in Cana. The celebration lasted late into the night.

Friday, August 15, A.D. 32 (Ab 19) This morning, in Edon, Jesus taught in front of the house where the wedding celebration had taken place. He taught about marriage. Then he returned to Cedar for the Sabbath. That evening, until about ten o'clock, he taught in an open place for prayer, a garden next to the synagogue. Then he went into the synagogue.

Saturday, August 16, A.D. 32 (Ab 20) During the day, Jesus taught in the synagogue and, that evening, in the garden next to the synagogue. He spoke again about marriage.

Sunday, August 17, A.D. 32 (Ab 21) This morning Jesus continued to speak in the synagogue about marriage. A divorced couple came to him. There were two groups: the husband and his relatives and the wife and her relatives. Jesus spoke with each group separately. Then the couple came together, held hands, and Jesus blessed them.

Monday, August 18, A.D. 32 (Ab 22) This evening Jesus visited a shepherd settlement north of Cedar. Many people went with him. It was a beautiful night and the stars shone brightly.

Tuesday, August 19, A.D. *32 (Ab 23)* Jesus and the three youths went further today. In the evening, they arrived at Sichar, a little town north of Cedar. Jesus was received as a guest in the house of Eliud, whose wife had been unfaithful. Eliud knew nothing of it. Jesus spoke alone with the wife who confessed her guilt and sank down weeping at Jesus' feet. Jesus blessed her and then spoke words of consolation to Eliud, but without mentioning his wife's infidelity.

Wednesday, August 20, A.D. *32 (Ab 24)* This morning Jesus took hold of Eliud's hands and spoke with him lovingly about the washing of the feet. Then he began to speak to Eliud of his destiny. Jesus told him that his children were not his, but had been conceived illicitly, and that his wife was again expecting a child that was not his. He said that his wife regretted this and wanted to make amends. He said that Eliud should forgive his wife. Eliud then cast himself down on the ground, smitten with anguish. Jesus stood in silent prayer. After a while, he raised Eliud up, comforted him, and washed his feet. Eliud became quiet and still. Jesus instructed him to call his wife, who came into the room. She was wearing a veil. Jesus took her hand, placed it in Eliud's hand, and blessed and comforted them. He raised the wife's veil, and bid her to send the children to him, whom he also blessed. From this time on, the couple remained true to one another. Afterward, Jesus went from house to house.

Thursday, August 21, A.D. *32 (Ab 25)* This afternoon Jesus taught beneath the porch of the town hall. He spoke in parables, referring to the bees, as there were many beehives kept by the people of the town. He spoke also of the vine and the vineyard, saying that he would produce the "wine of life" from the true vine.

Friday, August 22, A.D. *32 (Ab 26)* This morning Jesus visited many people of the town, teaching about the cultivation of the vine and drawing analogies with marriage and alluding to his work of love, wherever it may bear fruit. That afternoon he attended a wedding which took place in the open air, in front of the synagogue. With nightfall, as the stars shone above, they held the Sabbath in the synagogue.

Saturday, August 23, A.D. *32 (Ab 27)* Jesus taught in parables. He spoke of the prodigal son (Luke 15:11-32) and of the many rooms in his Father's house

(John 14:2). He again spoke about marriage and of the importance of regarding marriage as a spiritual task, one that included the spiritual education of children. Moreover, he alluded to himself as the spouse of a bride in whom all those gathered together would be reborn.

Sunday, August, 24, A.D. 32 (Ab 28) Jesus persuaded the people of Sichar to build a house for the newly-married couple close to the hill where the beehives were placed. He instructed the couple to cultivate a vineyard behind the house, in the area reaching up to where the bees were.

Monday, August 25, A.D. 32 (Ab 29) Jesus remained in Sichar.

Tuesday, August 26, A.D. 32 (Ab 30) Today began the Feast of the New Moon. It was celebrated in the evening in the synagogue. Afterward the people of Sichar gathered in the town hall to hear Jesus speak. He told them that he would not stay in Sichar, that he had no house, and that his kingdom would come later. First, he had to cultivate and water his Father's vineyard. He taught until late into the night.

> ELUL (29 days): August 26/27 to September 23/24, A.D. 32
> Elul New Moon: August 24 at 9:15 P.M., Jerusalem time.

Wednesday, August 27, A.D. 32 (Elul 1) Jesus stayed on in Sichar.

Thursday, August 28, A.D. 32 (Elul 2) Today Jesus visited the house where the bride's parents lived. Then he went to the place where the vineyard was to be cultivated. A trellis had already been set up. A large bunch of grapes was brought to him, and he selected five grapes. He dug up the ground, planted the grapes at a certain distance from the trellis and showed the people how the vine should be tied in a cross to the trellis. During this he taught concerning marriage, relating everything that takes place through nature and through cultivation of the vine to reproduction and spiritual fruit. Then they went to the synagogue and Jesus taught further about marriage. He talked of the dangers of intoxication.

Friday, August 29, A.D. 32 (Elul 3) This evening he went to the synagogue for the Sabbath and taught there.

Saturday, August 30, A.D. 32 (Elul 4) Today, Jesus taught again in the synagogue. He spoke of the bridegroom's house, which was delicate in construction. The bride groom was named Salathiel. Jesus said that one should not become too attached to the earth. Why build a house for the body, when this itself was a fragile house. The house of the soul should be purified and sanctified as a temple, and should not be desecrated. He also spoke of the Messiah and how to recognize him.

Sunday, August 31, A.D. 32 (Elul 5) Today Jesus spoke with a couple who wanted to marry. He told them that their plan to marry was motivated by the desire for property. They were shocked that he could read their thoughts, for they had not spoken with anyone about their secret intentions. Then they gave up their plans and believed in Jesus.

Monday, September 1, A.D. 32 (Elul 6) Jesus taught further today concerning marriage. He spoke of David, who had fallen into sin on account of the superabundance of forces within him, which he should have consumed within himself. He added that nothing is lost through continence, but rather through wastefulness. This afternoon he went about one hour east of Sichar to the house of a rich herd owner who had died suddenly in one of his fields. His wife and children were very sad and had sent for Jesus, begging him to come to the funeral. He came, accompanied by the three shepherd youths, by Salathiel and his wife, and about twenty-five other people from Sichar. After sending away the people of Sichar, apart from Salathiel and his wife, Jesus spoke with the wife of the dead man, whose name was Nazor. He said that if she and her son and daughter would believe in his teaching and follow him, and if they would keep silence on the matter, Nazor would be raised to life again. For, he said, Nazor's soul had not yet passed on to be judged but was still present over the place in the field where he had died. Jesus then went with them to the field. Praying, he called Nazor back to his body, saying to those present: "When we return, Nazor will be alive and sitting upright!" They then returned to the house to find Nazor sitting upright in his coffin, wrapped in linen cloths and with his hands bound. After being freed from the wrappings, Nazor climbed out of the coffin and cast himself down at Jesus' feet. Jesus told him to wash and purify himself, stay hidden in his room, and say nothing of being raised from the dead, until he (Jesus) had left the region. Jesus and the five people with him then stayed there overnight.

Tuesday, September 2, A.D. 32 (Elul 7) This morning, Jesus spoke with Nazor and washed his feet. He said that in the future he should think more of his soul and should put right the wrong he had done to some poor shepherds whose property he had unjustly confiscated. Jesus then blessed Nazor's wife and children. Afterward, he spoke with Salathiel and his wife, saying to Salathiel: "You have allowed yourself to be drawn by the beauty of your wife's body. But think how beautiful the soul must be, that God sends his Son to the Earth in order to save the soul through the sacrifice of his body." Jesus said that he wanted to teach on the Sabbath at the synagogue in Cedar, and that he would then leave this area and travel east through Arabia. They asked him why he wanted to go to those who worshipped the stars. He answered that he had friends there who had followed a star to greet him at his birth and that he wanted to seek them out in order to invite them, also, into the vineyard of the kingdom of his Father. That night, Jesus stayed at Nazor's house.

Wednesday, September 3, and Thursday, September 4, A.D. 32 (Elul 8–9) Jesus returned to Sichar, where a crowd of people had gathered. To the great astonishment of the crowd, Jesus then publicly healed the sick. All were filled with joy at these miraculous healings.

Friday, September 5, A.D. 32 (Elul 10) Today, at noon, Jesus taught in a house in Cedar. His theme was marriage. Salathiel and his wife were there. Jesus spoke of the conditions for living together in order to become good vine. All things between husband and wife should be dealt with lovingly. They should remain free of desire and should consider their motivation for each action in their marriage. If motivated by desire alone, a couple would reap bitter fruit. Jesus warned those present concerning overindulgence and instructed them to pray, exercise restraint, and guard against the intoxication of wine. After the onset of the Sabbath, Jesus spoke with a man, also called Nazor, who was responsible for the administration of the synagogue. He was a descendant of Tobias. Jesus then taught about the life of Tobias.

Saturday, September 6, A.D. 32 (Elul 11) Throughout the Sabbath, Jesus taught concerning the vine, the grain, bread, and wine. He spoke of Melchizedek as a forerunner, whose sacrifice was bread and wine; in himself, however, the sacrifice had become flesh and blood. Jesus indicated clearly that he was the Messiah, and said that they should follow him.

Sunday, September 7, to Monday, September 8, A.D. 32 (Elul 12–13) Jesus remained in Cedar.

Tuesday, September 9, A.D. 32 (Elul 14) Today, Jesus and the three shepherd youths left Cedar. About twenty people accompanied them to a place some distance from the town. Here Jesus blessed those who had accompanied them and then those who had accompanied them returned to Cedar. This was about midday. Jesus and the young shepherds went eastward and toward evening came to a settlement where the people lived in tents. Jesus and his traveling companions were invited to eat and stay there. Anne Catherine beheld a festival of star worship that took place there that night (it was the night after the Full Moon). The heathens cried out as the Moon rose or when other stars rose —later that night Mars rose, later still Jupiter, and then later still Saturn.

Wednesday, September 10, A.D. 32 (Elul 15) This morning Jesus taught the heathens, reprimanding them for their sacrificial practices, saying that they should pray to the Father who had created everything. He was well received. Then he left. As he was traveling further with the three shepherd youths, he remarked to them how well he had been received by the heathens.

Thursday, September 11, and Friday, September 12, A.D. 32 (Elul 16–17) Jesus and his three young traveling companions made rapid progress on their way. Around the onset of the Sabbath, they arrived at a well not far from a small shepherd settlement. Here they prayed together and held the Sabbath. Here Anne Catherine Emmerich remarked that the accusation on the part of the Pharisees that he did not sanctify the Sabbath simply was not true.

Saturday, September 13, A.D. 32 (Elul 18) Today some shepherds came to Jesus to hear him teach. He asked them if they had heard of the men who more than thirty years ago had been led to Judea by a star to greet the newborn King of the Jews? They replied: "Yes, yes!" Whereupon Jesus said that he was this King of the Jews and that he now wanted to visit these men again. (Anne Catherine Emmerich saw that the kings already knew, through dreams, that Jesus was coming to them.) That evening, after teaching, Jesus dined with the shepherds and blessed the meal that they ate together.

Sunday, September 14, A.D. 32 (Elul 19) Jesus taught the shepherds again today. He spoke of the creation of the world and of the Fall and of the promise of the restoration of all. During this discourse something wonderful took place. He appeared to catch a sunbeam with his right hand, and he made a luminous globe of light from it. It hung from the palm of his hand on a ray of light. While he was talking, the shepherds could see all the things he was describing in the globe of light. The Holy Trinity itself appeared there. At the end of this discourse, the globe of light disappeared, and the shepherds cast themselves down in sorrow. Jesus later taught them a wonderful prayer and how to worship God, the creator of all.

Monday, September 15, A.D. 32 (Elul 20) Today, Jesus stayed with the shepherds, teaching them about their flocks and also about various herbs.

Tuesday, September 16, and Wednesday, September 17, A.D. 32 (Elul 21–22) Today, Jesus and the three youths continued on their way. About twelve shepherds accompanied them. During the hottest part of the day, they rested. They made most rapid progress during the hours of darkness.

Thursday, September 18, A.D. 32 (Elul 23) Today Jesus and the three youths arrived at a settlement. They were led to a house where various fruits were brought to them. Meanwhile the other shepherds, who had received some food, made their way back home. Jesus asked the people in the house about the three kings. He was told that after they had returned from Judea, they had settled in a place not far away and had erected a "tent city" around a step-pyramid. They knew that the Messiah would visit them. Of the three kings, the eldest, Mensor, was alive and well. Theokeno, the next in age, was bedridden, while the third, Sair, had died about nine years before. His corpse lay undecayed in a tomb built in the form of a pyramid. (Note: in LBVM, p. 252, Anne Catherine describes Theokeno as being the eldest of the three kings.)[1]

Friday, September 19, and Saturday, September 20, A.D. 32 (Elul 24–25) The people, who believed Jesus to be an envoy of the King of the Jews awaited by the kings Mensor and Theokeno, sent a messenger to Mensor to inform him

---

1. Anne Catherine spoke of Mensor as the king who had brought the gift of gold to the child Jesus. She said that Sair had brought incense and Theokeno myrrh, and that the Mary had accepted these gifts with humble gratitude. She added that Mensor and Theokeno were baptized by the apostle Thomas three years after the ascension of Jesus. The two kings then left Chaldea and went to live on the island of Crete.

of Jesus' arrival. The tent city where Mensor and Theokeno lived was only a few hours away. With the onset of the Sabbath, Jesus and the three youths retired to a lonely hut where they remained until the close of the Sabbath. Afterward, Jesus taught the people of the place.

Sunday, September 21, A.D. 32 (Elul 26) Today Jesus went to the tent city of Mensor and Theokeno. As he approached, Mensor came to greet him, riding on a camel, accompanied by about twenty men. They were filled with joy as they went up to Jesus. Mensor climbed down from the camel, handed Jesus his royal scepter, and cast himself down before him. Jesus gave him his hand and raised him up. Mensor asked Jesus about the King of the Jews, believing Jesus to be an envoy of that king. They all went back to the tent city, where they dined together.

Monday, September 22, to Wednesday, September 24, A.D. 32 (Elul 27–29) Mensor went with Jesus to Theokeno, who on account of weakness and old age was no longer able to walk. He rested upon an upholstered bed. Jesus visited him daily with Mensor. Mensor and Theokeno related how they had seen the star which led them to the new-born child in Bethlehem. They asked Jesus why they had lost sight of the star as they had approached Jerusalem. Jesus replied: "To test your faith, and because it should not come across Jerusalem." With this, Jesus said that he was not the envoy of the King of the Jews but was himself that King. He added that he had come for Gentiles as well as for Jews, for all who believed in him. When Mensor and Theokeno said that they wanted to follow him back to Israel, Jesus said that his kingdom was not of this world. He said that they would be much upset and their faith sorely tried if they were to see how he would be despised and mistreated.

TISHRI (30 days): September 23/24 to October 23/24, A.D. 32
Tishri New Moon: September 23 at 2:00 P.M., Jerusalem time

Thursday, September 25, A.D. 32 (Tishri 1) Jesus visited the temple in the tent city. He also went to the tomb of Sair. Theokeno told Jesus how, according to their custom, they had placed a branch in front of the tomb; he said that a dove was often seen to settle on this branch and asked what this meant. Jesus asked Theokeno about Sair's faith. Theokeno replied: "Lord, his faith was like mine. Right up to his death, since we went to worship the King of the Jews, Sair always wanted only to think and do his will." Jesus explained to Mensor and Theokeno that the dove on the branch revealed that Sair had been baptized with the baptism of spiritual desire.

Friday, September 26, A.D. 32 (Tishri 2) Mensor and Theokeno told Jesus how they had first seen the star fifteen years before his birth. It was a vision of a virgin with a scepter in one hand and a pair of scales in the other, a beautiful ear of corn in one of the scales and a wine-grape in the other. [2] Since returning from Bethlehem, for three days each year they had celebrated a festival in honor of Jesus, Mary, and Joseph, who had welcomed them so lovingly.That evening, as the Sabbath began, Jesus and the three shepherd youths separated themselves from the others and prayed together.

Saturday, September 27, A.D. 32 (Tishri 3) This evening, at the close of the Sabbath, Jesus went into the temple where there was an idol of a dragon. As one of the women cast herself down before this idol to worship it, Jesus said: "Why do you cast yourself down before Satan? Your faith has been taken possession of by Satan. Behold whom you worship!" Instantly there appeared before her, visible to all, a slender, redfox-colored spirit with a hideously pointed countenance. All were horrified. Jesus pointed to the spirit and indicated that it was this spirit which had woken the woman from sleep each morning before the break of day. The woman had arisen each morning and cast herself down to pray in the direction of the dragon. Jesus said: "This awoke you. However, every person also has a good angel, who should wake you, and before whom you should cast yourself down and follow his advice." All then saw a radiant figure at the woman's side. At this approach of the good angel, the satanic spirit withdrew. Like the two kings, this woman later became baptized by the apostle Thomas and received the name Serena. Later, she suffered a martyr's death.

Sunday, September 28, A.D. 32 (Tishri 4) This morning Jesus went with Mensor to visit Theokeno. He bade Theokeno to arise. Taking him by the hand, Jesus raised him up, and Theokeno was able to walk. From this time on, Theokeno was no longer bedridden. Jesus then went with Mensor and

2. The night on which they had had this vision—December 7/8—was that of the Virgin Mary's immaculate conception and the three-day festival of commemoration of this began on December 8.

Theokeno to the temple, where he taught. After teaching the people, Jesus gave instruction to the two kings and the four priests of the temple. He explained that when the good angels withdraw, Satan takes possession of a temple service. He said that they should remove the various animal idols and teach love and compassion and give thanks to the Father in heaven. Jesus now took bread and wine, which had been prepared beforehand. Having consecrated the bread and wine, he placed them upon a small altar. He prayed and blessed everyone. Mensor, Theokeno, and the four priests knelt before him with their hands folded across their chests. Jesus laid his hands upon their shoulders and prayed over them. He blessed the bread and wine and said that they should partake of it once every three months. He taught them the words of blessing to use and said that they should begin taking the communion of bread and wine at Christmas time.

Monday, September 29, A.D. *32 (Tishri 5)* Jesus taught again today in the temple. He gave instruction to the women concerning prayer, saying also how they should bring up their children. Afterward, he blessed the children.

Tuesday, September 30, A.D. *32 (Tishri 6)* Before daybreak, Jesus left the tent city of the kings. Mensor begged him to remain with them, and wept profusely at Jesus' departure. Jesus and the three shepherd youths traveled far and that evening reached a shepherd settlement where they stayed that night.

Wednesday, October 1, A.D. *32 (Tishri 7)* Jesus and his traveling companions left the shepherd settlement before the break of day and journeyed again for the whole day. That night they slept in a hut made of earth and moss.

Thursday, October 2, A.D. *32 (Tishri 8)* Jesus and the three youths spoke with the people living at this place and accompanied them to their temple, where he taught. The name of the place was Atom and the chieftain of the people there was called Azaria. He was a son of one of Mensor's brothers. Jesus stayed that night in Azaria's house.

Friday, October 3, A.D. *32 (Tishri 9)* This evening, with the onset of the Sabbath, Jesus and the three shepherd youths went to the hut where they had stayed on their arrival in Atom. Here they prayed together. Later, in the temple, Jesus healed one of Azaria's wives, who was afflicted with an issue of blood. He also healed a woman possessed by a devil which had made her fall hopelessly in love with a youth. The youth's name was Caisar, and he was exceptionally pure. He had long had a presentiment of the coming of salvation and joined Jesus and the three shepherd youths to accompany them on their further journey. Jesus taught in the temple throughout the night until the break of day.

Saturday, October 4, A.D. 32 (Tishri 10) Jesus and the four youths spent the day in prayer. At the close of the Sabbath, they went to the temple. Jesus taught the people and then gave instruction to the priests concerning the communion of bread and wine. He consecrated the bread and wine, and blessed the priests.

Sunday, October 5, A.D. 32 (Tishri 11) Jesus and the four youths left Atom this morning, first traveling southward and then in an easterly direction. Toward evening they arrived at the Chaldean city of Sikdor. Here Jesus taught in the temple. He reproved them for their idolatry. He said that he was the vine whose blood would renew the world and that he was the grain of corn which would be buried in the earth and would rise again. The people here were very humble and believed that the Jews alone were the chosen people. Jesus comforted them and said that he had come for all human beings. He commanded them to destroy their idols and to give alms to the poor.

Monday, October 6, A.D. 32 (Tishri 12) Today Jesus and his four traveling companions left Sikdor. On the way, they stopped to eat bread and honey. They traveled all night.

Tuesday, October 7, A.D. 32 (Tishri 13) They journeyed on. Today, having already crossed the Euphrates, they crossed the Tigris. In the evening, they arrived at the city of Mozian, where they stayed the night.

Wednesday, October 8, A.D. 32 (Tishri 14) Jesus did not enter the temple in Mozian. He taught at a well in front of the temple. He strongly reprimanded the people on account of their idolatry. He left the city and traveled throughout the night in a southerly direction, recrossing the Tigris.

Thursday, October 9, A.D. 32 (Tishri 15) Jesus and his traveling companions continued their journey.

Friday, October 10, A.D. *32 (Tishri 16)* Traveling on, Jesus and the four youths recrossed the Euphrates. Toward evening, as the Sabbath began, they arrived at Ur, the birthplace of Abraham. Here they stayed in a house and held the Sabbath together in prayer.

Saturday, October 11, A.D. *32 (Tishri 17)* Jesus and his companions celebrated the Sabbath. Afterward, he taught in an open place. He spoke of Abraham.

Sunday, October 12, A.D. *32 (Tishri 18)* The people of Ur accompanied Jesus this morning and strewed branches on the street in front of him as he and the four youths left the city. They journeyed westward through the day and arrived that evening at a settlement. Here Jesus strongly inveighed against the people's worship. The chief of the settlement was deaf to Jesus' teaching and became enraged, even contradicting him. The chief lived in a house full of idols. Jesus said that on the anniversary of the night on which the star had appeared to the three kings, the idols would all break, the oxen idols would bellow, the dog idols would bark, and the bird idols would squawk. This would be proof of the truth of his words. The people listened to him in disbelief. Jesus told them that this would take place throughout Chaldea in the places that he had visited.

Monday, October 13, A.D. *32 (Tishri 19)* Today Jesus and the four youths set off on the long journey to Egypt, traveling westward through the Arabian desert. They traveled rapidly. In the course of this journey, which lasted some two and one-half months until the end of the year A.D. 32, Anne Catherine had a vision on Christmas night: she saw the journey of the Saviour through Chaldea, from Cedar to the tent city of the kings, to Atom, Sikdor, Mozian, Ur, and the last Chaldean settlement. Everywhere, she saw idols broken and animal idols crying out. Historically (in A.D. 32) this was probably the night of December 7/8, the anniversary of the immaculate conception of the Virgin Mary, on which night the three kings had first seen the star, fifteen years before the birth of Jesus.

TEBETH (29 days): December 22/23, A.D. *32, to January 19/20,* A.D. *33*
Tebeth New Moon: December 21 at 10:00 A.M., *Jerusalem time*

Wednesday, December 31, A.D. *32 (Tebeth 9)* Anne Catherine described the journey of Jesus and the four youths. She saw them coming from the Arabian desert and approaching Egypt; then, passing south of Mount Sinai, which they saw in the distance, they crossed the Sinai desert. She said that they traveled continuously through open, sandy desert, then crossed gently rolling hills, finally arriving in a land with more green. Then, in the evening, they arrived at the first Egyptian town. During the night, many idols fell to the ground.

Thursday, January 1, A.D. *33 (Tebeth 10)* This morning there was an uproar in the town, when the people discovered the broken idols. Jesus and the four youths hurriedly left the town, and as they did some children ran after them calling out: "These are holy people!" Jesus traveled further westward until he and his four young disciples reached a town that evening. Before entering the town they rested by a stream. When they entered the town, it was night. They made their way through the deserted streets, and then traveled on further.

Friday, January 2, A.D. *33 (Tebeth 11)* Around four o'clock this afternoon Jesus and his traveling companions arrived at Heliopolis. Here he met some Jews who had been friends of the Holy Family during the time of their stay in Heliopolis. With the onset of the Sabbath, Jesus was escorted to the synagogue by an aged man. In the synagogue, Jesus taught and prayed.

Saturday, January 3, A.D. *33 (Tebeth 12)* Today Jesus taught again in the synagogue of Heliopolis.

Sunday, January 4, A.D. *33 (Tebeth 13)* This morning Jesus left Heliopolis accompanied by the four youths and another youth named Deodatus, who was about eighteen years old. The mother of Deodatus had been childless, but the Virgin Mary had prayed for her when the Holy Family lived in Heliopolis and, later, Deodatus had been born. Jesus and the five youths made their way through the desert.

Monday, January 5, A.D. *33 (Tebeth 14)* This evening Jesus and his five young disciples arrived at a small town in the desert, where some Jews were living. He went to the town well, where he was greeted and then escorted to a house.

Tuesday, January 6, A.D. *33 (Tebeth 15)* In this little town, Jesus was held by the Jews to be a prophet. There was no synagogue, so Jesus taught in a house. He spoke of his approaching return to the Father. They could not believe him. When Jesus left, two more youths joined him, bringing his entourage to seven. One was about twenty years old, and the other was scarcely more than twelve years of age. Before he left, Jesus blessed the children of this place.

Wednesday, January 7 A.D. 33 (Tebeth 16) Today, Jesus and his seven young disciples proceeded rapidly through the desert.

MAP 38: *The Arrival at Jacob's Well*

Thursday, January 8, A.D. 33 (Tebeth 17) Jesus and the seven young disciples continued their journey. This evening, they arrived at the town of Beersheba where, at the town well, Jesus was received in a friendly way.

Friday, January 9, A.D. 33 (Tebeth 18) This morning, Jesus taught in the large synagogue in Beersheba. He formally declared who he was and spoke of his approaching end. Afterward, he blessed some children. Then he left the town, accompanied by his seven young disciples and five youths from Beersheba. They went to Bethain, not far from Abraham's grave in the cave of Machpelah, east of Mamre. As the Sabbath began, Jesus went to the synagogue in Bethain and taught there.

Saturday, January 10, A.D. 33 (Tebeth 19) Today, Jesus taught again in the synagogue in Bethain. Then he went from house to house, healing the sick. Finally, at the close of the Sabbath, he journeyed northward.

Sunday, January 11, and Monday, January 12, A.D. 33 (Tebeth 20–21) Jesus and his young disciples journeyed by night toward Sychar. They traveled under cover of darkness, so as not to provoke any disturbance among the people on account of Jesus' return to Palestine.

Tuesday, January 13, A.D. 33 (Tebeth 22) Today, at daybreak, Jesus arrived at Jacob's well, accompanied by sixteen young disciples, four having joined him in Bethain. Beholding their arrival, Anne Catherine suddenly called out in ecstasy: "O, he has arrived! How joyful they are to see him! He is at Jacob's well. They are weeping for joy. They are washing his feet and also the feet of the young disciples with him. There are about twelve of them, shepherd sons, who were with him as he went to Cedar—also Peter, Andrew, John, James, Philip, and one other! They were expecting him here." Jesus and his disciples stayed the day at Jacob's well. In the evening, he spoke of his approaching path of suffering.

Wednesday, January 14, A.D. 33 (Tebeth 23) Early this morning, Jesus arranged to meet with the apostles and disciples at the Sabbath in Sychar. Then he went with the sixteen young disciples to the settlement of the parents of the three shepherd youths—Eliud, Silas, and Eremenzear—a few hours away.

Thursday, January 15, A.D. 33 (Tebeth 24) Jesus taught here and there in the settlement among the shepherds and instructed the new disciples. He wished them to stay there for the time being.

Friday, January 16, A.D. 33 (Tebeth 25) Accompanied by the three shepherd youths—Eliud, Silas, and Eremenzear—Jesus returned to Sychar, leaving the other thirteen young disciples with the shepherds at the settlement. Jesus commanded the three youths not to tell anyone where they had been with him or what had taken place on this journey. Peter and John came to meet them on the way. Six more apostles were waiting for him at the entrance to Sychar. Together, they all went to a house in the town. At the beginning of the Sabbath, they went to the synagogue, but Jesus did not teach or do anything to draw attention to himself.

Saturday, January 17, A.D. 33 (Tebeth 26) The apostles wanted to hear from the three shepherd youths where they had been with Jesus for the past five months. They were much vexed when the youths refused to say anything. The apostles turned to Jesus and said that he should express himself more clearly, as they did not understand him. They also said that he should go to Nazareth once again to demonstrate his power through miracles there. Jesus replied that he did not want to do this, saying that miracles were of no use if people did not mend their ways. Peter and John agreed with him, but the others were unsatisfied by this reply. Jesus then said that he would go to Jerusalem and teach in the temple. That evening, after the meal, Jesus and all the disciples went to the synagogue. Here Jesus taught. Some of the Pharisees who were there were much vexed at his teaching and sent messengers to Jerusalem to report that Jesus was active again in Sychar.

Sunday, January 18, A.D. *33 (Tebeth 27)* The Pharisees at Sychar threatened to take Jesus into custody and deliver him to Jerusalem. Jesus replied that his time had not yet come. He said that he would go to Jerusalem of his own accord. Then he left Sychar, dismissing the apostles and disciples, keeping only the three "silent disciples"—Eremenzear, Eliud, and Silas— with him. Jesus and the three youths proceeded in a southeasterly direction toward Ephron. Meanwhile, his mother, the Holy Virgin, who was with her friends in Bethany, had received the news of Jesus' return to Israel. Jesus sent a messenger to her requesting her to meet him at an inn southwest of Ephron.

Monday, January 19, A.D. *33 (Tebeth 28)* On the way to the inn, Jesus healed and comforted various people in their homes. The apostles and disciples spread out to proclaim the nearness of Jesus. That evening Jesus and the three youths arrived at Ephron (John 11:54). Jesus went to various houses and healed the sick. There was a large synagogue in Ephron, where Jesus then taught concerning his near end. He spoke of the punishment that would come upon those who refused to believe. Meanwhile, in the evening, the Holy Virgin Mary, Mary Magdalene, Martha, Peter's wife and stepdaughter, Andrew's wife, Zacchaeus' wife and daughter, and two other holy women arrived at the inn they had rented between Jericho and Ephron.

Tuesday, January 20, A.D. *33 (Tebeth 29)* In the morning, the three silent disciples were sent by Jesus to the holy women to announce his coming. In the afternoon, the Holy Virgin, Mary Magdalene, Martha and a few women, accompanied by the three youths, came to greet Jesus. They waited for him at a well on the way to Ephron. He came with Peter, Andrew, and John, arriving at the well about two hours before sunset. The women cast themselves down before him and kissed his hand. They then returned to the inn together and Jesus spoke with all the women and also taught. Afterward there was a meal. The women ate alone and came afterward to hear Jesus speak. He and the other men did not stay at the inn but went to Jericho, where the other apostles and disciples were already waiting. The holy women followed them. In Jericho, Jesus healed many sick people. Then he went to the synagogue, where he taught. Mary and the holy women were also present in the synagogue and heard him teach. Afterward, Mary, Peter's wife and stepdaughter, and Andrew's wife left and returned to stay the night at the inn where they had been with Jesus.

SHEBAT (30 days): January 20/21 to February 18/19, A.D. 33
Shebat New Moon: January 19 at 9:00 P.M., Jerusalem time

Wednesday, January 21, A.D. 33 (Shebat 1) This morning, Jesus taught and healed in Jericho. The Virgin Mary, Peter's wife and stepdaughter, and Andrew's wife set off back to Galilee, and the other holy women also returned to their homes. There was a great throng of people in Jericho, as word had already spread that Jesus was there. The Pharisees were greatly disturbed by this and sent messengers to Jerusalem to report Jesus' presence in Jericho. Jesus, however, left the city and went to the place of baptism on the Jordan, accompanied by Peter, Andrew, and James the Lesser. There were many sick people waiting for him at the place of baptism. Jesus healed many, and then, as the throng of people grew, he and the apostles left and went to Bethel. They arrived in Bethel that evening and were met at an inn by Lazarus, Martha, Mary Magdalene, Nicodemus, and John Mark.

Thursday, January 22, A.D. 33 (Shebat 2) After healing many people in Bethel, Jesus went to a place north of Jericho, accompanied by Andrew, James the Lesser, and John. Jesus healed several people on the way.

Friday, January 23, A.D. 33 (Shebat 3) Having made a large detour, Jesus and the three apostles arrived today at their destination. It was shortly before the onset of the Sabbath. They went to the synagogue.

Saturday, January 24, A.D. 33 (Shebat 4) In the synagogue this morning Jesus taught briefly. Then he healed many people. The apostles also healed and blessed the people. After the close of the Sabbath, they all went to a nearby prisonhouse in Alexandrium. Here many people were imprisoned. Jesus secured the release of about twenty-five of them. Then, together, they all traveled through the night northward along the Jordan.

MAP 39: *Journey to the Final Passover*

Sunday, January 25, A.D. 33 (Shebat 5) Today, Jesus and those with him arrived in a town where many of the women and children of the released prisoners were living. They returned the released prisoners to them. Other released prisoners were from the region of Cedar. These crossed the Jordan to return to their homes. After dismissing the three apostles, Jesus then traveled alone in the direction of Tiberius. On the way, he met the three silent disciples—Silas, Eliud, and Eremenzear.

Monday, January 26, A.D. 33 (Shebat 6) Toward evening, Jesus and the three youths arrived in Capernaum. Here they were met by Peter, Andrew, and James the Lesser. Jesus went to the synagogue and taught. Many people were present. Afterward, the people on the streets of Capernaum called out: "Joseph's son is here again!"

Tuesday, January 27, A.D. 33 (Shebat 7) Jesus left Capernaum before day-break, traveling with several apostles and disciples to Nazareth. Arriving, he went straight to the synagogue. Here his presence caused much commotion. After teaching, Jesus and those with him went to an inn and stayed the night there.

Wednesday, January 28, A.D. 33 (Shebat 8) This morning Jesus went to various houses in Nazareth and healed. He also blessed the children. He sent the apostles on ahead to a mountain about sixteen miles south of Tiberius and then followed them there, accompanied by the remaining disciples. It was already night when he arrived at the "mount of the apostles." He found the apostles waiting for him at the top, grouped around a fire. Throughout much of the night, Jesus taught, giving the apostles and disciples instructions for the next period of time.

Thursday, January 29, A.D. 33 (Shebat 9) Around daybreak, Jesus and the disciples set off southward for Thanat-Silo, the apostles having gone on ahead. Jesus met up with the apostles—all twelve of them—at a well about one hour's distance from the town. They then proceeded together to Tha-nat-Silo. Here the Virgin Mary, Martha, Mary Magdalene, and some other holy women were waiting for them at an inn. In the evening, after a meal, Jesus taught.

Friday, January 30, A.D. 33 (Shebat 10) This morning, Jesus healed the sick and sent the apostles off to various places. The holy women left for Bethany. Jesus, accompanied by some disciples, followed in the same direction, arriv-ing at an inn before the onset of the Sabbath. Here, the disciples who had returned with him from his great journey were waiting for him. At this inn, Jesus celebrated the Sabbath together with about twenty disciples.

Saturday, January 31, A.D. 33 (Shebat 11) Jesus and the disciples remained at the inn for the Sabbath. They prayed, and Jesus gave them instructions about what they should do.

Sunday, February 1, A.D. 33 (Shebat 12) Today Jesus and the disciples proceeded on their way toward Bethany. Jesus taught the disciples as they went. He said that he would go to Jerusalem to teach, after which he would return to his heavenly Father. They arrived at an inn about an hour from Bethany. Here Mary, the holy women, and five apostles—Judas, Thomas, Simon, James the Lesser, and Judas Thaddeus—were waiting for him. There was a meal, and Jesus taught here.

Monday, February 2, A.D. 33 (Shebat 13) The five apostles and the sixteen disciples who had come with Jesus divided into two groups, one led by Judas Thaddeus and the other by James the Lesser. They went around the area and healed the sick. Jesus also went around healing, accompanied by the three silent disciples. Later, he went to Bethany, to the synagogue, and taught there.

Tuesday, February 3, and Wednesday, February 4, A.D. 33 (Shebat 14–15) Again, Jesus taught in the synagogue of Bethany and healed in the town.

Thursday, February 5, A.D. 33 (Shebat 16) Today, Jesus sent out the disciples in pairs to teach and to heal. Jesus went with the three silent disciples to a little place south of Bethany. Here he healed the sick.

Friday, February 6, A.D. 33 (Shebat 17) Having returned to Bethany, Jesus went to the synagogue for the beginning of the Sabbath.

Saturday, February 7, A.D. 33 (Shebat 18) Jesus taught in the synagogue.

Sunday, February 8, A.D. 33 (Shebat 19) Three secret disciples came from Jerusalem to see him. They reported that the high priests and Pharisees wanted to send out spies, so that they could capture him as soon as he came to Jerusalem. Jesus, accompanied by two young disciples, then left Bethany and traveled all night in a northerly direction.

Monday, February 9, A.D. 33 (Shebat 20) Early this morning, while it was still dark, Jesus arrived at Lazarus' property south of Alexandrium. Here he met with Lazarus, Nicodemus, Joseph of Arimathea, John Mark, and Jair. They ate a meal together.

Tuesday, February 10, to Saturday, February 14, A.D. 33 (Shebat 21–25) Jesus went with the two young disciples across the Jordan to Bethabara, where they celebrated the Sabbath.

Sunday, February 15, A.D. 33 (Shebat 26) Jesus and the two young disciples went from Bethabara to Ephron. Here Jesus healed two blind people. In the afternoon, Jesus was joined by the apostles Andrew, Judas, Thomas, James the Lesser, Thaddeus, and about ten other disciples. He healed the lame, the deaf and dumb, and drove a devil out of a possessed person.

Monday, February 16, A.D. 33 (Shebat 27) Today, Jesus went to a little place about an hour north of Jericho. Here there was a retreat house for the sick and needy. Jesus healed a blind man there through the power of the words he spoke.

Tuesday, February 17, and Wednesday, February 18, A.D. 33 (Shebat 28–29) Jesus returned to Lazarus' estate near Alexandrium.

Thursday, February 19, A.D. 33 (Shebat 30) In the morning, Jesus, accompanied by Lazarus, left Alexandrium and went to Bethany. The holy women came to meet him as he approached Bethany. In the evening, Jesus went to the temple in Jerusalem. He was accompanied part of the way by his mother, the Holy Virgin. Jesus told her that the time was drawing near when Simeon's prophecy—that a sword would pierce her soul—would become fulfilled. He stayed overnight in Jerusalem in the house of Mary Mark, the mother of John Mark.

ADAR (29 days): February 19/20 to March 19/20, A.D. 33
Adar New Moon: February 18 at 6:45 A.M., Jerusalem time

Friday, February 20, A.D. 33 (Adar 1) This evening, Jesus was at the temple for the celebration of the Sabbath. After the Pharisees had left, Jesus taught from the teacher's chair in the portico of Solomon, where he had taught at the age of twelve. All the apostles were present, and many people came to hear him. He spoke with great seriousness. For Jesus, the start of this month of Adar signified the beginning of his public teaching in the temple and of the way leading to the Cross. Inwardly, he was torn with sorrow at humanity's corruption.

Saturday, February 21, A.D. 33 (Adar 2) Today, Jesus taught again in the temple, beginning his teaching after the Pharisees had ended their's.

Sunday, February 22, A.D. 33 (Adar 3) Again, Jesus was in the temple.

Monday, February 23, A.D. 33 (Adar 4) From the morning on, Jesus taught in the temple. During the afternoon, he left to go to Bethany.

Tuesday, February 24, A.D. 33 (Adar 5) In the morning, Jesus made his way back to Jerusalem after visiting a little place, Bethphage, on the outskirts of the city.

Wednesday, February 25, and Thursday, February 26, A.D. 33 (Adar 6–7) Jesus continued to teach in the temple. He spoke of the parable of the field overgrown with weeds that had to be carefully uprooted so that the good grain would ripen and not be uprooted together with the weeds—meaning the Pharisees.

Friday, February 27, A.D. 33 (Adar 8) Today Jesus was in Bethany and spoke at length with his mother, the Holy Virgin, about his approaching suffering. This evening he went to the temple in Jerusalem for the onset of the Sabbath. After the Pharisees had left, Jesus taught late into the night.

Saturday, February 28, A.D. 33 (Adar 9) Jesus taught this morning in the temple. Around three o'clock, he shared a meal with about twenty of his apostles and disciples at the house of Mary Mark.

Sunday, March 1, A.D. 33 (Adar 10) Jesus taught again in the temple. He spoke of John the Baptist, and many pupils of John were present, but they did not display themselves openly. That evening he went to Bethany and spoke with the holy women. Afterward, he retired to sleep at Lazarus' house.

Tuesday, March 3, A.D. 33 (Adar 12) Jesus taught in the temple. He returned to sleep that night in Bethany.

Wednesday, March 4, A.D. *33 (Adar 13)* Jesus left Bethany and went to the temple in Jerusalem and taught there. He said that many did not believe in him but followed him only because of the miracles he performed. He added that they would forsake him in the hour of decision and that it would be better for them to leave him now. At this, many left. About one hundred people remained gathered around Jesus. Jesus wept on his way back to Bethany.

Thursday, March 5, A.D. *33 (Adar 14)* It was shortly before sunset as Jesus went to the temple. He was accompanied by six apostles and disciples. He taught that he would be leaving them soon.

Friday, March 6, A.D. *33 (Adar 15)* This afternoon Jesus came from Bethany to Jerusalem before the onset of the Sabbath. He ate at the home of John Mark. The holy women and Lazarus were also present. But Lazarus did not go with Jesus to the temple when the Sabbath began. Later, Jesus returned to Bethany.

Saturday, March 7, A.D. *33 (Adar 16)* Jesus taught in the temple again this morning and, after a short pause around midday, he continued teaching. He said that one should not hoard up perishable treasures (Matthew 6:19–21). He spoke, too, of prayer and fasting and of the danger of hypocrisy with regard to these practices (Matthew 6:5,16). He referred to his approaching end, indicating that he would make a triumphant entry into Jerusalem beforehand. Addressing the apostles, he revealed to them something of their future tasks. Peter, John, and James the Lesser would remain in Jerusalem; the others were to spread out and teach in various lands, e.g., Andrew in the region of Galaad, and Philip and Bartholomew around Gessur. Jesus told them that they would all meet again in Jerusalem, three years after his death, and that John and the Holy Virgin would then go to Ephesus. He taught many other things as well. The Pharisees were enraged by what they heard and wanted to stone Jesus as he made his way out of the temple. Jesus, however, managed to elude them and returned to Bethany. After this, he did not teach in the temple again for about three days.

Sunday, March 8, A.D. *33 (Adar 17)* Jesus remained hidden for three days in the house of Lazarus in Bethany. The apostles came to him and asked him about what he had taught in the temple on the Sabbath.

Monday, March 9, and Tuesday, March 10, A.D. 33 (Adar 18–19) Today Jesus stayed in Bethany. Three Chaldeans arrived to see him, having heard of his teaching in Chaldea. Jesus spoke with them only briefly and referred them to the centurion Cornelius in Capernaum.

Wednesday, March 11, A.D. 33 (Adar 20) Early this morning, Jesus went to the temple with about thirty disciples. He taught concerning his approaching suffering. Later, he returned to Bethany.

Thursday, March 12, A.D. 33 (Adar 21) Today, Jesus taught again in the temple and stayed in Jerusalem overnight.

Friday, March 13, A.D. 33 (Adar 22) This morning, all the disciples accompanied Jesus as he went to the temple. There were several vendors selling their wares in one of the forecourts to the temple. Jesus commanded them to leave. As they hesitated, he himself began to gather their things together, and some people carried them away. Later, in the afternoon, Jesus went to the house of John Mark. As the Sabbath began, he returned to the temple. He taught until late and stayed in Jerusalem that night.

Saturday, March 14, A.D. 33 (Adar 23) Today, Jesus cordoned off part of the teaching hall in the temple for himself and his apostles and disciples. He taught them concerning their future tasks.

Sunday, March 15, A.D. 33 (Adar 24) Jesus taught again in the temple concerning his approaching suffering (Matthew 20:17–19). The disciples were downcast.

Monday, March 16, A.D. 33 (Adar 25) Today, Jesus taught for about four hours in the temple. Once again, he described what would happen to him and how many of the disciples would forsake him. He spoke of his forthcoming triumphant entry into Jerusalem and said that he would then remain with them for fifteen days. The disciples did not understand the "fifteen days" and believed that he meant a longer period. Jesus repeated "three times five days."

Tuesday, March 17, A.D. 33 (Adar 26) The scribes and Pharisees, having been greatly disturbed by Jesus' teaching yesterday in the temple, met today at the house of Caiaphas. They proclaimed that henceforth it was forbidden for anyone to harbor Jesus or the disciples in their homes or anywhere else. Jesus went to Bethany to stay with Lazarus.

Wednesday, March 18, A.D. *33 (Adar 27)* Today, in a basement room in Lazarus' house, Jesus told Lazarus, Peter, James, and John that tomorrow would be the day of his triumphant entry into Jerusalem. The remaining apostles came and when all were gathered together, Jesus spoke with them at length. Then he went to a room where his mother, the Holy Virgin, and six other holy women were gathered. He told them a parable. Afterward, they all ate.

Thursday, March 19, A.D. *33 (Adar 28)* Early this morning Jesus instructed Silas and Eremenzear to go to Jerusalem, not by the main road, but along a secondary route via Bethphage. He told them to clear the way. He said that they would find a donkey and a foal in front of an inn at Bethphage and that they should tether the donkey to a fence. If asked what they were doing, they should reply that Jesus had need of these animals (Matthew 21:1–6). After the youths had been gone for a time, Jesus divided the disciples into two groups. Sending the older disciples on ahead, Jesus followed with the apostles and the younger disciples. His mother, the Holy Virgin, accompanied by six other holy women, followed at a distance. When they arrived at Bethphage, the two youths brought the donkey and the foal to Jesus. He took his seat on one of them. The apostles and disciples bore branches from palm trees. They began to sing. Thus they made their way into Jerusalem. The news spread quickly of the procession of Jesus and the disciples into the city, and people came from everywhere to see it. There was great jubilation. Jesus wept, and the apostles also wept, when he said that many of those now rejoicing would soon mock him. He wept too in beholding Jerusalem, which would soon be destroyed (Luke 19:41–44). When he arrived at the city gate, the jubilation grew and grew (Matthew 21:10–11). Jesus rode up to the temple and dismounted there. (Anne Catherine Emmerich saw that something took place in the temple, but she could not recall what. In all probability, Jesus taught there, surrounded by the apostles and disciples, in the presence of the priests and Pharisees and crowds of people.) The holy women returned to Bethany that evening, followed later by Jesus and the apostles (Matthew 21:17).

Friday, March 20, A.D. *33 (Adar 29)* Today, as Jesus and the apostles made their way to Jerusalem, Jesus was hungry. This was a hunger to convert the people and to fulfill his mission. As he passed by a fig tree, he cursed it when he saw that it had no fruit (Matthew 21:18–19). The fig tree symbolized the old Law and the vine the new Law. Then Jesus went to the temple. Many vendors were again selling their wares in the forecourt. Jesus drove them all out (Matthew 21:12–13). He taught in the temple. At this time, some travelers from Greece told the apostle Philip that they wished to see Jesus. Philip spoke with Andrew, who told Jesus. Jesus continued his teaching. With his hands folded, he gazed up to heaven. From a cloud of light, a ray descended upon him, and a voice like thunder resounded: "I have glorified him, and I will glorify him again" (John 12:20–36). Later, Jesus left the temple and disappeared into the crowd. He went to John Mark's house, where he met and spoke with the travelers from Greece. They were good and well-respected people. Hearing Jesus' words, they were converted. In fact, these Greeks were among the first to become baptized by the disciples after Pentecost. Jesus then went to Bethany for the beginning of the Sabbath and ate a meal with the disciples at the inn of Simon the leper, whom Christ had earlier healed of his leprosy. At the end of the meal, Mary Magdalene came up to Jesus from behind and poured a vial of costly ointment upon his head and feet. She then dried his feet with her hair and left the room. Judas was incensed by this, but Jesus excused Mary Magdalene on account of her love. That very night, Judas ran to Jerusalem to Caiaphas' house. This was Judas' first step toward the betrayal of Jesus.

NISAN (30 days): March 20/21 to April 18/19, A.D. 33
Nisan New Moon: March 19 at 3:30 P.M., Jerusalem time

Saturday, March 21, A.D. 33 (Nisan 1) This morning, as Jesus and some disciples made their way from Bethany to Jerusalem, the disciples were astounded to find the withered fig tree that Jesus had cursed the day before. John and Peter paused to look at the fig tree more closely. As Peter expressed his astonishment, Jesus said that if the disciples had faith, they would accomplish more than this, that even the mountains would cast themselves into the sea at their command (Mark 11:20–25). While he was teaching in the temple this morning, some priests and scribes came up and asked Jesus: "By what authority are you doing these things?" Jesus answered: "I will also ask you a question; and if you tell me the answer, then I will also tell you by what authority I do these things." He then addressed them as recorded in Matthew 21:23-32. During the afternoon he taught parables about the vineyard owner and the rejection of the cornerstone by the builders (Matthew 21:33-46). The Pharisees were enraged at Jesus' words and wanted to capture him, but they did not do so because of the people. That evening, after the close of the Sabbath, Jesus returned to Bethany.

Sunday, March 22, A.D. 33 (Nisan 2) Jesus taught in Bethany this morning. Later he went to the temple, where he taught for about three hours. He told the parable of the king who gave a marriage feast (Matthew 22:1-14). Afterward, he returned to Bethany.

Monday, March 23, A.D. 33 (Nisan 3) After teaching in Bethany, Jesus went to the temple to teach there. He was approached by five men who were in league with the Pharisees and Herodians. They asked him if they were allowed to pay tax to the emperor. Jesus replied as reported in Matthew 22:16-22. That afternoon, seven Sadducees came to him and asked him about the marriages of a woman after the death of her husband. Jesus answered as recorded in Matthew 22:23-33. He also said that love was the highest commandment (Matthew 22:34-40). Then he spoke of the Messiah (Christ) as being a "son of David" (Matthew 22:41–46). That evening, Jesus and the apostles dined with Lazarus, and he taught until late that night.

Tuesday, March 24, A.D. 33 (Nisan 4) Jesus taught in Bethany and then went to the temple. This morning the Pharisees were not present and he was able to teach the apostles and disciples undisturbed. They asked him about the meaning of the words: "Thy kingdom come." Jesus spoke at length about this. He also said that he and the Father were one (John 10:30) and that he would be going to the Father (John 16:16). The disciples asked why, if he and the Father were one, did he need to go to the Father? Jesus spoke of his mission, saying that he would withdraw from humanity, from the flesh, and that whoever—with him, through him, and in him—separated himself from his own fallen nature, would at the same time commend himself to the Father. The apostles were deeply moved by these words and cried out joyfully and full of enthusiasm: "Lord! We will spread your kingdom to the end of the world!" Jesus answered that whoever spoke like this would not accomplish anything. They should never boast: "I have driven out devils in your name!" or "I have done this and that!" Also, they should not carry out their work publicly. That afternoon a great many scribes and Pharisees were present. Jesus spoke the words recorded in Matthew 23:2–39. He added:

"You do not lay hands on me yet, as my hour has not yet come." At this, the Pharisees left the temple. It was already dark when Jesus made his way back to Bethany.

Wednesday, March 25, A.D. *33 (Nisan 5)* Today, Jesus spent the whole day with Lazarus and the holy women and the twelve apostles. During the morning, he taught the holy women. Then, around three o'clock in the afternoon there was a meal, after which they prayed together. Jesus spoke of the nearness of the time of delivery of the Son of Man, saying, too, that he would be betrayed. Peter asked why he always spoke as if one of them would betray him, as he, Peter, could testify for the twelve that they would not betray him. Jesus answered that if they were not to receive his grace and prayer, they would all fall, and in his hour of reckoning they would all forsake him. They also asked him about his kingdom. He said that he had to go to the Father and that he would send them the Spirit which proceeds from him and the Father. He said that he had come in the flesh for their salvation and that there was something material in his influence upon them, that the body works in a corporeal manner, and for this reason they could not understand him. However, he would send them the Spirit who would open up their understanding. He also spoke of the coming of a time of tribulation, when all would be filled with fear, and he referred to a woman in the pangs of giving birth. He spoke of the beauty of the human soul, created in God's image, and how wonderful it is to save souls and lead them to their salvation. He taught until late into the night. That night, Nicodemus and one of Simeon's sons came secretly from Jerusalem in order to see him.

Thursday, March 26, A.D. *33 (Nisan 6)* Early this morning, Jesus went to the temple. Today was a day of sacrifice for all who wanted to purify themselves for the feast of the Passover. Jesus and the apostles waited in the temple and watched the people coming with their contributions for the treasury. The last person was a poor widow. It was not possible to see what the people contributed, but Jesus knew what she had given. He said to the disciples that she had given more than anyone else, for she had given all that she had (Mark 12:41–44). That afternoon Jesus taught in the temple. Addressing some Pharisees, he said that they should not expect a peaceful Passover this year; they would not know where they should hide themselves; all the blood of the prophets whom they had murdered would be upon their heads. He also said that the prophets would arise from their graves and that the earth would quake. Later, Jesus went with the disciples to the Mount of Olives. On the way, a disciple showed Jesus the temple and spoke of its beauty. Jesus answered that not one stone would be left upon another (Matthew 24:1–2). On the Mount of Olives, Jesus sat down and some apostles asked him when the temple would be destroyed. Jesus spoke of his second coming, as recorded in Matthew 24:1–14. The last words he spoke here were: "Blessed is he who perseveres until the end."

Friday, March 27, A.D. *33 (Nisan 7)* Jesus and the apostles and disciples returned to the Mount of Olives early in the morning. Jesus spoke of the destruction of Jerusalem and of the end of the world (Matthew 24:15–31), referring, by way of analogy, to a fig tree standing there (Matthew 24:32–35). He also referred to his betrayal, saying that the Pharisees were longing to see the betrayer again. Judas listened with a smile. Jesus also warned the apostles not to be burdened with worldly cares. Later, he taught in the temple, employing the parables of the ten virgins (Matthew 25:1–13) and of the talents (Matthew 25:14–30). He also repeated his words to the Pharisees concerning the shedding of the blood of the prophets (Matthew 23:29–39). Jesus then spent the night at a place at the foot of the Mount of Olives.

Saturday, March 28, A.D. *33 (Nisan 8)* Early this morning, Jesus taught the apostles and disciples at the place at the foot of the Mount of Olives where he had spent the night. Then he went to the temple. There he spoke of his departure, saying that he was going to the Father. He described how the Fall into sin had begun in a garden and that it would end in a garden. His enemies would lay their hands on him in a garden. They had wanted to kill him, following the raising of Lazarus. He had gone away in order that everything could be fulfilled. He characterized the journey that he had made after the raising of Lazarus by dividing it into three parts, each several weeks long. (The journey had lasted five months.) He spoke also of Eve and said plainly that he was the Saviour who would free human beings from the power of sin.

Sunday, March 29, A.D. *33 (Nisan 9)* Today Jesus went with the disciples across the Cedron Brook to Gethsemane. He pointed out to the apostles the place where he would be seized and added that here they would forsake him. Jesus was very downcast as they went toward Bethany. That evening, they took a meal together at the house of Lazarus.

Monday, March 30, A.D. *33 (Nisan 10)* Early this morning, Jesus went with the disciples to Jerusalem. In the temple, he spoke of union and separation. He used the analogy of fire and water, which are inimicable. When water does not overpower fire, the flames become greater and more powerful. He spoke of persecution and martyrdom. By the flames of fire, he was referring to those disciples who would remain true to him, and by water he meant those who would leave him and seek the abyss. He spoke also of the mingling of milk and water; this symbolizes an inner union which cannot be separated. With this he meant his union with them. He referred to the mild and nourishing power of milk. He also spoke of the union of human beings in marriage. He said that there are two kinds of marriage: that of the flesh, where the couple become separated at death; and that of the spirit, where they remain united beyond death. He spoke also of the bridegroom and of the church as his bride and went on to refer to the union with them through the Last Supper, which union could never be dissolved. He spoke also of the baptism of John, which would be replaced by the baptism of the Holy Spirit, whom he would send, and gave instructions to the disciples to baptize all who came to them to be baptized. That evening he returned to Bethany.

Tuesday, March 31, A.D. *33 (Nisan 11)* Today, Jesus taught for the last time in the temple. He spoke of the truth and of the necessity of fulfilling what one teaches. He wished to bring his teaching to fulfillment. It was not enough to believe; one must also practice one's faith. Thus, he would bring his teaching to fulfillment by going to the Father. Before leaving his disciples, however, he wished to bestow on them all that he had; not money and property, which he did not have, but his power and his forces. These he wanted to give them, and also to found an intimate union with them to the end of the world, a more perfect union than the present one. He asked them to become united with one another as limbs of one body. By this, Jesus referred to that which was to be accomplished through the Last Supper, but without mentioning it. He also said that his mother, the Holy Virgin, would remain with them for a number of years after his ascension to the Father. As he left the temple that evening, he took leave of it, saying that he would never enter it again in this body. This was so moving that the apostles and disciples cast themselves down on the ground and wept. Jesus also wept. It was dark as he made his way back to Bethany.

Wednesday, April 1, A.D. *33 (Nisan 12)* Early this morning many disciples assembled at the home of Lazarus in Bethany to hear Jesus teach. In all, about sixty people were gathered together. Toward three o'clock that afternoon, tables were prepared for a meal at the house of Simon the leper. At the meal, Jesus and the apostles served, Jesus going from one table to the other, exchanging words with the disciples as he went. Mary was indescribably sad, as Jesus had told her that morning of the nearness of his approaching death. Jesus also spoke with the disciples of this, saying that one of them would betray him to the Pharisees for a sum of money. The disciples wept bitterly and were so downcast that they could no longer eat. But Jesus bid them to partake of the food. He also gave instructions as to what they should do and where they should go after his death. At the end of the meal, while Jesus was teaching, Mary Magdalene entered the room bearing a costly ointment that she had bought in Jerusalem that morning. She cast herself down at Jesus' feet, weeping, and anointed his feet with the costly ointment. Then she dried his feet with her hair. Jesus broke off what he was saying, and some of the disciples were irritated by this interruption. Jesus said: "Do not take offense at this woman!" Then he spoke quietly with her. Mary Magdalene took the remaining ointment and poured it upon his head and the fragrance filled the room. Some of the apostles muttered at this. Magdalene, who was veiled, wept as she made her way from the room. As she was about to walk past Judas, he held out his arm and blocked the way. Judas scolded her on account of the waste of money, saying that it could have been given to the poor. However, Jesus said that she should be allowed to go, adding that she had anointed him in preparation for his death and burial, and that afterwards she would not be able to do so again. He said that wherever the Gospel would be taught, her deed and also the disciples' muttering would be remembered (Matthew 26:13). Judas was quite furious and thought to himself that he could no longer put up with this kind of thing. He withdrew quietly and then ran all the way to Jerusalem. It was dark, but he did not stumble. In Jerusalem the high priests and Pharisees were gathered together. Judas went to them and said that he wanted to give Jesus over into their hands. He asked how much they would give him and he was offered thirty pieces of silver. After concluding this agreement by shaking hands, Judas ran back to Bethany and rejoined the others. That night Nicodemus came from Jerusalem to speak with Jesus, and he returned to Jerusalem before the break of day.

Thursday, April 2, A.D. *33 (Nisan 13)* Today, so-called Maundy Thursday, being Nisan 13 in the Jewish calendar, was the day prior to the Day of Preparation for the Passover. Shortly before daybreak Jesus called Peter and John and gave them instructions concerning the preparation for the Passover feast in the Coenaculum (Luke 22:7–13). They went to Heli, the brother-in-law of the deceased Zacharias of Hebron, who had rented the Coenaculum, which belonged to Nicodemus and Joseph of Arimathea. Heli showed Peter and John the room for the Last Supper. The two apostles then went to the house of the deceased priest Simeon, and one of Simeon's sons accompanied them to the marketplace, where they obtained four lambs to be sacrificed for the meal. They also went to Veronica's house and fetched the chalice to be used that evening by Jesus at the institution of the Holy Communion. Meanwhile Jesus spoke again to the disciples of his imminent death, and— in taking leave of her—talked at length alone with his mother, the Holy Virgin Mary. In Jerusalem Judas met again with the Pharisees and made the final arrangements for the betrayal of Jesus. Around midday, after taking final leave of Mary, his mother, the other holy women, and Lazarus, Jesus went to Jerusalem with the remaining nine apostles and a group of seven disciples. The disciples went to the Coenaculum to help with the preparations there, while Jesus walked with the nine apostles, teaching as he went, from the Mount of Olives to Mount Calvary and back again to the Valley of Josaphat. Here they were met by Peter and John, who summoned them to the Passover feast. Judas arrived just before the meal began. Jesus dined with the twelve apostles in the main hall of the Coenaculum; two groups of twelve disciples, each with a "house father," ate in separate side rooms. The house father of the first group, comprising older disciples, was Nathanael, and that of the second group was Eliachim, a son of Cleophas and Mary Heli. All subsequent events on this evening of the Last Supper, and the following events that night on the Mount of Olives, are described in each of the four Gospels.

Friday, April 3, A.D. 33 (Nisan 14) As described by Anne Catherine Emmerich, the Moon was not quite full as Jesus, accompanied by the eleven apostles, walked through the Valley of Josaphat up to the Mount of Olives. She recounted in detail the experiences undergone by Jesus in the Garden of Gethsemane, where his suffering began. Here he lived through, in his soul, all the future suffering of the apostles, disciples, and friends of the early church; and he also underwent the temptation which he overcame with the words: "Not my will, but thine, be done" (Luke 22:42). Around midnight Judas arrived at the Garden of Gethsemane accompanied by twenty soldiers and six officials. Judas went up to Jesus and kissed him, saying: "Hail, Master!" Jesus replied: "Judas, would you betray the Son of man with a kiss?"

(Luke 22:47–48). There then took place the capture of Jesus. Thus began Good Friday, the last day in the earthly life of Jesus Christ. The sequence of events summarizing his suffering (Passion) and culminating in his death on the cross was described by Anne Catherine Emmerich as follows:

The capture of Jesus shortly before midnight; Jesus presented to Annas around midnight; the trial by Caiaphas; Peter's denial; Jesus in the prison at Caiaphas' court; the sentencing of Jesus by Caiaphas; the suicide of Judas; Jesus presented to Pontius Pilate at around six o'clock that morning; Jesus presented to Herod Antipas; Jesus presented again to Pilate; the scourging of Jesus, which lasted about three-quarters of an hour and was over by about nine o'clock that morning; the crowning with thorns; Pilate handed over Jesus to be crucified and pronounced the death sentence upon him at about ten o'clock that morning; the carrying of the cross to Golgotha on Mount Calvary; after Jesus had fallen three times under the weight of the cross, Simon of Cyrene was compelled to help him carry the cross; Veronica came to mop the blood and sweat from the face of Jesus with her veil; Jesus fell to the ground for the fourth and fifth times—the fifth time in the presence of the "weeping daughters" of Jerusalem; Jesus, on his way up Mount Calvary, fell to the ground a sixth time, and then a seventh time shortly before reaching the summit—at this seventh time it was about 11:45 A.M. Jerusalem time; Jesus was disrobed for the crucifixion—at noon a reddish darkening appeared before the Sun; Jesus was nailed to the cross at about 12:15 P.M.; then the cross was raised up; and at 12:30 P.M. the trumpets sounded forth from the temple announcing the slaying of the Passover lambs; the two criminals were crucified—the repentant one to Jesus' right and the unrepentant one to his left; dice were cast for Jesus' clothes; Jesus, after being mocked, spoke the words: "Father, forgive them, for they know not what they do!"; shortly after 12:30 P.M., a darkening of the Sun took place, and the heavens grew darker and darker; the repentant criminal said: "Lord, let me come to a place where you may save me; remember me when you come into your kingdom," to which Jesus replied: "Truly, I say to you, today you will be with me in paradise!"; Jesus spoke the words to his mother, Mary, "Woman, behold, this is your son; he will be more your son than if you had given birth to him," and to John he said, "Behold! This is your mother!"; toward three o'clock that afternoon Jesus called out in a loud voice:

"Eli, Eli, Lama Sabachtani!" which means: "My God, my God, why hast thou forsaken me!"; Jesus spoke the words: "I thirst!"; the soldier Abenadar reached a sponge soaked in vinegar up to Jesus' mouth; Jesus spoke the words: "It is fulfilled!" followed by the words: "Father, into thy hands I commend my spirit!"; at these words Jesus died—it was just after three o'clock on that Good Friday afternoon, and an earthquake rent a gaping hole in the rock between Jesus' cross and that of the criminal to his left; the heavens were still darkened, and the radiant being of Jesus Christ descended into the gaping hole in the ground— thus began his descent into hell.

At the resurrection at dawn on Easter Sunday, April 5, A.D. 33 (Nisan 16), exactly 33 1/3 years less 1 1/2 days had elapsed since the birth of Jesus just before midnight on Saturday/Sunday, December 6/7, 2 B.C.

Alphabetical Index

to the geographical maps

The following index includes not only the names of places visited by Jesus Christ (which are in *italics*) but also gives translations of German and Arabic terms appearing on the geographical maps. For example, Tal is German for "valley" and Ain is Arabic for "spring." In cases where the German and English spelling of places differ, the English spelling is listed after the German, e.g., *Sichem* = *Sychar*, where Sichem is the German spelling and Sychar is the Biblical English equivalent. (The present Arabic name is Nablus and the Hebrew designation is Shechem.) In the case of many of the place names a translation (" ") is given of the name, relating to its meaning. Also the approximate location is indicated and the dates < > upon which Jesus Christ visited the place. The dates are written <year month day> so that, for example, <29 Dec.19> signifies December 19 in the year A.D. 29. In describing the location, place names are referred to as they appear on the maps in this book and, if known, present-day designations (Hebrew or Arabic) are given in parentheses. Note that all distances, given in miles, are approximate, even if this is not explicitly stated.

Abel-Mehola ("dance meadow"). Approximately 7 miles south of Scythopolis (Bet She'an). Birthplace of the prophet Elisha. <29 Dec.19; 30 Aug.28–30>

Abez, Ebez ("height" or "lead mine"). 6 miles northwest of Scythopolis (Bet She'an). Saul's well was immediately east of Abez. It was here that Saul was wounded and died. <30 Oct.31–Nov.1>

Abila, Abila Decapoleos. 16 miles southeast of the Sea of Galilee, 10 miles east of Gadara. Elijah's pillar of instruction was close by. <30 Sep.18–21>

Abram ("sublime father"). 11 miles west of the Sea of Galilee, north of present-day Eilabun. <30 Dec.19–23>

Adama ("red earth"). On the southwest shore of Lake Merom. <30 mid-June & Jul.4–15>

Adummim, Adommim ("red ascent"). Between Jerusalem and Jericho. <30 Jan.27–28>

Adventsherberge = Advent inn

Ädron Tal = Aedron valley

Ain = spring

Ainon ("spring" or "well"). 2 miles east of the Jordan and 2 miles south of Sukkoth = Succoth. Close to the first place of baptism of John the Baptist. <29 Oct.12; 30 Sep.4 & 29–30; 30 Oct.3>

Akrabis, Accrabata, Acrabeta, present-day Agraba. 8 miles south-east of Sichem = Sychar (Nablus). <30 Jan.11 & Oct.3–4>

Alexandrium (Berg-Festung = "mountain fortress"). 18 miles north of Jericho and 5 miles east of the Jordan. <33 Jan.24 & Feb.9 & 17–18>

Amichores-Libnath, Amead-Sichor, Sichor-Libnath, Sihor, Labanath. Sichor signifies the "Nile" and Labanath means "white" (the town was often flooded). 13 miles east of Ptolemais (Akko). <30 Jun.26–Jul.3>

Anathot (named after Anathot, the son of Bechor; see *Jeremiah* 1: 1). Present-day Anata, 3 miles northeast of Jerusalem. Birthplace of the prophet Jeremiah. <31 Jan.7>

Antipatris (built by Herod the Great and named after his father, Antipater). 10 miles northeast of Japha (Jaffa, near Tel Aviv). <31 Jan.4>

Apheke, Aphec ("stream"). Present-day Afula, 2 miles south-west of Naim (Nein). Place of birth of the apostle Thomas. <30 Mar.9>

Apostel-Berg = Mount of the Apostles. 16 miles south of Tiberias. <33 Jan.28>

Ard = land

Arga. Close to present-day Suf, about 3 miles northwest of Gerasa and 15 miles east of the Jordan. <30 Sep.8–10>

Argob. About 5 miles southeast of Lake Merom. <31 Mar.7–8; Jul.26–27>

Aruma, Ruma. 5 miles southeast of Sichem = Sychar (Nablus). <29 Oct.18; 30 Feb.7 & Oct.13–15>

Aser-Michmethat (Aser = "blessed", Michmethat = "hidden corner"). Present-day Tayasir, 12 1/2 miles south of Scythopolis (Bet She'an) and 11 miles north-east of Sichem = Sychar(Nablus). <30 Oct.18–22; 31 Jan.22>

Atharot ("glorious crown"?). Present-day ruins Attara, 19 miles east of the Mediterranean Sea and 3 miles northwest of Samaria (Sabastiya). <30 Jul.30; 31 Mar.30–31>

Attarus. Mount Attarus, southeast of Herod's fortress Machaerus and about 10 miles east of the Dead Sea. Jesus spent most of the forty days in the wilderness in a cave on Mount Attarus. <29 Oct.22–Nov.30>

Aussätzigen-Bezirk = lepers' territory

Aussichts-Berg = mountain lookout post

Azanoth. In the region of the Horns of Hittin, 6 miles northwest of Tiberias. <30 Dec.26; 31 Jun.10>

Azo. Present-day Ajlun, 12 miles east of the Jordan. <30 Sep.10–12. On Sep.12 Jesus Christ visited the fishing lake 3 miles north of Azo>

Bach = stream

Bade-Garten = bathing garden

Badeort = place for bathing

Bade-See = lake for bathing

Bahurim ("chosen"). East of the Mount of Olives, on the old road leading from Jerusalem to Jericho. <30 Apr.10–17; 31 Sep.28–30>

Bauern-Häuser = farmers' houses

Beerseba, Beersheba ("well of the seven"). <33 Jan.8>

Berg = mountain

Berg der Apostel-Wahl = Mount of the choosing of the apostles

Berg-Festung = mountain fortress

Berg der Tochter Jephtes = mountain of Jephtes' daughter

Bergwerk = mine

Bethabara ("house of crossing"). Just north of the point of influx of the Jordan into the Dead Sea. <29 Dec.3; 32 May 17–18; 33 Feb.10–14>

Bethagla. Present-day Ain Hajla, 4 1/2 miles south-east of Jericho. <30 Jan.21>

Bethain, Bethanoth ("house of Anoth"). The ruins Bet Enun, 2 1/2 miles northeast of Hebron. <31 Jan.10; 32 Jun. 25; 33 Jan.9–10>

Bethan. Close to present-day Akbara, 6 miles north-west of Capernaum. <30 Dec.15>

Bethanat. 2 1/2 miles east of Saphet (Safad, Zefat). <30 Jan.5–6 & Dec.13–14>

Bethanien = Bethany (Eizariya) ("house of the poor"). Place of residence of Lazarus. <29 May30 & Sep.21–22 & Oct.20–21: 30 Mar.19–Apr.17 & Apr.26–May2 & Jul.21–23; 31 Jan.7 & 18 & 20 & Mar.24–28; 32 Jul. 25–26; 33 Feb.2–4 & Feb.6–8 & Feb.19–Apr.2>

Beth-Araba ("house of the steppe"). 6 miles west of the Dead Sea and 12 miles north-east of Hebron. <29 Sep.28; 30 Jan.19–20>

Betharamphtha-Julias, Amatha. 16 miles east of the Jordan and 21 miles east of Scythopolis (Bet She'an). <30 Sep.15–18>

Bethel, Luz ("house of God"). Present-day Beitin, 10 miles north of Jerusalem. In the neighborhood of Bethel Jacob had his vision of the heavenly ladder (Genesis 28:12). <29 Sep.19–20; 33 Jan.21–22>

Bethel. 11 miles east of Jerusalem. A small place with a hospital, where Jesus spent the Sabbath after the baptism in the Jordan. <29 Sep.23–24>

Bethjesimoth, Bethsimoth ("desert houses"). Present-day ruins Suweima, about 1 mile north-east of where the Jordan flows into the Dead Sea. < 29 Dec.11–12; 32 May 23–27>

Beth-Lechem. Present-day Bet Lehem, 6 miles north-west of Nazareth. However, it does not seem likely that this Beth-Lechem is the place which, according to Anne Catherine Emmerich's description, Jesus Christ visited on June 10 in A.D. 31.

Bethlehem ("house of bread"). Birthplace of Jesus.<29 Sep.30; 30 Jan.18>

Bethoron, Beth-Horon ("house of caves"). Two towns: Upper and Lower Bethoron. Lower Bethoron is present-day Beit Ur et Tahta and Upper Bethoron is present-day Beit Ur el Fauqa, approximately 10 miles northwest of Jerusalem. <30 Jul.24; 31 Jan.5–6>

Bethsaida, Bezatha ("house of fishing or hunting"). Not to be confused with Bethsaida-Julias on the other side of the Jordan.The exact location of this little fishing village cannot be found, as the shoreline of the Sea of Galilee was changed significantly by an earthquake. From Anne Catherine Emmerich's description Bethsaida was on the shore of the Sea of Galilee about 2 1/2 miles southeast of Capernaum. Now the ruins of Capernaum are close to the shoreline on the north side of the lake. Bethsaida was the home town of the apostles Peter, Andrew and Philip. <29 Aug.5; 30 Aug.7 & Nov.23; 31 Mar.16 & Apr.7 & Jun.14–15 & 23; 32 Aug. 2–3>

Bethsaida-Julias. Present-day ruins at et-Tell on the east side of the Jordan, 2 1/2 miles north of the place of influx of the Jordan into the Sea of Galilee. <30 Nov.19; 31 Mar.7–17 & Apr.11 & Jun.25>

Bethsop ("house of Ysop"). 1 mile east of the Jordan and 23 miles north of the Dead Sea. <29 Oct.12>

Bethulia. A mountain stronghold about 6 miles west of Tiberias. <29 May29 & Aug.19–21; 30 Jan.3 & Feb.15–16 & Aug.20–22; 31 Jan.24 & Mar.19>

Bethzur, Bethsur ("home of rock"). Present-day Beit Sahur close to Bethlehem. The three kings passed through this place on their way from Jerusalem to Bethlehem. <31 Jan.16–17>

Bezech, Bezek. 1 mile west of the Jordan and 10 miles south of Scythopolis (Bet She'an). <30 Sep.1–3>

Bienenort = place with bee hives

Birkeh = lake

Boden = floor (of lake or sea)

Bosra, Beestra ("house of Astarte"). Present-day Busra, some 55 miles east of the Jordan, about 25 miles east of Edrai (Der'a).<31 Jul.2>

Brunnen = well

Caesarea-Philippi. Paneas (Baniyas) was the earlier name of this place, reminding us of the near-by grotto of Pan. The town was built by Philip, a son of Herod the Great, and was named Caesarea in honor of Emperor Tiberius. 5 miles north-west of Lake Phiala. <31 Mar.4–7>

Cana (see Kana)

Capernaum (see Kapharnaum)

Carmel. Mount Carmel (see Karmel)

Cedar. A heathen town about 100 miles northeast of the Sea of Galilee. There was a Jewish settlement in this town. <32 Aug.8–13 & 15–18 & Sep.5–9>

Chabul, Cabul, Chabalon. A stretch of land east of the Mediterranean, between Akko and Tyre, bordering onto Galilee. <30 end of May & Jul.1–2>

Chim. 16 miles southeast of Hepha (Haifa). <29 Sep.15>

Chirbet = ruin

Chorazin. Anne Catherine Emmerich saw two places: Great Chorazin and Little Chorazin. Great Chorazin she saw about 6 miles northeast of the place where the Jordan flows into the Sea of Galilee, and Little Chorazin approximately 1 mile from the place of influx of the Jordan. <29 Oct.15–16; 30 Nov.22; 31 Mar.11–12; 32 Aug.1>

Chytroi. Present-day Kythrea, northern Cyprus. <31 May4–8>

Cydessa, Cydassa, Cedesa. 11 miles northwest of Tiberias. <31 Feb.6>

Cypern = *Cyprus*. Island in the Mediterranean visited by Jesus Christ for five weeks. <31 Apr.26–May30>

Dabrath, Dabereth, Dabaritta. Present-day Dabburiya, 5 miles east of Nazareth, at the northwest side of Mount Tabor. <30 Nov.1–4>

Dalmanutha. "Jesus went to the district of Dalmanutha" (Mark 8:10). A small village at the southeast end of the Sea of Galilee, and close by a tax/customs place. <31 Jan.30 & Mar.15>

Damna, Dimnah. 2 miles west of Magdalum/Sea of Galilee. <30 Dec.27; 31 Jan.25 & Jun.11>

Dan ("judge"), previously named Lais (Lesem). 2 miles west of Caesarea-Philippi. <31 Jan.27–Feb.13>

Datheman, Dathema. Present-day Ataman, 4 1/2 miles north of Edrai (Der'a), 30 miles east of the Jordan. <31 Jul.8>

Davidstrasse = David's way, running south of Bosra (Busra)<31 Jul.6>

Dead Sea (see Totes Meer)

Die Besessenen aus Gergesa = the possessed men from Gergesa

Dibon. 5 miles east of the Jordan and 10 miles north of the Dead Sea. 1 mile west of Dibon was the suburb of Dibon. <29 Oct.10–11 & Dec.7–8>

Dion, Dium, Dia. 7 1/2 miles east of Scythopolis (Bet She'an), 3 miles east of the Jordan. <30 Sep.25–27>

Dothaim ("two wells"). 7 1/2 miles west of Tiberias. <29 Jun.15 & Aug.31; 30 Mar.2 & Dec.24–25; 31 Apr.4–5>

Dothan. 9 miles north of Samaria (Sabastiya). <30 Oct.27–29>

Dritte Taufstelle = third place of baptism, where the baptism in the Jordan took place, 3 miles north of the place of influx of the Jordan into the Dead Sea.

Dschebal = range of mountains

Dschebl = mountain

Ebene = plain or valley

Ebene Jezrael = Jezreel (Yizreel) valley

Edon. Heathen town with a Jewish settlement, east of Cedar. <32 Aug.13–15>

Edrai ("my strength"). Present-day Der'a, about 30 miles east of the place where the Jordan flows out of the Sea of Galilee, in the direction of Bosra (Busra), which is some 25 miles further east. <31 Jun.29–30>

Eleale, El'aleh ("God's path"). Present-day El'Al, 1 mile north-east of Hesbon (Hisban). <29 Dec.9–10>

Elias-Höhle = Elijah's cave

Elias-Säule = Elijah's pillar

Elisabeths Höhle = Elizabeth's cave

Elkasa, a village 2 miles northeast of Capernaum. <31 Feb.9>

Elkese, Elkosh. 5 miles northwest of Saphet (Zefat, Safad). Birthplace of the prophet Nahum. <30 Dec.14>

Endor, Ain-dor ("spring of Dor"). Present-day 'En Dor, 7 miles southeast of Nazareth. <29 Sep.8–10; 30 Oct.30>

Engannim ("garden spring"). 7 1/2 miles southwest of Scythopolis (Bet She'an). <30 Jul.31–Aug.1>

Ensemes, Ain-Semes ("spring of the sun"). 10 miles northeast of Bethlehem. <29 Sep.26>

Ephron. 8 miles east of the Jordan and 20 miles south of the Sea of Galilee. <30 Sep.13–14>

Ephron or Ephraim. Present-day Taiyiba, 14 miles west of the Jordan and 12 miles north of Jerusalem. <32 Aug.26; 33 Jan.19–20 & Feb.15>

Erntefeld = harvest field

Erste Taufstelle = first place of baptism, where John the Baptist first started baptizing people. Close to Ainon.

Essener = Essenes

Fasten Jesu = fasting of Jesus

Festung = fortress or fortified place

Fischerdorf = fishing village

Fisch-See = fishing lake

Fischteich = fishpond

Fluss = river

Furt = ford

Gabaa. 20 miles west of the Jordan and 14 miles north of Jerusalem. <30 Jul.25>

Gabara. Present-day ruins of Madin, 6 miles northwest of Tiberias. <30 Nov.6–9; and on the mount of instruction near Gabara on 30 Apr.18–20 & 31 Jun.21>

Gadara, Gadar. The present-day site Hamat Gader, 5 miles southeast of where the Jordan flows out from the Sea of Galilee. <30 Sep.21–24>

Galaad. 7 1/2 miles east of the Sea of Galilee. <30 Aug.14>

Galgala ("circle"). Close to the present-day site Gush Halav, 6 miles northwest of Saphet (Zefat, Safad). <30 Dec.14>

Garisma, Garis, Garsis. 14 miles west of the Sea of Galilee and 2 miles north of Sephoris (Zippori). <31 Apr.20–22>

Gärten = garden

Gath-Hepher, Gethepher (Geth = "wine-press"). 11 miles west of the Sea of Galilee and 3 miles east of Sephoris (Zippori). Present-day Mash-had. Birthplace of the prophet Jonas. <30 Jul.18 & Dec.28>

Gaulon, Golan ("exodus"). In the region of the present-day ruins of Summaka, 6 miles south of Caesarea-Philippi (Baniyas). <31 Feb.28>

Gebirge = mountain range

Gebirgsort = place in the mountains

Gennabris, Ginnabris, Sennabris. 2 miles west of the place where the Jordan flows out from the Sea of Galilee. Nathanael Chased lived here. <29 Dec.25; 30 Feb.14 & Aug. 25–26>

Gerasa. 5 miles east of where the Jordan flows into the Sea of Galilee. < 29 Oct.14; 30 Aug.16>

Gergesa. 5 miles east of the Sea of Galilee, approximately the location of present-day Eli'Al. <30 Dec. 6>

Gessur. Town with a Roman garrison, about 12 1/2 miles northeast of Caesarea-Philippi (Baniyas). <31 Feb.20–24>

Giah, Gibea, Gibeath ("hill"). Close to or perhaps identical with present-day Jaba, 6 miles north of Jerusalem. <29 Sep.21>

Gideons-Berg = Gideon's mountain

Gilgal. 2 miles southeast of Jericho. <29 Oct.7–8>

Ginää = *Ginea,* Ginnim, Ain-Gannim ("garden spring"). Present-day Jenin, midway between Nazareth and Sichem = Sychar (Nablus). An estate, which Lazarus had inherited from his father, was close to Ginea and was put at the disposal of the disciples. <30 Mar.14–16 & Jul.28–29; 32 Jul. 8–21>

Gischala, Gis-Halab. 3 miles west of Tiberias. Here there was a fortress with Roman soldiers. The birthplace of Antigonus (founder of the Sadducees) and of the rebel John of Gischala and also of Saul (later the apostle Paul). <30 Nov.5–6; 31 Feb.5>

Gophna. Present-day Jifna, 12 miles north of Jerusalem. <29 Sep.18–19>

Great Chorazin (see *Chorazin*)

Grenzgebiet = boundary region between two areas or countries

Gross-Chorazin = *Great Chorazin* (see *Chorazin*)

Gur. A village 2 miles southwest of Jezrael (Yizre'el), 15 miles west of the Jordan. <29 Sep.16–17>

Gutshof = farm estate

Hadad-Rimmon, Adaremmon, Maximianopolis. 5 miles southwest of Nazareth. <31 Apr.1–2>

Hafen = harbor

Hain = grove

Hain Mambre = Mambre grove. The site of the present-day sacred oak of Abraham, 3 miles north of Hebron. <31 Jan.10>

Hain Moreh = Moreh's grove ("Moreh's oak"). 2 1/2 miles northeast of Sichem = Sychar (Nablus). Here there was a sacred tree, where God appeared to Abraham. At this tree Mary prayed on her journey from Nazareth to Bethlehem. <30 Mar.17 & Oct.15 & 18>

Hanathon ("place of grace"). 5 miles north of Capernaum. <30 Jan.4–5 & Dec.10>

Handelstrasse = trade route

Hareth. A wood where David once sought refuge from Saul. 3 miles east of Sichem = Sychar (Nablus). <30 Oct.11>

Haus = house

Haus Mariä = Mary's house

Häuser = houses

Hay, ha'Ai ("pile of stones"). The present-day ruins Haiyan near Deir-Dibwan, 10 miles northeast of Jerusalem. <30 Jan.12>

Hazezon-Thamar, Asesonthamar ("row of palms"). An earlier name for En Gedi on the west shore of the Dead Sea. The town of Hazezon-Thamar was destroyed along with the destruction of Sodom and Gomorrha, which were located in the (what is now desert) region close to the Dead Sea. At the time of Jesus the ruins of Hazezon-Thamar still existed. <30 Jan.17>

Hebron ("friend of God"). 17 1/2 miles south of Jerusalem. The town of Abraham (= "friend of God"). See also Hain Mambre, Juta and Machpelah, all in the area of Hebron. <29 Jun.3; 30 Mar.30–31; 31 Jan.11–12>

Heidenort = heathen place

Heiden-Quartier = heathen quarter (of a town)

Heidenstadt = heathen town

Heliopolis. Present-day site adjoining Cairo in Egypt. Taking flight to Egypt, the Holy Family lived at Heliopolis (or close to Heliopolis) before returning to Israel. Jesus Christ visited Heliopolis three months prior to the crucifixion. <33 Jan.2–4>

Hepha. Present-day Haifa on the Mediterranean. Jesus Christ landed at the harbor of Hepha upon his return from Cyprus. <31 May31>

Herberge = inn

Hermon. Mount Hermon in the north, on the border between Lebanon and Syria, 27 miles south-west of Damascus, height 9,232 feet. Jesus passed by Mount Hermon on his journey to Sidon and Sarepta. <29 Jul.8>

Hieromax. A river flowing down from Galaad into the Jordan just south of the Sea of Galilee. <29 Jun.7>

Hippos, Hippene. Present-day site of Susitha, just east of 'En Gev on the east shore of the Sea of Galilee. <30 Jan.9>

Hirtenfeld = shepherds' field

Hirtenhaus = shepherd's house

Hirtenort = shepherds' place

Hirtental = valley of the shepherds

Hirtenturm = shepherds' tower

Historische Aiche = historic oak

Historischer Brunnen = historic well

Hoch-Plateau = high plateau

Hof = farm

Höhle = cave

Höhle Elisabeth = Elizabeth's cave

Höhle Ephraim = Ephraim's cave

Höhle Machpelah = Machpelah's cave (see Machpelah)

Hügel = hill

Hukok, Hucuca. Present-day Huqoq, 5 miles west of Capernaum. <30 Dec.11–13>

Inselstadt = island town

Irrenhaus = lunatic asylum

Ischariot = *Iscariot* ("man from Keriyot or Karioth"). In the region of present-day Aqaba, 12 miles west of the Jordan and 10 miles northeast of Sichem = Sychar (Nablus). Home town of Judas Iscariot. <30 Oct.27>

Jakob-Esau-Stätte = site of Jacob and Esau

Jakobsbrunnen = Jacob's well. One mile east of Sichem = Sychar (Nablus). Mentioned in John 4:6 as the place where the conversation between Jesus Christ and the Samaritan woman took place. <29 Jul.30; 30 Jul.26; 33 Jan.13>

Jakobs-Friedenslager = Jacob's site of peace

Jakobs-Stadt Bethel = Jacob's town Bethel (see *Bethel*)

Jericho. One of the most ancient archeological sites in the world, 5 miles west of the Jordan. Captured when its walls fell after the Hebrews marched around the city, it was destroyed by Joshua (Joshua 6). <32 May 29–Jun.10; 33 Jan.20–21>

Jerusalem, Salem ("peace"). <29 May31 & Nov.30; 30 Mar.20–Apr.9; 31 Jan.19–20 & Mar.25–28; 32 Jul. 27; 33 Feb.19–Apr.3>

Jezrael. Present-day Yizre'el, about 10 miles south of Nazareth. <29 Aug.27–28; 30 Feb.9 & 20>

Jogbeha ("high place"). 2 miles east of the Jordan and 24 miles south of the Sea of Galilee. <30 Sep.27–28>

Johanneshöhle = cave of John the Baptist

Josephs Erbe = Joseph's inherited place (Joseph's heritage)

Josephs Werkstatt = Joseph's work place

Jotopata, Jotapata. A town and fortress of the Herodians (followers of Herod). 3 miles northwest of Tiberias. <30 Aug.27>

Judenort = Jewish town or village

Jünger-Herberge = disciples' inn/guest house

Juta, Jutta. Present-day Yatta, 5 miles south of Hebron. Birthplace of John the Baptist. <31 Jan.8–9 & 13>

Kades-Nephthali (Kedes = "consecrated, holy"). 5 miles northwest of Lake Merom. <31 Feb.11>

Kafr = village

Kameltreiber = camel dealer

Kamel-Züchterei = breeding place for camels

Kamon. About 5 miles east of the Jordan and 29 miles north of the Dead Sea. <30 Sep.5>

Kana = Cana ("place of reeds"). Present-day Kafr Kanna, 3 miles northeast of Nazareth. Hometown of Nathanael the Bridegroom, at whose wedding Jesus Christ changed water into wine (John 2:1–11). <29 Jun.30 & Dec.25–31; 30 Aug.3; 31 Feb.4 & Jun.19–20>

Kapharnaum = *Capernaum*, Kafr Nahum ("village of Nahum"). The ruins of Capernaum are on the northwest shore of the Sea of Galilee. In the visions of Anne Catherine Emmerich she always saw Capernaum about 2 1/2 miles from the shoreline. She indicated that an earthquake significantly changed the shoreline of the Sea of Galilee: "The waters of the lake poured into the valley and came almost up to Capernaum, which previously was about half an hour from the shoreline. The house of Peter and that of the Holy Virgin—close to Capernaum, toward the lake—remained standing. The Sea of Galilee moved violently, the waters surging over the shoreline here and there, and receding elsewhere. The shoreline was changed significantly, approximating to its present form, and is no longer recognizable as it was." (WJW, 466) <29 May29, Jun.20, Aug.4 & 8–9, Dec.22–24; 30 Jan.1–2 & 6–7, Feb.10–13, Mar.l, mid–June, Jul.18–l9, Aug.4–7 & 9–ll, Nov.9–11 & 17–l9, Nov.24–Dec.10; 31 Jan.26–Feb.17, Apr.5–13, Jun.14–17 & 22; 33 Jan.26>

Kapharot. A small place 3 miles northwest of Tiberias. <31 Apr.20>

Karawanen-Lager = caravan site

Karmel = Mount Carmel. Mountain range near Haifa, overlooking the Mediterranean, rising to 1,730 feet above sea level. Elijah lived for some time on Mount Carmel and it was here that he defeated the prophets of Baal (I Kings 18:17–46). <29 Jul.23–24>

Keryneia. Town on the north side of the island Cyprus, which Jesus Christ visited in the spring of A.D. 31. <31 May25–26>

Kibzaim. 19 miles east of the Jordan and 25 miles north of Jerusalem. <29 Dec.16–17; 30 Jul.24>

Kimki, Chimki. A shepherd village 6 miles south of Nazareth.<29 Sep.2–4>

Kirjathaim. A Levite town 8 miles west of Capernaum. <30 Dec.17–19>

Kision, Kiseon, Kedes. A small place at the southern foot of Mount Tabor, 6 miles southeast of Nazareth. <29 Aug.25>

Kisloth-Tabor, Chesulloth. Present-day Iksal, west of Mount Tabor and 2 miles southeast of Nazareth. <29 Jul.25, Aug.31–Sep.1; 30 Feb.16–19; 30 Dec.28–29; 31 Apr.3>

Kition. Town with a near-by harbor on the southeast side of the island of Cyprus. Upon completion of his five-week stay on the island, Jesus Christ set sail from the harbor of Kition. <31 May23 & 30>

Klein-Chorazin = Little Chorazin (see *Chorazin*)

Klein-Sephoris = Little Sephoris (see *Sephoris*)

Korä = Kore. A small place between Edrai (Der'a) and Bosra (Busra), 38 miles east of the place where the Jordan flows out from the Sea of Galilee. <31 Jul.1>

Koreä = Korea. 15 miles west of the Jordan and 20 miles north of Jerusalem. <30 Oct.6–8; 31 Mar.22>

Krankenort Bethel = Hospital town of Bethel (see *Bethel*)

Krippenhöhle = cave of the nativity

Land-Chabul = land of Chabul

Landgut Lazari = Lazarus' estate

Landschaft = terrain

Lava-Erguss = overflow of lava

Lava-Strom = stream of lava

Lazari-Hof = Lazarus' country house

Lazari-Weinberg = wine orchards of Lazarus

Lebona. A small place at the southern foot of Mount Garizim, 17 miles west of the Jordan and 27 miles north of Jerusalem. <31 Jan.21>

Lebonah. Near present-day Lubban Shaqiya, 17 miles west of the Jordan and 20 miles north of Jerusalem. <31 Mar.21–22>

Leccum. One mile west of the Jordan and 8 miles north of the Sea of Galilee. <31 Apr.9–10>

Lehrberg = mount of instruction

Lehrberg der Seligkeiten = mount of beatitudes

Lehrberg der Speisung der 4000 = mount of the feeding of the 4,000

Lehrberg der Speisung der 5000 = mount of the feeding of the 5,000

Lehrhügel = hill of instruction

Lehrplatz = place of instruction

Lehrstuhl = seat of instruction

Leppe. A village west of Mallep (present-day Bellapaise) on the north side of the island of Cyprus. <31 May13>

Leviten-Stadt = town of Levites

Libnath, Libna, Lebna, Labana, Lobna. A town of Levites, 17 miles west of Hebron. <31 Jan.16>

Little Chorazin = *Klein-Chorazin* (see *Chorazin*)

Little Sephoris = *Klein-Sephoris* (see *Sephoris*)

Luz. Not to be confused with Jacob's town Bethel, present-day Beitin, formerly Luz. This place Luz was a village 9 miles west of the place of influx of the Jordan into the Dead Sea. <29 Sep.25>

m = meters (height of mountains). One meter = 3.3 feet.

Machpelah. Machpelah's cave is mentioned in Genesis 23:9 & 17; 49:29–30. A large cave located north of the old town of Hebron. The patriarchs Abraham, Isaac and Jacob, and also others, were buried in this cave. <31 Jan.10>

Madian, Midian. A large town of Madianites with a Jewish quarter, 12 miles east of the Dead Sea. <32 May 20>

Magdala ("tower"). On the east side of the Sea of Galilee in the region of present-day 'En Gev. <30 Dec.4–7>

Magdalum. Now generally referred to as Magdala, present-day Migdal, on the west side of the Sea of Galilee. <29 Aug.10>

Mahanaim. This historical town of Levites is on the north side of the River Jabbok (Yaboq), 6 miles east of the Jordan. <30 Sep.5>

Malachias Höhle = Malachi's cave

Mallep. A Jewish colony on the north side of the island of Cyprus. Present-day Bellapaise. It was here that Jesus Christ spent much of the time during his five-week visit to Cyprus. <31 May9–20 & 26–28>

Matthäi Haus = Matthew's house, on the northeast side of the Sea of Galilee.

Matthäi Zollstätte = Matthew's customs place, not far from his house on the northeast side of the Sea of Galilee.

Meer = sea

Megiddo, Magiddo. 17 miles southeast of Hepha (Haifa) on the southwest side of the Jezrael (Jezrael) valley. <30 Nov.14–15>

Merdsch = plain

Merom See = Lake Merom. Present-day Hula Reserve 12 miles north of the Sea of Galilee.

Meroz ("refuge"). 15 miles west of the Jordan and 30 miles north of Jerusalem. <30 Oct.23–26>

Misael ("who is like God"), also named Masal. An ancient Levite town 10 miles east of Akko, in the region of present-day Bet Kerem. <31 Jun.1–4>

Mitelländisches Meer = Mediterranean Sea

Mizpah ("lookout"), also named Maspha. Present-day Nabi Samwil (Shemu'el), supposedly the home town and place of birth and death of the prophet Samuel. <29 Oct.5>

Mozian. Ancient city east of the Tigris and Euphrates. <32 Oct.7–8>

Naasson ("big snake"). About 12 1/2 miles west of the place where the Jordan flows into the Sea of Galilee. <30 Dec.19>

Nach = to (in the direction toward)

Naim ("beautiful"), also named Nain. Present-day Nein, 6 miles southeast of Nazareth. The home town of the rich widow Maroni whose son was raised from the dead (Luke 7:11). Maroni became one of the holy women. <30 Aug.2, Nov.13–14; 31 Jun.7–9>

Nahr (abbreviated N.) = river

Naturbrücke = natural bridge

Nazara. A Samaritan town at the northwest end of the Jezrael (Jezreel) valley, 12 1/2 miles south-east of Hepha (Haifa). The Holy Family stopped here upon returning from Egypt. <30 Mar.13>

Nazareth. The home town of Jesus. According to Anne Catherine Emmerich Nazareth had five gates and the house of Joseph and Mary was close to the north gate. Joseph's carpentry was close by. <29 May29, Jul.31–Aug.2, Sep.5–7 & 11–14; 30 Mar.5–12, Aug.11–12; 33 Jan.27>

Nebo, Nabo. At the foot of Mount Nebo, 9 miles east of the north end of the Dead Sea. <30 Jan.29–30; 32 May 18>

Nephthali ("my battle"). A little place 4 miles west of Capernaum. <31 Feb.8>

Nobah. 14 miles northeast of Lake Merom. <31 Feb.25–27>

Nobah in Hauran. A heathen town with a Jewish quarter populated mainly by Rechabites who settled there upon returning from the Babylonian captivity. In the neighborhood of present-day Behem, 20 miles east of Bosra (Busra) and 8 miles northeast of Salcha (Salkhad). <31 Jul.3>

Noemis Hirtenort = Noemi's shepherd place

Ober = upper

Ober-Bethoron = Upper Bethoron (see *Bethoron*)

Obst-Tal = fruit valley

Oelberg = Ölberg = Mount of Olives

Ono. In the neighborhood of the present-day ruins of a Johannite monastery named Kasr el-Jehud, 1 mile northwest of the place of the baptism in the Jordan (see "Dritte Taufstelle") and 3 miles southeast of Jericho. <30 Jan.13–14, Feb.3–6>

Ophra, Ophera ("dust"?). In the region of present-day Mazra'at, some 16 miles north of Jerusalem. <30 Oct.8–9>

Ornithopolis ("bird town"). Located close to the shore of the Mediterranean Sea, between Sarepta (Sarafand) and Tyre (Sour). Pliny refers to the town Ornithon between Tyre and Sarepta (*Hist. nat.* V,18). Here there was a small Jewish colony north of the town. The Syrophoenecian woman, whose possessed daughter became healed (Matthew 15:22), lived in Ornithopolis. It was from the harbor of Ornithopolis that Jesus Christ set sail for his visit to the island of Cyprus on the evening of April 25, A.D. 31. <31 Feb.15–16, Apr.25>

Ort = place

Ozensara, Uzzen Se'ereh ("Sarah's town"). Between Jerusalem and Tel Aviv, 19 miles northwest of Jerusalem. <29 Sep.18; 31 Jan.4>

· Peräa = Perea. Stretch of land to the east of the Jordan, running down to the Dead Sea.

Petri Fischstelle = Peter's fishery

Petri Salz-Fischerei = Peter's salt fishery

Petrus = Peter

Phasael. Present-day El-Fasayil, 5 miles west of the Jordan and 22 miles northeast of Jerusalem. <29 Oct.19; 30 Feb.7>

Phiala-See = Lake Phiala. Present-day Berekhat Ram, 4 miles southeast of Caesarea-Philippi (Baniyas). <31 Feb.24–25>

Philippus = Philip

Plantage = plantation

Quarantania = Mount Quarantania. Present-day Quruntul, 7 1/2 miles west of the Jordan and 7 1/2 miles northeast of Jerusalem. It was here that Jesus Christ spent the first night of the forty days of temptation in the wilderness, before he went to Mount Attarus. <29 Oct.21>

Rama ("heights"). Present-day Ram, 5 miles north of Jerusalem. <31 Mar.28>

Ramoth-Galaad ("heights in Galaad"), also called Ramath-Mizpa, or sometimes Hag Gilead. Present-day Salt, 11 miles east of the Jordan and 25 miles north of the Dead Sea. <30 Sep.5–7>

Ras (abbreviated R.) = foothills

Rechob, Rehob. About 14 miles north of Lake Merom. <31 Feb.19>

Regaba. 10 miles southeast of Lake Merom. <31 Mar.1–4 & 9–10>

Rimon. About 2 miles southeast of Mount Tabor. <31 Jun.10>

Römer-Strasse = Roman road

Römische Garnison = Roman garrison

Rubens-Herberge = Ruben's inn

Ruinen = ruins

Salamis. Ancient port on the east coast of the island of Cyprus. It was here that Jesus Christ landed on April 26, A.D. 31 upon crossing the Mediterranean from the harbor of Ornithopolis. Salamis was destroyed by an earthquake in the fourth century A.D. <31 Apr.26–May1 & 29>

Salcha, Selcha. Present-day Salkhad in Hauran, 15 miles east of Bosra (Busra), 74 miles east of the Jordan and at a latitude corresponding to 12 1/2 miles south of the Sea of Galilee. <31 Jul.5>

Salem ("peace"). About 1 1/2 miles west of the Jordan and 24 miles north of the Dead Sea. According to Anne Catherine Emmerich, Melchizedek had built here prior to laying the foundations for another Salem (=Jerusalem). <30 Oct.11–12>

Saphet, Sephet. Present-day Safad/Zefat, 8 miles northwest of Capernaum. <30 Dec.15–17>; mount of instruction between Hanathon and Saphet: <30 Jan.4–5, Dec.10; 31 Jun.24>

Sarepta, Sarephat, Zarphat. Present-day Sarafand on the Mediterranean, north of Ornithopolis and Tyre (Sour). It was in Sarepta that the prophet Elijah raised the son of a widow from the dead (I Kings 17:9). <29 Jul.9 & 22; 31 Feb.17–18>

Sauls-Brunnen = Saul's well

Schiff Petri = Peter's boat

Schiffstelle = mooring place

Schlachtfeld = battlefield

Schloss = castle

Schloss-Festung = castle fortress

Schlucht = gorge

See = lake

See Genezareth = Sea of Galilee

See-Ufer = lake shore

Seil = stream

Seleucia. A garrison town of heathen soldiers about 3 miles southeast of Lake Merom. <30 mid-June & Jul.11>

Sephoris, Saphorim. Present-day ruins Zippori, 3 miles north of Nazareth. Sephoris had three synagogues: one for the Pharisees, one for the Sadducees, and one for the Essenes. Klein-Sephoris = Little Sephoris lay northeast of Greater Sephoris. Sephoris was the hometown of Anna, the mother of Mary of Nazareth. <29 Aug.14–18; 30 Mar.2–4; Little Sephoris: 30 Aug.8–10>

Serobabel = Zorobabel was the nobleman whose adopted son was healed by Jesus Christ (John 4:47). Jesus was often a guest at Zorobabel's estate at Capernaum. <30 Aug.20, Nov.9 & 11 & 17; 31 Jan.26 & 31, Apr.14, Jun.12 & 16>

Shiloh ("place of rest"). Present-day ruins of Shillo, 19 miles north of Jerusalem. <29 Dec.14–15; 30 Oct.4–5>

Sichar. A heathen town with a Jewish settlement, near Cedar, some 100 miles northeast of the Sea of Galilee. <32 Aug.19–Sep.4>

Sichem = Sychar. Present-day Nablus (Shechem). Jacob's well is located 1 mile east of Sychar. <29 Dec.17; 30 Jul.26–27; 33 Jan.16–17>

Sidon, Zidon ("fortress"). Present-day Saida on the Mediterranean, 21 miles north of Tyre (Sour). <29 Jul.8>

Siloh (see *Shiloh*)

Simons Haus = Simon's house

Sion. Not Mount Zion in Jerusalem but a small place southwest of Mount Tabor. <31 Jun.6–7>

Sogane. About 4 miles south of Caesarea-Philippi (Baniyas). <31 Mar.18–19>

Speisung = meal or feeding

Spiegel = surface (of lake or sea)

Stadt-Park = town park

Succoth (see *Sukkoth*)

Sukkoth = Succoth ("huts"). 2 miles east of the Jordan and 27 1/2 miles north of the Dead Sea. <29 Oct.12–13; 30 Oct.1–2>

Sumpf = swamp

Sunem. Present-day Sulam (Shunem), 9 miles southeast of Nazareth. <30 Feb.22–23; 31 Jan.1–2>

Sychar (see *Sichem*)

Tabor. Mount Tabor, 1,929 feet, located 5 miles southeast of Nazareth. It was on this mountain that the transfiguration took place (Matthew 17:1), around midnight April 3/4, A.D. 31. <31 Apr.3–4>

Tal = valley

Tal Zabulon = Zabulon valley, between Nazareth and Sephoris

Tarichäa = *Tarichea.* Located close to the place where the Jordan flows out from the Sea of Galilee. <29 Dec.20–21; 30 Aug.13; 31 Jan.30, Apr.16>

Taubental = valley of the doves, 6 miles northwest of Tiberias

Taufort = place of baptism (see "Dritte Taufstelle")

Taufstelle = place of baptism (see "Dritte Taufstelle")

Teich = pond

Tell (abbreviated T.) = hill or mountain-top

Terebenthe = hill of terebinth trees

Thaanach ("sandy ground"). Present-day ruins Ta'nakh, 13 miles southwest of Nazareth. <31 Jun.5>

Thänath-Silo = *Thanath-Silo.* Present-day ruins of Ta'na, 6 miles east of Sichem (Nablus). <30 Oct.16–18; 31 Jan.2–3, Mar.29; 33 Jan.29>

Thantia, Thainata. On the Roman road between Bosra (Busra) and Philadelphia (Rabbath Ammon), 22 miles south of Bosra, 33 miles northeast of Philadelphia, 46 miles east of the Jordan. <31 Jul.6–7>

Thebez. Present-day Tubas, 10 miles northeast of Sichem = Sychar (Nablus/Shechem). <29 Dec.18>

Thirza ("lovely"). Between Thebez (Tubas) and the Jordan, 15 1/2 miles northeast of Sichem = Sychar (Nablus/Shechem). <31 Jan.23>

Tierpark = zoo

Totes Meer = Dead Sea

Tyrus = *Tyre,* Zor ("rock"). Present-day ruins of Sour on the Mediterranean, 21 miles south of Sidon (Saida). Here there was a Jewish community, which Jesus Christ visited in the year A.D. 30. <30 Jun.20–25>

Ulama. Present-day village of Ullama, 5 1/2 miles southwest of the place where the Jordan flows out from the Sea of Galilee. <30 Feb.23–27>

Unter = lower

Unter Bethoron = *Lower Bethoron* (see *Bethoron*)

Ur. Ancient Chaldean city close to the Euphrates, about 160 miles northwest of the place where the Euphrates flows into the Persian Gulf. The home town of the patriarch Abraham. <32 Oct.10–12>

Valley of the Doves (see Taubental)

Verkl ärung = transfiguration

Villenort = place with villas

Vision Ezechiels refers to the battlefield of Ezekiel's vision

Von = from (leading away from a place or town)

Vorgebirge = foothills

Vorstadt = suburb

Wadi (abbreviated W.) = valley

Wald = wood or forest

Wandel auf dem See = walking on the water

Weide-Plätze = grazing ground

Weinberge = vineyards

Weisses Vorgebirge = foothills of the White Mountains

Westgaliläa = West Galilee

Wildnis = wilderness

Zabulon-Tal = Zabulon valley. Valley to the north of Nazareth, between Nazareth and Sephoris. <29 Aug.12 & 24; 30 Aug.10–11>

Zedad. A small town in Northern Galilee 12 1/2 miles west of Lake Merom. <30 Jul.16–17>

Zeltstadt der Könige = tent city of the three kings

Zollhäuser = publicans' houses

Zöllnerort = publicans' place (for payment of taxes or customs, etc.)

Zollort = tax or customs place

Zollstätte = tax or customs place

Zorobabel (see Serobabel)

Zuckerrohr-Plantage = sugar cane plantation

Zweite Lehre auf dem See = second time of instruction upon the lake

Zweite Taufstelle = second place of baptism. This was the second place where John the Baptist baptized people. (See Erste Taufstelle = first place of baptism and Dritte Taufstelle = third place of baptism.) The second place of baptism was located on the east side of the Jordan, more or less opposite (but slightly to the north of) the third place of baptism. It was at the third place of baptism, on the west side of the Jordan and close to the village of Ono, that the baptism of Jesus took place.

Zweiter Wandel auf dem See = second walking on the water

Some topographical corrections:

Map 25: Gath-Hepher should be shown 5 miles further to the northwest of the route.

On all the maps the place Koreä = Korea should be somewhat further northeast, adjoining Wadi Far'a = Far'a valley.

The village of Juta should appear on all the maps just southeast of Hebron.

The place Thänath-Silo = Thanath-Silo should appear a little further to the southeast on all the maps.

MAP 1: Journey to the Place Where John the Baptist Grew Up
MAY 29–JUNE 20, A.D. 29

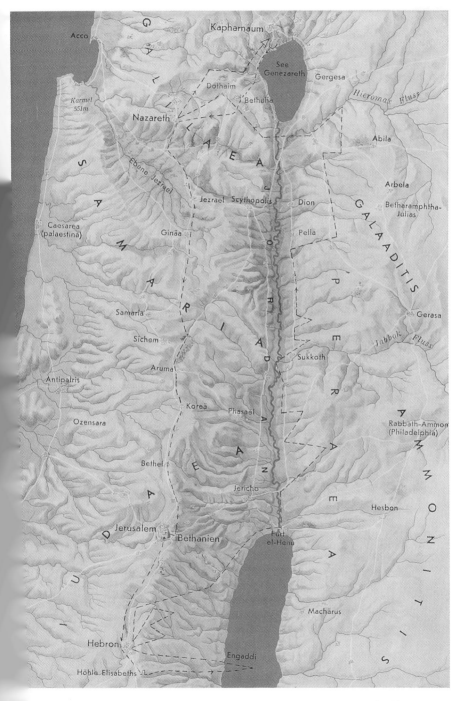

Capernaum—Bethulia—Nazareth—Bethany—Jerusalem—Hebron—Elizabeth's Cave—
Dead Sea—Hebron—Perea—Hieromax—Dothaim—Nazareth—Capernaum

MAP 2: Journey to Sidon, Mount Carmel, and Jacob's Well

JUNE 30–JULY 31, A.D. 29

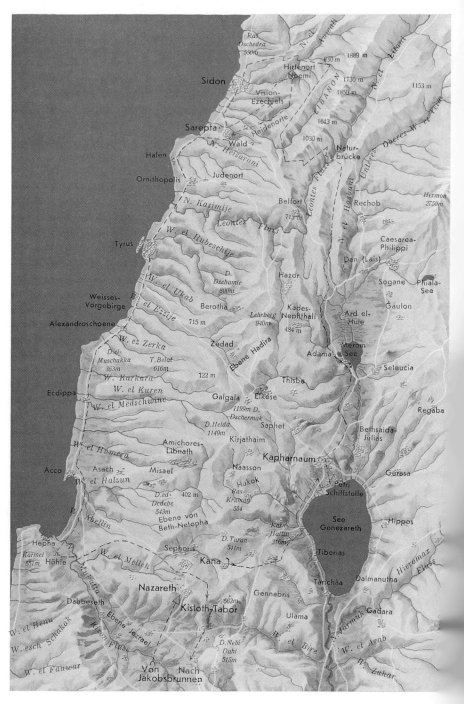

Cana—Peter's Fishery—Southern End of Lebanon—Sidon—Sarepta—
Battlefield of Ezekiel's Vision—Noemi's Shepherd's Place—Sarepta—Carmel—
Kisloth-Tabor—Jacob's Well—Nazareth

MAP 3: Travels in Southern Galilee
AUGUST 4–26, A.D. 29

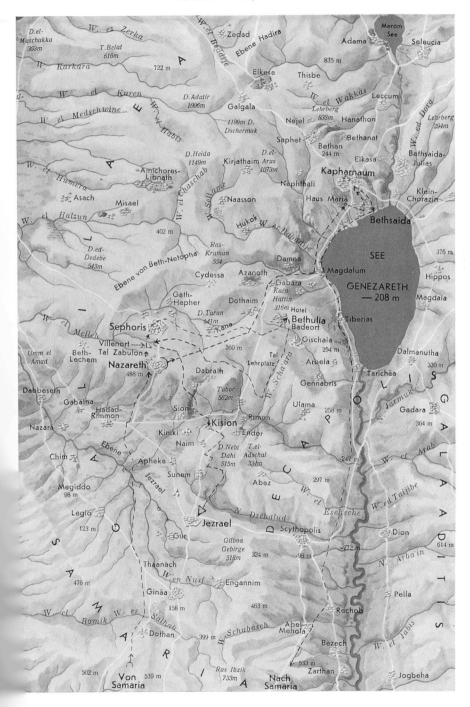

Nazareth—Capernaum—Bethsaida—Land of Samaria—Zabulon Valley—Sephoris—
Bethulia—Wadi Scha'ara—Zabulon Valley—Kision—Jezrael

MAP 4: Travels with Eliud in Lower Galilee

AUGUST 27–SEPTEMBER 17, A.D. 29

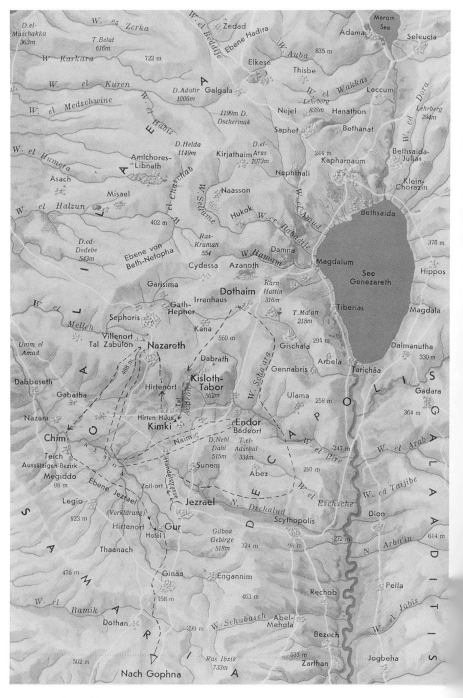

Jezrael—Publicans' Place—Dothaim—Kisloth-Tabor—Aedron Valley—Kimki—
Nazareth—Endor—Nazareth—Chim—Plain of Jezrael—Gur

MAP 5: Journey to the Baptism in the Jordan

SEPTEMBER 18–28, A.D. 29

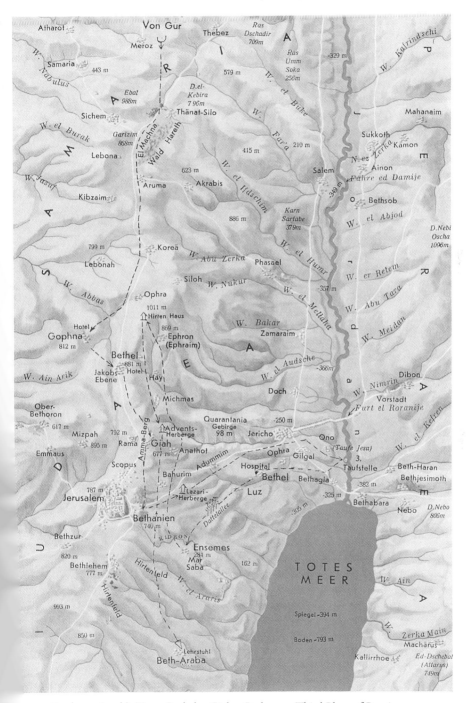

Gophna—Jacob's Town Bethel—Giah—Bethany—Third Place of Baptism—
ace of Convalescence Bethel—Luz—Ensemes—Shepherds' House—Advent Inn—Beth-Araba

MAP 6: Visit to the Valley of the Shepherds Near Bethlehem
SEPTEMBER 28–OCTOBER 10, A.D. 29

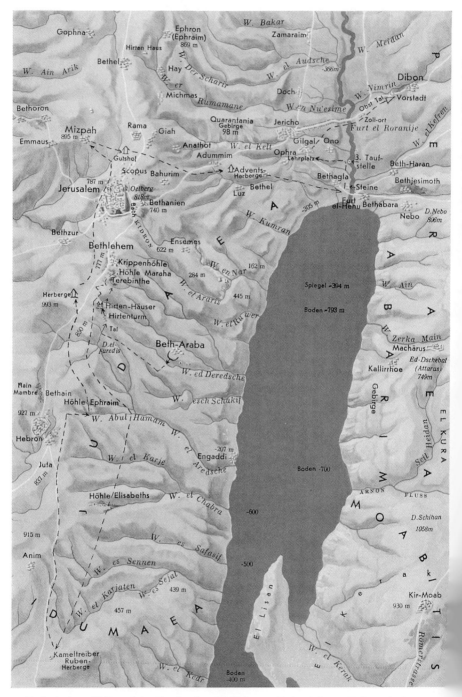

Beth-Araba—Valley of the Shepherds—Bethlehem—Ruben's Inn—Ephraim's Cave—
Mizpah—Third Place of Baptism—Gilgal—Publicans' Place—Suburb of Dibon

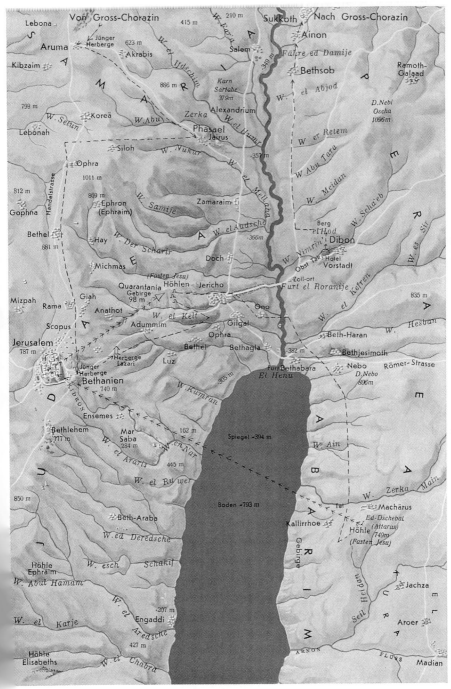

Suburb of Dibon—Bethsop—Ainon—Succoth—Gerasa—Near Great-Chorazin—
Aruma—Phasael—Bethany—Quarantania—Attarus—Jerusalem—Quarantania

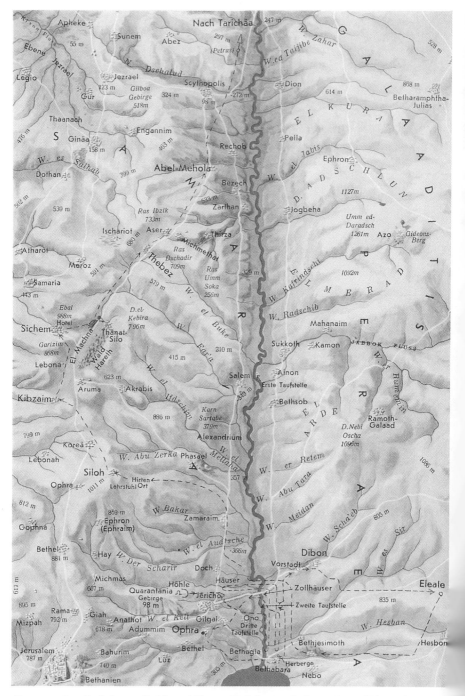

Quarantania—Bethabara—Publicans' Place—Bethabara—Ophra—Second Place of Baptism
—Suburb of Dibon—Eleale—Bethjesimoth—Siloh—Kibzaim—Sychar—Thebez—
Abel-Mehola

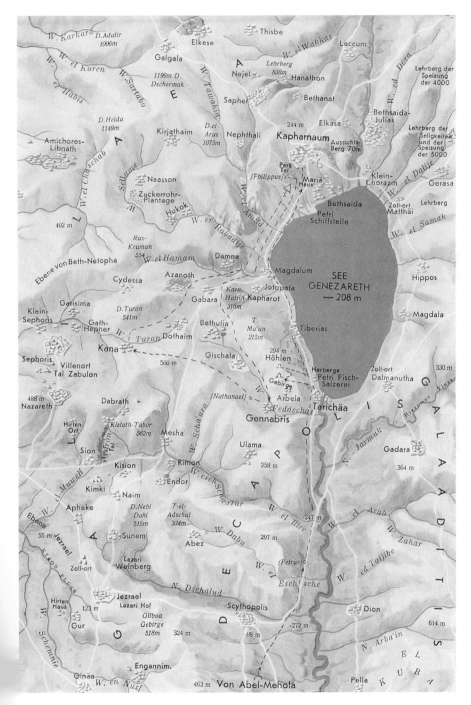

Tarichea—Capernaum—Gennabris—Cana—Capernaum

MAP 10: The First Sermon on the Mount
JANUARY 3–11, A.D. 30

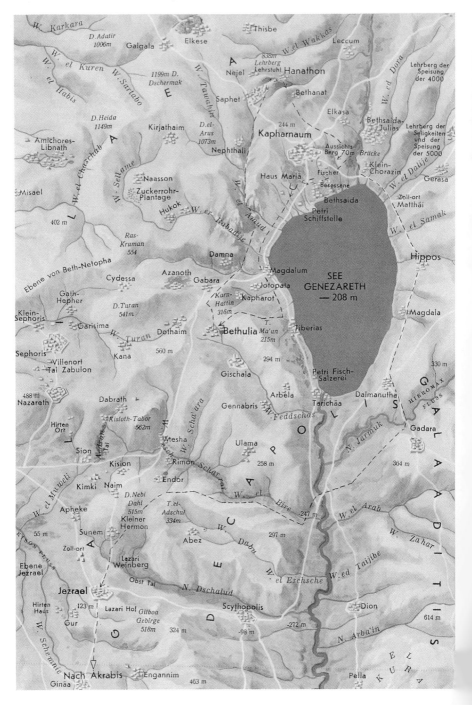

Capernaum—Bethulia—Hanathon—Mount of instruction—Bethanat—Capernaum—
Hippos—Jezrael—Akrabis

MAP 11: At the Place of Baptism

JANUARY 11–26, A.D. 30

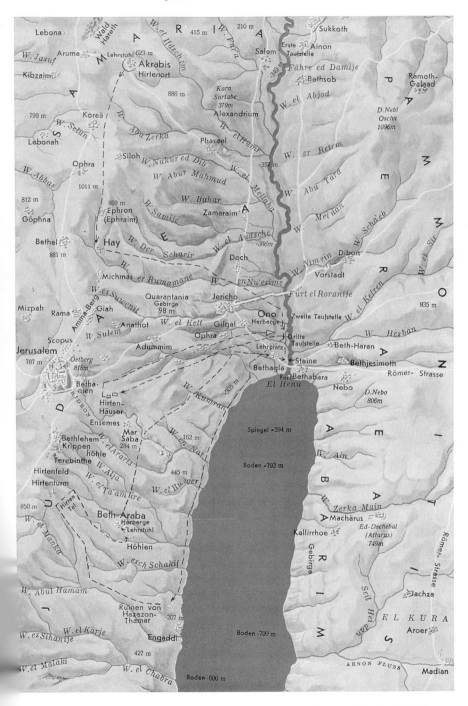

Akrabis—Hay—Third Place of Baptism —Ono—Hazezon-Thamar—Shepherds' Valley—
Beth-Araba—Bethagla—Third Place of Baptism

MAP 12: A Raising From the Dead

JANUARY 27–FEBRUARY 9, A.D.30

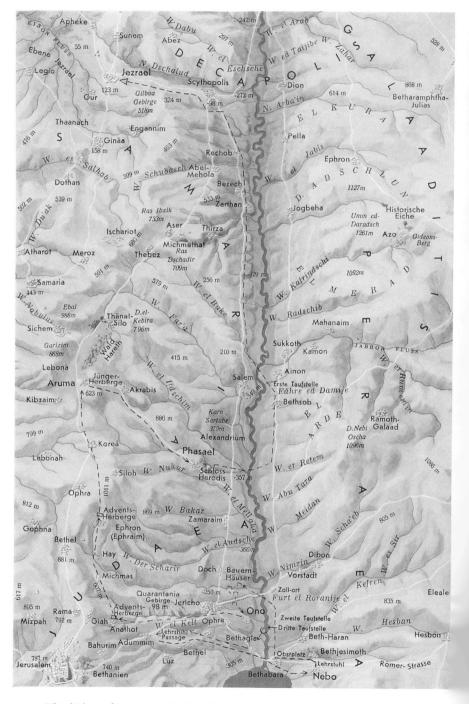

Third Place of Baptism—Wadi el-Kelt—Adummim—Nebo—Ono—Aruma—
Phasael—Jezrael

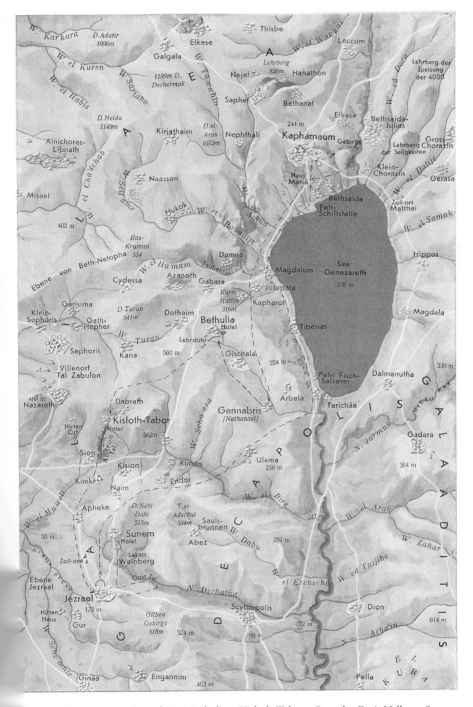

Jezrael—Capernaum—Gennabris—Bethulia—Kisloth-Tabor—Jezrael—Fruit Valley—Sunem

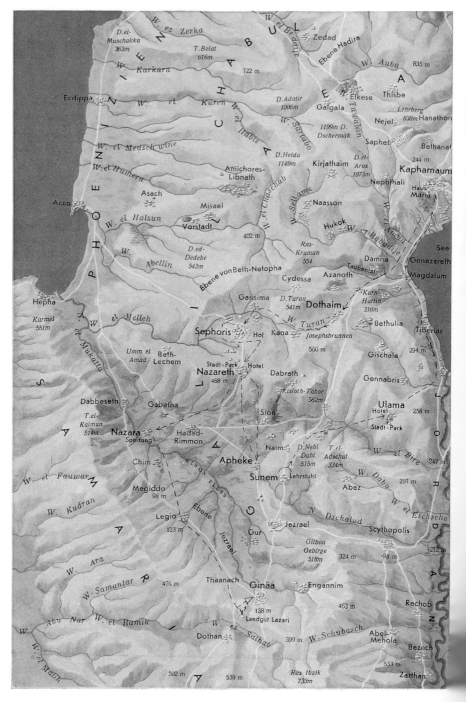

Sunem—Ulama—Capernaum—Dothaim—Sephoris—Nazareth—Apheke—Nazareth—
Nazara—Lazarus' Estate—Ginea

MAP 15: The First Passover

MARCH 16–MAY 26, A.D. 30

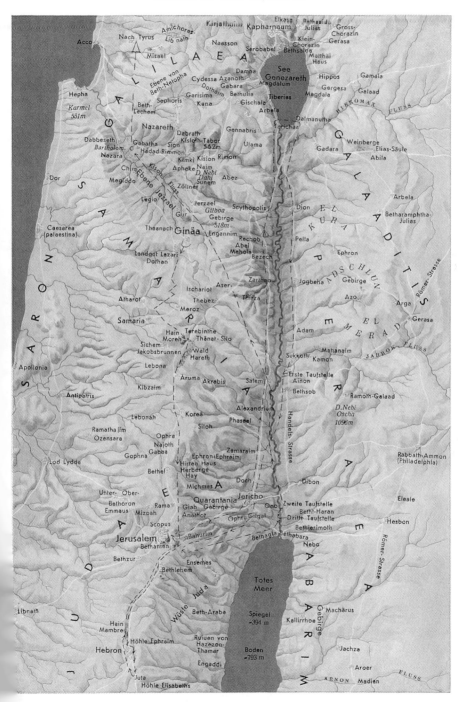

Ginea—Moreh's Grove—Bethany—Jerusalem—Juta—Hebron—Jerusalem—Bethany—
Bahurim—First Place of Baptism—Bethany—Third and Second Place of Baptism—
West Galilee

MAP 16: Travels in Northern Galilee
End of MAY–JULY 19, A.D. 30

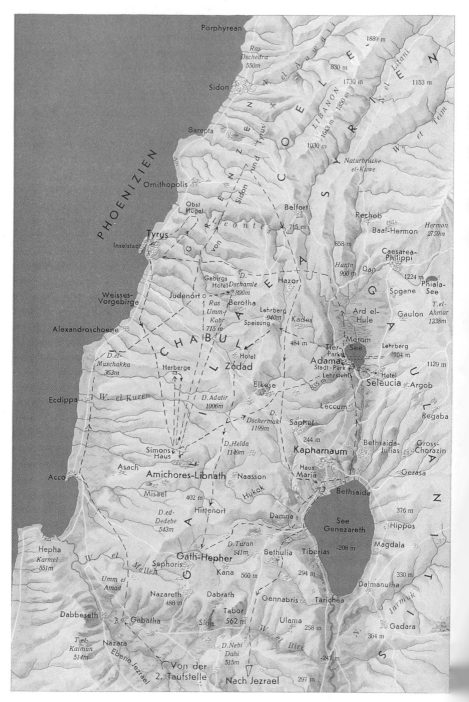

West Galilee—At the boundaries of Sidon and Tyre—Capernaum—
Adama and Seleucia—Tyre—Amichores-Libnath—Land of Chabul—Adama—Seleucia—
Adama—Mount of Instruction near Berotha—Zedad—Gath-Hepher—Capernaum

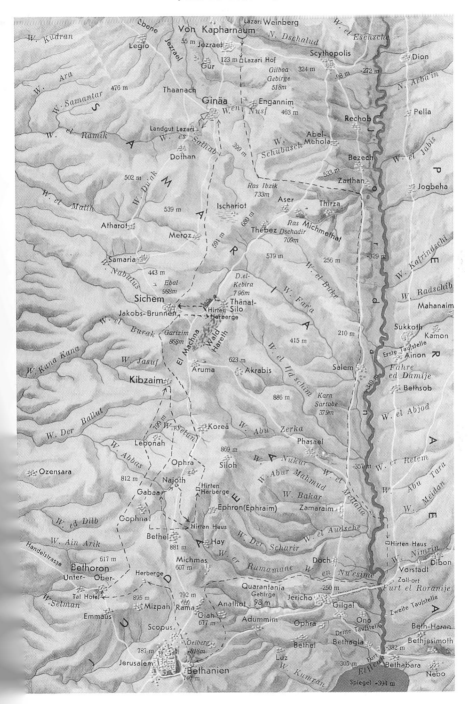

Capernaum—Lazarus' Estate near Jezrael—Bethany—Upper Bethoron—Kibzaim—
Boundary of Judea/Samaria—Jacob's Well—Sychar—Ginea

MAP 18: The Healing of the Nobleman's Son
JULY 29–AUGUST 7, A.D. 30

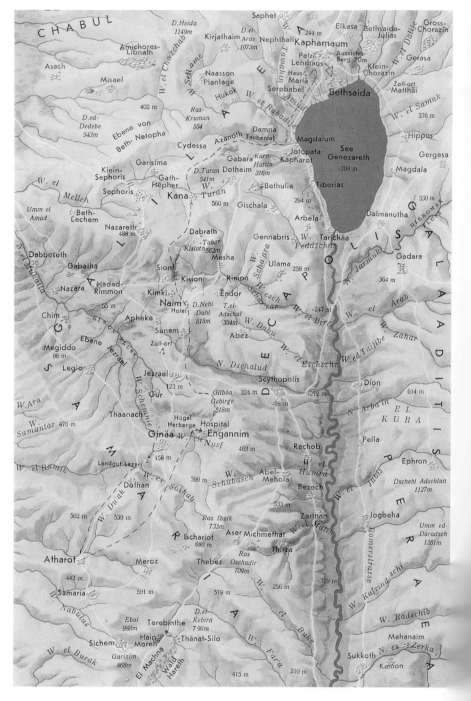

Ginea—Atharot—Engannim—Naim—Cana—Capernaum—Bethsaida

MAP 19: The Healings at Capernaum

AUGUST 8–26, A.D. 30

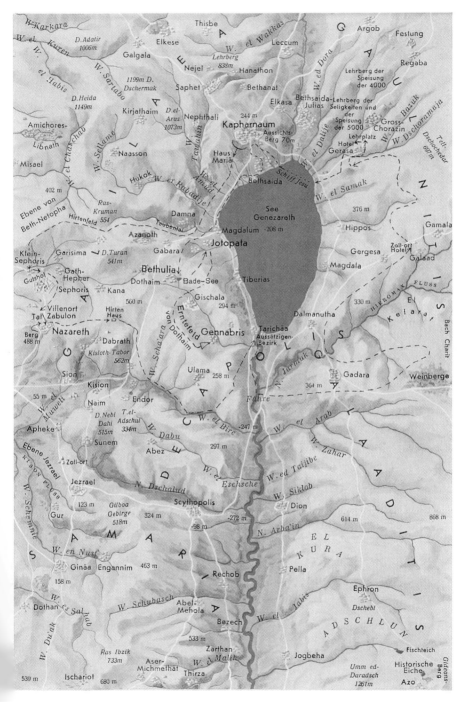

Capernaum—Little Sephoris—Zabulon Valley—Nazareth—Tarichea—
Publican's Place near Galaad—Gerasa—Bethsaida—Capernaum—Bethulia
—Jotopata—Gennabris

MAP 20: Journeys in Perea and Galaaditis
AUGUST 27–SEPTEMBER 27, A.D. 30

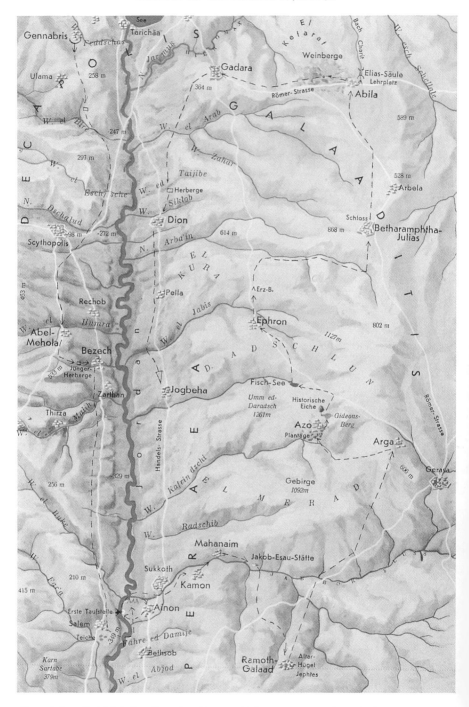

Gennabris—Abel-Mehola—Bezech—Ainon—Mahanaim—Ramoth-Galaad—Arga—Azo—
Ephron—Betharamphtha-Julias—Abila—Gadara—Dion—Jogbeha

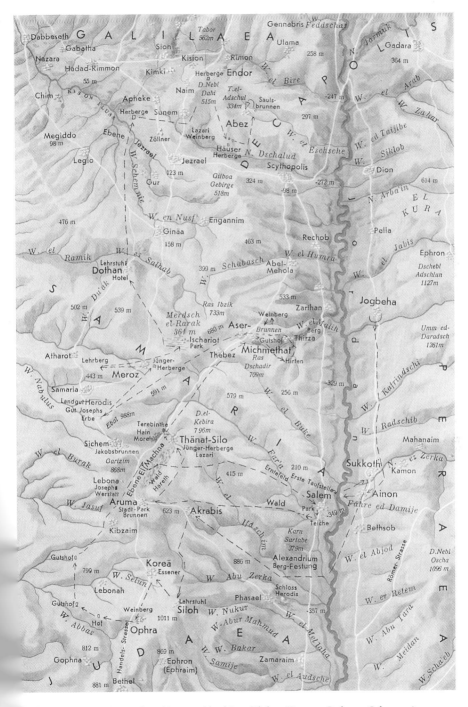

ogbeha—Ainon—Succoth—Ainon—Akrabis—Siloh—Korea—Ophra—Salem—Aruma—
Thanath-Silo—Aser-Michmethat—Meroz—Ischariot—Dothan—Abez

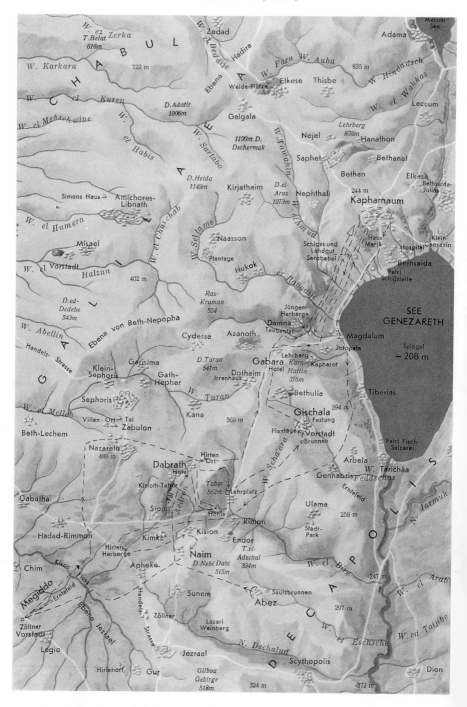

Abez—Dabrath—Malachi's Cave—Dabrath—Place of Instruction on Mount Tabor—
Gischala—Gabara —Mount of Instruction—Gabara—Zorobabel—Capernaum—Valley
of the Doves—Capernaum—Plain of Jezrael—Naim—Suburb of Megiddo—Capernaum

MAP 23: The Sermons on the Mount
NOVEMBER 19–DECEMBER 10, A.D. 30

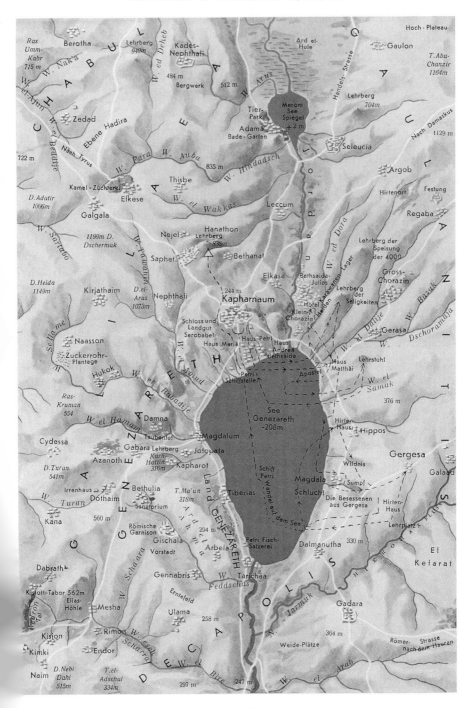

Capernaum—Matthew's House—Mount of Instruction near Gerasa—Bethsaida—
Mount of Beatitudes—Magdala—Gergesa—Capernaum—
Mount of Instruction near Hanathon

MAP 24: The Journey Through Middle Galilee

DECEMBER 10–27, A.D. 30

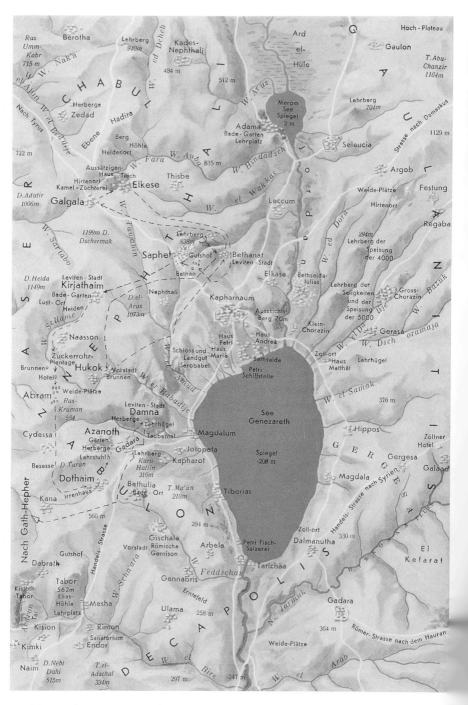

Mount of Instruction—Bethanat—Hukok—Bethanat—Galgala—Elkese—Bethan—
Saphet—Kirjathaim—Plantation near Naasson—Abram—Dothaim—Azanoth—Damna

MAP 25: The Third Journey to Hebron

DECEMBER 27, A.D. 30 – JANUARY 26, A.D. 31

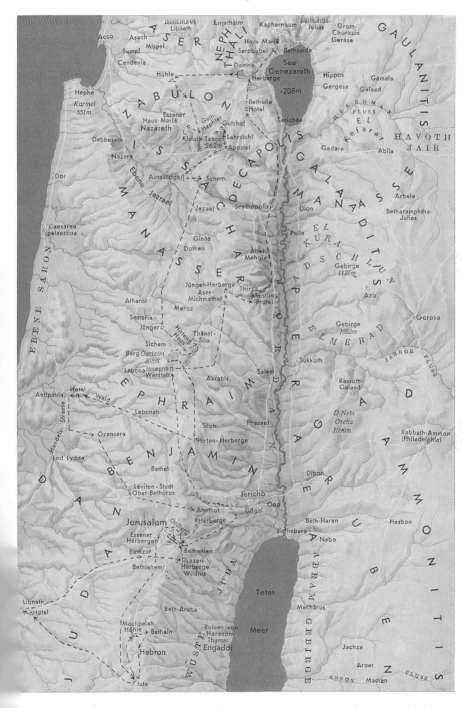

amna—Cave of John—Gath-Hepher—Kisloth-Tabor—Nazareth—Northwest Foot of Tabor—
Sunem—Thanat-Silo—Antipatris—Ozensara—Upper Bethoron—Anathot— Bethany—
Mount of Olives—Juta—Machpelah—Bethain—Hebron—Juta—Libnath— Bethzur—
Bethany—Jerusalem—Lebona—Aser-Michmethat—Thirza—Bethulia—Capernaum

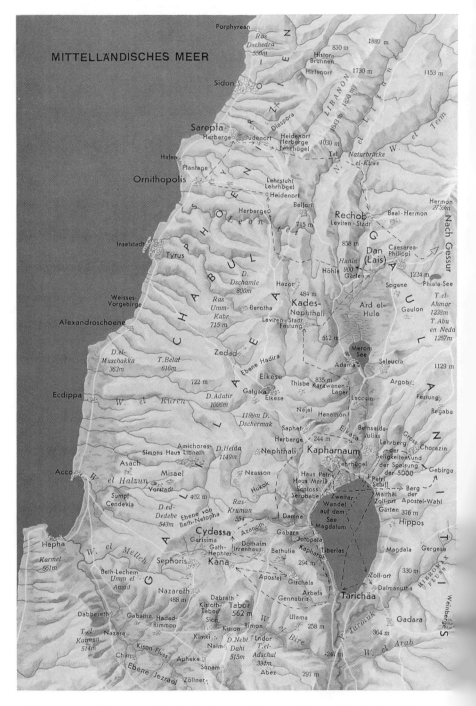

Capernaum—Mount near Matthew's Customs House—Mount of Beatitudes—Customs
Place near Dalmanutha—Tarichea—Lake Shore near Matthew's Customs House—
Capernaum—Hill of Instruction—Cana—Cydessa—Nephthali—Elkasa—
Kades-Nephthali—Dan—Hunin—Ornithopolis—Rechob

MAP 27: Journey to Gessur and Travels in Gaulanitis

FEBRUARY 19–MARCH 19, A.D. 31

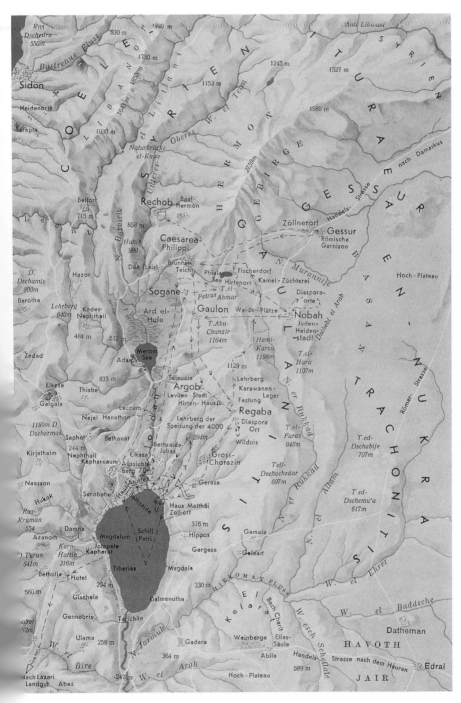

Rechob—Gessur—Phiala-See—Nobah—Gaulon—Regaba—Caesarea-Philippi —
rgob —Fortress of Regaba—Wilderness—Great Chorazin—Matthew's Customs House—
Bethsaida—Mount of the Feeding of the 4,000—Bethsaida—Bethsaida-Julias—Sogane—
Bethulia

MAP 28: Journey to the Second Passover
MARCH 20–APRIL 1, A.D. 31

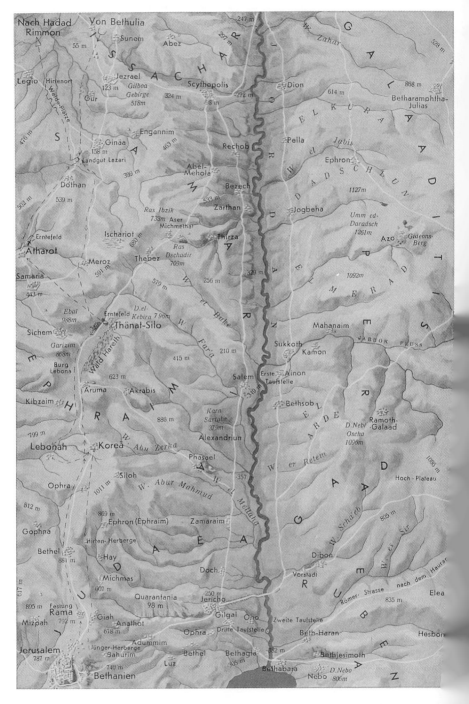

Bethulia—Lazarus' Estate near Ginea—Lebonah—Korea—Bethany—Jerusalem—Rama–
Thanat-Silo—Atharot—Lazarus' Estate near Ginea—Hadad-Rimmon

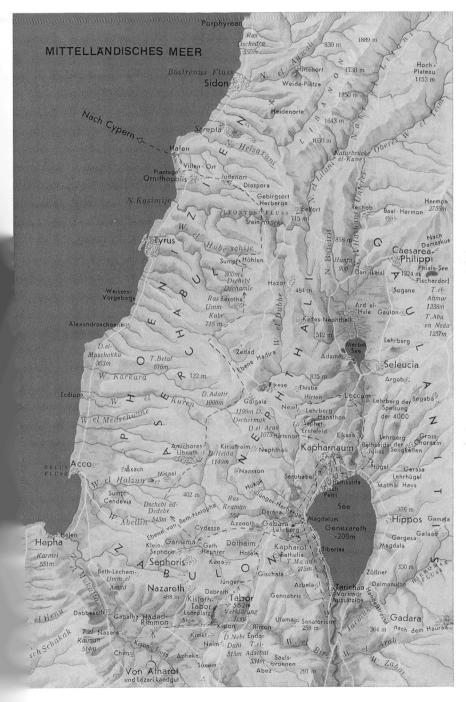

Porphyrean

MITTELLÄNDISCHES MEER

Bostrenus Fluss
Sidon

Nach Cypern

Screpta

Hafen

Villen · Ort
Plantage
Ornithopolis

N.Kasimije

Tyrus

Weisses-Vorgebirge

Alexandroschoene

D.el-Muschakka
363m

W. *Karkara*

Ecdippa

W. el Medschaume

Acco
BELUS
FLUSS

Hepha

Karmel
551m

el Henu

Dabbeseth

sch Schakak

Ras
Dschedra
350m

830 m   1889 m

el·Auuali   Hirtenort   1730 m
N.   Weide-Plätze
1850 m

Heidenorte

Heisarani
1643 m

1030 m

N. el Litani   *Oberes*
Judenort
Diaspora
Gebirgsort
Herberge
LEONTES FLUSS
Steinbrücke   715 m

Hube·schije
Sumpf·Höhlen

800m·i
Dschebl
Dschamle   Hazor

Ras Berotha
Umm-
Kabr
715 m

T.Belat
616m

122 m

Zedad
Ebene·Hadira

D.Adatir
1006m   Galgala
1199m D.
Dschermak

D.el-Arus
1073   Hirtenort

Amichores
Libnath   Kirjathaim
D.Heida   Nephthali
1149m

Asach
Misael   Naasson

W. el Halzun

Sumpf
Cendevia   402 m   Ras-
Dschebl ed-   *Beth-Nelopha*   Kruman
Dedebe   554

Abellin   543m

Ebene von   Azanoth
Cydessa   Gabara
Lehrberg

Klein   Garisima
Sephoris   Gath   Dothaim
Hephter   Hofen

Sephoris   Kana

Beth-Lechem-
Umm el   Jünger-
Amad   Nazareth   Dabrath
488 m   Kisloth-
Tabor   Tabor
562m
Lehrplatz   Verklärung
Gabatha   Hadad-   Sion   Jesu
Rimmon   Kisjon   Rimon

Tel Nazara   Kimki   D.Nebi Endor
Kaimun   Naim   Dahi   T.el-
514m   Kison Fluss   515m Adschul
China   Apheke   334m
Sünem   Abez

Von Atharot
und Lazari Landgut

1153 m

1030 m
Naturbrücke
el-Kuwe

Belfort   Rechob   Baal-Hermon   Hermon
2759m

858 m   G
N. Hasbani Unteres   Caesarea-
Hanin   Philippi
900   Dan (Lais)   1224 m   Phiala-See
Fischerdorf
484 m   Sogane   T.el-
Ahmar
Ard el-   1238m
Hule   Gaulon   T.Abu
Kades-Nephthali   en Neda
512 m   1257m

Lehrberg

Merom
See   Adama   Seleucia
835 m   Argob

Elkese   Thisbe
Hirten   Leccum   Regaba
Nejel   Lehrberg   Lehrberg der   Speisung
Sephet   Hanathon   der 4000
Erntefeld
Elkasa   Lehrberg   Gross-
Bethsaida-der   Chorazin
Julias   Seligkeiten
Hügel   Gerasa
Serobabel   Lehrhügel
Bethsaida   Matthäi Haus
Hukok   Petri
Jünger-Herberge   See   376 m
Dampa   Magdalum   Hippos   Gamala
Gabara   Genezareth   Gergesa   Galaad
Magdalum   -208m   Magdala

Kapharot   Tiberias
Bethulia
T.Ma'un   330 m
Gischala   215m   Zöllner
Arbela   Dalmanutha
Gennabris   Tarichäa   Aussätzige
Vorstadt   *nach dem Hauran*
Ulama   Sanatorium   Gadara
258 m   364 m
Souls-
brunnen   297 m

Kapharnaum

Hadir   Hukok

Naasson

Hirtenort

Kirjathaim

Dan (Lais)

W. el Arab

Bira

W. el Zahar

HIEROMAX FLUSS

Jarmuk

Hondschafele

MAP 30: The Journey to Cyprus
APRIL 26–MAY 30, A.D. 31

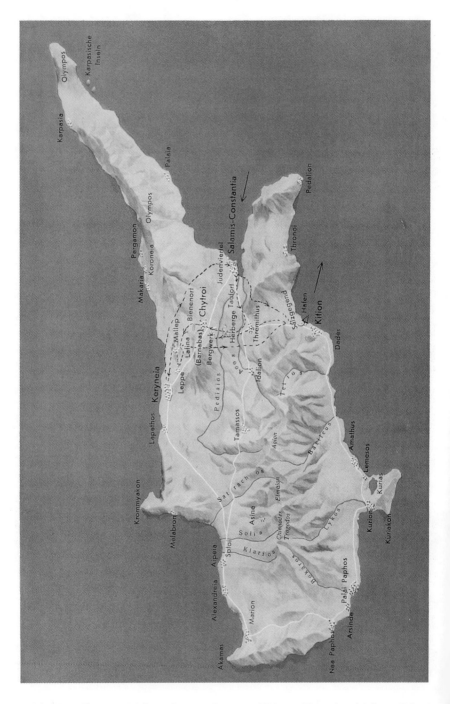

Salamis—Chytroi—Mallep—Leppe—Port near Kition—Keryneia—Mallep—Salamis—
Sea Harbor of Kition

MAP 31: Travels in Middle and Southern Galilee
MAY 31–JUNE 14, A.D. 31

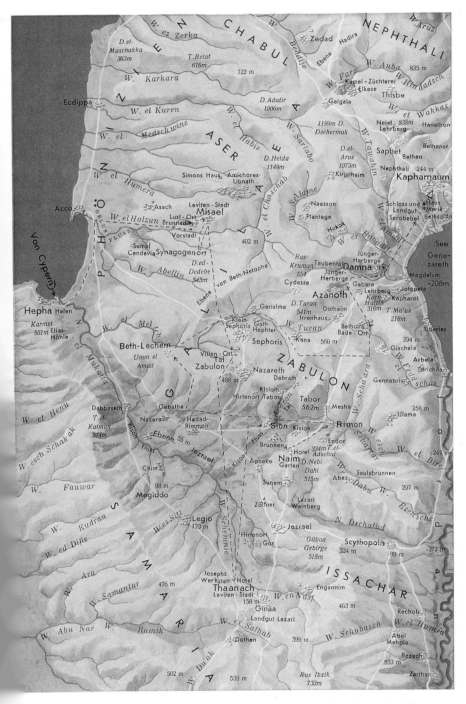

Harbor near Hepha—Misael—Place with Synagogue—Misael—Place with Villas
in Zabulon Valley—Thaanach—Sion—Naim—Rimon—Beth-Lechem—Azanoth—
Damna—Zorobabel—Capernaum

MAP 32: Travels in Galilee and Gaulanitis
JUNE 14–28, A.D. 31

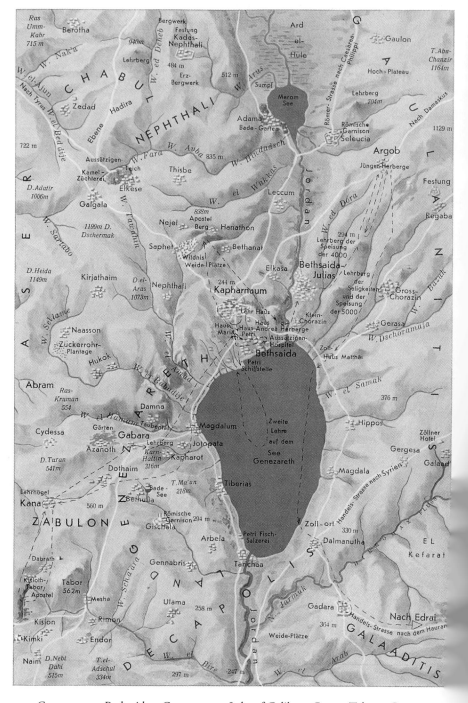

Capernaum—Bethsaida—Capernaum—Lake of Galilee—Cana—Tabor—Cana—
Mount of Instruction near Gabara—Capernaum—Bethsaida—Mount of Instruction near
Hanathon—Bethsaida-Julias—Mount of Instruction—Argob—Matthew's Customs House—
Customs Place near Dalmanutha

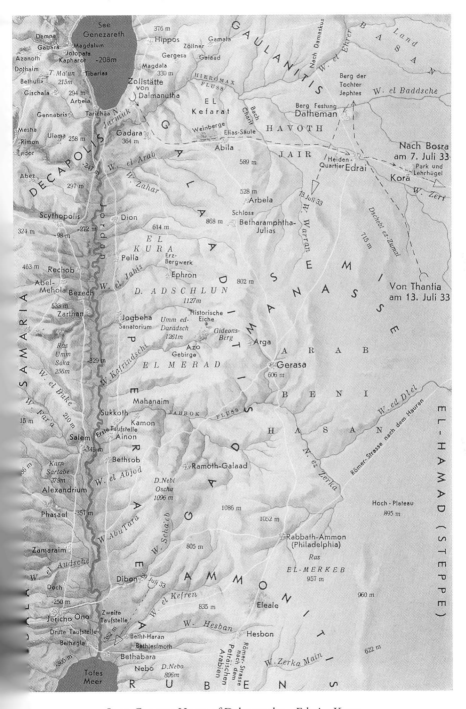

Start: Customs House of Dalmanutha—Edrai—Korea
End: Datheman—Terrain of Galaaditis—Bethabara

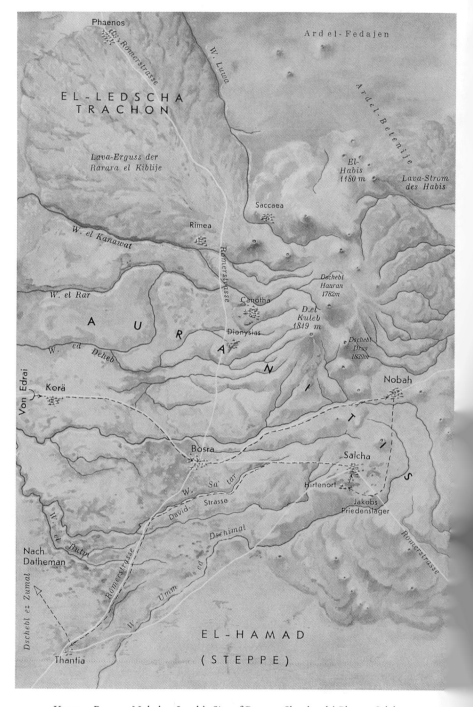

Korea—Bosra—Nobah—Jacob's Site of Peace—Shepherds' Place—Salcha—
David's Way—Thantia

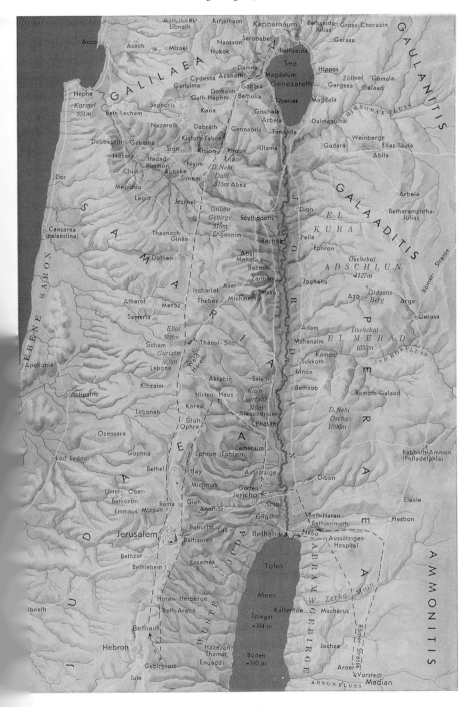

Bethabara—Hospital near Nebo—Suburb of Madian—Bethjesimoth—Jericho—
Shepherds' Fields in Southern Samaria—Shepherd's House near Hebron—
Place in the Mountains near Juta—Bethain—Capernaum

MAP 36: The Raising of Lazarus

Beginning of JULY–AUGUST 6, A.D. 32

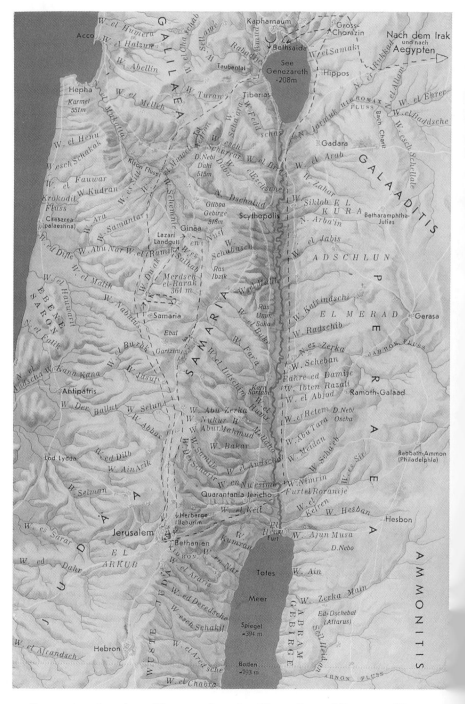

Capernaum—Jerusalem—Places near Samaria—Ginea—Lazarus' Estate near Ginea—
Ginea—Inn near Bahurim—Bethany—Jerusalem—Stretch of Land in Perea—
Great Chorazin—Bethsaida—In the Direction of Iraq

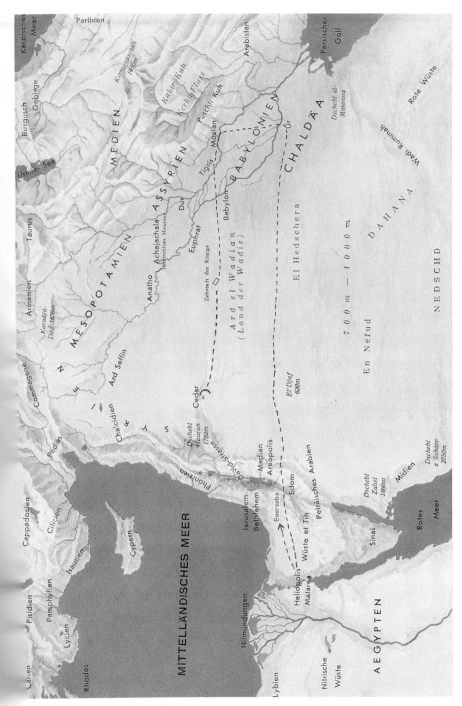

Cedar—Tent City of the Kings—Mozian—Ur—Heliopolis—Beersheba

MAP 38: The Arrival at Jacob's Well

JANUARY 8–24, A.D. 33

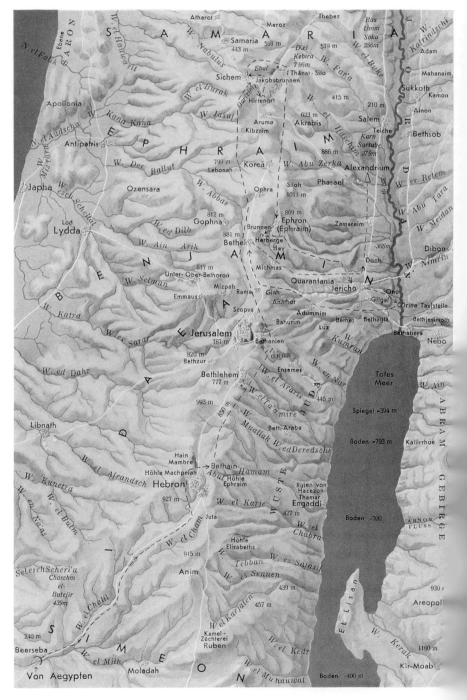

Beersheba—Bethain—Jacob's Well—Shepherds' Place in Samaria—Sychar—Ephron—
Jericho—Third Place of Baptism—Bethel—Doch—Alexandrium

MAP 39: The Last Journey to Jerusalem

JANUARY 24–FEBRUARY 19, A.D. 33

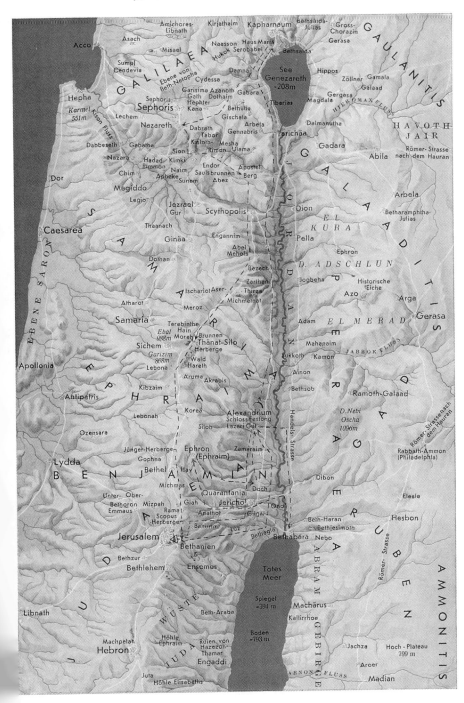

Alexandrium—Capernaum—Nazareth—Mount of the Apostles—Thanat-Silo—Bethany—
Ensemes—Bethany—Lazarus' Property near Alexandrium—Bethabara—Ephron—Doch—
Lazarus' Property near Alexandrium—Bethany—Jerusalem

Afterword

The 33 1/3-year rhythm

At the conclusion of his Gospel, Saint John wrote: "There are also many other things which Jesus did; were every one of them to be written, I suppose that the world itself could not contain the books that would be written" (John 21:25). In light of these words, any book about Christ Jesus and the mysteries surrounding him can be only a "drop in the ocean."

This book has been written with the intention of encouraging others to investigate further into the mysteries surrounding the life of Christ Jesus; it is an attempt to somewhat penetrate the circumstances surrounding his conception, birth, and death.

The prelude to this holy life was the "star of the Magi" referred to in the Gospel of Saint Matthew, and the accompanying conception and birth of the Solomon Jesus at the time of the triple conjunction of Jupiter and Saturn in 7/6 B.C. Then came the birth of Jesus of Nazareth (the Nathan Jesus) in 2 B.C., announced by the proclamation to the shepherds, as described in the Gospel of Saint Luke. The time interval between the birth of Jesus of Nazareth on the night of December 6/7, 2 B.C., and the resurrection at sunrise on Easter Sunday morning, April 5, A.D. 33, was 12,173 1/4 days. Rudolf Steiner spoke of the resurrection as the "birth" of Christ Jesus as the Risen One, and referred to the importance of the 33 1/3-year rhythm of the life of Christ Jesus leading up to this "birth." The time interval of 12,173 1/4 days is 33.329 years and is therefore almost exactly 33 1/3 years. The exact period of 33 1/3 years equals 33.333 and thus the life of Christ Jesus differed from this by only 0.004 years, which amounts to 1 1/2 days—that is, the exact length of the life of Christ Jesus from birth to the resurrection was 33 1/3 years less 1 1/2 days. Rudolf Steiner pointed out that, in addition to the various cosmic rhythms (the one-year rhythm of the Sun, the 29 1/2-year rhythm of Saturn, and so on), since the beginning of the Christian era a new rhythm—the 33-1/3 year rhythm of the life of Christ Jesus—has become one of the most important rhythms in the unfolding history of humanity and the Earth.[1] How does this rhythm manifest itself in our time?

---

1. See Ellen Schalk's article listed in the Bibliography.

Since the rhythm of 33 1/3 years occurs almost exactly three times in one hundred years, it is easy to follow it through the course of the centuries. But since the exact rhythm is 1 1/2 days less than 33 1/3 years, a slight adjustment must be made. Starting at midnight on December 6/7, 2 B.C., the first cycle was complete at the resurrection at dawn on April 5, A.D. 33. Adding 12,173 1/4 days, the second cycle—the first following the Mystery of Golgotha—lasted until mid-day on August 3, A.D. 66. Then, adding a further 12,173 1/4 days, the third cycle—the second since the Mystery of Golgotha—ended at sunset on December 1, A.D. 99.

Proceeding in this way through the centuries, the fifty-eighth cycle since the Mystery of Golgotha started on January 8, 1933 and lasted until May 9, 1966, followed by the fifty-ninth cycle—the present one—which will last until September 6, 1999.

According to Rudolf Steiner, this new rhythm, established through the life of Christ Jesus, is of the greatest possible significance for Earth evolution. One example Steiner gives is the point in time three hundred years after the Mystery of Golgotha, the year 333 (nine 33 1/3-year cycles), which he identifies as the central moment in the unfolding of the seven post-Atlantean cultural epochs, since it is the midpoint between the start of the first post-Atlantean civilization in 7227 B.C. and the end of the seventh post-Atlantean civilization in A.D. 7894 (see my book *Hermetic Astrology*, vol. I, Table 5). It was a turning point in the whole of humanity's spiritual evolution.[2] Other examples could be mentioned, such as the year A.D. 1899 referred to below.

With respect to this temporal rhythm, the reader may wonder why we take the moment of the resurrection and not the crucifixion as reference point. The whole intricate series of events we have tried to elucidate in this work led up to this moment. The resurrection, at dawn on Sunday, April 5, A.D. 33, was indeed the moment of *birth* of this being, the Risen *Christ* Jesus.

We have accounted for the rhythmic interval of 33 1/3 years, but can we understand in more detail the spiritual reality that lies behind it? In the case of a human being, the etheric body, together with the astral body and I (ego), separates from the physical body at the moment of death, leaving the physical body behind on the Earth as a corpse. The human being then lives on, not in his physical body, but in his etheric body, in which are inscribed all his life

---

2. Rudolf Steiner, *Three Streams in the Evolution of Humanity* (London: Rudolf Steiner Press, 1965), GA 184, lecture 6: Dornach, October 13, 1918.

experiences. Thus, for a short time (approximately three days) immediately following separation from the physical body, the human being beholds in a panorama the events of his life between birth and death. Rudolf Steiner describes how this panorama fades away as the etheric body gradually dissolves and is membered back into the universal ether. In the case of Christ Jesus, the etheric body did *not* dissolve but retained all his experiences, from the Mystery of Golgotha back to his birth in Bethlehem 33 1/3 years before. All these experiences were inscribed in this etheric body, which was preserved intact, and *this* is the basis of the 33 1/3-year rhythm. In fact, this etheric body was the source of the four Gospels. The evangelists Matthew, Mark, Luke, and John were four human beings able to experience the etheric body of Christ Jesus, in which the panorama of all the events of his life were inscribed. With this 33 1/3-year rhythm are connected profound mysteries. Most important for us is the mystery of the second coming, the so-called "Parousia," or return of Christ into the etheric world. We have mentioned the year 333, but we may follow the rhythm further to arrive at other significant dates. In the lectures already referred to, Rudolf Steiner mentions in particular the year 666.[3] Going further, we come to the year 966, which represents a turning point in the unfolding of the impulse of this Divine etheric organism. In 966, after twenty-eight cycles of 33 1/3 years, a "cosmic high point" was reached. Proceeding forward a further 28 cycles from the year 966, we come to the year 1899, the end of Kali Yuga. Here, from the year 1899 onwards, we find the beginning of the re-entry into the Earth organism of the etheric body of Christ Jesus.

Thus, the end of Kali Yuga, the Dark Age, was signaled by the return of Christ Jesus in the etheric, heralding the start of the New Age, the Age of Light. Underlying what is nowadays referred to as the New Age, starting in 1899, is a definite cosmic phenomenon, bound up with the 33 1/3-year rhythm of the etheric body of Christ Jesus. Let us try to attain a clearer understanding of this rhythm during the period leading up to 1899, starting A.D. 33.

Following the resurrection on April 5, A.D. 33, several appearances of the Risen One to the disciples are described in the Gospels. These appearances were not in the physical body but in the etheric body, which remained intact. With the ascension forty days later, on May 14, A.D. 33, these appearances ceased. Christ Jesus withdrew in his etheric body to cosmic spheres of existence. There then began an expansion of the etheric body outwards through

3. In the lectures referred to (see footnote 2), Rudolf Steiner indicates the year 666 in connection with the "beast" spoken of in Revelation 13:18.

the solar system. This expansion lasted until midway between A.D. 33 and 1899, i.e., 966. Then a contraction began, which continued between 966 and 1899. That is, we have twenty-eight 33 1/3-year cycles up to the year 966, to the "cosmic high point," and then a "descent" through a further twenty-eight 33 1/3-year cycles up to the year 1899.[4]

We can date this rhythm very precisely. As has been mentioned, the exact interval is not 33 1/3 years, but 1 1/2 days less, so that, making the necessary adjustment, we find that the end of Kali Yuga (denoting at the same time the start of what is called the "Satya Yuga," or Age of Light), which Rudolf Steiner dates to the year 1899, actually took place on September 10, 1899. Following this 33 1/3-year rhythm further, we find that the "integration" (incarnation) of this etheric organism into the Earth's aura was accomplished on January 8, 1933. One could say that the Age of the Second Coming began in an *earthly* sense on January 8, 1933, the New Age having begun in a *cosmic* sense on September 10, 1899. In fact, the whole of Rudolf Steiner's work itself may be seen in the light of the return of this etheric organism. We could say that anthroposophy was born out of the return of this etheric organism into the Earth's etheric aura. This is indeed a *raison d'être* of the impulse of anthroposophy. "In our age it is essential that Christ shall be proclaimed in his etheric form, and this is the task of anthroposophy."[5]

If we now examine the matter more closely, it becomes obvious that the most important time in the original "prototype" of the 33 1/3-year rhythm is the period from the baptism in the Jordan to the Mystery of Golgotha, its "crowning" so to say. It is interesting to note in this connection that Rudolf Steiner suggested that Christmas trees be decorated with thirty red roses, representing the thirty years of *Jesus'* life up to the baptism, and then three white roses crowning the tree, for the three years of the ministry of *Christ* from the baptism to the Mystery of Golgotha. The reliving of the time of this ministry is the most intense period in each repetition of the 33 1/3-year period—a time when an inner intensification or reawakening of the Christ impulse may take place.

In our own century we have—33 1/3 years after the end of the Kali Yuga on September 10, 1899—the start on the earthly plane of the Age of the

---

4. See my forthcoming book *The Sophia Mystery and the Christ Mystery* for a more detailed account. Briefly, the expansion of Christ's etheric body continued up to the outermost limit of the etheric cosmos. This was in 966. Then began the contraction from the outermost boundary, returning toward the earthly plane of existence.

5. Rudolf Steiner, *Esoteric Christianity and the Mission of Christian Rosenkreutz*, p. 112.

Second Coming on January 8, 1933, three days before the day of the Full
Moon. According to the research presented earlier in this book, the birth of
the Solomon Jesus took place on the night of a Full Moon. At his birth there
were no planets visible in the heavens other than the Full Moon, but the
Moon was in conjunction with the planet Pluto, with the Moon and Pluto
in opposition to the Sun. At the Full Moon on January 11, 1933, the Moon
was again in conjunction with Pluto, with both in opposition to the Sun,
"echoing," as it were, the night of the birth of the Solomon Jesus child. And,
just as at that earlier time the birth of the Solomon Jesus child was followed
by the evil king Herod the Great's Massacre of the Innocents, so in 1933
the inception of the Age of the Second Coming was followed by another
"massacre of the innocents"—the Holocaust. This was the background for
the onset of the second coming of Christ in this century. So the 33-1/3 year
rhythm in the life of Christ lies "behind the veil" of the events taking place
in our time, and it can help us find the inner spiritual heartbeat pulsing
behind these times, if we but know how to look.

The most important time during the 33 1/3-year cycle is, of course, the
last three and one-half year period, corresponding to the ministry of Christ
from the baptism in the Jordan to the Mystery of Golgotha. During this
three and one-half-year period, the Christ impulse is most active. On the
basis of what has been presented in this book, it is now possible to date this
three and one-half year period of the "Second Coming" exactly. Thus, June
29, 1929, signified the beginning and January 8, 1933, the end of the first
three and one-half year period of the working-in of the Etheric Christ—June
29, 1929, being the approximate date of the "etheric remembrance" of the
baptism and January 8, 1933, that of the resurrection. This was the first crucial three and one-half year period of the Etheric Christ in the twentieth century, that is, since the end of the Kali Yuga. It was a time when fierce
opposition to the Christ impulse began to emerge in the shape of National
Socialism (see below).

Moving forward from the unfolding of this etheric organism, the Parousia, the presence of Christ, on January 8, 1933, we come, 33 1/3 years later,
to May 9, 1966. The particularly significant three and one-half years of the
ministry therefore belong to the period going back three and one-half years
from this date. Looking at the world situation at that time, we see that this
was the time of the birth of a worldwide consciousness of peace and love.
Unfortunately, there also arose a "drug culture" which disturbed and
destroyed this new Christian impulse of love and peace, as will be discussed

in more detail below. And what about the end of the century, when the next cycle of 33 1/3 years will have been completed? This will occur on September 6, 1999; and so the three and one-half years prior to that, from 1996 through 1999, should be a period of tremendous significance for a new unfolding of the Christ impulse. This time is nearly upon us, and it is imperative that we use all the means at our disposal to prepare ourselves for it. This book, indeed, is a modest offering to this end—not to let the opportunity slip by unheeded.

How can we find a real connection with the new impulse of Christ in his etheric body (Etheric Christ) at this time? The chronicle of the life of Christ given in Part II offers a key, if it is transposed to the present time. Using the transposed chronicle, the possibility is opened up of entering into a relationship with the Etheric Christ, meditatively reliving the three and one-half years of Christ's ministry imprinted in his etheric body. Historically the three and one-half year period began with the baptism in the Jordan on Friday, September 23, A.D. 33. In terms of the rhythmically recurring 33 1/3-year rhythm of the etheric body of Christ Jesus, transposing to the present 33 1/3-year cycle, the following correspondences are found:

Baptism in the Jordan: Saturday, February 24, 1996
Resurrection: Monday, September 6, 1999

Since the chronicle given in Part II, based on the visions of Anne Catherine Emmerich, begins four months prior to the baptism, the first date in the chronicle corresponds to a 1995 date in the present cycle: Sunday, May 29, A.D. 29 = Monday, October 30, 1995. Taking this as the starting point, dates for the entire period covered by the chronicle can be transposed to modern dates (see tabulation in Appendix VI at the end of this book).

Making use of the Table in Appendix VI, an approximate guideline to the reliving of Christ's ministry in the present as an "etheric remembrance" of the historical Christ events is made available. The guideline is approximate since the actual etheric remembrance may vary slightly from the tabulated dates. Bearing this in mind, working with this tabulation in a sensitive way can help to enable an attunement to the Etheric Christ to become possible.

As the tabulation starts four months prior to the baptism in the Jordan, this allows for a period of preparation preceding the renewed activity of the Etheric Christ, beginning with the etheric remembrance of the baptism in the Jordan on February 26, 1996.[6] Transposing to modern dates, the tabulation starts on Monday, October 30, 1995, corresponding historically to Sunday, May 29, A.D. 29, on which day Jesus set off from Capernaum on a journey to the region of Hebron in Judea, where John the Baptist had grown up. Starting on Monday, October 30, 1995, the chronicle can be meditatively relived day by day, following the travels of Jesus leading up to the baptism by John, denoting the historical event of the union of Christ with Jesus. The etheric remembrance of the baptism in the Jordan, signifying the onset of a new three and one-half-year period of intensified activity by the Etheric Christ, occurs on or around Saturday, February 24, 1996.

The principle underlying the reliving in the present of events from the life of Christ is the "etheric return," or rather, the return of Christ in his etheric body. As stated above, this began in a cosmic sense in 1899, ushering in the New Age, and became more a reality within the earthly sphere from 1933 onwards. With the return of Christ in his etheric body, the 33 1/3-year rhythm has become the most important rhythm for the New Age, the Age of the Etheric Christ. And the last three and one-half years of each 33 1/3-year period represent the culmination, when the Etheric Christ works particularly intensively, bringing a new revelation. The question naturally arises: What is the nature of the new revelation of the Etheric Christ at the end of the twentieth century? And what kind of counter impulse can be expected to oppose the new Christ revelation?

Here it is possible to give only a brief indication in response to these questions. Looking at the three and one-half-year culminating periods within each 33 1/3-year cycle since the start of the New Age in 1899, the following dates emerge:

Period 1 : June 29, 1929 – January 8, 1933
Period 2 : October 27, 1962 – May 9, 1966
Period 3 : February 24, 1996 – September 6, 1999

In each case it is a matter of renewed activity of the Etheric Christ, at the same time countered by forces of opposition. (The background underlying

---

6. This does not mean that attunement to the Etheric Christ is restricted to the three and one-half year period under consideration, as it is possible—through grace—to have an experience of the Etheric Christ at any time. It is simply that the *intensity* of activity of Christ in his etheric body is greatly enhanced during the three and one-half year culminating period at the end of each 33 1/3-year cycle.

the oppositional forces is depicted later.) In Period 1 (1929–1933), Christ was working to inspire an awakening to the Divine Presence within each human being and to usher in a new era based on this awakening. Instead of awakening to the Divine Presence *within*, a temptation came from *without*, in the form of the *Führer* (leader), who promised the German people everything, "If you will fall down and worship me" (Matthew 4:9). This was the temptation of the "will to power." When this temptation was presented to Christ Jesus in the wilderness two thousand years ago, he replied: "You shall worship the Lord your God and him only shall you serve" (Matthew 4:10). These words could perhaps be expressed in modern terms as: "You shall seek the Divine Presence within and act only out of (its) moral intuitions to serve the good of the whole."

In Period 2 (1962–1966), the Etheric Christ was active in awakening love and community between people. This was the time in the 1960s when "flower power" was born. At the same time a new and powerful temptation arose in the shape of the drug culture. This temptation can be characterized as that of "casting oneself down from the pinnacle of the temple" (Matthew 4:5). It is the temptation of a hedonistic self-surrender to instinctual urges, often with the help and powerful inducement of intoxicating substances, to obliterate the clear light of conscience and reason ("pinnacle of the temple") and to cast oneself down by abandoning ego consciousness in favor of subconscious drives and impulses.

From this brief outline of the first and second periods—about which much more could be said—is it possible to anticipate something of the nature of the third period? In the sequence of three temptations, the archetype of which is to be found during the forty days of temptation in the wilderness, it is the temptation "to turn stones into bread" (Matthew 4:3) that is the keynote of the counter impulse during Period 3, extending from February, 1996, to September, 1999. This is the temptation to substitute lifeless matter, or *stones,* in the place of living substance, or *bread*; this applies not just on the physical level but also on other levels. The whole phenomenon of virtual reality, for instance, is a clear example of this: lifeless, computer-generated images are substituted for living reality. All in all, at the close of the twentieth century an exceedingly powerful temptation is being presented to humanity by the powerful means of technological science. In part, this temptation opposes—directly and also indirectly—the central thrust of the new Christ revelation, which is concerned with unveiling the living being of Nature, referred to in various traditions as the Divine Mother. Taking place worldwide is a growing awareness of the plight of Mother Nature, as well as a widespread awakening to the Divine Feminine in general. Underlying this is the renewed activity of the Etheric Christ, the culmination of which will be the new Christ revelation during the last three and one-half years of this century. It will be especially the unveiling of the Eternal Feminine in her various aspects— Mother Nature and Sophia, Divine Wisdom—which will be the central impulse of the Etheric Christ during Period 3.[7]

Of course, the 33 1/3-year rhythm will continue on into the future, and there will be a new impulse of the Etheric Christ in the next period (Period 4), signifying the etheric remembrance of the three and one-half-year period of the ministry at the culmination of the next 33 1/3-year period. Periods 4, 5, and 6 below indicate the times of major activity of the Etheric Christ in the course of the twenty-first century:

> Period 4 : June 23, 2029 – January 3, 2033
> Period 5 : October 22, 2062–May 4, 2066
> Period 6 : February 19, 2096 –September 1, 2099

The 33 1/3-year rhythm of the Etheric Christ is one of the most important rhythms for the future. As the primary rhythm of the New Age, the Age of the Etheric Christ, it will be of major significance until the year 4399, which is 2,500 years after the start of the New Age in 1899. The date 4399 falls close to the end of the Age of Aquarius—the next age, the Age of Capricorn, starts shortly after, in 4535, exactly 2,160 years after the start of the Age of Aquarius in 2375. Note that the length of the New Age, 2,500 years, is half that of the former Dark Age of Kali Yuga, which was 5,000 years long, from 3102 B.C. to A.D. 1899. In Hindu chronology, each successive Age is progressively shorter, indicating a qualitative speeding up in an evolutionary sense. The duration of the New Age (2,500 years) amounts to 75 cycles of the 33 1/3-year rhythm. At the end of these 75 cycles Christ will begin to work from a still higher plane of existence than the etheric, and a new impulse will enter around the time of transition from the Age of Aquarius to the Age of Capricorn.[8]

---

7. See Robert Powell, *The Most Holy Trinosophia*; also *Divine Sophia, Holy Wisdom*.
8. Robert Powell, *Hermetic Astrology, vol. I*, appendix II.

The 29 1/2-year rhythm

There is still another perspective concerning the present epoch of time, the end of the twentieth century/start of a new millennium, with its various temptations. This perspective entails looking at rhythms of the Cosmic Christ other than the 33 1/3-year rhythm of the Etheric Christ. How can we learn to live more consciously with the other cosmic rhythms relevant to the life of Christ?

As mentioned earlier, Rudolf Steiner often described that the Being of Christ was incarnated into the vehicle of the Nathan Jesus at the moment of the baptism in the Jordan. He likens this moment to that of conception, just as he likens the moment of resurrection to birth. The period from the baptism to the resurrection may therefore be considered the "embryonic period" of the Risen Christ Jesus.[9]

In the course of this work we frequently invoke the principle that the period between conception and birth is a time when a human being's destiny is woven into the etheric organism. This destiny then unfolds during the course of life in seven-year periods. This is the deeper background of the new science of astrological biography described in my book *Hermetic Astrology, vol. II,* and is applied in this book to the lives of Jesus, Mary, and John the Baptist.[10] In the case of Christ Jesus' "embryonic period," the period between the baptism and the resurrection amounts to exactly 1,290 days. Interestingly, this is also the number of days mentioned in the Book of Daniel (12:11). It is a period of three and one-half years. This period is also mentioned in the Apocalypse. In fact, three and one-half years is mentioned *four times* in The Revelation of Saint John and there are also other references to a period of three and one-half years (see Luke 4:25). This period of the ministry—three and one-half years, or 1,290 days—is indeed of the greatest significance. Rudolf Steiner describes how, during this period of the ministry, every action—literally, *each step*— of Christ Jesus was in perfect harmony with the whole cosmos: the perfect realization of the ancient hermetic saying, "as above, so below." This arche-typal "embryonic period" led to the birth of the God-Man; and just as the human being's destiny is prepared between conception and birth and then unfolds from the moment of birth in seven-year periods, so the destiny of the Being of Christianity, after its "embryonic period" between the baptism and

9. Rudolf Steiner, *The Spiritual Guidance of the Individual and Humanity*.
10. See Appendix V for the application of astrological biography to John the Baptist.

the resurrection, began to unfold according to its own specific cosmic rhythm (29 1/2 years, not seven, in this case—see below). If we can establish an exact chronology of this "embryonic period," if we know *what* took place *when* during these 1,290 days, we can then determine the cosmic correlates to the historical "biography" of the Being, Christianity, and understand the whole further course of Earth evolution as well as our own tasks within it! In the final analysis *this* is why it is relevant to work out the exact chronology of the life of Christ, as this book has tried to do.

The correlation between the movement of the heavenly bodies and the events occurring during the ministry of Christ is of great significance. Consider one example. As we have mentioned above, the rhythm of the unfolding of the Christ impulse in history is not the usual seven-year period applicable to human biography, but rather is connected with the planet Saturn, whose orbit through the zodiac takes approximately 29 1/2 years. Each day in Christ's ministry—that is, each day of the 1,290 days of this "embryonic period"—unfolds historically as one Saturn orbit of the zodiac. Measuring from the Mystery of Golgotha, one day of the ministry corresponds to 29 1/2 years historically.

The importance of the "Saturn period" has to do with Saturn's role as "guardian of cosmic memory." According to Rudolf Steiner, Saturn remembers everything, recording all that takes place. Therefore each day in Christ's life is inscribed in cosmic memory, the outer expression of which is the zodiacal realm of the fixed stars (the sidereal zodiac). We can conceive of this if we recall that, in the course of one day, as the Earth rotates upon its axis, any particular geographic location, e.g., Israel, is exposed to the rising of each of the twelve zodiacal signs in turn. However, since Christ is the "light of the world" (John 8:12), a day in the life of Christ is not like any other day in the life of the universe. From the Earth, the radiation of Christ's light shone out into the cosmos through Saturn—the guardian of cosmic memory—to be inscribed in the circle of the signs of the sidereal zodiac. Thus, Day 1, the 24-hour period following the baptism in the Jordan, was imprinted in the starry heavens; and then this cosmic memory was subsequently activated by Saturn's slow orbit through the zodiacal signs during the 29 1/2-year period following the Mystery of Golgotha. The content of Day 1 hence unfolded in accordance with the "time equation" of Saturn.[11] Then the content of Day 2 (the next

11. Bear in mind here the Greek name for Saturn, Chronos, meaning the ruler of the mystery of time.

24-hour period following the baptism) unfolded—activated during Saturn's second post-Golgotha orbit around the sidereal zodiac, the process continuing through history according to the following equation:

> one Earth day of 24 hours = one Saturn day of 29 1/2 years
> in Christ's ministry   starting from the Mystery of Golgotha

Note that the exact period of Saturn's orbit around the sidereal zodiac is 29.4578 years, that is, about 29 1/2 years. Whereas the 33 1/3-year rhythm relates to Jesus Christ's *etheric body*, i.e., to the biographical memories imprinted into this etheric body, the 29 1/2-year rhythm (as will emerge more clearly in the following) relates to Christ's *astral body* and what is imprinted in the astral (or "starry") world.

To readers unfamiliar with the hermetic mode of thought—thinking in terms of correspondences between the macrocosm and the microcosm—such "time equations" as the one above may seem arbitrary. To help clarify this, let us look at another example of a "time equation," namely, the correspondence between the cycle of the day and the cycle of the year: one day = one year.

Both the cycle of the day and the cycle of the year may be divided into four quarters. By this—in terms of hermetic correspondences—morning corresponds to spring, afternoon to summer, evening to autumn, and night to winter. This is one way of viewing this correspondence, one based on focusing our attention on the *quality* associated with a particular season of the year and the corresponding part of the day. In this case, it may be seen that sunrise, as the start of the morning period, corresponds to the spring equinox as the start of spring. (This applies to the northern hemisphere.) Similarly, the summer solstice, the beginning of summer, when the Sun is at its highest (maximum northerly declination in the northern hemisphere), corresponds qualitatively to the time of midday when the Sun is at its highest in the daily cycle. In the last analysis, however, such correspondences cannot be proven scientifically. Nevertheless, they can be inwardly tested by contemplating them over and over again—as "working hypotheses"—to see if they do not truly help to deepen an understanding of certain phenomena. In this spirit, the time equation relating to the 29 1/2-year Saturn period can also be tested.

As an example, let us take the beginning of the forty days in the wilderness, during which the three temptations took place. Using the methods previously employed we see from the Chronicle in Part II that the forty days began on the evening of the Sabbath, October 21, in the year 29 A.D.; that is, 28 1/3 days after the baptism. Applying the time equation, that is, taking each of these 28 1/3 days historically as 29 1/2 years (28 1/3 times 29 1/2) we arrive at 836 years. Adding this to A.D. 33 as the date of the Mystery of Golgotha we arrive at the date 869 as the start in humankind's historical "temptation in the wilderness."

Some readers will recognize 869 as a key date often referred to by Rudolf Steiner in connection with the Eighth Ecumenical Council (the fourth Council of Constantinople), which condemned Photius, who was thus made responsible for the schism between the Eastern and the Western Churches.[12] It was at this point in history that humanity began to lose sight of a truly spiritual conception of the human being. Seen in the light of the time equation that relates 869 to the start of the forty days in the wilderness, 869 was the point in time in the history of Christianity when the "temptation of humanity" began. In this sense, the year 2047 (see below) denotes the end of humanity's temptation. And, just as at the end of Jesus' forty days in the wilderness "angels came and ministered unto him" (Matthew 4:11), so, by the middle of the next century, there will be ministering angels to humanity in response to the overcoming of temptation. This accords with Rudolf Steiner's indication—in which he also draws attention to the need to overcome three temptations—of a new relationship between humankind and the angelic kingdom after the year 2000.[13]

Now, if the time equation relating to the 29 1/2-year Saturn period is true, the question arises as to precisely what it is. The 33 1/3-year period is the length of the life of Christ Jesus from the birth in Bethlehem to the Mystery of Golgotha—including the crucifixion and resurrection. Therefore, it can be readily understood as the rhythm of his etheric body, which contains all the memories of his entire biography. But what is the deeper significance of the time equation of 29 1/2 years?

Readers who have followed the argument so far will realize that there is an element relating to the future connected with the Saturn rhythm that we are considering. To express it succinctly: the 1,290-day period of the ministry contains in seed-form the future evolution of the Christ impulse as it will unfold through historical evolution. In other words, Christ lived out in advance, during the 1,290 days of the ministry, the entire future course of

---

12. See Robert Powell, "The Second Coming and the Approaching Trial of Humanity," *Shoreline*, vol. 5 (1992) pp. 27–34.
13. See Rudolf Steiner, *The Work of the Angels in Man's Astral Body*.

the world in archetypal form. This means that the "end of the world" will be the Mystery of Golgotha—death and resurrection—for the whole of humanity. It is even possible to date this event by projecting 1,290 days into the future in terms of the time equation of the Saturn rhythm of 29 1/2 years. Since 1,290 times 29 1/2 (or, more exactly, 29.4578) = 38,000, this locates the "end of the world" in the year A.D. 38,033 (taking, as our starting point, the Mystery of Golgotha in A.D. 33).

Such computation may seem unrealistic, but it is corroborated in an extraordinary way by Rudolf Steiner. In his lectures on *The Apocalypse of Saint John*, Steiner refers to the unfolding of the future in terms of 2,160-year periods ("cultural epochs") in relation to the seven letters, seven seals, and seven trumpets referred to in The Book of Revelation.[14] Each such period comprises 2,160 years, the seven letters representing the present cycle of seven cultural epochs in which humanity, at its present stage of evolution, is just over one-quarter of the way through the fifth cultural epoch, which is related to the zodiacal sign of Pisces. As I have indicated in *Hermetic Astrology*, vol. I (table 5), the fifth cultural epoch began in A.D. 1414. Taken together, the fifth, sixth, and seventh cultural epochs will last 3 times 2,160 = 6,480 years. Adding this to A.D. 1414, we arrive at A.D. 7894 (= 1,414 + 6,480), which date denotes the end of the seven letters and the start of the seven seals. The seven seals then unfold through 7 times 2,160 years = 15,120 years, terminating in A.D. 23014 (= 7,894 + 15,120). Then follow the seven trumpeters, again lasting 7 times 2,160 years = 15,120 years, i.e. until A.D. 38134 (= 23,014 + 15,120)—a date agreeing, to within one hundred years, with the date of A.D. 38033, determined by using the Saturn time equation.

At this point in evolution, after humanity's Mystery of Golgotha, which is the "end of the world," there will be a period of transition. This is indicated in the Book of Revelation by the seven "vials of wrath" that will lead over from the present Earth evolution to the future cosmic stage of evolution. It is referred to by the Book of Revelation as the "Heavenly Jerusalem" and in Rudolf Steiner's *Occult Science* as "future Jupiter."

We are now in a position to reflect further on the question of the significance of the Saturn time equation in relation to the future. Once again, thanks to Rudolf Steiner, it is possible to grasp something of what this means:

---

14. Rudolf Steiner, *The Apocalypse of Saint John*. The 2,160-year period also corresponds to one "Platonic month" of the Platonic year of 25,920 years.

for, on numerous occasions, Steiner spoke about *two streams* of time. Every human being stands in a flow of time extending from the past into the future. This has to do with the etheric body, which is the bearer of memory and biography. The second stream flows from the future into the past and has to do with the astral body, which is not only the bearer of passions and instincts, but also prophetically guides a person to the fulfillment of his or her destiny.[15] Against this background of the two streams of time, it is evident that, whereas the 33 1/3-year rhythm is that of Christ Jesus' etheric body, the 29 1/2-year Saturn time equation has to do with Christ's astral body.

After looking into the unfolding of this Saturn time equation into the distant future, let us now return to consider the present period of time.

Historically—that is, "biographically" with respect to the Being of Christianity—we are still today living in the period that correlates to the forty days in the wilderness and are, in fact, even now moving towards its climax. Christ Jesus spent the forty days in the wilderness on a mountain east of the Dead Sea—a lonely, deserted, and barren place. Here he fasted and was tempted three times. Indeed, the entire forty days was a period of trial leading up to the "three temptations"—culminating in the third temptation, representing Satan's final, concentrated onslaught.

Now, the forty "embryonic days" signify, historically, forty revolutions of the planet Saturn, or 1,180 years (40 times 29 1/2). Adding this to 869, we see that the end of the forty days, projected historically, will occur in the year 2049 (more precisely 2047, since Saturn's exact orbital period is slightly less than 29 1/2 years). Clearly, then, we are now living near the close of the historical correlate to the forty days in the wilderness; in fact, we are in the last two "days" of the temptation! Two "days" only—two Saturn cycles—remain.[16]

What are the three temptations? Firstly, the temptation of the *will to power*, something our century has witnessed to an unprecedented extent, especially in the thirties. Then the temptation of *plunging from the pinnacle of the temple*. Esoterically this means that clear ego-consciousness is tempted

---

15. During sleep, for example, the human being dwells in the astral body and is outside the physical and etheric bodies. It is then that dreaming takes place and, as is well known, dreams can sometimes be of a prophetic or future-oriented nature. This is not necessarily to recommend dream interpretation, for, if incorrectly interpreted, dreams can be highly misleading.

16. The significance of the fact that humanity is approaching the climax of the historically projected forty days of temptation is discussed in detail in *The Sophia Mystery and the Christ Mystery* (forthcoming).

to plunge down out of the realm of conscience and reason into that of the forces of instinct. And what clearer expression of this can there be than the "drug culture" of the sixties, with its unbridled sexuality and its "humanistic" and relativistic abrogations of humanity's very real "supraconscious" (not subconscious) responsibilities? Clearly this second temptation is still at work, and with incredible power; but now it is the third temptation that is coming more and more strongly to the fore, that of *turning stones into bread*. It is now feasible technologically to give to the non-living the appearance of life. Through technology the possibility is provided to change the dead and immaterial into the illusion of something living. There are countless examples of the working of this temptation through technology—presenting something that is actually completely mechanical, dead, and lifeless but imbuing it with the illusion that it is living. The "systematic" manifestation of this temptation is reductionism in all its forms. We can see how this third temptation is becoming more and more powerful. Just consider *virtual reality*, the latest "advance" in computer technology! Perceptive readers will certainly recognize that we are now approaching a time of intensification of the temptation to turn stones into bread.

Going back now to the original temptation in the wilderness, which started on the evening of Friday, October 21, A.D. 29, and extended forty days to sunset on Wednesday, November 30, A.D. 29, let us look at the cosmic circumstances during these forty days in order to establish some correspondences. The final temptation was overcome on the last day, Wednesday, November 30, A.D. 29, when it is reported that "angels came and ministered unto him" (Matthew 4:11). We should look at this more closely. On the preceding day, Tuesday, November 29, A.D. 29, there had been a conjunction between the Sun and Pluto at 9° sidereal Sagittarius. This conjunction between the Sun and Pluto formed, then, the cosmic culmination of the forty days in the wilderness.

Before proceeding further, it will be well to recall that the outer planets, Uranus, Neptune, and Pluto (as also indicated by Rudolf Steiner in the case of Uranus and Neptune), do not belong to our solar system in a full and proper sense, but are bearers of "extraneous" evil impulses. Consider the fact that the discovery of Uranus in 1781 was followed by the French Revolution, a period of untold suffering, and that the discovery of the planet Neptune in 1846 was shortly followed (in London in 1848) by the publication of the *Communist Manifesto* by Marx and Engels. At the same time, in many major cities throughout Europe, socialist revolutionary impulses emerged, culminating in the Russian Revolution in 1917, bringing with it misery and/or death to millions of human beings and leaving them with the most anti-human and atheistic "world-view" yet devised by those powers intending to subvert the true mission of humanity. With the discovery of Pluto there came an even more vicious mass movement—Pluto was discovered in the year 1930, shortly before Hitler rose to power under the banner of National Socialism. We can see therefore that these planets—Uranus, Neptune, and Pluto—are the bearers of what could be described as the *false glory,* the *false power,* and the *false kingdom.* The *true glory,* the *true power,* and the *true kingdom* are the gifts of the Holy Trinity. False glory, the "glory of the Republic" as proclaimed in the French Revolution, is connected with the planet Uranus. False power, "power to the people" as exemplified in the communist revolution, is connected with Neptune. And the false kingdom, such as it came to manifestation in the "third Reich," is connected with Pluto. We see here indeed the counter-impulses of evil working against the Holy Trinity.

As previously described, the culmination of the period of the temptation in the wilderness occurred under a conjunction between the Sun and Pluto. This took place in the sidereal zodiac at 9° Sagittarius. In the year 2010 Pluto will again be located at 9° Sagittarius, a sign for us that the three temptations are now moving rapidly towards this historic moment. At this time humanity will be confronted with a choice between Christ and Antichrist. This example illustrates again how our correlation of the years of the Ministry of Christ to the "biography" of the Being of Christianity yields results of practical significance.

We look back into the past in this way, not to bury ourselves nostalgically in an earlier historical period, but to come to terms with the real forces at work on the Earth and in humanity. We see our efforts as a prologue, a preamble to a modern, re-cast "science of the Magi," a science being called forth just now, we believe, especially by what Rudolf Steiner calls the Second Coming—the Parousia represented by the appearance of Christ in the etheric organism of the Earth. We have looked at this in relation to the 33 1/3-year rhythm of Christ's etheric body and the 29 1/2-year rhythm of his astral body. But are there further cosmic rhythms that are of significance in laying foundations for Cosmic Christianity?

Certainly, the 12-year Jupiter rhythm should be mentioned. We need only recall that the Nathan Jesus was born exactly as the planet Jupiter was rising (see Chart 4, p. 149), and that the Solomon Jesus united spiritually with the Nathan Jesus at the "temple event" (Luke 2:41–52) shortly after

Jupiter had made one complete orbit of the sidereal zodiac since the birth of the Nathan Jesus. Unfortunately, lack of space prohibits a deeper treatment of the 12-year Jupiter rhythm. Suffice it to mention here that research has shown the 12-year Jupiter rhythm to be connected with the rhythm of the Christ "I" or Self.[17]

Foundations of Cosmic Christianity: Transits

No doubt there are other rhythms—in addition to the 33 1/3-year rhythm of Christ's etheric body, the 29 1/2-year rhythm of his astral body, and the 12-year rhythm of his I—that are significant for Cosmic Christianity. Apart from these cosmic rhythms, however, there are two other fundamental principles that are of central importance in relation to cosmic aspects of the Christ impulse. One is the principle—well-known in astrology—of *transits*. In the context of the material presented in this book, a transit occurs whenever a planet crosses over a particular position in the sidereal zodiac that it (or another planet) occupied at the time of an event in Christ's life. Such events include those connected with this life, such as the conception, birth, and death of the two Jesuses, the two Marys, and John the Baptist.

The most common example of a transit is the yearly celebration of the "birthday." This occurs when the Sun transits the position in the zodiac that it held at someone's birth, a transit that occurs yearly, since it returns to the same zodiacal location at birth after one year. The transits of the Sun to its position in the sidereal zodiac for events that took place two thousand years ago can be readily followed if allowance is made for the shift of dates due to the precession of the equinoxes. This gives rise to modern "anniversary dates" as exemplified in the Excursus Table on page 143, which tabulates the present-day "solar transits" pertaining to the conception, birth, and death of the two Jesuses, two Marys, and John the Baptist. Further examples of this principle of transits in relation to the Christ events are discussed below.

The second fundamental principle—also well known in astrology—is that of *recurring aspects*. Generally speaking, an aspect is an angular relationship between two planets. There are many different aspects in astrology, the most striking being those of *conjunction,* when two planets occupy the same

---

17. See Robert Powell, "Sub-Nature and the Second Coming," *Shoreline*, vol. 4 (1991), pp. 25–52, which includes a study of the Jupiter rhythm in relation to the Christ impulse.

degree, or are close to the same zodiacal degree, and *opposition*, when they are 180 degrees (or close to 180 degrees) apart. For example, the New Moon, when the Sun and Moon are together in the same zodiacal degree, is a conjunction; and the Full Moon, when the Sun and Moon are opposite each other in the zodiac, denotes an opposition. Just as transits evidently reactivate cosmic memories of the Christ events, so do recurring aspects. An outstanding example of this is the opposition of the luminaries at the Mystery of Golgotha, since it was Full Moon at the crucifixion; in fact, the Moon was full in sidereal Libra. Every month, the Full Moon signifies a recurrence of this Golgotha aspect and thus, as it were, "commemorates" the death on the cross. This commemoration is especially potent at the Full Moon in sidereal Libra, which occurs once a year between mid-April and mid-May. Further examples of the principle of recurring aspects are given below. All of this belongs to Cosmic Christianity, newly arising in the twentieth century through the greatest mystery of our time, Christ's second coming.

Is there some way that each of us can move closer to this mystery of our time? Rudolf Steiner said that if we wish to understand and meet Christ we need to look to the cosmos. I am convinced that one aspect of this should be the birth of a new science of the stars in our time as a metamorphosis of the star wisdom of the Magi, giving rise to a new Christian star wisdom. Perhaps a further example will solidify the reader's conviction that this new science is concerned with concrete reality. Let us consider, then, the baptism in the Jordan and the events immediately preceding it.

John the Baptist was just approaching the age of thirty when, around the time of the Passover in the year A.D. 29, he received his spiritual mission. He left the wilderness where he had been living and began his travels throughout Israel, visiting various towns, such as Jericho, Tiberius, and Nazareth, proclaiming the imminent coming of the Messiah. Wherever he went he introduced himself as the son of Zechariah. Eventually, he came to a place on the Jordan between the towns of Salem and Ainon and began baptizing. Around this time—approximately the beginning of June in A.D. 29—Jesus made his first lengthy journey since having left Nazareth. He traveled down to Jutta (Yattah) near Hebron, to the place where John the Baptist had been born. This clearly intimates a spiritual link between Jesus and John. Jesus then went to John and was baptized that autumn, a few months after John had begun his baptizing activity. By this time John had moved further down the Jordan and was baptizing on the west bank near a small town called Ono, east of Jericho.

From the Chronicle in Part II, we see that on September 22, A.D. 29, the Virgin Mary visited the home of Lazarus in Bethany, and that afternoon and evening a profound conversation took place between Mary and Jesus, who was also visiting the home of Lazarus at that time. This is the conversation Rudolf Steiner refers to, during which there flowed an impulse between Jesus and Mary such that the individuality of the Solomon Jesus withdrew through an act of sacrifice.[18] Up to that point (after the "temple event"), the Solomon Jesus had been united with the Nathan Jesus. With this conversation on the eve of the baptism there came the realization on the part of the Solomon Jesus that he had to make way for the incarnation of the Christ Being. That very night the Solomon Jesus individuality withdrew into the spiritual world. The Nathan Jesus now knew that he had to go to the baptism in the Jordan.

Accompanied by Lazarus, he set out that night proceeding east toward the Jordan, arriving at the place of baptism around dawn the next morning. If it had been a clear night, they would have seen in the dawn sky the thin, waning crescent of the Moon in the middle of sidereal Leo. The Sun had just entered sidereal Libra (1°), and the waning crescent Moon was at 16° Leo at the time of the baptism. John the Baptist was preaching as they approached. Many people were gathered there, but John sensed the presence of Jesus among the crowd and spoke with special fervor that morning. Then he began baptizing. Many had already been baptized before Jesus came down to the baptismal place at around 10 o'clock that morning, Friday, September 23. At the baptism Christ descended in the form of a dove of light to unite with the Nathan Jesus. Thus the "conception" of the Being of Christ Jesus took place just as the Sun entered sidereal Libra; i.e., stood on the cusp.

It is no accident that so important an event fell just on the cusp, or demarcation, between two zodiacal signs; and this discovery shows clearly how the great rhythm of the ministry of Christ is attuned to the passage of the Sun through the sidereal signs of the zodiac. This becomes all the more apparent if we take seriously Rudolf Steiner's indication that the Christ Being came from the Sun. If we were to transpose ourselves from the Earth to the Sun just at the moment when the Sun was entering Libra, we would then see the Earth just entering Aries, the zodiacal point that has always signified the start of a new cycle. As previously mentioned, the forty days of fasting in the wilderness began 28 1/3 days later, on the evening of Friday, October 21, as the Sabbath was beginning. By this time the Sun had passed through Libra and

---

18. Rudolf Steiner, *The Fifth Gospel* (London: Rudolf Steiner Press, 1968), pp. 91–92.

was about to enter Scorpio. During the forty days in the wilderness the Sun progressed through sidereal Scorpio and the first ten degrees ("decan") of sidereal Sagittarius.

Again and again we find such correspondences in Christ's ministry (his "embryonic period") to the passage of the Sun through the sidereal signs of the zodiac. This synchronicity therefore provides the key to a profound experience of the ever-present archetypes of the events of this ministry. For example, since the stellar archetype of the baptism occurred on the cusp of Virgo/Libra in the sidereal zodiac, we shall be able to more intimately attune ourselves to this mystery by identifying the time in our own epoch when this cusp returns (October 18/19). This date, therefore, is of significance for Cosmic Christianity—many other examples are given in my *Christian Hermetic Astrology: The Star of the Magi and the Life of Christ.* Knowledge of the sidereal zodiac and of the cosmic correspondences in Christ's ministry—knowledge that requires the kind of precise dating that we have tried to make a start at determining in this book—makes possible the cosmic commemoration of these events in our time as a foundation for Cosmic Christianity.

Another example: at the birth of the Nathan Jesus on the night of December 6/7, 2 B.C., the Sun was at 16° Sagittarius. Although December 6, Saint Nicholas Day, is the day upon which the birth of the Nathan Jesus should be historically commemorated—and obviously this has a definite historical validity—the *cosmic* commemoration of this event in our day is January 1, when the Sun is at 16° Sagittarius sidereally (see Excursus Table on page 143).

Foundations of Cosmic Christianity: Recurring Aspects

We are now approaching the beginning of a new millennium, and January 1, A.D. 2000, will be the 2,000th "cosmic" anniversary of the birth of the Nathan Jesus. What depth this gives to our understanding of this turning point! Cosmic Christianity, as here developed—and we are only at the beginning of this work—will allow us to live more and more consciously with the very pulse of Christ's heart. It is this heartbeat that connects our lives with that of Christ—a union that we have also begun to discern in the script of the stars, the visible emblems of Divine messengers, the choirs of angels.

In speaking of Cosmic Christianity, it is only fitting at this juncture to mention Willi Sucher (1902–1985). Readers already familiar with his work will know how much this book owes to him. It is a kind of "white magic": one looks into the future, becomes aware of certain approaching cosmic configurations, brings them into consciousness in connection with the corresponding Christ event, and tries to make oneself receptive to the flowing in, from the etheric, of the Christ impulse—this was Willi Sucher's concern. How opposed this is to certain degenerate forms of modern astrology, where some astrologers—under the influence of destructive, negative beings—project the most terrible doomsday predictions into the future, effectively paralyzing the human will! The practice of Christian star wisdom counteracts this negative approach by forging a conscious connection to the new unfolding of the Christ impulse that has been taking place through the progressive incorporation of Christ's etheric body since the year 1933. The aim of this star wisdom is to actively live with the events proceeding out of the current manifestation of this 33 1/3-year rhythm, with the resolve to participate, outwardly and inwardly, with all that this implies for the future of humanity. This path, which is ultimately a true path of healing—for humanity, the Earth, and all Creation—entered a new phase through the trail-blazing work of Willi Sucher, and we render homage to him here—a true disciple of the Cosmic Christ.[19]

Readers of Sucher's work will know that, although he did work with traditional astrology, he also turned to the sidereal zodiac and worked with the movements of the planets through the zodiacal constellations (sidereal zodiac) in contradistinction to modern astrology, which generally takes no account of this approach. A second point to mention with regard to Sucher's work is his attention to the heliocentric movements of the planets; that is, the movements of the planets not as viewed from the Earth (geocentric), but from the Sun. It was a deep intuition that led Willi Sucher to this step. When one looks at the correspondences between cosmic events and the life of Christ, the extraordinary fact emerges that it is above all the *heliocentric* planetary movements that are of significance. As an example, let us look at the cosmic configuration at the moment of the baptism in the Jordan, when *heliocentrically* there was an exact conjunction between Mercury and Saturn at the feet of the Twins. What might this mean? What could be the significance of this heavenly configuration? Saturn can be described as the "portal to the Kingdom of the Father," and Mercury, the planet closest to the Sun, as the "Messenger." Further, the Twins symbolize the linking of the heavenly Higher Self (Christ) and the Earth-self (Jesus).

---

19. Willi Sucher, *Cosmic Christianity and the Changing Countenance of Cosmology* (Hudson, NY: Anthroposophic Press, 1993).

The conjunction between Mercury and Saturn at the moment of the baptism came to expression in the opening of the cosmic portal: the will of the *Father* was then fulfilled in the words, "This is my beloved son whom today I have begotten" (Luke 3:22). This was the birth of Christ, the Son of the Father, in union with Jesus, to whom Christ came from heavenly realms as the Messenger of the Father. "The words that I say to you I do not speak on my own authority; but the Father who dwells in me does his works," (John 16:10).

In a new, Christianized star wisdom not only will it be important to turn again, as the Magi did, to the zodiacal constellations, but it will also be necessary to take account of the heliocentric movements of the planets. Further, account must be taken of the fact that, through the Mystery of Golgotha, the Earth has become, in a *moral-spiritual* sense, the center of the solar system and that therefore a heliocentric conception with the Sun at the physical center is—on a higher, moral-spiritual level—not really true. For Christ, the Spiritual Sun, is now united with the Earth. Certainly, the heliocentric system will still have a validity from the point of view of the physical relationships between the planets; but as we human beings incarnate again and again on the Earth, it is here that we may enter fully into a relationship with Christ, the Spirit-Sun. Indeed, in a profound sense, full of significance for the future, the Earth itself is becoming a *Sun*, so that, in a higher sense, "geocentrism" is only a new "heliocentrism." Therefore, we have the somewhat complicated circumstance that the heliocentric movements of the planets—though of profound significance for entering into a relationship with the unfolding of the Christ impulse—must also be viewed from an Earth-centered perspective. The implications of this view have been systematically presented in Vol. I of the author's *Hermetic Astrology*, where attention is drawn to the astronomical system of Tycho Brahe, which, though heliocentric in one sense, also places the Earth at the *absolute center*. The Tychonic system thus helps provide a basis for a new Christian star wisdom. Moreover, Rudolf Steiner indicates in his lectures on occult history that the Tychonic system is something of profound significance; and our own investigations have also shown how important it is to make the step from the Copernican system to the Tychonic. In taking this step we begin to enter fully into the *Christ-centered* reality of our solar system and are offered the privilege of participating in the great work of redemption.

Before giving some examples of the significance of the modified heliocentric (or Tychonic) perspective, something else should be addressed. Mention was made earlier of the *negative* working of the planets Uranus, Neptune, and

Pluto; but other, more positive, aspects should also be pointed out. And the fact that these planets were only discovered within the last 200 years or so does not preclude our investigating their influence prior to their "discovery." Nero, for example, was born at a conjunction between the Sun and Pluto; and the culmination of the temptation in the wilderness, looked at cosmically, also corresponded to a conjunction between the Sun and Pluto. In the case of Nero we clearly have an individual who had fallen prey to the will to power, one aspect of Pluto; but this negative aspect was, for example, counterbalanced by the raising of the daughter of Jairus, which also took place during a conjunction of the Sun and Pluto. In fact, this raising occurred twice: on November 18, A.D. 30, and then again on December 1, A.D. 30 (see chronicle in Part II). The second was the occasion on which the Sun was in conjunction with Pluto. Here we have a preliminary indication that the Christ Being worked also with impulses from the planet Pluto, but in a positive sense (and a similar case could be made for Uranus and Neptune).

Having alluded, at least briefly, to the importance of the three outer planets, let us now return to the modified heliocentric (or Tychonic) perspective, prepared to consider them also in relation to the more traditional inner planets. To give a better picture, let us look again at the configuration at the baptism in the Jordan from the perspective of the Sun, at which time the planet Mercury, which is closest to the Sun, and the planet Saturn lined up together in the feet of the Twins, at 7° sidereal Gemini. Here we have the alignment Sun-Mercury-Saturn, and the remarkable thing is that this alignment occurs over and over again at other important events in Christ's life—for example, at the Adoration of the Magi.

At the Adoration of the Magi, on the evening of December 26, 6 B.C., there was a heliocentric conjunction between Mercury and Saturn in sidereal Aries. In studying these cosmic correspondences, what seems most important is the fact of *alignment*. A heliocentric conjunction between Mercury and Saturn means that Mercury and Saturn are in a line with the Sun— on the same side of the Sun. A heliocentric opposition would take place if Mercury were on one side of the Sun and Saturn on the other: Mercury-Sun-Saturn. And in fact, at the healing of the nobleman's son, the second miracle in the Gospel of Saint John, precisely this Mercury-Sun-Saturn alignment occurred. In other words, at the time of this miracle, which took place at 1:00 P.M. on Saturday, August 3, A.D.30 (see Chronicle in Part Two), there was a heliocentric opposition between Mercury and Saturn. This same opposition occurred again at the feeding of the five thousand, which, according to the chronicle took place between 4:00 and 6:00 P.M. on Monday, January 29, A.D. 31.

Another example: we know that the resurrection took place on the morning of Sunday, April 5, A.D. 33, and that the ascension followed forty days later. Adding these forty days, we arrive at Thursday, May 14, A.D.33. Looking at the cosmic configuration at this time, midday May 14, there was, heliocentrically, an opposition of Mercury and Neptune: that is, Mercury-Sun-Neptune. Neptune was at 1° sidereal Aquarius and Mercury at 1° sidereal Leo. Now, exactly the same cosmic configuration took place at the wedding at Cana. Again we have the alignment: Mercury-Sun-Neptune. The wedding at Cana took place on the morning of Wednesday, December 28, A.D. 29, at 9:00 A.M. Since the wedding meal directly followed, the time of the transformation of water into wine was about midday. At that time Mercury was, heliocentrically, at 24° Cancer and Neptune was opposite at 24° sidereal Capricorn. These few examples must suffice to illustrate the general point. Perhaps one day a more detailed study can be made of the close connection between Christ's life and astrological events as viewed from the Tychonic-heliocentric perspective.

Having considered the importance of the heliocentric perspective, let us go a step further; needless to say, traditional geocentric configurations are also significant in the life of Christ. For example, at the end of the forty days in the wilderness, as described in the Gospel of Saint Matthew (4:11) "angels came and ministered unto him." What is signified by these words? According to the spiritual tradition of the Knights of Malta, these were the angels of the twelve who were to become his apostles. Now we know—also from Rudolf Steiner—that the Moon sphere is the realm of the angels. So we would expect to find, at this moment, a planetary configuration involving the Moon; and, in fact, on that occasion—toward the evening of Wednesday, November 30, A.D. 29, at the end of the forty days in the wilderness—there was indeed a conjunction between the Moon and Jupiter. What took place? The angels poured out their blessing, signified cosmically by the alignment with Jupiter, planet of wisdom. They bestowed a cosmic benediction: a source of nourishment and sustenance radiated forth to fortify Christ Jesus at this moment just after he had met and overcome the three temptations.

One month later, Christ Jesus, together with about one hundred people, attended the wedding at Cana in Galilee. During the celebration following the wedding that morning, at which many of his own relatives were present, he performed his first public miracle—the transformation of water into wine. At that moment the Moon was again in conjunction with Jupiter, a fact that casts a remarkable light on this miracle. For what took place? The water—one could say the *water of wisdom*—is symbolized by the conjunction between the Moon and Jupiter. This *water* had flowed through the prophets of the people of Israel. Christ then came as the one who would fulfill this prophetic tradition. And what new thing did he bring to the water, the *wisdom*, the power of Yahveh that had flowed like a channel of inspiration since the time of Abraham and Melchizedek? He brought the *fire* of love. The water that was distributed to the wedding guests was mixed, not just with angelic blessing as at the end of the temptation in the wilderness, but with the Being of Christ himself, the *power of love*, the *fire of love* that transforms water into wine. When the guests drank of this water, they were imbued with the inner fire of love and devotion to the Christ. Those present recognized him as the emissary of the Divine. And this his first public miracle was followed by its "octave," the last miracle when—at the Last Supper on the night of Thursday, April 2, A.D. 33—with his twelve disciples he inaugurated the holy mystery of the sacrament of bread and wine; this spans the life of Christ. In living with the movements of the planets, this fact can inspire us: every month there is a recurring aspect when the Moon comes into conjunction with Jupiter; this aspect allows an echoing or reawakening inwardly of the mystery of the transformation of water into wine. In living with the cosmic correspondences of the Christ events, we can find a completely new relationship with the heavenly configurations taking place each month.[20]

There are many other examples that we could observe: for example, the descent of the Holy Spirit at Whitsun, which is celebrated ten days after the ascension. In the Hebrew calendar, the corresponding festival day is called the "Feast of Weeks." This event takes place fifty days after the Passover, which begins on the 15th day of the month of Nisan, the first month in the Jewish calendar. Fifty days later comes Pentecost, on Sivan 6/7, in the third month in the Jewish calendar. Many people were gathered together in Jerusalem for this festival of the Feast of Weeks, fifty days after the Passover in the year 33. The apostles and disciples, the holy women, and the Virgin Mary were gathered together in the Coenaculum, the house of the Last Supper on

---

20. Robert Powell and Michael Brinch, *Christian Star Calendar* (yearly) lists the cosmic correspondences of the Christ events through the twelve months of the year (distributed by Anthroposophic Press, Hudson, NY).

Mount Zion in Jerusalem. They were gathered together to unite in prayer. On that night, May 23, A.D. 33, the start of the sixth day of Sivan, the Feast of Weeks began. They met in the room of the Last Supper: the eleven apostles plus the newly chosen Matthias, who came in place of Judas Iscariot, together with the Blessed Virgin Mary. The other disciples and holy women were together in other parts of the house. During the night something very special began to take place—a mystery connected with the Blessed Virgin Mary. This then led to the descent of the Holy Spirit at dawn the next day, Sunday, May 24, A.D. 33—fifty days after Easter. At the Whitsun event, the Moon and Uranus were conjunct in the constellation of Leo. Each month there is a recurring aspect when the Moon again comes into conjunction with Uranus. When this aspect occurs, we can inwardly reawaken for ourselves this important event that actually signified the founding of the Church. We know that Peter and the apostles went down to the pool of Bethesda that day and baptized three thousand people (Acts 2:41).

Living with these cosmic configurations and correspondences to the time of the life of Christ can intensify our inner connection with the unfolding of the Christ impulse. In our *daily* lives we can cultivate an intimate relationship with these events of *eternal* significance. Christ said: "Heaven and Earth shall pass away, but my words will never pass away" (Matthew 24:35). How much more is this true, not just for the *words* of Christ, but for his *deeds*. These deeds were imprinted in the cosmic-etheric configuration of the universe; and through grace we can become attuned to them through the appropriate inner knowledge and orientation of will. This modern spiritual path is a metamorphosis of the path followed by the Magi two thousand years ago. Just as the Magi—fulfillers of the spiritual stream inaugurated by Zoroaster in Babylon in the sixth century B.C.—bore witness to the first coming of Christ, so there is today the need for a new *path of the Magi* leading to Cosmic Christianity, to a Christianized star wisdom, representing a metamorphosis of that ancient path. A true spiritual star wisdom, a true astrology, is needed in our time to enable us to draw closer to the second coming of Christ—to the coming of Christ in the etheric realm—just as the path of the Magi led to the coming of Christ in the physical realm. This is the true significance of the Christian star wisdom arising in our time, for which the Chronicle of the life of Christ provides a secure foundation. May our efforts stimulate others to join in the quest.

Appendices

Appendix I: The Date of the Crucifixion

Saint Matthew states that the hour of Christ's death was 3:00 P.M. in his Gospel (27:51), whereas Saint John in his Gospel indicates the day of preparation for the Passover, on Friday—prior to the commencement of the Sabbath (19:14,31). Taken together, it is apparent that the crucifixion occurred at 3:00 P.M. on Friday, Nisan 14. We also know that it took place when Pontius Pilate was procurator of Judea, so the date would be between A.D. 26 to 36, according to the Jewish historian Josephus (Antiquities 18:35, 89).[1]

We can determine which years Nisan 14 fell on a Friday—since Nisan 14 must occur on a Full Moon—the only years it could have been were 27, 30, 33, and 36.[2] Luke tells us that John the Baptist's ministry began in Tiberius' fifteenth year (3:1–2). As this equates with 28–29, the crucifixion could not have occurred in 27. Similarly, 36 is not plausible if the remark that Jesus "when he began his ministry was about thirty years of age" is taken seriously (Luke 3:23), for there is no indication in the Gospels that Jesus' ministry lasted six years.[3] This leaves only 30 and 33.

The ministry of John the Baptist, however, began in 28–29, thus the crucifixion could not have taken place in the year 30, which would mean that his ministry lasted little more than one year—from the baptism until the Passover in 29, and then one year to the Passover in 30. But since three Passovers are explicitly mentioned by Saint John, A.D. 30 is also unacceptable (2:13, 6:4, 11:55). This leaves the year 33 as the only possible year for the crucifixion. Astronomically, Nisan 14 in the year 33 equated with Friday, April 3. This date, determined by J.K. Fotheringham,[4] is the only possible

---

1. Ormond Edwards, *The Time of Christ* (Edinburgh: Floris Books, 1986), p.147; cf. also Harold W. Hoehner, "Chronological Aspects of the Life of Christ," *Bibliotheca Sacra* 131 (1974), p. 335.
2. J.K. Fotheringham, "Evidence of Astronomy and Technical Chronology for the Date of the Crucifixion," *Journal of Theological Studies* 35 (1934), pp. 146–162.
3. Hoehner, op. cit., p. 335.
4. Fotheringham, ibid.

date of the crucifixion according to astronomical chronology, as based on the indications in the Gospels. The date April 3, 33 was also indicated by Rudolf Steiner as the correct date for the crucifixion,[5] and it accords exactly with the account of the life of Christ Jesus given by Anne Catherine. She also stated that at the crucifixion the Moon was full (BL, 172). This was the case on April 3, 33. The exact moment of the Full Moon was 7:45 P.M. (Jerusalem time), just 4 3/4 hours after the death on the cross.

Appendix II: The Hebrew Calendar

During the time of the Babylonian captivity (sixth century B.C.), certain elements of Babylonian culture were assimilated by the Jewish people, one of which was the Babylonian lunar calendar. The months of both the Babylonian and the Hebrew calendars are determined by the Moon's cycle, and thus average about 29 1/2 days (the exact period from one New Moon to the next is 29.531 days). If a year contained exactly twelve lunar months its length would be about 12 x 29 1/2 = 354 days, some eleven days shorter than the solar year of 365 days. In order that the lunar calendar not fall out of step with the seasons of the solar year, the loss of these eleven days is compensated for by adding one extra lunar month approximately every three years. An intercalary year—a leap year—contains *thirteen* lunar months, and the Babylonians discovered that a nearly perfect concordance with the solar year could be established by distributing seven leap years within a cycle of nineteen lunar years. This principle also underlies the Jewish calendar, in which the 3rd, 6th, 8th, 11th, 14th, 17th, and 19th years of each 19-year cycle are leap years.

The names of the months of the Hebrew calendar are: Nisan, Iyyar, Sivan, Tammuz, Ab, Elul, Tishri, Marcheshvan (Heshvan), Kislev, Tebeth, Shebat, and Adar. In a leap year there are two months of Adar: Adar I and Adar II.

Normally the months comprise alternately 30 and 29 days, designated as *full months* and *hollow months* respectively. This yields the following (ideal) pattern: Nisan (30), Iyyar (29), Sivan (30), Tammuz (29), Ab (30), Elul (29), Tishri (30), Heshvan (29), Kislev (30), Tebeth (29), Shebat (30), Adar (29). This pattern would be adequate if the lunar month contained exactly 29 1/2 days; but, since the exact number is 29.531 days, there are deviations

---

5. Rudolf Steiner, *Kalendar 1912/13* (Berlin: Philosophisch-theosophischer Verlag, 1912), entry: April 3.

from this ideal. Thus, in a leap year, Adar I always has 30 days and Adar II 29 days. Moreover, Heshvan often becomes a full month of 30 days, and Kislev may in certain years become a hollow month of 29 days. Owing to the complex rules of this system, there is no easily recognizable pattern for the occurrence of Kislev and Heshvan as full or hollow months. But on average about 55% of Heshvan months are hollow and about 75% of Kislev months are full. The three possibilities in any given year are:

(1) Heshvan and Kislev both hollow (about 25% of the time)
(2) Heshvan hollow and Kislev full (about 30% of the time)
(3) Heshvan and Kislev both full (about 45% of the time)

This means that in the course of twenty years, on average, possibility (1) occurs five times, possibility (2) six times, and possibility (3) nine times. In the specification of the Hebrew calendar, the determination of whether possibility (1), (2), or (3) applies in any given year is completely independent of the 19-year cycle. It has nothing to do with whether the year in question is a common year or a leap year.

It was not until the fourth century A.D. that the patriarch Hillel II made public the system of calculating the Jewish calendar. Prior to this step, the determination of the calendar had been a closely guarded secret of the Sanhedrin, the supreme court in Jerusalem, and it is not known exactly when this system was first applied by them. From the calendar indications communicated by Anne Catherine, however, it proved possible—with the help of astronomical calculations—to reconstruct the Jewish calendar for much of the period of Christ's ministry. This reconstruction is presented in Appendix III, and shows that the Hebrew calendar at the time of Christ followed the pattern of full and hollow months described above, but with one exception: in the year A.D. 30, the month of Iyyar was full instead of hollow. Thus, it would seem that by the time of Christ the set of rules used by the Sanhedrin for determining the calendar had become more or less fixed, but not absolutely rigid.

Prior to the application of these rules, the beginnings of each month were sanctified and announced by the Sanhedrin after at least two witnesses had testified that they had seen the lunar crescent of the New Moon. Since each month had to contain 29 or 30 days, the search for the new lunar crescent started at dusk on the evening after the 29th day. If it was sighted and ratified by the Sanhedrin, the start of the new month was announced that evening throughout Israel by the kindling of night fires, sending out messengers, and hanging flags on the roofs of synagogues. The sanctification of the New Moon was celebrated in a festival lasting one day if the preceding month was hollow; otherwise the thirtieth day of the old month was counted (and was celebrated as the first day of a two-day New Moon festival), and the new month would begin on the following evening, in which case the New Moon festival lasted two days since it included the thirtieth day of the old month and the first day of the new one. (It should be remembered that the day in the Jewish calendar begins at dusk and extends to dusk the following evening). This ratification procedure ensured that the lunar months did in fact keep in step with the actual phases of the Moon.

When this observational system was replaced by a set of rules, it was essential that the rules ensure that months remain in step with the Moon's phases. This function was served by the Molad calculation (the determination of the conjunction of the Sun and Moon), and the Moladoth (the elapsed time from one Molad to the next). The Moladoth is calculated at 29 days, 12 hours, and 793 parts of an hour. It is also assumed that the very first Molad—the conjunction of the Sun and Moon at the time of the creation of the world on Tishri 1 of the year 1 of the Jewish world era—took place two days, 5 hours, and 204 parts of an hour after 6 P.M. (Jerusalem time) on the start of Tishri 1. By repeatedly adding multiples of the Moladoth to this original Molad, each new Molad could be determined. The first day of each month in the Jewish calendar begins close to the Molad—that is, close to the astronomical conjunction of the Sun and Moon. The exact rules concerning the relationship between the computed Molad and the start of day 1 of the month are complex; however, the basic intention of these rules was to adjust the start of day 1 (in relation to the Molad) so that it coincided with the day that would have been sanctified by the Sanhedrin, based on direct observation of the New Moon. In other words, the rules shifted the start of day 1 after the Molad in such a way as to approximate the time interval from the Molad to the evening on which the New Moon became visible in Jerusalem after the conjunction. In practice this means that the calendar date (civil calendar) on which day 1 of a given month starts is generally either the same as, or one or two days later than, the calendar date on which the astronomical conjunction between the Sun and Moon takes place.

Prior to the application of these rules for the Hebrew calendar, a special committee of the Sanhedrin had the task of determining leap years, in which a thirteenth month (Adar II) was inserted before Nisan to ensure that the Passover (starting Nisan 15) would take place in spring. Originally various signs were taken as indicators that spring had actually arrived—whether the barley was ripe, the fruit on the trees had grown properly, the winter rains had stopped, or the young pigeons were fledged. If these signs were fulfilled, there was no need for the intercalation of an extra month. In this way the Hebrew calendar was adjusted to keep in step with the passage of the actual seasons.

When the calendar rules were applied, the intention was to ensure its continued synchronization with the seasons. Since the vernal equinox—when the Sun begins its passage northward from the celestial equator—is the primary decisive astronomical factor for the onset of spring, the rules underlying the application of the 19-year cycle should specify that the Molad (conjunction of Sun and Moon) preceding day 1 of the month of Nisan should fall as close as possible to the vernal equinox. This is the theoretical basis of the Hebrew calendar. To make the 19-year cycle fit in practice, this theory, though generally correct, may occasionally not work. As Appendix III shows, the conjunction of the Sun and Moon preceding day 1 of the month of Nisan fell on March 22 in A.D. 30, March 12 in A.D. 31, March 30 in A.D. 32 and March 19 in A.D. 33. These dates nonetheless all fall relatively close to the date of the vernal equinox, March 22–23, during the time of Christ.

Appendix III: Reconstruction of the Hebrew Calendar for the Time of Christ's Ministry Based on Anne Catherine Emmerich's Calendar Indications

From the description of the Jewish calendar in Appendix II, it should be evident that the occurrence of the Molad (conjunction of Sun and Moon), which always falls close to the start of day 1 of a new month, is decisive for the specification of the calendar. A first step in reconstructing the Hebrew calendar is to compute the civil calendar date of the conjunction of the Sun and Moon in Jerusalem time each month, as listed in column 2 of the table below. The table lists a reconstruction of the months of the Hebrew calendar for the four years from June A.D. 29 to May A.D. 33, the time covering the 3 1/2 year period of Christ's ministry. In the first column the name of each month is given, together with an indication as to whether it was a *full* 30- day month, or a *hollow* 29-day month.

The pattern of full and hollow months conforms exactly with the description of the calendar in Appendix II, with the single exception that the month of Iyyar in A.D. 30 contained 30 days instead of 29 days. The second column lists the time (in Jerusalem) and the date (civil calendar) of the conjunction of Sun and Moon as computed astronomically. The third column gives the length of time (in days and hours) that elapsed from the conjunction to the start of day 1 of the corresponding lunar month. Here, for the sake of simplicity, day 1 is assumed to start at 6:00 P.M. Jerusalem time, on the given calendar date, though it actually starts at dusk. In the rare event that the astronomically computed conjunction of the Sun and Moon occurred *after* 6 P.M. on the given date, the time interval is prefixed with a minus (-) sign. Note that the civil calendar used in the Roman empire at the time of Christ was the Julian calendar, which is similar to, but not identical with, the modern Gregorian calendar now in use throughout the world. The fourth column gives the civil calendar date on which day 1 of the lunar month commenced, starting at dusk. Many of the dates in this column were determined from Anne Catherine's calendar indications, as described in the preceding text; the remaining dates were simply reconstructed on the basis of the usual pattern of full and hollow months.

RECONSTRUCTION OF THE JEWISH CALENDAR
from June A.D. 29 to May A.D. 33

MONTH	CONJUNCTION OF SUN AND MOON Time (Jerusalem time) & Date		TIME INTERVAL Days and Hours	START OF DAY 1 at dusk on:	
Sivan (30)	02:20 on 1 June	A.D. 29	-0d. 8h.	31 May	A.D. 29
Tammuz (29)	13:31 on 30 June	A.D. 29	0d. 4h.	30 June	A.D. 29
Ab (30)	23:10 on 29 July	A.D. 29	-0d. 5h.	29 July	A.D. 29
Elul (29)	08:01 on 28 August	A.D. 29	0d.10h.	28 August	A.D. 29
Tishri (30)	16:58 on 26 September	A.D. 29	0d. 1h.	26 September	A.D. 29
Heshvan (29)	02:51 on 26 October	A.D. 29	0d.15h.	26 October	A.D. 29
Kislev (30)	14:07 on 24 November	A.D. 29	0d. 4h.	24 November	A.D. 29
Tebeth (29)	02:46 on 24 December	A.D. 29	0d.15h.	24 December	A.D. 29
Shebat (30)	16:33 on 22 January	A.D. 30	0d. 1h.	22 January	A.D. 30
Adar (29)	07:15 on 21 February	A.D. 30	0d. 1h.	21 February	A.D. 30
Nisan (30)	22:41 on 22 March	A.D. 30	-0d. 5h.	22 March	A.D. 30
Iyyar (30)	14:31 on 21 April	A.D. 30	0d. 3h.	21 April	A.D. 30
Sivan (30)	06:06 on 21 May	A.D. 30	0d.12h.	21 May	A.D. 30
Tammuz (29)	20:40 on 19 June	A.D. 30	0d. 2h.	20 June	A.D. 30
Ab (30)	09:43 on 19 July	A.D. 30	0d. 8h.	19 July	A.D. 30
Elul (29)	21:20 on 17 August	A.D. 30	0d. 2h.	18 August	A.D. 30
Tishri (30)	08:07 on 16 September	A.D. 30	0d.10h.	16 September	A.D. 30

Heshvan (30)	18:45 on 15 October	A.D. 30	0d.23h.	16 October	A.D. 30
Kislev (30)	05:36 on 14 November	A.D. 30	1d.12h.	15 November	A.D. 30
Tebeth (29)	16:39 on 13 December	A.D. 30	1d. 1h.	15 December	A.D. 30
Shebat (30)	03:47 on 12 January	A.D. 31	1d.14h.	13 January	A.D. 31
Adar (29)	15:09 on 10 February	A.D. 31	2d. 3h.	12 February	A.D. 31
Nisan (30)	03:13 on 12 March	A.D. 31	1d.15h.	13 March	A.D. 31
Iyyar (29)	16:27 on 10 April	A.D. 31	2d. 1h.	12 April	A.D. 31
Sivan (30)	06:51 on 10 May	A.D. 31	1d.11h.	11 May	A.D. 31
Tammuz (29)	22:00 on 8 June	A.D. 31	1d.20h.	10 June	A.D. 31
Ab (30)	13:13 on 8 July	A.D. 31	1d. 5h.	9 July	A.D. 31
Elul (29)	04:02 on 7 August	A.D. 31	1d.14h.	8 August	A.D. 31
Tishri (30)	18:13 on 5 September	A.D. 31	1d. 0h.	6 September	A.D. 31
Heshvan (29)	07:46 on 5 October	A.D. 31	1d.10h.	6 October	A.D. 31
Kislev (30)	20:32 on 3 November	A.D. 31	0d.21h.	4 November	A.D. 31
Tebeth (29)	08:22 on 3 December	A.D. 31	1d.10h.	4 December	A.D. 31
Shebat (30)	19:08 on 1 January	A.D. 32	0d.23h.	2 January	A.D. 32
Adar I (30)	05:07 on 31 January	A.D. 32	1d.13h.	1 February	A.D. 32
Adar II (29)	14:49 on 29 February	A.D. 32	2d. 3h.	2 March	A.D. 32
Nisan (30)	00:54 on 30 March	A.D. 32	1d.17h.	31 March	A.D. 32
Iyyar (29)	11:54 on 28 April	A.D. 32	2d. 6h.	30 April	A.D. 32
Sivan (30)	00:10 on 28 May	A.D. 32	1d.18h.	29 May	A.D. 32
Tammuz (29)	13:51 on 26 June	A.D. 32	2d. 4h.	28 June	A.D. 32
Ab (30)	04:59 on 26 July	A.D. 32	1d.13h.	27 July	A.D. 32
Elul (29)	21:18 on 24 August	A.D. 32	1d.21h.	26 August	A.D. 32
Tishri (30)	14:08 on 23 September	A.D. 32	1d. 4h.	24 September	A.D. 32
Heshvan (29)	06:27 on 23 October	A.D. 32	1d.12h.	24 October	A.D. 32
Kislev (30)	21:14 on 21 November	A.D. 32	0d.21h.	22 November	A.D. 32
Tebeth (29)	10:03 on 21 December	A.D. 32	1d. 8h.	22 December	A.D. 32
Shebat (30)	21:04 on 19 January	A.D. 33	0d.21h.	20 January	A.D. 33
Adar (29)	06:43 on 18 February	A.D. 33	1d.11h.	19 February	A.D. 33
Nisan (30)	15:32 on 19 March	A.D. 33	1d. 2h.	20 March	A.D. 33
Iyyar (29)	00:03 on 18 April	A.D. 33	1d.18h.	19 April	A.D. 33
Sivan (30)	08:53 on 17 May	A.D. 33	1d. 9h.	18 May	A.D. 33

Crucifixion	Nisan 14	3 P.M.Friday	April 3	A.D. 33
Resurrection	Nisan 16	dawn Sunday	April 5	A.D. 33
Ascension	Iyyar 25	noon Thursday	May 14	A.D. 33
Whitsun (Pentecost)	Sivan 6	dawn Sunday	May 24	A.D. 33

Remarks concerning the reconstruction of the table of months of the Hebrew calendar from June A.D. 29 to May A.D. 33:

The reconstructed table of months of the Hebrew calendar may be divided into four periods:

(1) Sivan A.D. 29–Elul A.D. 29
(2) Tishri A.D. 29–Tammuz A.D. 31
(3) Ab A.D. 31–Ab A.D. 32
(4) Elul A.D. 32–Sivan A.D. 33

The first period covered by Anne Catherine's daily communications comprises the four months leading up to the baptism in the Jordan. It starts with the travels of Jesus after his move from Nazareth to Capernaum, and ends with his baptism on Elul 26. During this period the regular occurrence of the Sabbath is referred to by Anne Catherine, but she does not mention any festivals that can be linked to the Hebrew calendar. Her indications concerning the Sabbath enable the days of the week to be determined, but no explicit point of reference within the Hebrew calendar. The dating of her daily communications for this period is by way of extrapolation backwards from period (2), for which Anne Catherine *does* give explicit calendar indications. This extrapolation is effected simply by counting the seven-day Sabbath rhythm backward during the summer of A.D. 29. Similarly, the reconstruction of the Hebrew calendar for this period was made by extrapolating back from period (2), and is securely defined on the basis of statements made by Sister Anne Catherine.

Period (2) covers Anne Catherine's daily communications from the baptism to the start of the "missing period," where her communications were ended by her death. During this period she not only communicated the seven-day rhythm running through Christ's ministry, but also repeatedly referred to various Hebrew festivals. These references, together with the Sabbath rhythm, make it possible to reconstruct the calendar with great certainty. Almost all the calendar references given by Anne Catherine during this period are mutually supporting, so there can be little doubt concerning their authenticity. It would be virtually impossible to concoct such a set of consistent and mutually supporting calendar references and communicate them over a period of almost twenty-two months—Sister Anne Catherine was a simple woman of humble peasant origin with no knowledge of the intricacies of the Hebrew calendar.

Period (3) contains the missing period consisting of the 313 days absent in Anne Catherine's daily communications concerning Christ's ministry. Since there are no communications to go on, the Hebrew calendar is reconstructed by simply filling in the missing months between periods (2) and (4) through extrapolation forward from period (2) and backward from period (4).

Period (4) includes the time leading up to and immediately following the crucifixion, including Whitsun. This was the first period revealed by Anne Catherine when she began her daily communications, which were much shorter than her later communications belonging to periods (1) and (2). One possible reason for this is that, since Clemens Brentano initially had difficulty understanding her dialect, some things may not have been written down.

Unfortunately, the brevity of the communications during the period leading up to the crucifixion offer no indications concerning festivals in the Hebrew calendar. The sole exception is the time of the crucifixion itself, which was described (in agreement with the Gospel of Saint John) as taking place on the day of preparation for the Passover—Nisan 14 in the Hebrew calendar. Sister Anne Catherine indicates that the crucifixion of Jesus began at approximately 12:15 P.M. Jerusalem time and lasted until shortly after 3:00 P.M. (BL, 320, 346). Not long after the beginning of the crucifixion, she relates that trumpets sounded from the temple to announce the slaying of Passover lambs. This occurred at about 12:30 P.M. rather than the usual time of 3:00 P.M. because in A.D. 33 the day of preparation was on Friday, and the slaying had to be completed before the start of the Sabbath that evening (LJC iii, 281). The Gospel of Saint John also states that the day of preparation was on Friday. The date of the crucifixion was in fact Friday, April 3, A.D. 33 (see Appendix I). On the basis of the weekly Sabbath rhythm throughout the period of communications leading to the crucifixion, the dates of events during this period were determined by following the Sabbath rhythm back from the date of the crucifixion, with some modifications (see Appendix IV). Similarly, the months of the Hebrew calendar were extrapolated back from Nisan 14 on the day of the crucifixion, and the months of Iyyar and Sivan following after Nisan were added on. Thus, the Ascension took place at midday on Thursday, Iyyar 25 and Whitsun at dawn on Sunday, Sivan 6, the Feast of Weeks.

. . . .

Discussion of Anne Catherine Emmerich's Calendar Indications:

It is evident that the calendar indications of Anne Catherine during Period 2 are of key significance for dating Christ's ministry, as well as providing authenticity for her communications.

Taking a closer look, we see that the very first calendar indication she gave concerns the start of the Feast of Tabernacles on Monday evening after the baptism (LJ i, 186). Since the Feast starts on Tishri 15, and since three Sabbaths had occurred following the baptism, it is easy to determine that the baptism occurred at 10:00 A.M. on Friday, Elul 26, or September 23, A.D. 29 (see Table 2, p. 37). Therefore Tishri 1 began on the evening of Monday, September 26, A.D. 29 (as listed in column 4 of our reconstructed table of months, pp. 448–449).

The next calendar indication relates to the start of the Feast of Dedication, which coincides with Kislev 25 in the Hebrew calendar. According to Anne Catherine, Kislev 25 in that year began on a Sunday evening (LJ i, 248). Historically this must have been Sunday, December 18, A.D. 29, from which it follows that Kislev 1 started on the evening of Thursday, November 24, A.D. 29 (see column 4 of the Table).

Shortly after this, when Christ Jesus was in Cana for the wedding, she identified the start of the third day in Cana as Tebeth 4 (LJ i, 265). This began Tuesday evening, and on the following morning the wedding took place—the morning of Wednesday, December 28, A.D. 29. Thus Tebeth 1 commenced on the evening of Saturday, December 24, A.D. 29 (see column 4 of the Table). This is confirmed by the reference to the evening of the Sabbath (Friday) as the beginning of Tebeth 7 (LJ i, 281).

The New Moon festival celebrating the start of the month of Shebat fell on a Monday—beginning Sunday evening (LJ i, 300). She describes the flags for the New Moon festival hanging from long flagstaffs on the roof of the synagogue, and large knots tied at intervals on the staves, the number of knots signifying the month just begun—in this case eleven knots for Shebat, the eleventh month. This was the evening of January 22, A.D. 30 (see column 4 of the Table).

In the next month, Adar, the calendar indication given by Sister Anne Catherine refers to the start of the Feast of Purim, beginning on Adar 14, a Monday evening, or March 6, A.D. 30 (LJ i, 336). This means that Adar 1 commenced on the evening of Tuesday, February 21, A.D. 30 (see column 4 of the Table).

There is another calendar indication for the onset of the New Moon festival at the beginning of the month of Nisan, on a Wednesday evening, March 22, A.D. 30 (LJ i, 348).

There are no calendar communications, in the months of Iyyar and Sivan, until Tammuz 17, where Anne Catherine speaks of the day of fasting (Tammuz 17) commemorating the broken tablets of the Law on Mt. Sinai (LJ i, 401). The beginning of Tammuz 17 was on a Thursday evening, July 6, A.D. 30; Tammuz 1 therefore started on Tuesday evening, June 20, A.D. 30.

The New Moon festival of the month of Ab began on a Wednesday evening, on July 19, A.D. 30 (LJ i, 443). This is confirmed by the reference to the start of Ab 18 on Saturday evening after the Sabbath (LJ ii, 38).

Anne Catherine speaks of the onset of the New Moon festival of the month of Elul, on the start of the Sabbath (LJ ii, 84), August 18, A.D. 30 (see column 4 of the Table). This is confirmed by the reference to the morning of Elul 24 on a Monday morning (LJ ii, 191). The reference (LJ ii, 199) to Tishri 1 on Sunday, followed by the reference (LJ ii, 204) to the day of Tishri 2 on Monday, indicates the start of the month of Tishri on Saturday evening, which equated historically with Saturday, September 16, A.D. 30 (see column 4 of the Table). Similarly, she speaks of the start of the month of Marcheshvan on Monday evening (LJ ii, 283). This means that Heshvan 1 began on the evening of Monday, October 16, A.D. 30 (see column 4 of the Table).

The next calendar reference is to the onset of the New Moon festival on Wednesday evening (LJ ii, 401), signifying that Kislev 1 commenced on the evening of Wednesday, November 15, A.D. 30 (see column 4 of the Table). Up to this point, all of Anne Catherine's calendar indications are mutually supporting and consistent with one another and with the seven-day cycle of weekdays and with the Hebrew calendar for the period under consideration. But with the next reference, concerning the beginning of the Feast of Dedication, we encounter a one-day discrepancy:

> However, today was Friday, Kislev 24 and because this evening the Sabbath coincided with Kislev 25, the Feast of Dedication, the festival began already yesterday evening with the start of Kislev 24. (LJ ii, 486)

To be consistent with all her foregoing calendar indications, it is easily shown that Kislev 24 must have started on Friday evening and not, as the above statement implies, on Thursday evening. This is the first contradiction that emerges from Anne Catherine's statements concerning the calendar. It is clearly a matter of miscommunication, for the very next calendar indication definitely implies that Kislev 24 started on Friday evening. This reference (LJ ii, 503) mentions the coincidence of the New Moon festival with the Sabbath (i.e., Tebeth 1 started on the evening of Friday, December 15 A.D. 30). Thus Kislev 24, exactly one week prior to Tebeth 1, also commenced on Friday evening.

At present (1995), only the first two volumes (LJ i, ii) of the original notes by Clemens Brentano of Anne Catherine's account of Christ's ministry have been published. Thus the calendar indications cited henceforth derive from the original edition of Anne Catherine Emmerich's *Das Leben unseres Herrn und Heilands Jesu Christi* (LHHJC).

The next calendar indication concerns the New Moon festival, which is said to have started on Friday evening (LHHJC ii, 294). Here again there is a discrepancy of one day, for, to be consistent with the foregoing calendar statements, the first day of the month of Shebat must have started on Saturday evening, January 13 A.D. 31. However, it should be noted that as Anne Catherine generally communicated her visions either on the day she had them, or the day after, it is quite possible that a one-day discrepancy could occur occasionally in her narrative.

The next calendar indication states that the New Moon festival was celebrated "yesterday and today," referring to a Monday (LHHJC ii, 367), which can be taken to mean that Shebat 30 started on Sunday evening and Adar 1 on Monday evening. If this interpretation is correct, Adar 1 commenced on the evening of Monday, February 12 A.D. 31, in conformity with the preceding calendar dates. This is followed by a reference (LHHJC ii, 381) to the Purim festival starting on Monday (i.e., historically Monday, February 26, A.D. 31). Since the Purim festival starts on Adar 14, this implies that Adar 14 equated with Monday evening, whereas in fact Adar 15 started on Monday evening. (The Purim festival lasts for two days, Adar 14–15). Again there is a discrepancy of one day in Anne Catherine's communications with regard to the actual historical occurrence of the days of the Jewish calendar.

Then comes the calendar indication for the Passover meal, for which Jesus and his disciples gathered at Lazarus' castle. This feast, which is always on the evening of Nisan 15, was on Tuesday evening (LHHJC ii, 415), which equated with Tuesday, March 27, A.D. 31. This means that Nisan 1 began on the evening of Tuesday, March 13, A.D. 31, which agrees with our findings, thus confirming the authenticity of this calendar indication for the Passover.

The last calendar indication in period (2) concerns the start of the Feast of Weeks on Wednesday evening (LHHJC iii, 83). The Feast of Weeks occurs on Sivan 6–7. Since Sivan 6 started on Wednesday evening, May 16 A.D. 31, it follows that Sivan 1 commenced on the evening of Friday, May 11, A.D. 31— again in agreement with our findings.

In summary, it emerges from the above that of the twenty calendar indications given by Anne Catherine in period (2), only three do not fit exactly with the established pattern. In these three cases, however, there is only a one-day variation from the otherwise consistent calendar pattern. As mentioned already, this one-day difference may well be due to the fact that Anne Catherine communicated her visions either on the same day on which she had them or on the day after. Overall, the calendar indications are in fact virtually completely consistent—mutually supporting—in accord with the actual months of the Hebrew calendar for the period of Anne Catherine's description of the ministry of Christ Jesus—on the whole, historically accurate indeed.

If any reader remains skeptical here, it is worthwhile to consider the odds of the foregoing calendar indications being arbitrary. Summarizing the foregoing: the first thirteen calendar indications are correct, and of the last seven indications three display a one-day discrepancy. What is the probability of making a correct indication of the weekday for a given date? The answer is obviously one in seven. To give the correct weekday twice in a row is $1/7 \times 1/7$, i.e., one in 49. Similarly, to be able to say the correct day of the week for given historical dates three times in a row is $1/7 \times 1/7 \times 1/7 =$ one in 343. And the probability of indicating the correct weekday thirteen times in a row is one in 96,889,010,407 or almost one in 100 billion. Further, the probability of giving the sequence she did, in which seventeen of the twenty weekdays are correct, is one in 373,996,603,229,683. Technically the odds should be reduced by a factor of seven, since one of her weekday indications was pivotal in the correlation with the actual historical weekdays, but even reducing by a factor of seven, the odds are still enormous, the first figure being one in 13,841,287,201 (one in 14 billion) and the second one in 53,428,086,175,669 (one in 53 trillion). The only possible conclusion is that Anne Catherine's calendar indications are true (albeit sometimes with a one-day discrepancy). It is upon this scientifically verifiable foundation that the chronicle of the life of Christ presented in this book is based.

Appendix IV: A Summary of the Chronicle

In the following summary of Anne Catherine's chronicle of the ministry, it will emerge that the last part of the reconstruction of the chronicle discussed in Appendix III can be viewed in another way. In that appendix we specified four periods extending over four years, starting with Jesus' first major journey, which took place during the first half of the month of Sivan in A.D. 29:

> Period 1 : Sivan A.D. 29–Elul A.D. 29 (up to the baptism)
> Period 2 : Tishri A.D. 29–Tammuz A.D. 29 (up to the start of the
> missing period)
> Period 3 : Ab A.D. 31–Ab A.D. 32 (the missing period)
> Period 4 : Elul A.D. 32–Sivan A.D. 33 (up to Whitsun/Pentecost)

In the analysis of Anne Catherine Emmerich's calendar indications undertaken in Appendix III, it was shown she gave a number of calendar indications for Period 2 that are consistent and mutually supporting. These indications, taken together with her regular reference to the seven-day (Sabbath) rhythm running throughout the chronicle, enabled us to determine this part of the chronicle with great exactitude; e.g., it can be said with a high degree of certainty that the feeding of the five thousand took place on the afternoon of Monday, January 29, A.D. 31, the transfiguration on Mount Tabor on the night of April 3/4, A.D. 31, etc. Since Period 1 and Period 2 were communicated together, i.e. consecutively, with the seven-day (Sabbath) rhythm running throughout, it is not unreasonable to extend the Sabbath rhythm backwards in time from the securely defined Period 2 to Period 1. In this way, for example, the date of the baptism on the morning of Elul 26, equating with Friday, September 23, A.D. 29, is obtained (see Table 2 in the first part of this book). Comparing the derived historical dates for the events in Periods 1 and 2 with the calendar dates upon which Anne Catherine communicated these events, a pattern emerges:

EVENT	HISTORICAL DATE	CALENDAR DATE OF A.C.E
baptism	September 23	September 28
feeding of the 5000	January 29	February 3
transfiguration	April 3/4	April 8/9

It is evident that a simple five-day difference exists between the calendar date on which Anne Catherine made her communication and the historical date in the Julian calendar. This five-day difference holds throughout Periods 1 and 2. But it should be recalled here that during the last part of Period 2 Anne Catherine was obliged to re-narrate the course of the ministry after Clemens Brentano had been away for almost six months. The last eleven weeks of Period 2 were communicated in this way. For example, what she related on the morning of Sunday, December 7, 1823, referred to what she had seen the day before, and was a *repetition* of what she had seen *originally* on Saturday, June 14, 1823, during Clemens Brentano's absence. In this period of almost eleven weeks leading up to Anne Catherine's death, Brentano always dated the text with the earlier (original) date, thus maintaining continuity of dates throughout Period 2.

Is the account of the chronicle in these last eleven weeks of Period 2, as re-narrated almost six months later, as reliable as the account for the preceding part of the chronicle? This question has often been raised because it was during this time that Anne Catherine spoke of a journey Jesus undertook to Cyprus that lasted five weeks: from Wednesday, April 25, to Thursday, May 31, A.D. 31. (The dates recorded by Brentano were Wednesday, April 30, to Thursday, June 5, 1823). Since there is no record of such a journey in the Four Gospels, doubt has naturally been cast upon this account.

Of crucial importance for determining the reliability of Anne Catherine's account of this period is her communication concerning the celebration of the Feast of Weeks, which took place when Jesus was on the island of Cyprus. As with all her communications, the seven-day (Sabbath) rhythm forms the backbone of the chronicle because it specifies the weekdays. For the eleven weeks under consideration at the end of Period 2, the Sabbath rhythm continues on smoothly from the preceding part. On the morning of Thursday, November 13, 1823, Anne Catherine narrated her vision of the Feast of Weeks, which Brentano dated as representing a "repetition" of what she had experienced on Wednesday, May 21, 1823. Subtracting five days to obtain the historical date gives Wednesday, May 16, A.D. 31. Anne Catherine's description for this day included the preparations for the Feast of Weeks, which is celebrated on Sivan 6 and Sivan 7 in the Hebrew calendar, fifty days after Passover (Nisan 15). She saw Jesus at the town of Mallep, in the middle of the north side of Cyprus. There was a Jewish colony living there. Preparations were being made for the start of the Feast of Weeks that evening, which Jesus attended in the synagogue in Mallep. This would indicate that Sivan 6 started at dusk on the evening of Wednesday, May 16 A.D. 31; and indeed, it is evident from the table of the reconstructed Hebrew calendar in Appendix III that Sivan 6 A.D. 31 did start on a Wednesday evening. This strongly confirms that, despite the time-lag of almost six months in the reporting of her visions, Anne Catherine's account for the last eleven weeks of Period 2 is as reliable as her earlier revelations.

We now come to Period 3, the "missing period"—that part of the ministry unreported by Anne Catherine due to her untimely death. It was during this "missing period" that the events described in Chapters 7, 8, 9, and 10 of Saint John's Gospel took place, including the healing in Jerusalem of the man born blind. According to the description in Chapter 9 of the Gospel of Saint John, this healing took place on the Sabbath, i.e. either on a Friday evening, or on a Saturday morning or afternoon before sunset. As discussed in the first part of the book, the calendar indications given in Chapter 7 (Feast of Tabernacles) and Chapter 10 (Feast of Dedication) of Saint John's Gospel, permit us to establish that this healing took place after Friday, September 28, and before Thursday, November 29, A.D. 31. The earliest possibility would have been Saturday, September 29, A.D. 31; but this would entail compressing into the space of one day (before sunset) all that is described in Chapter 8 as well as the healing of the blind man in Chapter 9. Alternatively, the following dates (Friday/Saturday) are possible for this healing in A.D. 31: October 5/6, October 12/13, October 19/20, October 26/27, November 2/3, November 9/10, November 16/17, and November 23/24. Since Jesus was in Jerusalem at some time both before and after the healing, the first Sabbath (October 5/6) and the last Sabbath (November 23/24) seem more likely possibilities, as it is unlikely that he remained in Jerusalem the whole time, because of the persecution directed against him there. Further research will be necessary to penetrate more accurately into the details of the "missing period," but this example gives some indication of the method employed.

Let us now turn our attention to Period 4: the eight months leading up to the crucifixion and the following two months until Whitsun. It is only the eight months leading up to the crucifixion that will occupy us, since these belong to the ministry, and Anne Catherine communicated the seven-day (Sabbath) rhythm running more or less continuously throughout this period. Having determined the date of the crucifixion as Friday, April 3, A.D. 33 (see Appendix I), it is a simple matter to historically date Anne Catherine's account of Period 4 by retracing the Sabbath rhythm retrospectively. In this way, the raising of Lazarus, described in Chapter 11 of Saint John's Gospel, is found to have occurred on the morning of Saturday, October 11, A.D. 32. (However, as we shall soon see, this was not the correct date.)

As for Periods 1 and 2, where there is a correspondence between the historical dates and the actual calendar dates on which Anne Catherine made her communications—the historical dates being obtained simply by subtracting five days from the calendar dates—for Period 4, does this correspondence also seem to hold true? This is evident in the case of the following two examples:

EVENT	HISTORICAL DATE	CALENDAR DATE OF A.C.E
raising of Lazarus	October 11 A.D. 32	October 7
crucifixion	April 3 A.D. 33	March 30

The correlation shows that the historical date is given by adding four days to the calendar date on which Anne Catherine communicated the event in question. It will emerge that, whereas this correspondence holds good for the latter part of Period 4 leading up to the crucifixion, it becomes questionable for the early part of Period 4 to which belongs the raising of Lazarus.

If it is accepted that this simple correspondence (adding 4 days) applies to the whole of Period 4, it must be concluded that the date of the raising of Lazarus was October 11, A.D. 32, as just mentioned. In order to consider this date more closely, however, it is necessary to look at all of Period 4 leading up to the crucifixion. Let us do so on the assumption that October 11, A.D. 32, is the correct date—that is, let us assume that the correspondence (adding 4 days) applies to the whole of Period 4 just as the other correspondence (subtracting 5 days) applies to the whole of Periods 1 and 2.

After he raised Lazarus Jesus had to flee because the news caused a great uproar in Jerusalem that led to the Pharisees' determination to have him put to death. Anne Catherine described how he left Bethany and went with the apostles back to Galilee, travelling up the east side of the Jordan to the town of Chorazin, north-east of the Sea of Galilee. On October 12, 1820, she saw Jesus with his apostles and disciples in Chorazin. Adding four days, this would yield the historical date October 16, A.D. 32—five days after the raising of Lazarus. Here in Chorazin she heard Jesus describe to the apostles and disciples that he would now part company with them and go on a journey. He told them to which towns they should go and teach, and which towns they should avoid. According to Anne Catherine, he also said that he would be away for about three months, and that they should then meet him at Jacob's Well near Sychar. In the Jewish calendar the historical date October 16, A.D. 32, equates with Tishri 23; adding three months gives Tebeth 23, which equates with the historical date January 14, A.D. 33. Now, on January 9, 1821 Anne Catherine was in an ecstatic condition and suddenly cried out joyfully: "O! He has arrived there! How joyfully they go up to welcome him! He is at Jacob's Well. They are weeping for joy. They are washing his feet, and the feet of the disciples. There are about twelve here from this region, young shepherds who accompanied him to Cedar; also Peter, Andrew, John, James, Philip and one other! They were expecting him here" (LHHJC iii, 348). Adding four days gives as the historical date of Jesus' arrival at Jacob's Well, January 13, A.D. 33, equating with Tebeth 22. This corresponds exactly to the statement concerning a three-month period of absence owing to a journey, and seems to confirm the simple rule of four days taken as our basic assumption for Period 4.

This assumption becomes questionable, however, if Anne Catherine's account of the journey is taken seriously; it is evident that it would have been impossible to accomplish the journey in three months. In order to investigate this, let us look in detail at her description of the journey, determining dates simply by adding four days to the calendar dates on which she described its various stages. (Note: since this journey is not described in Helmut Fahsel's *Der Wandel Jesu in der Welt*, the original 1860 edition of *Das Leben unseres Herrn und Heilandes Jesu Christi nach den Gesichten der gottseligen Anna Katharina Emmerich aufgeschrieben von Clemens Brentano* has been consulted [abbreviated LHHJC].)

Preliminary remarks:

According to the correspondence described above, it was in Chorazin on Thursday, October 16, A.D. 32, that Anne Catherine Emmerich beheld a preview of the journey made by Jesus. After describing him visiting many towns (mostly unnamed), she said: "I also perceived that Jesus would go to Egypt and visit Heliopolis, where he had lived as a child. . . . He will return from the other side, via Hebron. . . . Jesus stated he would be away about three months. They would then definitely find him again at Jacob's Well near Sychar" (LHHJC iii, 251).

Further applying the correspondence of adding four days, we arrive at the following table of events belonging to the journey made by Jesus.

Dates obtained by applying the rule of adding four days; description of the main stages of Jesus' journey:

A.D. *32:*

Th. October 16. Jesus, in Chorazin, told the disciples he was going on a journey.

Sa. October 18. This evening Jesus went to Bethsaida with Andrew, Peter and Philip. They traveled by moonlight.

Mo. October 20. Jesus and the three apostles traveled the whole day and part of the night through East Galilee to the land of the Amorites (Basan).

Tu. October 21. In Basan three youths and a group of disciples met up with Jesus. Jesus said "that he and the three youths would travel alone through Chaldea and the land of Ur, where Abraham had been born, and would go through Arabia to Egypt. The disciples should spread out and teach here and there within the boundaries [of Palestine]; he would also teach wherever he went. Once again he specified that they would meet at Jacob's Well after three months." (LHHJC iii, 254)

We. October 22. At daybreak Jesus parted company with the apostles and disciples. They were much downcast. Jesus wanted to take only the three youths with him, who were sixteen to eighteen years old.

Fr. October 24. Jesus and the three youths arrived in Cedar, not far from the easternmost boundary of Israel, where they celebrated the Sabbath in the synagogue.

Tu. November 25. After teaching for one month in and around Cedar, Jesus and the three youths left Cedar and set off east across the desert.

Fr. December 12. Jesus arrived at the tent-city of the three kings, where they had settled after returning to Chaldea from Bethlehem. Only two of the kings (Mensor and Theokeno) were still alive, the third (Sair) died some years previously. Jesus was met by Mensor; Theokeno was bedridden.

Tu. December 16. Jesus left the two kings and journeyed further east, accompanied by the three youths.

Th. December 18. They arrived in the town of Atom, Chaldea.

Su. December 21. Jesus left Atom and traveled southeast, arriving at Sikdor that evening.

Mo. December 22. Jesus and the three youths, having been joined by a fourth youth, left Sikdor and, traveling past Babylon on the Euphrates, went east to Mozian on the Tigiris, arriving on the evening of Tuesday, December 23.

We. December 24. Jesus and his companions left Mozian and traveled south toward Ur, the birthplace of Abraham.

Fr. December 26. Toward evening they arrived in Ur, the journey time from Mozian to Ur being about thirty hours.

Su. December 28. This morning Jesus and the four youths left Ur and traveled west.

We. December 31. In the evening Jesus and the four youths arrived at a town in Egypt.

A.D. *33:*

Th. January 1.   They left this town and traveled toward Heliopolis.

Fr. January 2.   Around 4 P.M. they arrived in Heliopolis, where Jesus had been as a child.

Su. January 4.   In the morning they left Heliopolis and went east toward Palestine.

Th. January 8.   In the evening they arrived in Beersheba in Israel, and journeyed further the next morning toward Hebron.

Fr. January 9.   Toward evening they arrived at Bethain near Hebron, where they celebrated the Sabbath in the synagogue. They left Bethain after the close of the Sabbath on the evening of January 10, and traveled north toward Sychar.

Tu. January 13. Having traveled by night to avoid being seen, Jesus and the youths arrived by dawn at Jacob's Well.

A glance at the main stages of the journey to Chaldea and Egypt from Israel and back, as described by Anne Catherine, shows that the first part of the journey, from Cedar to Ur, could conceivably have been accomplished in the time stated, but that the journey from Ur to Egypt would have been impossible in the time allowed. According to the account, Jesus left Ur on the morning of Sunday, December 28, and arrived at a town in Egypt on the evening of

Wednesday, December 31, A.D. 32, *three days later.* Since the entire journey from Palestine to Ur, with stopovers at various places, took one month (from Cedar, November 25 to Ur, December 26), the far longer journey from Ur to Egypt could not possibly have been accomplished in so short a time-span.

It may be helpful to consider the approximate distances involved:

JOURNEY	DISTANCE	TIME ALLOWED IN A.C.E
Cedar to Ur	over 600 miles	31 1/2 days
Ur to Heliopolis	over 900 miles	5 1/2 days

As we contemplate this riddle, consider the following words of Anne Catherine, in which she describes the transition in her visions from Chaldea to Egypt: "Since yesterday evening I did not see Jesus and the youths stop anywhere. They traveled continuously, to begin with in the open, sandy desert, then traversing gently climbing hills, then in a land with more green..." (LHHJC iii, 341). It seems that the day-by-day account of the long journey through the Arabian desert is simply compressed into one night in her vision. The impression of a break at this point in the continuity of Anne Catherine's narrative is strengthened by the fact that up to this point the Sabbath is explicitly mentioned every seven days, whereas at Jesus' arrival in Heliopolis (according to her account on a Friday, shortly before the start of the Sabbath) the Sabbath is not mentioned. All that is said is that on that evening "the Lord was led into the synagogue by a very old man.... I saw Jesus teach and pray." And on the next day, "Jesus taught again in the synagogue" (LHHJC iii, 345). In fact, this probably was the Sabbath, since Jesus was in the synagogue that evening and the following morning, but it is not explicitly stated, whereas prior to this, throughout the journey to Ur in Chaldea, the Sabbath is explicitly referred to every seven days.

A closer scrutiny of the text, however, reveals a solution, but it means discounting the statement that Anne Catherine attributed to Jesus: that he would be away "about three months" (LHHJC iii, 251), and that the apostles should meet him at Jacob's Well near Sychar after three months (LHHJC iii, 254). The above-tabulated chronicle of Jesus' journey fits this specification of three months exactly. Nevertheless, the three months do *not* conform to another indication made by Anne Catherine, one that we have hitherto ignored on account of its uncertainty. This is the statement she made on Monday or Tuesday, November 6 or 7, 1820, referring to Jesus' stay in the town of Sichar-Cedar not far from the easternmost boundary of Israel:

> There began one of the first festivals which God commanded the Israelites to celebrate; I believe it was the New Moon festival. It was held that evening in the synagogue. (LHHJC iii, 273)

On the assumption that the rule of adding four days to Anne Catherine's calendar dates holds here also, Monday or Tuesday, November 6 or 7, would equate historically with Monday or Tuesday, November 10 or 11, A.D. 32. However, referring to the table of the reconstructed Hebrew calendar in Appendix III, it can be seen that these dates equate with Heshvan 18 or 19 in the Jewish calendar—nowhere near day 1 of the month! This statement concerning the New Moon festival (celebrated evening, at the commencement of day 1 at the start of a new Jewish month) does not fit then with the rule of adding four days.

But what if we take this problematic calendar indication seriously? If true, it would mean that Jesus was in Sichar-Cedar on a Monday or Tuesday on the evening of which day 1 of the new month in the Jewish calendar started. Let us therefore look through the table of the reconstructed Hebrew calendar in Appendix III to see if there was any Jewish month which started on a Monday or Tuesday in A.D. 32. We find two possibilities:

> Nisan 1, A.D. 32 started on the evening of Monday, March 31
> Elul 1, A.D. 32 started on the evening of Tuesday, August 26

The first case can be ruled out, since we may assume that Jesus must have been in Jerusalem for the Passover festival which started on Nisan 15 (April 15, A.D. 32). The second case is plausible, however, so let us assume that it is true, and, in light of this assumption, take a new look at Period 4.

As a starting point, we can reconsider the raising of Lazarus, which Anne Catherine described taking place on a Saturday morning, thirty-one days prior to the above-mentioned New Moon festival. Under our new assumption, the historical date of the raising of Lazarus would be thirty-one days prior to Tuesday, August 26—Saturday, July 26, A.D. 32. Under our old assumption (rule of adding four days) it took place on Saturday, October 11, A.D. 32, since, the calendar date on which Anne Catherine spoke of the raising of Lazarus was

Saturday, October 7. The old assumption was based on the rule: add four days; the new assumption yields the rule: subtract two months and twelve days (-73 days). The difference between the historical dates arrived at is therefore two months and sixteen days (-77 days). This period of two months and sixteen days is gained for the journey to Chaldea and Egypt if it is assumed that Anne Catherine's vision of the journey through the Arabian desert was compressed into one night. In other words, 2 1/2 months can be added to the journey time, so that the statement concerning a three-month absence can now be modified to 5 1/2 months. We need not go into the question whether 2 1/2 months was the actual journey time across the Arabian desert to Egypt, but it is certainly clear that the journey from Ur to Heliopolis and back to Beersheba in Israel becomes more plausible if two months and twenty-seven days are allowed rather than a mere eleven days.

There are two further minor points in Anne Catherine's description of the journey that support this new assumption. Referring to our summary of the main stages of the journey listed above, for the date Saturday, October 18, A.D. 32, we read: "This evening Jesus went to Bethsaida with Andrew, Peter and Philip. They traveled by moonlight." The thin waning crescent of the Moon rose on the eastern horizon only 3 3/4 hours before sunrise on the morning of Sunday, October 19, A.D. 32, so it was hardly possible to travel by moonlight that night. Under the new assumption, we have to go back two months and sixteen days from Saturday, October 18 to Saturday, August 2, A.D. 32. On that night the waxing Moon reached first quarter and so would have been high in the heavens at sunset, illuminating the journey that evening. For Tuesday, November 25, A.D. 32 (in our summary), we read: "Jesus and the three youths left Cedar and set off eastward across the desert." Anne Catherine also describes their arrival that evening at a heathen tent village, where a festival of star worship was being celebrated: "They cried out especially loudly as the Moon and other stars rose across the horizon" (LHHJC iii, 288). Since the waxing crescent of the New Moon was already visible above the horizon at sunset on the evening of Tuesday, November 25, A.D. 32, the foregoing statement does not really make sense. Under the new assumption, however, subtracting two months and sixteen days from November 25, we arrive at Tuesday, September 9, A.D. 32. On this evening the almost Full Moon rose across the eastern horizon some four hours after sunset.

There is yet another reason for believing that the new assumption is true. It concerns the raising of Lazarus, which, under this assumption, took place on Saturday morning, July 26, A.D. 32. Reading both Anne Catherine's account and that in the eleventh chapter of the Gospel of Saint John, one cannot help but get the impression that Jesus deliberately waited a few days before raising Lazarus from the dead. Why did he delay? As discussed in my book *The Star of the Magi and the Life of Christ*, there was a special cosmic configuration on the morning of Saturday, July 26, A.D. 32: a conjunction of the Sun and Moon with the Lion's heart (Regulus) in the constellation of Leo. It seems that Jesus deliberately waited for this special New Moon configuration before raising Lazarus from the dead. As described in my book, an earlier raising from the dead took place at Full Moon—again a special cosmic moment like the astronomical New Moon. This was the raising from the dead of the daughter of the Essene Jairus, which took place on February 7 A.D. 30, when the Moon was full in Leo.

But there is a complication. If the new assumption is accepted as true, Anne Catherine's report that Jesus said he would be away about three months does not hold good. In fact, however, there is a simple explanation for this statement about a three month absence; but in order to follow it we must take another look at Anne Catherine's entire revelation of the ministry, this time on the basis of the new assumption. Under these circumstances, a period of two months and sixteen days must be subtracted from all the dates prior to December 31, A.D. 32 in the above table listing the dates of Jesus' journey from Israel to Ur. Also, the four periods covered by her revelation need to be slightly amended as follows:

1) Sivan A.D. 29–Elul A.D. 29 (up to the baptism)
2) Tishri A.D. 29–Tammuz A.D. 31 (up to the start of the missing year)
3) Ab A.D. 31–Iyyar A.D. 32 (the missing period)
4a) Iyyar A.D. 32-Tebeth A.D. 32/33 (period including the raising of
      Lazarus and the journey to Chaldea and Egypt)
4b) Tebeth A.D. 32/33–Sivan A.D. 33 (from the return to Israel,
      to Pentecost /Whitsun, including the crucifixion)

Here the missing period, period (3), is reduced by 2 1/2 months; and period (4) is correspondingly lengthened by 2 1/2 months, which have been added to the journey time. Note that period (4) is now divided into two: 4a and 4b. The relationship between the calendar dates of Anne Catherine's communications and the historical dates, under the new assumption, is:

periods (1) and (2)   subtract 5 days
period (4a)   subtract 73 days (2 months and 12 days)
period (4b)   add 4 days

But how is it that the calendar dates of period (4a) of Anne Catherine's revelation of the ministry differ so much from the historical dates, whereas the calendar dates of most of her revelation harmonize so closely with the historical dates?

First, it should be noted that period (4a) was the very first period of the ministry communicated by Anne Catherine, starting in July 1820. But as early as September 1818 Clemens Brentano had been taking notes of much that Anne Catherine narrated from her visions. This period from September 1818 to July 1820 was plagued with difficulties that worked to prevent the free communication by Anne Catherine of her visions. (It must be remembered that she had visions from the Old and New Testaments almost continuously throughout her life.) It was only Brentano's patience and perseverance throughout all these difficulties that cleared the way and established the possibility of daily communications. During this time the visions communicated by Anne Catherine seem to have been drawn fairly randomly from the life of Christ. For example, on February 27, 1820, she had a vision of the transfiguration on Mount Tabor (LHHJC iii, 197–198), the historical date of which was the night of April 3/4, A.D. 31. Here the calendar date of her communication of this event is widely separated from the historical date. Then the regular daily communications of the ministry started suddenly on July 29, 1820, signifying the start of period (4a). It is not surprising, therefore, that the beginning of period (4a), which under the new assumption equates with the historical date May 17, A.D. 32, should also be widely separated in time from the calendar date of Anne Catherine's communications.

It was only during the course of the regular daily communications that a process of harmonization could take place, in which the calendar dates and the historical dates fell into step with one another, to become separated by a matter of only days. For this harmonization to take place, at some point a jump in the communications had to occur. All the evidence indicates that this was some time during the journey from Ur back to Israel (via Heliopolis). This "adjustment" entailed the loss of eleven weeks (77 days). Since 77 is a multiple of seven, the Sabbath rhythm could continue, as if in regular sequence; but the entire day-by-day account of the long journey through the Arabian desert was left out, having been compressed into a single day and night. Under this hypothesis the calendar indication (New Moon Festival) and details of astronomical phenomena referred to above are accounted for.

As Anne Catherine Emmerich often said, a higher intelligence was at work guiding her communications. Under the new hypothesis, it seems as though the omission of seventy-seven days was a calculated jump, planned in advance. And the statement concerning a three month absence from Israel does not refer to the actual journey time but to the calendar date on which Anne Catherine was to resume her description of the ministry after Jesus' return to Israel. What Anne Catherine saw was that in three months Jesus would be back in Israel at Jacob's Well near Sychar; but this refers to the timing of her visions. Since 2 1/2 months were omitted, the actual period of Jesus' absence was 5 1/2 months. However, as far as her *visions* were concerned it was three months, which would seem to explain her reference to a three month absence. This tentative conclusion will have to suffice until it is possible for further research in relation to the entirety of Emmerich's visions.

There still remain several questions concerning Jesus' journey to Chaldea and Egypt. For example, considering the great distance involved, would this journey have been physically possible? Anne Catherine repeatedly remarked, in her visions of Jesus' travels, her astonishment at the speed with which he walked. Although the distance from Israel to Ur to Heliopolis and back to Israel is great, it is not beyond the bounds of possibility that someone who was capable of walking swiftly for long distances could have accomplished the journey in 4 1/2 months. (4 1/2 months, since of the 5 1/2 months one month was spent at the beginning of the journey in and around Cedar not far from the easternmost boundary in Israel.) Nevertheless, other questions remain unanswered regarding the provisions needed by Jesus and his young traveling companions on their trek across the desert, a journey presumably made mainly by night because of the great heat. Why is there no mention of this journey in the Four Gospels or any other sources? And what could the purpose of this journey have been? Anne Catherine reported the following explanation given her by the intelligence (*angelos*) guiding her communications:

> I also received instruction as to why this journey of Jesus remained so concealed. I recall that Jesus said to his apostles and disciples that he wanted to withdraw somewhat in order to be forgotten. They themselves knew nothing of this journey. The Lord took only simple youths with him, who would not be outraged at the pagans and would not pay

attention to everything. I believe also that he strictly forbade them to speak about it, whereupon one of the youths responded naively: "Although you forbade the man born blind, after he received his sight, to say anything about it, he did so nevertheless, and he was not punished." Whereupon Jesus replied: "That took place to the glory of God, but this (journey) would give rise to much outrage." I understood that the Jews and even his apostles would have been outraged to a certain extent if they had learned that he had visited the pagans. (LHHJC iii, 330–331)

All that is said in the Gospel of Saint John, after the raising of Lazarus, is:

> Jesus therefore no longer went about openly among the Jews, but went from there to the country near the wilderness, to a town called Ephraim; and there he stayed with the disciples. Now the Passover of the Jews was at hand.... (John 11:54–55)

The impression here is that Jesus retreated for a time to a place near the desert, which is obviously the impression that the apostles and disciples had. But that he was away for 5 1/2 months, during which time he visited Chaldea and Egypt, is not in any way indicated in the text of *Saint John's Gospel* or in any other Gospel account. And after returning to Israel early in January A.D. 33, three more months elapsed before the Passover festival, at which the crucifixion and resurrection took place.

On the journey, according to Anne Catherine, Jesus gave instruction to the pagans and made it clear that he had come not only for the Jews but for them also. For the people of Israel, who were the pagans? The people of Egypt and Chaldea were the closest and most important ones. The father of Israel, Abraham, had been born in Ur in Chaldea, and the Jewish people had lived in Chaldea at the time of the Babylonian captivity. Chaldea was therefore of great significance to the people of Israel. Similarly, from the time of the patriarch Jacob, whose son Joseph had been sold as a slave and carried off to Egypt, the Jewish nation had lived in Egypt, until the exodus led by Moses. Jesus himself as a child had been obliged to flee Israel with his parents, because of Herod the Great, and the Holy Family had then lived for a time at Heliopolis in Egypt. So Egypt also represented an important station on the path of the people of Israel. The journey made by Jesus to Chaldea and Egypt retraced the path of the people of Israel, a path retraced immediately prior to the last three months of the life of the Messiah in Israel, leading

up to the Mystery of Golgotha. This journey by the Son of God was therefore a brief recapitulation of the steps made by God's chosen people just
before the sacrifice on Golgotha, which represented the culmination of the
history of Israel.

Another reason for this journey by Jesus was to visit the three kings who
had paid homage to him as a child. After the three kings had left Bethlehem,
they went south of the Dead Sea and returned east, toward Babylon, across
the desert. But before reaching Babylon they stopped at a place in pleasant
surroundings and settled there, living in tents. Just as they had been warned
in a dream not to return to Herod, so too they received instruction to settle
at this place and wait for the King of the Jews to visit them there. However,
when Jesus came, only two of the three kings were still alive: Mensor (Melchior) and Theokeno (Casper); the third king, Sair (Balthasar) had died nine
years before. Mensor and Theokeno, by now very old, were overjoyed when
Jesus told them that he was the child they had visited so many years ago.

Jesus told them that he had come for the pagans as well as for the Jews,
that he had come for all who believed in him. The two kings then said that
it was now time for them to leave their land; after having waited so long,
they wanted to accompany Jesus on his return to Judea. Jesus replied that
his kingdom is not of this world. Moreover, he said that they would only
take offense and be shaken in their belief if they were to see how he would
be despised and mistreated by the Jews. He spoke of his mission, now
approaching its end, and that it was a secret withheld from the Jews that he
was there with them. The Jews would have already murdered him if he had
not slipped away. But he had wanted to come and see the kings, because of
their faith, hope and love, before being delivered up and put to death. He
said that three years after his return to the Heavenly Father, he would send
his disciples to them. And indeed, three years later, the apostles Thomas and
Judas Thaddeus came to the two remaining kings and baptized them, as
well as others living there. According to the account by Anne Catherine,
Mensor was baptized *Leandor* and Theokeno was christened *Leo* (LHHJC
iii, 305–306, 318, 576–577).

Anne Catherine's account of Jesus' journey to the three (or rather, two)
kings, and thence to Ur and Heliopolis before returning to Israel, adds a new
dimension to our understanding of the life of the Messiah. The three kings
had been the first to recognize and acknowledge his coming, a fact that
implies he came not just as the Saviour of the people of Israel, but of all who
believe in him. And this is confirmed explicitly by Jesus' journey outside of

Israel, undertaken toward the end of his ministry, immediately prior to the last three months prior to his death.

Much of Jesus' last three months was spent in Jerusalem and Bethany, during which time the confrontation with the Pharisees built to a climax. At the start of the month of Adar, on the evening of Thursday, February 19, A.D. 33, six weeks prior to the Last Supper, Jesus went to Jerusalem, where he remained—either in Bethany or Jerusalem—until the crucifixion. Four weeks later, toward the end of the month of Adar, on the 28th (Thursday, March 19, A.D. 33), Jesus made his triumphant entry into Jerusalem. This event actually occurred two weeks prior to the Last Supper. (Traditionally it is celebrated on Palm Sunday, in the belief that it took place just four days prior to the celebration of the Last Supper on Maundy Thursday.) On the day of his triumphant entry into Jerusalem, there was a total eclipse of the Sun.

Jesus had taught at the temple in Jerusalem during much of this last six-week period, but intensified his teaching activity after making his triumphant entry into the city on a donkey. During these last two weeks he taught in two different ways, depending on the nature of his auditors. When the scribes and Pharisees were present, he attacked them for their hypocrisy and lack of humility, as, for example, in the words of Chapter 23 of the Gospel of Saint Matthew, that he spoke in the temple on Tuesday, March 24, A.D. 33. When speaking to his apostles and disciples alone, however, he gave instruction concerning the future, as in the words of Chapter 24 of the Gospel of Saint Matthew, that he spoke on the Mount of Olives on Thursday, March 26, A.D. 33. Sometimes he was able to teach the apostles and disciples in the temple without being disturbed by the presence of the scribes and Pharisees, as on the last occasion that he taught there (Tuesday, March 31 A.D. 33), when he spoke of the truth and fulfillment of his teachings. He went on to say that now he must *fulfill* what he had taught: It is not enough simply to believe; one must also fulfill one's belief. No one, not even the Pharisees, could accuse him of having taught anything false. Now, however, he wanted to fulfill the truth he had taught, and must ascend to the Father. Before departing, though, he wanted to bestow upon them all that he had. He had neither money nor possessions, but wanted to give them his might and his powers, to found a union with them to the end of time—a still more inward union than the present one. He wanted also to unite all of them together as members of one body (LHHJC iii, 415). Then, on the evening of the Last Supper, he instituted the holy sacrament, saying: "Now a new era and a new sacrifice is beginning, which will last until the end of the world" (BL, 83–84). With the Last Supper the ministry of Christ Jesus came to a close, and his Passion began, lasting until the following afternoon and culminating in the death on the cross at 3:00 P.M. on Friday, April 3 A.D. 33.

Appendix V: John the Baptist

According to the Gospel of Luke (1:26) the conception of Jesus took place six months after the conception of John the Baptist. For this reason, since the traditional date of celebration of the birth of Jesus is December 24/25, the birth of John is celebrated six months prior to this, on June 24. From the research presented in Part I of this book, the birth of the Nathan Jesus is dated to December 6/7, so the birth of John the Baptist probably took place about six months earlier, around June 6. Is it possible, however, to determine the birth date more precisely? The following offers an affirmative answer to this question, based on the astrological research described below.

Anne Catherine's statement that "the birth of John the Baptist would have happened at the end of May or the beginning of June" (LBVM, 163)—taken together with astrological considerations—indicates that his birth took place on June 4, 2 B.C., shortly after midnight (12:37 A.M. in Jutta). The birth of John the Baptist therefore took place almost exactly six months prior to the birth of the Nathan Jesus (Luke 1:36). At that time the Sun was at 12 1/2° Gemini, the Ascendant was 16 1/2° Pisces, and the Moon (3° Cancer) was in conjunction with Mercury (0° Cancer) and Mars (2° Cancer)—see Chart 13, p. 158. Applying the hermetic-astrological rule, the moment of conception can be computed retrospectively to 1:59 P.M. local time in Jutta on September 9, 3 B.C. At this moment the Ascendant was 3° Capricorn (opposite the Moon at birth), the Moon was at 16 1/2° Virgo (opposite the Ascendant at birth), and the Sun was at 17° Virgo (see Chart 14, p. 159). It is evident that the conception took place at New Moon (Sun conjunct Moon) in the middle of Virgo, and that the birth took place 267 1/2 days later, on June 3/4, 1 1/2 days after the day of the New Moon (June 2, 2 B.C.).

As in the case of the two Marys and the Nathan Jesus, the conception of John the Baptist was also, in a cosmic sense, an "immaculate conception," for it occurred at the New Moon. It took place when the Sun and Moon were aligned in the middle of the sidereal sign of Virgo. This same cosmic axis (middle of Virgo to middle of Pisces) aligns with the Full Moon (15°

Virgo) at the birth of the Solomon Jesus, the Sun (16° Virgo) at the birth of the Solomon Mary, the Sun (16° Pisces) and Moon (12° Pisces) at the conception of the Nathan Jesus, and the Sun (16° Pisces) at the birth of the Solomon Jesus. Moreover, the Sun (12 1/2° Gemini) at the birth of John the Baptist was on the opposite side of the sidereal zodiac to the Sun and Moon (18° Sagittarius) at the conception of the Solomon Mary and to the Sun (16° Sagittarius) at the birth of the Nathan Jesus. Thus a cosmic cross is formed in the heavens by the position of the Sun at the birth of John the Baptist, the Solomon Mary and the two Jesus children (see Figure below). One axis of the cross is established by the polarity: John the Baptist (12 1/2° Gemini) and the Nathan Jesus (16° Sagittarius); the other by the polarity: Solomon Mary (16° Virgo) and the Solomon Jesus (16° Pisces).

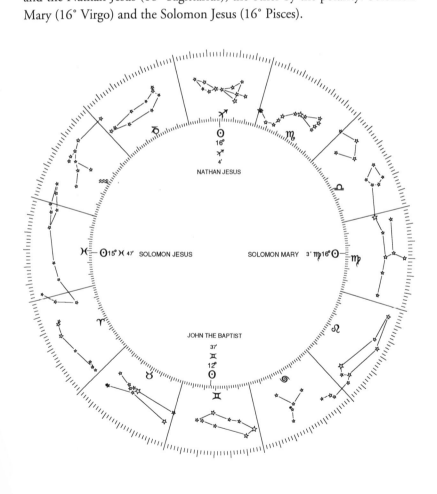

The reader may ask whether there are any textual sources that support the above dates of conception and birth of John the Baptist, derived by astrological research.

Given that the birth of the Nathan Jesus took place on December 6/7, 2 B.C., and given the statement that John the Baptist was six months older than the Nathan Jesus (Gospel of Saint Luke, 1:36), the date June 3/4 for the birth of John the Baptist is quite plausible. The striking planetary configuration of a conjunction between the Moon, Mercury and Mars on the night June 3/4 fits John the Baptist astrologically as the active, inspiring preacher. Concerning the conception of John the Baptist, Luke, 1:5,8 states that at the time of the annunciation of the conception, Zechariah, the father of John the Baptist, was serving in the Temple. According to Ormond Edwards, on the basis of his analysis of the reference to the "priestly course of Abijah" (Luke 1:5), this would have been in the period Elul 28 to Tishri 4 in the Jewish Calendar (TC, 83). Tishri 1 in the year 3 B.C. probably started when the new crescent Moon became visible on the western horizon on the evening of September 10. As the astronomical New Moon (conjunction of Sun and Moon) took place in the early afternoon of September 9, the conception of John the Baptist, assuming that it coincided with the New Moon, would have fallen on Elul 28 in the year 3 B.C. Presumably Zechariah had traveled from his home in Jutta on Elul 27 (during the day of September 8) in order to be at the Temple in Jerusalem for the commencement of his priestly duties on the evening of September 8 (the start of Elul 28). The annunciation of the conception of a son to Zechariah may well have taken place early on the evening of September 9—around the start of Elul 29—since the Gospel of Saint Luke (1:10) states that it was the "hour of incense." If this is true, the annunciation did in fact occur, according to the texts, shortly after the time of conception as determined astrologically.

Taking the horoscopes of conception and birth of John the Baptist as provisionally established, let us now apply the method of astrological biography to his life. The three central events referred to in the Gospels, are:

(1) The start of his ministry: "The word of God came to John the son of Zechariah in the wilderness; and he went into all the region about the Jordan, preaching a baptism of repentance for the forgiveness of sins" (Luke 3:2–3)

(2) The baptism of Jesus in the Jordan (Luke 3:21–23)

(3) The death of John the Baptist (Matthew 14:1–12)

With regard to (1), Anne Catherine Emmerich indicates that the start of the ministry of John the Baptist may be dated to the last day of the Passover festival in A.D. 29, which equates with April 24, A.D. 29. Similarly, in Part I the date of the baptism in the Jordan was determined to be Friday, September 23, A.D. 29. From the chronicle in Part II it is evident that the date of John's death, which took place on the evening of Herod Antipas' birthday, was January 3/4, A.D. 31.

For these three events, the following table lists the age of John the Baptist and the corresponding "embryonic age" in terms of the Moon's position in the sidereal zodiac.

AGE	MOON'S POSITION IN SIDEREAL ZODIAC	CORRESPONDING DATE IN EMBRYONIC PERIOD
1) 29 yrs 10 mos	4 orbits + 94° = 20 1/2° Sagittarius	January 4, 2 B.C., 3:00 P.M.
2) 30 yrs 3 1/2 mos	4 orbits + 118° = 14 1/2° Capricorn	January 6, 2 B.C., 12:00 P.M.
3) 31 yrs 7 mos	4 orbits + 184° = 20 1/2° Pisces	January 11, 2 B.C., 7:30 A.M.

At the embryonic correspondence (1), the corresponding embryonic zodiacal location of the Sun was 15° Capricorn, conjunct the conception position of Mars (14 1/2° Capricorn). This fits very well astrologically with the image of "the word of God" coming to John (Mars being the "planet of the word"), for John's was a ministry of preaching and baptizing. The *raison d'etre* of John's ministry was to prepare the way for the coming of the Messiah. It is he who is referred to—albeit indirectly—in the last passage of the last book of the Old Testament: "Behold, I will send you Elijah the prophet before the great and terrible day of the Lord comes" (Malachi 4:5). For, as Jesus said to James, Peter, and John after descending the Mount of Transfiguration: "I tell you that Elijah has already come, and they did not know him, but did to him whatever they pleased. So also the Son of Man will suffer at their hands. Then the disciples understood that he was speaking to them of John the Baptist" (Matthew 17:12–13). The Old Testament prophet Elijah (I Kings 17 –21, II Kings 1–11, II Chronicles 21:12–15), who lived in the ninth century B.C., reincarnated as John the Baptist in order to "prepare the way of the Lord, to make his paths straight" (Matthew 3:3).

The crowning point of the ministry of John the Baptist came at ten o'clock on the morning of Friday, September 23, A.D. 29, when Jesus came down to the Jordan to be baptized, and "the heaven was opened, and the

Holy Spirit descended upon him in bodily form, as a dove, and a voice came from heaven saying, 'Thou art my beloved Son, today I have begotten thee'" (Luke 3:21–22). At that moment Christ, the Logos, united with Jesus of Nazareth, and the ministry of the God-Man began.

In embryonic correspondence (2) of the astrological biography of John the Baptist, the Sun (17° Capricorn) and the Moon (14 1/2° Capricorn) were in conjunction, signifying the commencement of a new phase in his biography. Indeed, the further life of John the Baptist was devoted to proclaiming Christ Jesus, "the Lamb of God, who bears the sins of the world" (John 1:29). The position of the Moon at the embryonic moment in question was 14 1/2° Capricorn, in conjunction with the sidereal location of Mars (14 1/2° Capricorn) at the conception. Shortly after the baptism, John withdrew from the place of baptism (near Ono) and returned to another place on the Jordan (near Gilgal), and thence to a place still further north (near Ainon), where he had first commenced baptizing at the start of his ministry. He discontinued baptizing, but continued to preach, speaking always of Jesus. He also denounced Herod Antipas as an adulterer, thus arousing the fury of Herodias. Many of John's disciples went to join Jesus, whose own disciples had begun to baptize, and a controversy arose concerning differences in purity between the two baptisms. This controversy took place during May, A.D. 30. As Jesus now had so many disciples, John the Baptist's remaining few complained that everyone was going to Jesus (John 3:26). John's reply was that he had come to bear witness as the forerunner of the Messiah (John 3:26–36). It was on this occasion that he spoke the words: "He must increase, but I must decrease" (John 3:30). All of these events—the controversy, the testimony of John the Baptist, the multitude that flocked to be baptized by Jesus' disciples—also aroused the hostility of the Pharisees, who dispatched letters to the elders of all the synagogues throughout the land, directing them to take Jesus and his disciples into custody.

About this time Herod Antipas imprisoned John the Baptist in his castle at Callirrhoe, but let him go six weeks later. However, in the summer of A.D. 30, exactly 46 years after the birthnight of the Nathan Mary (July 17/18), Herod imprisoned John again, this time in his castle at Machaerus. At the festivities at Machaerus to celebrate Herod's birthday, Salome, the daughter of Herodias, danced. After beholding the wild spectacle of Salome dancing before him, Herod said to her: "Ask of me what you will, and I will give it to you. Yes, I swear, even if you ask for half of my kingdom, I shall give it to you." Salome hurriedly conferred with her mother, who instructed her to ask for the head of John the Baptist on a dish, and John was then beheaded (Mark 6:17–29). This took place during the night of January 3/4 A.D. 31, or Tebeth 20 (Herod's birthday) in the Jewish calendar.

Looking now at embryonic correspondence (3) to the death of John the Baptist, Venus and Jupiter were in opposition along the axis of the Moon's nodes (Venus conjunct the Moon's north node, and Jupiter conjunct the Moon's descending node); and the Moon itself was in conjunction with Uranus. In the planetary configuration of the actual death of John the Baptist on January 3/4, A.D. 31, the Sun was at 14 1/2° Capricorn, exactly conjunct the sidereal location of Mars (14 1/2° Capricorn) at the conception (see Chart 15, p. 160). And Mars (28 1/2° Pisces) was in conjunction with the location of Uranus (28 1/2° Pisces) at the birth of John the Baptist. Moreover, Mars (28 1/2° Pisces) was in opposition to the Moon (approximately 27° Virgo) at the death of John the Baptist. The Moon's longitude (27° Virgo) is accurate for midnight January 3/4. If the beheading occurred before midnight, it would have been less—that is, at 10:00 P.M. it would have been 26° Virgo—and correspondingly the opposition between the Moon and Mars would have been less exact. If the death occurred after midnight, the Moon's longitude would have been greater—at 2:00 A.M. it would have been 28° Virgo—and the opposition between the Moon and Mars would have been more exact.

It remains now to determine the dates of "cosmic commemoration" of the conception, birth and death of John the Baptist. Since at these three events the Sun's sidereal longitude was 17° Virgo, 12 1/2° Gemini, and 14 1/2° Capricorn respectively, the question is when, at the present time, does the Sun reach these sidereal locations in the zodiac? It reaches 14 1/2° Capricorn on January 29. This, then, is the date of the cosmic commemoration of the death of John the Baptist. Similarly, the date of the cosmic commemoration of his birth is June 28/29, when the Sun arrives at 12 1/2° Gemini. Lastly, the cosmic commemoration of the conception of John the Baptist takes place on October 4/5, on which date the Sun at the present time is located at 17° Virgo. The 2,000th anniversary of the cosmic commemoration of the conception of John will be October 5, 1998; of his birth, June 29, 1999; and of his death, January 29, 2031 (see Table, p.143).

*Appendix VI: Tabulation of Dates of the 3 1/2 Years of Christ's Ministry
Equated with Corresponding Modern Dates of the Last 3 1/2 Years within
the Present 33 1/3- Year Cycle at the End of the Twentieth Century*

Following is a tabulation of modern dates for the last part of the present 33
1/3-year cycle of the life of Christ in relation to the corresponding historical
dates. With the help of these dates it is possible to relive the Chronicle in a
meditative way day by day: for example, contemplating the baptism in the
Jordan (historical date: Friday, September 23 A.D. 29) on Saturday, February
24, 1996; the changing of water into wine at the wedding at Cana (historical
date: Wednesday, December 28 A.D. 29) on Thursday, May 30, 1996; and
so on; whereby the dates are an approximate guideline, since the actual
etheric recurrence may vary slightly from the given date.

In fact, for the sake of more readily enabling a reliving of the Chronicle
from day to day, the commemoration of events can be undertaken *on the
same weekday on which they occurred.* For example, as the baptism in the Jordan took place at about 10 o'clock on the morning of Friday, September 23
A.D. 29, a meditative contemplation of this event would be appropriate on
Friday, February 23, 1996. (Note here, in terms of months, that there is a
shift of five months from Friday, September 23 to Friday, February 23.)
Similarly, as the wedding at Cana occurred on the morning of Wednesday,
December 28 A.D. 29, the miracle of the changing of water into wine can be
commemorated on Wednesday, May 29, 1996. Effectively this means shift-
ing all the dates in the right-hand column of the following table forward by
one day so that the weekday coincides with the historical weekday in the left-
hand column. Why is it important to observe the weekdays?

It is a fact that Anne Catherine Emmerich's visions of the day-to-day
unfolding of Christ's ministry were attuned to the historical weekdays. Thus,
every Friday evening she beheld the commencement of the Sabbath. (The
Sabbath begins at dusk on Friday evening and extends to sunset on Saturday
evening.) Since the Sabbath day —as the seventh day—was the last day of
the week, for her every Friday evening signified the start of the Sabbath and
every Saturday evening denoted the commencement of the first day of the
week. (For the Semitic peoples of antiquity the "day" began at dusk and
lasted until sunset the following day.) Thus the weekdays were imbued with
meaning for Anne Catherine Emmerich on account of her attunement to the
life of Christ, and this was relevant—at least in some cases—to her experiences of the historical events on particular weekdays.

To give one example: let us consider the miracle of the healing of the paralyzed man at the pool of Bethseda in Jerusalem. This took place historically on Friday, January 19, A.D. 31. Anne Catherine Emmerich describes how, on the afternoon of this day, Jesus Christ and the disciples went to the pool of Bethesda and healed many people, including a number of blind people. On his way out from the pool of Bethesda Jesus healed a paralyzed man who had lain there for 38 years. According to Anne Catherine Emmerich's description, the Sabbath had just commenced. In other words, the sun had already set this Friday when the healing of the paralyzed man took place. It was this fact—that the healing of the paralyzed man occurred on the Sabbath—which led to the persecution of Jesus, "And this was why the Jews persecuted Jesus, because he did this on the Sabbath" (John 5:16). From this example it is possible to grasp something of the significance of the weekdays in the life of Christ's ministry, and hence to see their importance for a meditative reliving of the day-by-day unfolding of Christ's ministry. In the case of this example, therefore, it would be appropriate to contemplate it on Friday, June 20, 1997 (rather than on Saturday, June 21) in order to attune to the weekday of this event. In general, therefore, a meditative attunement to the chronicle of Christ's ministry is enhanced by taking the weekdays into account.

Su.May 29,29	=	Mo.Oct.30,1995	
Mo.May 30,29	=	Tu.Oct.31,1995	
Tu.May 31,29	=	We.Nov. 1,1995	
We.Jun. 1,29	=	Th.Nov. 2,1995	
Th.Jun. 2,29	=	Fr.Nov. 3,1995	
Fr.Jun. 3,29	=	Sa.Nov. 4,1995	
Sa.Jun. 4,29	=	Su.Nov. 5,1995	
Su.Jun. 5,29	=	Mo.Nov. 6,1995	
Mo.Jun. 6,29	=	Tu.Nov. 7,1995	
Tu.Jun. 7,29	=	We.Nov. 8,1995	
We.Jun. 8,29	=	Th.Nov. 9,1995	
Th.Jun. 9,29	=	Fr.Nov.10,1995	
Fr.Jun.10,29	=	Sa.Nov.11,1995	
Sa.Jun.11,29	=	Su.Nov.12,1995	
Su.Jun.12,29	=	Mo.Nov.13,1995	
Mo.Jun.13,29	=	Tu.Nov.14,1995	
Tu.Jun.14,29	=	We.Nov.15,1995	
We.Jun.15,29	=	Th.Nov.16,1995	
Th.Jun.16,29	=	Fr.Nov.17,1995	
Fr.Jun.17,29	=	Sa.Nov.18,1995	
Sa.Jun.18,29	=	Su.Nov.19,1995	
Su.Jun.19,29	=	Mo.Nov.20,1995	
Mo.Jun.20,29	=	Tu.Nov.21,1995	
Tu.Jun.21,29	=	We.Nov.22,1995	
We.Jun.22,29	=	Th.Nov.23,1995	
Th.Jun.23,29	=	Fr,Nov.24,1995	
Fr.Jun.24,29	=	Sa.Nov.25,1995	
Sa.Jun.25,29	=	Su.Nov.26,1995	
Su.Jun.26,29	=	Mo.Nov.27,1995	
Mo.Jun.27,29	=	Tu.Nov.28,1995	
Tu.Jun.28,29	=	We.Nov.29,1995	
We.Jun.29,29	=	Th.Nov.30,1995	
Th.Jun.30,29	=	Fr.Dec. 1,1995	
Fr.Jul. 1,29	=	Sa.Dec. 2,1995	
Sa.Jul. 2,29	=	Su.Dec. 3,1995	
Su.Jul. 3,29	=	Mo.Dec. 4,1995	
Mo.Jul. 4,29	=	Tu.Dec. 5,1995	
Tu.Jul. 5,29	=	We.Dec. 6,1995	
We.Jul. 6,29	=	Th.Dec. 7,1995	
Th.Jul. 7,29	=	Fr.Dec. 8,1995	
Fr.Jul. 8,29	=	Sa.Dec. 9,1995	
Sa.Jul. 9,29	=	Su.Dec.10,1995	
Su.Jul.10,29	=	Mo.Dec.11,1995	
Mo.Jul.11,29	=	Tu.Dec.12,1995	
Tu.Jul.12,29	=	We.Dec.13,1995	
We.Jul.13,29	=	Th.Dec.14,1995	
Th.Jul.14,29	=	Fr.Dec.15,1995	
Fr.Jul.15,29	=	Sa.Dec.16,1995	
Sa.Jul.16,29	=	Su.Dec.17,1995	
Su.Jul.17,29	=	Mo.Dec.18,1995	
Mo.Jul.18,29	=	Tu.Dec.19,1995	
Tu.Jul.19,29	=	We.Dec.20,1995	
We.Jul.20,29	=	Th.Dec.21,1995	
Th.Jul.21,29	=	Fr.Dec.22,1995	
Fr.Jul.22,29	=	Sa.Dec.23,1995	
Sa.Jul.23,29	=	Su.Dec.24,1995	
Su.Jul.24,29	=	Mo.Dec.25,1995	
Mo.Jul.25,29	=	Tu.Dec.26,1995	
Tu.Jul.26,29	=	We.Dec.27,1995	
We.Jul.27,29	=	Th.Dec.28,1995	
Th.Jul.28,29	=	Fr,Dec.29,1995	
Fr.Jul.29,29	=	Sa.Dec.30,1995	
Sa.Jul.30,29	=	Su.Dec.31,1995	
Su.Jul.31,29	=	Mo.Jan. 1,1996	
Mo.Aug. 1,29	=	Tu.Jan. 2,1996	
Tu.Aug. 2,29	=	We.Jan. 3,1996	
We.Aug. 3,29	=	Th.Jan. 4,1996	
Th.Aug. 4,29	=	Fr.Jan. 5,1996	
Fr.Aug. 5,29	=	Sa.Jan. 6,1996	
Sa.Aug. 6,29	=	Su.Jan. 7,1996	
Su.Aug. 7,29	=	Mo.Jan. 8,1996	
Mo.Aug. 8,29	=	Tu.Jan. 9,1996	
Tu.Aug. 9,29	=	We.Jan.10,1996	
We.Aug.10,29	=	Th.Jan.11,1996	
Th.Aug.11,29	=	Fr.Jan.12,1996	
Fr.Aug.12,29	=	Sa.Jan.13,1996	
Sa.Aug.13,29	=	Su.Jan.14,1996	
Su.Aug.14,29	=	Mo.Jan.15,1996	
Mo.Aug.15,29	=	Tu.Jan.16,1996	
Tu.Aug.16,29	=	We.Jan.17,1996	
We.Aug.17,29	=	Th.Jan.18,1996	
Th.Aug.18,29	=	Fr.Jan.19,1996	
Fr.Aug.19,29	=	Sa.Jan.20,1996	
Sa.Aug.20,29	=	Su.Jan.21,1996	
Su.Aug.21,29	=	Mo.Jan.22,1996	
Mo.Aug.22,29	=	Tu.Jan.23,1996	
Tu.Aug.23,29	=	We.Jan.24,1996	
We.Aug.24,29	=	Th.Jan.25,1996	
Th.Aug.25,29	=	Fr.Jan.26,1996	
Fr.Aug.26,29	=	Sa.Jan.27,1996	
Sa.Aug.27,29	=	Su,Jan.28,1996	
Su.Aug.28,29	=	Mo.Jan.29,1996	
Mo.Aug.29,29	=	Tu.Jan.30,1996	
Tu.Aug.30,29	=	We.Jan.31,1996	
We.Aug.31,29	=	Th.Feb. 1,1996	
Th.Sep. 1,29	=	Fr.Feb. 2,1996	
Fr.Sep. 2,29	=	Sa.Feb. 3,1996	
Sa.Sep. 3,29	=	Su.Feb. 4,1996	
Su,Sep. 4,29	=	Mo.Feb. 5,1996	
Mo.Sep. 5,29	=	Tu.Feb. 6,1996	
Tu.Sep. 6,29	=	We.Feb. 7,1999	
We.Sep. 7,29	=	Th.Feb. 8,1996	
Th.Sep. 8,29	=	Fr.Feb. 9,1996	
Fr.Sep. 9,29	=	Sa.Feb 10,1996	
Sa.Sep.10,29	=	Su.Feb.11,1996	
Su.Sep.11,29	=	Mo.Feb.12,1996	
Mo.Sep.12,29	=	Tu.Feb.13,1996	
Tu.Sep.13,29	=	We.Feb,14,1996	
We.Sep.14,29	=	Th.Feb.15,1996	
Th.Sep.15,29	=	Fr.Feb.16,1996	
Fr.Sep.16,29	=	Sa.Feb.17,1996	
Sa.Sep.17,29	=	Su.Feb.18,1996	
Su.Sep.18,29	=	Mo.Feb.19,1996	
Mo.Sep.19,29	=	Tu.Feb.20,1996	

Tu.Sep.20,29	=	We.Feb.21,1996	We.Nov.16,29	=	Th.Apr.18,1996
We.Sep.21,29	=	Th.Feb.22,1996	Th.Nov.17,29	=	Fr.Apr.19,1996
Th.Sep.22,29	=	Fr.Feb.23,1996	Fr.Nov.18,29	=	Sa.Apr.20,1996
Fr.Sep.23,29	=	Sa.Feb.24,1996	Sa.Nov.19,29	=	Su.Apr.21,1996
Sa.Sep.24,29	=	Su.Feb.25,1996	Su.Nov.20,29	=	Mo.Apr.22,1996
Su.Sep.25,29	=	Mo.Feb.26,1996	Mo.Nov.21,29	=	Tu.Apr.23,1996
Mo.Sep.26,29	=	Tu.Feb.27,1996	Tu.Nov.22,29	=	We.Apr.24,1996
Tu.Sep.27,29	=	We.Feb.28,1996	We.Nov.23,29	=	Th.Apr.25,1996
We.Sep.28,29	=	Th.Feb.29,1996	Th.Nov.24,29	=	Fr.Apr.26,1996
Th.Sep.29,29	=	Fr.Mar. 1,1996	Fr.Nov.25,29	=	Sa.Apr.27,1996
Fr.Sep.30,29	=	Sa.Mar. 2,1996	Sa.Nov.26,29	=	Su.Apr.28,1996
Sa.Oct. 1,29	=	Su.Mar. 3,1996	Su.Nov.27,29	=	Mo.Apr.29,1996
Su.Oct. 2,29	=	Mo.Mar. 4,1996	Mo.Nov.28,29	=	Tu.Apr.30,1996
Mo.Oct. 3,29	=	Tu.Mar. 5,1996	Tu.Nov.29,29	=	We.May 1,1996
Tu.Oct. 4,29	=	We.Mar. 6,1996	We.Nov.30,29	=	Th.May 2,1996
We.Oct. 5,29	=	Th.Mar. 7,1996	Th.Dec. 1,29	=	Fr.May 3,1996
Th.Oct. 6,29	=	Fr.Mar. 8,1996	Fr.Dec. 2,29	=	Sa.May 4,1996
Fr.Oct. 7,29	=	Sa.Mar. 9,1996	Sa.Dec. 3,29	=	Su.May 5,1996
Sa.Oct. 8,29	=	Su.Mar.10,1996	Su.Dec. 4,29	=	Mo.May 6,1996
Su.Oct. 9,29	=	Mo.Mar.11,1996	Mo.Dec. 5,29	=	Tu.May 7,1996
Mo.Oct.10,29	=	Tu.Mar.12,1996	Tu.Dec. 6,29	=	We.May 8,1996
Tu.Oct.11,29	=	We.Mar.13,1996	We.Dec. 7,29	=	Th.May 9,1996
We.Oct.12,29	=	Th.Mar.14,1996	Th.Dec. 8,29	=	Fr.May 10,1996
Th.Oct.13,29	=	Fr.Mar.15,1996	Fr.Dec. 9,29	=	Sa.May 11,1996
Fr.Oct.14,29	=	Sa.Mar.16,1996	Sa.Dec.10,29	=	Su.May 12,1996
Sa.Oct.15,29	=	Su.Mar.17,1996	Su.Dec.11,29	=	Mo.May 13,1996
Su.Oct.16,29	=	Mo.Mar.18,1996	Mo.Dec.12,29	=	Tu.May 14,1996
Mo.Oct.17,29	=	Tu.Mar.19,1996	Tu.Dec.13,29	=	We.May 15,1996
Tu.Oct.18,29	=	We.Mar.20,1996	We.Dec.14,29	=	Th.May 16,1996
We.Oct.19,29	=	Th.Mar.21,1996	Th.Dec.15,29	=	Fr.May 17,1996
Th.Oct.20,29	=	Fr.Mar.22,1996	Fr.Dec.16,29	=	Sa.May 18,1996
Fr.Oct.21,29	=	Sa.Mar.23,1996	Sa.Dec.17,29	=	Su.May 19,1996
Sa.Oct.22,29	=	Su.Mar.24,1996	Su.Dec.18,29	=	Mo.May 20,1996
Su.Oct.23,29	=	Mo.Mar.25,1996	Mo.Dec.19,29	=	Tu.May 21,1996
Mo.Oct.24,29	=	Tu.Mar.26,1996	Tu.Dec.20,29	=	We.May 22,1996
Tu.Oct.25,29	=	We.Mar.27,1996	We.Dec.21,29	=	Th.May 23,1996
We.Oct.26,29	=	Th.Mar.28,1996	Th.Dec.22,29	=	Fr.May 24,1996
Th,Oct.27,29	=	Fr.Mar.29,1996	Fr.Dec.23,29	=	Sa.May 25,1996
Fr.0ct.28,29	=	Sa.Mar.30,1996	Sa.Dec.24,29	=	Su.May 26,1996
Sa.Oct.29,29	=	Su.Mar.31,1996	Su.Dec.25,29	=	Mo.May 27,1996
Su.Oct.30,29	=	Mo.Apr. 1,1996	Mo.Dec.26,29	=	Tu.May 28,1996
Mo.Oct.31,29	=	Tu.Apr. 2,1996	Tu.Dec.27,29	=	We.May 29,1996
Tu.Nov. 1,29	=	We.Apr. 3,1996	We.Dec.28,29	=	Th.May 30,1996
We.Nov. 2,29	=	Th.Apr. 4,1996	Th.Dec.29,29	=	Fr.May 31,1996
Th.Nov. 3,29	=	Fr.Apr. 5,1996	Fr.Dec.30,29	=	Sa.Jun. 1,1996
Fr.Nov. 4,29	=	Sa.Apr. 6,1996	Sa.Dec.31,29	=	Su.Jun. 2,1996
Sa.Nov. 5,29	=	Su.Apr. 7,1996	Su.Jan. 1,30	=	Mo.Jun. 3,1996
Su.Nov. 6,29	=	Mo.Apr. 8,1996	Mo.Jan. 2,30	=	Tu.Jun. 4,1996
Mo.Nov. 7,29	=	Tu.Apr. 9,1996	Tu.Jan. 3,30	=	We.Jun. 5,1996
Tu.Nov. 8,29	=	We.Apr.10,1996	We.Jan. 4,30	=	Th.Jun. 6,1996
We.Nov. 9,29	=	Th.Apr.11,1996	Th.Jan. 5,30	=	Fr.Jun. 7,1996
Th.Nov.10,29	=	Fr.Apr.12,1996	Fr.Jan. 6,30	=	Sa.Jun. 8,1996
Fr.Nov.11,29	=	Sa.Apr.13,1996	Sa.Jan. 7,30	=	Su.Jun. 9,1996
Sa.Nov.12,29	=	Su.Apr.14,1996	Su.Jan. 8,30	=	Mo.Jun.10,1996
Su.Nov.13,29	=	Mo.Apr.15,1996	Mo.Jan. 9,30	=	Tu.Jun.11,1996
Mo.Nov.14,29	=	Tu.Apr.16,1996	Tu.Jan.10,30	=	We.Jun.12,1996
Tu.Nov.15,29	=	We.Apr.17,1996	We.Jan.11,30	=	Th.Jun.13,1996

Th.Jan.12,30	=	Fr.Jun.14,1996	Fr.Mar.10,30	=	Sa.Aug.10,1996
Fr.Jan.13,30	=	Sa.Jun.15,1996	Sa.Mar.11,30	=	Su.Aug.11,1996
Sa.Jan.14,30	=	Su.Jun.16,1996	Su.Mar.12,30	=	Mo.Aug.12,1996
Su.Jan.15,30	=	Mo.Jun.17,1996	Mo.Mar.13,30	=	Tu.Aug.13,1996
Mo.Jan.16,30	=	Tu.Jun.18,1996	Tu.Mar.14,30	=	We.Aug.14,1996
Tu.Jan.17,30	=	We.Jun.19,1996	We.Mar.15,30	=	Th.Aug.15,1996
We.Jan.18,30	=	Th.Jun.20,1996	Th.Mar.16,30	=	Fr.Aug.16,1996
Th.Jan.19,30	=	Fr.Jun.21,1996	Fr.Mar.17,30	=	Sa.Aug.17,1996
Fr.Jan.20,30	=	Sa.Jun.22,1996	Sa.Mar.18,30	=	Su.Aug.18,1996
Sa.Jan.21,30	=	Su.Jun.23,1996	Su.Mar.19,30	=	Mo.Aug.19,1996
Su.Jan.22,30	=	Mo.Jun.24,1996	Mo.Mar.20,30	=	Tu.Aug.20,1996
Mo.Jan.23,30	=	Tu.Jun.25,1996	Tu.Mar.21,30	=	We.Aug.21,1996
Tu.Jan.24,30	=	We.Jun.26,1996	We.Mar.22,30	=	Th.Aug.22,1996
We.Jan.25,30	=	Th.Jun.27,1996	Th.Mar.23,30	=	Fr.Aug.23,1996
Th.Jan.26,30	=	Fr.Jun.28,1996	Fr.Mar.24,30	=	Sa.Aug.24,1996
Fr.Jan.27,30	=	Sa.Jun.29,1996	Sa.Mar.25,30	=	Su.Aug.25,1996
Sa.Jan.28,30	=	Su.Jun.30,1996	Su.Mar.26,30	=	Mo.Aug.26,1996
Su.Jan.29,30	=	Mo.Jul. 1,1996	Mo.Mar.27,30	=	Tu.Aug.27,1996
Mo.Jan.30,30	=	Tu.Jul. 2,1996	Tu.Mar,28,30	=	We.Aug.28,1996
Tu.Jan.31,30	=	We.Jul. 3,1996	We.Mar.29,30	=	Th.Aug.29,1996
We.Feb. 1,30	=	Th.Jul. 4,1996	Th.Mar.30,30	=	Fr.Aug.30,1996
Th.Feb. 2,30	=	Fr.Jul. 5,1996	Fr.Mar.31,30	=	Sa.Aug,31,1996
Fr,Feb. 3,30	=	Sa.Jul. 6,1996	Sa.Apr. 1,30	=	Su.Sep. 1,1996
Sa.Feb. 4,30	=	Su.Jul. 7,1996	Su.Apr. 2,30	=	Mo.Sep. 2,1996
Su.Feb. 5,30	=	Mo.Jul. 8,1996	Mo.Apr. 3,30	=	Tu.Sep. 3,1996
Mo.Feb. 6,30	=	Tu.Jul. 9,1996	Tu.Apr. 4,30	=	We.Sep. 4,1996
Tu.Feb. 7,30	=	We.Jul.10,1996	We.Apr. 5,30	=	Th.Sep. 5,1996
We.Feb. 8,30	=	Th.Jul.11,1996	Th.Apr. 6,30	=	Fr.Sep. 6,1996
Th.Feb. 9,30	=	Fr.Jul.12,1996	Fr.Apr. 7,30	=	Sa.Sep. 7,1996
Fr.Feb.10,30	=	Sa.Jul.13,1996	Sa.Apr. 8,30	=	Su.Sep. 8,1996
Sa.Feb.11,30	=	Su.Jul.14,1996	Su.Apr. 9,30	=	Mo.Sep. 9,1996
Su.Feb.12,30	=	Mo.Jul.15,1996	Mo.Apr.10,30	=	Tu.Sep.10,1996
Mo.Feb.13,30	=	Tu.Jul.16,1996	Tu.Apr.11,30	=	We.Sep.11,1996
Tu.Feb.14,30	=	We.Jul.17,1996	We.Apr.12,30	=	Th.Sep.12,1996
We.Feb.15,30	=	Th.Jul.18,1996	Th.Apr.13,30	=	Fr.Sep.13,1996
Th.Feb.16,30	=	Fr.Jul.19,1996	Fr.Apr.14,30	=	Sa.Sep.14,1996
Fr.Feb.17,30	=	Sa.Jul.20,1996	Sa.Apr,15,30	=	Su.Sep.15,1996
Sa.Feb,18,30	=	Su.Jul.21,1996	Su.Apr.16,30	=	Mo.Sep.16,1996
Su.Feb.19,30	=	Mo.Jul.22,1996	Mo.Apr.17,30	=	Tu.Sep.17,1996
Mo.Feb.20,30	=	Tu.Jul.23,1996	Tu.Apr.18,30	=	We.Sep.18,1996
Tu.Feb.21,30	=	We.Jul.24,1996	We.Apr.19,30	=	Th.Sep.19,1996
We.Feb.22,30	=	Th.Jul.25,1996	Th.Apr.20,30	=	Fr.Sep.20,1996
Th.Feb.23,30	=	Fr.Jul.26,1996	Fr.Apr.21,30	=	Sa.Sep.21,1996
Fr.Feb.24,30	=	Sa.Jul.27,1996	Sa.Apr.22,30	=	Su.Sep.22,1996
Sa.Feb.25,30	=	Su.Jul.28,1996	Su.Apr.23,30	=	Mo.Sep.23,1996
Su.Feb.26,30	=	Mo.Jul.29,1996	Mo.Apr.24,30	=	Tu.Sep.24,1996
Mo.Feb.27,30	=	Tu.Jul.30,1996	Tu.Apr.25,30	=	We.Sep.25,1996
Tu.Feb.28,30	=	We.Jul.31,1996	We.Apr.26,30	=	Th.Sep.26,1996
We.Mar. 1,30	=	Th.Aug. 1,1996	Th.Apr.27,30	=	Fr.Sep.27,1996
Th.Mar. 2,30	=	Fr.Aug. 2,1996	Fr.Apr.28,30	=	Sa.Sep.28,1996
Fr.Mar. 3,30	=	Sa.Aug. 3,1996	Sa.Apr.29,30	=	Su.Sep.29,1996
Sa.Mar. 4,30	=	Su.Aug. 4,1996	Su.Apr.30,30	=	Mo.Sep.30,1996
Su.Mar. 5,30	=	Mo.Aug. 5,1996	Mo.May 1,30	=	Tu.Oct. 1,1996
Mo.Mar. 6,30	=	Tu.Aug. 6,1996	Tu.May 2,30	=	We.Oct. 2,1996
Tu.Mar. 7,30	=	We.Aug. 7,1996	We.May 3,30	=	Th.Oct. 3,1996
We.Mar. 8,30	=	Th.Aug. 8,1996	Th.May 4,30	=	Fr.Oct. 4,1996
Th.Mar. 9,30	=	Fr.Aug. 9,1996	Fr.May 5,30	=	Sa.Oct. 5,1996

```
Sa.May  6,30 = Su.Oct. 6,1996    Su.Jul. 2.30 = Mo.Dec. 2,1996
Su.May  7,30 = Mo.Oct. 7,1996    Mo.Jul. 3.30 = Tu.Dec. 3,1996
Mo.May  8,30 = Tu.Oct. 8,1996    Tu.Jul. 4.30 = We.Dec. 4,1996
Tu.May  9,30 = We.Oct. 9,1996    We.Jul. 5.30 = Th.Dec. 5,1996
We.May 10,30 = Th.Oct.10,1996    Th.Jul. 6.30 = Fr.Dec. 6,1996
Th.May 11,30 = Fr.Oct.11,1996    Fr.Jul. 7.30 = Sa.Dec. 7,1996
Fr.May 12,30 = Sa.Oct.12,1996    Sa.Jul. 8.30 = Su.Dec. 8,1996
Sa.May 13,30 = Su.Oct.13,1996    Su.Jul. 9.30 = Mo.Dec. 9,1996
Su.May 14,30 = Mo.Oct.14,1996    Mo.Jul.10,30 = Tu.Dec.10,1996
Mo.May 15,30 = Tu.Oct.15,1996    Tu.Jul.11,30 = We.Dec.11,1996
Tu.May 16,30 = We.Oct.16,1996    We.Jul.12,30 = Th.Dec.12,1996
We.May 17,30 = Th.Oct.17,1996    Th.Jul.13,30 = Fr.Dec.13,1996
Th.May 18,30 = Fr.Oct.18,1996    Fr.Jul.14,30 = Sa.Dec.14,1996
Fr.May 19,30 = Sa.Oct.19,1996    Sa.Jul.15,30 = Su.Dec.15,1996
Sa.May 20,30 = Su.Oct.20,1996    Su.Jul.16,30 = Mo.Dec.16,1996
Su.May 21,30 = Mo.Oct.21,1996    Mo.Jul.17,30 = Tu.Dec.17,1996
Mo.May 22,30 = Tu.Oct.22,1996    Tu.Jul.18,30 = We.Dec.18,1996
Tu.May 23,30 = We.Oct.23,1996    We.Jul.19,30 = Th.Dec.19,1996
We.May 24,30 = Th.Oct.24,1996    Th.Jul.20,30 = Fr,Dec.20,1996
Th.May 25,30 = Fr.Oct.25,1996    Fr.Jul.21,30 = Sa.Dec.21,1996
Fr.May.26,30 = Sa.Oct.26,1996    Sa.Jul.22,30 = Su,Dec.22,1996
Sa.May.27,30 = Su.Oct.27,1996    Su.Jul.23,30 = Mo,Dec.23,1996
Su.May.28,30 = Mo.Oct.28,1996    Mo.Jul.24,30 = Tu.Dec.24,1996
Mo.May.29,30 = Tu.Oct.29,1996    Tu.Jul.25,30 = We.Dec.25,1996
Tu.May.30,30 = We.Oct.30,1996    We.Jul.26,30 = Th.Dec.26,1996
We.May.31,30 = Th.Oct.31,1996    Th.Jul.27,30 = Fr.Dec.27,1996
Th.Jun. 1,30 = Fr.Nov. 1,1996    Fr.Jul.28,30 = Sa.Dec.28,1996
Fr.Jun. 2,30 = Sa.Nov. 2,1996    Sa.Jul.29,30 = Su.Dec.29,1996
Sa.Jun. 3,30 = Su.Nov. 3,1996    Su.Jul.30,30 = Mo.Dec.30,1996
Su.Jun. 4,30 = Mo.Nov. 4,1996    Mo.Jul.31,30 = Tu.Dec.31,1996
Mo.Jun. 5,30 = Tu.Nov. 5,1996    Tu.Aug. 1,30 = We.Jan. 1,1997
Tu.Jun. 6,30 = We.Nov. 6,1996    We.Aug. 2,30 = Th.Jan. 2,1997
We.Jun. 7,30 = Th.Nov. 7,1996    Th.Aug. 3,30 = Fr.Jan. 3,1997
Th.Jun. 8,30 = Fr.Nov. 8,1996    Fr.Aug. 4,30 = Sa.Jan. 4,1997
Fr.Jun. 9,30 = Sa.Nov. 9,1996    Sa.Aug. 5,30 = Su.Jan. 5,1997
Sa.Jun.10,30 = Su.Nov.10,1996    Su.Aug. 6,30 = Mo.Jan. 6,1997
Su.Jun.11,30 = Mo.Nov.11,1996    Mo.Aug. 7,30 = Tu.Jan. 7,1997
Mo.Jun.12,30 = Tu.Nov.12,1996    Tu.Aug. 8,30 = We.Jan. 8,1997
Tu.Jun.13,30 = We.Nov.13,1996    We.Aug. 9,30 = Th.Jan. 9,1997
We.Jun.14,30 = Th.Nov.14,1996    Th.Aug.10,30 = Fr.Jan.10,1996
Th.Jun.15,30 = Fr.Nov.15,1996    Fr.Aug.11,30 = Sa.Jan.11,1997
Fr.Jun.16,30 = Sa.Nov.16,1996    Sa.Aug.12,30 = Su.Jan.12,1997
Sa.Jun.17,30 = Su.Nov.17,1996    Su.Aug.13,30 = Mo.Jan.13,1997
Su.Jun.18,30 = Mo.Nov.18,1996    Mo.Aug.14,30 = Tu.Jan.14,1997
Mo.Jun.19,30 = Tu.Nov.19,1996    Tu.Aug.15,30 = We.Jan.15,1997
Tu.Jun.20,30 = We.Nov.20,1996    We.Aug.16,30 = Th.Jan.16,1997
We.Jun.21,30 = Th.Nov.21,1996    Th.Aug.17,30 = Fr.Jan.17,1997
Th.Jun.22,30 = Fr.Nov.22,1996    Fr.Aug.18,30 = Sa.Jan.18,1997
Fr.Jun.23,30 = Sa.Nov.23,1996    Sa.Aug.19,30 = Su.Jan.19,1997
Sa.Jun.24,30 = Su.Nov.24,1996    Su.Aug.20,30 = Mo.Jan.20,1997
Su.Jun.25,30 = Mo.Nov.25,1996    Mo.Aug.21,30 = Tu.Jan.21,1997
Mo.Jun.26,30 = Tu.Nov.26,1996    Tu.Aug.22,30 = We.Jan.22,1997
Tu.Jun.27,30 = We.Nov.27,1996    We.Aug.23,30 = Th.Jan.23,1997
We.Jun.28,30 = Th.Nov.28,1996    Th.Aug.24,30 = Fr.Jan.24,1997
Th.Jun.29,30 = Fr.Nov.29,1996    Fr.Aug.25,30 = Sa.Jan.25,1997
Fr.Jun.30,30 = Sa.Nov.30,1996    Sa.Aug.26,30 = Su.Jan.26,1997
Sa.Jul. 1.30 = Su.Dec. 1,1996    Su.Aug.27,30 = Mo.Jan.27,1997
```

```
Mo.Aug.28,30  =  Tu.Jan.28,1997      Tu.Oct.24,30  =  We.Mar.26,1997
Tu.Aug.29,30  =  We.Jan.29,1997      We.Oct.25,30  =  Th.Mar.27,1997
We.Aug.30,30  =  Th.Jan.30,1997      Th.Oct.26,30  =  Fr.Mar.28,1997
Th.Aug.31,30  =  Fr.Jan.31,1997      Fr.Oct.27,30  =  Sa.Mar.29,1997
Fr.Sep. 1,30  =  Sa.Feb. 1,1997      Sa.Oct.28,30  =  Su.Mar.30,1997
Sa.Sep. 2,30  =  Su.Feb. 2,1997      Su.Oct.29,30  =  Mo.Mar.31,1997
Su.Sep. 3,30  =  Mo.Feb. 3,1997      Mo.Oct.30,30  =  Tu.Apr. 1,1997
Mo.Sep. 4,30  =  Tu.Feb. 4,1997      Tu.Oct.31,30  =  We.Apr. 2,1997
Tu.Sep. 5,30  =  We.Feb. 5,1997      We.Nov. 1,30  =  Th.Apr. 3,1997
We.Sep. 6,30  =  Th.Feb. 6,1997      Th.Nov. 2,30  =  Fr.Apr. 4,1997
Th.Sep. 7,30  =  Fr.Feb. 7,1997      Fr.Nov. 3,30  =  Sa.Apr. 5,1997
Fr.Sep. 8,30  =  Sa.Feb. 8,1997      Sa.Nov. 4,30  =  Su.Apr. 6,1997
Sa.Sep. 9,30  =  Su.Feb. 9,1997      Su.Nov. 5,30  =  Mo.Apr. 7,1997
Su.Sep.10,30  =  Mo.Feb.10,1997      Mo.Nov. 6,30  =  Tu.Apr. 8,1997
Mo.Sep.11,30  =  Tu.Feb.11,1997      Tu.Nov. 7,30  =  We.Apr. 9,1997
Tu.Sep.12,30  =  We.Feb.12,1997      We.Nov. 8,30  =  Th.Apr.10,1997
We.Sep.13,30  =  Th.Feb.13,1997      Th.Nov. 9,30  =  Fr.Apr.11,1997
Th.Sep.14,30  =  Fr.Feb.14,1997      Fr.Nov.10,30  =  Sa.Apr.12,1997
Fr.Sep.15,30  =  Sa.Feb.15,1997      Sa.Nov.11,30  =  Su.Apr.13,1997
Sa.Sep.16,30  =  Su.Feb.16,1997      Su.Nov.12,30  =  Mo.Apr.14,1997
Su.Sep.17,30  =  Mo.Feb.17,1997      Mo.Nov.13,30  =  Tu.Apr.15,1997
Mo.Sep.18,30  =  Tu.Feb.18,1997      Tu.Nov.14,30  =  We.Apr.16,1997
Tu.Sep.19,30  =  We.Feb.19,1997      We.Nov.15,30  =  Th.Apr.17,1997
We.Sep.20,30  =  Th.Feb.20,1997      Th.Nov.16,30  =  Fr.Apr.18,1997
Th.Sep.21,30  =  Fr.Feb.21,1997      Fr.Nov.17,30  =  Sa.Apr.19,1997
Fr.Sep.22,30  =  Sa.Feb.22,1997      Sa.Nov.18,30  =  Su.Apr.20,1997
Sa.Sep.23,30  =  Su.Feb.23,1997      Su.Nov.19,30  =  Mo.Apr.21,1997
Su.Sep.24,30  =  Mo.Feb.24,1997      Mo.Nov.20,30  =  Tu.Apr.22,1997
Mo.Sep.25,30  =  Tu.Feb.25,1997      Tu.Nov.21,30  =  We.Apr.23,1997
Tu.Sep.26,30  =  We.Feb.26,1997      We.Nov.22,30  =  Th.Apr.24,1997
We.Sep.27,30  =  Th.Feb.27,1997      Th.Nov.23,30  =  Fr.Apr.25,1997
Th.Sep.28,30  =  Fr.Feb.28,1997      Fr.Nov.24,30  =  Sa.Apr.26,1997
Fr.Sep.29,30  =  Sa.Mar. 1,1997      Sa.Nov.25,30  =  Su.Apr.27,1997
Sa.Sep.30,30  =  Su.Mar. 2,1997      Su.Nov.26,30  =  Mo.Apr.28,1997
Su.Oct. 1,30  =  Mo.Mar. 3,1997      Mo.Nov.27,30  =  Tu.Apr.29,1997
Mo.Oct. 2,30  =  Tu.Mar. 4,1997      Tu.Nov.28,30  =  We.Apr.30,1997
Tu.Oct. 3,30  =  We.Mar. 5,1997      We.Nov.29,30  =  Th.May  1,1997
We.Oct. 4,30  =  Th.Mar. 6,1997      Th.Nov.30,30  =  Fr.May  2,1997
Th.Oct. 5,30  =  Fr.Mar. 7,1997      Fr.Dec. 1,30  =  Sa.May  3,1997
Fr.Oct. 6,30  =  Sa.Mar. 8,1997      Sa.Dec. 2,30  =  Su.May  4,1997
Sa.Oct. 7,30  =  Su.Mar. 9,1997      Su.Dec. 3,30  =  Mo.May  5,1997
Su.Oct. 8,30  =  Mo.Mar.10,1997      Mo.Dec. 4,30  =  Tu.May  6,1997
Mo.Oct. 9,30  =  Tu.Mar.11,1997      Tu.Dec. 5,30  =  We.May  7,1997
Tu.Oct.10,30  =  We.Mar.12,1997      We.Dec. 6,30  =  Th.May  8,1997
We.Oct.11,30  =  Th.Mar.13,1997      Th.Dec. 7,30  =  Fr.May  9,1997
Th.Oct.12,30  =  Fr.Mar.14,1997      Fr.Dec. 8,30  =  Sa.May 10,1997
Fr.Oct.13,30  =  Sa.Mar.15,1997      Sa.Dec. 9,30  =  Su.May 11,1997
Sa.Oct.14,30  =  Su.Mar.16,1997      Su.Dec.10,30  =  Mo.May 12,1997
Su.Oct.15,30  =  Mo.Mar.17,1997      Mo.Dec.11,30  =  Tu.May 13,1997
Mo.Oct.16,30  =  Tu.Mar.18,1997      Tu.Dec.12,30  =  We.May 14,1997
Tu.Oct.17,30  =  We.Mar.19,1997      We.Dec.13,30  =  Th.May 15,1997
We.Oct.18,30  =  Th.Mar.20,1997      Th.Dec.14,30  =  Fr.May 16,1997
Th.Oct.19,30  =  Fr.Mar.21,1997      Fr.Dec.15,30  =  Sa.May 17,1997
Fr.Oct.20,30  =  Sa.Mar.22,1997      Sa.Dec.16,30  =  Su.May 18,1997
Sa.Oct.21,30  =  Su.Mar.23,1997      Su.Dec.17,30  =  Mo.May 19,1997
Su.Oct.22,30  =  Mo.Mar.24,1997      Mo.Dec.18,30  =  Tu.May 20,1997
Mo.Oct.23,30  =  Tu.Mar.25,1997      Tu.Dec.19,30  =  We.May 21,1997
```

We.Dec.20,30	=	Th.May 22,1997		Th.Feb.15,31	=	Fr.Jul.18,1997
Th.Dec.21,30	=	Fr.May 23,1997		Fr.Feb.16,31	=	Sa.Jul.19,1997
Fr.Dec.22,30	=	Sa.May 24,1997		Sa.Feb.17,31	=	Su.Jul.20,1997
Sa.Dec.23,30	=	Su.May 25,1997		Su.Feb.18,31	=	Mo.Jul.21,1997
Su.Dec.24,30	=	Mo.May 26,1997		Mo.Feb.19,31	=	Tu.Jul.22,1997
Mo.Dec.25,30	=	Tu.May 27,1997		Tu.Feb.20,31	=	We.Jul.23,1997
Tu.Dec.26,30	=	We.May 28,1997		We.Feb.21,31	=	Th.Jul.24,1997
We.Dec.27,30	=	Th.May 29,1997		Th.Feb.22,31	=	Fr.Jul.25,1997
Th.Dec.28,30	=	Fr.May 30,1997		Fr.Feb.23,31	=	Sa.Jul.26,1997
Fr.Dec.29,30	=	Sa.May 31,1997		Sa.Feb.24,31	=	Su.Jul.27,1997
Sa.Dec.30,30	=	Su.Jun. 1,1997		Su.Feb.25,31	=	Mo.Jul.28,1997
Su.Dec.31,30	=	Mo.Jun. 2,1997		Mo.Feb.26,31	=	Tu.Jul.29,1997
Mo.Jan. 1,31	=	Tu.Jun. 3,1997		Tu.Feb.27,31	=	We.Jul.30,1997
Tu.Jan. 2,31	=	We.Jun. 4,1997		We.Feb.28,31	=	Th.Jul.31,1997
We.Jan. 3,31	=	Th.Jun. 5,1997		Th.Mar. 1,31	=	Fr.Aug. 1,1997
Th.Jan. 4,31	=	Fr.Jun. 6,1997		Fr.Mar. 2,31	=	Sa.Aug. 2,1997
Fr.Jan. 5,31	=	Sa.Jun. 7,1997		Sa.Mar. 3,31	=	Su.Aug. 3,1997
Sa.Jan. 6,31	=	Su.Jun. 8,1997		Su.Mar. 4,31	=	Mo.Aug. 4,1997
Su.Jan. 7,31	=	Mo.Jun. 9,1997		Mo.Mar. 5,31	=	Tu.Aug. 5,1997
Mo.Jan. 8,31	=	Tu.Jun.10,1997		Tu.Mar. 6,31	=	We.Aug. 6,1997
Tu.Jan. 9,31	=	We.Jun.11,1997		We.Mar. 7,31	=	Th.Aug. 7,1997
We.Jan.10,31	=	Th.Jun.12,1997		Th.Mar. 8,31	=	Fr.Aug. 8,1997
Th.Jan.11,31	=	Fr.Jun.13,1997		Fr.Mar. 9,31	=	Sa.Aug. 9,1997
Fr.Jan.12,31	=	Sa.Jun.14,1997		Sa.Mar.10,31	=	Su.Aug.10,1997
Sa.Jan.13,31	=	Su.Jun.15,1997		Su.Mar.11,31	=	Mo.Aug.11,1997
Su.Jan.14,31	=	Mo.Jun.16,1997		Mo.Mar.12,31	=	Tu.Aug.12,1997
Mo.Jan.15,31	=	Tu.Jun.17,1997		Tu.Mar.13,31	=	We.Aug.13,1997
Tu.Jan.16,31	=	We.Jun.18,1997		We.Mar.14,31	=	Th.Aug.14,1997
We.Jan.17,31	=	Th.Jun.19,1997		Th.Mar.15,31	=	Fr.Aug.15,1997
Th.Jan.18,31	=	Fr.Jun.20,1997		Fr.Mar.16,31	=	Sa.Aug.16,1997
Fr.Jan.19,31	=	Sa.Jun.21,1997		Sa.Mar.17,31	=	Su.Aug.17,1997
Sa.Jan.20,31	=	Su.Jun.22,1997		Su.Mar.18,31	=	Mo.Aug.18,1997
Su.Jan.21,31	=	Mo.Jun.23,1997		Mo.Mar.19,31	=	Tu.Aug.19,1997
Mo.Jan.22,31	=	Tu.Jun.24,1997		Tu.Mar.20,31	=	We.Aug.20,1997
Tu.Jan.23,31	=	We.Jun.25,1997		We.Mar.21,31	=	Th.Aug.21,1997
We.Jan.24,31	=	Th.Jun.26,1997		Th.Mar.22,31	=	Fr.Aug.22,1997
Th.Jan.25,31	=	Fr.Jun.27,1997		Fr.Mar.23,31	=	Sa.Aug.23,1997
Fr.Jan.26,31	=	Sa.Jun.28,1997		Sa.Mar.24,31	=	Su.Aug.24,1997
Sa.Jan.27,31	=	Su.Jun.29,1997		Su.Mar.25,31	=	Mo.Aug.25,1997
Su.Jan.28,31	=	Mo.Jun.30,1997		Mo.Mar.26,31	=	Tu.Aug.26,1997
Mo.Jan.29,31	=	Tu.Jul. 1,1997		Tu.Mar.27,31	=	We.Aug.27,1997
Tu.Jan.30,31	=	We.Jul. 2,1997		We.Mar.28,31	=	Th.Aug.28,1997
We.Jan.31,31	=	Th.Jul. 3,1997		Th.Mar.29,31	=	Fr.Aug.29,1997
Th.Feb. 1,31	=	Fr.Jul. 4,1997		Fr.Mar.30,31	=	Sa.Aug.30,1997
Fr.Feb. 2,31	=	Sa.Jul. 5,1997		Sa.Mar.31,31	=	Su.Aug.31,1997
Sa.Feb. 3,31	=	Su.Jul. 6,1997		Su.Apr. 1,31	=	Mo.Sep. 1,1997
Su.Feb. 4,31	=	Mo.Jul. 7,1997		Mo.Apr. 2,31	=	Tu.Sep. 2,1997
Mo.Feb. 5,31	=	Tu.Jul. 8,1997		Tu.Apr. 3,31	=	We.Sep. 3,1997
Tu.Feb. 6,31	=	We.Jul. 9,1997		We.Apr. 4,31	=	Th.Sep. 4,1997
We.Feb. 7,31	=	Th.Jul.10,1997		Th.Apr. 5,31	=	Fr.Sep. 5,1997
Th.Feb. 8,31	=	Fr.Jul.11,1997		Fr.Apr. 6,31	=	Sa.Sep. 6,1997
Fr.Feb. 9,31	=	Sa.Jul.12,1997		Sa.Apr. 7,31	=	Su.Sep. 7,1997
Sa.Feb.10,31	=	Su.Jul.13,1997		Su.Apr. 8,31	=	Mo.Sep. 8,1997
Su.Feb.11,31	=	Mo.Jul.14,1997		Mo.Apr. 9,31	=	Tu.Sep. 9,1997
Mo.Feb.12,31	=	Tu.Jul.15,1997		Tu.Apr.10,31	=	We.Sep.10,1997
Tu.Feb.13,31	=	We.Jul.16,1997		We.Apr.11,31	=	Th.Sep.11,1997
We.Feb.14,31	=	Th.Jul.17,1997		Th.Apr.12,31	=	Fr.Sep.12,1997

Fr.Apr.13,31	=	Sa.Sep.13,1997
Sa.Apr.14,31	=	Su.Sep.14,1997
Su.Apr.15,31	=	Mo.Sep.15,1997
Mo.Apr.16,31	=	Tu.Sep.16,1997
Tu.Apr.17,31	=	We.Sep.17,1997
We.Apr.18,31	=	Th.Sep.18,1997
Th.Apr.19,31	=	Fr.Sep.19,1997
Fr.Apr.20,31	=	Sa.Sep.20,1997
Sa.Apr.21,31	=	Su.Sep.21,1997
Su.Apr.22,31	=	Mo.Sep.22,1997
Mo.Apr.23,31	=	Tu.Sep.23,1997
Tu.Apr.24,31	=	We.Sep.24,1997
We.Apr.26,31	=	Th.Sep.25,1997
Th.Apr,26,31	=	Fr.Sep.26,1997
Fr.Apr.27,31	=	Sa.Sep.27,1997
Sa.Apr.28,31	=	Su.Sep.28,1997
Su.Apr.29,31	=	Mo.Sep.29,1997
Mo.Apr.30,31	=	Tu.Sep.30,1997
Tu.May 1,31	=	We.Oct. 1,1997
We.May 2,31	=	Th.Oct. 2,1997
Th.May 3,31	=	Fr.Oct. 3,1997
Fr.May 4,31	=	Sa.Oct. 4,1997
Sa.May 5,31	=	Su.Oct. 5,1997
Su.May 6,31	=	Mo.Oct. 6,1997
Mo.May 7,31	=	Tu.oct. 7,1997
Tu.May 8,31	=	We.Oct. 8,1997
We.May 9,31	=	Th.Oct. 9,1997
Th.May 10,31	=	Fr.Oct.10,1997
Fr.May 11,31	=	Sa.Oct.11,1997
Sa.May 12,31	=	Su.Oct.12,1997
Su.May 13,31	=	Mo.Oct.13,1997
Mo.May 14,31	=	Tu.Oct.14,1997
Tu.May 15,31	=	We.Oct.15,1997
We.May 16,31	=	Th.Oct.16,1997
Th.May 17,31	=	Fr.Oct.17,1997
Fr.May 18.31	=	Sa.Oct.18,1997
Sa.May 19,31	=	Su.Oct.19,1997
Su.May 20,31	=	Mo.Oct.20,1997
Mo.May 21,31	=	Tu.Oct.21,1997
Tu.May 22,31	=	We.Oct.22,1997
We.May 23,31	=	Th.Oct.23,1997
Th.May 24,31	=	Fr.Oct.24,1997
Fr.May 25,31	=	Sa.Oct.25,1997
Sa.May 26,31	=	Su.Oct.26,1997
Su.May 27,31	=	Mo.Oct.27,1997
Mo.May 28,31	=	Tu.Oct.28,1997
Tu.May 29,31	=	We.Oct.29,1997
We.May 30,31	=	Th.Oct.30,1997
Th.May 31,31	=	Fr.Oct.31,1997
Fr.Jun. 1,31	=	Sa.Nov. 1,1997
Sa.Jun. 2,31	=	Su.Nov. 2,1997
Su.Jun. 3,31	=	Mo.Nov. 3,1997
Mo.Jun. 4,31	=	Tu.Nov. 4,1997
Tu.Jun. 5,31	=	We.Nov. 5,1997
We.Jun. 6,31	=	Th.Nov. 6,1997
Th.Jun. 7,31	=	Fr.Nov. 7,1997
Fr.Jun. 8,31	=	Sa.Nov. 8,1997
Sa.Jun. 9,31	=	Su.Nov. 9,1997
Su.Jun.10,31	=	Mo.Nov.10,1997
Mo.Jun.11,31	=	Tu.Nov.11,1997
Tu.Jun.12,31	=	We.Nov.12,1997
We.Jun.13,31	=	Th.Nov.13,1997
Th.Jun.14,31	=	Fr.Nov.14,1997
Fr.Jun.15,31	=	Sa.Nov.15,1997
Sa.Jun.16,31	=	Su.Nov.16,1997
Su.Jun.17,31	=	Mo.Nov.17,1997
Mo.Jun.18,31	=	Tu.Nov.18,1997
Tu.Jun.19,31	=	We.Nov.19,1997
We.Jun.20,31	=	Th.Nov.20,1997
Th.Jun.21,31	=	Fr.Nov.21,1997
Fr.Jun.22,31	=	Sa.Nov.22,1997
Sa.Jun.23,31	=	Su.Nov.23,1997
Su.Jun.24,31	=	Mo.Nov.24,1997
Mo.Jun.25,31	=	Tu.Nov.25,1997
Tu.Jun.26,31	=	We.Nov.26,1997
We.Jun.27,31	=	Th.Nov.27,1997
Th.Jun.28,31	=	Fr.Nov.28,1997
Fr.Jun.29,31	=	Sa.Nov.29,1997
Sa.Jun.30,31	=	Su.Nov.30,1997
Su.Jul. 1,31	=	Mo.Dec. 1,1997
Mo.Jul. 2,31	=	Tu.Dec. 2,1997
Tu.Jul. 3,31	=	We.Dec. 3,1997
We.Jul. 4,31	=	Th.Dec. 4,1997
Th.Jul. 5,31	=	Fr.Dec. 5,1997
Fr.Jul. 6,31	=	Sa.Dec. 6,1997
Sa.Jul. 7,31	=	Su.Dec. 7,1997
Su.Jul. 8,31	=	Mo.Dec. 8,1997
Mo.Jul. 9,31	=	Tu.Dec. 9,1997
Tu.Jul.10,31	=	We.Dec.10,1997
We.Jul.11,31	=	Th.Dec.11,1997
Th.Jul.12,31	=	Fr.Dec.12,1997
Fr.Jul.13,31	=	Sa.Dec.13,1997
Sa.Jul.14,31	=	Su.Dec.14.1997
Su.Jul.15,31	=	Mo.Dec.15,1997
Mo.Jul.16,31	=	Tu.Dec.16,1997
Tu.Jul.17,31	=	We.Dec.17,1997
We.Jul.18,31	=	Th.Dec.18,1997
Th.Jul.19,31	=	Fr.Dec.I9,1997
Fr.Jul.20,31	=	Sa.Dec.20,1997
Sa.Jul.21,31	=	Su.Dec.21,1997
Su.Jul.22,31	=	Mo.Dec.22,1997
Mo.Jul.23,31	=	Tu.Dec.23,1997
Tu,Jul.24,31	=	We.Dec.24,1997
We.Jul.25,31	=	Th.Dec.25,1997
Th.Jul.26,31	=	Fr.Dec.26,1997
Fr.Jul.27,31	=	Sa.Dec.27,1997
Sa.Jul.28,31	=	Su.Dec.28,1997
Su.Jul.29,31	=	Mo.Dec.29,1997
Mo.Jul.30,31	=	Tu.Dec.30,1997
Tu.Jul.31,31	=	We.Dec.31,1997
We.Aug. 1,31	=	Th.Jan. 1,1998
Th.Aug. 2,31	=	Fr.Jan. 2,1998
Fr.Aug. 3,31	=	Sa.Jan. 3,1998
Sa.Aug. 4,31	=	Su.Jan. 4,1998

Su.Aug. 5,31	=	Mo.Jan. 5,1998		Mo.Oct. 1,31	=	Tu.Mar. 3,1998
Mo.Aug. 6,31	=	Tu.Jan. 6,1998		Tu.Oct. 2,31	=	We.Mar. 4,1998
Tu.Aug. 7,31	=	We.Jan. 7,1998		We.Oct. 3,31	=	Th.Mar. 5,1998
We.Aug. 8,31	=	Th.Jan. 8,1998		Th.Oct. 4,31	=	Fr.Mar. 6,1998
Th.Aug. 9,31	=	Fr.Jan. 9,1998		Fr.Oct. 5,31	=	Sa.Mar. 7,1998
Fr.Aug.10,31	=	Sa.Jan.10,1998		Sa.Oct. 6,31	=	Su.Mar. 8,1998
Sa.Aug.11,31	=	Su.Jan.11,1998		Su.Oct. 7.31	=	Mo.Mar. 9,1998
Su.Aug.12,31	=	Mo.Jan.12,1998		Mo.Oct. 8,31	=	Tu.Mar.10,1998
Mo.Aug.13,31	=	Tu.Jan.13,1998		Tu.Oct. 9,31	=	We.Mar.11,1998
Tu.Aug.14,31	=	We.Jan.14,1998		We.Oct.10,31	=	Th.Mar.12,1998
We.Aug.15,31	=	Th.Jan.15,1998		Th.Oct.11,31	=	Fr.Mar.13,1998
Th.Aug.16,31	=	Fr.Jan.16,1998		Fr.Oct.12,31	=	Sa.Mar.14,1998
Fr.Aug.17,31	=	Sa.Jan.17,1998		Sa.Oct.13,31	=	Su.Mar.15,1998
Sa.Aug.18,31	=	Su.Jan.18,1998		Su.Oct.14,31	=	Mo.Mar.16,1998
Su.Aug.19,31	=	Mo.Jan.19,1998		Mo.Oct.15,31	=	Tu.Mar.17,1998
Mo.Aug.20,31	=	Tu.Jan.20,1998		Tu.Oct.16,31	=	We.Mar.18,1998
Tu.Aug.21,31	=	We.Jan.21,1998		We.Oct.17,31	=	Th.Mar.19,1998
We.Aug.22,31	=	Th.Jan.22,1998		Th.Oct.18,31	=	Fr.Mar.20,1998
Th.Aug.23,31	=	Fr.Jan.23,1998		Fr.Oct,19,31	=	Sa.Mar.21,1998
Fr.Aug.24,31	=	Sa.Jan.24,1998		Sa.Oct,20,31	=	Su.Mar.22,1998
Sa.Aug.25,31	=	Su.Jan.25,1998		Su.Oct.21,31	=	Mo.Mar.23,1998
Su.Aug.26,31	=	Mo.Jan.26,1998		Mo.Oct.22,31	=	Tu.Mar.24,1998
Mo.Aug.27,31	=	Tu.Jan.27,1998		Tu.Oct.23,31	=	We.Mar.25,1998
Tu.Aug.28,31	=	We.Jan.28,1998		We.Oct.24,31	=	Th.Mar.26,1998
We.Aug.29,31	=	Th.Jan.29,1998		Th.Oct.25,31	=	Fr.Mar.27,1998
Th.Aug.30,31	=	Fr.Jan.30,1998		Fr.Oct.26,31	=	Sa.Mar.28,1998
Fr.Aug.31,31	=	Sa.Jan.31,1998		Sa.Oct.27,31	=	Su.Mar.29,1998
Sa.Sep. 1,31	=	Su.Feb. 1,1998		Su.Oct.28,31	=	Mo.Mar.30,1998
Su.Sep. 2,31	=	Mo.Feb. 2,1998		Mo.Oct.29,31	=	Tu.Mar.31,1998
Mo.Sep. 3,31	=	Tu.Feb. 3,1998		Tu.Oct.30,31	=	We.Apr. 1,1998
Tu.Sep. 4,31	=	We.Feb. 4,1998		We.Oct.31,31	=	Th.Apr. 2,1998
We.Sep. 5,31	=	Th.Feb. 5,1998		Th.Nov. 1,31	=	Fr.Apr. 3,1998
Th.Sep. 6,31	=	Fr.Feb. 6,1998		Fr.Nov. 2,31	=	Sa.Apr. 4,1998
Fr.Sep. 7,31	=	Sa.Feb. 7,1998		Sa.Nov. 3,31	=	Su.Apr. 5,1998
Sa.Sep. 8,31	=	Su.Feb. 8,1998		Su.Nov. 4,31	=	Mo.Apr. 6,1998
Su.Sep. 9,31	=	Mo,Feb. 9,1998		Mo.Nov. 5,31	=	Tu.Apr. 7,1998
Mo.Sep.10,31	=	Tu.Feb.10,1998		Tu.Nov. 6,31	=	We.Apr. 8,1998
Tu.Sep.11,31	=	We.Feb.11,1998		We.Nov. 7,31	=	Th.Apr. 9,1998
We.Sep.12,31	=	Th.Feb.12,1998		Th.Nov. 8,31	=	Fr.Apr.10,1998
Th.Sep.13,31	=	Fr.Feb.13,1998		Fr.Nov. 9,31	=	Sa.Apr.11,1998
Fr.Sep.14,31	=	Sa.Feb.14,1998		Sa.Nov.10,31	=	Su.Apr.12,1998
Sa.Sep.15,31	=	Su.Feb.15,1998		Su.Nov.11,31	=	Mo.Apr.13,1998
Su.Sep.16,31	=	Mo.Feb.16,1998		Mo.Nov.12,31	=	Tu.Apr.14,1998
Mo.Sep.17,31	=	Tu.Feb.17,1998		Tu.Nov.13,31	=	We.Apr.15,1998
Tu.Sep.18,31	=	We.Feb.18,1998		We.Nov.14,31	=	Th.Apr.16,1998
We.Sep.19,31	=	Th.Feb.19,1998		Th.Nov.15,31	=	Fr.Apr.17,1998
Th.Sep.20,31	=	Fr.Feb.20,1998		Fr.Nov.16,31	=	Sa.Apr.18,1998
Fr.Sep.21,31	=	Sa.Feb.21,1998		Sa.Nov.17,31	=	Su.Apr.19,1998
Sa.Sep.22,31	=	Su.Feb.22,1998		Su.Nov.18,31	=	Mo.Apr.20,1998
Su.Sep.23,31	=	Mo.Feb.23,1998		Mo.Nov.19,31	=	Tu.Apr.21,1998
Mo.Sep.24,31	=	Tu.Feb.24,1998		Tu.Nov.20,31	=	We.Apr.22,1998
Tu.Sep.25,31	=	We.Feb.25,1998		We.Nov.21,31	=	Th.Apr.23,1998
We.Sep.26,31	=	Th.Feb.26,1998		Th.Nov.22,31	=	Fr.Apr.24,1998
Th.Sep.27,31	=	Fr.Feb.27,1998		Fr.Nov.23,31	=	Sa.Apr.25,1998
Fr.Sep.28,31	=	Sa.Feb.28,1998		Sa.Nov.24,31	=	Su.Apr.26,1998
Sa.Sep.29,31	=	Su.Mar. 1,1998		Su.Nov.25,31	=	Mo.Apr.27,1998
Su.Sep.30,31	=	Mo.Mar. 2,1998		Mo.Nov.26,31	=	Tu.Apr.28,1998

```
Tu.Nov.27,31 = We.Apr.29,1998     We.Jan.23,32 = Th.Jun.25,1998
We.Nov.28,31 = Th.Apr.30,1998     Th.Jan.24,32 = Fr.Jun.26,1998
Th.Nov.29,31 = Fr.May  1,1998     Fr.Jan.25,32 = Sa.Jun.27,1998
Fr.Nov.30,31 = Sa.May  2,1998     Sa.Jan.26,32 = Su.Jun.28,1998
Sa.Dec. 1,31 = Su.May  3,1998     Su.Jan.27,32 = Mo.Jun.29,1998
Su.Dec. 2,31 = Mo.May  4,1998     Mo.Jan.28,32 = Tu.Jun.30,1998
Mo.Dee. 3,31 = Tu.May  5,1998     Tu.Jan.29,32 = We.Jul. 1,1998
Tu.Dec. 4,31 = We.May  6,1998     We.Jan.30,32 = Th.Jul. 2,1998
We.Dec. 5.31 = Th.May  7,1998     Th.Jan.31,32 = Fr.Jul. 3,1998
Th.Dec. 6,31 = Fr.May  8,1998     Fr.Feb. 1,32 = Sa.Jul. 4,1998
Fr.Dec. 7,31 = Sa.May  9,1998     Sa.Feb. 2,32 = Su.Jul. 5,1998
Sa.Dec. 8,31 = Su.May 10,1998     Su,Feb, 3,32 = Mo.Jul. 6,1998
Su.Dec. 9,31 = Mo.May 11,1998     Mo.Feb. 4,32 = Tu.Jul. 7,1998
Mo.Dec.10,31 = Tu.May 12,1998     Tu.Feb. 5,32 = We.Jul. 8,1998
Tu.Dec.11,31 = We.May 13,1998     We.Feb. 6,32 = Th.Jul. 9,1998
We.Dec.12,31 = Th.May 14,1998     Th.Feb. 7,32 = Fr.Jul.10,1998
Th.Dec.13,31 = Fr.May 15.1998     Fr.Feb. 8,32 = Sa.Jul.11,1998
Fr.Dec.14,31 = Sa.May 16,1998     Sa.Fep. 9,32 = Su.Jul.12,1998
Sa.Dec.15,31 = Su.May 17,1998     Su.Feb.10,32 = Mo.Jul.13,1998
Su.Dec.16,31 = Mo.May 18,1998     Mo.Feb.11,32 = Tu.Jul.14,1998
Mo.Dec.17,31 = Tu.May 19,1998     Tu.Feb.12,32 = We.Jul.15,1998
Tu.Dec.18,31 = We.May 20,1998     We.Feb.13,32 = Th.Jul.16,1998
We.Dec.19,31 = Th.May 21,1998     Th.Feb.14,32 = Fr.Jul.17,1998
Th.Dec.20,31 = Fr.May 22,1998     Fr.Feb.15,32 = Sa.Jul.18,1998
Fr.Dec.21,31 = Sa.May 23,1998     Sa.Feb.16,32 = Su.Jul.19,1998
Sa.Dec.22,31 = Su.May 24,1998     Su.Feb.17,32 = Mo.Jul.20,1998
Su.Dec.23,31 = Mo.May 25,1998     Mo.Feb.18,32 = Tu.Jul.21,1998
Mo.Dec.24,31 = Tu.May 26,1998     Tu.Feb.19,32 = We.Jul.22,1998
Tu.Dec.25,31 = We.May 27,1998     We.Feb.20,32 = Th.Jul.23,1998
We.Dec.26,31 = Th.May 28,1998     Th.Feb.21,32 = Fr.Jul.24,1998
Th.Dec.27,31 = Fr.May 29,1998     Fr.Feb.22,32 = Sa.Jul.25,1998
Fr.Dec.28,31 = Sa.May 30,1998     Sa.Feb.23,32 = Su.Jul.26,1998
Sa.Dec.29,31 = Su.May 31,1998     Su.Feb.24,32 = Mo.Jul.27,1998
Su.Dec.30,31 = Mo.Jun. 1,1998     Mo.Feb.25,32 = Tu.Jul.28,1998
Mo.Dec.31,31 = Tu.Jun. 2,1998     Tu.Feb.26,32 = We.Jul.29,1998
Tu.Jan. 1,32 = We.Jun. 3,1998     We.Feb.27,32 = Th.Jul.30,1998
We.Jan. 2,32 = Th.Jun. 4,1998     Th.Feb.28,32 = Fr.Jul.31,1998
Th.Jan. 3,32 = Fr.Jun. 5,1998     Fr.Feb.29,32 = Sa.Aug. 1,1998
Fr.Jan. 4,32 = Sa.Jun. 6,1998     Sa.Mar. 1,32 = Su.Aug. 2,1998
Sa.Jan. 5,32 = Su.Jun. 7,1998     Su.Mar. 2,32 = Mo.Aug. 3,1998
Su.Jan. 6,32 = Mo.Jun. 8,1998     Mo.Mar. 3,32 = Tu.Aug. 4,1998
Mo.Jan. 7,32 = Tu.Jun. 9,1998     Tu.Mar. 4,32 = We.Aug. 5,1998
Tu.Jan. 8,32 = We.Jun.10,1998     We.Mar. 5,32 = Th.Aug. 6,1998
We.Jan. 9,32 = Th.Jun.11,1998     Th.Mar. 6,32 = Fr.Aug. 7,1998
Th.Jan.10,32 = Fr.Jun.12,1998     Fr.Mar. 7,32 = Sa.Aug. 8,1998
Fr.Jan.11,32 = Sa.Jun.13,1998     Sa.Mar. 8,32 = Su.Aug. 9,1998
Sa.Jan.12,32 = Su.Jun.14,1998     Su.Mar. 9,32 = Mo.Aug.10,1998
Su.Jan.13,32 = Mo.Jun.15,1998     Mo.Mar.10,32 = Tu.Aug.11,1998
Mo.Jan.14,32 = Tu.Jun.16,1998     Tu.Mar.11,32 = We.Aug.12,1998
Tu.Jan.15,32 = We.Jun.17,1998     We.Mar.12,32 = Th.Aug.13,1998
We.Jan.16,32 = Th.Jun.18,1998     Th.Mar.13,32 = Fr.Aug.14,1998
Th.Jan.17,32 = Fr.Jun.19,1998     Fr.Mar.14,32 = Sa.Aug.15,1998
Fr.Jan.18,32 = Sa.Jun.20,1998     Sa.Mar.15,32 = Su.Aug.16,1998
Sa.Jan.19,32 = Su.Jun.21,1998     Su.Mar.16,32 = Mo.Aug.17,1998
Su.Jan.20,32 = Mo.Jun.22,1998     Mo.Mar.17,32 = Tu.Aug.18,1998
Mo.Jan.21,32 = Tu.Jun.23,1998     Tu.Mar.18,32 = We.Aug.19,1998
Tu.Jan.22,32 = We.Jun.24,1998     We.Mar.19,32 = Th.Aug.20,1998
```

Th.Mar.20,32	=	Fr.Aug.21,1998		Fr.May 16,32	=	Sa.Oct.17,1998
Fr.Mar.21,32	=	Sa.Aug.22,1998		Sa.May 17,32	=	Su.Oct.18,1998
Sa.Mar.22,32	=	Su.Aug.23,1998		Su.May 18,32	=	Mo.Oct.19,1998
Su.Mar.23,32	=	Mo.Aug.24,1998		Mo.May 19,32	=	Tu.Oct.20,1998
Mo.Mar.24,32	=	Tu.Aug.25,1998		Tu.May 20,32	=	We.Oct.21,1998
Tu.Mar.25,32	=	We.Aug.26,1998		We.May 21,32	=	Th.Oct.22,1998
We.Mar.26,32	=	Th.Aug.27,1998		Th.May 22,32	=	Fr.Oct.23,1998
Th.Mar.27,32	=	Fr.Aug.28,1998		Fr.May 23,32	=	Sa.Oct.24,1998
Fr.Mar.28,32	=	Sa.Aug.29,1998		Sa.May 24,32	=	Su.Oct.25,1998
Sa.Mar.29,32	=	Su.Aug.30,1998		Su.May 25,32	=	Mo.Oct.26,1998
Su.Mar.30,32	=	Mo.Aug.31,1998		Mo.May 26,32	=	Tu.Oct.27,1998
Mo.Mar.31,32	=	Tu.Sep. 1,1998		Tu.May 27,32	=	We.Oct.28,1998
Tu.Apr. 1,32	=	We.Sep. 2,1998		We.May 28,32	=	Th.Oct.29,1998
We.Apr. 2,32	=	Th.Sep. 3,1998		Th.May 29,32	=	Fr.Oct.30,1998
Th.Apr. 3,32	=	Fr.Sep. 4,1998		Fr.May 30,32	=	Sa.Oct.31,1998
Fr.Apr. 4,32	=	Sa.Sep. 5,1998		Sa.May 31,32	=	Su.Nov. 1,1998
Sa.Apr. 5,32	=	Su.Sep. 6,1998		Su.Jun. 1,32	=	Mo.Nov. 2,1998
Su.Apr. 6,32	=	Mo.Sep. 7,1998		Mo.Jun. 2,32	=	Tu.Nov. 3,1998
Mo.Apr. 7,32	=	Tu.Sep. 8,1998		Tu.Jun. 3,32	=	We.Nov. 4,1998
Tu.Apr. 8,32	=	We.Sep. 9,1998		We.Jun. 4,32	=	Th.Nov. 5,1998
We.Apr. 9,32	=	Th.Sep.10,1998		Th.Jun. 5,32	=	Fr.Nov. 6,1998
Th.Apr.10,32	=	Fr.Sep.11,1998		Fr.Jun. 6,32	=	Sa.Nov. 7,1998
Fr.Apr.11,32	=	Sa.Sep.12,1998		Sa.Jun. 7,32	=	Su.Nov. 8,1998
Sa.Apr.12,32	=	Su.Sep.13,1998		Su,Jun. 8,32	=	Mo.Nov. 9,1998
Su.Apr.13,32	=	Mo.Sep.14,1998		Mo.Jun. 9,32	=	Tu.Nov.10,1998
Mo.Apr.14,32	=	Tu.Sep.15,1998		Tu.Jun.10,32	=	We.Nov.11,1998
Tu.Apr.15,32	=	We.Sep.16,1998		We.Jun.11,32	=	Th.Nov.12,1998
We.Apr.16,32	=	Th,Sep.17,1998		Th.Jun.12,32	=	Fr.Nov.13,1998
Th.Apr.17,32	=	Fr.Sep.18,1998		Fr.Jun.13,32	=	Sa.Nov.14,1998
Fr.Apr.18,32	=	Sa.Sep.19,1998		Sa.Jun.14,32	=	Su.Nov.15,1998
Sa.Apr,19,32	=	Su.Sep.20,1998		Su.Jun.15,32	=	Mo.Nov.16,1998
Su.Apr.20,32	=	Mo.Sep.21,1998		Mo.Jun.16,32	=	Tu.Nov.17,1998
Mo.Apr.21,32	=	Tu.Sep.22,1998		Tu.Jun.17,32	=	We.Nov.18,1998
Tu.Apr.22,32	=	We.Sep.23,1998		We.Jun.18,32	=	Th.Nov.19,1998
We.Apr.23,32	=	Th.Sep.24,1998		Th.Jun.19,32	=	Fr.Nov.20,1998
Th.Apr.24,32	=	Fr.Sep.25,1998		Fr.Jun.20,32	=	Sa.Nov.21,1998
Fr.Apr.25,32	=	Sa.Sep.26,1998		Sa.Jun.21,32	=	Su.Nov.22,1998
Sa.Apr.26,32	=	Su.Sep.27,1998		Su.Jun.22,32	=	Mo.Nov.23,1998
Su.Apr.27,32	=	Mo.Sep.28,1998		Mo.Jun.23,32	=	Tu.Nov.24,1998
Mo.Apr.28,32	=	Tu.Sep.29,1998		Tu.Jun.24,32	=	We.Nov.25,1998
Tu.Apr.29,32	=	We.Sep.30,1998		We.Jun.25,32	=	Th.Nov.26,1998
We.Apr.30,32	=	Th.Oct. 1,1998		Th.Jun.26,32	=	Fr.Nov.27,1998
Th.May 1,32	=	Fr.Oct. 2,1998		Fr.Jun.27,32	=	Sa.Nov.28,1998
Fr.May 2,32	=	Sa.Oct. 3,1998		Sa.Jun.28,32	=	Su.Nov.29,1998
Sa.May 3,32	=	Su.Oct. 4,1998		Su.Jun.29,32	=	Mo.Nov.30,1998
Su.May 4,32	=	Mo.Oct. 5,1998		Mo.Jun.30,32	=	Tu.Dec. 1,1998
Mo.May 5,32	=	Tu.Oct. 6,1998		Tu.Jul. 1,32	=	We.Dec. 2,1998
Tu.May 6,32	=	We.Oct. 7,1998		We.Jul. 2,32	=	Th.Dec. 3,1998
We.May 7,32	=	Th.Oct. 8,1998		Th.Jul. 3,32	=	Fr.Dec. 4,1998
Th.May 8,32	=	Fr.Oct. 9,1998		Fr.Jul. 4,32	=	Sa.Dec. 5,1998
Fr.May 9,32	=	Sa.Oct.10,1998		Sa.Jul. 5,32	=	Su.Dec. 6,1998
Sa.May 10,32	=	Su.Oct.11,1998		Su.Jul. 6,32	=	Mo.Dec. 7,1998
Su.May 11,32	=	Mo.Oct.12,1998		Mo.Jul. 7,32	=	Tu.Dec. 8,1998
Mo.May 12,32	=	Tu.Oct.13,1998		Tu.Jul. 8,32	=	We.Dec. 9,1998
Tu.May 13,32	=	We.Oct.14,1998		We.Jul. 9,32	=	Th.Dec.10,1998
We.May 14,32	=	Th.Oct.15,1998		Th.Jul.10,32	=	Fr.Dec.11,1998
Th.May 15,32	=	Fr.Oct.16,1998		Fr.Jul.11,32	=	Sa.Dec.12,1998

Sa.Jul.12,32	=	Su.Dec.13,1998		Su.Sep. 7,32	=	Mo.Feb. 8,1999
Su.Jul.13,32	=	Mo.Dec.14,1998		Mo.Sep. 8,32	=	Tu.Feb. 9,1999
Mo.Jul.14,32	=	Tu.Dec.15,1998		Tu.Sep. 9,32	=	We.Feb.10,1999
Tu.Jul.15,32	=	We.Dec.16,1998		We.Sep.10,32	=	Th.Feb.11,1999
We.Jul.16,32	=	Th.Dec.17,1998		Th.Sep.11,32	=	Fr.Feb.12,1999
Th.Jul.17,32	=	Fr.Dec.18,1998		Fr.Sep.12,32	=	Sa.Feb.13,1999
Fr.Jul.18,32	=	Sa.Dec.19,1998		Sa.Sep.13,32	=	Su.Feb.14,1999
Sa.Jul.19,32	=	Su.Dec.20,1998		Su.Sep.14,32	=	Mo.Feb.15,1999
Su.Jul.20,32	=	Mo.Dec.21,1998		Mo.Sep.15,32	=	Tu.Feb.16,1999
Mo.Jul.21,32	=	Tu.Dec.22,1998		Tu.Sep.16,32	=	We.Feb.17,1999
Tu.Jul.22,32	=	We.Dec.23,1998		We.Sep.17,32	=	Th.Feb.18,1999
We.Jul.23,32	=	Th.Dec.24,1998		Th.Sep.18,32	=	Fr.Feb.19,1999
Th.Jul.24,32	=	Fr.Dec.25,1998		Fr.Sep.19,32	=	Sa.Feb.20,1999
Fr.Jul.25,32	=	Sa.Dec.26,1998		Sa.Sep.20,32	=	Su.Feb.21,1999
Sa.Jul.26,32	=	Su,Dec.27,1998		Su.Sep.21,32	=	Mo.Feb.22,1999
Su.Jul.27,32	=	Mo.Dec.28,1998		Mo.Sep.22,32	=	Tu.Feb.23,1999
Mo.Jul.28,32	=	Tu.Dec.29,1998		Tu.Sep.23,32	=	We.Feb.24,1999
Tu.Jul.29,32	=	We.Dec.30,1998		We.Sep.24,32	=	Th.Feb.25,1999
We.Jul.30,32	=	Th.Dec.31,1998		Th.Sep.25,32	=	Fr.Feb.26,1999
Th.Jul.31,32	=	Fr.Jan. 1,1999		Fr.Sep.26,32	=	Sa.Feb.27,1999
Fr.Aug. 1,32	=	Sa.Jan. 2,1999		Sa.Sep.27,32	=	Su.Feb.28,1999
Sa.Aug. 2,32	=	Su.Jan. 3,1999		Su.Sep.28,32	=	Mo.Mar. 1,1999
Su.Aug. 3,32	=	Mo.Jan. 4,1999		Mo.Sep.29,32	=	Tu.Mar. 2,1999
Mo.Aug. 4,32	=	Tu.Jan. 5,1999		Tu.Sep.30,32	=	We.Mar. 3,1999
Tu.Aug. 5,32	=	We.Jan. 6,1999		We.Oct. 1,32	=	Th.Mar. 4,1999
We.Aug. 6,32	=	Th.Jan. 7,1999		Th.Oct. 2,32	=	Fr.Mar. 5,1999
Th.Aug. 7,32	=	Fr.Jan. 8,1999		Fr.Oct. 3,32	=	Sa.Mar. 6,1999
Fr.Aug. 8,32	=	Sa.Jan. 9,1999		Sa.Oct. 4,32	=	Su.Mar. 7,1999
Sa.Aug. 9,32	=	Su.Jan.10,1999		Su.Oct. 5,32	=	Mo.Mar. 8,1999
Su.Aug.10,32	=	Mo.Jan.11,1999		Mo.Oct. 6,32	=	Tu.Mar. 9,1999
Mo.Aug.11,32	=	Tu.Jan.12,1999		Tu.Oct. 7,32	=	We.Mar.10,1999
Tu.Aug.12,32	=	We.Jan.13,1999		We.oct. 8,32	=	Th.Mar.11,1999
We.Aug.13.32	=	Th.Jan.14,1999		Th.Oct. 9,32	=	Fr.Mar.12,1999
Th.Aug.14,32	=	Fr.Jan.15,1999		Fr.Oct.10,32	=	Sa.Mar.13,1999
Fr.Aug.15,32	=	Sa.Jan.16,1999		Sa.Oct.11,32	=	Su.Mar.14,1999
Sa.Aug.16,32	=	Su.Jan.17,1999		Su.Oct.12,32	=	Mo.Mar.15,1999
Su.Aug.17,32	=	Mo.Jan.18,1999		Mo.Oct.13,32	=	Tu.Mar.16,1999
Mo.Aug.18,32	=	Tu.Jan.19,1999		Tu.Oct.14,32	=	We.Mar.17,1999
Tu.Aug.19,32	=	We.Jan.20,1999		We.Oct.15,32	=	Th.Mar.18,1999
We.Aug.20,32	=	Th.Jan.21,1999		Th.Oct.16,32	=	Fr.Mar.19,1999
Th.Aug.21,32	=	Fr.Jan.22,1999		Fr.Oct.17,32	=	Sa.Mar.20,1999
Fr.Aug.22,32	=	Sa.Jan.23,1999		Sa.Oct.18,32	=	Su.Mar.21,1999
Sa.Aug.23,32	=	Su.Jan.24,1999		Su.Oct.19,32	=	Mo.Mar.22,1999
Su.Aug.24,32	=	Mo.Jan.25,1999		Mo.Oct.20,32	=	Tu.Mar.23,1999
Mo.Aug.25,32	=	Tu.Jan.26,1999		Tu.Oct.21,32	=	We.Mar.24,1999
Tu.Aug.26,32	=	We.Jan.27,1999		We.Oct.22,32	=	Th.Mar.25,1999
We.Aug.27,32	=	Th.Jan.28,1999		Th.Oct.23,32	=	Fr.Mar.26,1999
Th.Aug.28,32	=	Fr.Jan.29,1999		Fr.Oct.24,32	=	Sa.Mar.27,1999
Fr.Aug.29,32	=	Sa.Jan.30,1999		Sa.Oct.25,32	=	Su.Mar.28,1999
Sa.Aug.30,32	=	Su.Jan.31,1999		Su.Oct.26,32	=	Mo.Mar.29,1999
Su.Aug.31,32	=	Mo.Feb. 1,1999		Mo.Oct.27,32	=	Tu.Mar.30,1999
Mo.Sep. 1,32	=	Tu.Feb. 2,1999		Tu.Oct.28,32	=	We.Mar.31,1999
Tu.Sep. 2,32	=	We.Feb. 3,1999		We.Oct.29,32	=	Th.Apr. 1,1999
We.Sep. 3,32	=	Th.Feb. 4,1999		Th.Oct.30,32	=	Fr.Apr. 2,1999
Th.Sep. 4,32	=	Fr.Feb. 5,1999		Fr.Oct.31,32	=	Sa.Apr. 3,1999
Fr.Sep. 5,32	=	Sa.Feb. 6,1999		Sa.Nov. 1,32	=	Su.Apr. 4,1999
Sa.Sep. 6,32	=	Su.Feb. 7,1999		Su.Nov. 2,32	=	Mo.Apr. 5,1999

Mo.Nov. 3,32	=	Tu.Apr. 6,1999		Tu.Dec.30,32	=	We.Jun. 2,1999
Tu.Nov. 4,32	=	We.Apr. 7,1999		We.Dec.31,32	=	Th.Jun. 3,1999
We.Nov. 5,32	=	Th.Apr. 8,1999		Th.Jan. 1,33	=	Fr.Jun. 4,1999
Th.Nov. 6,32	=	Fr.Apr. 9,1999		Fr.Jan. 2,33	=	Sa.Jun. 5,1999
Fr.Nov. 7,32	=	Sa.Apr.10,1999		Sa.Jan. 3,33	=	Su.Jun. 6,1999
Sa.Nov. 8,32	=	Su.Apr.11,1999		Su.Jan. 4,33	=	Mo.Jun. 7,1999
Su.Nov. 9,32	=	Mo.Apr.12,1999		Mo.Jan. 5,33	=	Tu.Jun. 8,1999
Mo.Nov.10,32	=	Tu.Apr.13,1999		Tu.Jan. 6,33	=	We.Jun. 9,1999
Tu.Nov.11,32	=	We.Apr.14,1999		We.Jan. 7,33	=	Th.Jun.10,1999
We.Nov.12,32	=	Th.Apr.15,1999		Th.Jan. 8,33	=	Fr.Jun.11,1999
Th.Nov.13,32	=	Fr.Apr.16,1999		Fr.Jan. 9,33	=	Sa.Jun.12,1999
Fr.Nov.14,32	=	Sa.Apr.17,1999		Sa.Jan.10,33	=	Su.Jun.13,1999
Sa.Nov.15,32	=	Su.Apr.18,1999		Su.Jan.11,33	=	Mo.Jun.14,1999
Su.Nov.16,32	=	Mo.Apr.19,1999		Mo.Jan.12,33	=	Tu.Jun.I5,1999
Mo.Nov.17,32	=	Tu.Apr.20,1999		Tu.Jan.13,33	=	We.Jun.16,1999
Tu.Nov.18,32	=	We.Apr.21,1999		We.Jan.14,33	=	Th.Jun.17,1999
We.Nov.19,32	=	Th.Apr.22,1999		Th.Jan.15,33	=	Fr.Jun.18,1999
Th.Nov.20,32	=	Fr.Apr.23,1999		Fr.Jan.16,33	=	Sa.Jun.19,1999
Fr.Nov.21,32	=	Sa.Apr.24,1999		Sa.Jan.17,33	=	Su.Jun.20,1999
Sa.Nov.22,32	=	Su.Apr.25,1999		Su.Jan.18,33	=	Mo.Jun.21,1999
Su.Nov.23,32	=	Mo.Apr.26,1999		Mo.Jan.19,33	=	Tu.Jun.22,1999
Mo.Nov.24,32	=	Tu.Apr.27,1999		Tu.Jan.20,33	=	We.Jun.23,1999
Tu.Nov.25,32	=	We.Apr.28,1999		We.Jan.21,33	=	Th.Jun.24,1999
We.Nov.26,32	=	Th.Apr.29,1999		Th.Jan.22,33	=	Fr.Jun.25,1999
Th.Nov.27,32	=	Fr.Apr.30,1999		Fr.Jan.23,33	=	Sa.Jun.26,1999
Fr.Nov.28,32	=	Sa.May 1,1999		Sa.Jan.24,33	=	Su.Jun.27,1999
Sa.Nov.29,32	=	Su.May 2,1999		Su.Jan.25,33	=	Mo.Jun.28,1999
Su.Nov.30,32	=	Mo.May 3,1999		Mo.Jan.26,33	=	Tu.Jun.29,1999
Mo.Dec. 1,32	=	Tu.May 4,1999		Tu.Jan.27,33	=	We.Jun.30,1999
Tu.Dec. 2,32	=	We.May 5,1999		We.Jan.28,33	=	Th.Jul. 1,1999
We.Dec. 3,32	=	Th.May 6,1999		Th.Jan.29,33	=	Fr.Jul. 2,1999
Th.Dec. 4,32	=	Fr.May 7,1999		Fr.Jan.30,33	=	Sa.Jul. 3,1999
Fr.Dec. 5,32	=	Sa.May 8,1999		Sa.Jan.31,33	=	Su.Jul. 4,1999
Sa.Dec. 6,32	=	Su.May 9,1999		Su.Feb. 1,33	=	Mo.Jul. 5,1999
Su.Dec. 7,32	=	Mo.May 10,1999		Mo.Feb. 2,33	=	Tu.Jul. 6,1999
Mo.Dec. 8,32	=	Tu.May I1,1999		Tu.Feb. 3,33	=	We.Jul. 7,1999
Tu.Dec. 9,32	=	We.May 12,1999		We.Feb. 4,33	=	Th.Jul. 8,1999
We.Dec.10,32	=	Th.May 13,1999		Th.Feb. 5,33	=	Fr.Jul. 9,1999
Th.Dec.11,32	=	Fr.May 14,1999		Fr.Feb. 6,33	=	Sa.Jul.10,1999
Fr.Dec.12,32	=	Sa.May 15,1999		Sa.Feb. 7,33	=	Su,Jul.I1,1999
Sa.Dec.13,32	=	Su.May 16,1999		Su.Feb. 8,33	=	Mo.Jul.12,1999
Su.Dec.14,32	=	Mo.May 17,1999		Mo.Feb. 9,33	=	Tu.Jul.13,1999
Mo.Dec.15,32	=	Tu.May 18,1999		Tu.Feb.10,33	=	We.Jul.14,1999
Tu.Dec.16,32	=	We.May 19,1999		We.Feb.11,33	=	Th.Jul.15,1999
We.Dec.17,32	=	Th.May 20,1999		Th.Feb.12,33	=	Fr.Jul.16,1999
Th.Dec.18,32	=	Fr.May 21,1999		Fr.Feb.13,33	=	Sa.Jul.17,1999
Fr.Dec.19,32	=	Sa.May 22,1999		Sa.Feb.14,33	=	Su.Jul.18,1999
Sa.Dec.20,32	=	Su.May 23,1999		Su.Feb.15,33	=	Mo,Jul.19,1999
Su.Dec.21,32	=	Mo.May 24,1999		Mo.Feb.16,33	=	Tu.Jul.20,1999
Mo.Dec.22,32	=	Tu.May 25,1999		Tu.Feb.17,33	=	We.Jul.21,1999
Tu.Dec.23,32	=	We.May 26,1999		We.Feb.18,33	=	Th.Jul.22,1999
We.Dec.24,32	=	Th.May 27,1999		Th.Feb.19,33	=	Fr.Jul.23,1999
Th.Dec.25,32	=	Fr.May 28,1999		Fr.Feb.20,33	=	Sa.Jul.24,1999
Fr.Dec.26,32	=	Sa.May 29,1999		Sa.Feb.21,33	=	Su.Jul.25,1999
Sa.Dec.27,32	=	Su.May 30,1999		Su.Feb.22,33	=	Mo.Jul.26,1999
Su.Dec.28,32	=	Mo.May 31,1999		Mo.Feb.23,33	=	Tu.Jul.27,1999
Mo.Dec.29,32	=	Tu.Jun. 1,1999		Tu.Feb.24,33	=	We.Jul.28,1999

```
We.Feb.25,33  =  Th.Jul.29,1999
Th.Feb.26,33  =  Fr.Jul.30,1999
Fr.Feb.27,33  =  Sa.Jul.31,1999
Sa.Feb.28,33  =  Su.Aug. 1,1999
Su.Mar. 1,33  =  Mo.Aug. 2,1999
Mo.Mar. 2,33  =  Tu.Aug. 3,1999
Tu.Mar. 3,33  =  We.Aug. 4,1999
We.Mar. 4,33  =  Th.Aug. 5,1999
Th.Mar. 5,33  =  Fr.Aug. 6,1999
Fr.Mar. 6,33  =  Sa.Aug. 7,1999
Sa.Mar. 7,33  =  Su.Aug. 8,1999
Su.Mar. 8,33  =  Mo.Aug. 9,1999
Mo.Mar. 9,33  =  Tu.Aug.10,1999
Tu.Mar.10,33  =  We.Aug.11,1999
We.Mar.11,33  =  Th.Aug.12,1999
Th.Mar.12,33  =  Fr.Aug.13,1999
Fr.Mar.13,33  =  Sa.Aug.14,1999
Sa.Mar.14,33  =  Su.Aug.15,1999
Su.Mar.15,33  =  Mo.Aug.16,1999
Mo.Mar.16,33  =  Tu.Aug.17,1999
Tu.Mar.17,33  =  We.Aug.18,1999
We.Mar.18,33  =  Th.Aug.19,1999
Th.Mar.19,33  =  Fr.Aug.20,1999
Fr.Mar.20,33  =  Sa.Aug.21,1999
Sa.Mar.21,33  =  Su.Aug.22,1999
Su.Mar.22,33  =  Mo.Aug.23,1999
Mo.Mar.23,33  =  Tu.Aug.24,1999
Tu.Mar.24,33  =  We.Aug.25,1999
We.Mar.25,33  =  Th.Aug.26,1999
Th.Mar.26,33  =  Fr.Aug.27,1999
Fr.Mar.27,33  =  Sa.Aug.28,1999
Sa.Mar.28,33  =  Su.Aug.29,1999
Su.Mar.29,33  =  Mo.Aug.30,1999
Mo.Mar.30,33  =  Tu.Aug.31,1999
Tu.Mar.31,33  =  We.Sep. 1,1999
We.Apr. 1,33  =  Th.Sep. 2,1999
Th.Apr. 2,33  =  Fr.Sep. 3,1999
Fr.Apr. 3,33  =  Sa.Sep. 4,1999
Sa.Apr. 4,33  =  Su.Sep. 5,1999
Su.Apr. 5,33  =  Mo.Sep. 6,1999
```

Bibliography

Bock, Emil. *Kindheit und Jugend Jesu* (Urachhaus: Stuttgart, 1939).

Edwards, Ormond. *A New Chronology of the Gospels* (Floris: London, 1972).

[Ferrari] d'Occhieppo, Konradin. *Der Stern der Weisen* (Herold: Vienna, 1977).

Finegan, Jack. *Handbook of Biblical Chronology* (University Press: Princeton, 1964).

Hughes, David. *The Star of Bethlehem Mystery* (Dent: London, 1979).

Josephus, Flavius. *Jewish Antiquities* (7 vols., Loeb Classical Library: 1930–1965).

Kepler, Johannes. *De Stella Nova* in: *Gesammelte Werke*, vol. 1 (C.H. Beck: Munich, 1938).

Krause-Zimmer, Hella. *Die zwei Jesusknaben in der bildenden Kunst* (Verlag Freies Geistesleben: Stuttgart, 1977).

Kudlek, M. and Mickler, E.H. *Solar and Lunar Eclipses of the Ancient Near East* (Butzon & Bercker Kevelaer: Neukirchen-Vluyn, 1971).

Kuhn, Karl Georg. "The Two Messiahs of Aaron and Israel," *The Scrolls of the New Testament* (ed. K. Stendahl, SCM: London, 1958), pp. 54–64.

Martin, Ernest L. *The Birth of Christ Recalculated* (FBR Publications: Pasadena, CA, 1978).

Novalis Werke (ed. G. Schulz, Verlag C.H. Beck: Munich, 1969).

Powell, Robert. *Christian Hermetic Astrology: The Star of the Magi and the Life of Christ* (Golden Stone Press: Great Barrington, MA, 1990) Distributed by Anthroposophic Press, Hudson, NY.

_____ *Christian Star Calendar* (yearly) (Vancouver, Canada: Suncross Press). Geocentric and heliocentric sidereal ephemeris computed by Michael Brinch; with commentary relating to the life of Christ by Robert Powell. Distributed by Anthroposophic Press, Hudson, NY.

_____ *Cosmic Aspects of the Foundation Stone* (Great Barrington, MA: Golden Stone Press, 1990) Distributed by Anthroposophic Press, Hudson, NY.

_____ *Divine Sophia, Holy Wisdom.* Written for the founding of the Sophia Foundation of North America, 1995 (Sophia Foundation, PO Box 712, Nicasio, CA, 94946).

_____ *Hermetic Astrology, vol. I: Astrology and Reincarnation/ vol. II: Astrological Biography* (Kinsau, West Germany: Hermetika, 1987, 1989). Distributed by Anthroposophic Press, Hudson, NY.

_____ *History of the Planets* (San Diego, CA: Astro Computing Services, 1989).

_____ *The Most Holy Trinosophia* (Great Barrington, MA: Golden Stone Press, 1990) Distributed by Anthroposophic Press, Hudson, NY.

_____ & Peter Treadgold. *The Sidereal Zodiac* (Tempe, AZ: American Federation of Astrologers, 1985).

_____ *The Zodiac: A Historical Survey* (Astro Computing Services: San Diego, CA, 1984).

Rosenberg, Roy A. "The Star of the Messiah Reconsidered," *Biblica* 53 (1972), pp. 105–109.

Schalk, Ellen. "Zur Frage der 33-jährigen Dauer des Jesus Christus Lebens", *Beiträge zu einer Erweiterung der Heilkunst* (Dornach, Switzerland: Med. Sektion am Goetheanum, 1983, pp. 1–7).

Schürer, Emil. *The History of the Jewish People in the Age of Jesus Christ* (2 vols.,: Edinburgh: T. & T. Clarke, 1973, 1979).

Steiner, Rudolf. *The Bhagavad Gita and the Epistles of Paul* (trsl. L.D. Monges and D.M. Bugbey, New York: Anthroposophic Press,1971).

_____ *Esoteric Christianity and the Mission of Christian Rosenbreutz* London: Rudolf Steiner Press, 1984).

_____ "Et incarnatus est" (a lecture held in Basel on December 23, 1917), (Spring Valley, NY: Mercury Press,1983).

_____ *The Fifth Gospel* (trsl. C. Davy and D.S. Osmond, London: Rudolf Steiner Press, 1968).

_____ *The Gospel of St. Luke* (trsl. D.S. Osmond and O. Barfield, London: Rudolf Steiner Press, 1975).

_____ *The Gospel of St. Matthew* (trsl. D.S. Osmond and M. Kirkcaldy, London: Rudolf Steiner Press, 1965).

_____ *How to Know Higher Worlds. A Modern Path of Initiation* (former title: *Knowledge of the Higher Worlds. How is it achieved?*) (Hudson, NY: Anthroposophic Press, 1994).

_____ *Intuitive Thinking as a Spiritual Path: A Philosophy of Freedom* (former title: *The Philosophy of Spiritual Activity*) (Hudson, NY: Anthroposophic Press, 1995).

_____ *The Science of Knowing* (Spring Valley, NY: Mercury Press, 1988).

_____ *The Spiritual Guidance of the Individual and Humanity* (Hudson, NY: Anthroposophic Press, 1992).

_____ *Truth and Science* (Spring Valley, NY: Mercury Press, 1993).

_____ *Zur Geschichte und aus den Inhalten der erkenntniskultischen Abteilung der Esoterischen Schule, 1904–1914,* GA265, (Dornach, Switzerland: Rudolf Steiner Verlag, 1987).

Sucher, Willi. *Cosmic Christianity and the Changing Countenance of Cosmology* (Hudson, NY: Anthroposophic Press, 1993).

Books translated into English by the Author:

(from the French) *Meditations on the Tarot: A Journey into Christian Hermeticism.* (Rockport, MA: Element Books, 1991)

(from the German, with James Morgante) Valentin Tomberg, *Covenant of the Heart* (Rockport, MA: Element Books, 1992).

ABOUT THE AUTHOR

ROBERT A. POWELL was born in 1947 in Reading, England, and studied mathematics at the University of Sussex, graduating with a Master's degree. At the same time, he developed an interest in astronomy and this, in turn, led him to explore the roots of astrology, the ancient science of the connections between the stars and human beings.

In the mid-seventies, while researching these fields at the British Museum in London, Powell discovered the Rudolf Steiner Bookshop and Library on Museum Street. From that moment on, Steiner's anthroposophy or spiritual science became the esoteric or spiritual context in which he was to work: a path and a guide. Steiner's many works provided the epistemological, cosmological, and Christological foundations he sought to continue his work. But Steiner's influence, though essential, was not the only one in these formative years. For, through Steiner, he was led to the work of both the astrosophist Willi Sucher (1902–1985) and the Russian anthroposophist, hermetic sophiologist, and (in his later years) Roman Catholic, Valentin Tomberg (1900–1973).

From 1978 to 1982, Powell, while continuing his research, was in Dornach, Switzerland, at the Goetheanum, where he completed a eurythmy training. Since graduating from eurythmy school, still continuing to study, research, and lecture on themes arising from the practice of esoteric Christianity and astrology, Robert Powell has lived and worked as a eurythmist and movement therapist at the Sophia Foundation in Kinsau, Germany.

The former editor of the *Mercury Star Journal*, a quarterly publication devoted to developing a new star wisdom, Robert Powell has written several books: on ASTRONOMY (*The Zodiac: A Historical Survey; The Sidereal Zodiac; A History of the Planets*); ASTROLOGY (*Hermetic Astrology*, vols. I and II; and *Christian Hermetic Astrology: The Star of the Magi and the Life of Christ*); and ANTHROPOSOPHY (*Cosmic Aspects of the Foundation Stone*; and *The Most Holy Trinosophia*). He is the co-author with Michael Brinch of the yearly *Christian Star Calendar* and a regular contributor to the Swiss journal, *Novalis*. In 1995, Powell co-founded the Sophia Foundation of North America.